Anonymus

The China Directory for 1874

Anonymus

The China Directory for 1874

ISBN/EAN: 9783743344723

Manufactured in Europe, USA, Canada, Australia, Japa

Cover: Foto ©ninafisch / pixelio.de

Manufactured and distributed by brebook publishing software (www.brebook.com)

Anonymus

The China Directory for 1874

THE
China Directory

FOR

1874.

Fourth Annual Publication.

NEW SERIES.

HONGKONG:
PUBLISHED AT THE "CHINA MAIL" OFFICE.
1874.

PRICE TWO DOLLARS.

PREFACE.

A SLIGHT delay in the issue of the present work has enabled the publishers to make it far more complete than would otherwise have been possible. Some idea of the changes it records may be gained from the fact that more than 2,030 names have been removed from, while 2,410 have been added to, the Alphabetical List in this edition, which may safely challenge comparison, as regards copiousness and accuracy, with any similar completion. The body of the work contains also a novel feature, a Singapore directory having, for the first time, been included.

The Appendix as usual, contains a vast amount of information, and the Index of Advertisements will afford useful hints to residents of all classes.

January, 14, 1874.

CONTENTS.

Agents for China Directory, ... —	Hankow Directory, ... **M**
Mail Steamers for 1874, ... —	Chefoo Do ... ... **N**
Anglo-Chinese Calendar, ... —	Taku Do. . ... **O**
List of Streets, &c., in Hongkong, ...	Tientsin Do. ... ... **P**
Alphabetical List of Foreign Residents, **1**	Newchwang Do. ... ... **Q**
Hongkong Directory, List of Compradores, &c., ... } **A**	Peking Do. ... . **R**
	Yedo Do. ... ... **s**
Hongkong Native Hong List, ... **s**	Yokohama Do. ... ... **S**
Macao Directory,... ... ... **B**	Osaka Do. ... ... **T**
Whampoa Do. ... ... **C**	Kobé, Hiogo Do. ... ... **U**
Canton Do. ... ... **D**	Nagasaki Do. ... ... **V**
Swatow Do. ... ... **E**	Hakodadi Do. ... ...
Amoy Do. ... ... **F**	Philippines Do. ... ... **W**
Formosa Do. ... ... **G**	Saigon Do. ... ... **X**
Foochow Do. ... ... **H**	Bangkok Do. ... ... **Y**
Ningpo Do. ... ... **I**	Singapore Do. ... ... **Z**
Shanghai Do. ... ... **J**	Borneo Do. ... ... **Za**
Chinkeang Do. ... ... **K**	Labuan Do. ... ... **Zb**
Kewkeang Do. ... ... **L**	

APPENDIX.

Postage and Money Order Regulations, ... } **A**	Philippine Passport Regulations for Foreigners, ... } **E**
Opium Sales at Calcutta, &c., ...	Signal Station at Victoria Peak, ... **F**
Table of Stamp Duties, ... **B**	London Agencies of Banks, and Companies connected with the Far East, ... } **G**
Hydrographic Memos, ...
Parcel Tariffs, ...
Legalized Scale of Fares for Chairs and Boats, ... ,	Hongkong Fire Brigade Establishment, **H**
	Index to Advertisements, ...i-ii
Canton Custom House Regulations, &c., **D**	Advertisements, ... **1**

AGENTS FOR THE CHINA DIRECTORY.

HONGKONG,	Messrs Lane, Crawford & Co.
CANTON,	Messrs Lane, Crawford & Co., Hongkong.
MACAO,	L. da Graja, Royal Hotel.
SWATOW,	Messrs Quelch & Campbell.
AMOY,	,, Wilson, Nicholls & Co.
FOOCHOW,	,, Hedge & Co.
SHANGHAI,	,, Lane, Crawford & Co.
NINGPO,	,, Lane, Crawford & Co., Shanghai.
TIENTSIN,	,, ,, ,,
CHEFOO,	,, ,, ,,
NEWCHWANG,	,, ,, ,,
PEKING,	,, ,, ,,
YANGTSZE PORTS,	,, ,, ,,
JAPAN PORTS,	,, ,, Yokohama.
MANILA,	S. J. Morris, Esq. (Messrs Morris, Barlow & Co.)
SAIGON,	Messrs Ribeiro & Co., Saigon Advertiser.
SINGAPORE,	,, H. Wilton & Co.
BANGKOK,	Rev. S. Smith, Siam Advertiser
LONDON,	Geo. Street, Esq., 80, Cornhill.
	F. Algar, Esq., 11, Clements' Lane, Lombard Street
	Messrs Bates, Hendy & Co., 4 Old Jewry, E.C.
AUSTRALIA, &c.,	,, Gordon & Gotch, Melbourne and Sydney.
SAN FRANCISCO,	,, White & Bauer.

BAIN & DENNYS, *Publishers*,
"*China Mail*" Office, Hongkong

MAIL STEAMERS FOR 1874.

THE ENGLISH MAILS.

Table shewing the dates of dep re of the English Ma.s from Hongkong, of their anticipated arrivals in Londor. and dates o return despatches:—

THE FRENCH MAILS.

Table shewing the dates of departure of the French Mails from Hongkong, of their anticipated arrivals in London, and dates of return despatches:—

Leaves Hongkong.	Arrives in London via Brindisi.	Answer Leaves London via Brindisi.	Answer due here.	Leaves Hongkong.	Arrives in London (via Marseilles.)	Answer Leaves London (via Marseilles.)	Answer due Here.
Jan. 8	Feb. 16	Feb. 20	Mar. 31	Jan. 1	Feb. 8	Feb. 13	Mar. 27
,, 22	March 2	March 6	April 14	,, 15	,, 22	,, 27	April 10
Feb. 5	,, 16	,, 20	,, 28	,, 29	March 8	Mar. 13	,, 21
,, 19	,, 30	April 3	May 12	Feb. 12	,, 22	,, 27	May 5
March 5	April 13	,, 17	,, 26	,, 26	pril 5	April 10	,, 19
,, 19	,, 27	May 1	June 9	Mar. 12	,, 9	,, 24	June 2
April 2	May 11	,, 15	,, 23	,, 26	Ma 8	May 8	,, 16
,, 16	,, 25	,, 29	July 7	April 9	,, 17	,, 22	,, 30
,, 25	June 8	June 12	,, 21	,, 23	,, 31	June 5	July 14
May 9	,, 22	,, 26	Aug. 4	May 2	June 14	,, 19	,, 28
,, 23	July 6	July 1	,, 18	,, 16	,, 28	July 3	Aug. 11
June 6	,, 20	,, 24	Sept. 1	,, 30	July 12	,, 17	,, 25
,, 20	Aug. 3	Aug. 7	,, 15	June 13	,, 26	,, 31	Sept. 8
July 4	,, 17	,, 21	,, 29	,, 27	Aug. 9	Aug. 14	,, 22
,, 18	,, 31	Sept. 4	Oct. 13	July 11	,, 23	,, 28	Oct. 6
Aug. 1	Sept. 14	,, 18	,, 27	,, 25	Sept. 6	Sept. 11	,, 20
,, 15	,, 28	Oct. 2	Nov. 13	Aug. 8	,, 20	,, 25	Nov. 6
,, 29	Oct. 12	,, 16	,, 27	,, 22	Oct. 4	Oct. 9	,, 20
Sept. 12	,, 26	,, 30	Dec. 11	Sept. 5	,, 18	,, 23	Dec. 4
,, 26	Nov. 9	Nov. 13	,, 25	,, 19	Nov. 1	Nov. 6	,, 18
			1875	Oct. 3	Nov. 15	Nov. 20	1875
Oct. 15	Nov. 23	Nov. 27	Jan. 8	,, 22	,, 29	Dec. 4	Jan. 1
,, 29	Dec. 7	Dec. 11	,, 22	Nov. 5	Dec. 13	,, 18	,, 15
Nov. 12	,, 21	,, 25	Feb. 5			1875	,, 29
	1875	1875		Nov. 19	Dec. 27	Jan. 1	Feb. 12
Nov. 26	Jan. 4	Jan. 8	Feb. 19		1875		
Dec. 10	,, 18	,, 22	Mar. 5	Dec. 3	Jan. 10	Jan. 15	Feb. 26
				,, 17	,, 24	,, 29	Mar. 12

ANGLO-CHINESE CALENDAR FOR 1874.

38th and 39th years of Queen Victoria. 12th and 13th years of Emperor Tung Chi.

JANUARY.—11th and 12th Moons.

PHASES OF THE MOON.

	d.	h.	m.	s.		d.	h.	m.	s.
Full Moon,	3rd	2	39	44 A.M.	First Quarter,	25th	8	19	2 A.M.
Last Quarter,	11th	3	31	44 A.M.	Apogee,	9th	11		A.M.
New Moon,	18th	3	36	88 P.M.	Perigee,	21st	5		A.M.

Notable Chronological Events.

Days of Month	Days of Week	Days of Moon	ENGLISH.	CHINESE.
1	Th	13	Circumcision. Osaka and Hiogo opened 1868. Overland Telegraph through Russia opened 1872.	(13.) Anniversary of the birth of Emperor K'ang-hi A.D. 1723. Mercury enters Aquarius between 5-7 a.m.
2	Fr	14	(2.) M. M. Str. "Donnai" arrived.	(16.) Festival of Kwan-yin (Avalokitesvara), the goddess of mercy, worshipped by Buddhists and Tauists, but chiefly by women.
3	Sa	15		
4	S	16	2nd Sunday after Christmas. Commiss. Yeh captured 1858.	(17.) Birth-day of Amitabha buddha, the ruler of the paradise in the West. Solar term "little cold." Sun in Taurus.
5	M	17		(18.) Day of ill luck.
6	Tu	18	Epiphany. P. M. Str. "Japan" arrived.	(19.) Day for obtaining heaven's forgiveness for sins.
7	W	19		
8	Th	20		(23.) Birthday of the spirit that grants progeny. Descent of the spirits of the southern bushel.
9	Fr	21		(26.) Birthday of the spirits of the different points of the compass.
10	Sa	22		
11	S	23	1st Sunday after Epiphany. Seaman's Church, West Point, opened 1872.	(27.) Birthday of a deified Buddhist priest.
12	M	24		(29.) Birthday of Surya-ehni Deva, a Buddhist deity. The earth spirit exercises his influence.
13	Tu	25		
14	W	26	Secretary to American Legation murdered at Yedo 1871. P. & O. Str. "Sumatra" arrived.	(1.) Twelfth Moon.
15	Th	27	(15.) Arsenic put in bread for H'kong resid. by baker Alum 1857.	(2.) The moon enters Aries between 1-3 p.m.
16	Fr	28	(16.) M. M. Str. "Peiho" arrived.	(3.) Solar term "great cold." Sun enters Aries between 11-1 p.m.
17	Sa	29		
18	S	1	2nd Sunday after Epiphany.	(5.) Venus enters Scorpio between 11-1 p.m.
19	M	2	Sailor's Home at Hongkong formally opened 1863.	(6.) Anniversary of the death of an Empress. Anniversary of Shakyamuni (B.C. 592) attaining to Buddhaship.
20	Tu	3	Hongkong ceded to Great Britain 1841. Licensed Gambling-houses closed in Hongkong 1872.	(8.) The annual brnt at the Peking Court.
21	W	4	(21.) Linguist of Brit. Legation murdered by the Japanese 1860.	
22	Th	5	(24.) Fatal collision between P. & O. Steamer "Bombay" and U. S. Corvette "Oneida" in Yokohama Bay, 120 lives lost 1870.	(10.) Mercury enters Scorpio between 11-1 p.m.
23	Fr	6		(11.) Anniversary of the death of an Empress.
24	Sa	7	P. & O. Str. "Geelong" arrived.	(12.) Anniversary of the death of an Empress.
25	S	8	3rd Sunday after Epiphany. Conversion of St. Paul.	
26	M	9	P. M. Str. "Alaska" arrived.	
27	Tu	10	(26.) British took possession of Hongkong 1841.	
28	W	11		
29	Th	12		
30	Fr	13		
31	Sa	14		

FEBRUARY.—12th and 1st Moons.

PHASES OF THE MOON.

	d.	h.	m.	s.			d.	h.	m.	s.
Full Moon,	1st	7	12	20 P.M.	First Quarter,		23rd	6	22	08 P.M.
Last Quarter,	10th	0	5	20 A.M.	Apogee,		6th	5		A.M.
New Moon,	17th	2	51	82 A.M.	Perigee,		18th	11		A.M.

Notable Chronological Events.

Days of Month	Days of Week	Days of Moon		Days of Moon	
			ENGLISH.		**CHINESE.**
1	S	15	*Septuagesima Sunday.* Inhabitants of Hongkong declared to be British subjects 1841. M. M. Str. "Meikong" arrived.	(15.)	Birthday of a deified warrior Wen-yuen of the Hemisphere.
2	M	16		(16.)	Official worship of Sha-teih, the gods of the land, and of the grain. Birthday of Nam-poh, the Tuaist god of the southern mountain. Birth of Leo-tze, the founder of Tauism
3	Tu	17	(2.) *Candlemas.* New German Club opened 1872		
4	W	18	Outrage on Foreigners at Kobe 1868.		
5	Th	19		(18.)	A solar term "spring sets in." Sun in Aries.
6	Fr	20		(20.)	Birthday of Lo-pan, the god of carpenters.
7	Sa	21		(21.)	Birthday of the supreme ruler of the heavenly dragon, a Tauist deity. (22.) Day of ill luck
8	S	22	*Sexagesima Sunday.* P. & O. Str. "Australia" arrived.		
9	M	23		(23.)	In the 6th ning general worship of the god of the hearth.
10	Tu	24		(24.)	Tsau-kwn, the god of the hearth, ascends to heaven to report on the domestic affairs of mankind.
11	W	25	Naval Court of Enquiry on "Oneida" catastrophe.	(25.)	Anniversary of the death of an Empress.
12	Th	26		(29.)	Birthday of Padma-vyuha, a fabulous Buddhistic Bodhisative. The gods of the northern bushel worshipped by Tauists. descend from heaven.
13	Fr	27	M. M. Str. "Sindh" arrived.		
14	Sa	28	*St. Valentine's Day.* New Chinese Hospital opened by Sir R. G. [MacDonnell 1872.	(30.)	All the Buddhas descend to search out good and evil in mankind. Auspicious time for worship and offerings.
15	S	29	*Quinquagesima Sunday.*		
16	M	30	Hongkong declared to be a free P c. 1841.		
17	Tu	1	*Shrove Tuesday.* Insurgents evacuated Shanghai 1855. P. M. Str. "China" arrived	(1.)	*First Moon.* For . . New Year's day.
18	W	2	(18.) *Ash Wednesday.* Year 1291 of Mahomedan Era commences.	(2.)	Dog day. Moon enters Pisces between 1-3 a.m. Jupiter enters Leo between 11-3 p.m. Birthday of Che-ta-yen-shwai, a deified warrior. The god of the hearth returns from heaven.
19	Th	3	"China Mail" newspaper established 1845.		
20	Fr	4	Ratification of first Treaty between U. S. Japan 1855. [rived.		
21	Sa	5	1st Sunday in Lent. Ember Week. P. & O. Str. "Ellora" arrived. Foundation Stone of Hongkong City Hall laid 1867. Emperor	(3.)	Pig day. A solar term "rain water." Sun enters Pisces between 1-3 a.m. Birthday of Maitreya, the Buddha of the future, and of Sun-ching-yin, deified physician. Anniversary of the death of Emperor Ki Jung A.D. 1736.
22	S	6			
23	M	7	Tung Chih assumed the reins of government.		
24	Tu	8	(24.) *St. Matthias.*	(4.)	Sheep day. (5.) Cow day.
25	W	9	(25.) *Ember Day.*	(6.)	Birthday of the god of wealth, worshipped by Tauists, and of Dipankara Buddha. (7.) Man day. Anniversary of the death of Emperor Yung-ching A.D. 1729.
26	Th	10	(26.) Bogue Forts destroyed by Sir G. Bremmer 1841.		
27	Fr	11	(27-8.) *Ember Days.*	(8.)	Grain day. Birthday of the judge of the fourth court in hell.
28	Sa	12		(9.)	Hemp day. Birthday of Yu-wang, the pearly emperor, the supreme God of the Tauists.
			(10.) Pea day. Birthday of some of the lares called dragon spirits of the five regions.		
			(111) Anniversary of the death of an Empress.		

MARCH.—1st and 2nd Moons.

PHASES OF THE MOON.

	d.	h.	m.	s.			d.	h.	m.	s.	
FULL MOON,	3rd	0	56	02	P.M.	FIRST QUARTER,	25th	6	7	5	A.M.
LAST QUARTER,	11th	5	10	20	P.M.	APOGEE,	6th	4			P.M.
NEW MOON,	18th	0	38	22	P.M.	PERIGEE,	18th	3			P.M.

Notable Chronological Events.

Days of Month.	Days of Week.	Days of Moon.	ENGLISH.
1	S	13	2nd Sunday in Lent. *St. David*
2	M	14	M. M. Str. "Provence" arrived.
3	Tu	15	Grand Duke Alexis left Hongkong 1872.
4	W	16	
5	Th	17	
6	Fr	18	P. & O. Str. "Travancore" arrived. P. M. Str. "Colombo" [arrived.
7	Sa	19	3rd Sunday in Lent. Commercial Treaty concluded between
8	S	20	United States and Japan 1854.
9	M	21	(9.) S. S. N. Co.'s Str. "Kiangloong" lost in the Yangtsze.
10	Tu	22	[died 1872.
11	W	23	Chinese Custom House closed at Macao 1849. Tseng-kwo-fan
12	Th	24	M. M. Str. "Hoogly" arrived.
13	Fr	25	
14	Sa	26	4th Sunday in Lent.
15	S	27	
16	M	28	St. Patrick's Day. P. & O. Str. "Deccan" arrived.
17	Tu	29	
18	W	1	Capture at Nankin by the Taipings 1853.
19	Th	2	
20	Fr	3	Vernal Equinox.
21	Sa	4	5th Sunday in Lent.
22	S	5	
23	M	6	
24	Tu	7	
25	W	8	Annunciation. *Lady Day*. Foundation of Seamen's Church
26	Th	9	laid 1871.
27	Fr	10	M. M. Str. "Tigre" arrived.
28	Sa	11	
29	S	12	Palm Sunday.
30	M	13	
31	Tu	14	

CHINESE.

(13.) Birthday of W:᎒ᐟ ᴋ Hü, two Cantonese warriors, chiefly worshipped in Fatshan.
(14.) Anniversary of death of Emperor Tao-kwang A.D. 1821.
(15.) The feast of lanterns. Birthday of the Taoist god Shang-yen, a heavenly ruler. "movement of larvæ." Sun in Pisces.
(18.) Venus enters Leo between 5-7 a.m. The Solar term
(19.) Birthday of Chang-chun, a deified physician.
(20.) Birthday of Shen-ts'ai, a Buddhist saint connected with the mythology of Kwan-yin (Avalokiteshvara). Auspicious day for worship if wealth is desired.
(21.) Anniversary of the death of an Empress.
(23.) Mercury enters Sagittarius between 11-1 a.m.
(29.) Anniversary of the death of an Empress.
(1.) *Second Moon.* Birthday of judge of first court in hell.
(2.) Moon enters Aquarius between 5-7 a.m. Birthday of one of the lares called gods of happiness. Plays performed in public. Fire-works. The remains of rockets presented as luck-bringing. Birthday of Mencius, the greatest rival of Confucius B.C. 371.
(3.) Birthday of the Confucianist star-god of literature.
(4.) The solar term "vernal equinox" Sun enters Aquarius between 1-3 a.m. patron for sins committed.
(6.) The vernal sacrifice. Auspicious day for obtaining heaven's
(6.) Day of ill luck. Birthday of the Taoist patriarch Tung wa-ti-kiun. [Chang-hien, a Taoist worthy.
(7.) Anniversary of the death of an Empress. Birthday of
(8.) Birthday of the judge of the fifth court in hell, and of the six Chinese patriarchs of the Buddhist church, Bodhidharma (A.D. 500,) being counted the first. [the ground.
(10.) Birthday of one of the dragon spirits, tutelary deities of
(11.) Anniversary of the death of an Empress. (see (the Pearl river.
(13.) Birthday of Hungshin, the Cantonese god of the souther:

APRIL.—2nd and 3rd Moons.

PHASES OF THE MOON.

	d.	h.	m.	s.			
Full Moon,	2nd	6	56	38 A.M.	Apogee,	1st	5 P.M.
Last Quarter,	10th	5	57	44 A.M.	New Moon,	16th	9 28 50 P.M.	Perigee,	16th	7 A.M.
First Quarter,	23rd	7	40	08 P.M.	Apogee,	28th	0 A.M.

Notable Chronological Events

ENGLISH.

Days of Month	Days of Week	Days of Moon	
1	W	15	
2	Th	16	Good Friday.
3	Fr	17	P. & O. Str. "Geelong" arrived.
4	Sa	18	Easter Sunday. Bogue Forts destroyed by Ge... ·l D'Aguilar 1847.
5	S	19	
6	M	20	P. M. Str. "Japan" arrived.
7	Tu	21	
8	W	22	
9	Th	23	M. M. Str. "Amazone" arrived.
10	Fr	24	
11	Sa	25	Sir R. G. MacDonnell left for Europe 1872.
12	S	26	Low Sunday.
13	M	27	37,000 Christians butchered in Japan 1638.
14	Tu	28	Str. "Roma" sunk by collision with Str. "Ava," great loss of life 1872. P. & O. Str. "Tanjore" arrived.
15	W	29	
16	Th	1	Sir A. Kennedy assumed government of Hongkong 1872. Total eclipse of the sun, invisible at Greenwich.
17	Fr	2	(17.) Telegraph to Shanghai opened 1871.
18	Sa	3	2nd Sunday after Easter.
19	S	4	
20	M	5	
21	Tu	6	
22	W	7	Termination of East Indn. Co.'s monopoly in China 1834.
23	Th	8	St. George's Day.
24	Fr	9	M. M. Str. "Ava" arrived.
25	Sa	10	St. Mark. Coolie Kwok Asing discharged by Chief Justice Smale 1871. Emperor of China, Tungo-chi, born 1857.
26	S	11	(26.) 3rd Sunday after Easter.
27	M	12	(27.) P. & O. Str. "Cathay" arrived.
28	Tu	13	
29	W	14	
30	Th	15	

CHINESE.

(15.) Fête-day of Lau-tsze, founder of Tauism, B.C. 604 and of Yoh-fi, a deified minister of the Sung dynasty. Anniversary of Shakyamuni Buddha's entrance into Nirwana, B C 543.

(16.) Venus enters Cancer between 11-1 p.m.

(18.) Solar term "Clear and bright." Sun in Aquarius. Tsing ming festival. Worship on the tombs.

(19.) Birthday of Kwanyin, the Buddhist goddess of mercy (Avalokiteshwara). Birthday of a goddess of the sea.

(20.) Birthday of Samanta-bhadra, the patron of the popular Buddhist sect called Lotus-school.

(22.) Mercury enters Scorpio between 9-1 a.m. Day of ill luck.

(25.) Birthday of Hiuen-tien-shin-fu, a Tauist deity, father of the god of the sombre heavens.

(26.) Anniversary of the death of an Empress.

(1.) Third Moon. Birthday of the judge of the second court in hell. Moon enters Capricorn between 9-1 a.m.

(3.) Birthday of Hiuen-tien-shang-ti or Peh-ti, supreme ruler of the sombre heavens, god of the North pole, a Tauist worthy deified by the Ming dynasty. The spirit of the earth exercises great influence.

(5.) Solar term "grain rain." Sun enters Capricorn between 1-3 p.m.

(6.) Birthday of Chang, a Tauist worthy.

(8.) Birthday of the judge of the sixth court in hell.

(10.) Birthday of a tutelary spirit of the ground.

(11.) Anniversary of the death of an Empress.

(12-15.) On or about the 14th of this moon is held the agricultural festival, when the Emperor ploughs a few furrows.

(13.) Birthday of some of the tutelar spirits of the ground.

(16.) Birthday of I-king tai-ti, a deified physician, and of Hiuentan, god of the sombre ail t, controller of disease, both worshipped by Tauists.

MAY.—3rd and 4th Moons.

PHASES OF THE MOON.

	d.	h.	m.	s.			d.	h.	m.	s.
FULL MOON	1st	11	45	02 P.M.	NEW MOON	16th	5	53	14 A.M.	FULL MOON	31st	2	22	50 P.M.
LAST QUARTER	9th	2	48	56 P.M.	FIRST QUARTER	23rd	10	55	20 A.M.	PERIGEE	14th	2 P.M.
										APOGEE	26th	8 P.M.

Notable Chronological Events.

Days of Month.	Days of Week.	Days of Moon.	ENGLISH.	CHINESE.
1	Fr	16	St. Philip and St. James.	(16.) Eclipse of the Moon (45 minutes and 6 seconds after midnight). Birthday of C'undee or Marichi, the Buddhist Durga.
2	Sa	17		(17.) Day of ill luck.
3	S	18	4th Sunday after Easter.	(18.) Birthday of Han-ti, goddess of the earth, worshipped behind the graves, and of Chung-yoh, god of the central mountain. Also birthday of one of the Tauist San Mau.
4	M	19		
5	Tu	20		(20.) Mercury enters Libra between 11-1 p.m. Birthday of Ta-tye-sun a Tauist goddess of progeny. Saturn enters Sagittarius between 5-7 a.m. (21.) Solar term "summer sets in." Sun in Capricorn. (28.) Birthday of H. I. M. the Emperor of China. of sailors. Also birthday of Tien-hau, a Tauist goddess
6	W	21	"Dolores Ugarte" burnt at sea, with 600 coolies, 1871. P. M.
7	Th	22	Hongkong Mint opened 1866. [S. S. "Alaska" arrived.
8	Fr	23	Half Quarter Day. British ship "Dunmail" wrecked entering
9	Sa	24	Hongkong Harbour with valuable cargo, 1870. M. M. str.
10	S	25	Rogation Sunday. ["Iraondaddy" arrived.
11	M	26		(26.) Birthday of Tsa-mun, the goddess of progeny.
12	Tu	27	P. & O. str. "Travancore" arrived.	(27.) Birthday of the judge of the seventh court in hell, also of Cha-ta-yoen-shuai, a god protecting money and valuables. Birthday of the six Evil Spirits of heaven, earth, the year, the month, the day and the hour. (28.) Birthday of Tsang-hieh, one of the inventors of the written character, and of Tung-yoh, the god of the eastern mountain, a Tauist divinity.
13	W	28	Old May Day.
14	Th	29	Ascension Day.
15	Fr	30	
16	Sa	1		(1.) Fourth Moon. Birthday of the judge of the eighth court in hell, and of Siau-pa-sien, a statesman of the Sung dynasty.
17	S	2	Sunday after Ascension.
18	M	3	M. M. str. "Peiho" arrived.
19	Tu	4		(2.) The Moon enters Sagittarius between 9-11 a.m. Mars enters Taurus at the same time. (4.) Birthday of Manôjushri, a fictitious Bôdhisattva, disciple of Shakyamuni. [p.m.
20	W	5	
21	Th	6	P. M. str. "China" arrived.
22	Fr	7	
23	Sa	8		(6.) Solar term "little full." Sun enters Sagittarius between 1-3 (8.) Day of conception of Shakyamuni Buddha. Gathering of the herb Yuen-se, used for charms against disease. Birthday of San-kai, god of the three worlds, chiefly worshipped at Fat-shan. Birthday of the judge of the ninth court in hell.
24	S	9	Whit Sunday. Ember Week. Queen Victoria born 1819.
25	M	10	Seamen's Hospital opened 1866.
26	Tu	11	
27	W	12	Ember Day. P. & O. str. "Mauslia" arrived.
28	Th	13	
29	Fr	14	Ember Day.	(10.) Birthday of Lü-sien, a deified Tauist physician. Mercury enters Virgo between 1-3 a.m. (16.) Birthday of Chung-li-sien, one of the eight genii worshipped by Tauists.
30	Sa	15	Ember Day.
31	S	16	Trinity Sunday. Hongkong Volunteers disbanded 1866. Str. "Drummond Castle" wrecked on Chusan Group, 1873.

JUNE.—4th and 5th Moons.

PHASES OF THE MOON.

	d.	h.	m.	s.			d.	h.	m.	s.
LAST QUARTER,	7th	8	54	32 P.M.		FULL MOON,	30th	2	24	26 A.M.
NEW MOON,	14th	2	28	50 P.M.		PERIGEE,	11th	10 A.M.		
FIRST QUARTER,	22nd	3	57	26 A.M.		APOGEE,	23rd	8 A.M.		

Notable Chronological Events.

Days of Month	Days of Week	Days of Moon	ENGLISH.	CHINESE.
1	M	17		(17.) Anniversary of the death of an Empress. Birthday of Kin-hwa the Cantonese goddess of parturition. Birthday of the judge of the tenth court in hell.
2	Tu	18	Hongkong connected with London by telegraph 1871.	
3	W	19	P. M. S. S. "Colombo" arrived. M. M. str. "Meikong" arrived.	
4	Th	20	Corpus Christi.	(19.) Birthday of Wa-to, deified physician, and of Tan-mi, the star god of malaria, both worshipped by Tauists.
5	Fr	21		(20.) Birthday of Yen-kwang, the holy mother of bright eyes, a Tauist goddess, worshipped by the blind. Day of ill luck.
6	Sa	22		
7	S	23	1st Sunday after Trinity.	(22.) Solar term "grain spiked." Sun in Sagittarius. Heaven grants absolution for sins committed. (28.) Birthday of Semintabadra, a fabulous Boddhistic Bodhisattva.
8	M	24		
9	Tu	25	P. & O. str. "Bokhara" arrived.	
10	W	26		
11	Th	27	St. Barnabas. Admiral Rogers' expedition to the Korea concluded 1871.	(28.) Birthday of Chung-chan a deified warrior of the Han dynasty. (28.) Day of ill luck. Birthday of Bodhisattva Yoh-wang, called Bhaichadyn radja, the Æsculapius of China.
12	Fr	28	Treaty between Russia and China signed 1858.	
13	Sa	29		
14	S	1	2nd Sunday after Trinity.	(29.) Anniversary of the death of an Empress.
15	M	2	Hope Dock, Aberdeen, opened 1867.	(1.) Fifth Moon. Birthday of Nan-kih, the ruler of the Southpole, a Tauist deity. Mars enters Aries between 11-1 a.m.
16	Tu	3	M. M. str. "Sindh" arrived.	
17	W	4	(18.) Treaty between U. S. and China signed 1858.	(3.) Moon enters Scorpio between 3-5 a.m. Death of an Empress.
18	Th	5	(20.) Accession. Queen Victoria succeeded the throne 1837.	(5.) The dragon boat festival. Noisy boat races and processions intended to terrify evil spirits and to ward off disease. Tradesmen clear off their accounts. Day of ill luck!
19	Fr	6	P. M. S. S. "Japan" arrived.—P. & O. str. "Bokhara" beached on Kowloong to save her, 1873. [igners at Tientsin 1870.	
20	Sa	7	3rd Sunday after Trinity. Proclamation. Massacre of fore-	
21	S	8	Canton blockaded by British 1840. P. & O. str. "Pekin" arr.	(8.) Birthday of one of the dragon spirits of the grounds. Solar term "summer solstice." Sun enters Scorpio between 11-1 a.m.
22	M	9	(24.) St. John Baptist. Midsummer Day. Admiral Hope repulsed at the entrance to the Peiho 1859.	(10.) Birthday of one of the dragon spirits of the ground. Venus enters Leo between 11-1 a.m. (11.) Day of ill luck. Birthday of the tutelary deity of every walled town.
23	Tu	10		
24	W	11	Taiping Wong beheaded 1864.	
25	Th	12	Treaty between Great Britain and China signed 1858.	(12.) Birthday of Ping-ling, a statesman of the Chow dynasty. (13.) Birthday of Kwan-ti, the national god of war, and of Kwan-ping his son, both deified warriors of the Three Kingdoms.
26	Fr	13	Treaty between France and China signed 1858	
27	Sa	14	4th Sunday after Trinity. Coronation.	
28	S	15	St. Peter. Emperor of China gave audience to representatives of foreign powers, 1873	(16.) Conjunction of heaven and earth. Day of general abstinence, fasting and repentance. Festival of Shakyamuni Buddha, the founder of Buddhism, and of Chang-tien-sze, the ruling head of the Tauist church.
29	M	16		
30	Tu	17		

JULY.—5th and 6th Moons.

PHASES OF THE MOON.

	d.	h.	m.	s.			d.	h.	m.	s.
Last Quarter,	7th	1	37	44 A.M.	Full Moon,		29th	12	19	14 P.M.
New Moon,	14th	00	04	26 A.M.	Perigee,		7th		1 P.M.
First Quarter,	21st	9	08	20 P.M.	Apogee,		21st		2 A.M

Notable Chronological Events.

Days of Month.	Days of Week.	Days of Moon.		
1	W	18		*ENGLISH.*
2	Th	19		Hakodadi, Kanagawa, and Nagasaki opened to trade, 1859.
3	Fr	20		
4	Sa	21		Declaration of U. S. Independence.
5	S	22		5th Sunday after Trinity.
6	M	23		Old Midsummer Day. P. & O. str. "Mirzapore" arrived.
7	Tu	24		
8	W	25		Perry's Squadron arrived at Japan 1853.
9	Th	26		P. M. S. S. "Quang-se" arrived.
10	Fr	27		
11	Sa	28		Treaty of Yeddo ratified 1859.
12	S	29		6th Sunday after Trinity. First English ship arrived in China 1635. Foreign Inspectorate of Customs established in Shanghai 1854.
13	M	30		M. M. str. "Hooghly" arrived.
14	Tu	1		St. Swithin. King of Cambodia arrived in Hongkong on a visit 1872. Simonoseki forts bombarded by a combined French, English and American squadron 1863.
15	W	2		
16	Th	3		
17	Fr	4		
18	Sa	5		(16.) British trade with China renewed 1842.
19	S	6		(18.) P. M. S. S. "Great Republic" arrived.
20	M	7		(19.) 7th Sunday after Trinity. Nankin captured by the Imperialists 1863.
21	Tu	8		(20.) P. & O. str. "Lombardy" arrived.
22	W	9		Str. "Esmeralda" lost on Fraile rocks.
23	Th	10		
24	Fr	11		St. James.
25	Sa	12		
26	S	13		8th Sunday after Trinity.
27	M	14		Canton opened to British 1849.
28	Tu	15		
29	W	16		Treaty between U. S. and Japan signed 1858
30	Th	17		M. M. str. "Tigre" arrived.
31	Fr	18		

CHINESE.

(18.) Birthday of Si-wang-mu, the royal mother of the West, a fabulous Taoist deity.
(19.) Birthday of Ma-tan-yang, a Taoist saint. A fast day among Taoists.
(23.) Anniversary of the death of an Empress.
(24.) A solar term "little heat." Sun in Scorpio. Birthday of Mayuraradja, a fictitious Buddha, invoked by exorcists and sorcerers.
(29.) Birthday of Hü-wei-hin, a statesman of the Tang dynasty.

(1.) *Sixth Moon.* Venus enters Cancer between 1-3 p.m.
(2.) The Moon enters Libra between 11-1 p.m.
(3.) Mars enters Pisces between 1-3 p.m. Birthday of the Bodhisattva Vida, the patron of all monasteries and nunneries, a Buddhistic divinity, adopted also by Taoists.
(6.) A day of ill luck. Birthday of Yang-si, a deified warrior, and of Tai-shan, the god of the great mountain in Shantung. Also birthday of Tsui-pan, an officer in the supreme court of hell. Festival of airing clothes.
(8.) The earth spirit reigns.
(10.) A solar term "great heat." Sun enters Libra between 9-11 a.m. Birthday of Liu-hai-sien, a Taoist worthy.
(12.) Birthday of Lung-wang, the dragon spirit of walls, fountains and mountain ridges, a Taoist divinity.
(13.) Birthday of Lu-pan, the god of carpenters and masons.
(15.) A day of ill luck.
(16.) Birthday of Wang-ing-kwan-shing, a deified statesman.

AUGUST.—6th and 7th Moons.

PHASES OF THE MOON.

	d.	h.	m.	s.			d.	h.	m.	s.
Last Quarter,	5th	6	23	0½ A.M.	First Quarter,	20th	2	29	26 P.M.	Perigee, 2nd 4 A.M.
New Moon,	12th	11	36	08 A.M.	Full Moon,	27th	9	05	02 P.M.	Apogee, 17th 9 P.M.
										Perigee, 29th 8 P.M.

Notable Chronological Events.

Days of Month	Days of Week	Days of Moon	ENGLISH.	CHINESE.
1	Sa	19	*Lammas Day.* Pier & Godown Co. ceased working, 1873.	(19.) Anniversary of Kwan-yin, attaining to the state of Bodhisattva. (23) Birthday of the god of horses, a Taouist deity. Heaven grants pardon for sins.
2	S	20	9th *Sunday after Trinity.* P. & O. str. "Geelong" arrived. Treaty between Portugal and Japan signed 1860.	(24.) Birthday of Fo-shin, the spirits of fire: of Wang-ling-kwan, a deified statesman; of Lui-tau, the father of thunder worshipped by Taouists; and of three Taouist genii called Hwo-chang-lin. Death of Kwan-ti, the god of war.
3	M	21		
4	Tu	22		(25) Solar term "autumn sets in." Sun in Libra. Birthday of the god of dogs.
5	W	23		
6	Th	24	P. M. Chartered S. S. "Magregor" arrived.	(29.) *Seventh Moon.* Anniversary of the death of Lau-tsze, the founder of Taouism.
7	Fr	25		(1-15.) All Souls Festival, lasting until the 15th of this moon, during which time Taouist and Buddhist priests are engaged reading masses, burning paper clothes and scattering food—all for the benefit of the dead. (2.) Moon enters Virgo between 7-9 a.m. Mars enters Aquarius between 3-5 a.m.
8	Sa	26		
9	S	27	10th *Sunday after Trinity.*	
10	M	28		
11	Tu	29	*Half Quarter Day.* [misfired.	(7.) The female genii: at the Pleiades descend. Birthday of the god and goddess of the bedstead, and of Kwai-sin, the star god of literature, both worshipped by Taouists.
12	W	1	(13.) Macao ceded to the Portuguese 1862; but concession not	
13	Th	2	(15.) Kagosima burnt by Admiral Kuper in the "Euryalus" 1863. M. M. str. "Amazone" arrived. [Siam signed 1866.	(8.) Heaven grants pardon for sins committed.
14	Fr	3	(16.) 11th *Sunday after Trinity.* Treaty between France and	(9.) Death of an Empress. (10.) Death of an Empress.
15	Sa	4	(18.) Treaty between the Netherlands and Japan signed 1858.	(12.) Solar term "cessation of heat." Sun enters Virgo between 3-5 p.m. (13.) Birthday of Tat-chang-chun, a Taouist saint, and of Mahasthama, one of the three Buddhistic sages of the West. (14.) A day of ill luck.
16	S	5	P. M. S. S. "China" arrived.	
17	M	6	(20.) Takn Forts taken by allied forces 1860.	
18	Tu	7	(21.) Governor Amaral murdered at Macao 1849. Treaty between Japan and Peru concluded, 1873.	
19	W	8		
20	Th	9	(22.) P. & O. str. "Malwa" arrived. (race proclaimed, 1873.	(15.) Birthday of Chung yen, the ruler of departed spirits, a Taouist deity, and of Maudgalyayana (Lo-puh), a Buddhist saint who went to hell to release his mother. Also birthday of Chang-po, a Taouist saint. (18.) Birthday of Sam-kwai, a Taouist deity. (19.) Birthday of Tai-sui, the gods of the cycle of 60 years, worshipped by Taouists.
21	Fr	10	(23.) 12th *Sunday after Trinity.* Chinese Emigration Ordinance	
22	Sa	11	(24.) St. Bartholomew. P. M. Str. "America" destroyed by fire in Yokohama Bay 1872. Macao coolie ships ordered to leave Hongkong Harbour, 1873.	
23	S	12		
24	M	13		
25	Tu	14		
26	W	15	(25.) Treaty between Great Britain and Japan signed 1868.	
27	Th	16	(26.) First Number of *China Review* published 1872.	
28	Fr	17	(27.) Road steamer successfully tried at Tientsin 1872. M. M. str. "Ava" arrived.	
29	Sa	18	(29.) First Chinese war with Great Britain ended by signing Treaty of Nanking 1842. Foochow opened to trade 1842.	
30	S	19	(30.) 13th *Sunday after Trinity.*	
31	M	20		

SEPTEMBER.—7th and 8th Moons.

PHASES OF THE MOON.

	d.	h.	m.	s.		d.	h.	m.	s.
Last Quarter,	3rd	0	30	33 P.M.	Full Moon,	26th	5	42	56 A.M.
New Moon,	11th	1	47	02 A.M.	Apogee,	14th	2	P.M.	
First Quarter,	19th	6	41	34 A.M.	Perigee,	27th	2	A.M.	

Notable Chronological Events.

Days of Month.	Days of Week.	Days of Moon.	ENGLISH.
1	Tu	21	
2	W	22	(2-3.) Severe Typhoon at H'kong, great loss to shipping, 1871.
3	Th	23	
4	Fr	24	P. M. S. S. "Colorado" arrived.
5	Sa	25	
6	S	26	14th Sunday after Trinity.
7	M	27	Prince Napolo's Batteries destroyed by an English, French, and Dutch fleet, 1864.
8	Tu	28	(8.) Shanghai taken by the Taipings 1853. M. M. Str. "Imomaddy" arrived.
9	W	29	
10	Th	30	[Aleria, 1872.
11	Fr	1	"Bredama" arrived in Hongkong, with Russian Grand Duke
12	Sa	2	15th Sunday after Trinity. Ember Week.
13	S	3	
14	M	4	Mr Richardson murdered by Satsuma's retainers, 1862.
15	Tu	5	Lord Macartney's Embassy arrived at Peking 1793. P. & O. Str. "Gwalior" arrived.
16	W	6	
17	Th	7	(16.) Ember Day. P. M. S. S. "Quang Se" arrived.
18	Fr	8	Ember Day.
19	Sa	9	Ember Day.
20	S	10	16th Sunday after Trinity.
21	M	11	St. Matthew. Chapel at Fatshan burned, native Christians maltreated 1870.
22	Tu	12	Autumnal Equinox.
23	W	13	
24	Th	14	
25	Fr	15	
26	Sa	16	Typhoon at Hongkong, great destruction of native craft and loss [of life 1870.
27	S	17	17th Sunday after Trinity.
28	M	18	P. & O. Str. "Sunda" arrived.
29	Tu	19	St. Michael.
30	W	20	

CHINESE.

(21.) Fête day of Pa-or', a deified Buddhist priest. (22.) Birthday of Ts'oi̯ Iu-tsai-shin, the Taoist god of wealth, the patron of trade. (24.) Festival of Shang-hwang, the tutelary deity of walled cities. Birthday of Ching-sien, a Taoist worthy; and of Negardjuna, the greatest philosopher and patriarch of the Buddhist church (A.D. 150). (25.) Death of Emperor Kia-king, A.D. 1821. (30.) Birthday of Ti-tang-wang, a Buddhist saint invoked on behalf of the dead. (1.) *Eighth Moon*. Beginning of the autumn festivities. Interchange of presents of moon cakes. (2.) Birth of She-toh-tai-wang, the prince of the agricultural deities; also of Hii-sun, a deified Taoist physician; and kin-kiah, the spirit of the golden armour, a god worshipped by the literati. (3.) Birthday of Tsau-kiun, the domestic god of the hearth; also descent of the gods of the northern bushel, worshipped by Taoists. Moon enters Leo between 1-3 a.m. Mercury enters Gemini at the same time. (5.) Birthday of Lui-shing, the Taoist god of thunder. (9.) Death of Emperor Tai-tsung-wen, A.D. 1644. [mountain. (10.) Birthday of Peh-yoh, the Taoist god of the northern (11.) Death of Emperor Tai-tsu-kao, A.D. 1627. (13.) Birthday of one of the dragon spirits of the ground. A solar term "the autumnal equinox." Sun enters Leo between 1-3 p.m. (15.) Mid-autumn festival, also feast of lanterns. Birthday of the regent of the moon. Oblations to the moon. Theatricals. Exchange of prsents of moon cakes. (16.) Birthday of Ta-tien, the monkey god, the Chinese Hanu-man, worshipped especially in Fatshan. Birthday of Chu-yuen-shui, a Taoist worthy. (18.) The autumnal sacrifice. (19.) Anniversary of Chundee (Durga) attaining to the state of Bôdhisattva.

OCTOBER.—8th and 9th Moons.

PHASES OF THE MOON.

	d.	h.	m.			d.	h.	m.
Last Quarter,	2nd	9	14	44 P.M.	Full Moon,	25th	9	57	20 P.M.
New Moon,	10th	6	38	08 P.M.	Apogee,	11th	10	P.M.
First Quarter,	18th	9	06	56 P.M.	Perigee,	25th	2	P.M.

Notable Chronological Events.

Days of Month.	Days of Week.	Days of Moon.	ENGLISH.	CHINESE.
1	Th	21	First battle of the Taiping Rebellion 1850. P. M. SS. "Japan" arrived.	(21.) A day of ill luck. (23.) Birthday of a fictitious Buddha called Dipankara. Anniversary of the death of an Empress.
2	Fr	22	*18th Sunday after Trinity.*	(24.) Tao-yue, a Tauist worthy, the inventor of pottery. (25.) Birthday of the regent of the sun. Sick people worship the sun by prostrations towards the East.
3	Sa	23	Cyclone at Calcutta 1864.	(27.) Anniversary of the death of Confucius, B.C. 478 [Note. The correct date is the 11th day of the 4th moon.]
4	S	24	Manila taken by British 1762. Looting of Summer Palace. ("Peiho" arrived.) Pekin 1860.	(28.) A solar term "cold dew." Sun in Leo.
5	M	25	Seizure of Lorcha "Arrow" by Chinese 1856. M. M. Str.	(1.) *Ninth Moon.* Mercury enters Taurus between 11-1 a.m. The spirits of the southern bushel descend. (1-9.) The spirits of the northern bushel descend. (1-30.) On a fortunate day of this moon the Empress with all the princesses worship the discoverer of "ho silkworm. (2.) Moon enters Cancer between 11-½ a.m. (3.) Birthday of a deified Tauist priest Wu-
6	Tu	26	Treaty between France and Japan signed 1858.	
7	W	27	Commercial Treaty concluded between China and Spain 1864.	
8	Th	28	Stamp Ordinance introduced 1867.	
9	Fr	29		
10	S	1		[wen.]
11	M	2	(11.) *18th Sunday after Trinity. Old Michaelmas Day.*	Mars enters Capricorn between 7-9 p.m.
12	Tu	3	(12.) Pekin taken by the allied forces 1860.	(9.) Birthday of a deified Tauist sun, a supposed incarnation of Chundoe (Dutze). Birthday of Chun juang, a Tauist patriarch; and of Fung-tu, an officer in hell. Anniversary of the ascension of Kwan-ti (god of war). Heaven grants pardon for sins committed. Visits to the tombs. Children fly kites.
13	W	4	(13.) Ningpo taken by British 1841. Mikado opened Yokohama and Yeddo railway 1872. (14.) P. & O. Str. "Orissa" arrived.	
14	Th	5	Emperor of China married 1872.	
15	Fr	6	St. John's Cathedral, Hongkong, dedicated 1849. P. M. SS. "Great Republic" arrived.	(11.) The earth spirit puts forth his energy. Birthday of Yuen-hwuy, the favourite disciple of Confucius, canonised A.D. 1630.
16	Sa	7		
17	S	8	(18.) *20th Sunday after Trinity. St Luke.*	(14.) A solar term "frost descends." Sun enters Cancer between 9-11 p.m. A day of ill luck. (15.) Birthday of Heituen lan, the Tauist god of the sombre ether, a controller of leprosy and pestilence. Birthday of Chuo-hi the father of modern philosophy A.D. 1131. (16.) Birthday of the spirit of the loom. (17.) Birthday of the golden dragon king, a Tauist deity of the ground ; and of Chao-wei, a Tauist god of wealth. Also birthday of Koh-kung, a deified Tauist physician and alchymist. (18.) Birthday of Tsui-shing one of the inventors of the written character, worshipped by Confucianists.
18	M	9	Canton evacuated by the allied forces 1861. Telegraphic line to Australia opened 1872. (23.) M. M. Str. "Meikong" arrived.	
19	Tu	10		
20	W	11		
21	Th	12		
22	Fr	13		
23	Sa	14	(24.) Kowloong ceded to Great Britain by Treaty of 1860.	
24	S	15	(25.) *21st Sunday after Trinity.* Ratification of Treaty between France and China 1860.	
25	M	16		
26	Tu	17	(27.) Sir M. Seymour opened fire on Canton 1856. The Tartar General of Canton vanied H.K., 1871. P. M. SS. "Ariel" wrecked near Yokohama, 1873.	
27	W	18		
28	Th	19	(28.) *Sts. Simon and Jude.* Inluam taken possession of by Great Britain 1848.	
29	Fr	20		
30	Sa	21		
31	S	22	(30.) About 200 houses burnt in H.K. 1866. (31.) Duke of Edinburgh arr. in H.K. 1869. P. & O. Str. "Zambesi" arr.	

NOVEMBER.—9th and 10th Moons.

PHASES OF THE MOON.

	d.	h.	m.	s.			d.	h.	m.	s.	
Last Quarter,	1st	9	36	20	A.M.	Full Moon,	24th	1	10	32	A.M.
New Moon,	9th	1	10	20	P.M.	Apogee,	7th	11	11	P.M.	
First Quarter,	13th	9	30	08	A.M.	Perigee,	23rd		2	A.M.	

Notable Chronological Events.

Days of Month.	Days of Week.	Days of Moon.	ENGLISH.	CHINESE.
1	S.	23	22nd Sunday after Trinity. All Saints Day.	(28.) Sa-ching-yin, a deified Taoist worthy.
2	M.	24	All Souls Day.	
3	Tu.	25	Great Britain commenced war with China by the naval action of	(26.) A day of ill luck.
4	W.	26	P. M. SS. "Alaska" arrived. [Chumphee 1839.	(28.) Birthday of Hwa-kwang, the Taoist god of fire; and of Ma-yen-shwai, a general of the god of the North Pole. Anniversary of the death of an Empress.
5	Th.	27	Pekin evacuated by allied powers 1860.	(29.) A solar term "winter sets in." Sun in Cancer.
6	Fr.	28	M. M. Str. "Sindh" arrived.	
7	Sa.	29		
8	S.	30	23rd Sunday after Trinity.	(30.) Tenth Moon. The Moon enters Gemini between 7-9 a.m. Mercury enters Aries between 3-5 a.m. Birthday of the ruler of the fire mountains. Descent of the nine Taoist gods of the great bear. Litanies for the dead.
9	M.	1	Prince of Wales born 1841.	(1.)
10	Tu.	2		(2.) Birthday of Chau, one of the attendants of the god of war, a Taoist deity.
11	W.	3	St. Martin. Half Quarter Day.	(3.) Birthday of San Men, three brothers, worshipped by Taoists. Mars enters Sagittarius between 11-1 a.m.
12	Th.	4	P. & O. Str. "Travancore" arrived.	
13	Fr.	5		(5.) Anniversary of the death of the first Chinese Patriarch Bodhidharma, a Hindoo who died in Canton A.D. 529.
14	Sa.	6		(6.) Birthday of the inferior spirits of all the heavens, worshipped by Taoists.
15	S.	7	24th Sunday after Trinity. [later" 1869.	(14.) A solar term "little snow." Sun enters Gemini between 7-9 p.m.
16	M.	8	H. R. H. the Duke of Edinburgh left Hongkong in the "Ga-	(15.) Birthday of Ha-yen, the Taoist ruler of the waters; of Tan-shin, the Taoist god of small pox; and of Wan-yen-shwai, a general of the god of the North-pole, worshipped by Taoists.
17	Tu.	9	Shanghai open to Foreign Commerce 1843.	
18	W.	10		(16.) Birthday of Wu-alan, the goddess of the bedstead.
19	Th.	11	P. M. SS. "China" arrived.	(17.) A day of ill luck.
20	Fr.	12		(20.) Birthday of Hsü-ching, a deified Taoist alchymist.
21	Sa.	13		
22	S.	14	25th Sunday after Trinity. St. Cecilia.	
23	M.	15		
24	Tu.	16	Snider Rifles first used in action at the capture of Anping, Formosa, by sailors of H.M. o.s. "Algerine" 1868.	
25	W.	17	General Chamber of Commerce formed in Canton 1836. P. & O Str. "Mirzapore" arrived 1872.	
26	Th.	18		
27	Fr.	19		
28	Sa.	20		
29	S.	21	1st Sunday in Advent.	
30	M.	22	St. Andrew's Day. New Boat-house and Gymnasium opened by H.E. the Governor 1872. St. Joseph's Church opened 1872.	

DECEMBER.—10th and 11th Moons.

PHASES OF THE MOON.

	d.	h. m. s.			d. h. m. s.
Last Quarter,	1st	2 05 32 a.m.	First Quarter,	16th	8 0 56 p.m.
New Moon,	9th	7 42 a.m.	Full Moon,	23rd	0 59 56 p.m.

				d. h. m. s.
Last Quarter,				30th 10 12 32 p.m.
Apogee,				5th 9 a.m.
Perigee,				21st 8 a.m.

Notable Chronological Events.

Days of Month.	Days of Week.	Days of Moon.	ENGLISH.
1	Tu	23	St. Francis Xavier died in San Chan 1552.
2	W	24	Seizure of Opium by Chinese authorities at Canton 1838. Hong-kong first lighted by Gas 1864.
3	Th	25	
4	Fr	26	[by Emperor of China 1839.
5	Sa	27	2nd Sunday in Advent. Intercourse with G. Britain prohibited
6	M	28	European Factories at Canton destroyed 1842.
7	Tu	29	
8	W	30	
9	Th	1	
10	Fr	2	Admiral Bell, U. S. Navy, drowned on Osaka Bar 1867.
11	Sa	3	
12	S	4	3rd Sunday in Advent. Ember Week.
13	M	5	Foreign Factories, Canton, burned by natives 1856.
14	Tu	6	
15	W	7	Ember Day.
16	Th	8	Club Lusitano inaugurated 1866.
17	Fr	9	Ember Day. Treaty between Holland and Siam signed 1860.
18	Sa	10	Ember Day.
19	S	11	4th Sunday in Advent.
20	M	12	St. Thomas.
21	Tu	13	
22	W	14	
23	Th	15	
24	Fr	16	Christmas Day.
25	Sa	17	St. Stephen.
26	S	18	1st Sunday after Christmas. St., John's Day.
27	M	19	Innocents. Canton bombarded 1857.
28	Tu	20	
29	W	21	
30	Th	22	
31		23	

CHINESE.

(26.) Birthday of the Supreme ruler of the five mountains, a Taoist deity.

(27.) Birthday of Tzu-wei, the star god of malaria, worshipped by Taoists.

(28.) Mercury enters Aries between 3-5 a.m.

(29.) A solar term "great snow." Sun in Gemini.

(30.) Birthday of Ma-tsien, one of the generals of the god of war.

(1.) *Eleventh Moon.* Moon enters Taurus between 11-1 p.m. Mars enters Scorpio between 9-11 a.m. A day of ill luck.

(4.) Birthday of Confucius, B.C. 550. (*Note.* Corrected date, the 21st day of the 10th moon). Birthday of Yeh-wang, the Supreme God of the Taoist pantheon; and of Si-yoh, the Taoist god of the western mountain.

(11.) Birthday of Ts'i ? b, a Taoist star god, the guardian of all sufferers.

(13.) Anniversary of the death of Emperor K'ang-hi A.D. 1723.

(14.) A solar term "winter solstice." Sun enters Taurus between 7-9 a.m. Officers worship the Emperor's tablet. The people worship the tutelary deities, exchange presents of cakes and settle their accounts.

(17.) Birthday of Amitabha Buddha, the ruler of the western paradise.

(19.) Birthday of a fictitious Bodhisattva called Kin-lin, "the nine Lotus flowers." A Buddhist fast day.

(29.) Birthday of the goddess of parturition.

LIST OF STREETS, ROADS, &c., IN HONGKONG,

with reference to their situations as far as obtainable.

Aberdeen Street, 押巴甸街 *Ap-pa-teen-kai*, (Queen's Road Central to Caine Road)
A Chung's Lane, 亞松巷 *A-chung-hong*, (Lower Lascar Row to Ng Kwa Lane)
Albany Road, 亞彬彌道 *A-pan-ne-to*, (Upper Albert Road to Peak Road)
Albany Street, 亞彬彌街 *A-pan-ne-kai*, (Queen's Road East to Praya East)
Albert Road, 亞厘畢道 *A-le-put-to*, (Wyndham Street to Parade Ground)
Albert Road, Upper, 亞厘畢上道 *A-le-put-sheung-to*, (Albert Road to Caine Road)
Alexandra Terrace, 亞厘山打拉街 *A-li-shan-ta-la-kai*, (Old Bailey to Shelley Street)
Arbuthnot Road, 亞畢諾道 *A-put-nok-to*, (Caine Road to Hollywood Road)
Asow's Lane, 亞秀巷 *Asow-hong*, (Market Street)
Astor Buildings, 同安里 *Tung-on-li*, (Staunton Street to Aberdeen Street)
Battery Path, 畢打厘徑 *Put-ta-lee-king*, (Murray Battery to Queen's Road Central)
Battery Road, 炮台道 *P'au-toi-to*, (Queen's Road West to Pokfulum Road)
Blacksmith's Lane, 打鐵巷 *Ta-tit-hong*, (Jardine's Bazaar)
Bonham Road, 文咸道 *Mun-ham-to*, (Caine Road to Pokfulum Road)
Bonham Strand, 文咸大街 *Mun-ham-tai-kai*, (Queen's Road Central to Bonham Strand West)
Bonham Strand West, 文咸西約 *Mun-ham-sai-yeuk*, (Bonham Strand to Praya West)
Bridge Street, 橋街 *Kiu-kai*, (Leighton Hill Road to Morrison Hill Road)
Bridges' Street, 必列者士街 *Pit-lit-ché-sz-kai*, (Sing Wong Street to Taipingshan Street)
Burd Street, 畢街 *Pat-kai*, (Mercer Street to Cleverley Street)
Burrows Street, 巴魯士街 *Pa-lo-sz-kai*, (Praya East to Wanchai Road)
Caine Road, 堅道 *Keen-to*, (Upper Albert Road to Bonham Road)

LIST OF STREETS, &c.

Canal Street East, 水坑東街 *Shui-hang-tung-kai*, (Garden Street to Praya)
Canal Street West, 水坑西街 *Shui-hang-sai-kai*, (Garden Street to Praya)
Canton Bazaar, 洋貨街 *Yeung-fo-kai*, (Queen's Road East, near H.M. Naval Yard)
Caroline Hill Road, 架老黎山路 *Ka-loo-lai-shan-loo*, (Round Caroline Hill)
Castle Road, 圍城道 *Wai-shing-to*, (Caine Road to Robinson Road West)
Castle Steps, 堆樓階 *Che-lau-kai*, (Seymour Road to Robinson Road)
Centre Street, 正街 *Ching-kai*, (Praya West to Bonham Road)
Chancery Lane, 晝時厘巷 *Chan-shi-le-hong*, (Arbuthnot Road to Old Bailey)
Cheung Hing Street, 長興街 *Cheong-hing-kai*, (Hollywood Road)
Cheung Kang Lane, 長庚里 *Cheung-kang-li* (Queen's Road East)
Cheung Sing Lane, 長勝里 *Cheong-shing-li*, (Caine Road, Taipingshan)
Chung Mau Lane, 松茂里 *Chung-mau-li*, (Praya West)
Chung Sau Lane, 松秀里 *Chung-sow-li*, (Queen's Road West to Praya)
Choong Woh Lane, 中和里 *Chung-wo-li*, (Staunton Street)
Circular Pathway, 弓弦巷 *Kung-yeen-hong*, (Gough Street Steps to Ladder Street)
Cleverley Street, 急庇利街 *Kup-pe-lee-kai*, (Praya Central to Queen's Road Central)
Cochrane Street, 閣麟街 *Kok-lun-kai*, (Queen's Road Central to Gage Street)
Cross Road, 交加道 *Kau-ka-to*, (Wanchai Road to Spring Gardens)
Cross Street, 交加街 *Kau-ka-kai*, (Albany Street to Wanchi Road)
Cross Lane, 交加巷 *Kau-ka-hong*, (Cross Street)
D'Aguilar Street, 德記拉街 *Tak-ke-la-kai*, (Queen's Road Central to Wyndham Street)
Duddell Street, 都爹厘街 *Too-te-li-kai*, (Queen's Road Central, next to Ice House Street)
Davis Lane, 爹庇士巷 *Tay-pih-sih-hong*, (Queen's Road East)
East Street, 太平山東街 *Tai-ping-shan-tung-kai*, (Queen's Road Central to Taipingshan Market)
Elgin Street, 伊裡近街 *Ee-lee-kun-kai*, (Staunton Street to Hollywood Road)
Elgin Terrace, 伊裡近台 *Ee-lee-kun-toi*, (Shelley Street to Caine Road)
Fat Hing Street, 發興街 *Fat-hing-kai*, (Hollywood Road to Queen's Road West)
First Street, 第一街 *Tai-yat-kai*, (New East Street to Pokfulum Road)
Fook Hing Lane, 福興巷 *Fook-hing-hong*, (Jardine's Bazaar)
Fuk On Lane, 福安里 *Fook-on-li*, (Market Street, Taipingshan)
French Street, 佛冷西街 *Fat-lan-sai-kai*, (Battery Road to Praya West)
Fung Un Lane, 逢源里 *Fung-un-li*, (Jardine's Bazaar)
Gage Street, 結志街 *Kit-che-kai*, (Lyndhurst Terrace to Aberdeen Street)
Gap Street, 鋤斷山街 *Cho-tün-shan-kai*, (Hollywood Road to Queen's Road West)

Garden Road, 花園道 *Fa-ün-to*, (Robinson Road to Albert Road)
Gibb's Lane, 闾士巷 *Gib-sz-hong*, (Queen's Road Central to Praya Central)
Gilman Bazaar, 機利文新街 *Kee-lee-mun-sun-kai*, (Queen's Road Central to Praya Central)
Gilman Street, 机利文舊街 *Kee-lee-mun-kau-kai*, (Queen's Road Central to Praya Central)
Gough Street, 歌賦街 *Ko-fu-kai*, (Aberdeen Street to Sing Wong Street)
Graham Street, 嘉咸街 *Ka-ham-kai*, (Queen's Road Central to Staunton Street)
Great George Street, 記列阻治街 *Ke-lit-cho-che-kei*, (Royal Mint Street to Sea Wall)
Gutzlaff Street, 郭士立街 *Kwok-sz-lap-kai*, (Queen's Road Central to Lyndhurst Terrace)
Heard Street, 喝街 *Hot-kai*, (Wanchai Road to Praya East)
Heung Street, 香街 *Heung-kai*, (Queen's Road to Bonham Street)
High Street, 高街 *Ko-kai*, (Bonham Road to Pokfulum Road)
Hill Lane, 山巷 *Shan-hong*, (From Hospital Hill Road)
Hill Road, 山路 *Shan-loo*, (Pokfulum Road to Middle Street)
Hill Street, 山街 *Shan-kai*, (Pokfulum Road to Shek-tong-tsui)
Hillier Street, 禧厘街 *He-le-kai*, (Praya Central to Queen's Road Central)
Hing Lung Street, (Endicott's Lane) 興隆大街 *Hing-lung-tai-kai*, (Praya Central to Queen's Road Central)
Hing Wan Street, 慶雲街 *Hing-wan-kai*, (Nullah Lane)
Hing Yan Lane, 興仁里 *Hing yan-li*, (Upper Station Street)
Hollywood Road, 荷李活道 *Ho-lee-wut-to*, (Pottinger Street to Fat Hing Street)
Hospital Hill Lane, 醫館山巷 *I-koon-shan-hong*, (Queen's Road West)
Hospital Road, 醫館道 *I-koon-to*, (Bonham Road to New East Street, Saiyingpoon)
How Fung Lane, 厚豐里 *How-fung-li*, (Ship Street)
Ice House Street, 冰厰街 *Ping-chong-kai*, (Praya Central to Albert Road)
Jardine's Bazaar, 渣甸墟 *Cha-teen-hü*, (Praya East to Sowkewan Road)
Jervois Street, 乍畏街 *Chu-wei-kai*, (Queen's Road Central to Morrison Street)
José's Lane, East, 佐士東巷 *Cho-sz-tung-hong*, (Ladder Street)
José's Lane, West, 佐士西巷 *Cho-sz-sai-hong*, (Tank Lane)
Kat On Street, 吉安街 *Kat-on-kai*, (From Nullah Lane)
Kai Ming Lane, 啟明里 *Kai-ming-li*, (Queen's Road East, opposite Naval Yard)
Kai Ün Lane, 溪源里 *Kai-un-li*, (Peel Street)
King Sing Street, 景星街 *King-sing-kai*, (Nullah Lane)
King Street, 王街 *Wong-kai*, (Pennington Street to Nullah)

King William Street, 威林王街 *Wai-lum-wong-kai*, (Pennington Street to Sea Wall, East Point)
Kin Sow Court, 乾秀里 *Kin-sow-li*, (Gage Street)
Kin Un Lane, 乾源里 *Kin-un-li*, (Praya East)
Koo Kee Alley, 高基 *Koo-ki*, (Stanley Street)
Kom-Ü-Lane, 甘雨街 *Kom-ü-kai*, (Queen's Road West)
Kwai Wa Lane, 貫華里 *Kwai-wa-li*, (Hillier to Cleverley Streets)
Kwong Fook Lane, 廣福里 *Kwong-fook-li*, (Upper Station Street to Lower Caine Road)
Kwong Fung Lane, 廣豐里 *Kwong-fung-li*, (Battery Road)
Kung Shan Lane, 拱辰里 *Kung-shan-li*, (First Street)
Kwong Yün Street, East, 廣源東街 *Kwong-ün-tung-kai*, (Bonham Strand to Wing Lok Street)
Kwong Yün Street, West, 廣源西街 *Kwong-ün-sai-kai*, (Bonham Strand to Wing Lok Street)
Ladder Street, 樓梯街 *Lau-tai-kai*, (Queen's Road Central to Bonham Road)
Lamont Lane, 黎文巷 *Lai-mun-hong*, (Jardine's Bazaar)
Lan Kwei Fong, 蘭桂坊 *Lan-kwai-fong*, (D'Aguilar Street)
Lascar Row, Upper, 摩羅上徑 *Mo-lo-sheung-king*, (Ladder Street to West Street)
Lascar Row, Lower, 摩羅下徑 *Mo-lo-ha-king*, (Ladder Street to Fat Hing St.)
Lau Yü Lane, 留餘里 *Lau-ü-li*, (High Street)
Leighton Hill Road, 禮頓山路 *Lai-tun-shan-lo*, (Round the Leighton Hill)
Lung On Street, 隆安街 *Lung-on-kai*, (Nullah Lane)
Leung Wa Tai Lane, 梁華帝里 *Leung-wa-tai-li*, (Queen's Road West)
Lyall's Lane, 禮義里 *Lai-yih-li*, (Queen's Road East, Praya East)
Lyndhurst Terrace, 麟檄士街 *Lun-hut-sz-kai*, (Wellington Street to Hollywood Road)
Mang Ming Lane, 孟明里 *Mang-ming-li*, (Queen's Road East)
Man Wa Lane, 文華里 *Man-wa-li*, (Bonham Strand to Praya Central)
Market Street, 街市街 *Kai-shi-kai*, (Ladder Street to Po-yan Street)
Matheson Street, 勿地臣街 *Ma-tee-sun-kai*, (Perceval Street to Show-ke-wan Road)
Mercer Street, 孖沙街 *Ma-sha-kai*, (Queen's Road Central to Bonham Strand)
Middle Street, 中街 *Chung-kai*, (Battery Hill to Shek-tong-tsui)
Ming Tak Lane, 明德里 *Ming-tak-li*, (Market Street)
Morrison Hill Road, 馬禮信山路 *Ma-li-sun-shan-loo*, (from Observation Place to the Wanchai Gap)
Morrison Street, 馬裡信街 *Ma-li-sun-kai*, (Bonham Strand to Queen's Road Central)

LIST OF STREETS, &c.   v

Mosque Junction, 摩羅廟交街 *Mo-lo-miu-kau-kai*, (Robinson Road to Shelley Street)
Mosque Street, 摩羅廟街 *Mo-lo-miu-kai*, (Robinson Road to Peel Street)
Mosque Terrace, 摩羅廟臺 *Mo-lo-miu-t'oi*, (Caine Road)
New East Street, 新東街 *Sun-tung-kai*, (Praya West to Bonham Road)
Ng Kwai Lane, 五桂坊 *Ng-kwai-fong* (From Upper to Lower Hollywood Road)
Nullah Lane, 石水渠街 *Shek-shui-kü-kai*, (Wanchai Temple to Praya)
Old Bailey, 澳老俾厘街 *O-lo-pai-lee-kai*, (Hollywood Road to Caine Road)
On Ning Lane, 安寧里 *On-ning-li*, (Battery Road)
On Woh Lane, 安和里 *On-woh-li*, (Queen's Road Central to Gough Street)
Pan Kwai Lane, 攀桂里 *Pan-kwai-li*, (Woh Fung Street)
Park Lane, 花園巷 *Fa-ün-hong*, (Square Street to Caine Road)
Parker Street, 伯架街 *Pak-ka-kai*, (Hollywood Road to Taipingshan Street)
Pechili Terrace, 必之厘台 *Pit-chi-li-t'oi*, (Peel Street to Shelley Street)
Pedder's Hill, 双旗山 *Sheung-ke-shan*, (Ice House Street)
Pedder's Street, 別打馬頭 *Pit-ta-ma-tou*, (Praya Central to Queen's Road Central)
Peel Street, 卑梨街 *Pi-li-kai*, (Queen's Road Central to Robinson Road)
Pennington Street, 邊寧頓街 *Pin-ning-tun-kai*, (Mint to Sow-ke-wan Road)
Perceval Street, 巴思華街 *Pa-sz-wa-kai*, (Sow-ke-wan Road to Praya East)
Pokfulum Road, 朴湖林道 *Pok-foo-lum-to*, (Queen's Road West to Pokfulum)
Pond Street, 潘街 *Poon-kai*, (Wanchai, Queen's Road East to Tung On Street)
Pottinger Street, 砵典乍街 *Put-tin-cha-kui*, (Praya Central to Hollywood Road)
Pound Lane, 旁巷 *Pong-hong*, (Hollywood Road to Rutter Lane)
Po Yan Street, 普仁街 *Po-yan-kai*, (from Gap Street)
Praya Central, 海旁中約 *Hoi-pong-chung-yeuk*, (Wardley Street to Harbor Master's Office)
Praya East, 海旁東約 *Hoi-pong-tung-yeuk*, (Eastern Market to East Point)
Praya West, 海旁西約 *Hoi-pong-sai-yeuk*, (Harbor Master's Office to Shek-tong-tsui)
Queen's Road Central, 皇后大道中約 *Wong-hau-tai-to-chung-yeuk*, (Parade Ground to West end of Hollywood Road)
Queen's Road, East, 皇后大道東約 *Wong-hau-tai-to-tung-yeuk*, (Parade Ground to Wanchai Market)
Queen's Road West, 皇后大道西約 *Wong-hau-tai-tou-sai-yeuk*, West end of Hollywood Road to Pokfulum)
Queen Street, 皇后街 *Wong-hau-kai*, (Praya West to Queen's Road West)
Rangel's Alley, 九江巷 *Kow-kong-hong*, (Hollywood Road)
Robinson Road, 羅便臣道 *Lo-peen-shun-to*, (Albany Road to Bonham Road)
Royal Mint Street, 鑄錢局街 *Chü-chin-kook-kai*, (Great George Street to Mint)

Rozario Street, 老些厘街 Lo-sha-li-kai, (Ladder Street to Tank Lane)
Russell Street, 剌士厘街 La-sz-li-kai, (Bowrington Canal to Perceval Street)
Rutter's Lane, 律打巷 Lūt-tu-hong, (Market Street)
Sai Lung Lane, 西隆里 Sai-lung-li, (Queen's Road West)
Sai On Lane, 西安里 Sai-on-li, (Battery Road)
Sai Woo Lane, 西胡巷 Sai-woo-hong, (Sai-ying-poon, Queen's Road West to Praya West)
Salt Fish Street, 鹹魚街 Ham-yü-kai, (New East Street)
Scott Lane, 士吉街 Si-kut-tai (Queen's Road Central to Praya Central)
Second Street, 第二街 Tai-ye-kai, (New East Street to Pokfulum Road)
Seymour Road, 西摩道 Sai-mo-to, (Robinson Road to Bonham Road)
Seymour Terrace, 西摩台 Sai-mo-toi, (Castle Steps to Seymour Road)
Sharp Street, East, 雲東街 Shap-tung-kai, (Bowrington Canal to Leighton Hill Road)
Sharp Street, West, 雲西街 Shap-sai-kai, (Bowrington Canal to Morrison Hill Road)
Shek Kai Lane, 石溪巷 Shek-kai-hong, (Wanchai)
Shek Kai Lane, 石溪里 Shek-kai-li, (Nullah Lane)
Shelley Street, 舍利街 She-li-kai, (Hollywood Road to Mosque Street)
Sheung Fung Lane, 常豐里 Sheung-fung-li, (Third Street to Second Street)
Shin Hing Lane, 善慶里 Shin-hing-li, (New East Street)
Ship Street, 洋船街 Yeung-shün-kai, (Praya East, across Queen's Road East)
Shung Hing Lane, 崇慶里 Shung-hing-li, (Queen's Road West, Praya)
Siemssen's Lane, 禪臣里 Seem-shun-li, (Poyan Street)
Sing Wong Street, 城隍街 Shing-wong-kai, (Caine Road to Gough Street)
Smithy Street, 士美地街 Sze-mi-ti-kai, (Jardine's Bazaar)
Soong On Lane, 崇安里 Shoong-on-li, (Queen's Road East.)
Sow-ke-wan Road, 筲箕灣道 Sau-ke-wan-to, (Leighton Hill Road to Sow-ke-wan)
Spring Garden's Lane, 景春花園巷 King-chun-fa-ün-hong, (Praya East to Queen's Road East.)
Square Street, 四方街 Sze-fong-kai, (Ladder Street to Market Street)
Stanley Street, 士丹利街 Sze-tan-le-kai, (D'Aguilar Street to Graham Street)
St. Francis' Street, 聖非蘭使士街 Sing-fe-lan-sz-sz-kai, (Queen's Road East to St. Francis' Hospital)
St. Francis' Lane, 聖化蘭些士巷 Sing-fa-lan-se sz-hong, (St. Francis' Street)
St. John's Place, 聖約翰之所 Shing-yeuk-hon-chi-sho, (Albert Road)
Station Street, 差館街 Chai-koon-kai, (Caine Road to Po-yan Street)

LIST OF STREETS, &c.

Station Street, Upper, 差館上街 Chai-koon-sheung-kai, (Caine Road to Bonham Road)
Staunton Street, 士丹頓街 Sz-tan-tun-kai, (Old Bailey to Bridges' Street)
Staveley Street, 時地華利街 She-te-wa-li-kai, (Queen's Rd. Central to Gage St.)
Stone Cutters' Lane, 石匠里 Shek-cheung-li, (Hollywood Road)
Sui Hing Lane, 瑞興里 Sui-Hing-li, (Caine Road, Taipingshan)
Sutherland Street, 沙打蘭街 Sha-ta-lan-kai, (Praya West to Queen's Road West)
Tak Sing Lane, 德星里 Tak-sing-li, (Second Street)
Tai Loi Lane, 泰來里 Tai-loi-li, (First Street)
Tai Ping Lane, 太平里 Tai-ping-li, (Taipingshan Street)
Tai Wong Lane, 大王里 Tai-wong-li, (Queen's Road East to Praya)
Tai Wong Street, 大王巷 Tai-wong-hong, (Praya East to Queen's Road East)
Taipingshan Street, 太平山街 Tai-ping-shan-kai (Bridges' Street to Po-yan St.)
Tai Wo Street, 太和街 Tai-wo-kai, (Wanchai Road to Praya East)
Tan Kwai Lane, 丹桂里 Tan-kwai-li, (Ladder Street)
Tank Lane, 水池巷 Shui-chi-hong, (Lower Lascar Row to Caine Road)
Tannery Lane, 劏皮巷 Yim-pi-hong, (Caine Road, Taipingshan)
Te Po Lane, 地步巷 Te-po-hong, (High Street)
Third Street, 第三街 Tai-sam-kai, (New East Street to Battery Road)
The Gap, 掘斷山 Kwat-tün-shan, (Wanchai Market to Morrison Hill Road)
Tik Loong Lane, 迪龍里 Tik-loong-li, (Queen's Road East)
Ting Lok Street, 庭樂街 Ting-lok-kai, (Praya East to Morrison Hill Road)
Toong Mun Lane, 同文街 Toong-mun-kai, (Queen's Rd. Central to Praya Central)
Triangle Street, 三丫街 Sam-a-kai, (Praya East to Wanchai Road)
Tse Mee Alley, 紫微街 Tsz-me-kai, (Queen's Road West to Praya West)
Tsing Chung Lane, 清松里 Tsing-chung-li, (Queen's Road East)
Tsing Kai Lane, 清溪里 Tsing-kai-li, (Nullah Lane to Albany Street)
Tsui Lung Lane, 聚龍里 Tsui-loong-li, (Queen's Road East)
Tsz Tung Lane, 紫桐里 Tsz-tung-li, (First Street)
Tuk Hing Alley, East, 德興東巷 Tuk-hing-tung-hong, (Queen's Road West to Praya West)
Tuk Hing Alley, West, 德興西巷 Tuk-hing-sai-hong, (Queen's Road West to Praya West)
Tung Hing Lane, 同慶里 Tung-hing-li, (Queen's Road to Bonham Strand)
Tung Lok Lane, 同樂里 Tung-lok-li, (Taipingshan Street)
Tung Lung Lane, 東隆里 Tung-lung-li, (Wanchi Road)
Tung Tak Lane, 同德里 Tung-tak-li, (Cochrane Street)
Tung Wo Lane East, 同和東里 Tung-woh-tung-li, (Middle Street)

Tung Wo Lane West, 同和西里 *Tung-woh-sai-li*, (Middle Street)
Ui Un Lane, Upper, 匯源上里 *Ui-un-sheung-li*, (Peel Street)
Ui Un Lane, Lower, 匯源下里 *Ui-un-ha-li*, (Peel Street)
U-Hing Lane, 餘慶里 *Yu-hing-li*, (Circular Pathway to Queen's Road)
U-Yam Lane, 餘蔭里 *Yu-yam-li*, (East Street)
Valley Road, 華利街 *Wa-le-kai*, (Round Wong-nei-chung Valley)
Village Street 鄉下街 *Heong-ha-kai*, (Leighton Hill Road to Jardine's Bazaar)
Wai Yan Lane, 懷仁里 *Wai-yan-li*, (Ladder Street, Taipingshan)
Wanchai Road, 灣仔道 *Wan-chai-to*, (Queen's Road East to Bowrington Canal)
Wardley Street, 滑梨街 *Wat-lee-kai*, (Queen's Road Central to Praya Central)
Water Lane, 水巷 *Sui-hong*, (Queen's Road Central to Market Street)
Webster's Bazaar, 威士打新街 *Wui-s:.-ta-san-kai*, Queen's Road Central to Praya Central)
Wellington Street, 威靈頓街 *Wai-ling-tun-kai*, (Wyndham Street to Queen's Road Central)
West Street, 太平山西街 *Tai-pin-shan-sai-kai*, (Queen's Road Central to Taipingshan Street)
West Terrace, 西台 *Sai-t'oi*, (Castle Road)
Western Street, 西便街 *Sai-pin-kai*, (Praya West to Bonham Road)
Wilmer Street, 威厘馬街 *Wai-lee-ma-kai*, (Praya West to Queen's Road West)
Wing Hing Lane, 永興里 *Wing-hing-li*, (Centre Street)
Wing Lok Street, 永樂街 *Wing-lok-kai*, (Praya Central to Praya West)
Wing On Lane, 永安街 *Wing-on-kai*, (Queen's Road Central to Praya Central)
Wing Wah Lane, 榮華里 *Wing-wa-li*, (D'Aguilar Street)
Witty Street, 滑地街 *Wat-tee-kai*, (Praya West to Middle Street)
Wo Fung Street, 和風街 *Wo fung-kai*, (Queen's Road West to Praya)
Wo Hing's Lane, 和興里 *Wo-hing-li* (Queen's Road West)
Woh On Lane, 和安里 *Wo-on-li* (D'Aguilar Street)
Wui Lung Lane, 匯龍里 *Wui-loon li*, (Bowrington)
Wyndham Street 雲咸街 *Wan-ham-kai*, (Queen's Rd. Central to Hollywood Road)
Yü Lok Lane, 餘樂里 *Yu-lok-li*, (Centre Street)
Yü Po Lane, East, 餘步東里 *Yu-po-tung-li*, (First Street)
Yü Po Lane, West, 餘步西里 *Yu-po-sai-li*, (First Street)
Yung Woh Lane, 雍和里 *Yung-wo-li*, (Pound Lane, Taipingshan)
Yan Shau Lane, 仁壽里 *Yan-shau-li*, (D'Aguilar Street)
Yap Chü Lane, 邑注巷 *Yap-chu-hong*, (Praya East)
Yee Wo Street, 怡和街 *Yee-wo-kai* (Near the Sugar Refinery)
Yee Yik Lane, 義益里 *Yee-yik-li*, (Middle Street)
Zetland Street, 泄蘭街 *Sit-lan-kai*, (Queen's Road Central to Ice House Street)

FOREIGN RESIDENTS IN CHINA, JAPAN
AND
THE PHILIPPINES, &c.

⁂ When the Name of the Town is omitted, Hongkong is to be understood.

A

Aastrome, C , Pilot, Bangkok
Abbot, J. C., chief officer (Str. *Yesso*)
Abbott, E., clerk (Gilman & Co.) Y'hama
Abbott, R. J., Assistant Customs, Chinkiang
Abbott, G. W., clerk (Olyphant & Co.) Shanghai
Abbs, M., (Naval College) Yedo
Abdolkhaluk, H. J. M., merchant (J. M. Abdolkhaluk & Co.) Gage Street (absent)
Abdool, K., Act. Hindustanee interpreter (Magistracy)
Abdoolalli, H. (A. Futtabhoy) Cochrane St.
Abdoolatiff, A. (A. Jafferbhoy & Co) B'bay
Abdoolcader, Hajee E., clerk (A. Jafferbhoy & Co.) Stanley Street
Abdoolraheem, G., clerk (D. Vassonjee & Co.) Stanley Street
Abdoolrahim, E., clerk (Ebrahim & Co.) Canton
Abdool, Kadar M., clerk (Ebrahim & Co.) Cochrane Street
Abdool Star, J. M., merchant
Abe, Rev. F. W., missionary, Sarawak
Abegg, F., merchant (Abegg, Borul & Co.) Yokohama
Abel, G., (Fischer & Co.) Hiogo
Abel, K., resident, Yokohama
Abell, H. J., clerk (Chart. Merc. Bank) Yokohama
Abell, J. C., bill broker, and secretary (Chamber of Commerce) Hiogo
Abendroth, H. agent (Hongkong and Shanghai Bank) Amoy
Aberdeen. A., sergeant (Legation Escort) Yedo
Aboobucker, A., clerk (A. Soab) Wellington Street
Abraham, A. E., clerk (D. Sassoon, Sons & Co.) Praya
Abraham, J., merchant (do.) Chefoo
Ackermann, B., 2nd officer (German str. *China*)
Adam, Lieut. —., French Marines, Y'hama
Adams, G., assist. (Farnham & Co.) S'hai

Adams, H. A., commander U.S N. (*Iroquois*)
Adams. J., M.D. Caine Road
Adams, K. D., clerk (Birley & Co.) Macao
Adams, M. C., baker (Adams & Co.) Nagasaki
Adams, Wm. Stanley, M.D., health officer, &c., Caine Road
Adams, M. J. constable, British Consulate, Kewkeang
Adamson, Jas., engineer R N. (*Avon*)
Adamson, A., asst. eng., U.S.N. (*Monocacy*)
Addicks, J. T., assistant paymaster, U.S.N. (*Ashuelot*)
Adds, C., coal merchant &c., Yokohama
Addyman, R. F., clerk (Hongkong & Whampoa Dock Co.)
Adkins, Thomas, British Consul & Danish Vice Consul, Newchwang (absent)
Adnams, W. T., storeman (Naval Yard)
Affourtit, F. C., steward to the 1st king (Bangkok)
Afsh, L., storeman (Naval Yard)
Agabeg, A. L., Jr., commission agent &c., (Jamieson & Barton) Hollywood Road
Agabeg, G. L., broker, Wyndham St.
Agius, Don J. J., intendant (Financial Department) Manila
Agnado, A., shipchandler, Yloilo
Aguedas, —., judge, Manila
Aguirre, F., merchant (Aguirre & Co.) Manila (absent)
Aguirre, Segundo, machinist (Morris, Barlow & Co.) Manila
Ahlmann, J. A., chief officer, *Fort William* (P. & O. S. N. Co)
Ahmed, Moosa, manager (Abdolkhaluk & Co.) Gage Street
Ahmed, M. merchant, Honam & Hongkong
Ahpaie, tailor, Bangkok
Ahrens, H., merchant (Ahrens & Co.) Y'kohama (absent)
Aitken, A. G., engineer (P. & O. S. N. Co.) Queen's Road West
Alabaster, Chaloner, Consul for Austria Denmark, Franco, Germany and Great Britain, Takow and Taiwan

Alabor, J., merchant (Meyer, Alabor & Co.) Stanley Street
Aladin, R., merchant, Honam & Hongkong
Albinson, Jos., merchant (Howell & Co.) Hakodadi
Alborado, A., constable (British Consulate) Taiwan
Alcuaz, C. S. de, clerk (Guichard & Fils) Manila
Alcuaz, José de, clerk (Guichard & Fils) Manila
Aldrich, A. S., chief account. (Japan Railway) Yokohama
Aledor, —, (V. A. Mauras) Saigon
Alegre, J., merchant (Cucullu & Co.) Manila
Alemão, D., clerk (Brandão & Co.)
Alexander, F., sub. Lieut. R.N. (*Rinaldo*)
Alexander, G., Lieutenant, R.N. (*Cadmus*)
Alexander, J. T. A., clerk (Tait & Co.) Amoy
Alexander, Hon. W. H., registrar (Supreme Court) Robinson Road
Alexandre, Dr. —., Dentist, Yokohama
Alexieff, Mrs. P, (Russian Hotel) Hiogo
Alezan, —., River Pilot, Saigon
Alford, E. P., clerk (Jardine, Matheson & Co.) Shanghai
Alford, Robert G., surveyor to Hongkong Fire Insurance Co., 15 Stanley Street
Algar, T., house agent (Barrington and Algar) and undertaker (Brown, Jones & Co.) Hollywood Road
Alladinbhoy, R., merchant (D. Alladinbhoy) (absent)
Allan, A., Engine driver (Govt. Railways) Yokohama
Allan, H. T., clerk (Elles & Co.) Amoy
Allan, J., assist. (Farnham & Co.) Shanghai
Allan, J. M., Engineer (Kiangnan Arsenal) Shanghai
Allan, W., junr. professor of Practical engineering, arsenal, Foochow
Allanson, M., Sister (The Convent) Caine Road
Allanson, W., clerk (Garcia y Garcia) Macao
Allard, G., importer, Yokohama
Allcook, G. H., clerk (Mourilyan, Heimann & Co.) Hiogo
Allcot, G., examiner Customs, Swatow
Allcot, J. H., tidewaiter, Customs, Swatow
Allemao, A. E., clerk (J. Quinn) Wellington Street
Allen, C. F. R., act. Consul for Denmark and assist. in charge, British Consulate, Chinkiang
Allen, G., captain.(tug *Woosung*) Foochow
Allen, G. L. B., student interpreter (Brit. (Legation) Peking
Allen, H., jr., commission agent, Yokohama
Allen, Herbert J., vice-consul (British Consulate) Shanghai
Allen, J. C., clerk (Olyphant & Co.) Shanghai
Allen, J. W., assistant (Lane Crawford & Co.) Shanghai
Allen, Mrs. J. W., manager (Watson & Co.) Shanghai
Allen, M., resident, Yedo
Allen, Rev. M., R. C. missionary, Yedo
Allen, R., wharfinger (Hunt's warf) S'hai
Allon, R. W., paymr. U.S.N. (*Idaho*)
Allen, Rev. Y. J., missionary, Shanghai
Allert, H., mariner (Jap. Govt.) Yedo
Alli, Boarding House keeper, Lower Lascar Row
Allier, Rev. R. P., Chaplain, Arsenal, Foochow
Allin L., clerk, (Wilson, Cornabé & Co.) Chefoo
Allison, J., engineer, (Novelty Iron Works)
Allocchio, T., sister (The Convent) Caine Road
Alloin, J. M, merchant, Bangkok
Allsop, C., engineer, R.N. (*Frolic*)
Allybhoy, K., manager (Dhurumsey, Poonjahboy, Shanghai
Allynshomed, A. T, clerk (Nowrojee & Co.) Hollywood Road
Almario, F S., compositor, (*Daily Press* Office) Bridges Street
Almeida, A. T. de, clerk (Holme, Ringer & Co.) Nagasaki
Almeida, J. A. de retired Lieut. Col. Macao
Alongo, J. Jr., clerk (Hongkong and China Gas Company)
Alongc, V., clerk (Hongkong and China Gas Company)
Alonzo, Teodoro, assayer (Mint) Manila
Aloya, Felix, clerk, (Heinszen & Co.) M'la
Alsiug, A H., in charge (receiving ships *Gauges* and *Sterling*) Kewkeang
Altum, W. E., clerk (Findlay, Wade & Co.) Shanghai
Alvares, M. F., prof. of English. (St. Joseph's College) Macao
Alvarez, J., clerk (Blanco, Domingo & Co.) Manila
Alvarez, Guerra, J., act. dist. magistrate, Manila
Alvarez, Manuel, administrative director (Mint) Manila
Alves, A. F., accountant (Treasury)
Alves, J. L. de. S., clerk (Harbor Master's Department)
Alves, J. M. S., clerk, Colonial Secretary's Department
Amade, —., chief artificer (Japan Govt.) Yedo
Amarinda, Dr. —., Osaka Hospital
Ameijeebhoy, Futtabhoy, merchant, Cochrane Street and Canton
Ameroodin, —., merchant C'ton and Hongkong

Ames, S. J. B., commis. of Police, Bangkok
Amiel, Major C. F., H.M.'s 80th regiment
Ammin, —., butcher (Manyn and Ammin) Bangkok
Amos, L. J. V., Solicitor, Judge's clerk (Supreme Court)
Amy, C., assist. light-keeper, Sha-wei-shan light-house, Shanghai
Anacleto, C., clerk (Casal Bros) Manila
Andersen, L. A. marine surveyor, Amoy
Andersen, R., pilot (Independence Pilot Co.) Shanghai
Andersen, S. P., master mariner, Bangkok
Anderson, A., clerk (Adamson, Bell & Co.) Shanghai
Anderson, Geo., pilot, Nagasaki
Anderson, H., clerk (Bavier & Co) Y'hama
Anderson, J., light-keeper (Sha-wei-shan Light-house) Shanghai
Anderson, J., proprietor (St Petersburg Hotel) Nagasaki
Anderson, J. Blacksmith (National S.S. Co. Nipon) Yokohama
Anderson, J. foreman carpenter (Pub. Works Dept.) Japanese Govt.
Anderson, John, engineer, R.N (Rinaldo)
Anderson, J. H., clerk, (Jardine, Matheson & Co.) Kewkeang
Anderson, John L., public tea inspector, Amoy
Anderson, Mrs. (Eureka Hotel) Shanghai
Anderson, N.P., commander (St. Kua Hsing) Customs, Shanghai
Anderson, R., merchant, Jardine Matheson
Anderson, T.C., supt. public works, Sarawak & Co. (Hankow)
Anderson, W., writer, Ryang outstation, Sarawak
Anderson, Wm. C. C. assistant (G. W. Collins & Co.) Taku and Tientsin
Anderson, W., assistant (Stephen & Stewart) Yokohama
Anderson, W. T., Lieut. H. M. 80th Regt.
Andrac, —., Chief Engineer (M. M. S. S. Donnai)
André, A., merchant (Melchers & Co.) Praya
Andreason, J., master mariner, Bangkok
Andreevsky, J. S. merchant (Andreevsky & Avramoff) Kalgan
Andresen, —., master mariner, Bangkok
Andreu, V., sister (maison de Jesus enfant) Ningpo
Andrew, J. clerk (Butterfield and Swire) Shanghai
Andrew, W. P., clerk (Japan railway)
Andrews, E., engineer (P. & O. S. N. Co.) Queen's Road West
Andrews, G. W., master (Str. Fire Queen) Shanghai
Andrews, H. J., merchant (Andrews & Co.) Manila
Andrews, Miss Mary E. (Amer. Board of Miss.) Peking (Tungchow)

Andrews, W. B., commander (P. & O. service.)
Andrieu, —., contractor, Saigon
Anduaga, Arturo, 3d valuator (Customs) Manila
Angart, M., clerk (Schultze, Reis & Co.) Hiogo
Angus, A. F., tea inspector (Jardine, Matheson & Co.) Foochow
Angus, J. K, clerk (Butterfield and Swire)
Añino, Manuel, 2d valuator (Customs) Manila
Annand, F., assist. (Lane Crawford & Co.) Shanghai
Annand, J., head foreman (Japan Railway) Yokohama
Annecke, W., consul (German Consulate) Shanghai (absent)
Annesley, A., British vice consul, Osaka, act. Br. vice consul, Hiogo
Anot, Rev. P.. R. C. missionary, Kewkeang
Antegnora, Juan, Rear Admiral and Com. in chief, Manila
Anthony, E. D., clerk (Russell & Co.) Shanghai and Kewkeang
Anthony, J., assistant (Hongkong Dispensary)
Anthony, T. T., storekeeper (Broadbear, Anthony & Co.) Praya
Antisell, Dr Thomas (Jap. Govt.) Yedo (Kaitikushi)
Antolini, —., soda water manufacturer, Saigon
Anton, —., Military Instructor (Jap. Govt.) Yedo
Anton, J. Ross, broker (Anton and Middleton) Belmont
Antonio, L., lighthouse keeper, Customs, Ningpo
Antonio, O., clerk (Tillson, Herrmann & Co.) Manila
Antunes, J., ensign, Military Depart., Macao
Anwarally, C., clerk (D. Vassonjee & Co.) Stanley Street
Apack, —., clerk (Hongkong & Shanghai Bank) Saigon
Apcar, M. T., assistant (Dry Dock Co.) Bangkok
Aphalo, —., aide com. de la marine, Saigon
Appassanry, clerk (M. Ribeiro & Co.) Saigon
Aquilar, L. E., provisor (Bishopric of Cebu) Manila
Aquino, E. H. d', clerk (Stamp Office)
Aquino, J. C., d', clerk (A. Heard & Co.) Shanghai
Aquino, J. F. d', compositor (A. H. de Carvalho) Shanghai
Aquino, P., assist. (Garchitorena & Smith) Manila
Aragones, H. E. Friar J. J., bishop (Nueva Segovia) Manila

Aranda, J., Paymaster General, Manila
Araujo, C. A. P. F., engineer (Tejo) Macao
Arbur, G., assist. Commissary (Control Depart.)
Arbuthnot, E. O., clerk (Rud. Evans & Co.) Shanghai
Arduse, —., River Pilot, Saigon
Arce, J., clerk (Ker & Co) Manila
Arone, J., student interpreter (French Consulate) Shanghai
Argo, J., 3rd. engineer (str. *Douglas*)
Ari, Lala, proprietor (French Hotel) Manila
Arjanee, F. H., assistant (N. Mody & Co.) Queen's Road
Arlegui, R , clerk (Peele, Hubbell & Co.) Manila (Leyte)
Armbruster, l'Abbe H., missionary, Yedo
Armistead, A. clerk (P. & O. Co.)
Armstrong, Geo., clerk (Smith, Bell & Co.) Manila
Armstrong, J. M., Government auctioneer, &c., The Hut, Castle Road
Armstrong, O., assistant (Farnham & Co.) Shanghai
Arndt, C , Interpreter, German Legation, Peking
Arnhold, Jacob, merchant (Arnhold, Karberg & Co.) (absent)
Arnhold, P., clerk (Arnhold, Karberg & Co) Canton
Arnold, A. A., Instructor (Govt. School) Nagasaki
Arnold, T., clerk (Aug. Heard & Co.)
Arnonx, F., proprietor " Café du Japon," Yokohama
Aroozoo, J. J , clerk (R. T. Rennie) Shanghai
Arrivat, L'abbé J., R. C. Missionary, Hiogo
Arrobas, A. M. B., Lieutenant Police Department, Macao
Arthur, A. M., C E., assist. (Public Works Depart.) Yedo
Arthur, Mrs., matron (Diocesan Home and Orphanage) Bonham Road
Arthur, O G. (Walsh, Hall & Co.) Hiogo
Arthur, Rev. J. H. (Am. Bap. Miss. Union)
Arthur, W. M. B., English master (Diocesan Home and Orphanage) Bonham Road
Arthur, William, flag captain, R.N. (H.M.S. *Iron Duke*)
Artindale, R. H , clerk (Bower, Hanbury & Co.) Shanghai
Ascnsi, Manuel, counsellor (War Department) Manila
Ashe, E. P., sub-lieut. R.N. (*Cadmus*)
Ashley, C. J., sailmaker, Shanghai
Ashmore, Rev. William, missionary (Amer Bap. Mission and vice-consul for U. S.) Swatow
Ashton, F., chief officer (str. *Kwangtung*)
Ashton, John, paymr., R.N. (*Rinaldo*)
Ashton, S , commander (steamer *Yesso*)

Assai, Mahomed, gunner (Elles & Co.) Taiwan
Assis, A. R., clerk (Frisby & Co.) Wellington Street
Assis, G , matron (Lock Hospital)
Assiter, W , assist. (H. B. M. Office of Works) Shanghai
Assumpção, J. C. P. de, act. chief clerk of Exchequer, Macao
Aston, W. G , interpreter and translator (British Legation) Yedo
Astorquia, A., merchant, Macao
Ateriana, F., Teacher (Jap. Govt,) Yedo
Atkins, E., melter (Mint) Kawasaki
Atkinson, A., officer (P. & O. service)
Atkinson, G L., lieut. R.N. (*Iron Duke*)
Atkinson, Hoff......... (Smith, Baker & Co)
Yokohama
Atkinson, Rev. —., Missionary, Hiogo
Atkinson, Robert, surgeon, R.N. (H. M. S. *Princess Charlotte*)
Aubert, F. J.. assist (Butterfield & Swire) Shanghai
Augier, Judge of 1st instance, Saigon
Auilia, A. L. Sanches del, Marine Sorter (General Post Office)
Auroju, F. D., master mariner, Bangkok
Aussonac, Eugene, clerk (Sigrist et Pradier) Yokohama
Austen, Geo., clerk (Russell & Sturgis) act U. S. Consular agent, Cebu
Austen, J. G., clerk (Russell & Sturgis) Secretary (U.S., Sweden and Norwegian Consulates) Manila
Austin, Hon. J. G., Colonial Secretary and Auditor General
Austin, —., prop. (Cosmopolitan Hotel) Saigon
Austin, J. H. (*Japan Gazette*) Yokohama
Austin, J. W. (Naval College) Yedo
Auzet, A., 2nd engineer (Chinese g.b. *Ching Tsing*) Canton
Avramoff, P. G., merchant (Andreevaky & Avramoff) Kalgan
Avril, P., resident, Hiogo
Ayers, J. G., asst. surg., U.S.N. (*Saco*)
Aylett, A., assist. (Santa Mesa Rope Factory) Manila
Aymeri, A. (Procure des Lazaristes) Shanghai
Aymonin, V., merchant (Aymonin & Co.) Yokohama
Ayres, C. A. S., clerk (Giles & Co) Amoy
Ayres, P. B. C., M.R.C.S.E. &c. Colonial Surgeon
Ayrton, Dr., resident, Yedo
Ayrton, W. S., assist. in charge of records (British Consulate) Shanghai
Azevedo, M. d', clerk (Caldwell and Brereton)
Azedo, C. M. D., ensign, Military Depart., Macao
Azevedo, A., purser (str. *Kiukiang*)

Azevedo, F. d', clerk (Deacon & Co.) Canton and Macao
Azevedo, F. H., clerk (Jardine, Matheson & Co.)
Azevedo, P. A. d', purser (receiving-ship Ariel) Shanghai

B

Baader, W., assist (Fahre & Co.) Y'hama
Baber, E. C., acting vice-consul (British Consulate) & acting consul for Austria and Germany, Yenoui
Babin H. J., assist. surgeon U.S.N. (Hartford)
Bacharach, N., merchant (Bacharach, Oppenheimer & Co.) Saigon (absent)
Bacon, A. C. A., Mid. R.N. (Iron Duke)
Baconnier, A., clerk (Nachtrieb, Leroy & Co.) Shanghai
Badaire, G., aide com. de la marine, S'gon
Bade, C. E., merchant (E. Schellhass & Co.) Shanghai
Badge, G., linen-draper, Hiogo
Baer, S., merchant (Baer & Co.) Manila
Baffey, G. W., assistant (P. M. S. S. Co. office) Praya West
Baffy, G. T. (Club Concordia) Shanghai
Bagnall, Rev. B, Missionary, Chinkiang
Bahunot, du Liscoet—Judge of 1st instance, Saigon
Bailey, C., constable (Police Force) Ningpo
Bailey, David H, consul (U. S. Consulate) Caine Road
Bailey, G., constable (Sailors' Home) S'hai
Bailey, J., clerk (A. Robinson) Shanghai
Baillie, A. (Naval College) Yedo
Baillie, C. W. (Naval College) Yedo
Bailie, H. C., engineer (Fire Brigade)
Bailly, —., general drapers and outfitters Saigon
Bain, A. W., clerk (Elles & Co.) Amoy
Bain, Geo. Murray, proprietor and general manager (Bain and Dennys) (China Mail Office) Wyndham Street (absent)
Bain, W. B., pilot (Independence Pilot Co.) Shanghai
Bains, J., assistant (Sayle & Co.) Alexandra Terrace
Bair, M. M, merchant (H. Ahrens & Co) Yokohama (absent)
Baird, Alex., coal hewer (Tanjong Kubong Mines) Labuan
Baird, C. W., clerk (Holliday, Wise & Co.) Praya Central
Baird, Jas., coal hewer (Tanjong Kubong Mines) Labuan
Baird, J. W., watchmaker (Falconer & Co.) Queen's Road
Bake, H., tide surveyor (Customs) S'hai
Baker, Colgate, merchant (Smith, Baker & Co.) Yokohama
Baker, D. F., mid., U.S.N. (Hartford)

Baker, E. M., public accountant, secretary Hongkong Hotel Co., Peddor's Hill
Baker, H. R. Lieut., U.S.N. (Iroquois)
Baker, J. H., Draper &c. (Baker & Co.) Queen's Road
Baker, Mrs., draper &c. (Baker & Co.) Queen's Road
Baker, R. B., manager (Chartered Mercantile Bank) Yokohama
Baker, R. C, dep. com. (Control Department) Labuan
Bakhmeteff, G., attaché (Russian Legation) Peking
Balaam, G., foreman mechanic (Japan Railway Works) Yokohama
Baldwin, J. C., merchant (McGregor & Co.) (absent)
Baldwin, Rev. C. C., missionary, Foochow
Baldwin, Rev. S. L., missionary (American Meth. Episc. mission) Foochow
Balfour, F. H, silk inspector (Balfour, Butler & Co.) Shanghai
Balfour, Wm., chief engineer, str. Hailoong
Ball, George, engineer, R.N. (Opossum)
Ball, W., chemist (China Dispensary) Praya
Ballagh, Rev. J. H., missionary, Yokohama
Ballance, T. F., merchant (Ballance & Co.) Hankow
Ballantine, G., examiner, Customs, Kewkeang
Baller, F., missionary (Nankin)
Balloy, R. de, secretary (French Legation) Peking
Balzano, M., constable (British Consulate) Amoy
Ban, S, student interpreter (Japanese Consulate) Shanghai
Banajee, N P., merchant (N. Kessowjee & Company)
Bandinel, J. J. F., clerk (J. Foster & Co.) Amoy
Bank, J., (New York House) Yokohama
Banyard, M., sub-acct. (Chartered Bank) Shanghai
Bao, Paul, professor (Educ. Inst.) Saigon
Baptista, J., ensign (Timor Corps) Macao
Baptista, L. J., (Municipal Council) Macao
Baptista, L M., clerk, (A. Heard & Co.)
Baptista, M. A., Jr., clerk (E. Sharp and Toller)
Baptista, M. A., drawing master (St. Saviour's College)
Baracho, F. de Mello, Administrador do Conselho (Macao)
Barbancon, Le, mechanist, (Japanese Govt.) Yokohama
Barbe, J., supt. (French Municipal Police) Shanghai
Barberot, —., chief artificer, (Jap. Govt.) Yedo
Barbier, Pere J. B., missionary (Roman Catholic Mission) Ningpo (Hangchow)

Barbier, —., engineer (Japanese Govt) Yokohama
Barbier, Rev. —., miss. (R. C. Mission) Bangkok (Petrin)
Barbosa, D. J. d'A., lieut.-col. commanding (Military Department) Macao
Barchet, Mrs. S. P., missionary, Ningpo
Barchet, S. P., miss. (Indep. Bap. Mission) Ningpo
Barclay, T., surgeon (P, & O. service)
Bareil, —., storekeeper (Bareil et Fils Freres) Saigon
Barelle, —., machinist (Yokoska Arsenal) Yokohama
Barff, S., assistant postmaster general (General Post-office) Arbuthnot Road
Barker, C. B., manager (Carlton House) Shanghai
Barker, W., chief officer (Sassoon's steamer *China*)
Barlow, H., merchant (Shaw & Co.) Yokohama
Barlow, H. J. E., clerk (Holliday, Wise & Co.) Shanghai
Barlow, J. S., c.e., engineer (Morris, Barlow, & Co.) Manila
Barnard, A., merchant (D. Sassoon, Sons & Co.) Yokohama
Barnard W., resident, Yokohama
Barnes, C. J., clerk (Hongkong and Shanghai Banking Corporation) Shanghai
Barnes, F. D., agent (P. & O. S. N. Co.) Shanghai
Barnes, J. P., merchant (Holliday, Wise & Co.) Shanghai
Barnett, B. S., assistant (Mrs J. Searle) Yokohama
Barnett, J B., commander R.N. (*Elk*)
Baron, J. S., ship and commission agent Shanghai
Barr, Geo., constable (Police Force) Ningpo
Barr, J., Carpenter, R.N. (*Cadmus*)
Barr, J., third officer (Sassoons's str. *China*)
Barr, J., engineer (P. & O. service)
Barradale, Rev. J. S., missionary (London Missionary Society) Tientsin
Barradas, E. C., writer (Naval Yard)
Barradas, F., Clerk (Union Insurance Society)
Barradas, J. M., marine sorter (General Post-Office)
Barradas, Z. M., sorter (General Post-Office)
Barrelot, J. H., watchmaker and com. merchant, Elgin Street (Hollywood Road)
Barrett, Rev. E. R., B.A. Missionary, S'hai
Barrett, J. surgeon (P. & O. Service)
Barretto, B. A., merchant (Barretto & Co.) Manila
Barretto, J., clerk (Olyphant & Co.) S'hai
Barretto, J. A., clerk (Jardine, Matheson & Co.) Aberdeen Street (absent)
Barretto, J. A., Jr., clerk (Jardine, Matheson & Co.) Foochow

Barretto, J. A., temporary clerk (Colonial Secretary's Department)
Barretto, M., sister (The Convent) Caine Road
Barretto, L., ensign (National Guard) Macao
Barretto, L. A., clerk (Findlay, Richardson & Co.) Manila
Barretto, L. F., clerk (Oriental Bank)
Barritto, Sister A. (The Convent) Caine Road
Barrington, T.W., Usher (Supreme Court) house agent &c., Wyndham Street
Barrois, —. Superior of Orphanage, C'ton
Barros, J. A. Le, clerk (Alloin & Co.) Bangkok
Barros, E. M., clerk (Novelty Iron Works)
Barros, F. J., clerk (Oriental Bank)
Carros, J. E. F., clerk (B S. Fernandes) Macao
Barros, V. de P., lieut. (Military Depart. Macao
Barrosa, M., secretary, (Sup. Court) Manila
Barry, Wm., assist. (Stephen & Stewart) Yokohama
Bartasheff, N. A., clerk (Matreninsky and Kazuutzoff) Kalgau
Bartasheff, J. A., clerk (A. D. Startseff) Tientsin
Bartesaghi, Carlo, assistant (Dell' Oro & Co.) Yokohama
Barthe, C. assistant (Gilman & Co.) Y'hama
Barthelemy, Madame, storekeeper, Saigon
Bartlett, H., fleet marine officer, U.S.N. (*Hartford*)
Bartolini, A., sergeant, Police Force (Customs) Foochow
Barton, C., clerk (H.K. and S. Banking Corporation) Shanghai
Barton, G., clerk (Municipal Council Office) Shanghai
Barton, G. K., M.D., Shanghai (absent)
Barucco, P. watchmaker, Yokohama
Bascombe, G. E. assist. eng R.N. (*Midge*)
Base, G., clerk (Casal Bros) Manila
Basto, Dr J. F. P., member of council (Public Instruction) Macao
Bastos, A., Jr., ensign (National Guard) Macao
Bastos, A. J., jun., advocate, Macao
Bastos, J. F. P., procurador, Macao
Batavus, E., merchant (Black, Batavus & Co.) Yokohama
Batcheldor, Capt., J. M., resident, Yedo
Bateman, S., commis. of Customs, Bangkok
Bateman, T. H., assistant (Watson, Cleave & Co.) Shanghai
Bates, Rev. J., missionary (Ch. Eng. Miss. Soc.) Ningpo
Bathgate, J., clerk (Olyphant & Co.) Foochow
Batt, E. W., merchant (Barnet & Co.) Shanghai
Batteke, Geo., merchant, Osaka

Batten, H., assistant (Hongkew Wharf) Shanghai
Batten, W., inspector (Police Dept.) Kowloong
Battles, W., commission merchant (Battles & Co.) Bank Buildings & Hongkong Hotel
Baud, —., contractor, Saigon
Baudran, Mdme , dressmaker, Saigon
Baudain, S., tidewaiter (Customs) Tamsui
Baudry, —., aide com. de la marine, Saigon
Bauduin, A. J. (Netherlands Trading Society) acting consul for Netherlands, & Sweden & Norway, Yokohama
Bauer, A. T., assistant (Ladage and Oelke) Yokohama
Bauermeister, H., clerk (Crasemann & Hagen) Chefoo
Bavier, Ant., merchant (Bavier & Co.) Yokohama (absent)
Bavier, Ed., merchant (Bavier & Co.) and Danish consul-general, Yokohama
Bavier, Earnest, merchant (Bavier & Co.) Yokohama
Bax, B. W., com. R.N (*Dwarf*)
Baxter, A. G. pilot, Taku (absent)
Bayet, —., sous com. de la Marine, Saigon (absent)
Bayley, G. J., tidewaiter (Customs) Takow
Bayley, O. E., tidewaiter, (Customs) Hankow
Bayley, W. V. Lieut., R.N. (*Ringdove*)
Bayly, Alfred, small arms dept. (Kiangnan Arsenal) Shanghai
Bayne, W. G., agent (N. Ch. Ins. Co.) Yokohama
Baynes, Rev. W. H., officiating Garrison Chaplain, Hongkong
Baziere, P., contractor, Saigon
Bazill, S., Boatswain, R N. (*Frolic*)
Bazing, Z., clerk (Pearson & Lawrence) Yokohama
Bean, A., clerk (Moffat & Co.) Shanghai
Bean, William, merchant, Chinkeang
Beangie, J., Hulk-keeper (*Sultan*,) Kewkeang
Beard, Rev. W. D., col chaplain, Labúan
Beart, E., secretary (Hongkong Club) Queen's Road
Beato, F., photographer, (Beato & Co.) Yokohama
Beattie, J. G. C., clerk (Holliday, Wise & Co.) Shanghai
Beauchamp, T. W., clerk (China & Japan Trading Co.) Yokohama
Beaudel, W., app. engineer (Novelty Iron Works)
Beaumont, J. M., M.R.C S., Customs medical attendant, Foochow (Nantai)
Beauregard, Mdlle., (Debit Lefebvre,) Saigon
Beazley, Henry, merchant (Beazley, Paget & Co.) Hankow

Bechr, H., merchant (Reimers, Bechr & Co.) Hiogo
Beck, M., clerk (De Bay, Gotte & Co) Bangkok
Becker, A. W., assist. light-keeper (North Saddle Light-house) Shanghai
Becker. H., clerk (Abegg, Borel & Co.) Yokohama
Beckett, W., clerk (Jardine, Matheson & Co.)
Beckhoff, J., overseer of roads, Shanghai
Beebe, C. G., merchant (Russell & Co) Acting Vice-Consul for Sweden and Norway, Ningpo
Beech, W. H., clerk (Findlay, Richardson & Co.) Manila (absent)
Beer, H. A , assist. (Mess. Mar. Co.) S'hai
Begeux, L., chief cook (Grand Hotel) Yokohama
Begier, Geo., assist. (China Merchants Steam Ship Co.) Nagasaki
Behn, C , clerk (Tastau & Co.)
Behn, O. C , merchant (Pustan & Co.) Shanghai
Behncke, A., merchant (Reis, Von der Heyde & Co.) Hiogo
Behncke, H., shipwright (Morrice, Behncke & Co.) Shanghai
Behre, Ernst, merchant (Bourjau & Co.)
Behrens, H., German Hotel, Chefoo
Behring, - -., Physician, Yedo
Belcher, A., clerk R.N. (*Thalia*)
Belcher, J W., M.D., assistant surgeon, Royal Artillery
Beliard, E., chief 2nd bureau, Saigon
Belilios, E. R., merchant, Caine Road
Bell, C. E., Lieut. R. N. (*Frolic*)
Bell, Capt G. E., hotel proprietor, Hankow
Bell, F H., merchant (Adamson, Bell & Co) Shanghai
Bell, T., chief engineer (National S. S. Co. of Nipon) Yokohama
Bell, W. H , lessee (*Daily Press* Office) Wyndham Street
Bellamy. A., assistant (Hudson, Malcolm & Co) Yokohama
Bellbin Ed , assist. (Shanghai Gas. Co.) Shanghai
Bellin, J., Foreman (Govt. Silk Factory) Yedo
Bellon, Rev. W., missionary (Evangelical Missionary Society of Basel) Lilong
Bellows, John (P. M. S. S. Co.) Yokohama
Belogolovy, A A. (N. A. Ivanoff & Co.) Tientsin
Beloin, —., overlooker (Arsenal) Foochow
Belt, J., quaarter-master, H. M. 80th Regt.
Beltran, P., clerk (Peruvian Consulate) Macao
Beltrão, I., boarding-house keeper, Jose's Lane
Beltras, P. A., compositor (*Hongkong Times*)
Béuaguet, P., contractor, Saigon

Bencke, G. A. C., engineer (Naval Yard)
Bender, Rev. H., missionary (Evangelical Missionary Society of Basel) Chonglok
Bendicht, W., merchant (W. Bendicht & Co.) Wellington St.
Benecke, O. merchant (Carlowitz & Co.) Praya
Benedictsen, T., master mariner, Bangkok
Benezech, A., tavern keeper, Saigon
Benjamin, A., merchant (Benjamin & Co.) Yokohama
Benjamin, B. D., clerk (E. D. Sassoon & Co.) Tientsin
Benjamin, D., clerk (D. Sassoon, Sons & Co.) Tientsin
Benjamin, R. J. K., merchant (Lucas and Waters) Hiogo
Benjamin, Sister M. (Asyle d- la Ste. Enfance) Queen's Road East
Bennary, F. H., chief officer (str. *Poyang*)
Bennett, A. G., clerk (Augustine Heard & Co.) Canton
Bennett, C. C., storekeeper (Mustard & Co.) Shanghai
Bennett, C R., clerk of works (British Consulate) Yokohama
Bennett, G. W., Captain (*Wellington*) S'hai
Bennett, H., (Naval College) Yedo
Bennett, M. E, tea inspector and vice-consul for Russia (A. Heard & Co) F'how
Bennett, P., clerk (Tillson & Co) Hiogo
Bennett, W. R., bill broker (Bennett & Brent) Yokohama
Bennett, W R. surgeon R.N. (*Princess Charlotte*)
Benney, C., clerk (Kirby & Co.) Yokohama
Benning, A., pilot, Canton, Whampoa and Hongkong
Benning, T. T., commander (str. *Kinkiang*)
Benoit, H., chief officer (M M. S. S. *Provence*)
Benson, E. S., municipal director, Y'hama
Benton, L., Surveyor (Lewes and Benton) Shanghai
Penton, Mrs L. E. Missionary Yokohama
Bentzon, E. W., master mariner, Bangkok
Berdsell, J. A., sailmaker U.S.N. (*Hartford*)
Beresford, J. S., overseer (Takasima Colliery) Takasima
Bergan, J., godown-keeper (L. Kniffler & Co.) Hiogo
Bergen, Mrs. G., milliner &c., Hiogo
Berger, —., foundry man (Yokoska Arsenal) Yokohama
Berger, E., watchmaker Yokohama
Berger, L., 2nd engineer, Chinese gunboat *Chun Hoi*
Berkeley, G. A., pilot, Bangkok
Berlingard, L., assist. engineer (Gas Company) Yokohama
Bernard, C., 1st engineer (gunboat *Chun Hoi*) Canton
Bernard, J., comdr. (P. & O. service)

Bernard, Theo., chief engineer (str. *Yesso*)
Bernhard, R., clerk (Gilman & Co.) Praya
Bernhardt, R., godown keeper (Capt. J. U. Smith) Nagasaki
Bernheim, A., clerk (Van Oordt & Co.) Yokohama
Bernom, Rev. A., French missionary, Swatow
Berns, H. L., proprietor (Berns' Hotel) Bangkok
Bernthal, H., assistant (Imp. Hotel) S'hai
Berrick, G P, news agent (Berrick Bros.) Yokohama
Berrick, L, news agent (Berrick Bros.) Yokohama
Berry, J. C., M.D., missionary, Hiogo
Berry, J. T., carpenter, R.N., (*Rinaldo*)
Berteau, —., sous com. de la marine, S'gon
Bertolli, M., sister, the Convent, Caine Road
Berthelier, F., auctioneer, Saigon
Berthemy, J minister for France, Yedo
Bertolutti, E., sister (the convent), Caine Road
Bertrau, Pedro, superior (Jesuits' College) Manila
Bertrand, C., principal agent (Messageries Maritimes) Caine Road
Bertrand, —., hair dresser, Saigon
Bertrand, Ch., importer and commission agent (Bertrand & Co.) Yokohama
Bertrand, G., harbor master, Saigon
Beruote, José, accountant general, Manila
Berwick, W., assistant (Boyd & Co,) S'hai
Besançon, —., forger (Arsenal) Foochow
Besant, E., chief clerk, Naval Yard
Besier, J. N., merchant (Hartmanns & Besier) Hioge
Bessard, F., commander (Chinese gun-boat *Ching-tsing*)
Beveridge, C. H, clerk (Hongkong and Shanghai Banking Corporation) S'hai
Beveridge, H, agent (Jardine, Matheson & Co.) Tientsin
Bevill, F. W., (School of Foreign Languages) Yedo
Bevitt, F, resident, Yedo
Bewick, G, shipbuilder (Thompson, Bewick & Co.) Hakodadi
Beyer, F, clerk (Pustau & Co.) Pottinger Street
Beyer, L., merchant (E. Schellhas & Co.) and Netherlands Consul, Wellington Street
Beyfuss, C., clerk (Pustau & Co.) Shanghai
Bezer, J., Proprietor (London Tavern) Nagasaki
Bezian, E., clerk (Denis Freres) Saigon
Bhoymeca, E., clerk (A. Ebrahim & Co.) Cochrane Street
Biagioni, F., clerk (Société Anonyme), Yokohama

Bibby, H. K., clerk (Peele, Hubbell & Co.) Manila
Bickmore, H. F., student interpreter (Brit. Consulate) Bangkok
Bidwell, H. S., (J. J. Buchheister), S'hai
Bielfield, A., clerk (Bush Bros.) N'chwang
Bigsby, W. F. D., broker, Shanghai
Bikoff, P. M., clerk (Matreninsky and Kasantzoff) Kalgan
Billequin, A., professor of natural history and chemistry (College) Peking
Bingham, Hon. Jno. A., U. S. minister, Yedo
Birglane, T., assist. (Chalmers & Co.) S'hai
Binos, L., Tax collector (French Secretary's Office) Shanghai
Birchal, E. F., clerk (Macleod, Pickford & Co.) Manila
Bird, E. A., clerk (Roe, Pratt & Co.) Hiogo (Yokohama)
Bird, E. T. P., acting inspector of machinery (Naval Yard)
Bird, R. W. M., barrister, Shanghai (absent)
Bird, S. G., clerk (Dodd & Co.) Amoy
Birt, W., agent (Wright, Burkill & Co.) Shanghai
Birt, W., merchant (W. Birt & Co) S'hai
Bisbee, Capt. A M., div. inspector, Customs, Foochow
Bischoff, J. J., watchmaker, Manila
Bischoff, J S., watchmaker (J. J. Bischoff) Manila (Yloilo)
Bishop, J. D., telegraph engineer, S'hai
Bishop, R, clerk (H. B. M.'s Supreme Court) Shanghai
Bismarck, C., interpreter and secretary (German Legation) Peking (absent)
Bisset, J., merchant (Strachan & Thomas) Yokohama
Bisset, J. P., sharebroker, &c. (Bissot & Co.) Shanghai
Bjøgreen, —, master mariner, Bangkok
Bjurling, A., manager (Malherbe, Jullien & Co.) Bangkok
Blachfood, B. F., pilot (Pilot Company) Newchwang
Black, A., engineer, Bangkok
Black, C. F., assist. surgeon, U.S.N. (Lackawanna)
Black, D., foreman (S. S. N. Co.'s Dock) Shanghai
Black, J., assist. (Sayle & Co.) Alexandra Terrace
Black, J. R., editor (Japan Gazette Office) Yokohama, and proprietor (Nishin-Shin-Ji-Shi) Yedo
Black, W., shipchandler (Black & Co.) Yokohama
Blackert, Sergt. H. J., Police force, Hankow
Blackett, F. C., lieut., R.N. (Thalia)
Blackhead, F. B., shipchandler (Blackhead & Co.) Queen's Road (absent)
Blacklock, F. sergeant, Police Force, Customs, Foochow
Blackmore, J. L., clerk (Customs) Shanghai
Blackwell, A. H., merchant (Blackwell & Co.) Osaka
Blackwell, G., engineer, R.N (Thistle)
Blackwell, R., clerk (Russell & Co.) Hermitage, Caine Road
Blackwood, H., clerk (Police Department)
Blain, John, merchant (Blain & Co.) S'hai
Blair, J. H., broker, Shanghai
Blaise, —., director (Mun. Educational Inst.) Saigon
Blake, J., assistant (Sayle & Co)
Blake, J., metallurgist (Borneo Co.) Sarawak
Blake, J. S., Fort adjutant (Army Staff)
Blakeley, Chas., clerk (Tillson, Hermann & Co.) Manila
Blakeman, A. N., secretary (Chamber of Commerce) and secretary (Indo-Chinese Sugar Co.) Wyndham Street
Blakeway, G., merchant (Societé Anonyme Franco-Japonaise) Yokohama
Blakiston, Thos., merchant (Blakiston, Marr & Co) Hakodadi
Blanchard, H. M., superintendent godowns (P. M. S. S. Co.) Yokohama
Blanchard, —., captain, Shanghai
Blanchet,—., chief engineer (M. M. S. S. Menzaleh)
Blancheton, E., actg. consul (French Consulate) Hankow and Shanghai
Blanco, J., merchant (Blanco, Domingo & Co.) Manila
Blancsubé, Jules, barrister, Saigon
Bland, O., Resident, Yokohama
Bland, C S, bill broker, Yokohama
Blass, M., assistant (Bush, Blass & Son) Yokohama
Blass, M. assist. (Herizog & Roth) Yokohama
Blass, M., storekeeper (Bush and Blass) Yokohama
Bleecker, A., assistant (Sailor's Home)
Blethen, C., assist. (Farnham & Co.) S'hai
Blethen, C. P., shipwright (S. C. Farnham & Co) Shanghai
Block, F. H., merchant (John Burd & Co.) (absent)
Blockley, A., police inspector (Japan Railway,) Yokohama
Blodget, Rev. Henry, D.D., miss. Peking
Blogg, J. A., clerk (Butterfield & Swire) Queen's Road
Bloodgood, D., fleet surgeon, U.S.N. (Hartford)
Bloom, Henry, master mariner, Bangkok
Bloom, J. H., manager (Saigon Advertiser, &c.) Saigon
Blow, H. McC., storekeeper (P. L. Laen & Co.) Tientsin

Blundel, A. W., assist. engineer (Govt. Railroad) Yokohama and Hiogo
Blundell, B., clerk (Japan Butchery) Yokohama
Blundell, Bryan, commission agent, Yokohama
Blydenburgh, W. J., merchant (Smith, Archer & Co.) Shanghai
Blyth, John, manager (Borneo Co.) B'kok (absent)
Blyth, P. L., clerk (Pickford & Co.) Cebu (absent)
Boad, Wm., pilot (tug-boat) Taku
Board, W. K. clerk (Japan railway)
Board, W. K., shipwright (Board & Co.) Hiogo
Boath, J. engineer (P. & O. service)
Bochu, Julius, hatter (Secker & Co.) Manila (Cebu)
Bœdinghaus, C. E., merchant, Nagasaki
Boehmer, L. (Jap. Govt.) Yedo (Kaitikushi)
Boehncke, A. W., act. light-keeper (West Volcano light-house) Shanghai
Boffey, William, tailor (Lane, Crawford & Co.) Queen's Road
Bogahhoy, C. manager (R. Alladinbhoy)
Bogel, F. L. W. N., commission merchant, Osaka
Bogel, N. F. W., resident, Hiogo
Böger, H., merchant (Kirchner, Böger & Co.) Shanghai
Bohdanoff, I. N., clerk (N. A. Nefedieff) Tientsin
Boblschau, P., clerk (E. Schellhass & Co) Shanghai
Bohn, P., undertaker and furnisher, Yokohama
Boinville, A. C. de, architect and assistant surveyor (Jap. Govt.) Yedo
Bois, J. C., clerk (Butterfield & Swire) Shanghai
Bojesen, C., electrician (Gt. Northern Ex. Tel. Co.)
Boldero, A. A., lieut. R.N. (*Thistle*)
Bollenhagen, E. clerk, (Kniffler & Co.) Yokohama
Bolles, T. D., master U.S.N. (*Ashuelot*)
Bolliet, John, secretary archivist (Chamber of Commerce) Saigon
Boldmida, G., merchant, Yokohama
Bolt, Chas. J., assist. paymr. in charge (*Kestrel*)
Bolton, Fred, clerk (Ker & Co.) Manila
Bolton, W., surgeon (P. & O. service)
Bomanjee, P. F., merchant (Cowasjee Pallanjee & Co.) Shanghai (absent)
Bomonjee, P., clerk (D. D. Ollia) Amoy
Bon, H., merchant (Bavier & Co.) Osaka
Bonand, E., watchmaker, Yokohama
Bond, G., tidewaiter, Customs, Swatow
Bond, W. H., Lieut Com., R.N. (*Mosquito*)
Bone, F. F., mid., R.N. (*Iron Duke*)
Boneboan, J., (Mussagorius Maritimes Co.)

Bonger, E., Navigating Officer (National S. S. Co. of Nipon) Yokohama
Bonger, M. C., architect, Hiogo
Bonger, W. C., architect, Hiogo
Bonhomme, L., chief engineer (M. M. S. S. *Provence*)
Bonifacio, V., secretary, bishopric of Yloilo, Manila
Bonnat, L., Hotel keeper (Oriental Hotel) Yokohama
Bonnefond, B., clerk (J. B. Lehmann) Saigon
Bonnell, S. R., instructor (Govt. School) Nagasaki
Bonney, N. B., broker (Bonney & Co.) Shanghai
Bonnissent, —., chief, 1st bureau, Saigon
Bono, C V., tidewaiter, Customs, Shanghai
Bonville, —., drill master (Yokoska Arsenal) Yokohama
Boone, Rev. W. S., missionary, Hankow (Wuchang)
Boordacheff, F. S., merchant, Tientsin
Booth, G., tailor (Lane Crawford & Co.) Yokohama
Borchardt, F., broker (Jurgens & Borchardt) Shanghai
Bordenave, D., Marine Surveyor to Lloyds (Manila)
Borel, A., accountant (Arsenal) Foochow
Borel, L., merchant (Abegg, Borel & Co.) Yokohama
Borel, L., clerk (Vrard & Co.) Tientsin
Borntraeger, F. (Borntraeger & Co.) S'hai
Borntraeger, J. M. (Borntraeger & Co.) Shanghai (absent)
Borries, W., apothecary, Manila
Borrodaile, J. F., Tidewaiter, Customs, Hankow
Bosch, J. de, vice-consul (British Consulate) Sual
Bosch, W., clerk (F. Peil) Pedder's Wharf
Bosma, H., clerk (Netherlands Trading Society) Hiogo
Boswell, J. B., Godown keeper (S. S. N. Co.) Shanghai
Botelho, A., apothecary (Civil Hospital) Hospital Road
Botelho, A. A., clerk (Olyphant & Co.)
Botelho, A. C., clerk (Harbour Master's Department)
Botelho, A. G., clerk (Frazar & Co.) Shanghai
Botelho, M. M., compositor (*Hongkong Times*)
Bothelo, D., assistant light keeper (Chapel Island) Swatow
Bottado, P., clerk (Norton & Lyall) Queen's Road
Bottomley, C. D., broker, Shanghai
Bouffier, —. Chief Artificer (Jap. Govt.) Yedo

Boulet, J. H., compradore (Woodruff & Co.) Yokohama
Boulineau, —, carpenter (Arsenal) Foochow
Boulle, E., Assistant (Oriental Hotel, Yokohama
Boulton, Wm. R., commander, R.N. (Kestrel)
Bourdon, G., commander (M. M. steamer Iraouaddy)
Bouret, H. A., compradore, Bangkok
Bourguignon, L. (Govt. Silk Reeling Factory) Yedo
Bouriau, A., merchant (Bourjau & Co.) (absent)
Bourke, H. G., Engineer, R. N. (Mosquito)
Bourke, R., clerk (Townend & Co.) Hankow
Bourlet, —, commis. de marine, Saigon
Bourne, W., auctioneer (Bourne & Co.) Yokohama
Boustead, E., Jr., merchant (Tillson, Herrmann & Co.) Manila
Boustead, R. N., assist. (Sayle & Co.) Alexandra Terrace
Boutefol, P. H. T., master mariner, Bangkok
Boutkes, P., clerk (M. J. B. Hegt) Yokohama
Bouverie, C. W. P., sub-lieut, R.N. (Frolic)
Bovet, A., merchant (Bovet, Bros. & Co.) Shanghai
Bovet, G., clerk (Bovet, Bros. & Co.) Shanghai
Bovis, F. de, clerk (B. K. & S. Banking Corp.)
Bowden, Frank, accountant (Caldwell and Brereton) Hollywood Road
Bowen, E., supt. (Sailors' Home) Shanghai
Bowers, S., merchant (Wm. Rees & Co) Ningpo
Bowers, W., light keeper (Public Works Department) Yokohama
Bowler, T. L., Resident, Hongkong
Bowman, C. G., master, U. S. N. (Yantic)
Bowman, G. F., agent (P. M. S. S. Co.) Shanghai
Bowman, J., engineer, R. N. (Curlew)
Bowra, E. C., com., Customs, Canton (on duty at Vienna)
Bowyer, Miss, missionary, Nankin
Boyce, R. H., C E., Surveyor (H. B. M.'s Office of Works) Shanghai
Boyd, M. W., (Chartered Bank) Queen's Road (absent)
Boyd, T. D., merchant (Boyd & Co.) Amoy (absent)
Boyé, C., Commissaire (M. M. S. S. Tigre)
Boyes, F. C., clerk (Dentjan & Co.) Praya
Boyle, R. V., chief engineer (Railways and Telegraphs) Yokohama
Boyol, H. V., clerk (Brown & Co.) Amoy
Boyol, J., tidewaiter, Customs, Shanghai
Bracegirdle, G., pattern maker (Imperial Arsenal) Tientsin

Brackenridge, J., asst. examiner, Customs, Tientsin
Braddon, H. E., bill and bullion broker, Hongkong Hotel
Bradfield, J., druggist (J. Llewellyn & Co.) Shanghai
Bradford, O. B., Deputy consul general (U. S. Consulate) Shanghai
Bradley, Dan. F., Assist. missionary, B'kok
Bradley, Miss. M. A., asst. missionary, Bangkok
Bradley, Mrs. M. C., missionary, Bangkok
Bradley, Mrs. S. B., missionary, Bangkok
Bradley, Rev. C. B., missionary, Bangkok
Bradley, W. M., assist. (Thorne Bros.) Shanghai
Bradshaw, J. L., captain, H.M. 80th Regt.
Brady, G., captain (str. White Cloud) Macao
Braga, C., assist. bookkeeper (Osaka Mint)
Braga, F., Proprietor (Nagasaki Express) Nagasaki
Braga, G. M, assist. (J. M. F. da Costa) Bangkok
Braga, J., assistant (Lane Crawford & Co.) Shanghai
Braga, J., merchant (L. Joseph & Co.) Hiogo
Braga, V. E., acct. (Osaka Mint)
Bramston, J., Attorney General
Bran, M., (School of Foreign Languages) Yedo
Brand, D., clerk (Brand Bros. & Co.) S'hai (absent)
Brand, E., pilot, Shanghai
Brand, J., clerk (Brand Bros.) Shanghai (absent)
Brand, J. T., silk inspector (Brand, Bros. & Co.) Shanghai
Brand, R., silk inspector (Brand Bros. & Co.) Shanghai (absent)
Brand, W., merchant (Westall, Brand & Co.) Shanghai
Brandão, A. C., (Tribunal of Commerce) Macao
Brandão, A. J., clerk (D. Sassoon, Sons & Co.)
Brandão, J. C., clerk (China and Japan Trading Co.) Shanghai
Brandt, Miss L., schoolmistress (Foundling House (West Point)
Brandt, M. von, Minister (German Legation) Yedo
Brandt, O., bill broker, Shanghai
Brandt, P., Supt. of Govt. Tailors, Yedo
Branth, A., clerk (Dircks & Krüger) S'tow
Branzell, A., agent in the provinces for Larrieu & Roque, Saigon
Bratmuller, —, Artisan (Japan Government) Yedo
Braund, J., private Mun. Police) Y'hama
Bray, Monsr. (French Mission) Kowkeang
Brécard, T., Assistant (Larrieu & Roque) Saigon
Breck, R. A., master U.S.N. (Yantic)

Bredon, Robert E., Chief Secretary, Customs, Peking
Breen, J., fresh water supplier, Nagasaki
Breese, J., assist. paymaster U.S.N. (Saco)
Bremer, L. J. (Fulton Market Butchery) Nagasaki
Bremner, C., Ship's Steward, Royal Naval Victualling Depôt, Yokohama
Bremner, J., paymaster, R.N. (Princess Charlotte) Naval Yard
Brenan, B., assistant (British Consulate) Shanghai (absent)
Brenan, E. V., chief officer (Chinese gunboat) Feihoo
Brennan, W., assist. Tide Surveyor (Chinhai Station) Ningpo
Brennwald, C., merchant (Siber & Brennwald) consul general for Switzerland, Yokohama
Brent, A., merchant (Hudson, Malcolm & Co., Yokohama
Brent, W., broker (Bennett & Brent) Yokohama
Brenton, R. O. B. C., Lieut. R.N. (Cadmus)
Brereton, Wm. H., solicitor (Caldwell and Brereton)
Bret, Pere J. B., missionary (Roman Cath. Mission) Ningpo (Tinghai, Chusan)
Bretonnière, —., machinist (Yokoska Arsenal) Yokohama
Breton, Leonard Le, tidewaiter, Customs, Takow
Bretschneider, Dr E., physician (Russian Legation) Peking
Brett, A. L., assistant, Customs, Hankow
Brett, J. C., chief officer (str Namoa)
Brett, W. R., chemist, Yokohama
Brewer, Rev. J., missionary (Wes. Mission Society) Hankow (Wuchang)
Brewer, Thos., assist. (J. Llewellyn & Co.) Shanghai
Bridgens, R. P., architect, Yokohama
Bridgford, S. T., capt. mar. artillery and control officer, Yokohama
Bridgman, W. B., lieut.-com., U.S.N. (Palos)
Brimley, Thomas, foreman machine shop (Kiangnan Arsenal) Shanghai
Brinkley, Lieut. F., R.A., gunnery instructor (Japan Government) Yedo
Brinster, —., director of artillery, Saigon
Brisbane, E., chief engineer (Chinese gunboat Fei-loong)
Brissonet, F., resident, Hiogo
Bristow, H., engine driver (Govt. Railway) Yokohama
Bristow, Henry B., acting interpreter (Brit. Consulate) Amoy
Bristow, H. W., head master, mission school, Sarawak
Bristow, W., publican (Diver's Arms) Queen's Road
Brito, J. M. de S. (Public Works Department) Macao

Britto, A. de, clerk (Jardine, Matheson & Co.)
Britto, C. A. de, clerk (P. & O. S. N. Co.) Praya
Britto, J. de, clerk (P. & O. Co.'s Factory) West Point
Britto, J. L., druggist (French Dispensary) Queen's Road
Broad, W., assist. engineer, R.N. (Dwarf)
Broadbent, T. W., clerk (Russell & Co.) Shanghai
Broadfield, J., (J. Thompson & Co.) Yokohama
Broadhead, C. A., officer (P. & O. service)
Broadhurst, R. C., drayman &c. (James & Wilson) Yokohama
Broadie, W. G., act. manager (Borneo Co.) Sarawak
Brockat, J., manager (H. K. & W. Dock Co.) Aberdeen
Brockett, T. clerk (Robertson & Co.) Foochow (Pagoda Anchorage)
Brodhurst, R. C., merchant, Yokohama
Broek, V. A. van den (Japan Government) Yedo
Broeschen, H., clerk (Hecht, Lilienthal & Co.) Yokohama
Bromley, J. R., clerk (Reiss & Co.) Shanghai
Broni, —., commis. de marine, Saigon
Brönsted, R., merchant, Hankow
Brook, —., resident, Yokohama
Brook, W., assistant (China Sub-marine Telegraph Co.)
Brooke, His Highness Chas. J., rajah of Sarawak
Brooke, H. H. fl., sub-lieut., R.N. (Cadmus)
Brooke, J. H., proprietor (Japan Herald Office) Yokohama
Brooks, C. W., assist. (L. Candrelier) Yedo (Tsukidji)
Broom, Aug., broker, Shanghai
Bröschen, W., clerk (Sander & Co.) Peel Street
Brosnahan, J. G., assistant engineer U.S.N. (Lackawanna)
Brossard, J. (Hotel des Colonies) Shanghai
Brossemeut, —., forger (Arsenal) Foochow
Broteland, L'Abbé C. A., R. C. Missionary, Yedo
Broughton, J. D., captain and paymaster R.M., Yokohama
Brower, T. L., chemist, Yokohama
Brown, A. N., clerk (Morris, Lewis & Co.) Shanghai
Brown, A. R., commander, steamer Thabor (Japanese Government) Yokohama
Brown, C., godown keeper (Holme, Ringer & Co.) Nagasaki
Brown, C., gunner (Harbour Master's Department)
Brown, Daniel, lieutenant (Chi. gun-boat Feiloong)

Brown, D. G., merchant (Brown & Co.) Amoy (absent)
Brown, E., proprietor (International Hotel) Canton
Brown, E. R., assistant paymaster, R.N. (*Curlew*)
Brown, F C., shipchandler (Wilson, Nichols & Co.) Amoy
Brown, G., student interpreter (British Legation) Peking
Brown, H., clerk (Nachtigal & Co) Hiogo
Brown, H. J., lieutenant (H.M. 80th Regt.)
Brown, H. O., acting commissioner, Customs) Chefoo
Brown, J., constable (British Consulate) Nagasaki
Brown, J., shoemaker (J. Kubik & Co.) Yokohama
Brown, J., clerk (*North China Herald* Office) Shanghai
Brown, J., clerk (Findlay, Richardson & Co.) Manila
Brown, J., godown-keeper (Russell & Co.) Hankow
Brown, Jno. J., bill collector (Hongkong Hotel)
Brown, Jas. L., barrister-at-law, D'Aguilar Street
Brown, J. McL., clerk (Customs) Shanghai
Brown, J. W., superintendent of coal yards (P. M. S. S. Co.) Yokohama
Brown, M., merchant (Findlay, Richardson & Co.) Yokohama (absent)
Brown, M., Jr., clerk (Findlay, Richardson & Co.) Yokohama
Brown, Peter, proprietor (Glenvue House) Chefoo
Brown, Rev. N., D D. (Amer. Bap. Miss. Union) Yokohama
Brown, Rev. S. R., D.D., missionary (Am. Reform Mission) Yokohama
Brown, R., tidewaiter (Customs) Kewkeang
Brown, R. C., broker, Shanghai
Brown, R. G., surgeon, R.N. (*Frolic*)
Brown, R. M., consul general for Hawaii, Yokohama
Brown, S., agent (Union Insurance Society of Canton) Shanghai
Brown, W., M B., med. missionary, Chefoo
Brown, W., watchmaker, Bangkok
Brown, W. (sloop *Corean Snake*) Chefoo
Brown, W., godown-keeper (Fergusson & Co.) Chefoo
Brown, W. (United States Naval Yard) Yokohama
Brown, W., godown-keeper (Takasima Colliery) Sagaritnatz
Brown, W. J, assistant (James & Wilson) Yokohama
Brown, W. T., clerk (R. C. Brodhurst) Yokohama
Browne, H. St. J., merchant (Browne & Co.) Hiogo

Browne, Miss M., missionary (Am. Meth. Epis. Miss.) Peking
Bruce, G., 2d engineer (Chinese gun-vessel *Anlan*) Canton
Bruce, James, clerk (Tait & Co.) Amoy
Bruce, R., chief engineer (P & O. service)
Bruce, R. H., tea inspector (Tait & Co.) Amoy (Tamsui)
Bruère, —., sous com. de la marine, Saigon
Brun, —., resident, Yokohama
Brun, F, teacher (First College) Yedo
Hrun, J., pilot, Ningpo
Brunat, Paul, director (Silk reeling Factory, Jap. Govt.) Yedo
Brunckhorst, E., clerk (Bourjau & Co.) Shanghai
Brundell, B., commission agent, Yokohama
Brunet, —., master of the "*Powerful*" Saigon
Brunet, —., pilot, Saigon
Brunet, P., capt·in (M. M. S *Provence*)
Bruni, F., vice-consul (Italian Consulate) Yokohama
Brunier, J., agent (China and Japan Trading Co.) Yokohama
Brunton, H. R., chief engineer (Japanese Government)
Bruse, A., clerk (Farnham & Co.) Shanghai
Brush, S. Jr., merchant (H. Church & Co.) Yokohama
Bryan, T., 2d engineer (str. *Yangtsze*)
Bryan, W., engineer, R.N. (*Growler*)
Bryant, C. (Naval College) Yedo
Bryant, C. J., tidewaiter, Customs, Canton
Bryant, N. E., clerk (Foochow Dock) Foochow
Brydon, J. H., engineer (P. & O. service)
Brynar, Julius, clerk (Walsh, Hall & Co.) Nagasaki
Bryner, J. A., clerk (Bourjau & Co.) S'hai
Bryson, Rev. T., missionary (London Miss. Society) Hankow, Woochang
Bryson, Rob., 2nd Coast Lights engineer, Customs, on duty at Foochow
Bubb, Rev. S. C., missionary, Sarawak
Buchanan, Jas., assistant (Bisset & Co.) Shanghai
Buchannan, J. R., resident, Hiogo
Buchard, —., secretary, Procureur of the Republic, Saigon
Buchheister, J. J., merchant, Shanghai
Buchholtz, L., master mariner, Bangkok
Buckle, C. E., commander, R.N. (*Frolic*)
Buckle, W. T., M.B., surgeon, Yokohama
Buckley, H. P., clerk (Shaw, Bros. & Co.) Shanghai
Buckley, J., staff surgeon, R.N. (*Rinaldo*)
Buckner, W. R. P., sub. lieut. (*Mosquito*)
Budd, U. A., clerk (Boyd & Co.) Amoy
Budde, C., mer. (Dreyer & Co.) Queen's Road (absent)
Budge, J., lightkeeper (Public Works Department) Yokohama

Budler, H., assistant, Customs, Ningpo
Buffam, C. H., clerk (Russell & Co) Kewkeang
Bulan, —., councillor (Court of Appeal) Saigon
Bull, J. H., ensign, U.S.N. (*Lackawanna*)
Bullock, T. L., assist. (Brit. Consulate) Takow and Taiwan
Bulwer, His Ex. S. H. A., Governor of Labuan
Bulwer, —., private secretary to the Governor of Labuan
Bumap, Geo. J., 1st asst. eng., U.S.N. (*Ashuelot*)
Bunker, A W., clerk (Russell & Sturgis) Manila (Albay)
Bunker, C. G., in charge (Dobie & Co.) Foochow
Burchard, E., clerk (Kirchner, Böger & Co.) Shanghai
Burchard, M., merchant (Simon, Evers & Co.) Yokohama
Burchardi, F., clerk (Pustau & Co.) S'hai
Burdon, Right Rev. bishop J. S.,
Burgess, P., M.A., M.B., Surgeon (H. M. Naval Hospital)
Burghignoli, Rev. G., Vice Prefect (Roman Catholic Church) Pottinger Street
Burjorjee, C., clerk (D. C. Tata) Hollywood Road
Burjorjee, D., clerk (D. C., Tata) Shanghai
Burke, J., M D., surgeon (Brit., U. S., Swedish and Norw. Consulates) Manila
Burke, P. W., drill master, Bangkok
Burkill, A. R., merchant (Wright, Burkill & Co) Shanghai
Burman, Andrew, clerk (Hogg Bros.) S'hai
Burmeister, E., accountant (Takasima Colliery) and accountant (Glover & Co., in liquidation) Nagasaki
Burmeister, E., clerk (E. Schellhass & Co.) Shanghai
Burn, Lieut. D. B. (H. M.'s 75th Regt.) aide-de-camp to H. E. the Lieutenant Governor
Burnett, J. H., examiner, Customs, Hankow
Burnie, Ed., commander (str. *Douglas*)
Burno, Rev. G., Missionary (R. C. Mission) Amoy
Burns, B. H., assist. accountant (Oriental Bank) Yokohama
Burns, G., inspector (Police Department) Showkewan
Burnside, Rev. H., Missionary, Nagasaki
Burr, W. A., pilot (Mercantile Pilot Company) Shanghai
Burrel, E. D., tidewaiter, Customs, Foochow
Burrell, Thos., clerk (Martin & Co.) Yokohama
Burrows, A., clerk (Butterfield & Swire) Shanghai

Burrows, E., book-keeper (Frisby & Co.) Wellington Street
Burrows, O. H., merchant (Burrows & Sons) St. John's Place
Burrows, S. E., Jr., merchant (Burrows & Sons)
Burrows, T. D., examiner, Customs. C'ton
Burte, —., contractor, Saigon
Burton, W., assistant (Sayle & Co.) Shanghai
Busch, C., Examiner, Customs, Pagoda Anchorage, Foochow
Busch, H., assist. (Bœddinghaus, Dittmer & Co.) Nagasaki
Busch, H., shipchandler (Busch, Schraub & Co.) Yokohama
Buschmann, R., clerk (E. Schellhass & Co.) Wellington Street
Buse, D., clerk (Carlowitz & Co.) Praya
Buse, J., clerk (F. Peil) Pedder's Wharf
Bush, Capt. J,, harbour master, manager (Bangkok Dock Co) Bangkok
Bush, E. D., clerk (Russell & Sturgis) Yloilo
Bush, F. D., clerk (Russell & Co) Shanghai
Bush, H., interpreter (U. S. Consulate) Bangkok
Bush, H. E., merchant (Bush Bros.) Newchwang
Bush, I., storekeeper (Bush, Blass & Son) Yokohama
Bush, L. L., clerk (Russell & Co.)
Bush, S., assistant (Bush and Blass) Yokohama
Bushell, S. W., M.D., physician (British Legation) Peking (absent)
Bushmann, John, pilot, Amoy
Butcher, G. M., Resident. Yedo
Butcher, Rev. C. H., chaplain (British Consulate) Shanghai
Butland, F., boatswain, U.S.N. (*Iroquois*)
Butler, G., merchant (Balfour, Butler & Co.) Shanghai
Butler, G. A., godown keeper (S. S. N. Co.) Shanghai
Butler, Miss, milliner (M. Garrett) Queen's Road
Butler, Rev. J., miss. (Amer. Presby. Miss.) Ningpo
Butt, N. F., hairdresser (W. P. Moore) Hongkong Hotel
Buur, A. H., Master Mariner, Bangkok
Buyers, W. B., 2nd engineer (str. *Poyang*)
Bye, J., constable (Brit. Consulate) Yedo
Byramjee, B., broker, Hollywood Road
Byramjee, M., clerk (D. S. Futtakia) Canton
Byrant, Rev. E., missionary (London Miss. Society) Tientsin
Byrne, E . resident, Hiogo
Byrne, E., draper (Watson & Co.) S'hai
Byrne, G., assistant (Sayle & Co.)

C

Cabeldu, P. S., tailor, Hiogo
Cabouret, —., finisher (Arsenal) Foochow
Cabral, F. A. de O., Commandant (*Tejo*) Macao
Cabral, J. A. R., professor of Latin (St. Joseph's College) Macao
Cabral, Lieut. F. A. C., Junta da Justica Militar, Macao
Cabreira, Major D. L., retired officer (Timor Corps) Macao
Canqueray, Catherine, Sister (Hospital St. Joseph) Ningpo
Cadell, G. B., merchant, (Smith, Bell & Co.) Manila (absent)
Caderdina, R., merchant, Cage St. (absent)
Cahill, D., engineer (National S. S. Co. of Nipon) Yokohama
Caill, —., master mason (Yokoska Arsenal) Yokohama
Caillens, J., Saddler, Yokohama
Cairns, R. H., marine surveyor, Mosque Terrace
Caldbeck, E. J., clerk (Gibb, Livingston & Co.) Shanghai
Calder, J. F., assistant (Boyd & Co) N'saki
Calder, John, chief officer, Chinese gunboat *Sui Tsing*
Caldeira, Jr., F. A. M., Attorney General, Macao
Caldwell, C., clerk (Laudstein & Co.)
Caldwell. Dr. R., Physician & Surgeon, Nagasaki
Caldwell, D. E., clerk (Caldwell & Brereton)
Caldwell, D. R., Chinese interpreter, Hollywood Road
Caldwell, H. C., solicitor and notary public (Caldwell & Brereton)
Caldwell, J., staff surgeon, R.M.L.I. Yokohama
Caldwell, R., assistant (McDonald & Co's patent slip) West Point
Calice, Henry de, chargé d'affaires and consul general in China, Japan and Siam (Austro Hungarian Consulate) Yedo
Calinaud, —., 2nd architect (Surveyor General's office) Saigon
Callagher, F., tide surveyor and Harbour Master, Tientsin
Callandar, A. F., mate, U.S.N. (*Idaho*)
Callinaud, —., chief civil engineer, Saigon
Callwell, W. H., sub, Lieut. R.N. (*Cadmus*)
Calver, E. V., tidewaiter, Customs, Amoy
Cama, F. B., merchant Peel Street
Camajee, D. N., merchant (Camajee & Co.) Shanghai
Cameron, E., manager (H'kong. and S'hai. Bank'g. Corp.) Shanghai
Cameron, O. S., commander, R.N. (*Hornet*)
Caminha, C. R., Sub-Lieut. (*Principe Dom Carlos*) Macao
Camp, H. O. de la, merchant (Heinemann & Co.) Yokohama
Campana, —., com. de la marine, Saigon
Campbell, A., assist. (Smith & Co.) Yedo
Campbell, A., merchant (Campbell & Co) Shanghai
Campbell, A., clerk (Olyphant & Co.) S'hai
Campbell, D., tidewaiter, Customs, Foochow
Campbell, D. C, pilot (Black Ball Pilot Company) Shanghai
Campbell, James, manager (National Bank of India) Queen's Road
Campbell, Mrs., resident, Yokohama
Campbell, P., ship-chandler (Quelch and Campbell) Swatow
Campbell, Rev. W., missionary, Taiwan
Campbell, S, clerk, Customs, Shanghai
Campbell, T., light-house keeper, Chefoo
Campbell, Thos. M., "Cosmopolitan Hotel," Chefoo.
Campbell, Wm., M. D., British Consulate, Bangkok
Campos, B. P., foreman (Noronha & Sons)
Campos, E. P., clerk (P. & O. S. N. Co.)
Campos, F. N. P. do, assistant (Messageries Maritimes) Shanghai
Campos, J. P., clerk (A. A. de Mello & Co. Macao
Campos, L. P., clerk (P. & O. S. N. Co.)
Camrun, C, "Union Tavern," Whampoa
Canal, —., Copyist, Trib. 1st instance, S'gon
Cance, W., clerk (Little & Co.) Shanghai
Candau, V., clerk (Larrieu & Roque) Saigon
Candido, da Silva, apprentice engineer (H'kong & W'poa Dock Co.) Aberdeen
Candrelier, L., store-keeper, Yedo
Cañete, —., judge (Court of Appeal) Manila
Cann, J. J., commission agent, Shanghai
Canny, J. M., merchant and French consular agent, (absent)
Caño, J. A. M. del, consul for Spain, Macao
Canse, R. M. C., restaurant keeper, Yedo
Cantelli, V., cashier (Comptoir d'Escompte de Paris) Yokohama
Cape, J. S., assistant dispenser (H. M. Naval Hospital)
Cape, Thos, engineer R.N. (*Teaser*)
Capello, H. C. de B., 2nd com. (*Tejo*) Macao
Capitaine, —., machinist (Yokoska Arsenal) Yokohama
Capp, Rev. E. P., miss., Chefoo (absent)
Capron, Gen. H. (Japan Government) Yedo (Kaitikushi)
Caraman, F., wine merchant, Saigon
Carani, F., assistant (W. Saunders) S'hai
Carballo, J., clerk (Ker & Co.) Manila (Yloilo)
Carbollo, José, clerk (G. v. P. Patel & Co.) Manila
Cardi, J. Senior, M.D., Ice manufacturer, Saigon
Cardi, J., Apothecary, Saigon

Cardoza, A. L., assist. (Nagasaki Express) Nagasaki
Cardwell, Rev. J. E., and Mrs., missionaries, Kewkeang
Cargill, W., assist. (Pitman & Co.) Yokohama
Cargill, W. W., director of telegraphs, Yokohama
Carion, F. D., compositor (H'kong Times)
Carion, L. J. F., compositor (H'kong Times)
Carles, W. R., 3rd assistant, (British Legation) Peking
Carlisle, E., chief engineer (National S. S. Co. of Nipon) Yokohama
Carlmann, T., shoemaker (F. H. Smith) Yokohama
Carlos, B., pilot, (Pilot Co.) Newchwang
Carlos, S. A., clerk (Andrews & Co.) Manila
Carlotta, C., clerk (Russell & Sturgis) Surigao
Carlowitz, R. v., merchant (Carlowitz & Co.) (absent)
Carlson, W., light keeper, Customs (Woosung Bar) Shanghai
Carlton, I. O., clerk (Smith, Archer & Co.) Shanghai
Carmac, C., chief officer (M. M. S. Donnai)
Carmichael, A., assist. (Farnham & Co.) Shanghai
Carmichael, A. T., manager (Chartered Bank) Shanghai
Carmichael, James, engineer (str. Maggie Lauder) Shanghai
Carmichael, J. R., M.D., (Carmichael & Myers) Chefoo
Carmody, R. E., Lieut. U S. N. (Ashuelot)
Curmons, —., judge, Manila
Carneiro, B. E., merchant, Macao
Carnforth, J., chief engineer (str. Douglas)
Carnie, F., (J. M. Canny & Co.) Chinkeang and Shanghai
Carpenter, A , Lieut. R. N. (Iron Duke)
Carr, Henry J. H., "British Inn," Queen's Road West
Carr, J. H., tidewaiter, Customs, Swatow
Carr, R. P., tidewaiter, Customs, Newchwang
Carrall, J. W., assistant, Customs, Canton
Carréro, F., Sister (Maison de Jesus Enfant) Ningpo
Carrier, E. (Pillon & Co) Yokohama
Carrigan, A. C., (Dr. Macgowan) Shanghai
Carrington, Rev. J., missionary (American Presbyterian Mission) Bangkok
Carrion, M., clerk (Macleod, Pickford & Co. Cebú
Carroll, A., Engine driver (Govt. Railway) Yokohama
Carroll, Chas., vice-consul (British Consulate) Pagoda Anchorage, Foochow (absent)
Carroll, J., head teacher, nav. school (Arsenal) Foochow
Carroll, J. D., shipchandler (J. D. Carroll & Co.) Yokohama
Carroll, R., captain (steamer Poyang)
Carrothers, Rev. C., missionary, Yedo
Carte, E. L., engineer, R. N. (Iron Duke)
Carter, P., mail boat proprietor (Carter's Hotel) Bangkok
Carter, W., private (Municipal Police) Yokohama
Carter, W. H., silk broker (Carter & Co.) Shanghai
Cartier, Adjt. (Jap. Govt.) Yedo
Carvalho, A. de, bailiff (Procurador's Dept.) Macao
Carvalho, A. C. M. de, aide-de-camp to the Governor of Macao
Carvalho, A. H. de, printer, Shanghai
Carvalho, G. M. de, clerk (Oriental Bank) Hicgo
Carvalho, J., clerk (Olyphant & Co.) S'hai
Carvalho, J. A., cashier (Treasury) Hollywood Road
Carvalho, J. C. de, bailiff (Procurador's Department) Macao
Carvalho, J. H. de (Municipal Council) Macao
Carvalho, J. L. de, bailiff (Procurador's Department) Macao
Carvalho, L. F. de, writer (Naval Yard) Wyndham Street
Carvalho, M. A. de, clerk (H. and S. Banking Corporation) Shanghai
Carvalho, M. do (Turner & Co.) Wellington Street
Carvalho, P. M. de, clerk (Oriental Bank) Shanghai
Carvalho, P. M. de, clerk (Procurador's Department) Macao
Carvalho, Rev. A. L. de, president (St. Joseph's College) Macao
Carvanza, José, captain (Naval Department.) Manila
Cary, A. G., commander (steamer Kinshan)
Casal, A. P., timber merchant (Casal Bros.) Manila
Casal, J. de, timber merchant (Casal Bros.) Manila
Case, A. M., clerk (Gibb Livingston & Co.) Shanghai
Casembrost, L G. de, resident, Yokohama
Cass, J. G., agent (Elles & Co.) Tamsui and Keelung
Cass, F., clerk (Elles & Co) Amoy
Cassambhoy, E. merchant, Lyndhurst Terrace
Cassell, D., lieut. commander, U.S.N. (Ashuelot)
Cassels, J. T., clerk (Ker & Co.) Manila
Castle, W. C., tidewaiter (Customs) Shanghai
Castello, Branco, major H. G. de L., Governor of Timor Corps, Macao
Castera, —., river pilot, Saigon

Casteren van Cattenburch, H. W., assist. (Netherlands Trading Society) N'saki
Castillo, S. P., clerk (*Emily Jane*) S'hai
Castro, A., tidewaiter, Customs, Kewkeang
Castro, C. C. de, tidewaiter, Customs, T'sin
Castro, Dr. H. de, colonial secretary, Macao
Casumji, G., manager (A. Futthabhoy) Cochrane Street
Caswell, Jas. G., merchant, British consul (Wm. G. Hale & Co) Saigon (absent)
Caswell, S., fitter (Japan Railway)
Caswell,—., machinist (Jap. Govt.) Yedo
Catel, L., chief officer (M. M. S. S. *Hoogly*)
Catoire, A., shipwright, Saigon
Cauchfert, E., clerk (Kaltenbach, Engler & Co.) Saigon
Cavendish, J., tidewaiter (Customs) S'hai
Caw, Thos., merchant (Findlay, Richardson & Co.) Manila
Cawasjee, S , clerk (Hongkong Hotel)
Cawley, G., general assistant (Govt. college of engineering) Yedo
Caylor, A., steward (Grand Hotel) Y'hama
Cazeaux,—., tinman, Saigon
Cazelles,— , director of arsenal, Saigon
Ceely, C. H., paymaster, R.N. (*Cadmus*)
Célard, Madeleine,sister, H'pital St.Joseph, Ningpo
Colestin, F., Gaoler (U. S. consulate) Amoy
Cembrano, J., clerk (Ker & Co.) Manila
Center, A., agent (P. M. S. S. Co.) Hiogo
Centurioni, C., baker, Yokohama
Cerle, —., forger (Arsenal) Foochow
Chaalons, Mdlle., Ladies Academy, Saigon
Chaberisner, Victoire (Govt. Silk Reeling Factory) Yedo
Chagas, F. Z. das, clerk (Surveyor General's Department) West Point
Chagas, M. J., clerk (E. R. Handley) Praya West
Chagneau, R. (Messageries Hotel) Shanghai
Chaignou, —., notary public, Saigon
Chalker, A., assist. (Sayle & Co) Shanghai
Chalmers Rev. J., M.A., missionary (London Missionary Society) Canton
Chalmers, J. C., painter and glazier (Chalmers & Co.) Shanghai
Chalmers, James L., assistant (Customs) Tientsin
Chamaison, L'abbé J. B., Miss. Apost., Yokohama
Chambers, A. F., clerk (Jardine, Matheson & Co.) Queen's Road
Chambers, H. J. J., tea inspector (John Forster & Co.) Amoy
Chambers, Right Rev. Walter, bishop, Labuan and Sarawak
Chambers, T., agent (Army and Navy Scripture Readers Society)
Champenois, C., commander (M. M. S. S. *Amazone*)
Champon, M., butcher, Saigon
Chandler, J. H., interpreter, Bangkok

Chape, George, clerk (McEwen, Frickel & Co.) Queen's Road
Chapin, Miss Jane E. (American Board of Miss.) Peking
Chapin, Rev. L. D., missionary, Peking
Chapman, F., merchant (Chapman, King & Co) Shanghai (absent)
Chapman, T., Tidewaiter (Customs) Canton
Chapman, T. H., public tea inspector, Foochow
Chapman, T. S., resident (Kaluka Outstation) Sarawak
Chapsal, J., clerk (Messageries Maritimes) Yokohama
Charay, Mlle. M. (Govt. Silk Reeling Factory) Yedo
Chariot, —., engineer of bridges, Saigon
Charleson, Geo., light-keeper (Japanese Government) Yokohama
Charlesworth, G., clerk (Japan Railway)
Charuieh, J. N , clerk (Haminoff, Rodinoff & Co.) Hankow
Charpentier, E., slaughter house farmer, Saigon
Charrier, A. (French Livery Stables) S'hai
Chart, A., engineer &c. (J Inglis & Co.) Praya East
Chartin, T., tidewaiter (Customs) S'hai
Chastel, E., merchant (Dubost & Co.) Queen's Road
Chatelain, —., sous com. de la Marine, Saigon
Chater, C. P., broker, Caine Road
Chater, J. T., share broker, Caine Road
Chatron, Rev. D. (R. C. Church) Nagasaki
Chatron, J. (govt. silk reeling Factory) Yodo
Chaumet, Rev. B. M., R. C. missionary, Bangkok
Cheesman, W. E., assist. (Public Works Dept.) Yedo
Cheetham, J. C., captain (Takasima tug boat) Nagasaki
Chenenaille, —., chief cantonnier, municipality, Saigon
Cherami, J. (govt. silk reeling Factory) Yedo
Cherepanoff, T., clerk (Okooloff & Tomakoff) Hankow
Cherest, V., merchant (Guichard & Fils) Manila
Cheshire, F. D., clerk (Augustine Heard & Co.) Canton
Cheshire, W., average stater (Cheshire & Co.) Yokohama
Chessney, J., 2nd engineer (str. *Kinshan*
Chester, F., sergeant (Mun. Police) Y'hama
Cheverton, J. H., clerk (Jardine, Matheson & Co.) Shanghai
Chevillard, Rev.—., missionary (French R. C. Mission) Bangkok (Thakhien)
Chevrior,—., (Catholic Mission) Peking
Cheyne, A., clerk (Jardine, Matheson & Co.)

Child, F. A., clerk (Japan Railway)
Child, Thos., gas engineer, Customs, P'king
Chinchon, Rev. A., missionary (Roman C. Church) Amoy and Formosa
Chipman, H. S., merchant (Chipman, Stone & Co) Yokohama
Chipp, Wm., (Naval College) Yedo
Chisholm, E. A., engineer (Takasima tugboat) Nagasaki
Chivers, J., tidewaiter Customs, Bangkok
Chomercau, Lamotte, Act. Sec. to Governor, Saigon
Chomley, F., merchant (Brown & Co.) Amoy
Christians, J. H., pilot, Bangkok
Christiansen, C., master mariner, Bangkok
Christiansen, F. C. clerk (Gt. N. Teleg. Co.) Amoy
Christiansen, K. L., master mariner, B'kok
Christie, W., naval architect (Kiangnan Arsenal) Shanghai
Christien,—., resident, Yokohama
Christison, John (Naval College) Yedo
Christy, F. C., resident, Yedo
Christy, F. C., Locomotive superintendent (Government Railroad) Yokohama
Christy, W., clerk (Elles & Co.) Amoy
Chrystall, W., clerk (lyphant & Co.) S'hai
Chun Ayin, reporter (China Mail) and editor Chinese Mail, Hollywood Road
Church, E. J., commander, R.N. (Curlew)
Church, H., merchant, Yokohama
Church, T., clerk (N. C. Insurance Co.)
Churton, C. S., chemist (British Dispensary) Shanghai
Cinatti, D., officer (Tejo) Macao
Ciret, —., aide com. de la marine, Saigon
Clans, J., clerk (Knoop & Co.) Shanghai
Clark, A., assistant (Stentz, Harvey & Co.) Yokohama
Clark, C. A., ensign, U.S.N. (Saco)
Clark, C. B., clerk of works (Engineer's Office) Shanghai
Clark, E. W., A.M., French and English instructor (Japanese Govt.) Yedo
Clark, J. S., Col. Secretary, &c., Labuan
Clark, R., general assistant (Government Engineering College) Yedo
Clark, S. (Japanese Government) Yedo (Kaitikushi)
Clark, W., commission agent (Ice House) Yokohama
Clark, W. T., assistant freight clerk (P. M. S. S. Co.) Shanghai
Clarke, B. A., clerk (Jardine, Matheson & Co.) Shanghai
Clarke, F. S., assistant (Borneo Company) Bangkok
Clarke, G., chief engineer (P. & O. service)
Clarke, Geo., examiner, (Customs) Newchwang
Clarke, Geo., clerk (David Sassoon, Sons & Co.) Shanghai
Clarke, H. S., sub-lieut. R.N. (Iron Duke)

Clarke, J., boatswain, R.N. (Opossum)
Clarke, R., proprietor, (Yokohama Bakery) Yokohama
Clarke, R. H., assistant paymaster, R N. (Cadmus)
Clarke, W., sen., chief engineer (Kwangtung)
Clarke, W., jun., chief engineer (Numwa)
Clarke, W. E., butcher (Burgess & Co.) Y'hama
Clarke, W. J., merchant (Fergusson & Co.) Chefoo
Clarke, W. L., assistant (Watson, Cleave & Co.) Shanghai
Claro, S., assistant (Eugster & Co.) Manila
Clasen, H. G., clerk (O. Stammann) T'tsin
Claude, C. S., assistant accountant (Oriental Bank) Osaka
Clausen, ?. (Hook and Ladder Brigade) Yokohama
Cleland, M, provision dealer, Yedo
Claussen, F. E., clerk (E. Schellhass & Co.) Shanghai
Claussen, P., proprietor, "Union Saloon," Yokohama
Clayson, W. H., captain (Chinese gunboat Fei hoo)
Cleeve, S. W., chemist (Watson, Cleeve & Co.) Shanghai
Cleeve, C. K., assistant controller (Control Department) West Terrace
Clément, —., contractor and boardinghouse keeper, Saigon
Clément, Mdme., storekeeper, Saigon
Clemente, E., official, Post Office, Manila
Cleonie, —, assistant registrar, trib. of 1st instance, Saigon
Clifford, A., surgeon (P. & O. service)
Clifford, J., clerk (Gilman & Co.) Shanghai
Clifton, A. S. T., assistant (North China Insurance Company) Shanghai
Clifton, C., constable (British Consulate) Shanghai
Clohn, —, master mariner, Bangkok
Clodd, W. E., tidewaiter (Customs) S'hai
Clouth, Chas., M.D., Physician to German Consulate, Wyndham Street
Clow, R. H., private (Mun. Police) Y'hama
Clunis, J., civil architect, Bangkok
Clyatt, W. B. (Clyatt & Co.) Newchwang
Coales, T., magazine foreman (Control Department)
Coare, Fred. W., merchant (Coare, Lind & Co.) Canton
Coate, T. A., assistant (J. Llewellyn & Co.) Shanghai
Coates, A., merchant (Ker & Co.) Manila
Coates, J. E., pilot to P. & O. Co., S'hai
Cobb, C. E., tidewaiter (Customs) S'ghai
Cobden, C. H. (E. Fischer & Co.) Hiogo
Coch, F., clerk (Paul, Ehlers & Co.) Praya
Cochin, Dr. H. (Japanese Govt.) Yedo
Cochran, A., lieut., R N. (Midge)
Cochrane, Revd. G., missionary, Yokohama

Cooker, T. E., captain (Chinese gunboat Ling-fing)
Cocking, S., jr., merchant (Cocking and Singleton) Yokohama
Codevilla, José, treasurer general, Manila
Cowlry, E., chief government architect, Saigon (absent)
Cody, B. A., coroner, Labuan
Coffin, J. M. (North Saddle light-house) Shanghai
Cohen, C. C., merchant (C. C. Cohen & Co.) D'Aguilar Street
Cohen, H., merchant, Burd's Lane
Cohen, S. H. D., clerk (E. R. Belilios) Lyndhurst Terrace
Cohn, B., storekeeper, Kobe
Coifier, sub-lieut., French Marines, Yokohama
Coit, F., merchant (Coit & Co.) Ningpo
Coker, J. J. ("Nucleus" billiard rooms) Shanghai
Colaban, W. H., M.D., surgeon, R.N. (Hornet)
Colberg, M. T., master mariner, Bangkok
Cole, C. C., lieut., H. M.'s 80th Regt.
Cole, T., police inspector (Govt. Railways) Yokohama
Cole, W. F., engineer, R.N. (Thalia)
Coleman, J., barman, "Union Saloon," Yokohama
Coles, Chas., chief officer (str. Thales)
Coles, F. W., tea inspector (Margesson & Co.) Macao
Coles, G., clerk, civil service (H. M. Naval Hospital)
Colhoun, E. R., chief of U. S. Naval Staff
Colin, A. McV., surveyor general (Public Works Department) Yedo
Collago, H., clerk (Messageries Maritimes)
Collago, F. C., clerk (J. S. Hook, Son & Co.)
Collago, J., insp. of junks (Harbour Master's Department)
Collago, L. F. A., clerk (J. F. Scheffer) Praya
Collago, Major F. X., retired officer, Macao
Collago, M. A., clerk (Police Department)
Collago, R. S. ("Hiogo and Osaka Herald office) Hiogo
Collago, T., app. engineer (Novelty Iron Works)
Colleau, Oscar, consul (French Consulate) Yokohama
Coller, R. L., merchant (Holliday, Wise & Co.) Manila
Collin, J., commissaire (French Consulate) Shanghai
Collingwood, Geo., agent (Smith, Bell & Co.) Manila (Camiguin)
Collinga, C. E., clerk, 23 Queen's Road
Collins, C. (Naval College) Yedo
Collins, G. W., pilot and storekeeper (G. W. Collins & Co.) Taku and Tientsin

Collins, Henry, foreman (Japan Mail office) Yokohama
Collins, James, clerk and marriage registrar (Police Magistrates' Department) Wyndham Street
Collins, J., assistant (Eureka Saloon) Hiogo
Collins, J., tidewaiter (Customs) Tientsin
Collins, J. (Naval College) Yedo
Collins, Rev. W. H., missionary, Peking
Collins, V. D., dental surgeon, Arbuthnot Road
Collyn, J. E., assistant (Douglas & Co.) Yokohama
Colomb, F., merchant, Osaka
Colomb, J., foreman mechanic (Govt. Railroad) Yokohama
Colomb, J., merchant (J. Colomb & Co.) Yokohama
Colomb, P., clerk (Colomb & Co.) Yokohama
Colombet, Rev E. A., R. C. missionary, Bangkok
Colombo, L., clerk (Bavier & Co.) Y'hama
Colomer, Rev. Miguel, missionary, Amoy and Formosa
Colquhoun, W., clerk (Macleod, Pickford & Co.) Cebú
Coltbrup, G. J., assist. (Maltby & Co.) Nagasaki
Colvocoresses, G. W. P., master, U.S.N. (Lackawanna)
Combs, Miss L. L., M.D. (Am. Meth. Epis. Miss.) Peking
Comi, V., merchant, Yokohama
Commélerant, C., tavern-keeper, Saigon
Compagnotti, Claudia, sister (The Convent,) Caine Road
Compton, —., livery stables, Shanghai
Conard, A., teacher, Yedo
Conil, A., agent (Messageries Maritimes) Yokohama
Connell, Robert, 3rd engineer (str. Appin) Shanghai
Conners, Jno. R., supt. carpenter (P. M. S. S. Co.) Yokohama
Connor, J., private (Mun. Police) Y'hama
Considine, D., assist. undertaker (Brown, Jones & Co.) Queen's Road
Consterdine, H., naval contractor, Chefoo
Contenson, Comte G. de, attaché militaire (French Legation) Peking
Conwell, T., foreman mechanic (Govt. Railway) Yokohama
Cook, H., shipwright, Yokohama
Cook, H., (P. M. S. S. Co.) Yokohama
Cook, H. L., news agent, Yokohama
Cook, J. H., engineer, Bangkok
Cook, L., fitter (Govt. Railway) Yokohama
Cook, Mrs D., milliner, Yokohama
Cook, M. H., sailmaker, &c., Shanghai
Cook, R. H., assist. acct. (Hongkong and Shanghai Bank) Yokohama
Cook, W., shipwright (H. Cook) Yokohama

Cooke, J. E., controller (Police Force) and commandant (Anglo-Chinese Force) Ningpo
Coombe, J., boatswain, R.N. (*Ringdove*)
Coombs, J. T., engineer, R.N. (*Dwarf*)
Cooper, Chas., engineer (Witte & Co.) M'la
Cooper, D., resident, Shanghai
Cooper, H., gunner, P. & O. Service, Shanghai (Pootung)
Cooper, H. N., merchant, Honam & Hongkong
Cooper, H. V. C., boatswain, R.N. (*Iron Duke*)
Cooper, J., clerk (Cumine & Co.) Shanghai
Cooper, J. E., foreman mechanic (Govt. Railway) Yokohama
Cooper, T. W., deputy control paymaster (Control Department)
Cooper, W., commission agent, Shanghai
Cooper, W. M., acting consul (British Consulate) Chefoo
Cooverjee, H., merchant (C. Pallanjee & Co.) Lyndhurst Terrace
Cooverjee, M., merchant (Pallanjee & Co.) Lyndhurst Terrcae
Cooverjee, R., merchant (C. Pallanjee & Co.) Shanghai
Cope, A. E., clerk (H. K. & S. Bank)
Cope, Herbert, acting manager (Hongkong & Shanghai Banking Corp.) Yokohama
Corbach, W. van, pilot (Independence Pilot Company) Shanghai
Corbett, J. W., assistant (Crown & Anchor) Hiogo
Corbett, Rev. H., missionary, Chefoo
Cordeiro, A. A., clerk (Russell & Co.) Canton
Cordeiro, L. M. G., compositor (Typographia Mercantil) Macao
Cordeiro, M., tidewaiter, Customs, F'chow
Corder, G., 2nd engineer, Chinese gunboat (*Chentu*)
Cordes, A. C., merchant (Cordes & Co.) Tientsin (absent)
Cordes, A. S., clerk (Cordes & Co.) Tientsin
Cordes, C. D. H., clerk (Bourjau & Co.) Praya
Cordes, J. F., merchant and German Consul (Pustau & Co.)
Cordier, H., clerk (Russell & Co.) S'hai
Cordova, J. de, clerk (Reid, Evans & Co.) Shanghai
Coridon, —., commis. de marine, Saigon
Corion, Capt. —., French marines, Yokohama
Cornaqé, W. A., consul for Netherlands, Norway & Sweden, and U. S., and merchant (Wilson, Cornabé & Co.) Chefoo
Cornell, Rev. I. H., missionary (Am. Neth. Epis. Church Mission) Yokohama
Corner, A., captain (str. *Yangtsze*)
Corner, Geo. R., Reuter's agent Shanghai

Corner, G. N., officiating secretary (Chamber of Commerce) Shanghai
Cornes, F., merchant (Cornes, & Co.) Yokohama (absent)
Cornan, A., clerk (Ed. Renard & Co.) Saigon
Cornu, E., merchant (Ed. Renard & Co.) Saigon (absent)
Corominas, B., president, San Juan de Letran (Ecclesiastical Dept.) Manila
Correia, J. L., messenger (Revenue Dept.) Macao
Corrie, A. L. B., assist paymaster in charge (*Midge*)
Corte, Real, F. G., captain-fiscal (Police Department) Macao
Corter, J., act. marshal, (U. S. Consulate) Hankow
Cortey., —, judge, Manila
Corveth, C., assist. (Mess. Mar.)
Coryell, J. R., clerk (U. S. Consulate) Shanghai
Coryell, M., supt. (S. S. N. Co.) Shanghai
Cosieng, José, interpreter (Spanish Consulate) Amoy
Costa A. P. da, clerk (D. Sassoon, Sons & Co.
Costa, D, A. da, marine sorter (General Post-office)
Costa, F. G., compositor (De Souza & Co.) Hollywood Road
Costa, H. A. F. da, clerk (Colonial Government) Macao
Costa, G., compositor) De Souza & Co.) Hollywood Road
Costa, J. M. F. da, Inspr. (Customs) Bangkok
Costa, J. da, clerk (Gilman & Co.)
Costa, J. da (St. Joseph's College) Macao
Costa, J. A. da, Lieut (Timor Corps) Macao
Costa, J. M. da, notary public, Macao
Costa, J. P. da (H. K. soda water man. Co.)
Costa, J. P. da, clerk (Jardine, Matheson & Co,)
Costa, Lourenco da, Foreman (Typographia Merchantil) Macao
Costa, P. A. da, clerk (A. Heard & Co.)
Costard, Gabriel, 1st engineer (Chinese gunboat *Ching-tsing*)
Coste, Rev. J., vice-procurador (French Roman Catholic Mission) Staunton Street
Cottam, J. P., assistant (Mrs. J. Searle) Yokohama
Cottle, T., store issuer (H. M. Naval Yard) Shanghai
Cotton, Nathaniel, lieut. R.N. (*Curlew*)
Cotbrail, L. W., Marshal (U. S. Consulate) Hiogo
Cotwal, H. R., Cotton broker (D. C. Tata) Hollywood Road
Couder, J., assist. (Pignatel & Co.) Nagasaki

Coudroy, de Laurial, registrar Court of Appeal, Saigon
Coughtrie, J. B., secretary (China Fire Insurance) Albany Road
Couper, Ivie A., engineer, R.N. (Naval Yard)
Cour, F P. de la, tidewaiter (Customs) Shanghai
Court, A., assist. paym. in charge, R. N. (*Frolic*)
Court, S. V., interpreter to International Court, Bangkok
Courtan, A., assistant, Customs, Chinkeang
Courtenay, F., tidewaiter (Customs) Shanghai
Courtier, —., commis. de marine, Saigon
Coutel, J. B., clerk (F. Jame) Saigon
Cousin, l'Abbé J., R. C., missionary, Osaka
Cousins, E., clerk, (Ferguson & Co) Chefoo
Coutinho, M. d'A., captain (Military Department) Macao
Coutu, E. J., clerk (Jardine, Matheson & Co.) Shanghai
Coutris, A., contractor, Chefoo
Coutts, G. W., merchant (Coutts & Co.) Shanghai
Coutts, J. C., merchant (Coutts & Co.) Shanghai (absent)
Covil, Thos., tea inspector (Boyd & Co.) Amoy
Cowasjee, F., assistant (D. Nowrojee) Queen's Road
Cowasjee, H., assistant (D. Nowrojee) Queen's Road
Cowderoy, J., clerk (Hall & Holtz) Shanghai
Cowderoy, W., clerk (Hall & Holtz) S'hai
Cowie, F., assist. (Larrieu & Roque) Saigon
Cowie, G. J. W., solicitor, sec. (Shanghai Dock Co.) Shanghai
Cowie, Rev. H., missionary (English Presb. Mission) Amoy (absent)
Cowley, W. H., supt. purser (P. & O. S. N. Co.)
Cowper, I. A., engineer R. N. (Naval Yard)
Cox, J. H., clerk (Turner & Co.) Queen's Road
Cox, John S., storekeeper, &c. (Lane, Crawford & Co.) Queen's Road
Cox, Rev. Josiah, missionary (Wes. Miss. Society) Hankow (Wuchang)
Cox, Wm, constable (British Consulate) Shanghai
Coxon, A., broker, Robinson Road
Cozon, J., silk inspector (Mestern & Hulse) Canton
Crace, E. L. H., merchant (Augustine Heard & Co.) Canton (absent)
Craddock, G. T., engineer, R N. (*Frolic*)
Craddock, J., inspector of police (Police Department) Central Station
Craig, capt. (str. *Legislator*)

Craig, Robt., merchant (Boyd & Co) vice-consul Sweden & Norway, Amoy
Craig, W. G., 3rd officer (str. *Numoa*)
Craigie, W., M. A., professor of English (Jap. Govt.) Yedo
Cramer, F., assistant (Walsh, Hall & Co.) Yokohama
Crane, H. A., auctioneer (Commercial Sales Room) Yokohama
Crane, W. A., piano tuner, Yokohama
Cranston, D., mechanic (Shanghai and Pootung Foundry) Shanghai
Crasemann, E., merchant (Crasemann and Hagen) Chefoo
Craufurd, F. B N., captain, H. M. 80th Regt.
Crawford, D. R., storekeeper, &c. (Lane, Crawford & Co.) (absent)
Crawford, H., clerk (Lane, Crawford & Co.) Queen's Road
Crawford, J., surgeon, R.N. (*Iron Duke*)
Crawford, J., chief engineer (Chinese str. *Peng-chao-hai*)
Crawford, J. D., assist. in charge of accts. (British Consulate) Shanghai
Crawford, Rev. T. P., missionary, Chefoo
Crawford, Wm., clerk (Carter & Co.) S'hai
Crawley, —., engineer, Bangkok
Creagh, captain C. A., H. M. 80th Regt.
Creagh, C. V., deputy superintendent (Police Department) Central Station
Cremazy, —. (V. A. Mauras) Saigon
Crescini, D., clerk (her & Co.) Manila
Crespiguy, C. C. de, resident, (Muka out-station) Sarawak
Cressy, E. P., (First College, Jap. Govt.) Yedo
Creswell, W. R., Sub. Lieut. R.N. (*Thalia*)
Cresswell, P. E., Sub. Lieut. R.N. (*Thalia*)
Crety, C. H. de, clerk (Comptoir d'Escompte) Shanghai
Crighton, R. T., master (Langshan light vessel) Shanghai
Crinlzi, G., clerk (G. Bolmida) Yokohama
Cripps, G. fitter (Govt. Railway) Yokohama
Cristian, —., barkeeper (Hotel de la Marine) Yokohama
Crittenden, F., proprietor, "Brooklyn Hotel," Yokohama
Croad, A., assistant harbour master, (Customs) Shanghai
Croal, R., commander (receiving-ship *Ariel*) Shanghai
Croal, T. P., assist. (Hunt's Wharf) Shanghai
Crocker, A., dep. surgeon gen. of hospitals (Mil. Med. Dept.)
Crocker, J., (Naval College) Yedo
Crocker, W., commander, (steamer *Bertha*) Sarawak
Crocker, W. M. (Sarawak Trading Co.) Sarawak
Crofts, J., Shanghai Horse Bazaar, S'hai

Croix, Sœur P. de la, superioress (Asyle de Sainte Enfance) Queen's Road East
Croker, John W., engineer (Novelty Iron Works) Praya West
Cromartie, M. H., broker (Guam)
Crombie, D. A J., acting agent (Oriental Bank) Hiogo
Crombie, Rev. G., and family, missionary, Ningpo
Cromie, C., silk inspector, Shanghai
Cromwell, J. B., clerk (P. M. S. S. Co.) Praya West
Croome, L. J., engineer, R.N. (*Midge*)
Cropley, J. P. P., chief engineer (gunboat *Heartsease*) Sarawak
Crosby, Miss Julia, missionary, Yokohama
Croset, —., military instructor, Yedo
Cros, —., Adjt. (Japan Government) Yedo
Cross, R. H., gunner, U.S.N. (*Hartford*)
Cross, T., fitter (Government Railway) Yokohama
Crossan, J., engineer (P. & O. Service)
Crossette, Rev. J. F., missionary, Chefoo
Crossland, Rev. W., missionary, Sarawak
Crouch, J., tidewaiter, Customs, Chinkeang
Crouch, Miss L. H., missionary, (American Pres. Board) Canton
Crouchley, F. (*Hiogo & Osaka Herald* Office) Hiogo
Crowell, J., captain (str. *Millet*) Shanghai
Crowninshield, A. S, lieut.-commander, U.S.N. (*Lackawanna*)
Cruckshanks, W, clerk (McEwen, Frickel & Co) Queen's Road
Cruickshank, B, M.D., assistant surgeon, H.M. 80th Regiment
Cruikshank, Hon. J. B., resident (Rejang outstation) Sarawak
Cruikshank, W. J., clerk (Smith, Archer & Co) Yokohama
Cruise, W., clerk (Control Department)
Crutch, S. J., tea inspector (Reiss & Co)
Cruz, A. A. da, assistant (Falconer & Co.) Queen's Road
Cruz, A. da, assistant (Sayle & Co.) Shanghai
Cruz, D. J. da, clerk (China Dispensary)
Cruz, E. da, clerk (Arnhold, Karberg & Co.) Praya
Cruz, F. A. da, clerk (A. A. de Mello & Co.) Macao
Cruz, J. M., compositor (*Saigon Advertiser*) Saigon
Cruz, O. A. da, clerk (Aug. Heard & Co.)
Cruz, S. da, clerk (A. A. de Mello & Co.) Macao
Cruz, Th. da, clerk (J. das Neves e Souza & Co.) Macao
Cuartero, M., bishop of Yloilo (Ecclesiastical Department) Manila
Cuchen, C., clerk (French Post Office) Yokohama

Cuculiu Jose de, merchant (Cucullu & Co.) Manila
Cuddy, W., sailmaker (*Lackawanna*)
Culbertson, Rev. J. N., missionary (Amer. Pres. Mission) Bangkok
Cullen, J. P., clerk (Brand, Brothers & Co.) Shanghai
Culty, A., hairdresser, Yokohama
Cumberland, R., officer (P. & O. Service)
Cumine, A. G. T., clerk (Cumine & Co.) Shanghai
Cumine, C., merchant (Cumine & Co.) Shanghai (absent)
Cumming J., reporter (*Daily Press* office)
Cummins, F., clerk (Carter & Co.) Shanghai (absent)
Cundall, C. H., clerk (Smith, Bell & Co) Manila (Cebu)
Cunha, A. d'A. E., Jr., Ensign, Public Works Department, Macao
Cunha, F. da., Resident, Hiogo
Cunha, J. oa, clerk (Naval Yard)
Cunha, J. de, assist. (Euzicre & Co) Hiogo
Cunniffy, P., gunner, Chinese gun-vessel (*Chento*)
Cunningham, E., merchant (Russell & Co.) (absent)
Cunningham, H. M , clerk (Russell & Co.) Hankow
Cunningham, J , assist. (Lano, Crawford & Co.) Shanghai
Cunningham, J. W., pilot (Independence Pilot Co.) Shanghai
Cunningham, T. B., merchant (Russell & Co.) Canton, vice-consul for Sweden and Norway
Curballo, E , assist. (Findlay, Richardson & Co.) Manila
Cursetjee, S. J., clerk (Pallanjee & Co.) Lyndhurst Terrace
Cursetjee, V. R , merchant (Pallanjee & Co.) Lyndhurst Terrace
Curtin, J., inspector of cargo boats (Harbour Master's Department)'
Curtis, A. W., Jr., assistant (International Hotel) Yokohama
Curtis, H., Teacher (Jap. Govt.) Yedo
Curtis, H. L., reporter (*Hongkong Times*) 5, Duddell Street
Curtis, W., prop. (*Hongkong Times*) 5, Duddell Street
Curtis, W., proprietor (International Hotel) Yokohama
Cussum, K., trader, Shanghai
Cuthbertson, R. B., assistant (Lane, Crawford & Co.) Shanghai
Cuthill, W., chief engineer (Chinese g.-b. *Anlan*)
Cutting, J., assist. (Spring & Co.) Manila
Cuyugan, Vicente, notary general (Ecclesiastical Department) Manila
Czarnewsky, C., assist. (G. N. Teleg. Co.) Nagasaki

Daa   FOREIGN RESIDENTS.   Dav   23

D

Daae, J. M., clerk (Customs) Shanghai
Daberley, J. G., Mid., R N. (*Iron Duke*)
Dabry de Thiersant, P., French Consul, Canton
Da Costa, J. M. F. inspector (Customs) and merchant, Bangkok
Da Costa, N. T., broker (Da Costa & Co) Shanghai
Dadabhoy, B., broker, Shanghai
D'Addosio, —., Catholic Miss., Peking
Dagron, —., chief artificer (Jap. Govt.) Yedo
Dalden, M. C. van., Consul for Belgium and Denmark) Nagasaki
Dalgarno, A., issuer of stores (Control Department) Queen's Road East
Dalgas, C., 3rd Officer (str. *Hailoong*)
Dalgleish, W. H., clerk (Carter & Co) Shanghai
Dallas, Barnes, Broker, Shanghai
Dallas, C. H., Teacher (Jap. Govt) Yedo
Balliston, J. J. R, M D, Yokohama
D'Almada e Castro, J. M, clerk (Colonial Secretary's Department) Caine Road
D'Almada e Castro, L., clerk of councils (Colonial Secretary's Depart) Staunton Street
Dalmeida, E. F., clerk (Russell & Co) Shanghai
D'Almeida, J., clerk (Russell & Co.)
D'Almeida, J. V., secretary in charge (Portuguese Consulate) Bangkok
D'Almeida, T. M., clerk (Comptoir D'Escompte)
Dalrymple, H. L., tea inspector (Birley & Co.) Foochow
Dalrymple, L.D., pilot (Independence Pilot Co.) Shanghai
Daly, A. M., clerk (A. Heard & Co.) F'chow
Daly, S., broker, Shanghai
Damas-Ribeiro, —commis. de marine, S'gon (absent)
Dames, M., clerk (Netherlands Trading Co.) Yokohama
Damström, O. P., propr. (Glenvue House) Chefoo
Danby, W., clerk of works (S'veyor General's Office)
Danenberg, C., clerk (Reiss & Co.)
Danenberg, H., clerk (Naval Yard)
Danenberg, J., assist. (Drysdale, Ringer & Co) Shanghai
Danenberg, V., clerk (Naval Yard)
Danican, —., treasurer, Saigon
Daniel, H. W., clerk (Gibb Livingston & Co) Shanghai
Daniel, Rev., S., provicaire (Catholic Miss.) Bangkok
Daniel, Robert, mil. foreman of works (Royal Engineer Dept.)
Daniell, W. H. M., sub-Lieut., R.N. (*Dwarf*)

Daniels, G. R., light-keeper (Chapel Island) Amoy
Danielsen, J. W., merchant (H. A. Petersen & Co.) Amoy
Dantra, Dr. H. B., G.G.M.C, Robinson road
Dantra, R. B., broker, Peel Street
Dantra, R. D., broker, 24 Peel Street
Darby, W. H. F., clerk (Gibb, Livingston & Co) Aberdeen Street
Daré, A , commissaire (M. M. S. S *Peiho*)
Dare, A. H., clerk (Strachan & Thomas) Yokohama
Dare, G. M., bill broker (McDonald & Dare) Yokohama
Dare, J. J., secretary, Chamber of Commerce, Yokohama
Darling, D. A., agent (Brown & Co) T'sui
D'Arnoux, Vte. G., assistant (Customs) Amoy
Da Silva, F. R., clerk (Ziegler & Co.) Yokohama
D'Assis, F., boarding house keeper, Tank Lane
D'Assumpção, J. S., compositor (*China Mail*)
Daure, L , chief account. (Comptoir d'Escompte)
Dauver, H. R., merchant (Dauver & Co.) Amoy
Dauverchaine, O., sister (Maison de Jesus enfant) Ningpo
Davearn, B., merchant (B. Davecurn)
Davenport, R. G., master, U.S.N. (*Saco*)
Davey, W, R., engineer, R.N. (*Iron Duke*)
David, A., clerk (A. G. Hogg & Co) Saigon
David, C., clerk (Lacroix, Cousins & Co.) Shanghai
David, D. W , merchant, Chinkeang
David, S. J., merchant (E. D. Sassoon & Company)
David, —., carpenter (Yokoska Arsenal) Yokohama
Davidson, Chas., M.D., surgeon, R.N. (*Kestrel*)
Davidson, Duncan, mer. (Brown & Co.) Amoy
Davidson, F. G., assistant (P. & O. S. N. Co.) Yokohama
Davidson, G. R., tidewaiter, Customs, Amoy
Davidson, J., assistant cap factory foreman (Imperial Arsenal) Tientsin
Davidson, J., clerk (Grand Hotel) Y'hama
Davidson, J., Fitter (Govt. Railroad) Yokohama
Davidson, P., clerk (Davidson & Co.) N'po
Davidson, R. M., merchant (Davidson & Co) Ningpo
Davidson, W., merchant (Davidson & Co.) Ningpo
Davidson, W. R., merchant (Davidson & Co.) Ningpo
Davies, B., merchant, 2 Pedder's Wharf

Davies, C. F., commander (P. & O. service) Seymour Terrace
Davies, J., apothecary (Military Medical Department) Queen's Road East
Davies, O. A., chief eng., R.N. (*Thetis*)
Davies, T., clerk (Haliday & Co.) Newchwang
Davies, T., (school of foreign languages) Yedo
Davies, T., trooper (British Legation Guard) Yedo
Davila, —., judge, Manila
D'Avila, J. A., 2nd Com. (*Principe dom Carlos*) Macao
Davis, D., general merchant, Yokohama
Davis, Edward, clerk (Olyphant & Co.) Foochow
Davis, Edward, H. M., lieut., R N. (*Elk*)
Davis, H. W., merchant (Thos. Howard & Co.) West Point and agent for Purdon & Co.
Davis, J., assist. (Lake & Co.) Nagasaki
Davis, J. K., Act. Secretary (North China Insurance Co) Shanghai
Davis, J. M. C., master mariner, Bangkok
Davis, J. W. C., master mariner, Bangkok
Davis, L., general trader, Yokohama
Davis, Mrs. E., milliner and dressmaker, Yokohama
Davis, Rev. G. R., missionary, Tientsin
Davis, Rev. J., missionary, Hiogo
Davis, T., road inspector (Japanese Government) Yokohama
Davison, J., merchant (Davison & Co) Yokohama
Davison, Rev. J C., Missionary, Nagasaki
Dawbarn, A. H., clerk (D. Sassoon, Sons & Co.) Hankow
Dawson, Fred , tide-surveyor, Customs, Whampoa
D'Audigier, F.; chief, 3rd Bureau, Saigon
Day, J. E. asst. engineer (Imp. Govt. Railways) Yokohama
D'Azevedo, F., clerk (Deacon & Co) Macao
D'Azevedo, J. J., secretary, Military Hospital, Macao
D'Azevedo, J. J., captain (National Guard) Macao
D'Azevedo, J. J., acting bookkeeper (Revenue Department) Macao
Deacon, E., merchant (Deacon & Co.) Macao, acting consul for Portugal, Canton
Deacon, Richard, bill broker, agent (Foochow Dock Co.) College Gardens
Deacon, Sydney, merchant (Deacon & Co.) Macao and Canton
Dean, Rev. William, D. D., missionary, Bangkok
Deane, W. M., superintendent (Police Department) Central Station
Dess, J., mate (tug *Woosung*) Foochow
De Ath, A. (De Ath & Co.) Hiogo
De Ath, W. H. (resident) Hiogo
De Bay, H. A., merchant (De Bay, Götte & Co.) Bangkok
De Beer, G., constable (Police Force) Hiogo
Deblois, J. E., clerk (Peele, Hubbell & Co.) Manila
De Butler, captain (M. M. S. S. *Donnai*)
Decauchuis,—., founder (Arsenal) Foochow
De Cruz, José, assist. usher (Magistracy)
Deetjen, Ed., merchant (Deetjen & Co) Praya
De Gaillaude, —., com. de la marine, S'gon (absent)
Degenaer, F., merchant, D'Aguilar Street
De Greeuw, N., manager (Ling a King & Co.) Chefoo
Degron, H., director, (French Post Office) Yokohama
Deguria, R. N., (Deguria & Co) Gage Street and Canton
Deidenbach, J. clerk (Langfeldt & Mayers) Yokohama
Deighton Braysher, C., assistant Harbour Master (Customs) Shanghai
De Jong, C. G., Dr., M.D., Yokohama and Yedo
De Kerlan, Rev. —., Saigon
Delafon,—., sons com. de la marine, Saigon
De Lano, M. M., consul (U. S. & German Consulates) Foochow
Delaplace, Msgr L. G , bishop (Mission Catholique) Peking
Delboy, captain, U., P.N., Consul General for Peru, Macao
Delemasure, l'Abbé.—., R. C. missionary, Tientsin
Delemasure,—., Mission Catholique, P'king
Delestre, E , tidewaiter, Customs, F'chow
Dell 'Oro, I., merchant (Dell 'Oro & Co) Yokohame
Dell 'Oro, J., merchant (Dell Oro & Co.) Yokohama
De Longueville, C., captain (Chinese gunboat *Tien po*)
Demara, — , chief telegraphist, Saigon
Demée, F., apprentice engineer (Novelty Iron Works)
Demée, O. F., captain (Chinese gunboat *Chun-hoi*)
De Mérendol, assistant registrar, Trib. 1st instance, Saigon
Demetrius, G , purser (Sassoon's str. *China*)
Demetts, T., tidewaiter, Customs, Ningpo
Demianoff, A., clerk (Malherbe, Jullien & Co.) Bangkok
De Montesquieu, Fezensac, aide-de-camp to Government, Saigon
De Montgolfier,—., accountant (Yokoska Arsenal) Yokohama
De Montjon, M. A., commissaire adjoint, Saigon
Doneeke, C., clerk (Pustau & Co.)
D'Engente, Du M., sous commissaire, S'gon

Deniaud, —., coppersmith (Yokoska Arsenal) Yokohama
Danis, Alphonse, clerk (Denis Fréres), Saigon (absent)
Denis, E., merchant (Denis Fréres) Saigon
Denis, Gustav, merchant (Denis Fréres) and secretary (Chamber of Commerce) Saigon
Denison, H. W., deputy consul (U. S. Consulate) Yokohama
Denison, N., postmaster &c., Sarawak
Denny, J. S. H., assist. eng. R.N. (*Cadmus*)
Denny, B. St. L., lieut., R.M., Yokohama
Denny, J., foreman merchanic (Government Railroad) Yokohama
Dennys, H. L., solicitor, 1 Wyndham Street
Dennys, N. B., proprietor (Bain & Dennys) and editor (*China Mail*), secretary, City Hall, 1 Wyndham Street
Dent, A., merchant (A. Dent & Co.) S'hai
Dent, H. F., silk inspector (Birley & Co.) Canton
Dent, John, merchant (Dent & Co.) S'hai
De Poli, —., commissaire (M. M. steamer *Provence*)
De Reuter, Miss (Jap. Govt.) Yedo (Kaitikushi)
Derisley, Martin, paymaster R.N., S'hai
Dermer, T. M., clerk (Adamson, Bell & Co.) Foochow
De Sa, Caetano, apprentice engineer (H. & W. Dock Co.) Aberdeen
Descharmes, Captain (Jap. Govt.) Yedo
De Russett, W., clerk (P. & O. S. N. Co.) Praya
Desbois, Antoine, storekeeper (M. M. Co.) Saigon
Desconnet, Captain —., French Marines, Yokohama
Desgranges, F., chief engineer (M. M. Str. *Meikong*)
Desgraz, vise, missionary, Chinkeang
Deshoulieres, —., aide com. de la marine, Saigon
Deslandes, E. J., captain (*Emily Jane*) Shanghai
Deslandes, F., broker, Chinkeang
Des Vallons, —., aide com. de la marine, Saigon
Desmazes, —., aide com., Saigon
De Souza, S. R. (*Nagasaki Gazette*) Nagasaki
Dessaut, —., Finisher, Arsenal, Foochow
De St. Peru, —., aide com. de la marine, Saigon
De Tersannes, —., sous com. de la marine, Saigon (absent)
Dethlofsen, —., master mariner, Bangkok
Detmering, H., clerk (Pustan & Co.) S'hai
Detmering, W., clerk (W. G. Hale & Co.) Saigon
De Trentenian, —., commandant of troops, Saigon

Detring, G., commissioner (Customs, Chinkeang (absent)
Devenny, B. M., clerk (Foster & Co.) Foochow
Devens, R., clerk (Pustau & Co.) Canton
Deveris, G., interpreter (French Legation) Peking
Deveze, A., merchant (Aymonin & Co.) Yokohama
Devlin, H., constable, U. S. Consulate, Swatow
Devine, J. G., mate, *Tung-sha* light-ship, Shanghai
Devine, R., assistant (C. H. Schmidt & Co.) Yokohama
De Vo., H., constable (Police Force) Hiogo
Dewing, J. A., assistant engineer (Japan Railway Works)
Dexter, Rev. G. M., missionary, Osaka
D'Hont, Rev. —., missionary (French R. C. Mission) Bangkok (Chantaboun)
Dhunjeeshaw, R., merchant (F. Hormusjee & Co.) (absent)
Dhurumsey, P., merchant, Shanghai
Diack, D., assistant engineer (Japan Railway Works)
Diamont, Miss Naomi, missionary, Kalgan
Dias, L. P (St. Joseph's College) Macao
Diaz, F., timber merchant, Iloilo
Diaz, J. M., H. E., Civil Governor, Manila
Dick, J., shipwright (Shanghai and Pootung Foundry) Shanghai
Dick, Joseph light keeper (Japanese Government) Yokohama
Dickon, Frederick R., flag-lieutenant, R.N. (H.M.S *Iron Duke*)
Dickens, F. V., barrister-at-law, Yokohama
Dickie, H., manager (China Sugar Refinery) East Point
Dickie, Miss, Missionary, Chefoo
Dickins, F. W., Lieut. U.S.N. (*Monocacy*)
Dickinson, D., assist. surgeon (U. S. Naval Hospital) Yokohama
Dickman, Geo., clerk (China and Japan Trading Co.) Shanghai
Dickson, M., M.D., med. missionary, Taiwan
Didier, —., sub. chief, 4th bureau of interior, Saigon
Diercks, F., assistant examiner (Customs) Tientsin
Dierx, E., merchant, Saigon
Dierx, L., clerk (E. Dierx) Saigon
Dietrich, O., clerk (Telger, Nölting & Co.) Shanghai
Dieu, P., Constable, French Consulate, Bangkok
D'Iffanger, F., merchant (Adamson Bell & Co.) Yokohama (absent)
Digby, H. A., lieut., R.N. (*Iron Duke*)
Dillon, A., assistant, Customs, Tientsin
Dillon, B. E., Assayer (Mint) Osaka
Dillon, Chas., consul (French Consulate) Tientsin (absent)

Dillon. E., trooper (British Legation Guard) Yedo
Dillon, H. D., Mid. R N. (*Iron Duke*)
Dillon, J. G. B., clerk (Little & Co.) S'hai
Dillon, O., mate, lightship, Newchwang
Dillon, W., police inspector (Government Railroad) Yokohama
Dilthey, Rev. W., Rhenish Miss. Society, Fumun
Dimitri. —., Café keeper, Saigon
Diniz, A J., clerk (Hongkong & Shanghai Banking Corporation) Shanghai
Diniz, A. J., compositor (typographia mercantil) Macao
Diniz, S. J., clerk (Provand & Co) Shanghai
Dinnen, —., 2nd engineer gun-boat *Ping-chao-hoi*
Dinnis, H A. D , foreman (*Hongkong Times*)
Dinsdell, G K , clerk (Macpherson & Marshall) Yokohama
Dittmer, F. C., clerk (Snider & Co.) Peel Street
Dittmer, J., merchant (C. Bœdenghaus, Dittmer & Co) Nagasaki
Divers, E , M D , F C.s , Professor of Chemistry (Jap Govt) Yedo
Dix, W., examiner, Customs, Hankow
Dixon, J. A., carpenter, U.S.N. (*Hartford*)
Dixwell, G. B., merchant (A. Heard & Co.)
Doane, Mrs., missionary, Hiogo
Dobbyn, W. A., pilot (Independence Pilot Co.) Shanghai
Dockrell, H. J., nav. mid., R.N. (*Iron Duke*)
Dodd, John, merchant (Dodd & Co.) and Netherlands Vice-Consul, Amoy (T'sui)
Dodd, Rev. S., missionary (Am. Pres. Miss.) Ningpo (Hangchow)
Dodds, J., Chamber of Commerce, Y'hama
Dodds, J., clerk (Butterfield & Swire) Yokohama
Dods, Geo., M.D., College Gardens
Doel, P., police inspector (Govt. Railways) Yokohama
Doenitz, Dr. W (Jap. Govt.) Yedo
Doherty, F., fitter (Govt. Railways) Y'hama
Dohmen, M., acting consul (British Consulate) Yedo
Dolan, W., sailmaker and shipchandler (MacEwen, Frickel & Co.) Queen's Road
D'Oliveira, J. F., quarter-master, Military Department, Macao
Dolling, R., clerk (Schmidt, Westphal & Co.) Hiogo
Domingo, F., merchant (Blanco, Domingo & Co.) Manila
Domoney, G., butcher (Domoney & Co.) Yokohama and Hiogo
Donald, T., superintendent of fittings (Hongkong and China Gas Co.)
Donaldson, C. M., storekeeper (Donaldson & Co.) Shanghai

Donaldson, C. P. M., (H. B. M. Office of Works) Shanghai
Donaldson, D., (Naval College) Yedo
Donegan, H., nav. sub. lieut., R.N. (*Thistle*)
Donner, C. M., clerk (Pustau & Co.)
Donnet,—., pastry-cook, Saigon
Donovan, Revd. J., missionary (Ganking)
Donovan, Revd. J., missionary, Kewkeang (Ganking)
Dorabjee, D., joint lessee (H'kong Hotel) Queen's Road
Dorabjee, D., assistant (Nowrojee & Co.) Queen's Road
Dorabjee, P., clerk (D. Hosungjee & Co.) Amoy
Doral, P., clerk
Dorel, C , clerk (Société Anonyme Franco-Japonnaise) Yokohama
Dores, R da, lieut. (Timor Corps) Macao
Dorn, C. J. von, architect (Jap. Govt.) Yedo
Dorrink, J. J., clerk (E. Schellhass & Co.) Wellington Street
D'Ormay,—., physician in chief, Saigon
D'Ormer, C. F., asst. wharf clerk (S. S. N. Co.) Shanghai
Douglas, A. L., (Naval College) Yedo
Douglas, F., superintendent (Victoria Gaol)
Douglas, Fred., butcher (Douglas & Co.) Yokohama
Douglas, Rev. Carstairs, missionary (Eng. Pres. Miss.) Amoy
Douglas, Wm., act. superintendent (Japan Govt. Patent Slip) Nagasaki
Dourille, P., clerk (Hecht, Lilienthal & Co.) Yokohama
Dousdebes, A., interpreter of English and Spanish (French Consulate) Yokohama
Douw, Miss D. M., (Women's U. Missionary Society) Peking (absent)
Doyen, Rev. J. T. (American Bap. Miss. Union) Yokohama
Dow, Jas., broker, Shanghai
Dowdney, H. B., 3rd officer (Str. *Thales*)
Downes, J., midshipman, U.S.N. (*Hartford*)
Downey, Miss, asst. (Sayle & Co.)
Downing, Miss. C. B., missionary, Chefoo
Downs, V. B., clerk (Peele, Hubbell & Co.) Manila
Dowson, P. S., engineer (Whitefield & Dowson) Yokohama
Drake, C., assistant (Smith, Baker & Co.) Yokohama
Dredge, G. H., tidewaiter, Customs (Hunt's Wharf) Shanghai
Drell, —., Contractor, Saigon
Dreuche, H. von, clerk (A. Cordes & Co.) Tientsin
Drewer, A., clerk (Robertson & Co.) Pagoda Anchorage, Foochow
Dreyer, F., merchant (Dreyer & Co.) Queen's Road

Dreyer, H., general agent (Great Northern Telegraph Company) Shanghai
Driscoll, W., tailor, Hiogo
Driscoll, W. F., tailor (Driscoll & Co.) Yokohama, Kobé, and Hongkong and comp. (Frisby & Co) Wellington Street
Drishaus, O., clerk (Pasedag & Co) Amoy
Driver, A. J., clerk (Govt. Telegraph) Yokohama
Drouart, L'abbé de Lezey, R.C. Missionary, Yedo
Drought, J A. H., clerk (Westall, Galton & Co) Foochow
Drown, T. P, commission agent (Vincent & Co.) Swatow
Drummond, A., agent (China and Japan Trading Co.) Osaka
Drummond, J., master (National S. S. Co. of Nipon) Yokohama
Drummond, J., clerk (Holliday, Wise & Co.) Manila
Drummond, —., mariner (Jap Govt.) Yedo
Drummond, W. V., barrister-at-law (Rennie and Drummond) Shanghai
Drury, C C., lieut., R.N. (Iron Duke)
Drury, Fred. R.B., lieutenant, R M , Y'hama
Druse, R., baker, Yokohama
Drysdale, Thos. M , merchant (Drysdale, Ringer & Co.) Hankow
Dubarry, P. R., tidewaiter (Customs) Foochow
Dubief, L. (A. Real & Co.) Osaka & Hiogo
Dublane, L., com. de la Marine, Saigon
Dubois, —., machinist (Yokoska Arsenal) Yokohama
Dubois, —., clerk to harbour master, S'gon
Dubois, J., examiner (Customs) Chinkeang
Dubost, G., merchant (G. Dubost & Co.) Queen's Road
Dubost, J., silk inspector (Russell & Co.) Canton
Du Bousquet, Capt. A., Attaché au Conseil d'etat de S. M. le Tenno, Yedo
Duc, F., hotel manager, Saigon
Ducroux, —., auditor, sup. court, Saigon
Dudfield, J. B., harbour master's clerk, (Customs) Shanghai
Dudgeon, John, M.D. (London Missionary Society) professor of anatomy (College of Peking)
Dudley, Dr. D. E., surgeon, Manila
Dudley, Miss, missionary, Hiogo
Dufourg, C., watchmaker, Saigon
Dufresne, —., écrivain de marine, Saigon (absent)
Duff, A., store issuer (P. & O. Coal Depôt) Queen's Road West
Duffus, Rev. Wm., missionary (Eng. Pres. Church) Swatow
Duggan, C., inspector (Police Department) Stanley
Duivenenbode, Dr. W. K. M. van L. van (Jap. Govt. H'pital) Nagasaki

Du Jardin, F., clerk (Russell & Co.) S'hai
Dulcken, A. C., editor (Daily Press Office)
Dumaresq, P. K , clerk (Russell & Co.) Shanghai
Dumas, —., Commissaire (M. M. S. S. Amazone)
Dumelin, A., clerk (Ziogler & Co.) Yokohama
Dumphy, W., engineer (Novelty Iron Works) Praya West
Dunbar, D., 3rd engineer (Str. Hindostan)
Dunbar, W., chief engineer (Str. Hindostan)
Duncan, A., proprietor (Oriental Hotel) 4 Wellington Street
Duncan, And , tidewaiter (Customs) Whampoa
Duncan, J., engineer (P. & O. Service)
Duncan, R., secretary (H.K. & W. Doc'k Co.) 7, West Terrace
Dunk, T., inspector (Government Telegraphs) Yedo & Yokohama
Dunlop, C. G., clerk (Findlay, Richardson & Co.) Yokohama
Dunlop, J., M.D., surgeon, R.N. (Avon)
Dunn, C. A. L., Shanghai
Dunn, Col., resident, Yedo
Dunn, Miss S., milliner (Rose & Co.) Wellington Street
Dunn, Thos., merchant (Hedge & Co.) Foochow
Dunn, W. E. H., assistant (Lane, Crawford & Co.) Queen's Road
Dunne, R., clerk (Turner & Co.) Foochow
Dunnill, J., assistant (W. Watson & Co.) Shanghai
Dunnon, T. W., assistant (L. Candrelier) Yedo (Tokidji)
Duparc, sister Josephine (Mais. de la Presentation) Ningpo
Duplaquet, G., clerk (Real & Co.) Hiogo
Dupond, Right Rev. F. A. A., bishop of Azoth, Bangkok
Dupont, Geo., auctioneer, Bangkok
Dupré, His Excellency Jules Marie, governor, Saigon
Dupuis, J., merchant, Hankow
Duruflé, G. P. L., acting French consul, Bangkok
Bussutour, A., auctioneer. Saigon
Dutouquet, —., sous com. de la marine, Saigon (absent)
Dutras, Rev. José, missionary (Roman Catholic Church) An Poa, Amoy
Dutrouilh, Mad., superioure (Mais. de St. Vincent) Ningpo
Dutton, G., proprietor, The "Bee-hive," Yokohama
Duus, J. H., merchant and Danish Consul, Hakodadi
Duval, A. T., clerk (Tate and Hawes) Shanghai
Du Year, J., M. D., acting physician, British Legation, Peking

Duzac, —., River Pilot, Saigon
Dwarford, Jno., Lieut. R. N. (*Rinaldo*)
Dyce, Chas. M., clerk (Westall, Brand & Co.) Shanghai
Dyer, Atkins, pilot, Bangkok
Dyer, H., C. E., M. A., B. SC., (Imp. Engineering College) Yedo
Dyer, Henry, storekeeper (Hall & Holtz) Shanghai
Dymstan, —., resident, Yokohama

E

Eager, R., fitter (Govt. Railway) Yokohama
Eagling, E., employé (U. S. Naval Hospital) Yokohama
Eales, R., gunner, R.N. (*Iron Duke*)
Eames, I. B., barrister, Shanghai
Earnshaw, —., engineer (Wilks & Earnshaw) Manila
Eastlack, R. F., clerk (Frazar & Co.) S'hai
Easton, S., engineer (Easton & Co.) East Point
Eaton, F. C., clerk (Peele, Hubbell & Co.) Manila (Leyte)
Eaton, G., teacher mathematical surveying (Jap. Govt.) Yedo
Eaton, J., teacher, Osaka College
Ebell, H., merchant (Ebell & Co.) consul for Germany and Netherlands, Macao
Ebrahim, A., merchant (Ebrahim & Co.) Cochrane Street and Honam
Ebrahimbhoy, P., broker, Shanghai
Ega, D. A. d' (Hongkong Soda-water Man. Co.) 15, Graham Street
Ecclestone, G., pilot, Bangkok
Echemann, Captn. (Jap. Govt.) Yedo
Echevarria, D. F., acct., Customs, Manila
Echevarria, Prudencio, d. E., chief justice, Manila
Eckard, Rev. L. W., missionary, Chefoo
Eckfeldt, T. W., clerk (Russell & Co.) Shangh i
Eckford, A. M., merchant (Wi'son, Cornabé & Co.) Chefoo
Eckhold, M., mate, Lang-shan light-ship, Shanghai
Eckhouse, H., clerk (Elles & Co.) Taiwan
Eckman, C., engineer (tug *Pathfinder*) Taku
Eckstrand, J., master (National S. S Co. of Nipon) Yokohama
Edbrook, C., farrier, &c., Shanghai
Ede, J. M., clerk (An lrews & Co.) Manila
Ede, N. J., secretary (Union Ins. Society of Canton)
Edes, B. C., lieut. U.S.N. (*Yantic*)
Edge, Rev. Ch., London Missionary Society
Edkins, Rev. J., B.A., missionary, Peking (absent)
Edmond, E. M., R.W.D., commander (P. & O. service)
Edwardes, D. J., assistant (British Consulate) Bangkok

Edwards, E. J., chief officer (Steamer *Hindustan*)
Edwards, G., clerk (U. S. Consu'ate) T'kow
Edwards, J., storekeeper, Yokohama
Edwards, J., assistant examiner (Customs) Shanghai
Edwards, O. E., merchant and Danish consul (Peele, Hubbell & Co.) Manila (absent)
Edwards, R., assist. (Whitfield & Dowson) Yokohama
Edwards, Rev. J. C., chaplain and N. I., R. N. (*Iron Duke*)
Edwards, St. J. H., clerk, U. S. Consulate, Amoy
Edwards, T. H., officer (P. & O. service)
Edwards, W., foreman mechanic (Japan Railway Works) Yokohama
Edwards W. C., shipwright (W. B. Spratt & Co.) Praya East
Edwards, W. T. H., midshipman, R.N. (*Cadmus*)
Edyvean, W. H. mid., R.N. (*Iron Duke*)
Egan, O. G., assist. eng., R.N. (*Hornet*)
Egart, H., lightkeeper (Japanese Government) Yokohama
Eggert, J., tidewaiter (Customs) Chinkeang
Eglin, J., chief engineer (str. *Yangtsze*)
Eguares, R., clerk (Smith, Bell & Co.) Manila
Ehlers, Paul, merchant (Ehlers & Co.) Honam (absent)
Eimbcke, A., merchant and Peruvian Consul
Eitel, Rev. E. J., missionary, M.A., PH.D. (Lon. Miss. Soc.) Aberdeen Street
Ela, F. P., 2nd lieut. mar., U.S N. (*Hartford*)
Elder, S. J., assistant accountant (Oriental Bank) Yokohama
Eldridge, C. J., examiner (Customs) Hankow (absent)
Eldridge, Dr. Stuart (Jap. Govt.) Yedo (Kaitikusbi)
Eldridge, H., tide-surv. (Customs) Canton
Elfen, H., clerk (Kniffler & Co.) Yokohama
Elias, E. E. J., clerk (J. A. Solomon) Cochrane Street
Elias, E. J., clerk (E. D. Sassoon & Co.) Queen's Road
Elias, J. B., clerk (E. D. Sassoon & Co.)
Elias, S. J., carpenter, R.N. (*Princess Charlotte*)
Elio, J., clerk (Russell & Sturgis) Manila (Camiguin)
Elio, S., judge (Superior Court of Appeal) Manila
Elles, James, clerk (Elles & Co.) Amoy
Elles, Jamieson, merchant (Elles & Co.) Amoy (absent)
Ellie, —., registrar of the Tribunal de Commerce, Saigon
Elliott, G., clerk (Japan Railway)
Elliott, G. J., tidewaiter (Customs) S'hai

Elliott, J. R., assist. (Alt & Co.) Nagasaki
Elliott, M., assist. (L. Candrelier) Yedo (Tsukidji)
Elliott, W. P., mid., U.S.N. (Lackawanna)
Elliott, W. St. G., M.D.. D D S., dentist, Yokohama
Ellis, Alex., gunner, R.N. (Thalia)
Ellis, L., merchant (Barnet & Co.) Shanghai (absent)
Ellis, E. W., wharf clerk (S. S. N. Co.) Shanghai
Ellis, G., Fitter (Govt. Railways) Yokohama
Ellis, G. A., lieut., R.N. (Princess Charlotte)
Ellis, G. J., broker (Stewart & Ellis) S'hai
Ellis, J., chief engineer (National S. S. Co. of Nipon) Yokohama
Ellis, Miss, assistant (Millinery & Drapery Establishment) Yokohama
Ellis, S. J., asst. carpenter (Naval Yard)
Ellman, S., proprietor ("Crown & Anchor") Yokohama
Elmer, W., deputy marshal (U. S. Consulate) Yokohama
Elmore, J. F., Dr., secretary (Peruvian Legation) Yedo
Elphick, F., assist. (Lewes & Benton) S'hai
Elshout, J. M., tidewaiter (Customs) Ningpo
Elwin, Rev. A., missionary (Ch. Eng. Miss. Society) Ningpo (Haugchow)
Elye, —., tailor (Elye & Kesam) Bangkok
Emamoodeen, S., broker, Gage Street
Emanuel, B. E., book-keeper (Hongkong Times)
Emanuel, J. M., shipwright (Spratt & Co.) Praya East
Emerson, —., Engineer (Jap. Govt.) Yedo
Emery, David A., U. S. vice-consul, and commission agent (Wadleigh & Emery) Chinkeang
Emory, G. B., assistant (P. M. S. S. Co.) Praya West
Emory, W. H., flag lieut., U S.N. (Hartford)
Enperanza, J. J. de, consul (Spanish Consulate) Shanghai
Encarnação, A. L., 2nd officer, Fort William (P. & O. S. N. Co.)
Endicott, C. E., clerk (A. Heard & Co.) Shanghai
Endicott, H. B., clerk (Butterfield & Swire) Shanghai
Endicott, J., foreman, hose carriage (Am. Fire Brigade) Yokohama
Endicott, J. R., clerk (Peele, Hubbell & Co.) Manila (Albay)
Endicott, S., clerk (Smith, Archer & Co.) Yokohama
Enevino, J., clerk (J B. Eames) Shanghai
Eng, C. S., clerk (Engwat, Brother & Co.) Amoy
Engel, —., chief artificer (Japan Govt.) Yedo
Engelhardt, —., assist. (Davison & Co.) Yokohama

Engholm, V., chemist (China Dispensary) Praya
England, J., chief assistant engineer, (Govt. Railroad) Yokohama and Hiogo
Engler, A., clerk (Kaltenbach, Engler & Co.) Saigon
Engler, F., merchant (Kaltenbach, Engler & Co.) Saigon (absent)
English, A., teacher (Jap. Govt.) Yedo
Engwat, S., merchant (Engwat Bro. & Co.) Amoy
Enrique, M., third secretary (Spanish Legation) Yedo
Enslie, J. J., acting vice-consul (British Consulate) Osaka and assist. (British Consulate) Hiogo
Ephrem, Sœur St., Sister of Charity, Yokohama
Erdmann, C., merchant (Landstein & Co.) Queen's Road
Erevegniac, G. L., French Private (Mun. Police) Yokohama
Ernst, J. E., merchant (Russell & Sturgis) Manila
Escalaute, A., clerk (Rocha & Co.) Manila
Escalera, José, attorney general, Manila
Esdale, O., (Kirby & Co) Hiogo
Esdale, C., assistant (Whitfield & Dowson) Yokohama
Esdale, James, tailor, Yokohama
Esdale, J. T., assistant (Wilkin & Robinson) Yokohama
Esmail, M. S. H., merchant, 17, Gage Street
Espin, F., harbour master (Naval Department) Cavite, Manila
Espina, Mariano, constable (Spanish Consulate) Amoy
Espinosa de los Monteros, Narciso, district magistrate, Manila
Esprit, A , —., 84 Bluff, Yokohama
Esquer, —., substitute Proc. Gen., Saigon
Esson, B., 2nd engineer (steamer Haivong
Estarico, E., proprietor (Hotel D'Europe) Hollywood Road
Estienne, G., clerk (Fabre & Co.) Yokohama
Estienne, M., Ch. Subs. (French Consulate) and clerk (Arsenal) Foochow
Estruch, Alberto, engraver (Mint) Manila
Estublier, Dr. A. D. (French Legation) Peking
Estvelde, E. van, Student (Customs) Peking
Eugster, Ed., assistant (Eugster & Co.) Manila
Eugster, J., merchant (L. Eugster & Co.) Manila
Eugster, Ph., assistant (Eugster & Co.) Manila
Eugster, R., assist. (Eugster & Co.) Manila
Eusden, R., consul (British Consulate) Hakodadi (absent)

Eustace, G. O., assistant (Sayle & Co.) Shanghai
Euxiere, —., master mariner, Bangkok
Euziere, J, hairdresser (Euziere & Co.) Hiogo
Evans, H., shipchandler and brewer (H. Evans & Co.) Shanghai
Evans, J. H., merchant (Evans, Pugh & Co.) and consul for Portugal, Hankow
Evans, J. R., merchant (Holme, Ringer & Co.) Hiogo
Evans, Miss J., missionary, Tungchow
Evans, M. P., merchant (Reid, Evans & Co.) Shanghai
Evans, Mr and Mrs. H., teachers (Japanese Govt) Yedo
Even, —., founder (Yokoska Arsenal) Yokohama
Everall, Henry, storekeeper (Hall & Holtz) Shanghai
Everett, A. H., assistant, Rejang outstation, Sarawak
Everett, H. H., Supt. of antimony mines, Busan, Sarawak
Evers, A., merchant (Simon, Evers & Co.) Yokohama
Every, J., master mariner, Bangkok
Evrard, L'abbé F., miss. apost., Yokohama
Ewald, L., sub. manager (Comptoir d'Escompte) Shanghai
Ewart, W., accountant, Yokohama
Ewart, W., resident, Yedo
Ewer, F. H., examiner (Customs) Canton
Exton, T., clerk (Mourilyan, Heimann & Co) Hiogo
Eydner, A., apothecary (Zobel and Nohr) Manila
Eyton, J. L. O., shipbroker (M. Hegt) Yokohama
Ezekiel, M. D., clerk (E. D. Sassoon & Co.) Queen's Road
Ezra, A., clerk (D. Sassoon, Sons & Co.) Newchwang
Ezra, I., agent (E. D. Sassoon & Co.) C'foo
Ezra, N. S., clerk (D. Sassoon, Sons & Co.) Praya

F

Faber, H., commission merchant (Faber & Voigt) Hiogo
Faber, Rev. E., miss. (Rhenish Mission) Fumoun, Canton
Fabie, F. R., clerk (Martin, Dyce & Co.) Manila
Fabre, —., Hair dresser, Saigon
Fabre, A., merchant (Fabre & Co.) Yokohama
Fabro, A., 2nd Lieut. (Gunboat *Chun Hoi*) Canton
Fabris, E. A., broker, Shanghai
Fabris, Frank, assist. (J. J. Buchheister) Shanghai

Fabris, J., assistant (Mun. Council Offices) Shanghai
Fafont, Francisco C. E., director and assayer (Mint) Manila
Fagan, C. S. F., lieut, R.M, Yokohama
Fahrer, M., teacher, Yedo
Fail, Chas. C., engineer (Boyd & Co.) S'hai
Fairbairn, John, storekeeper, &c. (Lane, Crawford & Co.) Queen's Road
Fairbairn, Thomas, clerk (Lane, Crawford & Co.) Shanghai
Fairburn, J. U., engineer (P. & O. S. N. Co. Factory) Praya West
Fairlie, H. G., lieut., R N (*Opossum*)
Fajard, E., silk inspector, Shanghai
Fakeera, M., boarding-house keeper, Upper Lascar Row
Falck, C. (Falck's Hotel) Bangkok
Falck, C, godown keeper (Kniffler & Co.) Nagasaki
Falcon, Y., clerk (Witte & Co.) Manila
Falconer, Alexander, third-master (Central School)
Falconer, George B., watchmaker and jeweller (G. Falconer & Co.) Queen's Road
Falconer, J., M.R.C.S., Hankow
Farazona, Rev. M., R. C. missionary, Taiwan
Farbridge, C. W., merchant (Holliday, Wise & Co.) (absent)
Farfara, G., merchant (Farfara and Grenet) Yokohama (absent)
Fargeot, Mme., milliner, Saigon
Farinole, J. B., "Bureau d'encaissements &c" Saigon
Farley, G., Jr., merchant (Augustine Heard & Co.) Yokohama
Farmer, C., Teacher of Engineering (Public Works Department) Yokohama
Farmer, J. M., Clerk (Wilson, Cornabe & Co.) Chefoo
Farnham, Rev. J. M. W., missionary (Board For. Miss. Pres. Church) S'hai (absent)
Farnham, S. C., shipwright (Farnham & Co.) Shanghai
Farmer, J., livery stable keeper (Cobb & Co.) Yokohama
Farr, Fred. (Sodawater Manufactory) Shanghai
Farrar, A. A. G., clerk (Provand & Co.) Shanghai
Farron, S, 3rd engineer (str. *Yesso*)
Farrow, J. manager and secretary (Amoy Dock Co.) Amoy
Farthing, J., corporal, river police, Shanghai
Fatakia, D B., clerk (F. B. Cama) Peel St.
Fatakia, D. B., merchant (R. N. Deguria & Co.) Honam, Hongkong
Faucon, ?., Commissaire (M.M.S.S. *Volga*)
Fauque, Rev. Joseph A., missionary, B'kok

Faure, J., 1st engineer, Chinese gun-boat Chun-hoi
Faure, Vincent, sister (Maison de St. Vincent) Ningpo
Faurie, L'Abbé U., R. C. Missionary, Hiogo (Nugata)
Fautra', —, chief draughtsman (Yokoska Arsenal) Yokohama
Fauvel, A., assistant, Customs, Chefoo
Favacho, V. A., clerk (P. M. S. S. Co.) Praya West
Favie, —, missionary (French Mission) Peking
Favre, V, lessee (Hotel de l'Universe)
Favre-Brandt, C., watchmaker (C. & J. Favre-Brandt) Yedo and Osaka (absent)
Favre-Brandt, J., watchmaker (C. & J Favre-Brandt) Yokohama, Yedo and Osaka
Fawcett, Thos, mechanic, (Customs) S'hai (Pootung)
Fay, Miss L. M., missionary, Shanghai (Hongkew)
Fearon, J. S., clerk (A. Heard & Co.) Shanghai
Fearon, R. I., merchant (A. Heard & Co.) Shanghai
Featherstone, T, constable (British Consulate) Tientsin
Fo d'Ostiani, Conte Allessandro, Italian Minister, Yedo
Fehrs, H., shipwright (Meyer & Fehrs) Swatow and Chefoo
Feibel, Tho., accountant (Comptoir d'Escompte) Shanghai
Feliciano, B., assist. (Tutuban Rope Factory) Manila
Feliciano, M., assist. (Eugster & Co.) Manila
Feltham, C., Surgeon, R.N. (Cadmus)
Fennell, H. J., Fitter (Govt. Railways) Yokohama
Fenning, W., examiner, Customs. Shanghai
Fenton, J. W., band-master (Jap. Govt) Yedo
Fenton, R. B., clerk (Boyd & Co) Amoy
Fentum, Geo. B., organist (Trinity Church) piano tuner, Shanghai
Fenwick, J. M., manager (Borneo Company) Tegora, Sarawak
Féraud, —, sous com. de la marine, Saigon
Ferguson, J., constable, River Police, S'hai
Ferguson, J. H., consul general (Netherlands Legation) Peking
Fergusson, R, manager (Chartered Mercantile Bank) Shanghai
Fergusson, T. T., merchant (Fergusson & Co.) Chefoo
Fergusson, W. S., clerk (Bradley & Co.) Swatow
Fernandes, B. de S, merchant and consul for Siam, Macao
Fernandes, F. (St. Joseph's College) Macao
Fernandes, F. F., assistant (Hawkins' Horse Repository)
Fernandes, M. de S., bailiff (Municipal Council) Macao
Fernandes, N T., proprietor Typographia Mercantil) Macao
Fernandez, J. V., assistant (J. B. Roxas) Manila
Fernandez, Rev. V., Vice Procurator (Dominican Mission) Caine Road
Fernandez, Y, assist (J. B. Roxas) Manila
Fernando, A, ensign (Timor Corps) Macao
Ferrand, —, Baker, Saigon
Ferrario, V., Sister (The Convent) Caine Road
Ferraz, J. A., assistant (Oriental Bank)
Ferreira, A. A., secretary (Public Works Department) in charge of Bomparto Fort, Macao
Ferreira, C. J., assist. (P. M. S. S. Co.) Nagasaki
Ferreira, F., barrack clerk (Control Department) Shelley Street
Ferreira, J. A., ensign (Police Department) Macao
Ferreira, L. A., advocate, Macao
Ferrier, Mdme., Café proprietor, Saigon
Fesfield, G, Resident, Yedo
Fettes, D., 1st engineer, Chinese gunboat Lingfeng
Feyerabend, R., clerk (Dircks & Krüger) Swatow
Fiburcio, R. y M., Chargé d' affaires for Spain, Yedo (absent)
Fielde, Miss A. M., Am Bap Mission, S'tow
Fielder, J. W. (Ocean Tavern) Nagasaki
Fielding, C , machinist (Amoy Dock Company) Amoy
Figgins, A. F., Light-keeper (Public Works Department) Yokohama
Figueiredo, H. C. V. da, clerk (Aug. Heard & Co.)
Figueiredo, J. A. (Alt & Co.) Nagasaki
Figuerredo, J. A , Chancellor (Portuguese Consulate) Nagasaki
Filatrian, —., Copyist, Trib. 1st instance, Saigon
Finch, R. F. C. S , Foreman, Sulphuric Works (Osaka Mint)
Findlay, Chas. B., merchant (Findlay, Richardson & Co.) Yokohama
Findlay, J., merchant (Findlay, Wade & Co) Shanghai
Findlay, J., merchant (Findlay, Wade & Co.) Shanghai (absent)
Findlayson R., draughtsman (P. & O. S. N. Co.'s Factory) Praya West
Finke, H., assist. (L Haber) Yokohama
Fioritti, —., Mission Catholique, Peking
Firman, Fred., military clerk, Royal Engineer Dept.
Firmin Marrot, Mdme. V., store-keeper, Saigon

Fischer, A., merchant (Fischer & Co) Osaka
Fischer, E , commission agent, Hiogo
Fischer, F. von. merchant (Hecht, Lilienthal & Co) Hiogo
Fischer, G., clerk (Meyer, Alabor & Co.) Stanley Street
Fishe, Rev. C. T., missionary, Chinkeang (Yangchow)
Fishe, Rev. E. and Mrs., missionary, Chinkeang (Yang-chow)
Fishe, Rev. E. miss. Ningpo (T'aichow)
Fisher, A. A., house carpenter, &c. (Müller & Fisher) Shanghai
Fisher, Chas. L., M D., Hawaiian Consul, U. S Vice-Consul, Nagasaki
Fisher, E , clerk (Townend & Co) Hankow
Fisher, E , barman (Hongkong Hotel)
Fisher, F., commission agent, Kobé
Fisher, H. J., assistant, Customs, Foochow (absent)
Fisher, S., clerk (Lammert, Atkinson & Co.)
Fisher, S., assistant chief engineer (Japanese Government) Yokohama
Fisk, F., inspector (Japan Telegraphs) Himeji & Onomedu
Fisler, L. F., photographer, Shanghai
Fitch, Rev. G. F., missionary, S'hai (S'chow)
Fitch, H. W., chief engineer, U.S.N. (Lackawanna)
Fitz, W. S., merchant (Russell & Co., and Vice-Consul for Netherlands) Hankow
Fitzgerald, M., storekeeper (China & Japan Trading Co.) Osaka
Fitzgerald, M. O., clerk (Dickinson & Co) Shanghai
FitzHenry, D., acting cashier (Comptoir d'Escompte) Shanghai
Fitzmaurice, Hon. J., commander, R.N. (eazer)
Flambeau, A., captain (M M. S. Volga)
Fleischer, H M , assist. (Hecht, Lilienthal & Co) Yokohama
Fleming, J. M., clerk (Smith, Bell & Co.) Manila
Flemming, T. P., chief officer (Str. Hailoong)
Flemming, M., engineer (Tanjore Kubong mines) Labuan
Fleuriais, H., Capt (M. M. S. S. Ava)
Fleury, J. A. interpreter (Gas Company) Yokohama
Flint, Weston, U. S consul, Chinkeang
Floros, C., compositor (Hongkong Times)
Flowers, Marcus O., British consul, & act. consul for Austria & France) Nagasaki
Floyd, W. P., photographer (Victoria Photographic Gallery) Wellington Street
Foache, G., commander (M.M.S. Meikong)
Fobes, A. S., agent (China and Japan Trading Company) Hiogo
Focho, Dr. actg. German consul, Hiogo
Focken, F. W., pilot, Swatow
Fölser, Jno., pilot, Taku

Folsom, W. A., Boarding Officer, Customs, Swatow
Fonseca, A. J., da, merchant, Macao
Fonseca, A. Jr., clerk (Lane, Crawford & Co.)
Fonseca, E. F., clerk (Lammert, Atkinson & Co.) Queen's Road East
Fonseca, F., clerk (Heard & Co.)
Fonseca, F. V. da, clerk (Evans Pugh & Co.) Hankow
Fonseca, J. A., da, clerk, Deutche bank, Yokohama
Fonseca, J. B., clerk (Butterfield & Swire) Shanghai
Fonseca, José M. da, shipchandler, Macao
Fonseca, J., vice-rector, St. Tomas College (Ecclesiastical Department) Manila
Fonseca, R. R., clerk (Aug. Heard & Co.) Shanghai
Fonseca, V P., purser (receiving ship Wellington) Shanghai
Fontaine, G , (Imperial College) Yedo
Fontaine, H. C., professor of Literature (First College) Yedo
Fontayne, J., assistant (China and Japan Trading Co.) Nagasaki
Foot, M , assist (Thabor & Co) Hiogo
Foote, C , manager (Foote's Club) Y'hama
Foque, P. (Imperial College) Yedo
Forbes, D. M., merchant (Ker & Co.) M'la
Forbes. F. B., merchant (Russell & Co) and consul general for Sweden and Norway, Shanghai
Forbes, H. de C , merchant (Russell & Co.) Shanghai
Forbes, J. M., jun., mer. (Russell & Co.)
Forbes, P. S., merchant (Russell & Co.) (absent)
Forbes, W. H., merchant (Russell & Co.)
Ford, A. R. stevedore (Ford & Co.) N'saki
Ford, C. McKenzie, assist. and postal agent (British Consulate) Swatow
Ford, Chas., superintendent (Government Gardens) Albany Road
Ford, J. D , assist. engr. U S N. (Hartford)
Ford, Mrs., stewardess (Grand Hotel) Yokohama
Ford, R A., reporter (Nagasaki Express and Nagasaki Gazette) Nagasaki
Forno, Dr. M., surgeon in charge (L' Hopital Jaures) Yokohama
Forrest, R. J., act. consul for Austria and Great Britain and act. vice-consul for France and Germany, Swatow
Forrest, T., accountant (Char. Bank of I. A. and China)
Forrest, Thomas, lightkeeper (Japanese Government) Yokohama
Forsaith, G. A , tidewaiter, Customs, S'tow
Forssblad, Bernhard, M. C., proprietor, (Chefoo Medical Hall) Chefoo
Forster, John, merchant (J. Forster & Co.) Foochow

Fortant, —., chief-artificer (Jap. Govt.) Yedo
Foss, H , clerk (Borneo Company Limited) Dinder, Caine Road
Foster, C. A., mid U.S.N. (*Lackawanna*)
Foster, F. E., merchant (Peele, Hubbell & Co.) Manila
Foster, F. T. P., clerk (Birley & Co.) Queen's Road
Foster, J. T., 1st asst. supt. (Govt. Telegraph) Shimonoseki
Foster, Rev. A., miss. (London Miss. Soc.) Hankow (Hanyang)
Foster, R. W., lieut. R.N. (*Dwarf*)
Foster, W., tidewaiter, (Customs) Shanghai
Fouesnel, —., chief officer (M. M. S. S. *Nil*)
Fourgade, J. J., storokeeper, Yokohama
Fournier, J., clerk (French Post Office) Shanghai
Fowler, W., police inspector (Central Station) Shanghai
Fox, —., 2nd engineer (Str. *Hindostan*)
Fox, C. E., midshipman, U.S.N. (*Hartford*)
Frachtenberg, S. T., teacher (Gaim'cho) Yedo
Frager, L., commissaire (M. M. S. S. *Menzaleh*)
Fraissinet, J., clerk (Rand & Co.) Y'hama
Framjee, C., clerk (Framjee Hormusjee & Co.) Shanghai
Framjee, C., clerk (N. Ollia) Amoy
Francis, F., proprietor (Oriental Hotel) 4, Wellington Street
Francis, M. H., assistant (Cobb & Co.) Yokohama
Francis, M. H., clerk (J. L. Liebermann) Yokohama
Francis, R , merchant (R. Francis & Co.) Shanghai and Kewkeang
Francisco, Pedro A., assist. (J. B. Roxas) Manila
Francke, O., clerk (Kniffler & Co.) Hiogo
Franco, Don Antonio, municipal magistrate, Manila
Franco, F. M., clerk (Olyphant & Co.
Franco, J. F., clerk (Colonial Government) Macao
François, —., adjt (Jap. Govt.) Yedo
François, —., sub-engineer (Yokoska Arsenal) Yokohama
Frank, H., merchant, Sual
Franklin, J., master U.S.N. (*Saco*)
Franklyn, L. H., medical attendant (Customs) Whampoa
Fraser, E. J., clerk (Fraser & Co.) Y'hama
Fraser, J. A., merchant (A. Heard & Co.) Yokohama
Fraser, J. C., merchant (Fraser & Co.) Yokohama (absent)
Fraser, J. P. M., assistant (British Consulate) Hankow
Fraser, M. F. A., student Interpreter (British Legation) Peking
Fraser, L., clerk (Gilman & Co.) Hankow
Frasque, —., sous com. de la Marino, Saigon
Frazar, E., merchant (Frazar & Co.) Shanghai (absent)
Frazar, John, L.R.C.P., Medical Officer, Tientsin
Fream, C., Resident, Yeao
Fredricksen, F., master mariner, Bangkok
Freeman, R., Teacher (Jap. Govt.) Yedo
Freerks, R., shipchandler (Freerks, Rodatz & Co.) Praya
Freeth, G., lightkeeper, Customs, Foochow
Freidrich, R., chemist (P. Sartorius) Manila
Freire, F., clerk (A. G. Hogg & Co.)
French, H. S., merchant (Jackson, French & Co.) Manila
French, W., signalman, Customs, Taku
Freudenberg, — ., master mariner, Bangkok
Freudenthaler, —., clerk (Maron & Co.) Yokohama
Freudenthaler, M., (School of Foreign Languages) Yedo
Freund, —., "Café de Marseille" Saigon
Freusberg, C., interpreter and act. Germ. consul, Canton
Frewin, Henry, merchant (Frewin & Co) Swatow
Freyre, Lieut. O., attaché (Peruvian Legation) Yedo
Fricke, P. H., merchant (Renard & Co) Consular agent for Switzerland, Hiogo
Fricot, A., storekeeper, Saigon
Friedrich, O., shipchandler (Lammert, Atkinson & Co.) Arbuthnot Road
Friedrichsen, A., pilot (Newchwang Pilot Company, Newchwang
Friend, A. F., Captain (str. *Honan*) S'hai
Frigerio, Luigia, sister (The Convent) Caine Road
Frischling, C. J., draper (Driscoll & Co.) Yokohama
Fritsche, Dr. H., astronomer (Russian Observatory) Peking (absent)
Fritz, J., assistant (S. S. N. Co.'s Wharf) Shanghai
Frome. Captain (*Sadkia*) Yedo
Frontil, F., sister (Maison de Jesus enfaut) Ningpo
Frost, A., (Scott and Frost) Hiogo
Frost, F., boatswain (P. & O. S. N. Co.) Praya West
Fry, F. W., clerk (J. Silverlock & Co.) Foochow
Fry, J. G., merchant (J. Silverlock & Co.) Foochow (absent)
Fry, J. O., supt. (Govt. Telegraph) Nagasaki
Fryer, H., gunner, (P. & O. Service,) Shanghai (Pootung)
Fryer, J., teacher and translator (Kiangnan Arsenal) Shanghai
Fuentes, M. de la, clerk (Martin, Dyce & Co.) Manila

Fukir, M., manager (P. Ebrahimbhoy) Shanghai
Fuller, J. O., clerk (Olyphant & Co.) S'hai
Fulmer, D. M., engineer U.S.N. (*Ashuelot*)
Funfgeld, E., clerk (Kaltenbach, Engler & Co.) Saigon
Funk, Dr. H. (Jap. Govt.) Yedo
Furber, E. G., barge "Shamrock" Nagasaki
Furumatz, S., clerk (Grand Hotel) Yokohama
Furze, J., clerk (China Sub. Tel. Co.)
Futtakis, D. S., merchant, Canton
Fyfe, James S., merchant (Loney & Co.) Yloilo

G

Gabain, P., merchant (Russell & Co.) vice-consul for Germany, Ningpo (absent)
Gabrié, —., écrivain de marine, Saigon
Gaidrich, F., merchant (L. Vrard & Co.) Tientsin
Gainza, F. A., bishop of Nueva Cáceres (Ecclesiastical Department) Manila
Gair, W. T., inspector (Police Department) Central Station
Gale, S. R., asst. tax collector (Mun. Council Offices) Shanghai
Galerié, —., sous com. de la marine, Saigon (absent)
Galian, M., clerk (Smith, Bell & Co.) Cebu
Gallagher, James, sergeant (Anglo-Chinese Police) Pagoda Anchorage, Foochow
Gallatz, T., clerk (Mourylian, Heimann & Co.) Hiogo
Galle, P. E., M.D., Shanghai
Galles, F. W., clerk (Farnham & Co.) S'hai
Galloway, H., chief quartermaster (Royal Naval Victualling Depot) Yokohama
Galloway, W., M.D., asst. surgeon, R.N. (*Elk*)
Gallstell, —., resident, Yokohama
Galpin, Rev. F., missionary (Eng. Meth. F. Church) Ningpo
Galt, J., med. miss. (Ch. Eng. Miss. Soc.) Ningpo (Hangchow)
Galt, R. W., engineer, U.S.N. (*Yantic*)
Galton, W. P., public tea inspector (Westall & Galton) Foochow
Galwey, W., traffic manager (Govt. Railroad) Yokohama
Galy, A., resident, Yedo
Games, R., engineer (Novelty Iron Works)
Gamman, E., clerk (Aug. Heard & Co.) Foochow
Gammell, W., assist. com. (Control Depart.)
Gamwell, F. R., silk broker, Shanghai
Gangjee, M., clerk (D. Vassonjee & Co.) Stanley Street
Garchitorena, A. M., coachbuilder (Garchitorena & Smith) Manila
Garchitorena, V. M., coachbuilder (Garchitorena & Smith) Manila
Garcia, A. J., captain (Macao Battalion)

Garcia, Dr. V., provisor and vicar-general, Nueva Cáceres (Ecclesiastical Department) Manila
Garcia-y-Garcia, captain A., minister for Peru, Yedo (absent)
Garcia-y-Garcia, N., merchant, Macao
Gargin, A., clerk (Reis, von der Heyde & Co.) Yokohama
Gardiner, C., chief engineer (Chinese gunboat *Feiho*)
Gardiner, T. J., assist. accountant (Oriental Bank) Shanghai
Gardiner, W. A., clerk (Loney & Co.) Cebu
Gardner, C., interpreter and act. vice-consul (British Consulate) Canton
Gardner, Chas., Lieut., R.N. (*Kestrel*)
Gardner, H. A., constable (British Consulate) Bangkok
Gardner, J. P. W., clerk (H'K. and S. Bank)
Gardner, L., resident, Yedo
Gardner, Mrs. F. E., storekeeper (Gardner & Co.) Chefoo
Gardner, T. S., master (Sassoons' steamer *China*)
Gardner, W., (boarding house keeper) Queen's Road West
Garland, G., attaché (Peruvian Legation) Yedo
Garnier, B., French Consul, Bangkok
Garnier, L., master mariner, Bangkok
Garraway, C., assist. (Astor House) Shanghai
Garrett, Miss M., milliner, Queen's Road
Garrett, W. R., clerk (Control Department) Queen's Road
Garrette, Miss M. R., milliner (Watson & Co.) Shanghai
Garrigue, —., Mission Catholique, Peking
Gartner, H , engineer, Bangkok
Gartshore, N., blacksmith (Tanjore Kubong Minus) Labuan
Gaskell, J. M., clerk (Russell & Sturgis) Manila
Gaston, Vicomte de S. S. de B., student interpreter (French Legation) Peking
Gattrell, M., chief engineer (P. & O. service)
Gaucho, Federico, sorter (Postal Department) Manila
Gauld, Wm., M.D., missionary (Eng. Pres. Mission) Swatow
Gaupp, Chas, watchmaker (C. J. Gaupp & Co.) (absent)
Gaupp, E., watchmaker (C.J. Gaupp & Co.) (absent)
Gaupp, H., watchmaker (C. J. Gaupp & Co.) Hollywood Road (absent)
Gauvain, —., commissaire (M. M. S. S. *Nil*)
Gavey, J. J. C., supt. (China Sub. Tel. Co.) Bonham Road
Gavini, —., river pilot, Saigon
Gay, A. O., merchant (Walsh Hall & Co.) Kobe
Gearing, J. G., merchant, Chinkeang

Geary, H. S., merchant (Olyphant & Co.) Yokohama
Gebauer, R., secretary (German Consulate)
Geerty, Dr. A. J. (Jap. Govt. Hospital) Nagasaki
Gedes, J., master mariner, Bangkok
Geffeney, C., hairdresser, Yokohama
Geffroy, E., sister (Maison de Jesus enfant) Ningpo
Gehlsen, H. J., barkeeper, "German Tavern," Queen's Road West
Gehmeyer, A., clerk (Behre & Co.) Saigon
Geisenheimer, F., merchant (Hecht, Lilienthal & Co.) Yokohama
Gélase, Sœur St., Sister of Charity, Yokohama
Geller, R., merchant (Pula & Co.) Shanghai
Genato, M., auctioneer (Genato & Co.) Manila
Genth, Ad. S., clerk (Renard & Co.) Hiogo
Genton, F., clerk (Peele, Hubbell & Co.) Manila
Geofroy, M. de, minister plenipotentiary (French Legation) Peking
Georg, E., clerk (Siemssen & Co.) Queen's Road
George, E., chief superintendent (Government Telegraphs) Yedo (absent)
George, E., clerk (Holliday, Wise & Co.)
George, Edgar, resident, Yedo
George, W. D., assistant (Spring & Co.) Manila
Gepp, A. M., merchant (Gibb, Livingston & Co.) Canton
Gerard, A., navy waterworks office, Yokohama
Géraud, —., baker and wine merchant, Saigon
Gerlach, J., M.D., Wyndham Street
Germann, Chas., merchant and consul for Switzerland, Manila
Gerrard, John, clerk (Registrar General's Department) Mosque Street
Gervais, L., engineer, &c., Shanghai
Gest, —., aide commissaire and director (Imprimerie Nationale) Saigon
Ghandy, Dinshaw D., merchant (M. D. Ghandy & Co.) (absent)
Ghira, A.A., sub-lientenant (Camoes) Macao
Giaretto, J. (Marine Hotel) Yokohama
Giassoodin, A., clerk (A. Jafferbhoy & Co.) Stanley Street
Gibarta, Rev. S. F., missionary, Bangkok
Gibb, H. B., merchant (Gibb, Livingston & Co.) (absent)
Gibbs, J. B., proprietor ("The Snug") Yokohama
Gibbs, J. H., accountant (Customs) Peking
Gibert, Des Vallons, sous com. de la marine, Saigon
Gibson, G., mate (str. Kiukiang)
Gibson, Rev. J., missionary (Wes. Meth. Miss. Soc.) Canton

Gibson, T., assist. (Butterfield and Swire) Shanghai
Gibson, T., wharfinger (Kung-tsing Wharf) Shanghai
Gifford, C. E., asst. paymaster, R.N., clerk to sec. (H.M.S. Iron Duke)
Gifford, Patrick, tea inspector (Gifford & Co.) Canton
Gika, N. D., tidewaiter (Customs) Hankow
Gilbert, G. M., Resident, Yedo
Gilbert, S. S., clerk (Russell & Co.) S'hai
Gilbie, W., storeman (Naval Yard)
Giles, H. A., interpreter (British Consulate) Ningpo
Giles, J., assist. (Farnham & Co.) Shanghai
Giles, John, shipchandler (Giles & Co.) Amoy
Gill, C. B., lieut., U. S. N. (Hartford)
Gill, E. H., clerk (Gu'schow & Co.) Yokohama
Gill, H. S., teacher, Eurasian School, Shanghai
Gill, John, foreman of works (H. K. Gas Co.)
Gill, Mrs H. S., teacher, Eurasian School, Shanghai
Gilles, G. H., draughtsman (Kiangnan Arsenal) Shanghai
Gillespie, J., coal heaver (Tanjong Kubong mines) Labuan
Gillett, B., clerk (J. S. Robison) Shanghai
Gillies, J., coal heaver (Tanjong Kubong mines) Labuan
Gillingham, A. W., clerk (Mourylian, Heimann & Co.) Hiogo
Gillingham, J., clerk (Aug. Heard & Co.) Hiogo
Gilman, F., merchant (Gilman & Co.) Shanghai
Gilman, R. S., merchant (Gilman & Co.) (England)
Gilmour, D., public silk inspector (Skeggs & Co.) Shanghai (absent)
Gilmour, Rev. J., M.A., missionary, Peking
Gillpatrick, W. W., lieut. U S. N. (Yantic)
Gimenes, Rev. F., missionary, Amoy and Takan
Gimeno, R., bishop of Cebú (Ecclesiastical Department) Manila
Ginart, M., comdr. Engineers of Arsenal, Manila
Gingell, J., moulder (Naval Yard)
Ginsburgh, S. L., merchant (Ginsburgh & Co.) Yokohama
Giolitti, E., merchant, Chinkiang
Gioranni, E., Boulangerie Française Yokohama
Gipperich, E., merchant, Shanghai
Giquel, J., secretary interpreter (Arsenal) Foochow
Giquel, P., director-in-chief (Arsenal) Foochow

Girard, —., watchmaker, Saigon
Girard, —., founder (Yokoska Arsenal) Yokohama
Girard, P. C. E., chief commissioner (Police Department) Saigon
Giraud, —., chief engineer (M. M. str. *Volga*)
Gissing, T. S., (Naval College) Yedo
Gittins, J., Public Tea Inspector (Newman & Co.) Foochow
Giudicelli, T., Tax collector (French Municipal Council) Shanghai
Giussani, C., silk inspector (Aymonin & Co.) Yokohama
Glackmeyer, G., commission agent, &c., Yokohama
G'anville, R., (Naval College) Yedo
Glass, D., clerk (Jardine, Matheson & Co.) Shanghai
Glass, H., lieut., U.S.N. (*Iroquois*)
Glasse, G., chemist (Victoria Dispensary) Pedder's Wharf
Glehn, E. von, clerk (Smith, Bell & Co.) Manila
Gleizes, —., écrevain de marine, Saigon
Glénat, L., sub-accountant (Comptoir dEscompte de Paris) Yokohama
Glennie, A. W., clerk (Gilman & Co.) Yokohama (absent)
Glover, Alex. B., (Takasima Colliery) Takasima
Glover, Alfred, B., (Takasima Colliery) Nagasaki
Glover, Capt. T. G., (Jardine, Matheson & Co.) East Point (absent)
Glover, Geo. B., commissioner, Customs, Shanghai
Glover, T. B., Trustee, (Glover & Co. in liquidation) Nagasaki
Glover, W., clerk (Barnet & Co.) Shanghai
Goble, Rev. J. (Am. Bap. Miss. Union) Yokohama
Goddard, F. D., 3rd officer (str. *Douglas*)
Goddard, Rev. J. R., miss. (Amer. Bap. Miss.) Ningpo
Godeaux, E., Consul general for France, Shanghai
Godenrath, H., baker (Godenrath & Co.) Shanghai
Godsil, J., captain (Chinese g.-b. *Anlan*)
Godt, C., 3rd officer (German str. *China*)
Godwin, A. A., Tidewaiter (Customs) S'hai
Goetz A., clerk (F. Peil) Shanghai
Goldenberg, —., store-keeper, Nagasaki
Golding, T. B., Superintendent (Police Force) Ningpo
Goldman, S., store-keeper, Hiogo
Goldsmith, Henry C., engineer, R.N. (Naval Yard)
Goldsmith, L. R., mer. (Browne & Co.) Hiogo
Goldsmith, Mrs. proprietor ("City of Hamburg") Yokohama

Goldspink, R. J., tide-surveyor (Customs) Chinkeang
Goldstein, —., "Café de London" Saigon
Goltze, W., assistant (Lohmann, Kuchmeister & Co.) Yokohama
Gomar, Rev. V., R. C. missionary, Taiwan
Gomara, F., assist. engineer (Witte & Co.) Manila
Gombert, C., watchmaker, Shanghai
Gomes, A. J., merchant (Brandão & Co.) Wellington Street
Gomes, F. A., merchant (Brandão & Co.) Wellington Street
Gomes, J. (Welcome Tavern) Queen's Road West
Gomes, J., Jun., merchant (Brandão & Co.) Wellington Street
Gomes, M., clerk (Hongkong & Whampoa Doc: Co.) Kowloon
Gomes, N. J., clerk (E. R. Belilios)
Gomez, F. N. H., clerk (Harbour Master's Office) Macao
Gonner, A. vol., clerk (Pustau & Co.) Shanghai
Gonsalves, C. J., clerk (Hongkong & S'hai Banking Corporation) Wyndham Street
Gonsalves, F. M., clerk (Rozario & Co) Stanley Street
Gonsalves, Major J. M., retired officer, Macao
Gonsalves, R., clerk (F. Degenaer)
Gonsalvez, B. F., clerk (J. J. dos Remedios & Co.) Gough Street
Goode, F. P., 2nd officer (str. *Kwangtung*)
Goodenough, R. B., inspector (Police Court) Sarawak
Goodfellow, J. F., clerk (Russell & Co.) Shanghai
Goodison, F. S., assistant (Walsh, Hall & Co.) Yokohama
Goodrich, Rev. Chauncey, miss., Peking (Tungchow)
Goodridge, R., tidewaiter (Customs) F'chow
Goodwin, A., boilermaker (P. & O. S. N. Co.) Queen's Road West
Goodwin, C. W., assistant judge (H.B.M.'s Supreme Court) Shanghai
Goodwin, W., assistant (Watson & Co.) Shanghai
Goolamhoosein, A., clerk (F. Amijibhoy) Canton
Goosmann, J., clerk (Melchers & Co.) Praya
Gordes, A., photographer (Gordes Brothers) Osaka and Hiogo
Gordes, H., photographer (Gordes Brothers) Osaka and Hiogo
Gordo, A. F., proprietor (Mercantile Printing Office) Yokohama
Gordo, F. J. F., assistant book-keeper (Revenue Department) Macao
Gordo, W. F., clerk (Chartered Mercantile Bank) Yokohama

Gordon, C. W., clerk (Gordon Brothers) Hankow
Gordon, H. L., clerk (China and Japan Trading Company) Shanghai
Gordon, Rev. M. L., M.D., missionary, Osaka
Gordon, Rev. R, missionary, Amoy
Gordon, W., accountant (Dock Co.) Amoy
Gordon, W. G., commission agent (Gordon Brothers) Hankow
Gore Booth, R. H., broker, Shanghai
Gorham. A, M D., surgeon R N. (Ringdove)
Gorman, H. J., clerk (Nachtigal & Co.) Hiogo
Gosselin, —., boilermaker and coppersmith (Arsenal) Foochow
Gosset, F., lieutenant, R. E.
Gottburg, Dr W., Shanghai
Götte, R., merchant (De Bay, Götte & Co.) Bangkok
Göttlinger, L., resident, Hiogo
Goty, W., in charge of hulk Cæsar (Elles & Co.) Tamsui
Götze, W., clerk (Rodewald, Schönfeld & Co.) Shanghai
Goudard, —, off. d'ordonnance, Saigon
Gough, Rev. F. F., Missionary, Ningpo
Gouilloud, L., clerk (Gilman & Co.) Yokohama
Gouin, —., aide commissaire, Saigon
Gouineau, —., pilot, Saigon
Goularte, J. B., clerk (Procurador's Department) Macao
Gould, E. B, assistant (British Consulate) Bangkok
Goulding, T., 2nd officer, Ch. gun-boat Feihoo
Goup, P., clerk (L. Vrard & Co) Tientsin
Gourdin, A. O'D., clerk (Olyphant & Co.) Canton
Goutagny —., superior, Orphanage, French Mission, Canton
Gowan, Peter, M B , surgeon. Bangkok
Gower, A. A. J., consul (British Consulate) Hiogo
Gower, E. (Jap. Govt.) Yedo (Sado)
Gower, S. J., merchant (Jardine, Matheson & Co.)
Gowland, W., metallurgist (Osaka Mint)
Grabe, O., clerk (O. Stammann) Tientsin
Graça, F M. de, clerk (J. A. Tuton and Sons) Macao
Graça, L. A. de, auctioneer and manager (Royal Hotel) Macao
Graça, V. A. de, merchant, Macao
Graham, G., 4th engineer (Sassoon's str. China)
Graham, Geo. G., manager (American Miss printing office) editor (Daily Advertiser) Bangkok
Graham, J. W., clerk (Elles & Co.) Amoy
Graham, W. J., barge master (I. M. S. S. Co.) Hiogo
Grain, E. M., lieut. col. commdg., Royal Engineers, West Terrace
Granados, G., assist. (J. B. Roxas) Manila
Grandon, J., 2nd officer (str. Kua Hsing) Customs, Shanghai
Grandpré, C., clerk (J. B. Lehmann) Saigon
Grandpré, Madame (Bon-marché Store) Saigon
Grange, Alex., marine surveyor, Nagasaki
Granger, A., pilot, Saigon
Granier de Cassagnac, —., commis. de marine, Saigon (absent)
Grant, A. T., smith (Naval Yard)
Grant, Cardross, merchant 'Bradley & Co.) Swatow
Grant, C. Lyall, merchant (Adamson, Bell & Co.) Shanghai
Grant, David, engineer, R.N. (Elk)
Grant, F. G., boatswain, R.N. (Teaser)
Grant, J F. G., commander, R.N. (Midge)
Grant, J., clerk (Iohn Burd & Co.) Queen's Road
Grant, P. V., engineer (Boyd & Co.) S'hai
Grant, R. (Naval College) Yedo
Grauert, H., resident, Yokohama
Graves, P. W., commander (str. Feiwan) laid up at Canton
Graves, Rev. R. H., missionary (South. Bap. Con. U. S. A.) Canton
Gray, D., fitter (Japan Railway)
Gray, E. O. B., Capt., R.M., Yokohama
Gray, G. H., A.M., M.D. (First College, Jap. Govt.) Yedo
Gray, H. N., captain (str. Hirado) S'hai
Gray, James, steward, steamer Thabor (Japanese Government) Yokohama
Gray, J., Fitter (Govt. Railways) Y'hama
Gray, R. M., silk inspector (Reiss & Co.)
Gray, T., assistant engineer (Japan Railway Works)
Gray, Ven. Archdeacon, M.A., chaplain Christ's church, Canton (absent)
Gray, W., tidewaiter, Customs, Chinkeang
Gray, W., tidewaiter (Customs) Chinkeang
Greave, V., manager (London Inn) 126, Queen's Road Central
Greaves, E. E., nav. sub. lieut., R.N. (Cadmus)
Green, A., diver, (Customs) Shanghai (Pootung)
Green, F. J., assist. (W. Miller) Shanghai
Green, F. J., clerk (Gilman & Co.) S'hai
Green, —, serjeant, police force (Customs) Foochow
Green, J. G., lieut. com., U.S.N. (Saco)
Green, Mrs. M. E. (Hiogo Hotel) Hiogo
Green, S. A. A., clerk (Gt. N. Teleg. Co.) Amoy
Green, Thos., superintendent engineer (P. & O. S. N. Co.) Arbuthnot Road
Greenberg, M., assist. (Greenberg & Co.) Yokohama
Greene, Rev. D. C., missionary, Kobé

Greenleaf, F. W., lieut. U S N. (*Monocacy*)
Greenough, H., jun., clerk (Peele, Hubbell & Co.) Manila
Greensward E., assistant, "British Queen" Yokohama
Greeven, G. A., teacher (First College) Yedo
Greeven, G. A., merchant (Greeven, Seges & Co.) Yedo
Greffrier, —., commis. do marine, Saigon
Gregoire, —., resident, Yedo
Grégoire, Sœur St (Sisters of Charity) Yokohama
Gregorie, Sœur M., sister (Asile de la Sainte enfance) Queen's Road, East
Gregorio, C., assistant (Casal Brothers) Manila
Gregory, J., purser (Sassoon's str. *Hindostan*)
Gregory, W., acting consul (Brit. Consulate) and acting consul for Austria, France, Denmark and Germany, Taiwan
Greig, J., assistant (Dodd & Co.) Tamsui
Greig, Jas., chief manager (Hongkong and Shanghai Banking Corporation) Wardley House
Greig, J., clerk (P. O. S. N. Co.)
Greig, M. W., clerk (J. Forster & Co) Foochow
Greig, Wm. G., accountant (Hongkong and Shanghai Bank) Shanghai
Grencer, W., clerk (China Sugar Refinery) East Point
Grenet, J. J., merchant (Farfara and Grenet) Yokohama
Grenot, A., storekeeper, Shanghai
Gretton. Rev. H., missionary (Ch. Miss. Society) Peking
Grey, Alfred, warden (Victoria Gaol)
Grey, E., baker, Chefoo
Grey, H , agent (P. & O. S. N. Co) Nagasaki
Grey, T., inspector (Police Department) Central Station
Gribble, H., agent (P. & O. S. N. Co.) Nagasaki
Gribble, Henry, merchant (H. Gribble & Co.) Nagasaki
Gribble, T. (Naval College) Yedo
Gribooshin, G., clerk (Okoololf & Tomakoff) Hankow
Griflis, W. E., A.M., professor of Chemistry (Jap. Govt.) Yedo
Griflith, D. K., assistant (W. Saunders) Shanghai
Griffiths, J. H., carpenter, R.N. (*Thetis*)
Grigor, John, M., assistant (Hongkong and Shanghai Banking Corp.) Shanghai
Grimani, E. H., student, (Customs,) Peking
Grimble, P., foreman (Control Department) Queen's Road
Grimes, J., inspector (Police Department) Central Station

Grimm, B., dispenser (Pharmacie de l'Union) Shanghai
Grimmen, L., architect, Yedo
Grinberg, Mrs., "Crown and Anchor," Hiogo
Grinsen, H., merchant, Yedo
Grobien, F., merchant (Sander & Co.) Queen's Road
Grobien, J., clerk (Sander & Co.) Queen's Road
Groeneveldt, W. P., secretary (Netherlands Legation) Peking
Groenewout, J. A. A., merchant (Schüt, Scheuten & Co.) Hiogo (absent)
Gromoff, K. S., merchant, Kalgan
Groom, A. H., clerk (Mourylian, Heimann & Co.) Hiogo
Groom, Francis A., broker, Shanghai
Groombridge, Rev. F., missionary, K'keang
Groos, J. H., broker, Hongkong Hotel
Groote, C. de, Belgian Minister (not arrived)
Grosclaude, E., watchmaker (E. & U. Grosclaude) Hankow and Hiogo
Grosclaude, U., watchmaker (E. & U. Grosclaude) Hiogo and Hankow
Grösser, E., merchant (Grösser & Co.) Yokohama
Grösser, F., clerk (Grösser & Co.) Yokohama
Grossmann, C. F., merchant (Kirchner, Büger & Co)
Grosvenor, Hon. T., second secv. (British Legation) Peking
Grote, M., clerk (Melchers & Co.) Praya
Groth, A., clerk (Heinszen & Co.) Manila
Groth, J., merchant (Groth & Co.) Ningpo
Groundwater, A., 2nd officer (str. *Thales*)
Groupiere, F., 2nd commis. (French Consulate) Yokohama
Grove, T. G , lieut. U.S.N. (*Monocacy*)
Groves, T. J., tailor (Driscoll & Co.) Yokohama and Kobé
Gruet, J., clerk (Blanco, Domingo & Co.) Manila
Grün, F., merchant (Kaltenbach, Engler & Co.) Saigon
Grunauer, L., clerk (E. Vincent & Co.)
Grundy, A., clerk (Holliday, Wise & Co.) Manila
Grunwald, F., assistant (Morf & Co.) Yokohama
Grupe, G., dispenser (Zobel & Nohr) Manila
Gsell, E., photographer, Saigon
Gubbay, E. S., clerk (David Sassoon, Sons & Co.) Ningpo
Gubbay, M. S., merchant (David Sassoon, Sons & Co.) Shanghai
Gubbins, W. H , clerk (Jardine, Matheson & Co.) Shanghai
Gubbins, J. H., student interpreter (British Legation) Yedo
Gue, G., tide-surveyor, Customs, Takow

Guedes, F. D., clerk (Dubost & Co.) Queen's Road
Guedes, J. M., Jr., auctioneer, Mosque Street
Guégo, Rev., —., missionary (French R. C. Mission) Bangkok (Bang Plasoi)
Gueri , —., Patternmaker (Arsenal) F'chow
Guérin, —., hairdresser. Saigon
Gueritz, Geo., act. resident, Sarebas, Sarawak
Guerrero, Scarnichia Eduardo, Adm. Ger. Postal dept. Manila
Guevarra, B., clerk (Guichard & Fils) Manila
Guichard, A., merchant (Guichard & Fils) Manila (absent)
Guichard, Eug., merchant (Guichard & Fils) Manila (absent)
Guichard, Fr., merchant (Guichard & Fils) Manila (absent)
Guichard, J. A., merchant (Guichard & Fils) Manila (absent)
Guierry, F., monseigneur vic. apostolique (R. C. Mission) Ningpo
Guigne, A. de, assistant (Mess. Mar.)
Guild, Chas. F , paymr. in charge, U. S. Naval Depot, Praya East
Guillemin, Right Rev. Z., bishop, Canton (absent)
Guillet, de Grois —., Proc. general, Saigon
Guillot, Pere A., missionary (R. C. Mission) Ningpo (Kiukiang)
Guimarães, J. da S., lieut. (Police Department) Macao
Guimarães, J. M. T., commandor (Camões) Macao
Guimard, A., chief engineer (M. M. S. S. Hoogly)
Guion, Ch., chief engineer (M. M. S. Peiho)
Guiraud, L., gen sec. of Interior, Saigon
Guiraud, —., carpenter (Arsenal) Foochow
Guirrini, N., resident, Yokohama
Guitard, Madame L. (European Laundry) Hiogo
Guixa, Rev. N., missionar; (R. C. Mission, Lam-pi-lau) Amoy
Gulsmally, S., clerk (Ebrahim & Co.) Cochrane Street
Gulick, Rev. C. H., missionary, Osaka
Gulick, Rev. John T., missionary, Kalgan
Gültzow, A., clerk (Siemssen & Co.) F'chow
Gundorph, F., assistant (C. Gombert) Shanghai
Gundry, R. S., editor (*North China Herald* Office) Shanghai
Gunther, C., harbour master (Customs) Swatow
Gurlitt, H., merchant (Reis, Von der Heyde & Co.) Hiogo
Gusman, S. A., hairdresser (W. P. Moore) Hongkong Hotel
Gussman, Rev. G. A., miss. (Evan. Miss. Soc. Basel) Lilong

Gutbrod, —., clerk (German Consulate) Hiogo
Guterres, A. P., clerk (Harbour Master's Department)
Guterres, F., clerk (Scott & Co.) Hiogo
Guthrie, Miss L. M., missionary, Yokohama
Gütschow, O., merchant (Gütschow & Co.) Yokohama and Hiogo (absent)
Gütschow, P., merchant (Gütschow & Co.) Yokohama and Hiogo
Gutteres, R. A., clerk (J. A. Tuton & Sons) Macao
Gutterres, D. M., clerk (Hongkong and Shanghai Bank) Shanghai
Gutterrez, F. B., clerk (Olyphant & Co.) Shanghai
Guttierrez, A. O., clerk (P. &. O. S. N. Co.) Wyndham Street
Guttierrez, J. A., clerk (Russell & Co.)
Guttierrez, J. G., clerk (Olyphant & Co.)
Guttierrez, L. J. (Gifford & Co.) Gough Street
Guttierrez, M. clerk (Surveyor General's Department)
Guttierrez, Q. A. (Russell & Co.)
Guttierrez, Q. O., clerk (Russell & Co.)
Guttierrez, R. F., printer, Wyndham Street
Guttierrez, S. C., clerk (Colonial Secretary's Department) Wyndham Street
Guttierrez, S. J., clerk (M. J. D. Stephens) Wyndham Street
Guttierrez, V , mer hant, Wyndham Street
Guyomar, —., sous com. de la marine, Saigon
Guyon, —., off. d'ordonnance, Saigon
Guzder, A. R., clerk (Nowrojee & Co.) Hollywood Road
Guzder, B. N., merchant (Nowrojee & Co.) Hollywood Road
Guzder, C. B., merchant (Nowrojee & Co.) (Calcutta)
Guzman, G., assist. (Casal Bros.) Manila
Gwanho, T., clerk (Dauver & Co.) Amoy

H

Haas, Joseph, interpreter (Austro-Hungarian Consulate) Peking (absent)
Habgood, T. E., tidewaiter (Customs) Canton
Haber, L., merchant, Yokohama
Habibbhoy, A., merchant, Shanghai
Habibbhoy, A., merchant C'ton & H'kong
Habibbhoy, R., merchant, Canton and Hongkong
Habibbhoy, R., merchant, Shanghai
Habiboolla, A., clerk (Ebrahim & Co.) Cochrane Street
Hackett, T., assist. engineer (Osaka Mint)
Hackman, A., nav. lieut., R.N. (*Thalia*)
Haddy, George A., assist. Eng. R. N., (*Cadmus*)

Haden, C. S., clerk (Gilman & Co) Praya
Hadler, —., captain (str. *Rocket*) Shanghai
Hadley, A., Boilermaker (Naval Yard)
Haenni, C., clerk (Siber and Brennwald) Yokohama
Haffenden, John, clerk (Russell & Sturgis) Manila
Hagart, H. W., merchant (Hagart & Co.) Hiogo
Hagedorn, F. W., merchant (Vogel Hagedorn & Co) (absent)
Hagelstange, G. Emil, clerk (Thorne Rice & Co.) Shanghai
Hagen, C., merchant (Crasemann and Hagen) vice-consul for Germany, C'foo
Hagens, E., assist. (Grössel & Co.) Y'hama
Hager, R , assist. (Ladage & Oelke) Y'hama
hagge, H., clerk (Bourjau & Co) Praya
Hague, E. P., clerk (Thorne Brothers & Co) Shanghai
Hague, F. M., clerk (Coutts & Co.) S'hai
Hague, W. A., public ten. inspector, Shanghai
Hahn, A., piano tuner, Yokohama
Haille, M. Ch. de la, engineer, Shanghai
Hainard, —., watchmaker, Saigon
Hajee, F. A., clerk (B. A. Ismael) Canton
Hake, T. H., merchant (Ahrens & Co.) Yokohama
Hake, Th., assistant (H. Ahrens & Co.) Yedo
Hakimna, H. R., assistant (N. Mody & Co.) Queen's Road
Hale, Wm. G , merchant (Wm. G. Hale & Co.) Saigon (absent)
Hales, G., clerk (Birley & Co.) Foochow
Hall, A., engineer (Takasima Colliery) Takasima
Hall, C. F., resident, Yedo
Hall, C. P., clerk (Walsh, Hall & Co.) Yokohama
Hall, G. W., assist. eng., U.S.N. (*Yantic*)
Hall, J., clerk (Butterfield & Swire) S'hai
Hall, J., fitter (Govt. Railroad) Yokohama
Hall, J. C., Act. Registrar and Interpreter H. M.'s Provincial Court, Yokohama
Hall, J. H., tidewaiter (I. M. Customs) Keelung
Hall, J. W., average adjuster (Cheshire & Co.) Yokohama
Hall, M. E., master, U.S.N. (*Iroquois*)
Hall, Rev. Henry H., missionary, K'keang (absent)
Hall, Rev. W. N., missionary (Meth. Miss. Society) Tientsin (absent)
Hall, S. T., teacher (Jap. Govt.) Yedo
Hall, T., clerk (Butterfield & Swire) Queen's Road
Hall, Thos. W., assist. pay. R.N. (*Thalia*)
Hallaban, J., gunner, R.N., (*Princess Charlotte*)
Hallifax, T. E., assist. supt. (Govt. Telog.) Toyohashi

Hallorau, J., inspector (Police Department) Central Station (absent)
Halsey, J. S., tide surveyor, Customs, Shanghai
Halsey, W., Foreman Mechanic (Govt. Railroad) Yokohama
Hamilton, E., tidewaiter (Customs) Chefoo
Hamilton, G., clerk (Fraser & Co.) Yokohama
Haminoff, J. S., merchant (Haminoff, Rodionoff & Co.) Hankow (Irkutsk)
Hamlin, Thos., chief officer (str. *Appin*) Shanghai
Hamlyn, J., tidewaiter (Customs) Newchwang
Hammersley, Wm., godown keeper (Dodd & Co.) Tamsui
Hammond, F. (Naval College) Yedo
Hammond, W. H. (Skipworth, Hammond & Co.) Hiogo
Hamonic, H., engineer (Hamonic Freres) Saigon
Hamonic, J., engineer (Hamonic Frères) Saigon
Hampshire, S., foreman (China Sugar Refinery) East Point
Hams, Mrs. —., milliner (Miss M. Garrett) Queen's Road
Hanbury, T., merchant (Bower, Hanbury & Co.) Shanghai (absent)
Hancaster, —., teacher (Jap. Govt.) Yedo
Hance, E. W. (Pacific Mail S. S. Co.) Yokohama
Hance, H. F., PH.D., vice-consul (British Consulate) Whampoa
Hancock, H. S., agent and tea inspector (Gibb, Livingston & Co.) Hankow
Handel, H., clerk (Hall & Holtz) Shanghai
Handley, E. R., gas-fitter, Praya West
Handley, P. A., barrister at law
Hanlon, M., proprietor (Carlton House) Shanghai
Hanna, John, merchant, Tientsin (absent)
Hannen, N. J., act. ass. judge (H. M.'s Provincial Court) Yokohama
Hansen, A. C. W., master mariner, B'kok
Hansen, H. A. D., master mariner, B'kok
Hansen, J. G. R. C., master mariner, Bangkok
Hansen, L., assist. (Tillson & Co.) Hiogo
Hansen, N. P., master mariner, Bangkok
Hansen, O. S., master mariner, Bangkok
Hansen, H. H., master mariner, Bangkok
Hansen, H. P., merchant (A. Dent & Co.) act. consul general for Portugal, S'hai
Hansen, P., publican, Chefoo
Hanus, G. C., mid., U.S.N. (*Palos*)
Happer, Miss Lillie B., missionary, Canton
Happer, Rev. Dr. A. P., missionary (Amer. Presbyterian) Canton
Harber, G. B., master, U.S.N. (*Lackawanna*)
Hardcastle, E. J., manager (Comptoir d'Escompte) Shanghai

Hardee, —., machinist (Jap. Govt.) Yedo
Harder, J., paymaster's clerk, U. S. Naval depôt, Praya East
Hardey, E. P., medical missionary (Wes. Mission Society) Hankow
Hardie, D., agent (H. K. & S. Banking Corp.) Saigon
Hardie, J., act. manager (Borneo Company) Sarawak
Hardie, Jas. D., agent (Tait & Co.) Amoy (Takow)
Harding, Geo. asst. engineer, R.N. (Teazer)
Harding, H., police inspector (Govt. Railroad) Yokohama
Harding, J. W., clerk (Birley, Worthington & Co.) Shanghai
Harding, M., assist. (L. Candrelier) Yedo (Shiba)
Harding, T., reporter (Japan Herald) Yokohama
Harding, W. J. (Naval College) Yedo
Hardman, C. R., clerk (Hudson, Malcolm & Co.) Yokohama
Hardoon, E. A., clerk (D. Sassoon, Sons & Co.) Chefoo
Hardoon, S. A., clerk (D. Sassoon, Sons & Co.) Praya
Hardwick, W. O., assist. (Domoney & Co.) Yokohama
Hardy,—., chief of staff, Saigon
Hardy, C., assistant engineer, (Government Railways) Yokohama
Hardy, George S., tea inspector (Birley & Co.) Canton
Hardy, J. T., C.E., assistant (Public Works Department) Yedo
Hare, A. J. (Hare & Co.) Yedo
Hare, D. J., (Hare & Co.) Yedo
Hare, H. T., asst. engineer (Customs) S'hai
Harkness, T. G., clerk (Boyd & Co.) Amoy
Harlet,—., Park guardian, Saigon
Harley,—., resident, Yokohama
Harley, J., proprietor (Old Brown Jug) Yokohama
Harman, G., examiner, (Customs,) S'hai
Harmon, Joseph, master (str. Fusiyama) Shanghai
Harr, Miss L. H., missionary, Osaka
Harries, W. H., agent (H'K. & S. Bank) Hiogo
Harris, Chas., lightkeeper (Japanese Govt.) Yokohama
Harris, G. L., supt. engineer (P. M. S. S. Co.) Yokohama
Harris, J., M.D. (Govt. Railroad) Hiogo and Yokohama
Harris, P., officer (P. & O. service)
Harris, R., assist. eng., R.N. (Rinaldo)
Harris, Revd. S. D., missionary (Am. meth. Epis. miss.) Pekin
Harris, T. A., agent (P. M. S. S. Co.) Bonham Road
Harris, U. W., sergeant, river police, S'hai

Harris, W., shipwright (Harris & Co.) Swatow
Harris, W., constable (Municipal Council) Nagasaki
Harris, W. H., second officer (str. Yangtze)
Harris, W. R. J., clerk (Lane, Crawford & Co.) Shanghai
Harrison, H., eng. R.N. (Ringdove)
Harrison, G. E., sub-lieut., R.N. (Iron Duke)
Harrison, Miss E., assist. (Mrs. G. Bergen) Hiogo
Harrison, W.D., clerk (Butterfield & Swire)
Harrison, W. G., tidewaiter (Customs) Kewkeang
Harrold, F., engineer (steamer Kiuliang)
Harryman, F., storekeeper (M. J. B. Hoyt) Yokohama
Hart, G. M., assist. (Mun. Council Offices) Shanghai
Hart, J., clerk (Turner & Co.) Shanghai
Hart, J. H., com. (Customs) Takow
Hart, Rev. V. C., and wife, missionaries Kewkeang
Hart, Robert, inspector general, (Customs,) Peking
Hart, Thomas, police reporter (Daily Press Office) Wyndham Street
Hart, W., merchant (Marmelstein & Co.) Hiogo
Hart, W., merchant (Hart & Co.) Ningpo
Hartley, H., storekeeper (Hartley & Co.) Yedo
Hartley, J., merchant (Hartley & Co.) Yokohama, Osaka and Yedo
Hartman, H. A., fitter (Government Railway) Yokohama
Hartmann, G. W., clerk (Deutsche Bank) Shanghai
Hartmans, W. L., merchant (Hartmans & Besier) Nagasaki
Harton, C. F., clerk (Gilman & Co.) Foochow
Harton, W. H., clerk (Gilman & Co.) S'hai
Hartwell, Rev. C., missionary, Foochow
Hartwell, Rev. J. B., missionary, Chefoo
Harvey, A. S., vice-consul for Great Britain and Denmark, Newchwang
Harvey, C. J., clerk (Little & Co.) S'hai
Harvey, H. J., paymaster, R.N. (Princess Charlotte)
Harvey, H. P., assistant surgeon, U.S.N. (Palos)
Harvey, J., compradore (Stentz, Harvey & Co.) Yokohama
Harvey, J., second officer (Chinese gunboat Antan)
Harvey, J. R., engineer, R.N. (Naval Yard)
Harvey, W. V., 3rd engineer (Str. Namoa)
Harvin, J. A., shipchandler (Lane. Crawford & Co.) Shanghai
Harwood, J., gunner (Arsenal) Foochow
Harwood, W., solicitor, Shanghai (absent)
Hase, W., manager (Kaga Foundry) Hiogo

Haselwood, A. H. C., clerk (Hongkong and Shanghai Banking Corporation) Shanghai
Haager, M. E., merchant, 17, Gage Street
Haskell, F. E., local agent (China & Japan Trading Company) Shanghai
Haskell, H. B., clerk (Walsh, Hall & Co.) Yokohama
Haslam, R. H., merchant (John Silverlock & Co.) Foochow
Haslam, W. H., tea inspector, Shanghai
Haslem, J., writer (Sarawak Trading Company) Sarawak
Haslem, W., engineer (str. *Bertha*) Sarawak
Hassall, J. G. T., clerk (Birley & Co.) Queen's Road
Hassoll, J., manager (Japan Butchery) Yokohama
Hastings, R., tidewaiter (Customs) Taiwan
Hatch, J. J., Commission agent (J. Hanna) Tientsin
Hatton, Mrs. A., laundress, Yokohama
Haudoin, O., teacher (Jap. Govt.) Yedo
Hauenstein, G., pilot, Amoy
Hauschild, H., Engineer, Bangkok
Hauschild, Louis, broker, sec. (German Consulate)
Hauschild, R., clerk (Meyer, Alabor & Co.) Stanley Stuct
Hauschildt, O., miller (Markwald & Co.) Bangkok
Hausmann, Capt. T., secretary, German Consulate, Bangkok
Hawes, —., U. S. Consul, Hakodadi
Hawes, J. A., merchant (Tate and Hawes) Shanghai
Hawes, Lt. R., M.A., gunnery instructor (Jap. Govt.) Yokohama
Hawke, Richard F., accountant (Naval Yard) (absent)
Hawkins, C. E., boatswain, U.S.N. (*Lackawanna*)
Hawkins, H., assist. (China Sub. Tel. Co.)
Hawkins, H. J., clerk (Heinemann & Co.) Yokohama
Hawkins, T. E., farrier, rear of Murray Barracks
Hawtrey, M., clerk (Chapman, King & Co.) Shanghai
Haxty, R., clerk (F. Lucheinger) Yloilo
Hay, C. E., clerk (Martin, Dyce & Co.) Manila
Hay, C. W., assist, (Boyd & Co.) Nagasaki
Hay, D., storekeeper (China and Japan Trading Co.) Osaka
Hay, R. M., act. manager (Borneo Co.) Bangkok
Hayan, W., Professor of Russian and German (College) Peking
Hayden, G. W., Lightkeeper (Gutzlaff Lighthouse) Shanghai
Hayes, A. A. Jr., merchant (Olyphant & Co.) Shanghai

Hayllar, Hon. T. C., Act. Attorney General (Supreme Court House) Arbuthnot Road
Hayne, R. B., clerk (P. M. S. S. Co.) Yokohama
Hays, J., gunner, U. S. N. (*Lackawanna*)
Hazlett, A., inspector of nuisances (Medical Department) Central Station
Head, A., pilot, Foochow (Anchorage)
Head, F. S., clerk (A. Heard & Co.)
Head, R. G., merchant (Lindsay & Head) Shanghai
Head, R. L., clerk (Ferguson & Co.) C'foo
Head, R. S. B., staff surgeon R.N. (*Thalia*)
Healey, W. L., naval instructor, R.N. (*Thalia*)
Heard, Augustine, merchant (A. Heard & Co.) (absent)
Heard, A. F., merchant (A. Heard & Co.) Caine Road
Heard, G. F., merchant, acting Russian vice-consul (A. Heard & Co.) (absent)
Heard, John, merchant, consul for Russia (A. Heard & Co.) (absent)
Hearn, H. R., clerk (F. R. Gamwell) Shanghai
Hearne, A., clerk (E. James) Yokohama
Hearns, H., steward (International Hotel) Yokohama
Heaton, A. McG., merchant (D. Lapraik & Co.) Caine Road
Heaton, W., 3rd eng. (Sassoon's str. *China*)
Hebhú, —., clerk (Maron & Co.) Yokohama
Hebrard, Scipion, chancellor (French Consulate) Manila
Hedge, T. B., merchant (Hedge & Co.) Foochow
Beenskerk, C., clerk (Walsh, Hall & Co.) Yedo
Heenzager, C., chief engineer (M. M. S. S. *Irrawaddy*)
Heeren, O., acting Peruvian consul, Yedo
Heermann, C. O., assistant (C. J. Gaupp & Co.) Queen's Road
Hegt, M. J. B., storekeeper, Yokohama
Heguembourg, Miss S. K. M., missionary, Yokohama
Heimann, C. A., merchant (Mourylian, Heimann & Co.) Hiogo (absent)
Heimann, M., clerk (Kirchner, Böger & Co.)
Heimsoht, —., master mariner, Bangkok
Heinemann, F., merchant, Shanghai
Heinemann, P., merchant (Heinemann & Co.) Yokohama
Heinemann, S. L., shipbroker, Bank Buildings, Queen's Road
Heinszen, C., merchant (Heinszen & Co.) Manila (absent)
Heinszen, J. N., merchant (C. Heinszen & Co.) Manila
Huise, G., clerk (Russell & Co.) Ningpo
Heiss, W., machinist (Jap. Govt.) Yedo
Hoitmann, J. C., merchant (Smith, Archer & Co.) Canton

Helby, F. T., Nav. Lieut. R.N. (*Coelmus*)
Held, R., clerk (Vogel, Hagedorn & Co.) Praya
Helland, A., clerk (John Burd & Co.) Praya
Hellendoal, P. J., yardsman (Jap. Railway)
Hellyer, F., clerk (Alt & Co.) Nagasaki
Helms, L. V., manager (Borneo Company) Sarawak (absent)
Helyer, Giles, commander gunboat (*Heartsease*) Sarawak
Hember, Samuel, general manager (*Daily Press* Office)
Henderson, C., assistant (Domoney & Co.) Hiogo
Henderson, D. M., coast lights engineer (Customs) Shanghai
Henderson, E., M.D. (health officer) S'hai
Henderson, F., clerk (Russell & Co.)
Henderson, G., clerk (Hongkew Wharf Co.) Shanghai
Henderson, J., merchant, Tientsin
Henderson, J. J., consul for U. S., Amoy
Henderson, J. W., clerk (Walsh, Hall & Co.) Kobe
Henderson, J. V., clerk (Lane, Crawford & Co.) Yokohama
Henderson, P., fitter (Govt. Railway) Yokohama
Henderson, W. A., med. miss., Chefoo
Henderson, W. D., acting accountant (Chartered Mercantile Bank) Yokohama
Hendrick, C. E., pilot (Independence Pilot Company) Shanghai
Hendricks, R., interpreter (German Consulate) Bangkok
Hendricks, W. H., jailer (U. S. Consulate) Shanghai
Hendriks, N. F., clerk (Harbour Master's office) Bangkok
Henley, H. H., clerk (P. & O. S. N. Co.) Yokohama
Hennequin, A., agent (Messageries Maritimes) Shanghai
Hennessy, William Pope, supt. Police, Labuan
Henninger, T. (Ogoe Tannery) Yedo
Hennings, P. H., master (German steamer *China*)
Henningsen, J., clerk (G. N. Teleg. Co.) and agent for Reuter, Amoy
Henningsen, S. H., master mariner, B'kok
Henri, S., commissaire (M. M. steamship *Meikong*)
Henriot, C., assistant (M. M. Co.'s office) Saigon
Henriques, W. (Tillson & Co.) Hiogo
Henriques, W. A. L., sub-lieut., R.N. (*Thetis*)
Henry, Alex. A., inspector, native affairs, Saigon
Henry, J. P., tidewaiter (Customs) Ningpo
Henry, M., clerk (Russell & Sturgis) Manila
Henry, P., dispenser (Borneo Co.) Sarawak

Henry, Rev. B. C., missionary (Am. Pres. Board) Canton
Hens, J. F., in charge (Belgian Consulate) Manila
Hensen, —. (School of Foreign Languages) Yedo
Henson, J., clerk (Hartley & Co.) Yokohama & Osaka
Henson, —, mariner (Jap. Govt.) Y o
Hepburn, Dr. J. C., medical miss., Y'hama
Hepper, F. H., clerk (MacCloud, Pickford & Co.) Manila (Cebu)
Herbert, H. G., asst. paymaster, R.N., clerk to secretary (H.M.S. *Iron Duke*)
Herb, F., clerk (Alloin & Co.) Bangkok
Herbst, E., clerk (McEwen, Frickel & Co.) Queen's Road
Herce, Rev. F. B., missionary (Roman C. Church) Dominican Mission, H'kong
Herdman, W. G., clerk (Brand Brothers) Shanghai
Herdman, J., superintendent of works (Public Works Department) Yokohama
Herhausen, O., merchant, Osaka
Heris, T., teacher (Japanese Govt.) Yedo
Hermann, F., clerk (Lehmann, Hartmann & Co.) Osaka and Hiogo (absent)
Hermann, J., acting consul for North Germany & Russia, and merch. (Schmidt, Westphal & Co.) Nagasaki
Hermann, M. A., German consul and merchant (Tillson, Hermann & Co.) Manila (absent)
Hernandez, J., clerk (Martin, Dyce & Co.) Manila
Heron, F. G., merchant (Russell & Sturgis) Manila
Herreva, José de, assistant (Loney & Co.) Surigao
Herring, F., assistant (James & Wilson) Yokohama
Herring, T., clerk (R. C. Broadhurst) Yokohama
Hertz, A., clerk (Carlowitz & Co.) Canton
Hertzog, —., merchant (Hertzog & Roth) Yokohama
Heseltine, G. A., lieut. R.M., Yokohama
Heuermann, F. W., clerk (MacEwen, Frickel & Co.) Queen's Road
Heuschell, J. H., clerk (Peel, Hubbell & Co.) Manila
Hewat, W., captain (str. *Sri Sarawak*) Sarawak
Hewetson, C., bandmaster to 2nd King, Bangkok
Hewett, W., clerk (Lane, Crawford & Co.) Shanghai
Hewlett, A. R., assist. Chinese secretary (British Legation) Peking
Hewlett, W., R.N., master attendant, Naval Yard
Hey, F., clerk (Knoop & Co.) Shanghai
Heyden, F. E., merchant (F. Peil) Shanghai

44　　Hey　　FOREIGN RESIDENTS.　　Hol

Heymann, J., clerk (Baer & Co.) Manila
Heymanson, B. (Havana Cigar Co.) Yokohama
Heywood, H. C., clerk (A. Heard & Co.) Seymour Terrace
Hinto, C., teacher (Jap. Govt.) Yedo
Hickling, A., clerk (Turner & Co.) Hankow
Hickling, H., merchant (Phipps, Hickling & Co.) Foochow
Hicks, G. W., pilot, Taku
Hidalgo, A., Portuguese consul and merchant (Aguirre & Co.) Manila
Higgin, J., British vice-consul and merchant, Yloilo
Higginbotham, Joseph, clerk (Whitfield & Dowson) Yokohama
Higgins, J. (Naval College) Yedo
Higgins, W. J., master mariner, Bangkok
Hildalgo, D. D., 1st off. (Customs) Manila
Hilgendorff, Dr. F. (Jap. Govt.) Yedo
Hill, A., captain and adj., R.M., Yokohama
Hill, B. G., in charge of Berwick Walls, Shanghai
Hill, C. E. (Hunt's Wharf) Shanghai
Hill, Geo. B., surgeon, R.N. (Iron Duke)
Hill, G. W., barrister, legal adviser (Saibansho) Yokohama
Hill, J., assist. (Pootung Foundry) S'ghai
Hill, Jno. C., pilot, Taku
Hill, Rev. David, missionary (Wes. Miss. Society) Hankow (Wusuch)
Hill, Robt. H., clerk (Bradley & Co.) Swatow
Hillier, H. M., clerk, Customs, Shanghai
Hillier, Walter C., assistant (British Consulate) Canton
Hilston, Duncan, M.D., medical off. (Royal Naval Hospital) Yokohama
Himly, K., interpreter (German Consulate) Shanghai
Hinckley, N. B., clerk (Russell & Co.)
Hind, J., draper (Thompson & Hind) Queen's Road (absent)
Hingkee, joint-lessee (Hongkong Hotel)
Hinz, E., constable (German Legation) Peking
Hippisley, A. E., clerk (Customs) Shanghai
Hirsbrunner, J., watchmaker (Hirsbrunner & Co.) Hankow und Shanghai
Hirsbrunner, J., assistant (Vrard & Co.) Shanghai
Hirth, Dr. F., PH.D., assistant, (Customs) Canton
Hirzel, F., clerk (Carlowitz & Co.) Praya
Hitch, F. D., merchant (Russell & Co.) Shanghai
Hitchcock, F., foreman (S. Easton & Co.) East Point
Hitzeroth, Gustav, merchant (Carlowitz & Co.) Canton
Hoar, J., pilot, Ningpo
Hobson, H. E., commissioner (Customs) Tamsui

Hobson, R. M., assist. (Customs) Chefoo
Hochreuter, H., master mariner, Bangkok
Hock, L. C., assistant (Hoiloo & Enam) Shanghai
Hock, L. C., clerk (Bisset & Co) Shanghai
Hockmeyer, F., clerk (Siemssen & Co.) Queen's Road
Hodge, Rev. W. B., missionary, Tientsin
Hodges, G., proprietor, "United Service Sailors' Home," Yokohama
Hodges, H., constable (British Consulate) Shanghai
Hodgkins, J. R., clerk (Aug. Heard & Co.)
Hodgkins, W. R., purser (Kinshan)
Hodgson, John G., acting account. (Hongkong & Shanghai Bank) Yokohama
Hoffmann, Dr. Ph. (Jap. Govt.) Yedo
Hoffmann, G., assist. (Water Works office) Yokohama
Hoffmann, H., master mariner, Bangkok
Hoffmeyer, V., electrician (Great Northern Teleg. Co.) Shanghai
Hogarth, J. B., clerk (Holliday, Wise & Co.)
Hogg, A. G., merchant (Hogg & Co.) Saigon
Hogg, E. J., merchant (Hogg Brothers) Shanghai
Hogg, G. S., engineer (P. & O. service)
Hogg, James, merchant (Hogg Brothers) Shanghai (absent)
Hogg, Jas., master (str. Chinkiang)
Högquist, M., auctioneer (Högquist & Co.) Shanghai
Höhing, Rev. A. C., missionary, Hankow
Hohn, G., clerk (Vogel, Hagedorn & Co.) Shanghai
Höhne, A., clerk (Vogel, Hagedorn & Co.) Shanghai
Hohnholz, H. W, storekeeper (Hohnholz & Co.) Yokohama
Hoiler, Y., manager (Hoiloo & Enam) Shanghai
Holcombe, Rev. C., missionary. (Am. B. Com. For. Miss.) Peking
Holding, J., clerk (Ker & Co.) Manila (Leyte)
Holdsworth, E., public silk inspector, S'hai
Holland, C. J., 2nd officer (str. Hailoong)
Holland, W., student interpreter (British Legation) Peking
Holleben, Baron von, Chargé d'Affaires (German Legation) Peking
Holliday, J. F., merchant (Holliday, Wise & Co.) (absent)
Holliday, John, merchant (Holliday, Wise & Co.) (absent)
Hollingworth, H. G., merchant (Olyphant & Co.) Shanghai
Hollins, H. H., clerk (Customs) Shanghai (absent)
Hollowell, Thos., proprietor (Star Tavern) Queen's Road

Holmblad, J., assistant (O. N. T. Co.) Nagasaki
Holme, E., merchant (Holme, Ringer & Co.) Nagasaki (absent)
Holme, Ryle, merchant (Holme, Ringer & Co.) Hiogo
Holmes, E. R., general broker, corner of Bank Buildings
Holmes, Geo., ship broker, Pedder's Hill (agent for Oriental Telegram Co.)
Holmes, Henry J., solicitor, clerk of court (Supreme Court) Kowloong
Holmes, Mrs., missionary Chefoo
Holmes, M. G., commission agent (Holmes, Wadman & Co.) Chefoo and Shanghai
Holstius, O., tidewaiter, Customs, Shanghai
Holt, V., resident, Yedo
Holt, N. W. (Jap. Govt.) Yedo (Krilikushi)
Holtham, E. G., assistant engineer (Govt. Railroad) Yokohama
Holton, C. F., agent (Tudor Company) Ice House Street
Holttum, W. W. (Hiogo & Osaka Herald) Hiogo
Holwill, E. T., clerk (Customs) Shanghai
Holz, —., teacher (First College) Yedo
Holz, V. (Jap. Govt.) Yedo
Homan, J. A., manager (Naconchaisee Factory) Bangkok
Homarth, Chas. engineer, Bangkok
Honey, G. A. K., merchant (Smith, Bell & Co.) Manila
Honiss, Albert, merchant (Honiss & Co.) Manila
Hood, W., assistant (P. & O. Coal Depôt) Yokohama
Hook, J. S., shipping agent, &c. (J. S. Hook, Son & Co.) Praya
Hook, T. R. S., shipping agent, &c. (J. S. Hook Son & Co.) Praya
Hooper, A., chief officer (Str. Yangtsze)
Hooper, C. F., merchant (Hooper Bros.) Hiogo and Yokohama
Hooper, E. A., furnisher, Shanghai
Hooper, H. J., merchant (Hooper Bros.) Yokohama
Hooper, J., clerk of Works (British Consulate) Yokohama
Hooper, J., resident, Yedo
Hooper, T. B., commander (Jardine's str. Takü)
Hopkins, G. G., clerk (A. Heard & Co.) Shanghai
Hopkins, W., butcher, Shanghai
Hoppius, H., merchant (Siemssen & Co.) Queen's Road
Hopton, H., (Naval College) Yedo
Horo, T., chief usher (H. B. Supreme Court) Shanghai
Hore, T., clerk (A. Myburgh) Shanghai
Hore, T., clerk (R. W. M. Bird) Shanghai
Horowalla, M. S., manager (Mc ly & Co.) 40, Queen's Road

Hormann, J., clerk (Fabre & Co.) Y'hama
Hormusjee, C., clerk (Camajee & Co.) Shanghai
Hormusjee, F., manager (F. Hormusjee & Co.) Shanghai
Hornby, Sir Fd., judge (H. B. M.'s Supreme Court) Shanghai
Horne, P., teacher (Jap. Govt.) Yedo
Horne, T. W., godown-keeper (Bradley & Co.) Swatow
Horsley, A. J., midshipman, R.N. (Cadmus)
Horspool, G., inspector (Police Department) Central Station
Horton, W., assist. insp. of brothels (Med. Department)
Hoskings, F. J., tidewaiter (Customs) Sh'ai
Hoskyn, R. F., clerk (Loney & Co.) Yloilo
Hosungjee, D., merchant (D. Hosungjee & Co.) Amoy
Hosungjee, N., merchant, Amoy and Hollywood Road
Hottinger, J., engineer, Bangkok
Houery, Rev. —. (Procu. French Mission) Canton
Hough, B. F., 2nd officer (Str. Douglas)
Houghton, A. R., resident, Sadong, S'wak
Houghton, E. P., M.D., medical officer (Medical Department) Sarawak
Houghton, H., foreman (Govt. Railways) Yokohama
Houles, Joseph, sister (Mais on de Jesus enfant) Ningpo
Housden, J., Taoutri's constable, Chefoo
House, E E., Professor of Literature (Jap. Govt.) Yedo
House, J. B., master, U.S.N. (Palos)
House, Rev. S. R., M.D., missionary, B'kok
Housman, C. V., clerk (Gibb, Livingston & Co.) Shanghai
Houston, N. T., master, U.S.N. (Ashuelot)
Houstoun, W., engineer (str. Kien Hsing,) Customs, Shanghai
Houy, Miss L H., missionary, Kowkeang
Hovenburg, G. W. van, butcher (Burgess & Co.) Yokohama
How, A. J., resident, Shanghai
Howard, F., resident, Yedo
Howard, F., clerk (P. M. S. S. Co.) Hiogo
Howard, W. C., tide surveyor and har. master, (Customs,) Chefoo
Howard, J. J., clerk (Russell & Co.) H'kow
Howard, The Hon. J. R., registrar, M.L.C. &c., Labuan
Howard, T., merchant (Howard & Co.) West Point
Howe, H. A., junr., assistant (Walsh, Hall & Co.) Nagasaki
Howe, Miss Gertrude, missionary, Kowkeang
Howell, B. W., clerk (Gilman & Co.) S'hai
Howell, G. H., sub-editor (Japan Mail) Yokohama
Howell, J., constable, river police, S'hai

Howell, W. G., proprietor (*Japan Mail Office*) Yokohama
Howell, W., monitor, mission school, Sarawak
Howes, C. P., captain (*Shingking*) Shanghai
Howes, J., inspector of nuisances, S'hai
Howie, R., broker, Shanghai
Howie, R., silk inspector (Deacon & Co.) Canton and Macao
Howie, W., clerk (Birley, Worthington & Co.) Shanghai
Howlett, T., roller (mint) Osaka
Howlett, —., captain (str. *Tunsin*) S'hai
Hoyland, J. P., chief officer (str. *Kinshan*)
Hoyrup, Mrs. J. C., hotel-keeper, Chefoo
Hoyt, Rev. S., missionary, Hankow (Wuchang)
Huard, L., aide com. de la marine, Saigon
Hubback, H. W. J., lieut. and act. adjutant, Royal Artillery
Hübbe, P G, clerk (Siemssen & Co.) Queen's Road
Hubib, H. E. H., merchant (A. Soab) (absent)
Hubener, F. W., merchant (Lehmann, Hartmann & Co.) Hiogo
Huber, A., commr. (Customs) Tientsin
Hubert, —, storekeeper, Saigon
Hubert-Delisle, —., asst. registrar, Trib. 1st instance, Saigon
Hübler, A., clerk (Möller, Maitland & Co.) Shanghai
Hübner, M., cashier, Deutsche Bank, Yokohama
Hubrig, Rev. F., missionary (Chinese Evangelical Society, Berlin) Canton
Hüchting, Fred., merchant (Russell & Co.) and act. Netherlands consul, Ningpo
Hudoffsky, H., clerk (Gutschow & Co.) Hiogo and Yokohama
Hudson, A. J., 1st engineer (Chinese gun-vessel *Chen-to*)
Hudson, J., merchant (Hudson, Malcolm & Co.) Yokohama (absent)
Hudson, J. S., merchant (Hudson & Co.) Ningpo
Hudson, Rev. T. H., missionary (English Bap. Mission) Ningpo
Huffam, F. S., deputy registrar (Supreme Court) West Terrace
Huggan, J. G., resident, Osaka
Huggan, R., manager (Kobé Iron Works) Hiogo
Hugh, Antony, writer, Sarawak
Hughes, Geo., commissioner (Customs) Amoy
Hughes, J. R., assistant accountant (Chartered Mercantile Bank)
Hughes, P., watchmaker, Manila
Hughes, P. J., consul (British Consulate) and Austro-Hungarian and Danish do. Hankow
Hughes, R., merchant (Hughes & Co.) Osaka

Hughes, T. F., clerk (Customs) Shanghai (absent)
Hughes, V. D., sub lieut., R.N. (*Kingdom*)
Hughes, W. K., broker, Gough Street
Hüllimann, G., clerk (Reiss & Co.) Y'hama
Hull, W. M., assistant (Watson & Co.) Shanghai
Hulse, R., tidewaiter (Customs) Chefoo
Hülse, W., public tea inspector (Mestern & Hülse) consul for Netherlands, Canton
Human, W. H., barman, The "Beehive," Yokohama
Humblot, —. (Catholic Mission) Peking
Humby, John (Empire Tavern) Queen's Road West
Hume, A., clerk, r.N. (*Rinaldo*)
Humphreys, J D, chemist, &c. (Hongkong Dispensary) Queen's Road
Humphreys, W. G., assistant (Sayle & Co.) Alexandra Terrace
Hungerford, Lieut. T. E., acting quartermaster, R.M.L.I., Yokohama
Hungerford, S. A., sub-lieut., R.N. (*Thalia*)
Hunsicker, J. L., midshipman, U.S.N. (*Hartford*)
Hunt, H. I., merchant (Alt & Co.) N'saki
Hunt, J. H., clerk (Wm. Rees & Co.) Ningpo
Hunt, Phineas R., superintendent of mission press, Peking
Hunt, Rev. M. W., missionary (Am. Board Com. For. Mission) Peking
Hunt, W. E., clerk (David Sassoon, Sons & Co.) Shanghai
Hunt, —., master mariner, Bangkok
Hunter, D. L., merchant (Holliday, Wise & Co.) Praya Central
Hunter, E. H., clerk (Kirby & Co.) Hiogo
Hunter, G. W., assayer silver bullion (mint) Osaka
Hunter, H., assist. (Boyd & Co.) Nagasaki
Hunter, J., M.D., Newchwang
Hunter, R. P., clerk (Heard & Co.) Foochow
Hunter, W., 2nd officer (str. *Yesso*)
Hunter, W. L., merchant (Adamson, Bell & Co.) Foochow
Huntington, S. E., merchant (Smith, Archer & Co) Praya
Huot, C., assistant (C. & J. Favre Brandt) Yokohama
Hurdle, W., light-keeper (Japanese Government) Yokohama
Hurlburt, S., clerk (Russell & Co.) S'hai
Hurlbut, G., merchant (Smith, Archer & Co.) Yokohama
Hurt, Thos., fitter (Govt. Railroad) Yokohama
Hurst, R. W., student interpreter, (British Legation) Peking
Huskisson, S. G., capt., H. M. 80th Regt.
Hutchings, C. H., broker, Shanghai
Hutchins, John, gunner, R.N. (*Thistle*)

Hutchinson, Rev. A. B., church miss., West Point
Hutchinson, St. J., silk inspector (Olyphant & Co.) Canton
Hutchinson, Wm. L., M.D., Bangkok
Hutchison, A., merchant (Deacon & Co.) Macao and Canton
Hutchison, W. B., R N., sec. to com.-in-chief (H. M. S. *Iron Duke*)
Hutton, M. L., merchant (Hughes & Co.) Hiogo
Hyde, E. L., merchant (Hudson, Malcolm & Co.) Yokohama
Hyde, W., merchant (Woodruff & Co.) Yokohama
Hyndman, F., teacher of English (elementary) St. Joseph's College, Macao
Hyndman, H., book-keeper (China Sugar Refinery) East Point
Hyndman, J., clerk (Silva & Co.) Macao
Hyndman, J. A., clerk (Chinese Emigration Macao
Hyndman, João, substitute (Judicial Department) Macao
Hyslop, W., clerk (Helbling & Co.) Shanghai
Hyver, J. P., storekeeper (J. P. Hyver & Co.) Nagasaki

I

Ibanez, F. Bautista, assistant (Loyzaga & Co.) Manila
Ibanez, Pablo Bautista (Loyzaga & Co.) Manila
Icaza, Y., rope manufacturer, Manila
Iffland, A., tidewaiter (Customs) Chefoo
Ilbert, A., broker, Shanghai
Illies, C., merchant (Kniffler & Co.) Hiogo
Imbert, A., assistant (Customs) Swatow
Impey, G., Foreman mechanic (Govt. Railways) Yokohama and Osaka
Ing, Rev. J. & Wife, missionaries, Kewkeang
Inglis, D. D., agent (China and Japan Trading Co.) Nagasaki
Inglis, G., chief engineer (P. & O. Service)
Inglis, J., engineer (Victoria Foundry) Spring Gardens and Alexandra Terrace
Innes, J., clerk to council, Sarawak
Innes, R., assistant acct. (Oriental Bank)
Innes, Thomas, clerk (Loney & Co.) Leyte
Innes, W. F., chief eng., R.N. (*Thalia*)
Innocent, Rev. J., and family, missionary (Meth. Mission Society) Tientsin
Irminger, F. C. G., assist. (Great Northern Tel. Co.) Shanghai
Irvine, G. J., surgeon, R.N. (*Iron Duke*)
Irving, J. Bell, (Jardine, Matheson & Co.'s Insurance Office)
Irwin, R. W., merchant (Walsh, Hall & Co.) Yokohama
Isaac, J. D., surgeon, R.N. (*Dwarf*)
Isaacs, A., wine and spirit merchant, Yedo

Isaacs, E. M., merchant (Benjamin & Co.) Yokohama
Isaacs, I., gen. merchant (Isaacs Brothers) Yokohama
Isaacs, M., clerk (Isaacs Brothers) Yokohama
Isaacs, R., general merchant (Isaacs Bros.) Yokohama
Isaacs, S., merchant (Isaacs & Co.) Hiogo
Ismael, H. A., merchant, Canton and Hongkong
Ismael, —., boarding house keeper, Circular Pathway
Ivanoff, N. A., merchant, Foochow
Ivanoff, N. A., merchant and vice-consul for Russia (Ivanoff & Co.) Hankow
Iversen, A., clerk (Bourjau & Co.) S'hai
Iveson, E., merchant (Bower, Banbury & Co.) Shanghai
Ivey, H., assistant (Farnham & Co.)
Iwersen, C., merchant (Langgard, Kleinwort & Co.) Hiogo

J

Jack, E., 3rd engineer (str. *Kwangtung*)
Jack, John, shipwright (Patent Slip) East Point (absent)
Jack, Y., ship's compradore, Hiogo
Jackson, Ed., merchant (Jackson, French & Co.) Manila
Jackson, H. B., midshipman, R.N. (*Cadmus*)
Jackson, J., missionary, Ningpo
Jackson, —., mariner, (Jap. Govt.) Yedo
Jackson, T., manager (Hongkong & Shanghai Banking Corporation) Yokohama (absent)
Jackson, W., manager (Chartered Mercantile Bank)
Jacobs, F. S., resident, Yokohama
Jacobsen, F., tidewaiter (Customs) S'hai
Jacobsen, P., shipchandler (C. Gerard & Co.) Amoy
Jacque, —., commis. de Marine, Saigon
Jacquemin, Rev. J. B. C. (French miss.) Swatow
Jafferbhoy, A., merchant, Canton & H'kong
Jaffray, A. (livery stables) Yokohama
Jaffray, R., assist. (A. Jaffray) Yokohama
Jaffray, W., clerk (Jardine. Matheson & Co.) Shanghai
Jaffrey, W., engineer, Bangkok
Jairaz, J., manager (R. Habibhoy) Wellington Street
Jalland, Wm., Secretary, Municipal Council, Nagasaki
Jalland, Wm., Proprietor (Kagasaki Medical Hall) Nagasaki
Jamesjee, J., broker, Gage Street
Jamaux, E., copying clerk (French Secretary's Office) Shanghai
Jamault, Rev. D. (R. C. Church) Nagasaki
Jame, F., merchant, Saigon

James, Captn, Military instructor (Jap. Govt.) Yedo
James, F. S., assistant (Hoard & Co.) Yokohama
James, H. G., clerk (Jardine, Matheson & Co.) East Point
James, N. T., mid., U.S.N. (*Yantic*)
James, W., (Naval College) Yedo
Jameson, J. N., clerk (Olyphant & Co.) Praya
Jamieson, C., clerk (Customs) Shanghai
Jamieson, Geo. Acting interpreter (British Consulate) Shanghai
Jamieson, R. Alex., M.D. (Customs) S'hai
Jamieson, W., assistant (Cornes & Co.) Yokohama
Jamieson, W. B., merchant (Jamieson & Co.) Shanghai
Jan, Mohamed, A. merchant, Honam
Jansen, De Witt C. manager (Astor House) Shanghai
Jansen, J. E., clerk (Muller & Co.) S'hai
Jansyan, P., Foreman (P. M. S. S. Co.) Yokohama
Japp, —., mariner (Jap. Govt.) Yedo
Jaquemot, C. R., merchant (J. M. Jaquemot) Yokohama
Jaquemot, J. Jr., clerk (Abegg, Dorel & Co.) Yokohama
Jaquemot, J. M., merchant, Yokohama
Jaques, J., clerk (Customs) Shanghai
Jardine, Rob. (Jardine, Matheson & Co.) (England)
Jarvis, David, mil. foreman of works (Royal Engineer Department)
Jaudon, A., Commissaire (M. M. S. S. *Donnai*).
Jaudon, F., Teacher (Gaim'sho) Yedo
Jaudon, P., Teacher (Gaim'sho) Yedo
Jauncey, H. H. sub-lieut, R.N. (*Iron Duke*)
Jaurias, Sœur, superieure (St. Vincent de Paul) Peking
Jauris, —., Chief Artificer (Jap. Govt.) Yedo
Javair, N., manager (Goolamhoosein & Co.)
Javier, J., clerk (Tillson, Hermann & Co.) Manila
Jeffries, H. U., merchant (Russell & Sturgis) Manila
Jenke, C., draper (Jenke & Co.) Shanghai
Jenkins, A., boarding house keeper, Lower Lascar Row
Jenkins, F. H. B., commission agent, S'hai
Jenkins, M., A., vice-consul and interpreter (U. S. Consulate) Hankow
Jenkins, Rev. H., missionary (American Baptist Mission) Ningpo (absent)
Jenkins, T. O. S., clerk (A. Heard & Co.) Shanghai
Jenkins, W., engineer in charge (National S. S. Co. Nipon) Yokohama
Jenkins, W., examiner, Customs, Pagoda Anchorage Foochow (on leave)

Jennings, B. (The Snug) Hiogo
Jensen, M., sergeant, police Force, (Customs) Foochow
Jensen, Rud., merchant, consul for Denmark and Sweeden and Norway (John Burd & Co) Bonham Road
Jerdein, M. S., merchant, Chinkeang
Jessen, C., master mariner, Bangkok
Jessen, J. P., master mariner, Bangkok
Jesus, F. M. do, clerk (Windsor, Redlich & Co.) Bangkok
Jesus, J. A. de, clerk (Turner & Co.) Arbuthnot Road
Jesus, J. G. de, clerk (L. A. Graça) Macao
Jesus, J. de, Jun., storekeeper (Hongkong and Whampoa Dock Company) W'poa
Jesus, J. V. de, clerk (Hongkong and Whampoa Dock Company) Whampoa
Jewell, R. G. W., U. S. consul, Canton
Jeyes, H. O., clerk (Butterfield & Swire) Yokohama
Jims, T., assist. (Empire Brewery) Shanghai
Jocquel, adjt. (Jap. Govt.) Yedo
Jocquil, —., chief artificer (Jap. Govt.) Yedo
Johannes, S. P., merchant, Queen's Road and Canton
Johanssen, F., clerk (Russell & Co.) S'hai
John, Rev. G., missionary (London Missionary Society) Hankow
Johns, P., miner (Borneo Co.) Sarawak
Johnsford, A., assistant (A. Dent & Co.) Shanghai
Johnson, A B., solicitor and Managing clerk (Sharp & Toller)
Johnson, B. R., tidewaiter, (Customs,) Foochow
Johnson, C., pilot, Nagasaki
Johnson, F., pilot, Foochow (Anchorage)
Johnson, F. B., merchant (Jardine, Matheson & Co.) acting Danish consul, S'hai
Johnson, G. C., captain (str. *Hupeh*) S'hai
Johnson, G. F., clerk (P. & O. Co.'s Office) Praya
Johnson, H., pilot, Swatow
Johnson, H , inst. boatswain, (Arsenal) Foochow
Johnson, J. H., proprietor (Snug Hotel and Bowling Saloon) Nagasaki
Johnson, Mrs L. W. (Am. Bap. Mission) Swatow
Johnson, O., student interpreter (British Legation) Peking
Johnson, R. M., consul (U. S. Consulate) Hankow and Kewkeang
Johnson, W. G., auctioneer (Johnson & Co.) Hiogo
Johnson, W. G. (*Hiogo News* Office) Hiogo
Johnston, G. R., clerk (Hongkong and Shanghai Banking Corporation) S'hai
Johnston, H. B., clerk (A. G. Hogg & Co.) Saigon

Johnston, J., Dep. Com. (Control Department)
Johnston, Jas., M.D , Shanghai
Johnston, Jas., assist (Boyd & Co) S'hai
Johnston, R., assistant (Sayle & Co) S'hai
Johnston, Sir W., assistant acct. (Oriental Bank Corporation) Shanghai
Johnston, W., clerk (Martin Dyce & Co.) Manila
Johnston, W. C., merchant (Tait & Co.) Amoy
Johnstone, R., merchant (Findlay, Richardson & Co.) Yokohama
Johnstone, W., tidewaiter (Customs) Whampoa
Join, —., coppersmith (Yokoska Arsenal) Yokohama
Jok Lin, manager (Ice and Soda-wrter Manufactory) Amoy
Jolly, L., pro. prefect apostolique (French Mission) Canton
Jonas, F. (Havana Cigar Co.) Yokohama
Jones, A. E., assistant (Municipal Council) Shanghai
Jones, B., assistant (Thabor & Co.) Yokohama
Jones, Charles M., F.R.C.S. (Jones, Müller and Manson) Amoy
Jones, C. P. (Naval College) Yedo
Jones, D. G., captain, Royal Engineers, West Terrace
Jones, D. W., engineer (P. & O. S. N. Co)
Jones, Ed., coal hewer (Tanjong Kubong mines) Labuan
Jones, E. B., assistant (Hudson, Malcolm & Co.) Yokohama
Jones, F., 2nd engineer (str *Thabor*) Yokohama
Jones, G., examiner (Customs) Canton
Jones, Jas., clerk (Custom-) Shanghai
Jones, J. H., constable (British Consulate) Whampoa
Jones, R. R. O., Teacher Mathematical Surveying (Jap. Govt.) Yedo
Jones, R. S., assistant paymaster in charge, R.N. (*Elk*)
Jones, R W., engineer, R.N. (*Kestrel*)
Jones, T., clerk (Russell & Co.) Foochow
Jones, T. M. R., assist. engineer (Gov. Railroads) Yokohama
Joole, P., compositor (*Japan Gazette*) Yokohama
Jooniff, A. I., clerk (Matreninsky & Kasantzoff) Kalgan
Joost, A., mer. (Siemssen & Co.) Queen's Road
Jorge, A., clerk, Caine Road
Jorge, C., interpreter (Procurador's Department) Macao
Jorge, E. A., clerk (L. A. Graça) Macao
Jorge, F., clerk (Russell & Co.)
Jorge, H., clerk (Comptoir d'Escompte) Shanghai

Jorge, Pompilio, clerk (Peele Hubbell & Co.) Manila
Jorgensen, C. L., master mariner, Bangkok
Jorgensen, E., master mariner, Bangkok
Jorgensen, J , master mariner, Bangkok
José, F., light-house keeper. (Customs) Ningpo
Joseph, B., sister (Asyle de la Ste. Enfance) Manila
Joseph, D., clerk (E. D. Sassoon & Co.) Shanghai
Joseph, H. H., clerk (P. & O. Co.) Shanghai
Joseph, I., agent (E. D. Sassoon & Co.) Newchwang
Joseph, J. S , clerk (E. D. Sassoon & Co.) Shanghai
Joseph, M., merchant (L. Joseph & Co.) Hiogo
Josephs, L., clerk (Empire Brewery) Shanghai
Jourdan, Capt. (Jap. Govt.) Yedo
Jourdan, P., Coal. Dépôt, Messageries Maritimes) Yokohama
Jourde, A., clerk (Denis Frères) Saigon
Jouslain, —., Councillor (Sup. Court) S'gon
Jouvet, A., public accountant, Saigon
Jouvet, E., civil engineer (Arsenal) Foochow
Joyner, H. B., C.E., chief assist. (Public Works Dept.) Yedo
Jubin, C., clerk (Société Anonyme Franco-Japonaise) Yokohama
Jubin, E., merchant, (Societé Anonyme Franco Japonaise) Yokohama (absent)
Jucker, A., manager (Malherbe, Jullien & Co.) Bangkok
Judd, Rev. C. H., and Mrs., missionaries, Nankin
Judd, W., clerk (China Sub. Tel. Co.)
Juery, H., clerk (Messageries Maritimes) Yokohama
Julien, H., clerk (U. S. Consulate) Takow
Jullien, St. Cyr, merchant (Malherbe, Jullien & Co.) Bangkok (absent)
Jumatjee, M., shopkeeper, Peel Street
Jumsetjee, P., broker, 10 Peel St.
Jungbanns, Dr., Physician (Jap. Govt.) Yedo
Junkin, N. B., carpenter, U.S.N. (*Lackawanna*)
Junquito, Manuel Gonzales, first district magistrate (acting) Manila
Jurgens, H. J., broker (Jurgens & Borchardt) Shanghai
Jurgenson, J., pilot (Black Ball Pilot Co.) Shanghai
Just, H. Z., clerk (Arnhold, Karberg & Co.) Praya
Juster, John, publican (Hamburg Tavern) Queen's Road
Justinien, —., copyist (Procureur General) Saigon
Juvet, L., importer (L. Juvet) Shanghai

K

Kaffen, ---, artisan (Jap. Govt.) Yedo
Kahler, W. R. clerk (Hall & Holtz) S'hai
Kuhn, L., merchant (Reiss & Co.)
Kalb, M., merchant (Reiss & Co) Shanghai
Kaltenbach, G., merchant (Kaltenbach, Engler & Co) Saigon (absent)
Karberg, P., merchant (Arnhold, Karberg & Co.) Praya
Kasantzoff, P. J., merchant (Matreninsky & Kasantzoff) Kalgan
Kasby, J., boiler maker (National S. S. Co. of Nipon) Yokohama
Kassburg, A., compradore (Kassburg & Co.) Nagasaki
Kauppe, S., employé (Royal Naval Hospital) Yokohama
Kavanagh, M. R , clerk (Tait & Co.) Amoy (Taiwan)
Kay, J. R., engineer (P & O. service)
Kaye, Wm., manager (Chartered Bank of India, Australia and China)
Keele, O. R., inspector of markets, Shanghai (absent)
Keeshaw, Z., linguist (Municipal Engineer's Office) Shanghai
Keetch, J. R., assist. (Vulcan Iron Works) Hiogo
Keeton, A., engineer (Imperial Arsenal) Tientsin
Keg, J. C., assist. (Netherlands Trading Society) Nagasaki
Keg, J. J., Secretary (Netherlands Consulate) Nagasaki
Keir, W., asst. (Taylor & Bennett) S'hai
Keischer, H. M., merchant (Hecht, Lilienthal & Co.) Hiogo
Keiser, J., watchmaker (C. J. Gaupp & Co.) Hollywood Road
Keller, E., clerk (Lutz & Co.) Manila
Keller, Jno., assistant (Sailor's Home)
Kelly, J. F., bookseller (Kelly & Co.) S'hai
Kelly, J. M , news-agent (Kelly & Co.) Shanghai
Kelvie, M., master of the "Attalo" Saigon
Kempermann, S., Secretary (German Legation) Yedo
Kendall, C. C., wharf clerk (S. S. N. Co.) Shanghai
Kennedy, F., constable (British Consulate) Foochow
Kennedy, H. E. Sir A. E., governor of Hongkong
Kennedy, Sergt., acting inspector of Markets, Shanghai
Kennedy, W., clerk (Govt. Telegraph) Nagasaki
Kennelly, T. F., resident, Hiogo
Kenrick, H. E.; tidewaiter (Customs) Shanghai
Kent, J., boatswain, R.N. (Cadmus)
Kent, J., master mariner, Bangkok
Kent, W. K., clerk (Butterfield & Swire) Shanghai
Kent, W. P., merchant, Yokohama
Ker, W. G., merchant (Loney & Co.) Yloilo
Kerdraon, ---, draughtsman (Arsenal) Fo chow
Kergariou, Comte Ph. de, attaché libre (French Legation) Peking
Kermath, J. S., Shanghai Hotel, Shanghai
Kerr, C. D., merchant (Dodd & Co) Amoy
Kerr, C. Morland, accountant (Oriental Bank) Queen's Road (absent)
Kerr, G., engine driver, Fire Brigade
Kerr, J., engineer (P. & O. Service)
Kerr, J. G., M.D., secretary (Medical Mission Society) Canton
Kerr, R. J., clerk (Gibb, Livingston & Co.) Shanghai
Kerrimar, E., shipmaster (Jap. Govt.) Yedo
Kesam, ---, tailor (Elye & Kesam) B'kok
Kessowjee, N., merchant (N. Kessowjee & Co.) Lyndhurst Terrace and Shanghai
Kestell, J. T., carpenter, R.N. (Iron Duke)
Keswick, J. J., clerk (Jardine, Matheson & Co.) Shanghai
Keswick, W., merchant (Jardine, Matheson & Co) consul for Hawaii, East Point (absent)
Keymer, W. J., tidewaiter (Customs) Hankow
Khakeebhoy, C., manager (R. Habibhoy) Shanghai
Khamise, ---, boarding house keeper, Lower Lascar Row
Khetsey, J., clerk (Kessowjee & Co.) Lyndhurst Terrace
Khetsey, K., clerk (Kessowjee & Co.) Lyndhurst Terrace
Khetsey, M., clerk (Kessowjee & Co.) Lyndhurst Terrace
Khruminh, J., 2nd Interpreter, French Consulate, Bangkok
Kiaer, H., merchant and commission agent
Kidd, Rev. R. Hayward, M.A., colonial chaplain, Albany Road
Kidner, W., architect, Shanghai
Kieffer, Rev. F. H., R. C. missionary, Bangkok
Kierulff, P., merchant and interpreter to Danish Consulate, Tientsin
Kilby, E. F., clerk (Hudson, Malcolm & Co.) Yokohama
Kiley, J. D., sailmaker, Yokohama
Killeen, Chas., clerk (H. Consterdine) Chefoo
Kilner, W., clerk (Hall & Holtz) Shanghai
Kimber, J. (J. Thompson & Co.) Yokohama
Kimpton, B. T., clerk (Browne & Co.)
Kindblad, A., tidewaiter (Customs) H'kow
Kinder, C. (Railway Department) Osaka

Kinder, C. W., assistant engineer (Government Railroads) Yokohama
Kinder, E., sub lieut., R.N. (*Iron Duke*)
Kinder, T. W., master (Mint) Kawasaki
King, A., modeller (Govt. Engineering College) Yedo
King, C. J., merchant (Chapman, King & Co.) Shanghai (absent)
King, G., clerk (P. & O. S. N. Co.) Praya
King, G., foreman mechanic (Japan Railway Works) Yokohama
King, H. E., resident, Yedo
King, J. D., clerk (Drysdale, Ringer & Co.) Hankow
King, J. D., printing office, Hankow
King, R., fitter, (Govt Railways) Y'hama
King, Wm., inspector of Brothels (Medical Department)
King, W. E., British vice consul & consul for Austria and Denmark, Kewkeang (absent)
King, W. M., surgeon in charge, (U. S. Naval Hospital) Yokohama
King, W. W., merchant (Shaw, Ripley & Co.) Hankow
Kingdon, N. P., merchant (Kingdon, Schwabe & Co.) Yokohama
Kingselle, F., clerk (D. Noronha & Co.) Yokohama
Kingsmill, H, M A., barrister at law, 2 Club Chambers
Kingsmill, T. W., civil engineer, Shanghai
Kinnear, H. R., clerk (Westall, Galtou & Co.) Foochow
Kip, Rev. L. W., missionary (Reformed Church) Amoy
Kirby, —, captain (str. *Bunker Hill*) S'hai
Kirby, E. C., merchant (Kirby & Co.) Yokohama and Hiogo
Kirby, R., clerk (Kirby & Co.) Osaka
Kirby, W., clerk (Jardine, Matheson & Co.)
Kirchhoff, H., merchant (Vogel, Hagedorn & Co.) Shanghai
Kirchmann, Henry, (Rising Sun Tavern) Queen's Road West
Kirchmann, L., proprietor ("Land We Live In" Tavern) Queen's Road Central
Kirchner, A., merchant (Kirchner, Böger & Co.) Queen's Road (absent)
Kirk, James, engineer (str. *Samson*) S'hai
Kirk, W., commander, (str. *Royalist*) Sarawak
Kirkham, J., engineer (National S. S. Co. Nipon) Yokohama
Kirkwood, J., 2nd engineer (Chinese revenue steamer *Fei Hoo*)
Kirschstein, J. C., storekeeper (Siotas & Co.) Chefoo
Kitching, F. W., clerk (John Forster & Co.) Foochow
Klasen, A. J., C.E., assist. (Public Works Dept.) Yedo

Kleczkowski, A., clerk (Aug. Heard & Co.) Shanghai
Klein, J. C., trader, Osaka
Kleinmann, J., (Steam Aerated Water Works) Hiogo
Kleinwächter, F., commissioner (Customs) Canton
Kleinwort, C., merchant (Langgaard, Kleinwort & Co.) Hiogo
Kliene, A. tide-surveyor (Customs) Ningpo Point
Klinck, C., engineer (Santa Mesa Rope Factory) Manila
Klint, H., master mariner, Bangkok
Klitzke, E., pastor (Foundling House) West Point
Klopfer, Emil, clerk (Heinszen & Co.) Manila
Klopp, H., clerk (De Bay, Gotte & Co.) Bangkok
Klotz, F., sec. int: (French Legation) Yedo
Klyne, L., compositor (*Japan Gazette*) Yokohama
Knäpel, M. F. G., ("Hamburg Coffee House") Ningpo
Knecht, Emile, chancellier (French Consulate) Bangkok
Kneebone, G. A., stock and bullion broker, 9, Seymour Terrace
Kniffler, Alex., clerk (L. Kniffler & Co.) Yokohama
Kniffler, H., clerk (Kniffler & Co.) N'saki
Kniffler, L., merchant (Kniffler & Co.) Yokohama, Nagasaki and Osaka (absent)
Knight, A. M., vice-consul for U. S., Newchwang (absent)
Knight, F. P., vice-consul for Germany France and consul for U. S., merchant (Knight & Co.) Newchwang
Knight, R. H., foreman (*Hongkong Times*)
Knight, W., (Yeutai Butchery) Chefoo
Knights, A. E., merchant, Shanghai
Knipping, E., teacher (Japan Govt.) Yedo
Knoblock, A., von, No. 1, assist. German Legation, Yedo
Knoblock, A., von, No. 2, assist. German Legation, Yedo
Knoop, H. A., shipchandler (Knoop & Co.) Shanghai
Knott, R., pilot to P. M. S. S. Co., S'hai
Knott, T., assist. (Evans & Co.) Shanghai
Knowles, J. S., sec. (Victoria Recreation Club)
Knowlton, Rev. M. J., missionary (Amer. Bap. Miss.) Ningpo
Knox, H. A., midshipman, R. N. (*Cadmus*)
Knox, J. (Jardine's receiving ship *Berwick Halls*) Shanghai
Knox, T. G., consul general (British Consulate) Bangkok
Köbke, F. C. C., Danish consul, Bangkok
Koch, C., clerk (Deetjen & Co.) Praya Central

Koch, W., clerk (Siemssen & Co.) Shanghai
Kock, C. (Army and Navy Tavern) Queen's Road West
Kock, M., constable (German Consulate) Shanghai
Koffer, Th., manager (Medical Hall) Q s Road
Kofœl, E. C., pilot, Shanghai
Kofoed, P. J., master mariner, Bangkok
Koloboff, J. A., clerk (Matreninsky & Kusantzoff) Kalgan
Kolwig, F., assist. (Great North. Tel. Co.) Shanghai
Kopp, C. O., shipchandler (C. Gerard & Co.) Amoy
Kopsch, H., commissioner, Customs, Kewkeaug
Korthals, W. C. (Netherlands Trading Society) Hiogo
Kossehin, J. A., clerk (Ivanoff & Co.) Hankow
Kosminski, J., merchant (Kosminski & Co.) Shanghai
Koss, F., tailor (Koss & Co.) Queen's Road
Kotwal, D. R., clerk (R. Davecurn) Hollywood Road
Koyauder, A., secy. (Russian Legation) Peking
Kraal, F., clerk (Mess. Mar. Comp:)
Kraal, G. F., Clerk (Royal Hotel) Macao
Kraal, P. C., clerk (Elles & Co.) Taiwan
Kraal, S. A., clerk (Dobie & Co.) Foochow
Kraemer, H., resident, Yokohama
Kraetzer, E., chancellier (French Consulate) Yokohama
Krager, H., godown keeper (Customs) Shanghai (Pootung)
Kragh, C. H., Clerk (G. N. Teleg. Co.) Amoy
Kramer, J., silk inspector (Arnhold, Karberg & Co.) anton
Kramer, W. A. T., master mariner, Bangkok
Krasnopolsky, J. A., Clerk (Raminoff, Rodio ioff & Co.) Hankow
Kraul, W., master, Tungsha lightship, Shanghai
Krause, Adolph, clerk (Heinszen & Co.) Manila
Krause, O., resident, Yokohama
Krauss, A., clerk (lease & Co.) Canton
Krauss, A. A., merchant (Shaw, Brothers & Co.) Shanghai
Krebs, C., clerk (Melchers & Co.) Praya
Krebs, F., resident, Osaka
Krein, T., assist (German Legation) Yedo
Kresser, Victor, partner (China Sugar Refinery) East Point
Krey, W., assistant (Customs) Foochow
Kreyer, C. T., teacher (Kiangnan Arsenal) Shanghai
Kritsch, K., assistant (German Consulate) Yokohama

Kross, J., master mariner, Bangkok
Krug, A., watchmaker (J. C. Kruse) Q'n's Road
Krug, E., accountant (Deutsche Bank) Shanghai
Kruger, C., merchant (Dircks & Krüger) vice-consul for Germany, Swatow (abs.)
Krummel, C. (Schmidt, Westphal & Co) Hiogo (absent)
Kruse, J. C., jeweller, &c., (Kruse & Co.) Queen's Road, Central
Kruse, —, master mariner, Bangkok
Kubic, J., shoemaker (Kubic & Co.) Yokohama
Kuchmeister, A., tailor (Lohmann, Kuchmeister & Co.) Yokohama
Kufahl, C. T., clerk (W. G. Hale & Co.) Saigon
Kuhhardt, A. M., merchant (Faber and Voight) Hiogo
Kuhlmann, H., jeweller &c. (Kruse & Co.) Queen's Road
Kuhn, M. M., importer, Yokohama
Kumashiro, T., Chinese interpreter (Japanese Consulate) Shanghai
Kummel, C. (Schmidt, Westphal & Co.) Nagasaki (Hamburg)
Kunaring, T., resident, Yedo
Kurchis, D., teacher (Jap. Govt) Yedo
Kurtzhalss, A., clerk (Markwald & Co.) Bangkok
Kurumsey, H., merchant (N. Kessowjee & Co.,
Kyle, D., engineer (China Sugar Refinery) East Point
Kyle, J., engineer (Kyle & Bain) Hongkong I e Co., East Point
Kyle, Thomas, D., ice-maker (Kyle & Co.) Foochow

L

Laackmann, J. C. N., clerk (Hesse & Co.)
Labhart, J. C., merchant (Labhart & Co.) Manila
Laborde, C., clerk (French Post Office) Shanghai
Lacant, —., boarding house keeper, Saigon
Lacaze, A., hotel keeper, Saigon
Lacaze, A., storekeeper, Saigon
Lacerda, A. P. C., clerk (Col. Govt.) Macao
Lacôte, Vincent, sister (Maison de la Presentation) Ningpo
Lacouture, —., com. de la marine, Saigon
Ladage, H., tailor (Koss & Co.) Queen's Road
Laen, P. L., storekeeper, Tientsin
Lafitte, Benjn., French corporal (Mun. Police) Yokohama
La Forest, Ch. O. L. de, chancellier and vice-consul for France, Alex. Terrace
agden, C. W., (School of Foreign Languages) Yedo

Lagueras, G., clerk (Loney & Co.) Cebu
Laidlaw, W., tea inspector (Boyd & Co.) Amoy (Tamsui)
Laidrich, F., storekeeper (Vrard & Co.) Tientsin
Laiyon, J., news agent and storekeeper, Yokohama
Lake, E., compradore (Geo. W. Lake & Co.) Nagasaki
Lake, Geo. W., compradore (Geo. W. Lake & Co.) Nagasaki (absent)
Lalande, C., storekeeper (Messageries Maritimes)
Lalcact, E. P., general broker, Shanghai
Lallemand, —., secretary, municipality, Saigon
Lalor, J. P., broker, Fooch w
Lamache, E., merchant, (J. M. Ailoin & Co.) Bangkok
Lamb, J. '., post office clerk (U. S. Consulate) Yokohama
Lamber, E. B., schoolmaster, Yedo
Lambert, A. G., manager (Green Point, Pootung & S. S. N. Co.'s Dock) S'hai
Lambert, A. J., naval architect (Marine Department) Kiangnan Arsenal, S'hai
Lambert, W. M., lieut., R.M.A. (*Iron Duke*)
Lambuth, Rev. J. W. (Meth. Miss.) S'hai
Lammert, G. R., storekeeper (Lammert, Atkinson & Co.) Queen's Road East
Lamont, J., chief engineer R.N. (*Iron Duke*)
Lamout, Rev. J., Union Chapel, and Prus. Chap. to Forces
Lamour, —., écrivain de marine, Saigon
Lamoza, clerk (Tillson, Herrmann & Co.) Manila
Lampe, L., pilot, Bangkok
Lancaster, W. S., constable (British Consulate) Hiogo
Lancken, F., merchant (Wm. Pustau & Co.) Pottinger Street (absent)
Land, J. M., examiner (Customs) Keelung
Landeshut, S. S., accountant, Yokohama
Landstein, W. R., merchant (Landstein & Co.) Queen's Road (absent)
Lane, G. E., agent (P. M. S. S. Co.) Yokohama
Lane, H., 1st officer (Chinese gun-boat (*Peng chau-hoi*)
Lane, R. A., clerk (Peele, Hubbell & Co.) Manila
Lang, Arch., chief engineer (str. *Appin*) Shanghai
Lang, C. V., chief engineer (str. *Kinshan*)
Lang, H., editor (*Evening Courier*) Shanghai
Lang, W., mert t (Butterfield & Swire) Shanghai
Lange, A. E., 2nd clerk, imp. & exp. office, Sarawak
Large, H., master mariner, Bangkok
Langelier, John B., 1st officer (Chinese gun-vessel *Chento*)

Langfeldt, A., shipchandler (Langfeldt & Mayers) Yokohama
Langhorne, M. B., book-keeper (P. M. S. S. Co.) Shanghai
Langlais, L'abbé A. J., Miss. Apost., Yokohama
Lanigan, S. W., 2nd engineer (str. *White Cloud*)
Lannes, C. B., com. police, Saigon
Lanning, H., M.D., missionary, Osaka
Lant, T. J., tidewaiter (Customs) Amoy
Lapraik, John S., merchant (Douglas Lapraik & Co.)
Lapsley, W., sugar boiler (China Sugar Refinery) East Point
Lapuente, A., clerk (Russell & Sturgis) Manila
Large, G., gunner, R.N. (*Rinaldo*)
Lark, O. S., assist. paymr in charge, R.N. (*Avon*)
Lark, D. J., examiner (Customs) Amoy (absent)
Larken, M., tea inspector (Dodd & Co.) Tamsui
Larkin, Thos. J., assist. supt. (Govt. Telegraph) Kobe
Larnaudie, Rev. F. L., R. C. Miss., B'kok
Larrieu, C. M., third commissioner of police, Saigon
Lary, J., cook. (Silver & Brennwald) Yokohama
Lascelles, Hon. J. C., lieut., R.N. (*Thalia*)
Lasher, O. F., mid., U.S N. (*Yantic*)
Lasseu, H. P. C., broker, corner of Wyndham and Wellington Streets
Lassere, —., chief artificer (Jap. Gov't.) Yedo
Latham, O., exchange broker, Foochow (absent)
Latouche, —., carpenter (Arsenal) Foochow
Laucaigne, Rev. J. (R. Catholic Church) Nagasaki
Laude, —., President of the Court, Saigon
Laufenberg, L , carpenter (Watson Hall & Co.) Yokohama
Launay-Cephas, E. G., 2nd commissioner of police, Saigon
Laurence, H. A., accountant, Shanghai
Laurence, Miss M., supt. (C. M. S. School) Ningpo
Laurence, S. A., (Pearson and Laurence) Yokohama
Laurent,—., supplier to M. M. str. Saigon
Laurent,—., professor (Yokoska Arsenal) Yokohama
Laurie, P. G., clerk (Jardine, Matheson & Co.) Foochow
Laurie,—., chief artificer (Jap. Govt.) Yedo
Lauriol, S., chief engineer (M. M. S. S.) *Ava*)
Lauritzen, S., clerk (Great North. Telegraph Co.) Shanghai
Lauritzen, —., master mariner, Bangkok

Lautier, —., hair-dresser, Saigon
Laval,—., 3rd commiss. police, Saigon
Lavalle, Don José, A. de, Spanish Consul, (absent)
Lavers, E. H., merchant (Gilman & Co.) Shanghai
Lavers, R. H., engineer, R.N. (*Cadmus*)
Law, W., chief engineer (str. *White Cloud*)
Law, W. C., manager (Pootung Lumber Yard) Shanghai
Lawless, Wm. J., steward (Royal Naval Hospital) Yokohama
Lawrence, C. W., second secy. (Brit. Legation) Yedo
Lawrence, J., foreman (China Sugar Refinery) East Point
Lawrence, S. F., constable (British Consulate) Hakodadi
Lawson, J., asst. (Alfred Dent & Co.) S'hai
Lay, A., assistant, (Customs) Hankow
Lay, U. S., clerk (Eugwat Bros. & Co.) Amoy
Lay, W. H., consul (Brit. Consulate) and Aust-o-Hungarian consul, Chefoo (absent)
Lay, W. T., assistant (Customs) Foochow
Layton, B., clerk (Gibb, Livingstone & Co.) Aberdeen Street
Leão, J. M, compositor (*Foochow Herald*) Foochow
Lebedeff, J. R., clerk (Ivanoff & Co.) Hankow
Lebedeff, N. R., clerk (Ivanoff & Co.) Hankow
Leblanc L'Abbé R., R. C. missionary, Hakodadi
Lebon, Captain (Jap Govt.) Yedo
Le Boucher, —., commis. de marine, Saigon
Lechler, Rev. R., missionary (Evangelical Miss. Society of Basel) Bonham Road (absent)
Leckie, John, clerk (Wilkin & Robison) Yokohama
Leclercq, Flore Josephine, sup. (Maison de la Presentation) Ningpo
Lecointre, L., Captain (M. M. S. S. *Tigre*)
Lee, E. W., tidewaiter (Customs) S'hai
Lee, J., inspector of brothels (Medical Department) Wanchi
Lee, James T., gunner, R.N. (*Avon*)
Lee, K. B., interpreter, German and U. S. Consulates, Foochow
Lees, Rev. J., missionary (London Miss. Society) Tientsin (absent)
Leesemann, Miss P., (German Foundling House) West Point
Loesen, F. von, clerk (L. Kniffler & Co.) Nagasaki
Leet, H. K., commander, R.N. (*Thistle*)
Legar, Madame F. (A. R. Marty) 92 and 24 Queen's Road
Legardeur, —., chief artificer (Jap. Govt.) Yedo

Le Garnison, —., commis. greffier, trib. ler. instance, Saigon
Le Gendre, General Chas. W., teacher (Gaim'sho) Yedo
Legg, H, light-keeper (Public Works department) Yokohama
Legge. Rev. James, D D., LL D., minister (Union Church) (absent)
Legludic, —., river pilot, Saigon
Legrand, A., 1st lieut. (Chinese gunboat *Chun-hoi*) Canton
Legrand, L, tax-collector (French Municipal Council) Shanghai
Legros, —., "Café de la Marine," Saigon
Le Hérisson, —., cordier (Yokoska Arsenal) Yokohama
Lehmann, C., merchant (Lehmann, Hartmann & Co.) Osaka
Lehmann, J. B., agent for A. Cahuzac, Bordeaux, and Steam Service between Saigon & Cholon, Saigon
Leicester, S. C., clerk, court establishment, Sarawak
Leicester, H., second clerk, post office, Sarawak
Leiria, A., sorter (General Post-Office)
Leiria, R. A., clerk (J. J. dos Remedios & Co) Gough Street
Leiser, —., master mariner, Bangkok
Leitch, R M., assist. (North Ch. Ins. Co.) Shanghai
Leite, A M., 2nd comdr. (gun-boat *Camoes*)
Leite, J. P., lieut. col. (Police Department) Macao
Leite, L. P., secretary (Council Public Instruction) Macao
Le Jemble, —., co judge, Sup. Court, Saigon
Lemaire, —, Farmer to Market, Saigon
Lemaire, G, French Consul, Foochow (absent)
Lemann, H. B., merchant (Gilman & Co) Praya
Lemann, Wm., merchant (Gilman & Co.) Foochow
Lemarchand, F. W., manager (Agra Bank) Shanghai
Le Marchand, —., optician (Arsenal) Foochow
Le Mare, J., assistant (Cornes & Co.) Yokohama
Lemattre, E., Watchmaker, Amoy
Lembke, J. P., clerk (Ehlers & Co) Praya
Lemcke, W., Telegraphist (Gt. Northern Ext. Tel Co)
Lemos, José de, judge's clerk, Macao
Lemos, José C., clerk (Colonial Government) Macao
Lemos, V. de P. da C., wardmaster (Military Hospital) Macao
Lent, J. R., assistant, Customs, Taiwan
Lent, W. broker, Shanghai
Leatz, A., merchant, Hiogo

Leuzy, A., interpreter (Russian Legation) Peking
Leon, L., do, clerk (Blanco, Domingo & Co.) Manila
Leon, M. P. de (Botica de San Gabriel) Manila
Leonce, —., commis. de marine, Saigon
Le Peltier, —., aide com., Saigon
Le Petit de Si uques, —., commis de marine, Saigon
Lepissier, E., professor of mathematics (First College) Yedo
Lepissier, E. L., assistant (Customs) Hankow
Le Pontois, —., aide com. de la marine, Saigon (absent)
Leppar, Thos , (E. Fischer & Co.) Hiogo
Lepper, H. F. G., accountant (Great Northern Tel. Co.) Shanghai
Lepper, T., agent (Walsh, Hall & Co.) Osaka and Yedo
Lequerre, P., Chief Officer (M. M. S. S. Irraouaddy)
Lerma, M. L., clerk (Russell & Sturgis) Manila
Leroy, E , drapers &c., Saigon
Leroy, E , merchant (A Nachtrieb & Co) Shanghai
Le Roux, 1st officer, Chinese gun-boat Ching-tsing
Le Sage, E., assist. (Zobel & Nohr) Manila
Lescasse, J., civil engineer, Yokohama
Lescaudron, —., pilot, Saigon
Leslie, J., chief engineer (Sassoon's Str. China)
Leslie, S., assistant, Customs, Tamsui
Lesaler, P., merchant (A. Markwald & Co.) Bangkok
Lessmann, G. W., assist. (A. H. Maertens) Shanghai
Lestang, —., sous com. de la marine, Saigon (absent)
Lester, H., architect, Shanghai
Lethbridge, G., act. accountant (Oriental Bank) Shanghai
Lethbridge, Tyndall, M D , hewkeang
Lethimonnier, M., sister (Maison de St. Vincent) Ningpo
Le Troter, —., smith (Yokoska Arsenal) Yokohama
Levin, C., mate U.S.N., (Hartford)
Levitski, Gerontius, missionary (Greek Church Mission) Peking
Levy, A., clerk (Landstein & Co.) Queen's Road
Levy, O., conductor (Echo du Japon) Yokohama
Levysohn, A. C., merchant (Arnhold, Karberg & Co.) Canton
Lewes, W. F., marine surveyor (Water Witch) Shanghai (absent)
Lewis, A. J., assistant (China Fire Insce. Company)

Lewis, E., watchman (Surveyor General's department) Pokfolum
Lewis, E., prop. "Far East" Tavern, Yokohama
Lewis, F. E., clerk (Adamson, Bell & Co.) Shanghai
Lewis, G., ship and general broker (Morris & Lewis) Shanghai
Lewis, Henry (Am. Rice Mill) Bangkok
Lewis, H., engineer, Bangkok
Lewis, J. K , chaplain, U.S N. (Hartford)
Lewis, J. N., proprietor (Rajah's Arms) Sarawak
Lewis, J W. M , clerk (Treasury) Sarawak
Lewis, W. H., lieut., R.N. (Thalia)
Leyenberger, Rev. J. A., and family miss. (Am. Pres. Mission) Ningpo
Leyva, J., assist. (Garchitoreua & Smith) Manila
Libson, Wm. (Naval College) Yedo
Licavo, P., hotel keeper (Oriental Hotel) Yokohama
Liccioni, —., maitre de manœuvres (Yokoska Arsenal) Yokohama
Lichagoff, K. F., clerk (N. A. Nefedieff) Tientsin)
Lichtenstein, L., importer, Yokohama
Liddell, J. G., supdt. (H.K. & W. Dock Co.) Kowloong
Liebermann, J. L., commission merchant and furniture broker, Yokohama
Liebich, R., clerk (Prehn & Co.) Manila
Liedcke, L., tidewaiter (Customs) W'poa
Lienhardt, C. E., clerk (Simon, Evers & Co.) Yokohama
Liger, F. P., assistant (French Dispensary)
Lilburn, S., lieut., R N. (Rinaldo)
Lilieuthal, J , engineer apprentice (H. K. & W. Dock Co.) Aberdeen
Lilley, B., draper and storekeeper, Lyndhurst Terrace
Lilley, J. S., fitter (Japan Railway)
Lillibridge, H. P., clerk (P. M. S. S. Co.) Yokohama
Lima, F. M., book-keeper (De Souza & Co.) Hollywood Road
Lima, J. M. O., clerk (Holliday, Wise & Company)
Lima, M C. da S. surgeon (Tejo) Macao
Limby, H. J., broker (Limby & Co.) S'hai
Limjee, D., clerk (S. Visram) Gage Street
Linch, J. H., assistant (A. R. Ford & Co) Nagasaki
Lincoln, R., chief officer (steamer Royalist) Sarawak
Lind, A , assist. (P. & O. Co. Office)
Lind, A. A., merchant (Coare, Lind & Co.) Canton
Lindesay, A. H., sub. lieut., R.N. (Midge)
Lindo, F., resident, Yedo
Lindo, T., architect (Jap. Govt.) Yedo
Lindsay, G., chief officer (Emily Jane) Shanghai

Lindsay, G. A., merchant (Lindsay & Head) Shanghai
Lindsley, J., merchant (Frazar & Co.) Shanghai
Lines, A. J., clerk (H. Fogg & Co.) S'hai
Linstead, T. G., merchant (A. G. Hogg & Co.) and consul for Italy, Alexandra Terrace
Lionel, G., clerk (A. Olano) Macao
Lippe, J. E., assistant (Jenko & Co.) S'hai
Lipscott, W., steward (Yokohama Club)
Lisle, R. M., lieut. U.S.N. (*Ashuelot*)
Lister, A., interpreter and act asst. harbour master, West Terrace
Lister, W., constable (British Consulate) Newchwang
Little, A. J., merchant (Little & Co.) S'hai
Little, L. S. M D., Shanghai
Little, R W., merchant (Little & Co.) S'hai
Livick, E., foreman mechanic (Govt. Railways) Yokohama
Livingston, J., inspector of markets
Livingston, R. F., proprietor (British Queen) Yokohama
Livingston, T., pilot, Taku
Livingstone, H. W., clerk (Aug. Heard & Co.) Kobé
Llopez, A., assist (Casal, Bros.) Manila
Llorenti, Juan, clerk (Loney & Co.) Yloilo
Llyas, J. E., staff-surgeon, R.N. (*Cadmus*)
Loam, W. B., Tidewaiter (Customs) Amoy
Lobo, A. F., Public Works Department, Macao
Lobo, F. da C., advocate (Judicial department) Macao
Lobo, L. M (British Crown Tavern) Queen's Road West
Lock, H. J., assist. engineer, R.N. (*Iron Duke*)
Lockhead, J. H., M.D., Elgin Street
Lockyer, Mrs. E., milliner, Yokohama
Loercher, Rev. J. G., missionary (Evangelical Mission Society of Basel) Bonham Road
Logan, F. H., sub-lieut., R.N. (*Teazer*)
Logan, J. H., tidewaiter (Customs) C'ton
Lohmann, H., tailor (Lohmann, Kuchmeister & Co.) Yokohama
Lohr, G., chief engineer (German Str. *China*)
Loiscleur, —., contractor (— Mulaton) Saigon
Loney, R., merchant (Loney & Co.) Yloilo (Negros)
Loney, W. M D., dep insp. gen., R.N. (H. M. Naval Hospital)
Long, B., compositor (*Japan Herald*) Yokohama
Longford, J. H., 2nd assistant (British Consulate) Yokohama
Longo, Rev. V., miss. (R. C. Church) and R. C. Chaplain to forces, Pottinger Street

Loo, C. G., clerk (Engwat Bros. & Co.) Amoy
Loomis, Rev. H., missionary, Yokohama
Lopes, A. C., steward (St Joseph's College) Macao
Lopes, C. J., clerk (Tait & Co) Takow
Lopes, C. V., ensign (National Guard) Macao
Lopes, E. G., clerk (Caldwell & Brereton)
Lopes, F. A., purser (Str. *White Cloud*)
Lopes, L. J., clerk (Estate of E. J Sage)
Lopez, C. J., clerk (Tait & Co) Amoy
Lopez, E (Tribunal of Commerce) Macao
Lopez, F. Purser (Str. *White Cloud*) Macao
Lopez, J. de B., lieut., R.N. (*Thetis*)
Lopez, J. J, actg. chancellor (Spanish consulate) Macao
Lord, C. A., assistant (Customs) Amoy
Lord, F., gunner, Chinese g. b. (*Chento*)
Lord, Mrs. E. C, missionary, Ningpo
Lord, Rev. E. C., consul (U. S. Consulate) Ningpo
Lording, W. S, 1st clerk (Harbour Master's Department) Hongkong Hotel
Lorestcare, —., Chief Cantonnier (Municipality) Saigon
Loring, H. S., U.S. vice consul, Hollywood Road and Seymour Terrace
Loring, R. F., clerk (Olyphant & Co.) Foochow
Lorne, Dupuy de, in charge of Spanish consulate, Yokohama
Lösch, E., clerk (Russell & Co.) Tientsin
Lotz H., prop. (North German Hotel) Yokohama
Louis, —., draughtsman (Arsenal) Foochow
Louis, Rev. W., miss. (Rhenish Mission) Fukwing
Loup, P., assist. (Vrard & Co.) Tientsin
Lourdeault, —., apothecary, Saigon
Loureiro, A, printer (*Nagasaki Gazette* office) Nagasaki
Loureiro, E., consul (Portuguese Consulate) Yokohama and consul general for Portugal (Yedo)
Loureiro, P., manager (Ching Foong printing office) Shanghai
Lourenço, C. J., advocate, Macao
Lourtis, Miss, assist (Sayle & Co.) S'ghai
Louvier, M, merchant (Lacroix, Cousins & Co.) Shanghai
Louy, Louise, sister (Maison de Jesus Enfant) Ningpo
Louzada, J. do R., ward-master (Military Hospital) Macao
Lovatt, W. N., tide-surveyor (Customs) Kewkeang
Love, J. Jr., merchant (Rothwell, Love & Co) Shanghai
Love, S. C., clerk (Rothwell, Love & Co.) Shanghai
Lovett, H. F., tidewaiter (Customs) Newchwang

Lovett, W. W., clerk (Russell & Co.) Kewkeang
Low, C. P., clerk (Smith, Archer & Co.) Praya
Low, E. G., clerk (Augustine Heard & Co.) Shanghai
Low, F., merchant (Heard & Co.) acting Belgian consul, Osaka
Low, F., clerk (Heard & o.) Kobe
Low, G. W., surgeon, R.N. (Rinaldo)
Low, H. B., cadet (Rejang Out-Station) Sarawak
Low, Hon. Frederick F., U. S. minister, Peking (absent)
Low, Hon. H., magistrate and M. L. C. Labuan
Low, W., engineer (Steamer *White Cloud*) Macao
Lowcock, Henry, merchant (Gibb Livingston & Co.) Glenealy, Caine Road
Lowder, F., legal adviser (Imp. Japanese Customs) Yokohama
Lowder, G. G., clerk (Customs) Shanghai (absent)
Lowe, J., examiner (Customs) Chinkeang
Lowe, R., acting tide-surveyor (Customs) Foochow (Nantai)
Lowe, W., broker (Lowe & Co.) Shanghai
Lowndes, R. W., merchant, Queen's Road East
Lowry, Rev. H. H., missionary (American Meth. Mission) Peking
Lowtrop, S. K., assistant (Walsh, Hall & Co.) Yokohama
Loxley, W., assistant (Sayle & Co.)
Loyzaga, J. de, printer (J. de Loyzaga & Co.) Manila
Lubbes, H., clerk (Siemssen & Co.) Foochow
Lucas, Clement, merchant (Blain & Co.) Shanghai
Lucas, H., merchant (Lucas & Waters) Hiogo
Luce, A. E., freight clerk (P. M. S. S. Co.) Shanghai
Luchsinger, F., merchant, Yloilo
Luciano, M., sister (The Convent) Caine Road
Lucy, A., instructor in English (Japan Government) Yedo
Lüders, J., pilot (tug-boat) Taku
Ludewig, George, apothecary, Manila
Ludlam, T. E., clerk (Tait & Co.) Amoy
Ludwig, H., clerk (Bavier & Co.) Y'hama
Lueder, C., consul for Germany, Canton (acting at Shanghai)
Lugden, W., nav. sub. lieut., R.N. (*Elk*)
Lugo, C., clerk (Kaltenbach, Eugler & Co.) Saigon
Luhra, C., storekeeper (F. A. Schultze & Co.) Newchwang
Lumsden, A., manager (Tanjore Kubong Mines) Labuan

Luna, F. J., lieut.-col. (director of public works) Macao
Lunau, C., merchant (Lunau & Polano) Hiogo
Lungrana, E. D., merchant (Deguria & Co.) (absent)
Luperne, —., pilot, Saigon
Luscan, Angelique, sister (Hôpital St. Joseph) Ningpo
Luther, H., clerk (Schmidt, Westphal & Co.) Hiogo
Luther, W. H., examiner (Customs) Foochow
Lütkens, L., clerk (Pustau & Co.) Pottinger Street
Lutz, C., merchant (C. Lutz & Co.) Manila
Luz, A. J. F. da, clerk (Portuguese Consulate) Bangkok
Luz, C. S., compositor (*Saigon Advertiser*) Saigon
Luz, D. F. da (Tribunal of Commerce) Macao
Luz, F. da, bailiff (Procurador's department) Macao
Luz, F. M., clerk (H. K. & S. Banking Corp.)
Luz, F. de P. da, captain (Macao Battalion)
Luz, J. A. da, clerk (Olyphant & Co.)
Luz, J. A. da, printer (Commercial Printing office) Graham Street
Luz, V. E. da, linguist (Procurador's department) Macao
yall, Robert, merchant (Norton & Co.) Queen's Road
Lyell, T., marine surveyor, Chefoo
Lyman, B. G., marshal (U. S. Consulate) Foochow (absent)
Lynill, C. S. S., clerk (Strachan & Thomas) Yokohama
Lyon, J. M., superintendent (Borneo Co. Steam Rice Mill) Bangkok
Lyon, Rev. D. N., miss. (American Presb. Miss.) Ningpo (Hangchow)
Lyons, E., 3rd engineer (str. *Yangtsze*)
Lyons, J., manager (Grand Hotel) Y'hama
Lyra, Rev L., professor of Chinese (St. Joseph's College) Macao

M

Macaire, —., judge (Tribunal de Commerce) Saigon
Macaire, J., inspector in charge (M. M. Company) Saigon
Macallen, A., chief engineer (str. *Royalist*) Sarawak
MacArthur, H., assistant (Hudson, Malcolm & Co.) Yokohama
MacBean, J., resident, Shanghai
MacClymont, A., clerk (Russell & Co.) Praya
Macdonald, Rev. J. A., prefect (St. Saviour's English School)

MacDonald, T. J., clerk (Reid, Evans & Co.) Shanghai
MacDonnell, H., Medical Officer (R. N. Hospital) Yokohama
MacEwen, A. P., clerk (Holliday, Wise & Co.) Wyndham Street
MacGibbon, Thos., merchant (Loney & Co.) Yloilo
Macgowan, D. J., M D., Shanghai
Macgowan, Rev. John, missionary (London Miss. Society) Amoy
Macgregor, D. R., manager, Oriental Coal Co., Labuan
Macgregor, J., clerk (Jardine, Matheson & Co.) Shanghai
Machado, F., clerk (Harbour Master's Department)
Machado, F. G., postmaster (British Postal Agency) Yokohama
Machado, J. M. E., sorter (Gen. Post-office)
Machado, M. M., compositor (Hongkong Times)
Machefer, F., apothecary, U. S. A., Yokohama
Machenhauer, B., clerk (Gutschow & Co.) Yokohama
MacIntyre, Rev. J. (U. P. church of Scotland) Chefoo
MacIvor, A., clerk (Jardine Matheson & Co.) Shanghai
Mackay, G., upholsterer, Shanghai
Mackay, G. G., constable (British Consulate) Taku
Mackay, J., tidewaiter (Customs) Shanghai
Mackay, J., upholsterer (G. Mackay & Co.) Shanghai
Mackay, Rev. G., missionary, Tamsui
Mackellar, M. R., broker and secretary (Municipal Council) Hankow
Mackenzie, —, mariner (Jap. Govt.) Yedo
Mackenzie, F. W., 3rd officer (str. Kwangtung)
Mackenzie, G., merchant (Smith, Bell & Co.) Manila
Mackenzie, H., assist. accountant (Oriental Bank) Yokohama
Mackenzie, J., secretary (Pootung foundry) Shanghai
Mackenzie, J., storekeeper (Mackenzie & Co.) Shanghai (absent)
Mackenzie, J., fitter (Govt. Railways) Yokohama
Mackenzie, J. H., M.D. Ningpo
Mackenzie, M., assist. (Pootung Foundry) Shanghai
Mackenzie, R., storekeeper Mackenzie & Co.) Shanghai
Mackenzie, Rev. H. L., missionary, Swatow
Mackenzie, Wm., clerk (Boyd & Co.) Amoy
Mackorsie, W., clerk (Carter & Co.) S'hai
Mackey, J., assistant (Customs) Ningpo
Mackie, J. B., merchant (Martin, Dyce & Co.) Manila

Mackie, J. H., manager (Olyphant's Wharf) Shanghai
Mackillop, J., clerk (Canny & Co.) 'S'hai
Mackintosh, E., clerk (Butterfield & Swire) Shanghai
Mackintosh, L., bill broker, Shanghai
Maclagan, R., assist. eng. (Osaka Mint)
Maclay, R. H., clerk (Russell & Co.) S'hai
Maclay, Rev. Robert S., D.D., missionary (Amer. Meth. Epis. Mission) Y'hama
Maclean, D., merchant (Clyde Steam Saw Mill) Bangkok
Maclean, G. F., commission merchant, Albany Road (absent)
Maclean, H. C., clerk (Jardine, Matheson & Co.)
Maclean, John, merchant (Clyde Steam Saw Mill) Bangkok
Maclean, P., merchant (Maclean & Co.) Shanghai
Maclean, W. S., public tea inspector, S'hai
Maclehose, Jas., clerk (R S. Walker & Co.)
Macleod, A., second officer (Sassoon's str. China)
Macleod, A. Y., clerk (Macleod, Pickford & Co.) Manila
Macleod, N., merchant (Macleod, Pickford & Co.) Manila (Cebu)
Macomber, Wm. H., at Adamson, Bell & Co. Shanghai
Macmahon, J. P., Editor and Proprietor Foochow Herald, Foochow
Macnab, J., asst. acct. (H. K. & S Banking Corp.) Yokohama
Macphail, T., constable (Customs River Police) Shanghai
Macpherson, A., commis. (Customs) H'kow
Macpherson, A. J., merchant (Macpherson & Marshall) Yokohama
Macpherson, M. T. B., clerk (Browne & Co.) Hiogo
Macrae, K., Commission Agent, Yokohama
Macroin, —, Mariner (Jap. Govt.) Yedo
Macvicar, C. Y., clerk (Birley, Worthington & Co.) Shanghai
Madar, A. R., clerk (Treasury) Shelley St.
Madar, Ismail P., clerk (Hongkong Hotel)
Maertens. A. H., silk inspector, Shanghai (absent)
Magill, W., M.D., staff surgeon, R N. (Thetis)
Magnan, A., Commissaire (M. M. S. S. Sindh)
Magniac, Herbert St. L., merchant (Jardine, Matheson & Co.) consul for Denmark at Canton
Magruder, A. F., assistant surgeon, U.S.N. (Iroquois)
Maher, J., adjutant, National Guard, Macao
Maher, J., coal agent (Dodd & Co.) Tamsui
Maher, J., J., ensign, Military Depart., Macao
Maher, M. N., clerk (M. A. dos Remedios) Macao

Mahnz, H., clerk (Spahn & Co.) Osaka
Mahon, J., tidewaiter, Customs, Canton
Mahood, Rev. J. E., miss. (Eng. Ch. Miss.) Foochow
Maignan, H. C., director (French Post office) Shanghai
Mailber, M. C., physician (Jap. Govt.) Yedo
Maillot, X., Professor of Chemistry (First College, Jap. Govt.) Yedo
Mainland, F., master shipwright (Kiangnan Arsenal) Shanghai
Maitland, J., 2nd officer (gun-boat *Ling Feng*) Swatow
Maitland, J., merchant (Moller, Maitland & Co.) Shanghai
Maitland, J. A., mercha.t (Thorne Bros. & Co.) Shanghai
Maitland, T. W., tidewaiter, Custems, Kewkeang
Major, E., commission agent and manager (*Shun Pum*) Shanghai
Major, F., merchant (Major & Smith) Hankow and (Major & Co.) Nagasaki
Maloher, H. A., assistant paymaster, R.N. (*Iron Duke*)
Malcolm, G. W., (Telegraph Department) Yedo
Malcolm, J. W., teacher at Telegraph School, Yedo
Malcolm, J., mechanic (Customs) Shanghai (Pootung)
Malcolm, W. A., merchant (Hudson, Malcolm & Co.) Yokohama (absent)
Malcolmson, W. L., coal merchant, S'hai
Maleschal, —., commis. de Marine, Saigon
Malet, Rev. A. S., B.A., R N. (*Cadmus*)
Malherbe, L., merchant (Malherbe, Jullien & Co.) Bangkok (absent)
Maligen, A. P., clerk (A. D. Startseff) Tientsin
Mallard, M. G. C., assistant paymaster, R.N. (*Thetis*)
Mallory, L., clerk (Burrows & Sons) Praya East
Maloney, H., assistant (Imperial Hotel) Shanghai
Maltby, J., merchant (Maltby & Co.) Nagasaki
Maltby, S, merchant (Maltby & Co.) N'saki
Malteau, G, clerk (Pustau & Co.) S'hai
Mama, H. P., broker, 30, Feel Street
Mammelsdorff, J., manager Deutche Bank, Yokohama
Man, Captain A. J., commissioner, Customs, Newchwang
Mancini, N., roller (Mint) Kawasaki
Mange, —., machinist (Yokoska Arsenal) Yokohama
Manger, A. T., clerk (Douglas Lapraik & Co.) D'Aguilar Street
Manger, J. E., clerk (D. Lapraik & Co.) D'Aguilar Street

Mangue, A, blacksmith, Yokohama
Mangum, W. P., consul (U. S. Consulate) Nagasaki
Mann, J., master (str. *Vine*) Labuan
Mann, J. A., clerk (Thomas & Mercer) Canton
Manners, Thomas N., tidewaiter, Customs, Tientsin
Mannich, J., agent (Brown & Co.) Takow
Manook, E., clerk (Control Department) Hollywood Road
Manookjee, merchant, Canton
Mansfeldt, J., von, Physician (Jap. Govt.) Yedo
Mansfield, R. W., assistant, Brit. consulate Canton
Manson, D., M.D. (Jones, Müller & Manson) Amoy
Manson, D. C. M., M.D Takow
Manson, J. B., clerk (Reid, Evans & Co.) Shanghai
Manson, P., M.D (Jones, Müller & Manson) Amoy
Manthei, J., wharfinger (Gibb's wharf) S'hai
Manyn, —., butcher (Manyn, & Aumin) Bangkok
Manz, J., assistant (Hirsbrunner & Co.) Shanghai
Manzoto, G., sister teacher (The Convent) Caine Road
Marcaida, A. de, clerk (Smith, Bell & Co.) Manila
Marçal, E. M., clerk (Colonial Treasury) Macao
Marçal, F. de P., acting assistant bookkeeper (Revenue department) Macao
Marçal, F. P. S., clerk (Iwiss & Co.) S'hai
Marçal, J. de C., interpreter (Procurador's Department) Macao
Marçal, S. A., compositor, Typographia Mercantil, Macao
Marchi, Rev. Pere, R. C. missionary, C'foo
Marcus, A., storekeeper (Marcus & Co.) Yokohama
Marcus, E., storekeeper (Marcus & Co.) Yokohama
Marcus, S., storekeeper (Marcus & Co.) Yokohama
Mardfeldt, J. F., clerk (Molchers & Co.) Praya
Marechal, Revd J. L., (R. C. Church) Nagasaki
Marey, A. de L. de, sub chief, 2nd Bureau, Saigon
Mariano, F., "Liverpool Arms" tavern
Marians, J., merchant (Isaacs & Co.) Hiogo
Marin, L'abbé J. M., (R. C. missionary) Yedo
Marin, —., pilot, Saigon
Marinelli, E., storekeeper (Marinelli & Co.) Shanghai
Marjary, A. R., actg. interpreter, (British Consulate) Chefoo

Markwick, R., clerk (Customs) Shanghai
Marmelstein, E., storekeeper (Marmelstein & Co.) Hiogo
Marmelstein, J., assistant (G. Moritz) Yokohama
Maron, J. H., merchant (Maron & Co.) Yokohama
Marquand, P. le, constable (Brit. Consulate) Canton
Marquant,— pilot, Saigon
Marquerie, Lieut. Col. (Jap. Govt.) Yedo
Marques, A. G., Jr., clerk (Baker & Co.) Bridges Street
Marques, A. O., interpreter (Chinese Emigration office) Macao
Marques, C. V. M., clerk (Reiss & Co.) Yokohama
Marques, D. S., clerk (J. M. Armstrong)
Marques, E., clerk (Miss M. Garrett) Aberdeen Street
Marques, E., interpreter (Procurador's Department) Macao
Marques, E. J., clerk (Oriental Bank Corporation) Yokohama
Marques, E. P., clerk (L. Marques) Macao
Marques, F. J., professor of mathematics (St. Joseph's College) Macao
Marques, I. M., 2nd class interpreter (Procurator's Department) Macao
Marques, J. G., porter (Col. Govt) Macao
Marques, J. M., clerk (Frazar & Co) S'hai
Marques, L. A., merchant (Pres. Mun. Chamber) Macao
Marques, L. J. M., ensign (National Guard) Macao
Marques, P., secretary (Municipal Council) Macao
Marr, Thos., military clerk (Royal Engineer Department)
Marsan,—., secretary (Procureur General's) Saigon
Marsh, G., clerk (Bourne & Co.) Yokohama
Marsh, S., clerk (Gilman & Co.) Shanghai
Marshall, D. H., M A., professor of mathematics, Yedo
Marshall, J., harbour master, Hiogo
Marshall, J R T., nav mid. (Cadmus)
Marshall, R., clerk (Smith, Bell & Co.) Manila
Marshall, T., accountant (Evening Courier) Shanghai
Marshall, W. A., midshipman, U.S.N. (Hartford)
Marshall, W. D., overseer (Br. W. I. E. Soc) Canton
Martens, J., clerk (Netherlands Trading Society) Hiogo
Marthe, Sœur St., Sister of Charity, Yokohama
Marthon, J., lieut., U.S.N. (Idaho)
Martin, C. F., chief engineer, R N. (Cadmus)
Martin,—., plumber & tinman, Saigon
Martin, E., fitter (Govt. Railways) Y'hama

Martin, F., storeman (Naval Yard)
Martin, J., coal merchant, Yokohama
Martin, J. Jr., coal merchant, Yokohama
Martin, J. P., postmaster (British Post-Office) Shanghai
Martin, M., aide commissaire (L'Hôpital Janres) Yokohama
Martin, M., clerk (Harwood and Wainwright) Shanghai
Martin, Madame (Café de Paris) Saigon
Martin, P., assistant (Customs) Ningpo
Martin, Revd. T., missionary, Bangkok
Martin, Rev. T. P., R. C. missionary, B'kok
Martin, W. A. P., D. D., president and professor of natural philosophy, College of Peking
Martínez, G. M., archbishop (Ecclesiastical Department) Manila
Martinez, P., act. com. of arsenal, Manila
Martinez, R. J., clerk (Holliday, Wise & Co.) Manila
Martinez, V., clerk (Macleod, Pickford & Co.) Cebu
Martinot, G., assistant (Vrard & Co) Tientsin
Marty, A. R., Japanese ware storekeeper, 92 and 24 Queen's Road
Marty, P., assistant (A. R. Marty) 92 and 24, Queen's Road
Marvin, A. T., clerk (Peele. Hubbell & Co.) Manila (Albay)
Marx, L., government supplier (L. Marx & Co.) Saigon
Marzaudin,—., resident, Yokohama
Marzin,—., carpenter (Arsenal) Foochow
Mas, C., tinman, Saigon
Mascañana, R., merchant, Yloilo
Masefield, W. J., clerk (Blackwell & Co.)
Masius, W., merchant (Markwald & Co.) and consul for Austria, Bangkok
Massey, Dr., physician (Jap. Govt.) Yedo
Massie, J. S., proprietor (International Hotel) Nagasaki
Masson, James, clerk (Tait & Co.) Amoy (Tamsui)
Master, L. H., sub. lieut., H.M. 80th Regt.
Mateer, Rev. C. W., missionary, Chefoo
Mather, H., signalman (Harbour Master's Department) Victoria Peak
Mathews, E., engineer (National S. S. Co. of Nipon) Yokohama
Mathews, W. G., assist. (Wheelock & Co.)
Mathisen, William, clerk (F. Degunaer) D'Aguilar Street
Matias, Francisco, clerk (Barretto & Co.) Manila
Matreninsky, V. J., merchant (Matreninsky & Kasantzoff) Kalgan
Matthews,—., engineer (Jap. Govt.) Yedo
Matthews, A. E., storekeeper (Matthews & Co.) Hankow
Matthews, N. foreman mechanic (Govt. Railways) Yokohama

Maturin, W. M., sub. lieut., R.N. (*Iron Duke*)
Mauras, C., clerk (Vve. A. Mauras,) Saigon
Mauras, F., lawyer, Saigon
Mauras. Vve. A., storekeeper Saigon
Mawhood, F., livery stables (Edbrook & Co.) Shanghai
Maxwell, F., asst. resident, Sarebus, Sarawak
Maxwell, J., coal hewer (Tanjong Kubong Mines) Labuan
Maxwell, John, 2nd engineer (str. *Appin*) Shanghai
Maxwell, J. L., M.D., missionary, Taiwan (absent)
Maxwell, R., coal hewer (Tanjong Kubong Mines) Labuan
May, Chas., police magistrate and acting colonial treasurer (Police Magistrate's Court) The Castle
May, F. N , assistant, Customs, K'keang
May, Henry, (Victoria Hotel) 9 Gage St.
May, J. C., merchant (Mourilyan, Heimann & Co.) Osaka
May, J. H., tide surveyor, (Customs) Hankow
Mayer, A , contractor, Saigon
Mayers, E. G., assist paymaster (Control Department) Hongkong Hotel
Mayers, J. L., clerk (Langfeldt & Mayers) Yokohama
Mayers, S., storekeeper (Langfeldt & Mayers) Yokohama
Mayers, W. F., Chinese secretary (British Legation) Peking
Mayhew, J., clerk (Govt. Telegraph) Kobe
Maymo, J., captain, flag ship, Manila
Mayne, G G , manager (Hongkew Wharf Co.) Shanghai
Mazziole, A., assist. light keeper, Kintoan light house, Shanghai
McAllister, D., tea inspector (Morris & Co.) Shanghai
McBean, Thos R., bailiff (Supreme Court) Lyndhurst Terrace
McBeth, —., police inspector (Harbour Master's Dept.) Aberdeen
McCallum, A., assist. (Boyd & Co.) S'hai
McCallum, John, clerk (Lane, Crawford & Co.) Queen's Road
McCartee, D. B., A M., M. D., (First College, Jap. Govt.) Yedo
McCarthy, J., asst. eng. R N. (*Thalia*)
McCarthy, Rev. J., and fam., missionary Chinkeang
McCaslin, C. H., captain (Steam-tug *Orphan*) Shanghai
McCaslin, R. J., pilot, Shanghai
McCauley, E. Y., capt. U.S.N. (*Lackawanna*)
McClatchie, H. P., interpreter (British Consulate) Hankow
McClellan, W., inspector of junks (Harbour Master's Department)

McClement, F., M.D., assistant surgeon, R.N. (*Curlew*)
McClosky, Jas. H., col. surgeon, Labuan
McClure, —., chief engineer (str. *Sri Sarawak*) Sarawak
McClymont, A., clerk (Russell & Co.)
McColen, F., officer in charge of str. *Spark* (laid up)
McConachie, Alex., assistant (McEwen & Co.) Arbuthnot Road
McCoy, Rev. D. C., missionary (Pres. Board of Miss.) Peking
McCulloch, D., clerk (Turner & Co.)
McCulloch, J. B., clerk (Holliday, Wise & Co.) Manila
McDaniel. C. A., paym., U.S.N. (*Iroquois*)
McDermott, R. H., clerk (Treasury) L'buan
McDonald, Alex., surgeon (H. M. Naval Hospital)
McDonald, J., manager (McDonald & Co.) Patent slip, West Point
McDonald, J., tidewaiter, Customs, T'tsin
McDonald, Rev. M , Missionary, Yokohama
McDonald, Rev. Noah A., missionary, Bangkok
Mc Donald, W., bill broker (McDonald & Dare) Yokohama
McDonald, Wm , Lloyd's surveyor, Y'hama
McDougal, C. S., commr., U.S.N. (*Saco*)
McFall, D. C., surgeon major, H. M. 80th Regt.
McFarland, Rev. Sam. G., missionary, Bangkok (absent)
McGavin, J. P., assist. (Findlay, Richardson & Co) Manila
McGiffic, J. D., tidewaiter (Customs) Swatow
McGilvray, Rev. D., missionary, Bangkok (absent)
McGregor, G., engineer (P. & O. Service)
McGregor, H., clerk, (Paul Heinemann & Co) Yokohama
McGregor, J., watchmaker (Geo. Falconer & Co) Queen's Road
McGregor, Rev. W,, missionary (English Pres. Miss.) Amoy (absent)
McIlvaine, Rev. J. S., missionary, Peking
McIlwraith, R., supt. (Imperial Arsenal) Tientsin
McIntosh, H. P., mid., U.S.N. (*Lackawanna*)
McIntosh, J., light-keeper, Shaweishan Light House, Shanghai
McIntyre, A., engineer (P. & O. Service)
McIntyre, A., 2nd engineer (str. *Thales*)
McIver, A., supt. (P. & O. S. N. Co.) St. John's Place
McKay, Geo. S., (Hongkong & Whampoa Dock Company) Whampoa
McKean, E., Professor of English (College of Peking) Peking
McKechnie, A G., Lieut., R.N. (*Cadmus*)
McKenzie, D., Proprietor (Snug Tavern) Yokohama

McKenzie, R., broker (Miller, McKenzie & White) Shanghai (absent)
McKenzie, R M., accountant, treasury, Sarawak
McKinnon, A , Farmer (Jap. Govt) Yedo
McLane, Louis, clerk (Pacific Mail S. S. Co.) Yokohama
McLatchie, T. R. H., 2nd assistant (British and Austrian Consulates) Hiogo
McLeod, A., merchant (Gibb, Livingston & Co.) Shanghai
McLeod, E , overseer of works (Surveyor General's Department)
McLeod, J., clerk (Gibb, Livingston & Co.) Aberdeen Street
McLeod, N., resident, Osaka
McLoughlin, E., broker, Shanghai
McMicken, W., accountant (Oriental Bank) Foochow
McMicking, T., clerk (Ker & Co.) Manila
McMillan, J., local postmaster, Shanghai
McMinnies, H. H., clerk (Elles & Co.) Amoy
McMurdo, R., marine surveyor, Excelsior, Seymour Road
McMurtrie, D., surgeon, u.s.n. (*Ashuelot*)
McNab, A F., chief engineer (str. *Thabor*) Yokohama
McNulty, John (British Hotel) Queen's Road West
M'cQueen, H., commander (str. *Glengyle*)
McRitchie, J., assistant engineer, coast lights, Yokohama
McThorne, H., pilot (Pilot Co.) Newchwang
Meade, H. J., chief tide surveyor (Customs) Shanghai
Meadows, J. A. T., consul for Denmark and Netherlands, Tientsin
Meadows, Rev. J. and family, missionary (G'au-king) Chinkeang (absent)
Mechain, E. consul (Fch. Consulate) Manila
Medard, L , professor of mathematics (Arsenal) Foochow
Medeiros, Rev. A. J. de, prof. of elementary Portuguese (St. Joseph's college) Macao
Medhurst, W. H., consul (British Consulate) Shanghai
Medina, João de C. (Royal Oak Tavern) Queen's Road West
Medlen, G. A., architect (Rawling, Medlen & Co.) (absent)
Meech, Rev. S. E., missionary (London Missionary Society) Peking
Mees, R A., clerk (Netherlands Trading Company) Yokohama
Meesenmecker, —, com. de la Marine, Shanghai (Woosung)
Mehta, B. M., assistant (N. Mody & Co.) Queen's Road
Mehta, B. S., merchant (D. D. Ollia & Co.) Amoy

Mehta, D M., merchant (Ghandy & Co.) Hollywood Road
Mehta, M. M., assistant (Ghandy & Co.) Hollywood Road
Mehta, M M., clerk (Framjee Hormusjee & Co.)
Mehta, R D., merchant (R. Dhunjebhoy & Co.)
Meier, A., (A. Meier & Co.) Yokohama
Meier, L., assistant (A. Meier & Co.) Yokohama
Meilhan, A., baker (Boulangerie Provençale) Shanghai
Meily, J. U., clerk (Chartered Bank, and Vice Consul for Switzerland, Manila
Mein, P. W , cut. acct. (Chartered Bank)
Meincke, G., clerk (Telge, Nölting & Co.) Shanghai
Meira, X., clerk (McEwen Frickel & Co.
Meisner, C. F., shipchandler (Moller and Meisner) Bangkok
Melbye, Emil, clerk (John Burd & Co.) Praya
Melchers, H., merchant (Melchers & Co.) Praya
Moldrum, A., pilot, Ningpo
Mellhuish, C. F., clerk (Gilman & Co.) Yokohama
Melizan, E., commissaire (M. M. S. S. *Irrawaddy*)
Melizan, G., commander (M. M. S. *Sindh*)
Meller, H., auctioneer (Meller & Co.) S'hai
Melling. Robert, boatswain (Naval Yard)
Mollo, A. A de (Visconnt do Cereal) merchant (A. A. de Mello & Co) Consul for Brazil, Macao
Mello, A., compositor (*Saigon Advertisir &c*) Saigon
Mello, Antonio de (Barão do Cereal) merchant (L. A. de Mello & Co) Consul for Belgium, France and Italy, vice-consul for Brazil, Macao
Mello, P. M., compositor (*Foochow Herald*) Foochow
Melville, M., assistant (Vulcan Iron Works) Hiogo
Melvin, Wm., 2nd officer (steamer *Appin*) Shanghai
Mendel, L., clerk (Arnhold, Karberg & Co.) Praya
Mendelson, J., merchant (Mendelson Brothers) Yokohama
Mendelson, S., merchant (Mendelson Brothers) Yokohama
Mendes, A. N., advocate, Macao
Mendes, A. N., jr., clerk (Margesson & Co.) Macao
Mendonga, L. M de, compositor (Typographia Mercantil) Macao
Menzies, A. B., Examiner (Customs) Chinkiang
Menzies, A., Librarian (Shanghai Library) Shanghai

Mercer, James, engineer (National S. S. Co., Nipon) Yokohama
Mercer, T., engineer (National S. S. Co., Nipon) Yokohama
Mercer, T., public tea-inspector (Thomas & Mercer) Canton and Macao
Merlande, F., French vice-consul, Chefoo
Merle, —., River Pilot, Saigon
Merredew Miss M. A., milliner (Rose & Co.) Wellington Street
Merrilees, A. G., foreman printer (N. C. Daily News) Shanghai
Merriman, J., Auctioneer (Merriman and Stevenson) Yokohama
Merriman, W., clerk (Cheshire & Co.) Yokohama
Merritt, Chas., Garrison Sergeant Major (the Staff)
Mertz, A., mid. U.S.N. (Yantic)
Merve, S., Sister (Maison de Jesus enfant) Ningpo
Merwanjee, —., merchant, Canton
Merwanjee S., broker, Gage Street
Mesney, J., Examiner (Customs,) Hankow
Meauey, Rev. W., missionary, Sarawak
Mesnier, P. G., private secretary to the Governor of Macao
Mesquita, Lieut. Col. V. N. de (Monte Fort) Macao
Mostern, C. J., public tea inspector (Mestern & Hülse) Canton
Mestres, B., auctioneer (Mestres y Hermano) Manila
Mestres, F., auctioneer (Mestres y Hermano) Manila
Metherall, W., storeman (Naval Yard)
Methvin, Jas., clerk (Russell & Sturgis) Manila
Metta, E. N., merchant, Canton
Metta, S. F., clerk (E. N. Met.a) Canton
Metta, S. M., clerk (Pallanjee & Co.) Lyndhurst Terrace and Shanghai
Metzner, W., Teppozu, Yedo
Meunier, —., sub. lieut. French Marines, Yokohama
Meuser, O. clerk (P. Ehlers & Co.) Honan
Meyer, A. E., merchant (Meyer, Alabor & Co.) Stanley Street
Meyer, B. F., assist. paymaster in charge, U.S.N. (Dwarf)
Meyer, E., merchant (O. Stammann) Tientsin
Meyer, H. B., clerk (Siemssen & Co.) Queen's Road
Meyer, J. D., shipwright (Meyer & Fehrs) Swatow
Meyer, J. E., clerk (D. Sassoon Sons & Co.) Shanghai
Meyerink, H. F., clerk (Meyer, Alabor & Co.) Stanley Street
Meyers, A., importer, Yokohama
Meylan, —., chief engineer (M. M. S. S. Amazone)

Meynard, H., (Meynard, Cousins & Co.) Shanghai (absent)
Meyn, M. C., clerk (Raynal & Co.) Stanley Street
Michel, G., engineer (Naval Yard)
Michel, J., tavern keeper, Saigon
Michel, —., pilot, Saigon (absent)
Michel, Louis, modeller (Yokoska Arsenal) Yokohama
Michel, —., chief officer, (M. M. S. S. str Volga)
Michell, G. N. H., engineer, R.N. (Naval Yard)
Michelot, L., acct. (Comptoir d'Escompte) Saigon
Michelsen, L., clerk (Petersen & Co.) Amoy
Michie, A., merchant (Chapman, King & Co.) Shanghai
Mickley, J. P., asst. eng., U.S.N. (Lackawanna)
Middleton, J. T., acting vice-consul (Brit. Consulate) Takú
Middleton, O., storekeeper, Chinkeang
Middleton, P., clerk (Sarabus Station) Sarawak
Middleton, W., shipwright (Shanghai & Pootung Foundry) Shanghai
Middleton, W. N., broker (Anton & Middleton) The Brook
Midon, L'abbé Felix, miss. apost. Y'hama
Mielanhausen, E., assistant (Lndage, and Oelke) Yokohama
Mightom, G., foreman mechanic (Govt. Railways) Yokohama
Miguieis, T. D'A, retired clerk and notary public, Macao
Miles, Henry A., constable (Brit. Consulate) Hiogo
Milisch, C., Austrian vice-consul, merchant (Raynal & Co.) Macao
Milisch, J., clerk (Knight & Co.) Newchwang
Militzer, Max., merchant (Schmidt, Westphal & Co.) Nagasaki
Millar, A., plumber (A. Millar & Co.) Queen's Road East
Millar, C., constable (Police Fore) Y'hama
Miller, A., clerk (P. & O. S. N. Co.) Queen's Road
Miller, A., forman (Japan Gazette) Office) Yokohama
Miller, H. M., appraiser (Japanese Customs) Yokohama
Miller, D. A., clerk (Drysdale, Ringer & Co.) Hankow
Miller, Mrs. E. R., missionary Yokohama
Miller, Rev. E. R., missionary, Yokohama
Miller, J. A., commander (Sassoon's steamer Hindustan)
Miller, J., asst steward (Yokohama General Hospital) Yokohama
Miller, J., light-keeper (North Saddle Light House) (Customs) Shanghai

Miller, J. J, broker (Miller, McKenzie and White) Shanghai
Miller, N., stevedore (P. M. S. S. Co.) Yokohama
Miller, P. J., boatswain, U.S.N. (*Hartford*)
Miller, R , clerk (Behre & Co) Saigon
Miller, R., general broker (Miller, McKenzie & White) Shanghai
Miller, T. T. R., midshipman, R.N. (*Iron Duke*)
Miller, W. A., ballast master, Yokohama
Miller, W., clerk (Gilman & Co.) Shanghai
Milley, W., foreman (*Evening Courier*) S'hai
Millot, E., merchant (E. Millot & Co.) Shanghai
Milles, H , asst. foreman (Hook and Ladder Brigade) Yokohama
Mills, H., proprietor (Imperial Hotel) Shanghai
Mills, Rev. C. R , missionary, Chefoo
Milne, A., clerk (Walsh, Hall & Co.) Yokohama
Milsom, A., merchant (Valmale, Schoene and Milsom) Yokohama
Milton, A., boatswain, R.N. (*Mosquito*)
Minden, P., master mariner, Bangkok
Miranda, Antonio, apprentice engineer (Hongkong & Whampoa Dock C'pany) Whampoa
Miranda, F. F. da, ensign (Timor Corps) Macao
Miranda, Major M. C. G. d'O., inspector of war material, Macao
Mitchell, A., clerk (Curnow & Co.) Yokohama
Mitchell, F. W., postmaster general and acting police magistrate (General Post-Office) Queen's Road
Mitchell, F. W., Jr., clerk (Hongkong and Shanghai Bank) Hankow
Mitchell, Geo., pilot, Taku (absent)
Mitchell, Geo. N., vice-consul (U. S. Consulate) Yokohama
Mitchell, J, engineer (Novelty Iron Works)
Mitchell, T., engineer (P. & O. service)
Mitchell, W. pilot (Anchorage) Foochow
Mitchell, Wm., mechanic (Shanghai & Pootung Foundry) Shanghai
Mitchell, Wm. share-broker, &c. (Bisset & Co.) Shanghai
Mitford, B. A., clerk (Forster & Co.) Foochow
Modesto, F., clerk (Rocha & Co.) Manila
Mody, A. N., merchant (Mody & Co.) (absent)
Mody, H. N., auctioneer, &c., Lyndhurst Terrace
Mody, J. N., merchant (Mody & Co.) (absent)
Mody, N. B., merchant (Mody & Co.) (absent)
Mody, P. C., general broker, Shanghai
Moeriko, G., assistant (P. Sartorius) Manila
Moffatt, R. C. D., merchant (Moffatt & Co.) Shanghai (absent)
Moisy, L., sub. chief 1st bureau (Direction of Interior) Saigon
Molchanoff, J. M., agent (Botkin & Sons) Kalgan
Molin, O., assistant (Lohmann, Kuchmeister & Co.) Yokohama
Mollendorff, Otto von., student (German Legation) Peking
Moller, H. A., shipchandler (Moller & Meisner) Bangkok
Moller, S. H., master Mariner, Bangkok
Müller, J., clerk (Alloin & Co) Bangkok
Moller, J. J. C. (Moller, Maitland & Co.) Shanghai
Molthchanoff, J. M., clerk (Ivanoff & Co.) Hankow
Möller, L P., examiner, Customs. S'hai
Moller, Nils, auctioneer, Shanghai
Müller, R., bro'.er (Nils Möller) Shanghai
Mollison, J. P., merchant (Fraser & Co.) Yokohama
Molloy, E., tidewaiter (Customs) Whampoa
Mompeon, J., sorter, Post Office, Manila
Monat, A. R. D., clerk (Provand & Co.) Shanghai
Mondy, E. F., A.R.S.M , professor of drawing (Jap. Govt.) Yedo
Mongan, J., consul (British and Austro-Hungarian Consulates) Tientsin
Monier, Mdlle. L. (Govt. Silk Recling Factory) Yedo
Mounier, —., Café de la Marine, Saigon
Monro, G. A., tea inspector, Shanghai
Monro, J. D., clerk (Bradley & Co.) Swatow
Montagneux, Père, P. (Roman Catholic Missionary) Ningpo
Montant, G., private (Mun. Police) Yokohama
Montfalconnet, R. Mdme., Café de la Regence, Saigon
Montgomery, G. L., clerk (Jardine, Matheson & Co.) Yokohama
Montigny, Remi de, merchant, Shanghai (absent)
Montjon, M. A. de, secretary to Government, Saigon
Montojo, Vicente, harbour master (Naval Department) Manila
Montresor, W. H. H., mid., R.N (*Iron Duke*)
Moon, Miss E., missionary, Chefoo
Moon, Miss L., missionary, Chefoo
Mooney, Captn. J., Resident, Queen's Road East
Mooney, J. K., pilot (Black Ball Pilot Co.) Shanghai
Moor, A. F., trader, Bangkok
Moore, A. (Am. Steam Rice Mill) Bangkok
Moore, A. M., assist. surgeon U.S N. (*Saco*)
Moore, C. F., examiner (Customs) Kewkeang

Moore, E., assist. (Olyphant & Co.) Praya
Moore, F., tidewaiter (Customs) Canton
Moore, H., clerk (Hk. & Sh. Bank)
Moore, J., freight clerk (*Shamrock*) N'saki
Moore, J. W., fleet engr., U.S N. (*Hartford*)
Moore, L., general broker, Shanghai
Moore, L P., merchant (Moore & Co.) Yokohama
Moore, M. G., clerk (Russell & Co) and vice-consul for Sweden and Norway, Tientsin
Moore, W. H., storekeeper (Lammert, Atkinson & Co) Queen's Road
Moore, W. P., hair dresser Hongkong Hotel
Moorehead, T., examiner (Customs) Taku and Tientsin
Moorhead, R. B., assist.-in-charge (Customs) Swatow
Moorman, J. B., paymr., R.N. (*Thetis*)
Moran, R , exam (Customs) An,oy (absent)
Morando, —., secretary, municipality, Saigon
More, M , assist. (L. Candrelier) Yedo (Tekidji)
Moreau, —., park guardian, Saigon
Morehouse, W. N., assist. (Customs) Canton
Morejon, Sr. Don Carlos O , Spanish consul, Amoy
Morel, E., bill broker and consul for Belgium, Shanghai
Moreno, J., sorter, Post Office, Manila
Morf, H. C., merchant (Morf & Co.) Yokohama
Morgan, Chas. H., auctioneer and broker, Caine Road
Morgan, F. A , assist (Customs) Canton
Morgan, J., tidewaiter (Customs) Shanghai
Morgan, W. M., broker, Pedder's Hill
Morice, —., general drapers and outfitters, Saigon
Morin, L , chief, 1st bureau, Saigon
Morison, W. O., clerk (Gibb, Livingston & Co) Foochow
Moritz, C., hatter (M. Secker & Co.) Manila
Moritz, G., storekeeper, Yokohama
Morone, S., compositor (*Hongkong Times*)
Morphew, J. S , clerk (G. Smith & Co.) agent , *Straits Times Extra*, Shanghai
Morricé, T , shipwright (Morrice, Behncke & Co) Shanghai
Morris, A , clerk (F. Fisher) Hiogo
Morris, A. G , ship and general broker, Pechili Terrace
Morris, Rev. A. R . missionary, Osaka
Morris, B. J , merchant, Foochow
Morris, —., Mineralogist (Jap. Govt) Yedo
Morris H. S , secretary (North China Insurance Company) Shanghai (absent)
Morris, J., assistant superintendent (Govt. Telegraph) Yedo & Yokohama
Morris, John, ship and general agent (Morris & Lewis) Shanghai (absent)

Morris, S., assist. (Domoney & Co.) Yokohama
Morris, S. J., engineer (Morris, Barlow & Co.) Manila
Morris, Thos. assist eng. R.N. (*Ringdove*)
Morris, W. J., 3rd officer (str. *Hindostan*)
Morrison, J., act. agent (Chartered Mercantile Bank) Hankow
Morrison, J., clerk (H. K. & S. Banking Corp.) Gough Street
Morrison, John, assistant (Whitfield & Dowson) Yokohama
Morriss, H , bill broker, Shanghai
Morse, A. H , comr. (str. *Nanking*) S'hai
Morse, W. H., merchant (Smith, Baker & Co) Hiogo
Mortimer, H. W., assist. (China Sub. Tel. Co.)
Mortley, J., printer, Sarawak
Morton, Andrew, clerk (Lane, Crawford & Co.) Shanghai
Morton, Rev. Thomas F., chaplain, R.N. H. M. Naval Hospital
Moses, D. E., clerk (D. Sassoon, Sons & Co) Shanghai
Moses, J. S., clerk (E. D. Sassoon) S'hai
Moses, S. E., clerk (E. D. Sassoon & Co.) Shanghai
Moses, S. M., merchant (D. Sassoon, Sons & Co.) Shanghai
Moset, —., artisan (Jap. Govt.) Yedo
Moshergen, W., book keeper " Rajah's arms" Tarwak
Moss, C. D , book-keeper (*Japan Gazette* office) Yokohama
Moss, E. J., manager (*Japan Gazette* office) Yokohama
Moss, H., proprietor (Japan Hotel) Y'hama
Moss, John, godown-keeper (Dodd & Co.) Tamsui
Mostyn, R. B., superintendent of police, &c. (Municipal Council) Tientsin
Mott, G. B., chief officer (str. *White Cloud*)
Motz, R., interpreter (The Suibansho) Yokohama
Mouat, J., clerk (Walsh, Hall & Co.) Yokohama
Mougeol, —., in charge of trees, Saigon
Mouillesaux, A., clerk (Customs) Shanghai
Moule, Rev. A. E., missionary (Ch. Eng. Mission Society) Ningpo
Moule, Rev. G. E., missionary (Ch. Eng. Mission Society) Ningpo (Hangchow)
Moulins, —., chief armourer (Japanese Government) Yedo
Moulls, J., tidewaiter (Customs) Taku
Moultron, E., vice-consul for Belgium, Yokohama
Mountain, J. J., engineer (Naconchaisee Factory) Bangkok
Mourilyan, W., merchant (Mourilyan, Heimann & Có.) Osaka
Mourrut, P., captain (M. M. str. *Mensaleh*)

Mowat, R. A., registrar (H.B.M. Supreme Court) Shanghai
Mowe, S., writer (Rejang Outstation) Sarawak
Mowjeebhoy, G. manager (P. Jairazbhoy)
Moysey, F. A., lieutenant, U.N. (*Thalia*)
Mudgett, E., teacher (Japanese Government) Yedo
Mueller, Dr. L. (Japanese Government) Yedo
Muffitt, J., chemist (Canton Dispensary) Canton
Muggeridge, J. S., sub-lieut., R.N. (*Kestrel*)
Mühlenfold, H., clerk (Deusche Bank) Yokohama
Mühlensteth, J. A., clerk (Great Northern Telegraph Company) Amoy
Muir, G. W., paymaster, R.N., secretary to Commodore.(*Princess Charlotte*)
Muirhead, D., superintendent (Pootung Dock Company) Shanghai
Muirhead, Rev. W., missionary, Shanghai
Mulaton, —., contractor, Saigon
Mulcahy, E., assist. surgeon, R.N. (*Thistle*)
Mulership, S. (Takasima Colliery) Ta'sima
Mullan, D. W., lieut.-commander, U.S.N. (*Saco*)
Müller, Aug., M.D. (Jones, Müller & Manson) Amoy
Müller, C., clerk (Siber & Brennwald) Yedo
Müller, F., clerk (Pickenpack, Thies & Co.) Bangkok
Müller, G. F., clerk (Customs) Shanghai
Müller, J. (Tungsha Light Vessel) Shanghai
Müller, J. (City of Hamburg Tavern) Hiogo
Müller, J. W., merchant (Muller & Co.) Shanghai
Müller, O., clerk (Muller & Co.) Shanghai
Müller, W., clerk (Pickenpack, Thies & Co.) and acting consul for Netherlands, Bangkok
Mulior, —., patternmaker (Arsenal) F'chow
Mullins, D., constable (Customs) Foochow
Mullis, J., engineer (P. & O. Service)
Munchau, —., master mariner, Bangkok
Muncherjee, D., manager (F. Hormusjee & Co.) Hollywood Road
Muncherjee, E. (Nowrojee & Co.) Queen's Road
Muncherjee, E., clerk (Joolamhoosein & Co.)
Munday, N., assistant (Sayle & Co.)
Munn, D., clerk (Ker & Co.) Yloilo
Munro, D., commission merchant, Amoy
Munrou, B. S. (Japanese Government) Yedo (Kaitikuishi)
Munz, J., assistant (Eugster & Co.) Manila
Murly, —., Teacher (Jap. Govt.) Yedo
Murphy, D., engineer (steamer *Poyang*)
Murphy, J. J., barkeeper (Royal Oak Tavern) Queen's Road
Murphy, M. W. (Mariner's Home) Shanghai

Murray, —., captain (steam-tug *Pokelin*) Shanghai
Murray, D. G., clerk (Customs) Shanghai
Murray, E. D., assistant (Fraser & Co.) Yokohama
Murray, J., M.D., assistant surgeon, H.M. 80th Regiment
Murray, John B., chief officer (Chinese gunboat *Anlan*)
Murray, M. E., merchant (Margesson & Co.) Macao
Murrow, Y. J., proprietor, *Daily Press* (absent)
Murton, N., tea inspector (Heard & Co.) Amoy
Musliah, M. H., clerk (E. D. Sassoon & Co.) Shanghai
Mustard. R. W., commission agent (Mustard & Co.) Shanghai
Myburgh, A., barrister (R. W. M. Bird) Shanghai
Myers, Mrs., resident, Yokohama
Myers, T. D., asst. surgeon, U.S.N.(*Monocacy*)
Myers, W. W., M.B. (Carmichael & Myers) Chefoo
Mylne, H. A., clerk (Adamson, Bell & Co.) Shanghai
Myres, C., contractor (Coutris & Co.) C'foo

N

Naber, F. W., mid., U.S.N. (*Palos*)
Nachtigal, G., stevedore (Nachtigal & Co.) Hiogo
Nachtrieb, A., merchant (Nachtrieb, Leroy & Co.) Shanghai
Nacken, Rev. J., miss. (Rhenish Mission) Fairlea, Bonham Road
Nagle, C. F., assist. eng. U.S.N. (*Monocacy*)
Nail, C. H., clerk (C. & J. Trading Co.) Shanghai
Nail, W. H., clerk (Borneo Co.) Sarawak
Nakoda, I. Solomanjee, proprietor (Model Rice Mill) Bangkok
Nales, J., clerk (Blanco, Domingo & Co.) Manila
Namazy, H. A. A., clerk (Hajee Ali Asgar & Hajee Esmail) Gage Street
Nash, H., clerk (Russell & Co.) Shanghai
Nash, H. M., surgeon, R. N. (*Thetis*)
Nathan, E. E., clerk (E. D. Sassoon & Co.) Tientsin
Nathan, S. A., clerk (D. Sassoon, Sons & Co.) Newchwang
Nathan, E. J., clerk (E. D. Sassoon & Co.) Shanghai
Nathan, J. A., clerk (D. Sassoon, Sons & Co.) Shanghai
Nathan, J., clerk (E. D. Sassoon & Co.) Shanghai (Tientsin)
Nathan, M., merchant, Shanghai
Nathan, S. A., agent (D. Sassoon, Sons & Co.) Newchwang

Nathan, S. J., clerk (E. D. Sassoon & Co.) Chefoo
Naudin, N., clerk (Kniffler & Co.) Hiogo
Naudin, V., assistant light-house keeper, Chapel Island, Amoy
Navarro, José de, vice-consul for Spain, (absent)
Nazor, B. W., court repor'er (*Hongkong Times*)
Nazer, J S., clerk (Inglis & Co)
Nazel, R. H., 3rd officer (str. *Yesso*)
Neate, S. R., inspector of buildings (Surveyor General's Office)
Nefedieff, A. A., clerk (N. A. Nefedieff) Tientsin
Nefedieff, N. A., merchant and agent Tientsin
Negro, A. F., merchant (Rand & Co.) Yokohama
Nelson, H. H., act. agent (Ch. Merc. Bank) Foochow
Nelson, J. H., resident, Lundu, Sarawak
Nelson, Rev. R., missionary, Shanghai (Hongkow)
Nels n, T., clerk (Olyphant & Co.) Praya
Nelson, T., lieut. commdr., U.S.N. (*Idaho*)
Nemtchinoff, F. J., clerk (Ivanoff & Co.) Hankow
Nemtchinuff, M. J., clerk (Ivanoff & Co.) Hankow
Nemtchinoff, W. J., clerk (Ivanoff & Co.) Hankow
Nepea , A. O., lieutenant, R.M. Yokohama
Nesbit, C , harbour reporter (*Hongkong Times*)
Ness, G. P., barrister at law, Yokohama
Nethersole, H., aerated water manufactory, Yokohama
Nethersole, H. Jr., assistant, aerated water manufactory, Yokohama
Neves, C. L. das, ward-master (Military Hospital) Macao
Nevin, Rev. J. C., missionary, Canton
Nevius, Rev. J. L., D.D., miss., Chefoo
Newbiggin, W. C., clerk (Barnet & Co.) Shanghai
Newbury, J., tidewaiter (Customs) Shanghai
Newcombe, E., assistant engineer (Govt. R ilroads) Yokohama
Newitt, W. T., clerk-in-charge (China Sub. Telegraph Co.) Bonham Road
Nowman, E., manager, Chefoo Family Hotel, Chefoo
Newman, Mrs., Chefoo Family Hotel, C'foo
Newman, Rev. J., missionary, Yedo
Newman, W., public tea-inspector, F'chow
Newman, W. H., interpreter, (British Consulate) Bangkok
Newton, A., manager (Hongkong & China Gas Co) West Point
Newton, C., foreman mechanic (Govt. Railways) Yokohama

Newton, H. B., nav. sub-lieut., R.N. (*Cadmus*)
Ng Achau, manager Chinese paper (*Daily Press* Office)
Nicaise, H., consul for Belgium and Siam, manager (Borneo Company, Limited) Dinder, Caine Road
Nicholls, B., shipchandler (Wilson, Nicholls & Co) Amoy
Nichols, C. W. (Naval College) Yedo
Nichols, H. E., lieut , U.S.N. (*Idaho*)
Nicholson, C., clerk (Shaw Brothers & Co.) Shanghai
Nicholson, C. S., sub-lieut., R.N. (H.M.S. *Avon*)
Nicholson, C. W., clerk (Jardine, Matheson & Co.) Foochow
Nickels, J. A. H., ensign, U S.N. (*Ashuelot*)
Nickels, M. C., clerk (Russell & Co.)
Nickle, A., Constable, Municipal Council, Nagasaki
Nickle, Mrs. C. J., proprietor ("Falcon Hotel") Nagasaki
Nicolayson, N. O., steward (Yokohama General Hospital) Yokohama
Niederberger, G., consul for Germany, merchant (Behre & Co.) Saigon
Niedhardt, E., chemist &c., (Medical Hall) Queen's Road
Nields, H. C., lieut., U.S.N. (*Lackawanna*)
Nielsen, C. P., superintendent (G. N. Teleg. Co.) Amoy
Nielsen, F. C. C., assistant (G. N. Teleg. Co.) Nagasaki
Nielsen, J., telegraph engineer (G. N. Telegraph Co.) Shanghai
Nielsen, J., tidewaiter (Customs) Shanghai
Niewerth, R. (Japan Govt.) Yedo
Niobey, —., lawyer, Saigon
Nissen, A., pilot, Swatow
Nissen, F., merchant (Siemssen & Co.) Shanghai
Nissen, W., merchant (Siemssen & Co.) (absent)
Nissle, G., clerk (Behre & Co) Saigon
Nisted, F., master mariner, Bangkok
Noac, C., clerk (Jardine, Matheson & Co.) Foochow
Nobile, N. B., Consul for Italy, Yokohama
Noble, A. K., assistant (Domoney & Co.) Yokohama
Noble, C. J., assistant (Hongkong Dispensary) Queen's Road
Noble, J., assistant (G. Falconer & Co.) Queen's Road
Noël, L'Abbé André Léonard
Noetzli, G. H., deputy commissioner (Customs) Hankow
Nogueira, F. D. G. de, chief clerk (Treasury) Macao
Nogueira, V., wharfinger (H. K., C. & M. steamboat Co.) Macao
Nohr, J., apothecary (Zobel & Nohr) Manila

Nölting. J., merchant (Telge, Nölting & Co.) Shanghai
Noodt, Emil, clerk (Raynal & Co.) Stanley Street
Noodt, Oscar, clerk (Kirchner Böger & Co.)
Norbert, Sœur St., Superieure (Sisters of Charity) Yokohama
Norcock, C. J., lieut., R.N. (*Iron Duke*)
Nordenstadt, N. N., assist. engineer (Govt. Railroads) Yokohama
Noronha, Delfino, manager (Noronha & Sons) Hollywood Road
Noronha, D. L., agent for Manila lottery, Yokohama
Noronha, L., printer (Noronha & Sons) Oswald's Terrace
Noronha, S. A., compositor (Noronha & Sons) Oswald's Terrace
North, C. J., assis. eng., R.N. (*Elk*)
North, J. (Yokohama Dispensary) Y'hama
North, Miss M. B., missionary, Peking
Norton, Ed., merchant (Norton & Co.) Queen's Road
Notley, W. H., merchant (Rob. S. Walker & Co.) Gough Street
Novion, A., acting commissioner (Customs) Chinkeang
Nowrojee, C., clerk (D. Hosunpjee & Co.) Amoy
Nowrojee, D., baker (D. Nowrojee & Co.) Yokohama and Hongkong
Noyer, G., clerk (Bavier & Co.) Yokohama
Noyes, Miss H., (Amer. Presb. Mission) Canton
Noyes, Miss M., missionary (Amer. Presb. Board) Canton
Noyes, Rev. H. V., missionary (American Presb.) Canton
Nully, R. de, clerk (Lane, Crawford & Co.) Yokohama
Nunes, A. A., clerk (Hook, Son & Co)
Nunes, A., Jr., clerk (A. R. Marty) Queen's Road
Nunes, L., act. 2nd clerk (Revenue Department) Macao
Nunn, Chas., constable (British Consulate) Chiukeang
Nunn, C. F., clerk (Gibb, Livingston & Co.) Aberdeen Street
Nuthall, E. S., lieutenant, R.N. (*Rinaldo*)
Nuthoobhoy, E., merchant (R. Alladinbhoy)
Nyberg, W., master (str. *William Miller*) Labuan
Nye, G., Jr., merchant (Nye & Co.) Canton
Nysten, G., auctioneer (Hogquist & Co.) Shanghai

O

Oakey, F., clerk (Russell & Sturgis) Manila
Oastler, J., supt. of works, lighthouse service (Japanese Government) Yokohama
Oastler, Wm., assist. (Stephen & Stewart) Yokohama
Obadaya, J. E., clerk (E. D. Sassoon & Co.) Queen's Road
O'Brien, M. J., clerk (Customs) Shanghai
O'Brien, M. J., B.A., professor of English (College of Peking)
O'Brien, R. A., M.D., Arbuthnot Road
O'Brien, T., inspector of nuisances (Medical Department)
O'Brien, W. F., clerk (Government Telegraph) Kobé
O'Callaghan, Capt. Cor. (1st W. I. Regt) A.D.C. to H. E. the Governor
Odell, John, merchant (Purdon & Co.) Foochow
Odell, W. L., clerk (Purdon & Co.) Foochow
Oelke, J. D. W., clothier (adage, Oelke & Co.) Shanghai and Yokohama (absent)
Oelrich, H., clerk (Siemssen & Co) S'hai
Oeltze, C., pilot, Foochow (Anchorage)
Oestmann, A., clerk (Kniffler & Co.) Yokohama
O'Flaherty, T. H. (Praya Hotel) Praya Central
Ogden, J., clerk (H. J. Andrews & Co.) Manila
O'Geran, E. H. B., lieut., H.M. 80th Regt.
Ogilvie, J., clerk (Ker & Co.) Manila
Ogilvie, T , clerk (Martin, Dyce & Co.) Manila
Ogle, H. A., sub-lieut R.N. (*Curlew*)
Ogle, R. G., clerk (Birley, Worthington & Co.) Shanghai
Ogle, W. S. A., sub-lieut., R. N. (*Thetis*)
O'Hara, H., clerk (E. D. Sassoon & Co.) Shanghai
Ohl, H., Yokohama
Ohl, lieut. (Jap. Govt.) Yedo
Ohlinger, Rev Franklin, missionary, Foochow
Ohlmer, E., clerk (Customs) Peking
Ojeda, Emilio de, Spanish Chargé d'Affaires ad. int. (edo)
Olano, A., merchant, Macao
Oliveira, A. M. de, general broker
Oliveira, A. S., assist. purser (*Wellington*) Shanghai
Oliveira, V. dos S. e, porter (Revenue Department) Macao
Oliver, E. H., municipal engineer, S'hai
Oliver, Geo., clerk (Heard & Co.) Foochow
Oliver, J. W., naval store issuer, Shanghai
Ollard, H. J., assist. paymr., R. N. (*Cadmus*)
Ollia, D. D., merchant, Amoy
Ollia, N. D., commission agent, Amoy (absent)
Olmsted, F. H. (P. M. S. S. Co.) Y'hama
Olsen, A., tidewaiter (Customs) Swatow
Olsen, J., stevedore (Nachtigal & Co.) Hiogo
Olsen, J., proprietor (National Tavern) Queen's Road West

Olsen, M. P., master mariner, Bangkok
Olyphant, T., merchant (Olyphant & Co.) Shanghai
O'Malley, A. B., pilot (Newchwang Pilot Comp.) Newchwang
Oomar, Mahomed, merchant, Canton and Hongkong
Onslow, G. R., gunner, Chinese gunboat *Feiloong*.
Oosman, A., clerk (A Soab) Wellington St.
Oppenheimer, G., merchant (Bachurach & Oppenheimer) Saigon (absent)
Opstelten, J. C., clerk (Kaltenbach, Engler & Co.) Saigon
Orcel, Captain (Jap. Govt.) Yedo
Orieux, —., river pilot, Saigon
Orley, G., inspector (Police Dept.) Eastern district
Orme, P., clerk (Jardine, Matheson & Co.) Shanghai
Orny, V., storekeeper, Yokohama
Orr, W. S., clerk (Boyd & Co.) Amoy
Orsted, A. S., assistant (Gt. Northern Tel. Co.) Shanghai
Ortega, M., clerk (Tilson, Hermann & Co.) Manila
Ortmans, H. A., clerk (Wachtels & Co.) Hio,o (absent)
Orton, G., master mariner, Bangkok
O'Ryan, J., assistant (A. McDonald & Co.'s Patent Slip) West Point
Osborne, . H., assistant (Watson & Co.) Shanghai
Osgood, D. W., M.D., medical missionary, Foochow
O'Shaughnessy, Captain W. C., assist. mil. secy. to General Whitfeild, Seymour Terrace
Osmund, Chas., clerk (Registrar General's Department) Rozario Street
Osouf, Rev. P. M, procureur (French R. Catholic Mission) Staunton street
Osset, Don Juan, provisor (Bishopric of Nueva Segovia) Manila
Osterholen, L, tidewaiter (Customs) S'hai
Ostiani, Conte F. de, minister (Italian Legation) Peking (absent)
Oswell, Thoma J., midshipman, R.N., (*Cadmus*)
Otadiu, F. de O., clerk (Peele, Hubbell & Co.) Manila
Otin y Mesias, F., chargé d'affaires (Span. Legation) Peking
O'Toole, P., compositor (*Japan Herald*) Yokohama
O'Toole, P. F., resident
Ott, Rev. R., missionary (Evangelical Society of Basel) Chonglok
Ottaway, E. F., tidewaiter (Customs) C'foo
Otto, J. H., assist. (J. Steward's Boarding House) Queen's Road
Ottomeier, P. A. W., clerk (Mestern & Hulse) Canton

Oueda, C., assistant interpreter (French Consulate) Yokohama
Ouspensky, V., secretary (Russian Consulate) Tientsin
Overbeck, G. v., consul-general (Austrian Consulate) Pedder's Hill, and Austrian Consul for Macao (absent)
Overbeck, B., merchant (Overbeck & Co.) Shanghai
Owens, J., assistant (Vulcan Iron Works) Hiogo
Owens, J., mer. (Hughes & Co) Hiogo
Owens, L., mer. (L. Owens & Co.) Manila
Owston, A., clerk (Lane, Crawford & Co) Yokohama
Oxenham, E L., assist. (British Consulate) Hankow (absent)
Oxlad, Miss teacher, Staunton Street
Oxlade, George, agent (Eastern Extension Aust. and China Tel Co.) Shanghai
Oxley, C., (*Hiogo News* Office) Hiogo
Oxley, E. G., resident. Shanghai
Ozorio, C. A., Jr., clerk (Jardine, Matheson & Co)
Ozorio, C. J., clerk (G. von Overbeck) Wyndham Street
Ozorio, F. A., foreman (*Foochow Herald*) Foochow

P

Paasch, C. W., clerk (Siemssen & Co.) Shanghai
Pacheco, A. A., advocato, Macao
Pacheco, D. C., clerk (B. du S. Fernandes) vice-consul for Siam, Macao
Pacheco, P. A., (Municipal Council) Macao
Pacquetet, —., commis de marine, Saigon
Padsha, H. M, merchant, Canton and Hongkong
Paes, A. M., clerk (Hongkong and Whampoa Dock Co.) Aberdeen
Pagden, H., sailmaker, Yokohama
Paget, T. G., merchant (Beazley Paget & Co.) Hankow (absent)
Paillet, —, Forger, Arsenal, Foochow
Palamountain, B., manager, (Customs printing office) Shanghai
Palladius,—., Rt. Rev. archimandrite(Greek Church) Peking
Pallas, —., pilot, Saigon
Pallister, E, clerk (Smith & Co.) Shanghai
Palm, J. L. E, assistant in charge, (Customs) Chefoo
Palmer, A, asst. engineer, R N. (*Iron Duke*)
Palmer, C. H., captain (Chinese str. *Pengchuo-hai*)
Palmer, H. N., merchant (Peele, Hubbell & Co.) Manila (absent)
Palmer, Rev. E. S, O.S.B. Rector (St. Saviour's English College)
Palmer, Rev. R. N., missionary (Ch. Eng. Miss. Society) Ningpo (absent)

Puloma, L., secretary (Ecclesiastical Department) Manila
Paltonwoek, G., 2nd lieut. (Chinese gunboat *Tieupo*)
Pan, E. del, clerk (Pan & Co.) Manila
Pan, J. F. del, merchant (J. F. del Pan & Co.) Manila
Pandorf, F., clerk (Pustau & Co.) Shanghai
Pantou, W., 2nd engineer (str. *Kwangtung*)
Papillon, F., lieut., R N. (*Juno*)
Papps, W., broker and wine merchant (H. J. Limby & Co) Shanghai
Parada, E., sister (Maison de Jesus Enfant) Ningpo
Paranchin, G. P., assist. (Russian Hotel) Hiogo
Pardun, W., merchant (Kniffler & Co.) Yokohama
Parish, J. E., commodore, H. M. S. *Princess Charlotte*
Parke, Miss M., missionary, Yedo
Parker, C. E., merchant (A. Heard & Co.) West Terrace,
Parker, E. H., acting interpreter in charge, Brit. Consulate, Kowkeang
Parker, J., M D., Ningpo
Parker, James, proprietor (Canton printing office) Canton
Parker, J. B., asst. surgeon, U.S.N. (*Yantic*)
Parker J. H. P., mate (receiving ship *Wellington*) Shanghai
Parker, T , assistant (Hongkong and China Gas Company)
Parkes, Rev. H., missionary (Wes. Meth. Miss. Soc.) Canton
Parkes, Sir Harry S , K. C. B., minister (British Legation) Yedo
Parkhill, S., tidesurveyor (Customs) Canton
Parkin, W. W., merchant (Olyphant & Co.) (absent)
Parlane, W., chief engineer (str. *Thales*)
Parlati, A., clerk (Marinelli & Co.) Shanghai
Parr, E., merchant (Tillson, Herrmann & Co.) Manila (absent)
Parr, Richard B., merchant (Tillson, Hermann & Co) act. Ger. Consul, Manila
Parrott, E. G., rear admiral, U. S. Com. in chief
Parry, Rev. W. W., Chaplain, R.N. (*Thetis*)
Parson, Geo., commander, R.N. (*Rinaldo*)
Partridge, F. P., marshal (U. S. Consulate) Bangkok
Partridge, General F. W., consul (U. S. Consulate) Bangkok
Partridge, Rev. S. B., missionary (Amer. Bap. mis.) Swatow
Pasch, W., clerk (China and Japan Trading Co.) Hiogo
Pascoal, J. P., clerk (Thomas and Mercer) Canton
Pasedag, C. J., merchant (Pasedag & Co.) Amoy

Pasquier, Catherine, superieure (Maison de Jesus Enfant) Ningpo
Passmore, J H., chief officer (str. *Kwa Hsing*) Customs, Shanghai
Passos, J. M. dos, assist. (French Dispensary)
Patch, J. M., officer (P. & O. service) atell, P. N., broker, Wellington Street
Paterson, A., act. manager (Oriental Bank Corporation) Shanghai
Paterson, D., pilot, Amoy
Paterson, Geo, assist. (Boyd & Co) S'hai
Paterson, J., merchant (Tait & Co.) vice-consul for the Netherlands, Amoy
Paterson, J. W., tidewaiter (Customs) Swatow
Paterson, T., resident, Yokohama
Paterson, W., agent (Jardine, Matheson & Co.) Foochow
Paton, W. Y., surgeon, R.N. (*Teazer*)
Patow, W, commis. agent, Yokohama
Patriat, Rev. Ch. E., directeur du sanatorium, French Mission, Pokefoolum
Patterson, J. C., commander, R.N. (*Avon*)
Patterson, W. F., commander (steamer *Chili*) Shanghai
Paul, E. B , student interpreter (British Legation) Yedo
Paul, John, Colporteur
Paul, R., compradore, Shanghai
Paul, S., clerk (ustoms) Shanghai
Paula, F. de (Administraçao do Conselho) Macao
Paulin, M. M., cook, Yokohama
Pauline, J., cook (United Club) Yokohama
Paulser, C., master mariner, Bangkok
Payne, Th., clerk (Comptoir d'Escompte) Shanghai
Payne, W., barkeeper (Crown and Anchor) Queen's Road West
Paynter, captain (str. *Dragon*) Shanghai
Payson, Miss A. M., missionary, Foochow
Peacock, P., inspector (British Legation Guard) Yedo
Peacock, T., draper (Watson & Co.) S'hai (absent)
Pearce, A., clerk (Loney & Co.) Yloilo (Negros)
Pearce, E. W., emigration agent, Macao
Pearce, J., supt. of works, light-house service (Jap. Govt.) Yokohama
Pearse, H., assist. (Geo. Polite) Shanghai
Pearse, J. B., assistant (Thomson & Hind) Queen's Road
Pearse, Mrs., assistant (Thomson & Hind) Queen's Road
Pearson, G. C., merchant (Pearson & Laurence) Yokohama
Pearson, J., tidewaiter (Customs) Shanghai
Pearson, T., godown-keeper (Landstein & Co.) Queen's Road East
Peat, J., chief officer (str. *Chinkiang*)
Pebany, E., merchant, Canton & Hongkong

Pedder, W. H., consul (British Consulate) consul for Austria & Germany, Amoy
Pedro, J., wardmaster (Military Hospital) Macao
Peerbhoy, Jairabhoy, merchant, Canton & Hongkong
Pegemsky, J. P., clerk (Haminoff Rodionoff & Co.) Hankow
Peil, F., merchant, Shangbai, & Pedder's Wharf
Pejemsky, J. P., clerk (Audreevsky & Avramoff) Kalgau
Pejemsky, J. P., clerk (N. A. Ivanoff & Co.) Tientsin
Pelegrin, H. (Meynard, Cousins & Co.) Shanghai (Yokohama)
Pellew, H. M. G., engineer, R. N. (*Kestrel*)
Pellew, H. W. R., assist. engineer, R. N. (*Opossum*)
Pellicot, —, écrivain de marine, Saigon
Pellisser, V., timber merchant, Saigon
Peltzer, T., Tailor (Lohmann, Kuchmeister & Co.) Yokohama
Pélu, L'abbé A., Roman Catholic Missionary, Kobe
Pender, John, engineer, Chinese gun-boat *Sui-tsing*
Pendred, J., chief officer (S.S. *Thabor*) Yokohama
Penfold, C., superintendent (Police Force) Shanghai
Pemberton, T., assist. (Shanghai Tug & Lighter Co.) Shanghai
Penrose, J. H., tidewaiter (Customs) Amoy
Penrose, J. H., broker, Shanghai
Pepperill, Geo. (Naval College) Yedo
Pequignot, —, lively stable keeper (Pequignot & Co.) Yokohama
Peralta, Manuel, dean (Ecclesiastical Department) Manila
Peray, Victor, 1st valuator, (Customs) Manila
Perboyre, Gabriel, sister (Maison de la Presentation) Ningpo (Tingbai)
Percebois, C., overseer, French Concession, Shanghai
Percival, R. H., clerk (Reiss & Co.) S'hai
Percival, W. H., assist. (North Ch. Ins. Co.) Shanghai
Percival, Osborn, Foreign Secretary (The Kencho) Yokohama
Pereira, A. A., clerk (H.K. and Shanghai Banking Corporation)
Pereira, A. sister, (The Convent) Caine Road
Pereira, A. E., compositor (Typographia Mercantil) Macao
Pereira, A. F., clerk (Landstain & Co.) Wyndham Street
Pereira, A. L. G., clerk (National Bank of India)
Pereira, A. M. R., clerk (P. M. S. S. Co.) Cochrane Street

Pereira, A. S., compositor (Noronha & Sons) Bridges Street
Pereira, B., clerk (Russell & Co.) Foochow
Pereira, B. A., merchant, chancellor (Belgium Consulate) Macao
Pereira, C. d'A., lieutenant (*Tejo*) Macao
Pereira, E., clerk (E. Schellhaas & Co.)
Pereira, E., assistant (Lewes & Benton) Shanghai
Pereira, E. F., assistant (Bisset & Co.) Shanghai
Pereira, E. J., clerk (Hongkong and Shaughai Bank) Hiogo and Osaka
Pereira, F. G., writer (Naval Yard)
Pereira, F. P., Manila lottery ticket seller, Tank Lane
Pereira, H., compositor (A. H. de Carvalho) Shanghai
Pereira, H. E. Juan M., envoy extraordinary and minister plenipotentiary (Spanish Legation) Peking (absent)
Pereira, I. P., clerk (ng. Beard & Co.) Gough Street
Pereira, J., overseer (Borneo Co.) Sarawak
Pereira, J. A. (Victoria Sodawater Manufactory) Hollywood Road
Pereira, J. C. da C., clerk (Chinese Emigration Office) Macao
Pereira, J. L., clerk (Oriental Bank) S'hai
Pereira, L., proprietor (Victoria bakery) Wellington Street
Pereira, M. C., paymaster (*Tejo*) Macao
Pereira, M. L., clerk (Hongkong & Shanghai Bank) Shanghai
Pereira, P., assistant (D. Nowrojee & Co.)
Pereira, R., overseer (Borneo Co.) Muka, Sarawak
Pereira, R. J., ensign (Timor Corps) Macao
Pereira, R. N., clerk (Mello & Co.) Macao
Pereira, T. S., compositor (A. H. de Carvalho) Shanghai
Pereira, V. S., advocate, Macao
Peres, B. A., clerk (Oriental Bank) Yokohama
Peres, M., Jun., lieutenant quarter-master (National Guard) Macao
Peres, D. M., notary general (Ecclesiastical Department) Manila
Perham, Rev. John, missionary, Sarawak
Perkes, A., 2nd officer (steamer *Yesso*)
Pernay, E. D. de, sub-chief 3rd Bureau, Saigon
Perpetuo, A. V., compositor (Typographia Mercantil) Macao
Perpetuo, J. E., court writer, Macao
Perpigna, Arthur de, instructor (Govt. School) Nagasaki
Perrauz, Rev. R. C. missionary, Bangkok
Perregeaux, F., Yedo
Perr.que, J. de F., wardmaster (Military Hospital) Macao
Perrichon, L., contractor, Saigon
Perrimond, —., "Café Restaurant," S'gon

Perrin, A., clerk (Hongkong and Shanghai Bank) Saigon
Perrin, ., restaurateur, Saigon
Perrin, E., hair'r sser, Yokohama
Perry, J. S., clerk (E. D. Sassoon, Sons & Co.) Newchwang
Perry, M., carpe ter, Yedo
Pestonjee, D., clerk (H. Framjee & Co.) Shanghai
Pestonjee, J., storekeeper (D. Nowrojee) Y. kohama
Petel, G. v. P., merchant (G. van Polanel, Petel & Co.) Netherlands Consul, Manila
Petel, G. v. P., Jr., merchant (G. van Polanel Petel & Co.) Manila
Peter, —, carpenter (Arsenal) Foochow
Peter, —, assist. (M. C. Adams & Co.) Nagasaki
Peters, G., clerk (Siemssen & Co.) S'hai
Peters, H., shipchandler (Knoop & Co.) Shanghai
Petersen, —, lightkeeper, Customs, F'chow
Petersen, C. F. W., proprietor (German Tavern) Queen's Road W., and shippingmaster (German Consulate)
Petersen, F. C., master mariner, Bangkok
Petersen, H., boot and shoe maker, N'saki
Petersen, H. A., merchant (H. A. Petersen & Co.) and consul for Demark, Amoy
Petersen, J., clerk (Great Northern Telegraph Co.) Nagasaki
Petersen, P. L., pilot, Foochow
Petersen, P. M., pilot, Ningpo
Petersen, F., pilot, Bangkok
Peterson, G., sergeant (Police Force) Hiogo
Peterson, Peter, barman ("Land We Live In" Tavern) 204, Queen's Road West
Pethick, W. A., clerk (A. Heard & Co.) Peking
Pethick, Wm. N., U.S. vice-consul and interpretor, Tientsin
Petijean, Rt. Rev. F. T. (Roman Catholic Bishop) Yokohama
Petrie, D.; merc'aut, (Thomas Howard & Co.) West Point
Pettier, L'Abbe A. E., mis. apost., Yokohama
Peynet, H., physician (Jap. Govt.) Yedo
Pfaff, I., watchmaker (Muller & Co.) S'hai
Pfaff, L., assistant (Knoop & Co.) Shanghai
Pfaff, L., watchmaker (Muller & Co.) S'hai
Pfaff, R., watchmaker (Muller & Co.) S'hai
Pfoundes, C., director (national S. S. Co. of Nipon) Yokohama
Philidor, D., treasurer, Saigon
Philippe, A., act. manager (Comptoir d'Escompte) Queen's Road
Philips, C., carpenter, R.N. (Thalia)
Phillip, J. W, lieut. commander, U.S.N. (Monocacy)
Philuppi, —, chief artificer (Jap. Govt.) Yedo

Phillips, Chas., master mechanic (Government Railroad) Yokohama
Phillips, G., acting British vice-consul, Foochow
Phillips, P. W., colonel commanding (Royal Artillery)
Phillipps, R. (School of foreign languages) Yedo
Phillips, S. T. L., assistant (Westall, Brand & Co.) Shanghai
Phipps, A. L., merchant (Phipps, Hickling & Co.) Foochow
Phipps, H. G., clerk (Phipps, Hickling & Co.) Foochow
Phœnix, Richard, marshal (U. S. Consulate) Shanghai
Piatkoff, M. T., clerk (Ivanoff & Co.) Hankow
Piazzoli, Rev. L., Roman Catholic Mission, Wellington Street
Picault, —, inspector, Municipality, S'gon
Pichat, J., chief officer (M.M.S. Sindh)
Pichon, L., D.M.P., assistant (Dr. Galle) Shanghai
Pickenpack, V., merchant (Pickenpack, Thies & Co.) and Netherlands Consul Bangkok (absent)
Pickford, C. R. B. P., merchant (Macleod, Pickford & Co.) Cebu (absent)
Pierce, Geo. Henry, merchant (Peele, Hubbell & Co.) and in charge, Danish Consulate, Manila
Pierce, T., "Fulton Market House" Tavern, Yokohama
Piercy, Rev. G., missionary (Wesl. Meth. Miss. Society) Canton (absent)
Pierre, J. B., director, Botanical Gardens, Saigon
Pierdorff A. L., pilot, Swatow
Pierson, Mrs L. H., missionary, Yokohama
Pierson, Rev. Isaac, missionary. Peking
Pietra, A., sister (The Convent) Caine Road
Pigeon, F., teacher (Japanese Government) Yedo
Pigeon, J., drainage foreman, Shanghai
Pigeon, M. (school of Foreign Languages) Yedo
Pigman, G. W., lieutenant com., U.S.N. (Shuclot)
Pignatel, C., storekeeper (Pignatel & Co.) Nagasaki (Saga)
Pignatel, J., general trader, Chefoo
Pignatel, V. L., storekeeper &c. (Pignatel & Co) Nagasaki
Pike, C. H., examiner, Customs, Hankow
Pike, J., captain (Steam-tug Orphan) S'hai
Pike, O. O., clerk (Macleod, Pickford & Co.) Cebu
Pila, V., merchant (Pila, Ulysse & Co.) Shanghai (absent)
Pilcher, Rev. L. W., missionary, Peking
Pilkington, J., bandmaster (Jap. Govt.) Yedo

Pilliet, A., merchant (Ed. Renard & Co.) Saigon (absent)
Pillon, A., merchant (Pillon & Co.) Yokohama
Pim, J. F., manager (*Japan Herald*) Yokohama
Pim, T., merchant (Olyphant & Co.) and acting consul for Netherlands, F'chow
Pinckvoss, J. H., clerk (Siemssen & Co.) Shanghai
Pinel, John, Jr., clerk (A. Heard & Co.) Yokohama
Pinna, F. F. de, compositor (Noronha & Sons)
Pinna, J. de, writer (Naval Yard)
Piñol, Francisco, valuator (Customs) Manila
Pinto, A., hair dresser, Yokohama
Pinto, R., organist and teacher of music (Roman Catholic Church) Mosque Junction
Pinto, Rev. J. F. (Com. of estate of St. José's College) Macao
Pioch, Ainé, —., river pilot, Saigon
Pioch, Jeune, —., river pilot, Saigon
Piotranski, K. de, commission merchant, and agent for Reuter, Hiogo
Piper, Rev. John, Church missionary, Yokohama
Piquet, E., clerk (Walsh, Hall & Co.) Yokohama
Pirie, H. R., employé (U. S. Naval Hospital) Yokohama
Pirkis, A. E., accountant (British Legation) Peking
Piron, —., finisher (Arsenal) Foochow
Piry, P., clerk, Customs, Shanghai
Piry, T., clerk (Arsenal) Foochow
Pistorius, A. A., clerk (Van Oordt & Co.) Yokohama
Pistorius, P. E., agent (Netherlands Trading Society) Yokohama
Pitman, G. D., com. (str. *Kwangtung*) Mosque Terrace
Pitman, John, agent (Japan Railway) Yokohama
Pitman, R., commander, R.N. (*Ringdove*)
Pitman, W. J., constable (Anglo-Chinese Police) Pagoda Anchorage, Foochow
Piton, —., master of the "*Vaico*," Saigon
Piton, Rev. C. P., missionary (Evangelical Missionary Society of Basel)
Pitter, V. P. S., (Council of the Province) surgeon, National Guard, Macao
Pittman, F., R.N., accountant and storekeeper, Royal Naval Victualling Depôt, Yokohama
Placé, A. F., bailiff, Macao
Placé, A. M., sorter (General Post Office)
Placé, C., clerk (Procurador's Department) Macao
Placé, E. W., 2nd officer (str. *Namoa*)
Placé, F. L., clerk (Comptoir d'Escompte de Paris) Queen's Road

Placé, J. L., clerk (P. & O. S. N. Co.) Praya Central
Plate, F., clerk (Renard & Co.) Hiogo
Playfair, G. M. H., student interpreter (British Legation) Peking
Plazuelos, C., employé (Post Office) Manila
Plessis, L'Abbé, M. J., R. C. Missionary, Hakdadi
Plettner, —., master mariner, Bangkok
Plichon, H., Elève Consul (French Consulate) Yokohama
Plitt, C., dispenser (Zobel & Nohr) Manila
Plotnikoff, K., clerk (Matreninsky & Kasantzoff) Kalgan
Plumb, Rev. Nathan J., missionary, F'chow
Plummer, A., butcher (Domoney & Co.) Yokohama
Plunket, J., pilot, Newchwang
Plunkett, J., private (Municipal Police) Yokohama
Ply, F., resident, Yokohama
Poate, T. P., resident, Yedo
Poate, W. H., writer (Naval Yard) Pedder's Wharf
Pocock, J. J., midshipman, R. N. (*Cadmus*)
Pockley, W. N., commander (P. &. O. Service)
Pode, W. Y., accountant (Chartered Bank) Shanghai
Poe, G. L., lieutenant, R.N. (*Cadmus*)
Poesnecker, L., clerk (Arnhold, Karberg & Co.) Praya
Poffin, J., tidewaiter (Customs) Amoy
Pohl, H., government supplier (Pohl Frères) Yokohama
Pohl, J., government supplier (Pohl Frères) Yokohama
Pohl, S., assistant (Pohl Frères) Y'hama
Poirier, Rev. B. (Roman Catholic Church) Nagasaki
Poitevin, L., confectioner, Yokohama
Pol, L. v. de, storekeeper, Nagasaki
Polano, L., merchant (Lunau & Polano) and Danish consul, Hiogo
Pole, G. H., secretary to Engineer in Chief (Government Railroad) Yokohama
Pole, W., consulting engineer (Government Railroad) Yokohama
Polishwolla, M. B., broker (F. B. Cama) Peel Street
Polkinghorne, S., lieut., R.N., Yokohama
Pollard, Edward H., Q.C., barrister, Club Chambers (absent)
Pollard, F. L., clerk (Strachan & Thomas) Yokohama
Polley, S. E., clerk (Wilkin and Robison) Yokohama (absent)
Pollock, A. J., clerk (Chapman, King & Co.) Shanghai
Pollock, W., tidewaiter (Customs) S'hai
Pomeroy, S. W., Jr., merchant and vice-consul for Sweden and Norway (Russell & Co.) Foochow

Pond, J. A., assistant (Municipal Council) Shanghai
Pons, —., pattern-maker (Arsenal) F'chow
Ponti, F. de, assistant (V. Comi) Y'ham
Popoff, P., assist. chinese secretary (Russian Legation) Peking
Portaria, V. de P., merchant (V. de P. Portaria & Co.) Macao
Portoons, H. L., clerk (Ker & Co.) Manila
Porter, A. P., marine surveyor, Hakodadi
Porter, C. E., pilot, Foochow (Anchorage)
Portor, J. C., examiner (Customs) K'keang
Porter, Miss M. (Am. Meth. Epis. Miss.) Peking
Porter, Miss M. H. (Am. Board Com. For. Missions) Peking
Porter, Rev. H. D., missionary, Tien'sin
Portes, Rev. A., R. C. missionary, K'keang
Postel, —., Councillor, Sup. Court, Saigon
Pot, J. J., van der, Italian & Netherlands Consul, and manager (Takasima Colliery) Nagasaki
Pott, —., chief of secretariat (Procureur General's) Saigon
Potts, L. C., lieutenant, H. M. 80th Regt.
Poucelet, H., organist, Sarawak
Poujade, A., physician (Arsenal) Foochow
Poulsen, C. H. O., telegraphist (Gt. Northern Tel. Co.)
Poulsen, O., Electrician (Great Northern Telegraph Co.) Shanghai
Poulson, E. A., telegraphist (Great Northern Tel. Co.)
Powcock, J. G., chief officer (str. Douglas)
Powell, C. S., clerk (Forster & Co.) F'chow
Power, E., engine-driver, Fire Brigade
Power, W., clerk of works (H. B. M. Office of Works) Shanghai
Powers, R. B., marshal (U. S. Consulate) and assistant (Kasaburgh & Co.) Nagasaki
Powrie, James, assist. (Mackenzie & Co.) Shanghai
Powys, Ed., draper (Driscoll & Co.) Yokohama
Poynton, H., lightkeeper (North Saddle Light House) Shanghai
Pradier, A., storekeeper (Pradier & Co.) Yokohama
Prann, W., (Japan Government) Yedo
Prat, Paul, foreman (Govt. Silk Reeling Factory) Yedo
Pratt, R. H., fancy store (Roe, Pratt & Co.) Yokohama
Pratt, N., captain (str. Kiangse) Shanghai
Preciado, T., assist. (J. J. Bischoff & Co.) Manila
Prehn, L. O., merchant (Prehn & Co.) Manila
Prémond, M., assistant (Larrieu & Roque) Saigon
Prentice, J., shipwright (Pootung Foundry) Shanghai
Prestage, Ward. clerk of works (Surveyor General's Department) Albany Road
Preston, Rev. C. F., missionary (American Presb. Miss.) Canton
Preston, Rev. J., missionary (Wes. Meth. Miss. Society) Canton
Preysler, G., merchant (Pan & Co.) Manila
Price, Alex., bill broker, Hankow
Price, C. J., Examiner, (Customs) Amoy
Price, J. M., F. G. S. Surveyor General
Price, R. E., teacher, Osaka College
Price, S., draughtsman (Kiangnan Arsenal) Shanghai
Price, W. G., clerk, act. vice-consul for Denmark (Gilman & Co.) Foochow
Priebee, C., clerk (M. J. B. Hegt) Y'hama
Priego, Don J. C. y, vice-consul in charge for Spain, M'cao
Prieto, L., clerk (S. Baer & Co.) Manila
Prime, E. S., master, U.S.N. (Monocacy)
Primrose, Geo. A., sub. lieut., R.N. (Elk)
Primrose, J. A., merchant (Primrose & Co.) Shanghai
Primrose, W. M., broker, Shanghai
Pringle, Thos., engineer, R.N. (Thistle)
Prior, J. E. H., lieut., H. M. 80th Regt.
Prior, L., assistant accountant (Oriental Bank) Queen's Road
Pritchard, A. T., clerk (Walsh, Hall & Co.) Hiogo
Pritchard, J., fitter (Government Railways) Yokohama
Pritzsche, Rev. C., Rhenish Missionary Society, Longhou
Prockter, —., pilot, Saigon
Prophet, W. W., 4th engineer (str. Douglas)
Provand, A., merchant (A. Provand & Co.) Shanghai
Provost, —., carpenter (Yokoska Arsenal) Yokohama
Provost, —., (Catholic Mission) Peking
Prowse, F., storekeeper (Japan Telegraphs) Yedo
Pruyn, Mrs M., missionary, Yokohama
Pryer, H., merchant (Adamson, Bell & Co.) Yokohama
Pryer, W. B., clerk (Thorne Brothers & Co.) Shanghai (absent)
Puertas, F. Diaz y, printer (Loyzaga & Co.) Manila
Pugh, W., merchant (Evans, Pugh & Co.) Hankow
Pulsipher, C. H., pilot (Newchwang Pilot Co.) Newchwang
Punchard, J. E., master (str. Hailoong)
Pun Lun, photographer, Saigon
Purcell, P. U., tidewaiter, (Customs) H'kow
Purcell, T. A., principal medical officer (Japan Railway) Yokohama
Purchase, E., foreman (China Sugar Refinery) East Point
Purchase, J. W., commander Fort William (P. & O. S. N. Co.)

Purdon, John G., merchant (Purdon & Co.) Shanghai
Purvis, Capt. J. R., R.N., harbour master, Yokohama
Purvis, J., assistant (Lane, Crawford & Co.) Shanghai
Pustau, Wm., merchant (Pustau & Co.) (absent)
Puthon, —., chron. shop (Arsenal) F'chow
Putsey, W. H., surgeon, R.M.L.I., Yokohama
Pye, Edmund, merchant and consul for France and vice-consul U.S. (Elles & Co.) Amoy (Tamsui)
Pye, R. H., merchant (Elles & Co.) Amoy
Pyke, T., merchant (Birley & Co.) Caine Road
Pyne, F., clerk (Government Telegraphs) Nagasaki

Q

Quedons, H. G., pilot, Swatow
Quekett, J. F., clerk, (Adamson, Bell & Co) Shanghai
Quelch, C. B., shipchandler (Quelch & Campbell) Swatow
Quénson, —., carpenter (Arsenal) Foochow
Queri, M., auctioneer (Genato & Co.) Manila
Quick, W. H. (Naval College) Yedo
Quillien, —., caulker (Yokoska Arsenal) Yokohama
Quin, J., tailor, corner of d'Aguilar and Wellington streets
Quin, J. J., interpreter (British Consulate) Nagasaki
Quinby, Revd. G. H., missionary, Osaka
Quintana, P. P., clerk (Blanco, Domingo & Co.) Manila

R

Rabardelle, Rev. —., Roman C. missionary, Bangkok (Banchang)
Rabillié, —., Forger (Arsenal) Foochow
Race, Revd. J., missionary (Wes. Soc.) Hankow (Wusueh)
Rälecker, R., merchant (Krummenacher & Co.) Stanley Street
Rademaker, —., master mariner, Bangkok
Rae, W., assistant, (Llewellyn & Co.) Kobé
Rae, W., examiner (Customs) Chefoo
Rae, W. H., assist. paymaster, R.N. (Teazer)
Raffeneau, —., carpenter (Arsenal) F'chow
Rahimbhoy, F. M., merchant (R. Alladinbhoy)
Rahinsky, Rev. Johannes, miss. (Greek Church Mission) Peking
Raimondi, Very Rev. T. pref. apos. (Roman Catholic Church) (absent)
Rainbow, B., broker, Shanghai
Raitt, P. C., mid., R.N. (Thalia)

Ralston, W., 2nd engineer (Chinese gunboat Sui Tsing)
Ramee, P. A. (Smith, Baker & Co.) Yokohama
Ramiez, Don Simon, counsellor, Ecc. dept., Manila
Ramirez, D. R., counsellor (Bishopric of Yloilo) Manila
Ramirez y Giraudia, publisher, (Diario de Manila) Manila
Ramnaramjee, S., manager (B. Davccan) Hollywood Road
Ramos, J., boarding-house keeper, Jose's Lane
Ramsay, H. F., merchant (Gilman & Co.) Hankow
Ramsay, J., engineer (P. & O. service)
Ramsay, J. S., assistant paymaster, R.N. (Princess Charlotte)
Ramsay, R., fitter (Govt. Railway) Y'hama
Rand, A., clerk (Rand & Co.) Yokohama
Rand, J. (Rand & Co.) Yokohama
Randal, T., pilot, Foochow (Anchorage)
Randell, J., storeman (Naval Yard)
Ranfaing, Rev. R., miss., Bangkok (Chautaboon)
Rangan, W., resident, Yokohama
Rangel, Antonio, accountant (Judicial Par'ment) Macao
Rangel, Q. A., clerk, Treasury
Rangel, S. G., clerk (H. K. & S. Banking Corp.) Shanghai
Ranken, A. A., merchant (Bower, Hanbury & Co.) (absent)
Raonkilde, W., master mariner, Bangkok
Rapalje, Rev. D., miss. (Reformed Church) Amoy
Rapp, F., storekeeper (Blackhead & Co.) Queen's Road
Rappard, C. H. A. (Netherlands Trading Society) Osaka
Rappeport, J. M. (W. Rangan) Yokohama
Rappolt, Chr., merchant (Chs. Germann) Manila
Rasch, C., agent (Textor & Co.) Nagasaki
Rasch, Jacob M., assistant (Thorne, Bros) Shanghai
Rasmussen, N. C., foreman mechanic (Govt. Railway) Yokohama
Raspe, H. (Kniffler & Co.) Hiogo
Raspe, M., clerk (Kniffler & Co.) Osaka
Rastoul, E., commissionaire (M. M. S. S. Ava)
Rateniz, Baron R. Stillfried, photographer (Stillfried & Co.) Yokohama
Rathbone, W., watchmaker (Falconer & Co.) Queen's Road
Rathborne, C. A., M.D., R.N. (Thalia)
Raud, —., aide com. de la marino, Saigon (absent)
Rautenberg, T. H., clerk (Bourjau & Co.) Praya
Ravallo, F., assistant (Hiogo Hotel) Hiogo

Ravel, —, contractor, Saigon
Raven, E. A., clerk (Sander & Co.) Peel St.
Ravetta, F., resident, Hiogo
Ravioli, A., sister (The Convent) Caine Road
Rawlinson, C. J., assistant (Watson & Co.) Shanghai
Ray, E. C., clerk (Russell & Co.) Praya
Ray, J. J., clerk (Russell & Sturgis) Manila
Ray, W. H., clerk (A. Heard & Co.) China Traders' Ins. Office
Raymond, B., (Osaka Hotel) Osaka
Raynal, G., merchant (Raynal & Co.) Stanley Street
Rayner, J. M., captain (steamer *Ningpo*)
Raynor, —, mariner (Jap. Govt.) Yedo
Real, A., merchant (A. Real & Co.) Osaka
Reardon, J. H., assistant (Mariner's Home) Shanghai
Rebbeck, J. G., master, spare light vessel (Customs) Shanghai
Rebello, S., dispenser (Oriental Dispensary) Peel Street
Rech, M., assistant (Gaupp & Co.) Queen's Road
Reddelien, A. (Reddelien & Co.) Nagasaki
Reddelien, G., merchant (L. Kniffler & Co.) Yokohama
Reddie, A. C., clerk (Holliday, Wise & Co.)
Reddie, J., clerk (Holliday Wise & Co.) Shanghai
Reddock, G., lightkeeper (Public Works Department) Yokohama
Redfield, J. B., asst. paymr. U.S.N. (*Monocacy*)
Reding, J. E., consul for Russia, clerk (Heard & Co.) Shanghai
Redlich, A., merchant (Windsor, Redlich & Co.) Bangkok
Reed, W., assistant (Japan Butchery) Yokohama
Reed, W. E. E., clerk R N. (*Cadmus*)
Reeks, A. J., tidewaiter, (Customs) Kewkeang
Rees, C. A., clerk (Carter & Co.) Shanghai
Rees, Wm., merchant (Wm. Rees & Co) Ningpo
Reeve, H., trooper, (British Legation Guard) Yedo
Reeve, J., constable (Sailor's Home) S'hai
Reeve, R., steward (Sailor's Home) Shanghai
Reeves, G., Examiner, (Customs) Ningpo
Reeves, J., chief officer (P. & O. service)
Reeves, W. M., clerk (Westall, Galton & Co.) Foochow
Regenberg, Julius, importer, Yokohama
Rego, A. A., Ensign, Military Department, Macao
Rehders, E., clerk (Pustau & Co.) Canton
Rehematool, A. S. J. M. E., merchant, Canton

Rehfues, M. de, minister plenipotentiary (German Legation) Peking (absent)
Rehemtoola, E., clerk (J. M. Abdool Star)
Reiche, Th. M. (Jap. Govt.) Yedo
Reichert, T., bookkeeper (Blackhead & Co.) Queen's Road
Reid, A. G., M.D. Medical Officer (Customs) Hankow
Reid, D., merchant (Reid, Evans & Co.) Shanghai
Reid, D., chief officer (str. *Powan*)
Reid, E. J., assistant accountant (Oriental Bank) Yokohama
Reid, F., clerk (Olyphant & Co.) Shanghai
Reid, G., assist. (James & Wilson) Y'hama
Reid, G. G., foreman, machine shop (Kiangnan Arsenal) Shanghai
Reid, W., second engineer (str. *Kiukiang*)
Reiff, R., clerk (Carlowitz & Co.) Praya
Reilly, F. E., clerk, (Thompson & Co)
Reimann, F., broker, Wyndham Street
Reimers, C. F., clerk (Jardine, Matheson & Co.) Yokohama
Reimers, O., merchant (Reimers, Bechor & Co.) Hiogo
Reimers, O., clerk (Siemssen & Co.) Queen's Road
Reina, F. S., proprietor (Reina's Hotel) Bangkok
Reiners, W., merchant (Melchers & Co.) Praya
Reis, A., merchant (Reis, Von der Heyde & Co.) Yokohama (absent)
Reis, Ad., merchant (Schultze, Reis & Co.) Hiogo (absent)
Reis, J. S. da S., adjutant (Police Department) Macao
Reiyter, J. S., clerk (Schmidt, Westphal & Co.) Hiogo
Relph, Henry, storekeeper and auctioneer (Lane, Crawford & Co.) Shanghai
Remé, Wm., merchant (Wm. Remé & Co.) Shanghai
Remedios, A., clerk (D. Lapraik & Co.) D'Aguilar Street
Remedios, A. dos, clerk (M. A. Remedios) Macao
Remedios, A. A. dos, clerk (Vogel Hagedorn & Co.)
Remedios, A. A. dos, clerk (J. J. dos Remedios)
Remedios, A. F., clerk (D. Lapraik & Co.)
Remedios, A. F., dos, clerk (Butterfield & Swire) Shanghai
Remedios, C. O. dos, clerk (Remedios & Co.) Gough Street
Remedios, D. A. dos, clerk (Remedios & Co.) Gough Street
Remedios, F. dos, clerk (Union Insurance Society)
Remedios, F. dos, clerk (E. H. Pollard) Shelley Street

Remedios, F. J., clerk (D. Lapraik & Co.) D'Aguilar Street
Remedios, F. T. dos, clerk (Wilkie & Robison) Yokohama
Remedios, G. dos, clerk (Jardine Matheson & Co.)
Remedios, G. M, dos, clerk (Walsh, Hall & Co.) Yokohama
Remedios, J. dos, clerk (Vogel, Hagedorn & Co.) Praya
Remedios, Jaa. A. dos, clerk (Butterfield & Swire)
Remedios, J. A. dos, merchant (Remedios & Co.) Gough Street
Remedios, J. C., dos, clerk (Remedios & Co.) Gough Street
Remedios, J. G., clerk (Chartered Bank)
Remedios, J. H. dos, merchant (J. J. dos Remedios & Co.) Gough Street
Remedios, J. J. dos, merchant (J. J. dos Remedios & Co.) consul general for Portugal, Gough Street
Remedios, J. M. dos, clerk (J. J. dos Remedios & Co.) Gough Street
Remedios, M. A. dos, merchant, Macao
Remedios, M. A. dos, Jr., clerk (M. A. Remedios) Macao
Remedios, S. A., clerk (Butterfield & Swire) Shanghai
Remedios, S. B., clerk (Knoop & Co.) Shanghai
Remedios, V., clerk (J. M. Armstrong)
Remerchiad, —., artisan (Jap. Govt.) Yedo
Remiannikoff, S. J., clerk (Haminoff, Rodionoff & Co.) Hankow
Remusat, M., musician, Shanghai
Renard, Ed., merchant (Renard & Co.) Hiogo (Paris)
Renard, Ed., merchant (Ed. Renard & Co.) Saigon (absent)
Ronfry, A. H., assist. eng., R.N. (Hornet)
Rennell, E., silk inspector (Coare, Lind & Co.) Canton
Rennell, T. B., harbour master (Customs) Newchwang
Rennie, R. T., barrister-at-law, Shanghai
Renucoli, J., constable (French Municipal Council) Shanghai
Repenn, J. A., godown-keeper (Maltby & Co.) Nagasaki
Resident, Jas., master mariner, Bangkok
Restalio, A., assistant (Mess. Mar.)
Retz, F., watchmaker (Schwartz & Co.) Yokohama
Reuchlin, —., "Café Militaire," Saigon
Reusch, Rev. Ch. G. (Evangelical Missionary Society of Basel) Lilong
Reuter, H., assistant (Burgess & Co.) Yokohama
Revest, C., assistant (Mess. Maritimes) Yokohama
Rey, C., draughtsman (Kiangnan Arsenal) Shanghai

Rey, J., clerk (Arsenal) Foochow
Reyes, A., clerk (Rocha & Co.) Manila
Reyes, F., shipchandler (Reyes & Co.) Manila
Reyes, F., clerk (Smith, Bell & Co.) Manila
Reyes, G., clerk (Smith, Bell & Co.) Manila
Reyes, José, shipchandler (Reyes & Co.) Manila
Reyes, M., hairdresser (W. P. Moore) Hongkong Hotel
Reynaud, J., merchant (Maron & Co.) Yokohama
Reynell, H., clerk (Turner & Co.) Shanghai
Reynell, S., assistant (Municipal Council Offices) Shanghai
Reynier, A., chief officer (M. M. S. Tigre)
Reynier, J. B., chief officer (M. M. S. Peiho)
Reynolds, R. A., Pootung Point, Shanghai
Reynolds, W. H. H., pilot, Bangkok
Reynvaan, J. M., merchant (Van Oordt & Co.) Yokohama
Rhein, H. H. G., usher (Netherlands' Consular Court) Shanghai
Rhein, J., assistant (Netherlands Legation) Peking
Rhinehart, B. F., mid., U. S. N. (Yantic)
Rhodes, P., clerk (D. Sassoon, Sons & Co.) Foochow
Risch, John, shipbuilder, &c. (Boyd & Co.) Shanghai
Ribeiro, A. A. V., foreman compositor (Daily Press Office)
Ribeiro, A. F., clerk (Borneo Co., Limited)
Ribeiro, A. V., clerk (Jardine, Matheson & Co.)
Ribeiro, F. A. V., chief clerk (Recebedoria das Decimas) Macao
Ribeiro, F. V., clerk (Auditor General's Department)
Ribeiro, F. V., secretary (Junta dos Langamento das Decimas) Macao
Ribeiro, J. da S., ensign (Timor Corps) Macao
Ribeiro, J. M. V., Hiogo News office, Hiogo
Ribeiro, J. S. V., clerk (Hook, Son & Co.)
Ribeiro, J. V., clerk (A. Astorquia) Macao
Ribeiro, L. V., purser (str. Poyang)
Ribeiro, M. J. V., consul for Portugal (Imprimerie Commerciale) Saigon
Ribert, F., assistant (Vrard & Co.) Shanghai
Ribiere, —., forger (Arsenal) Foochow
Ribiero, F. C. C., clerk (Japan Railway)
Rice, E. W., commission agent (Thorne Rice & Co.) Shanghai
Ricci, T., Sister (The Convent) Caine Road
Rice, J., Engineer R.N., (Mosquito)
Rice, N. E., Interpreter, U. S. Legation, Yedo
Rich, H. B., Lieut., R.E.
Richard, Mdme., dressmaker &c. Saigon
Richard, P., boatswain, R.N. (Rinaldo)
Richard, Rev. T., missionary, Chefoo

Richards, C. W., assist. (Mackenzie & Co.) Shanghai
Richards, F. J., lieut. colonel commanding, R.M., Yokohama
Richard, G. C., pilot (Pilot Company) Newchwang
Richards, Mrs., assistant (Sayle & Co.) S'hai
Richardson, F., merc' ant (Findlay, Richardson & Co.) Yokohama (absent)
Richardson, S. B., master (Tug Fame)
Richardson, T. W., commission merchant (Bradley & Co.) consul for Netherlands, Swatow
Richie, R., Resident, Yedo
Richaud, F., chief, 4th bureau, Saigon
Richmann, J., clerk (Markwald & Co.) Bangkok
Richmond, T. G., clerk (Lane, Crawford & Co.) Yokohama
Richten, —., (Falck's Hotel) Bangkok
Richter, G., clerk (E. Schellhass & Co.)
Richter, G., clerk (Richter & Co.) Hiogo
Richter, R. storekeeper, Hiogo
Rickard, G. P., chief clerk (Naval Yard)
Rickards, F., barman ("Rising Sun" Tavern) Queen's Road, W.
Rickards, F., assist. (P. Smith's Boarding House) Queen's Road
Ricke, Th., clerk (Muller & Co.) Shanghai
Ricket, C. B., assistant acct. (H'kong and S'kai Banking Corporation) Yokohama
Ricketts, G. T., consul (British Consulate) Manila
Rickett, John, agent (P. & O. S. N. Co.) Yokohama
Ricou, W., clerk (Renard & Co.) Saigon
Riddle, C. (Jap Railway) Osaka
Rider, H., assistant (Sayle & Co.) S'hai
Ridez, Sister Jeanne (Hôpital St. Joseph) Ningpo
Ridings, G. E., assist. (Boyd & Co.) S'hai
Riener, —., teacher (Jap. Govt.) Yedo
Rietschler, R., watchmaker (C. Gombert) Shanghai
Rieutord, N., assist. (M. M. Co.'s Office) Saigon
Rifkens, C., watchmaker, Sarawak
Rigby, G., eng., R.N. (Thetis)
Rigodit, F., commander (M. M. S. Peiho)
Ring, A. R., chief officer (Chinese gunboat Ling-feng)
Ringer, F., merchant (Holme, Ringer & Co.) Nagasaki
Ringer, J. M., assist. (Drysdale, Ringer & Co.) Shanghai
Rio, E. A. de, lieutenant (Tejo) Macao
Rios, M. R. de los, treasurer (Mint) Manila
Ristelhubert, M., acting consul, French consulate, Tientsin
Ritchie, Rev. H., missionary, Takow
Ritchie, J., engineer, R.N (Iron Duke)
Ritchie, J., assist. examiner (Customs) S'hai
Ritter, H., Ph. D. (Imperial College) Yedo

Rival, J., chief officer (M. M. S. S. Ava)
Rivasseau, —., founder (Arsenal) Foochow
Rivington, Chas., agent China Tel. Co. and merchant, Shanghai
Rizzi, Pere J., missionary (Roman Catholic Mission) Ningpo (Taichow)
Roa, R., broker, Shanghai
Roach, H., merchant (C. Adds) Yokohama
Roach, Rev. N. A., London Miss. Soc., Canton
Roberts, J. T., linguist (Procurador's Department) Macao
Roberdeau, —.; teacher (Arsenal) Foochow
Roberdeau, —., commis. de marine, Saigon
Robers, W. von, clerk (Pustau & Co.) Pottinger Street
Robert, J. (Normal School) Saigon
Roberton, R C., clerk (Ker & Co.) Manila
Roberts, C., compositor (Hongkong Times)
Roberts, E., fitter (Gov. Railways) Yokohama
Roberts, J., boatswain, R.N. (Midge)
Roberts, A. S., silk inspector (Coare, Lind & Co.) Canton
Roberts, H. (Govt. Railway) Yokohama
Roberts, H., constable, Hankow
Roberts, J. H., clerk (Gilman & Co.) Praya
Roberts, H M., clerk (J. D. Carroll & Co.) Yokohama
Roberts, J. P., surveyor, Shanghai
Roberts, —., engineer (Jap. Govt.) Yedo
Roberts, W., carpenter, R.N., Naval Yard, Shanghai
Robertson, A., assist. (Boyd & Co.) N'saki
Robertson, A. L., clerk (C. & J. Mar. Ins.) Shanghai
Robertson, Sir Brooke, C B., consul (British Consulate) Canton
Robertson, Geo., captain (Chinese gunboat Chen-to)
Robertson, H. G., shipchandler (Robertson & Co.) Foochow
Robertson, J., agent (Oriental Bank) Yokohama
Robertson, James, clerk (Lane, Crawford & Co.) Queen's Road
Robertson, James, Fitter (Government Railroad) Yokohama
Robertson, J. A. surgeon, R.N. (Mosquito)
Robertson, P., clerk (Smith, Archer & Co.) Shanghai
Robertson, P., engineer, R.N. (Avon)
Robertson, Russell, consul (British Consulate) Yokohama
Robertson, T., clerk (Reid, Evans & Co.) Shanghai
Robertson, Wm., inspector (Glover & Co. (in liquidation) Nagasaki
Robertson, W., iron founder (Boyd & Co.) Nagasaki
Robeson, W., founder, Arsenal, Foochow
Robilliard, W. S., clerk (Chart. Merc. Bank) Yokohama

Robin, —., carpenter (Arsenal) Foochow
Robins, —., furniture dealer, Shanghai
Robinson, A., solicitor, Shanghai
Robinson, C. N., sub-lieut, R.N. (*Teaser*)
Robinson, John, broker, Morrison Hill
Robinson, J. S., draper (Rose & Co.) Wellington Street
Robinson, W. J., clerk (Butterfield & Swire) Foochow
Robison, J. S., silk inspector, Shanghai
Robison, R. D., merchant (Wilkin & Robison) Yokohoma (absent)
Rocha, A. A. da, purser (Hongkong, Canton and Macao Steam-boat Company)
Rocha, C. V. da, colonial treasurer, capt. Macao Battalion, Macao
Rocha, J. G. da, accountant (General Post-office)
Rocha, V. C. da, chief clerk (Recebedoria das Decimas) Macao
Rocha, V C., Jun., clerk (Naval Yard)
Rocha, V. F. da, clerk (David Sassoon, Sons & Co.)
Rocha, Y., merchant (Y. Rocha & Co.) Manila
Roche, H.C., nav. sub. lieut., R N. (*Cadmus*)
Roché, —., sub. inspector, Municipality, Saigon
Rochechouart, Comte J. de, 1st Secretary (French Legation) Peking
Rocher, L., clerk (Customs) Peking
Rochkugel, A., assistant (L. Haber) Yokohama
Rock, W B., engineer, R.N. (*Iron Duke*)
Rockett, H. S., asst. eng., R.N. (*Thetis*)
Rodatz, G. C. F., shipchandler (Freerks, Rodatz & Co.) Praya
Roddier, Sister Louise (Maison de St. Vincent) Ningpo
Rodewald, J. F., merchant (Rodewald & Schönfeld) Foochow and Shanghai
Rodgers, J. A., master, U.S.N. (*Hartford*)
Rodionoff, A. L., merchant (Haminoff, Rodionoff & Co.) Hankow
Rodionoff, N. L., merchant (Haminoff, Rodionoff & Co.) Hankow
Rodrigues, A. J., sorter (Post Office)
Rodrigues, B. V., compositor (*Nagasaki Gazette*) Nagasaki
Rodrigues, F. P., clerk (Club Lusitano)
Rodrigues, J., 2nd clerk (Recebedoria das Decimas) Macao
Rodrigues, J. S., clerk (Stamp Office)
Rodrigues, M., compositor (De Souza & Co.)
Rodrigues, S. M., constable (U. S. Consulate) Foochow
Rodrigues, Theo. J., prof. philosophy (St. Joseph's College) Macao
Rodway, W. H., acting resident, Sarawak
Roelofs, J. J., student interpreter (Netherlands Legation) Peking
Roeser, P. A. (Imperial Copper Works) Hiogo

Rogers, E., clerk (China & Japan Trading Company) Shanghai
Rogers, F. R., clerk (Lammert, Atkinson & Co.)
Rogers, J., clerk (Martin, Dyce & Co.) Manila
Rogers, J., dentist, Arbuthnot Road
Rogers, R. W. S., sub-lieut., R.N. (*Iron Duke*)
Rogers, W., assist. engineer (Government Railroads) Yokohama
Rogerson, W. J., clerk (Lane, Crawford & Co.) Queen's Road
Roggers George, tax-collector (Municipal Council) Shanghai
Roglin, —., engineer and coppersmith, Saigon
Rohde, C., clerk (Reis, Von der Heyde & Co.) Yokohama
Röhl, E., assistant (S. C. Farnham & Co.) Shanghai
Röhl, E., clerk (Russell & Co.) Shanghai
Röhl, G. (Hunt's Wharf) Shanghai
Röhr, W., clerk (Kniffler & Co.) Nagasaki
Roldan, J. C., draftsman (Morris, Barlow & Co.) Manila
Rollet, Madame, storekeeper, Saigon
Rolls, J., superintendent engineer (Marine Department) Kiangnan Arsenal, S'hai
Roman, G., gunner (*Waterwitch*) Shanghai
Romano, A. G., vice-consul (Portuguese Consulate) Gough Street
Rondard, —., saddler, Saigon
Ronnenkamp, W. H., clerk (Great North. Teleg. Co.) Amoy
Rooks, A. J., general assistant (*Evening Courier*) Shanghai
Roper, H., moulder (P. & O. S. N. Co.) Queen's Road West
Ropke, C. K., stevedore (P. M. S. S. Co.) Yokohama
Roque, H., clerk (Larrieu & Roque) Saigon (in the interior)
Roque, V., merchant (Larrieu & Roque) Saigon (absent)
Roquerbe, H., manager (Comptoir d'Escompte de Paris) Saigon
Rosa, M. d'A., ensign, National Guard, Macao
Rosanquet, S. S., sub-lieut., R.N. (*Thetis*)
Rose, E., assistant (E. R. Handley) Praya West
Rose, Edward N., clerk (Boyd & Co.) Amoy
Rose, G., clerk (Whitfield and Dowson) Yokohama
Rose, J. F., clerk (Control Department) and draper (Rose & Co.) Wellington St.
Rose, Miss J., milliner (Rose & Co.) Wellington Street (absent)
Rose, S. C., clerk (Russell & Co.) U. S. Consular agent and vice consul for Netherlands, Kewkeang (absent)

Rose, T. J., clerk (Borneo Co. Limited) Queen's Road
Rose, W., assist. (Hiogo Iron Works) Hiogo
Rosenbaum, Jos., merchant, Chefoo
Rosenstand, A., resident, Yedo
Rosenthal, J. W., resident, Yokohama
Ross, D., assistant (Vulcan Iron Works) Hiogo
Ross, G., clerk (Whitfield & Dowson) Yokohama
Ross, J., light-keeper, White Dog Light House, Foochow
Ross, J., tidewaiter, Customs, Shanghai
Ross, John, merchant (Ker & Co.) and Belgian consul, Manila (absent)
Ross, Rev. J., missionary (United Presb. Mis.) Newchwang
Ross, William, watchmaker (G. Falconer & Co.) Queen's Road
Ross, W. M., hairdresser, Nagasaki
Rossich, A., keeper of the bridge of boats, Ningpo
Rost, W., clerk (Carlowitz & Co.) Canton
Roth, T., merchant (Hertzog & Roth) Yokohama
Rothwell, A. W., tea inspector (Olyphant & Co.) Foochow
Rothwell, T., merchant (Rothwell, Love & Co.) Shanghai
Rotschke, C. A., merchant (Andrews & Co.) Manila (absent)
Rouet, —., watchman (Mess. Mar.) Saigon
Rouger, Rev. F., R.C. missionary, K'keang
Rouhaud, H., chancelier (French Consulate) Shanghai
Roule, —., resident, Yokohama
Roumain, de la Touché, councillor, Sup. Court, Saigon
Roupell, S. B., sub-lieut., R.N. (*Thistle*)
Rouqette, G. de, 2nd secretary (French Legation) Peking
Rousseau, Rev., P. L., missionary (French R. C. Mission) Bangkok
Rousset, L., prof. of chemistry (Arsenal) Foochow
Roussin, L., chief engineer (M. M. S. S. *Tigre*)
Roux, —., pilot, Saigon
Röver, B., clerk (Bohre & Co.) Saigon
Rovira, —., judge, Manila
Rowband, C. F., asst. sect. (Chart. Merc. Bank) Shanghai
Rowbotham, W., asst. eng., U.S.N., (*Palos*)
Rowe, Alfred, clerk (Thomas & Mercer) Canton
Rowe, Miss. (Wes. Meth. Miss. Soc.) C'ton
Rowe, N., engineer, R.N. (*Dwarf*)
Rowett, Hon. R., merchant (Holliday, Wise & Co.) Wyndham Street
Roxas, J. B., rope manufacturer, Manila
Roxas, P. P., assist. (J. B. Roxas) Manila
Roy, H. L., 2nd officer (Sassoon's Str. *Hindostan*)

Roy, J. A., clerk (Lane, Crawford & Co.) Yokohama
Roza, A. B. da, clerk (Birley & Co.)
Roza, B. M. A., retired lieut. colonel, Macao
Roza, B. M. das N. A., surgeon (Police Dept.) Macao
Roza, E. da, 2nd class interpreter (Procurador's Dept.) Macao
Roza, F. da, compositor (Nishin-shin-ji-shi) Yedo
Roza, F. H. da, assist. treasurer (Municipal Council) Macao
Roza, J. da, barber (J. da Roza & Co.) Wellington Street
Roza, J. F. da, clerk (Birley & Co.)
Roza, J. M. da, clerk (St. Joseph's College) Macao
Roza, J. M. da, junr., clerk (St. Joseph's College) Macao
Roza, M. da, clerk (Birley & Co.)
Roza, S. da, compositor (St. Joseph's College) Macao
Roza, S. V., assistant (Chinese Emigration Office) Macao
Rozario, A. A. do, printer (Mercantile Printing Office) Shanghai
Rozario, A. E. do, bailiff (Mun. Council) Macao
Rozario, A. F. do, compositor (Typographia Mercantil) Macao
Rozario, A. F. do, manager (Canton Hotel) Canton
Rozario, A. J. do, assist. (D. Sassoon, Sons & Co.)
Rozario, C., master mariner, Bangkok
Rozario, C. do, clerk (Melchers & Co.)
Rozario, C. E. do, printer (Mercantile Printing Office) Shanghai
Rozario, E. F. (D. Sassoon Sons & Co.) Praya
Rozario, F., chemist, Shanghai
Rozario, F. de, writer, Rejang outstation, Sarawak
Rozario, F. J. do, clerk (M. A. Remedios) Macao
Rozario, H. do, compositor (*China Mail* Office)
Rozario, J. de, writer (Bintulu outstation) Sarawak
Rozario, Januario J. do, overseer (*China Mail* Office) Bridges Street
Rozario, J. E, clerk (Chartered Mercantile Bank) Shanghai
Rozario, J. M., clerk (Chartered Bank)
Rozario, J. P., de, compositor (*Japan Mail* Office) Yokohama
Rozario, L. A., clerk (P. M. S. S. Co.) Praya West
Rozario, L. do, clerk (E. Sharp and Toller)
Rozario, L. M. do, messenger (Municipal Council) Macao
Rozario, M. C. do, merchant (Rozario & Co.) Stanley Street

Rozario, M. das N do, clerk (Chinese Emigration office) Macao
Rozario, M. J. do, clerk (H. & W. Dock Co.) Kowloong
Rozario, P. H. do, clerk (Holliday, Wise & Co.) Shanghai
Rozario, R. A. do, interpreter (Supreme Court) D'Aguilar Street
Rozario, R do, clerk (J. J. dos Remedios & Co) Gough Street
Rozorio, R. M., assistant (Eastern Ex. Aust. and China Tel. Co.) Shanghai
Rozorio, S. R. do, manager (Frisby & Co.)
Roze, T., capitaine d'armement (Larrieu & Roque) Saigon
Ruas, A. J., ensign (Tim. 'r Corps) Macao
Rubery, Henry, assist. (Customs) Swatow, (absent)
Rudland, Rev. W. D. and family, Missionary, Ningpo
Ruel, J. (Hotel des Colonies) Yedo
Ruff, T., silk inspector (Carlowitz & Co.) Canton
Ruiz, Don J., consul for Spain, Saigon
Ruiz, V., clerk (Loney & Co.) Cebu
Ruppaner, J , clerk (Labhart & Co.) Manila
Ruprecht, W., secretary (German Consulate) Shanghai
Ruschenberger, C. W., master, U.S.N. (Iroquois)
Rusden, A. W. G , public tea inspector, Foochow (absent)
Russell, G. W., sub-lieut., R.N. (Iron Duke)
Russel, H., clerk (Bacherach, Oppenheimer & Co) Saigon
Russell, H. V., commander (steamer Appi)
Russell, J., junior police magistrate (absent)
Russell, Jonathan, merchant (Russell & Sturgis) vice consul, U.S., Sweden and Norway, Manila
Russell, Joseph, accountant (Oriental Bank) Yokohama (absent)
Russell, M., storekeeper (J. Curnow & Co.) Yokohama
Russell, R. P., clerk (A. Dent & Co.) Shanghai
Russell, Rt. Rev. W. A., bishop (Ch. Eng. Miss. Society) Ningpo
Russell, R., broker, Shanghai
Russell, T., supt. (Great Northern Tel. Co.) Nagasaki
Russell, T. O., auctioneer and commission agent, Nagasaki
Russell, W. B., student (Customs) Peking
Rustomjee, C., merchant (Cawasjee, Pallanjee & Co.) Shanghai
Rustomjee, P., merchant (Cawasjee, Pallanjee & Co.) Shanghai
Ruthven, J., tidewaiter, (Customs) Canton
Ruttmann, H , clerk (Arnhold, Karberg & Co.) Praya
Ruttmann, Theo., clerk (Labhart & Co.) Manila
Ruttonjee, M., clerk (Framjee, Hormusjee & Co.) Shanghai
Ruttonjee, R., merchant, Foochow
Ruttunjee, B., shopkeeper (M. Jumsetjee) Peel Street
Ruttunjee, D., merchant (D. Ruttunjee & Co.) Lyndhurst Terrace
Rnyter, L., clerk (Schmidt, Westphal & Co.) Nagasaki
Ryan, W. S., clerk (Russell & Sturgis) Manila
Ryan, Thos., wardmaster (Civil Hospital)
Ryder, F. H., master (steam tug Maggie Lauder) Shanghai
Rye, J., carpenter (Chinese str. Peng-chao-hai)
Ryle, —., assist. ("Snug Hotel and Bowling Saloon") Nagasaki
Rylander, G., tidewaiter (Customs) Shanghai
Ryrie, Hon. Phineas, merchant (Turner & Co.) Queen's Road

S

Sá, A. F. de, clerk (Jardine, Matheson & Co.) Shanghai
Sá, F., de, clerk (Lane, Crawford & Co.) Tank Lane
Sá, H. de, interpreter (Portuguese Consulate) Bangkok
Sá, L. J., de, clerk (Walsh, Hall & Co.) Yokohama
Saboureau, —., aide com. de la marine, Saigon
Sackerman, E., clerk (Tillson, Hermann & Co.) and secretary (German Consulate) Manila
Sadewasser, O., clerk (Thorel & Co.) Yokohama
Sadler, Rev. J., missionary (London Miss. Society) Amoy
Sagar, Thomas, chief engineer, R.N. (Rinaldo)
Sage, H., constable (British Consulate) Swatow
Sagor, E. M., clerk (R. Dunjeebhoy & Co.) Hollywood Road
Saillant, —., clerk (Ed. Renard & Co.) Saigon
Sake, N. K., clerk (Engwat, Brother & Co.) Amoy
Saladin, Rev. S., missionary (French Roman Catholic Mission) Bangkok
Sales, Sister F. de, Asyle de la Ste. Enfance
Sales, V. A., interpreter (French Consulate) Canton
Sallardo, A., lieut. col. (Mar. Art.) Manila
Salmon, Rev. A. (R. C. Church) Nagasaki
Salter, A. E., vice consul for Netherlands, and commission agent, Chinkeang
Saltzkorn, E., merch. (Behre & Co.) Saigon
Salvaire, —., tinman, Saigon

balvan, Pere H., missionary (Roman Cath. Mission) Shanghai
Salway, W., architect (Wilson and Salway) Queen's Road
Sam Januario, H. E. Viscount de, Governor of Macao
Samat, —., captain (M. M. S. S. *Nil*)
Sambuck, J., proprietor (Eureka Hotel) Nagasaki
Sami, V., assistant steward (General Hospital) Yokohama
Sampaio, E. P., officer, Macao
Sampaio, M. de C., captain (Military Department) Macao
Sampson, A. F., boarding officer (Harbour Master's Department) Praya West
Sampson, E., master of the *Saltee*, Saigon
Sampson, Theo., agent (British West India Emigration Society) Canton
Sams, W. F. B., partner (China Sugar Refinery) East Point
Samson, D., inspector (Municipal Council) Osaka
San Buenaventura, A., assistant (Loyzaga & Co.) Manila
Sanches, J. M., druggist (French Dispensary) 131a Queen's Road
Sanches, V. F. D., clerk (Chartered Mercantile Bank) Shanghai
Sancho, José, engraver (Mint) Manila
Sandeman, F., teacher of English (Public Works Department) Yokohama
Sander, F., merchant (Sander & Co.) Peel Street (absent)
Sanders, W., assist. examiner (Customs) Shanghai
Sandford, W. Graham, second secy. (British Legation) Peking
Sandilands, J. A., broker, Wyndham Street
Sandner, E., Judge (Tribunal de Commerce) and Consul for Belgium, Saigon
Sandred, —., ecrivain de marine, Saigon
Sands, G. U., marine supdt. (Hongkong, Canton and Macao Steamboat Company) Castle Road
Sands, W. G., merchant (Hughes & Co.) Osaka and Hiogo
Sandwith, J. H., lieut. and adjutant, R. M., Yokohama
Sangster, C. F. A., cathedral organist, and clerk (Registrar General's Department)
Sangster, T., signalman (Customs) Shanghai (Pootung)
Santos, A. F. dos, compositor (*Daily Press* Office)
Santos, E. dos, clerk (Brown & Co.) Taiwan
Santos, J. M., compositor (*Japan Mail* Office) Yokohama
Santos, Rev. M. A. dos, vice-rector (St. Joseph's College) Macao
Sapoorjee, E., clerk (Nowrojee & Co.) Yokohama
Sapoorjee, E., clerk (P. & O. S. N. Co.)

Sarda, G., assist (Gas Company) Yokohama
Sarda, —., professor (Yokoska Arsenal) Yokohama
Sardinha, F. P., lieut. (Police Department) Macao
Sargent, T., engineer (P. & O. Service)
Sarloff, V., merchant, Hiogo
Sarthou, —., catholic missionary, Peking
Sartorious, P., chemist, Manila
Sass, —., master mariner, Bangkok
Sassi, Rev. P., R. C. missionary, Sewkeang
Sassoon, E. E. clerk (E. D. Sassoon & Co.)
Sassoon, F. D., merchant (D. Sassoon, Sons & Co.)
Sassoon, J. E., merchant (E. D. Sassoon & Co.) Shanghai
Sassoon, S. D., merchant (D. Sassoon, Sons & Co.) Praya
Satow, E. M., Japanese secretary (British Legation) Yedo
Sauger, P. M., clerk (Dauver & Co.) Amoy
Saul, G. M., clerk (Ker & Co.) Yloilo
Saul, J. S., clerk (D. Sassoon, Sons & Co.) Shanghai
Saul, M. M., clerk (D. Sassoon, Sons & Co.) Praya
Saunders, A., lieut. and adjutant, H. M. 80th Regiment
Saunders, Capt. J. C., marine surveyor, (chup Min) and Arsenal, Foochow
Saunders, G., sexton (St. John's Cathedral) and usher, Police Magistrates' Court, Arbuthnot Road
Saunders, H. C., assistant (Wm. Saunders) Shanghai
Saunders, W., photographer, Shanghai
Saunderson, J. P., assistant tide-surveyor, (Customs) Foochow
Sauné, B., Tax Collector (French Secretary's Office) Shanghai
Saupivius, —., mission Catholique, Peking
Saura, C., clerk (Sietas & Co.) Chefoo
Sauze, —., commander (*Fleurus*) Saigon
Savacho, D., assist. (Macleod, Pickford & Co.) Manila
Savatier, —., surgeon (Yokoska Arsenal) Yokohama
Sawyer, F. E., mid., U.S.N. (*Hartford*)
Saxthorph, W., master mariner, Bangkok
Sayce, J. N., clerk (Phipps, Hickling & Co.) Foochow
Sayle, D., assist. (Sayle & Co.) Alexandra Terrace (absent)
Sayle, R., draper (Sayle & Co.) (absent)
Sayle, T. H., assist. (Sayle & Co.) S'hai
Sayle, W. J., examiner (Customs) Hankow
Sayn, Henri (Sayn & Co.) secretary (French Municipal Council) Shanghai
Saymac, —., chief engineer (M. M. S. S. *Nil*)
Scarborough, Rev. Wm., missionary (Wes. Miss. Society) Hankow
Scarutchia, J. E., harbour master, Macao

FOREIGN RESIDENTS.   Sch   Sco   83

Schaab, W., clerk (Pickenpack, Thies & Co.) Bangkok
Schaal, Ferd, assistant (Hecht, Lilienthal & Co.) Yokohama
Schaar, R, clerk (Dreyer & Co.) Queen's Road
Schaefer, L., electrician (Govt. Telegraphs) Yedo
Schaeffer, A., clerk (Reis, Von der Heyde & Co.) Yokohama
Schaefer, F., clerk (Hecht, Lilienthal & Co.) Yokohama
Schaumlöffel, H., tidewaiter (Customs) Swatow
Schaeffer, G., clerk (Overbeck & Co.) S'hai
Scheffer, J. F., shipchandler, Praya
Scheidecker, —., finisher (Arsenal) F'chow
Schellhass, Edward, merchant (E. Schellhass & Co) (absent)
Schenck, W. S., clerk, (Customs) Shanghai
Schenk, C., teacher (First College) Yedo
Schenk, W. S., 2nd lieut. mr'ines, U.S.N. (Lackawanna)
Scheppelmann, C., accountant and bookkeeper, Shanghai
Schereschewsky, Rev. S. J. J., missionary (Am. Board Prot. Epis. Church) Peking
Scherzer, F., chancelier interpreter (French Legation) Peking
Scherzinger, L. S., assistant (Windsor, Redlich & Co.) Bangkok
Scheuten, H. A., merchant (Schutt, Scheuten & Co.) Hiogo
Schilles, —., chief artificer (Japan Govt.) Yedo
Schinnie, O., commission agent, Yokohama
Schjoth, F., assistant, (Customs) N'chwang
Schleming, C., overseer (Naconchaisée Sugar Factory) Bangkok
Schlick, R, consul for Austro-Hungary, Shanghai and Chinkeang
Schluter, P., compradore (Schluter & Strandt) Hakodadi
Schmid, E., merchant (H. Ahrens & Co) Yokohama (absent)
Schmid, P., teacher (Gaim' sho) Yedo
Schmidt,—., engineer (tug Algerine) Taku
Schmidt, C. (For. Mis. Pres. Ch., U.S.A.) Shanghai (Soochow)
Schmidt, C. H., stevedore, Yokohama
Schmidt, C W., assistant (Pootung Lumber Yard) Shanghai
Schmidt, Edouard, resident, Yokohama
Schmidt, H. clerk,(Arnhold, Karberg & Co.) Praya
Schmidt, J. M., merchant, bill collector &c., Shanghai
Schmidt, N. C., assist. (Great North. Tel. Co.) Shanghai
Schmidt, T. P., assistant (Eureka Bowling Saloon) Yokohama
Schmidt, W., gunsmith (W. Schmidt & Co.) Queen's Road
Schmidt, W., secretary (C. and J. Marine Ins. Co-) Shanghai
Schmitt, Rev.—., missionary, Bangkok (Petrin)
Schneider, T.; clerk (Vogel, Hagedorn & Co) Praya
Schnell, T., clerk (F. Peil) Peddar's Wharf
Schner, S, furniture depot, Yokohama
Schoene, F., merchant (Valmale, Schoene & Milsom) Yokohama
Schoenke, F., watchmaker, &c., Foochow
Schofield, R., general broker, Shanghai
Schofield, W. K., surgeon, U. S. N. (Lackawanna)
Schoker, H. J. A. C., M.D., Hiogo
Schomburg, A., clerk (E. Schellhas & Co.) Shanghai
Schonfeld, F., merchant (Rodewald, Schonfeld & Co.) Foochow
Schönhard, G. clerk (Nachtrieb, Leroy & Co.) Shanghai
Schonhardt, H., clerk (Lane, Crawford & Co.) Yokohama
Schöning, H., merchant (Reis, Von der Heyde & Co.) Hiogo
Schoyer, E. A., merchant (Sitwell, Schoyer & Co.) Yokohama
Schrader, H. L, watchmaker, Shanghai
Schraub, E, shipchandler (Busch, Schraub & Co.) Yokohama
Schriever, W., clerk (Siemssen & Co) Queen's Road
Schröder, E, storekeeper (Sietas & Co.) Chefoo
Schroeder, A., clerk (K. Schroeder) Saigon
Schroeder, K., merchant, Saigon
Schroeder, Miss F., (German Foundling House) West Point
Schultz, C. A., assistant (Gt. Northern Tel. Co.) Shanghai
Schultz, G., chief officer (German str. China)
Schultz, H. M., clerk (Bourjau & Co.)
Schultze, Ad., merchant (Schultze, Reis & Co.) Hiogo
Schultze, F. A., shipchandler and storekeeper (Schultze & Co) Newchwang
Schuster, J. T., Steward, Sailor's Home
Schütt, J., merchant (Schütt, Seheuten & Co.) Hiogo
Schütze, C. H. F., merchant (Wm. Remé & Co.) Shanghai
Schutze, F. S., merchant (Margesson & Co.) Macao (absent)
Schwabe, R. S., merch. (Kingdon, Schwabe & Co.) Yokohama
Schwartz, F., watchmaker (E. Schwartz & Co.) Yokohama
Scoble, J. W., engineer, R. N. (Iron Duke)
Scoti, Scoto, resident, Yokohama
Scotland, J. J., 3rd engineer (str. Hailoong)
Scott, A. B., nav. sub-lieut., R. N. (Tenzer)
Scott, B. C., asst. paymaster, R. N. (Thistl)

Scott, C. M., M.D. (Scott & Scott) Swatow
Scott, Capt. D , marine surveyor & shipping reporter, Yokohama
Scott, D., assistant (W. McDonald) Yokohama
Scott, E. J., M.D. (Scott & Scott) Swatow
Scott, George O., acting acct. (Oriental Bank) Queen's Road
Scott, J., engineer (Jap. Govt.) Yedo
Scott, J., engineer, Hakodadi (Sado Isld.)
Scott, J., student interpreter (British Legation) Peking
Scott J. (Scott & Frost) Hiogo
Scott, J. H., clerk (Butterfield & Swire) Queen's Road (absent)
Scott, J. K. (Ahrens & Co.) Yedo
Scott, J. L., clerk (Birley, Worthington & Co.) Shanghai
Scott, John M., commission agent (Scott & Co.) Hiogo
Scott, M., proprietor ("Brooklyn Hotel") Yokóhama
Scott, M. M., teacher (First College) Yedo
Scott, T., shipwright and blacksmith, C'foo
Scott, T., resident, Shanghai
Scott, W., 3rd engineer (steamer *Yesso*)
Scott, W., clerk (Inglis & Co)
Seabra, F. A., clerk (A Heard & Co.)
Seabrook, Wm , chief clerk (Shanghai Gas Co.) Shanghai
Seabrook, W., clerk (J. S. Baron) S'hai
Seabury, S., mid., U.S.N. (*Iroquois*)
Seaman, J. F., merchant (Olyphant & Co.) Albany
Searle, J., Shanghai Hotel, Shanghai
Searle, J., Boatswain, R.N. (*Kestrel*)
Searle, Mrs. J., draper, Yokohama
Becker, E., hatter (M. Secker & Co) Manila
Sedgewick, E. W., 2nd officer (*Wellington*) Shanghai
Sodgwick, Robert, clerk (Heard & Co.)
Sednoff, N. N., clerk (A. D. Startseff) T'sin
Seó,—., postmaster, Saigon
Seel, A. B., clerk (Hall and Holtz) S'hai
Segar, H., assist. (Customs) Takow
Seger, P., merchant (Greeven, Seger & Co.) Yedo
Seger, P., teacher (First College) Yedo
Segonzac, E. D. de, clerk (Customs) Canton
Segonzac, L. D. de, sub-director (Arsenal) Foochow
Seimund, C. H. E., storekeeper (Broadbear, Anthony & Co) Praya
Seisson, A., assistant (Hotel des Colonies) Shanghai
Seitz, C., lightkeeper (Public Works Department) Yokohama
Selby, Rev. T. G., missionary (Wes. Meth. Miss. Society) Canton (Fatshan)
Seligmann, E., Deutsche Bank, Shanghai
Semanne, H., chief of secretariat, editor (*Independant de Saigon*) Saigon
Semanne. P., lawyer, Saigon

Senior, T., fitter (Japan Railway)
Senna, A. P. da, clerk (J. das N. e Souza & Co.) Macao
Senna, C. M., clerk (Stephenson & Co.) Shanghai
Senna, F., assist. (Nagasaki Express) N'saki
Senna, F. P., clerk (Margesson & Co.) Macao
Senna, J. de, clerk (Duboat & Co.) Queen's Road
Senna, V. P. de, clerk (Ebell & Co.) Macao
Sequeira, E. P., clerk (E. R. Belilios) Lyndhurst Terrace
Sequeira, F. P., advocate, Macao
Sequeira, N., foreman (*China Mail* Office) Mosque Junction
Sequeira, P. A., piano-forte tuner and repairer, corner of Hollywood Road and Aberdeen Street
Sere, Ch., sub-chief of secretariat, Saigon
Serié, Jean, 1st Lieut. Chinese gunboat *Tienp.*
Serreau, A. Forger, (arsenal) Foochow
Serreau, C., forger (arsenal) Foochow
Seth, A., clerk (Police Ma_istracy) Peel St.
Séth, B. P., clerk (Wilson, Cornabé & Co.) Chefoo
Seth, S. A., trader, Peel Street
Setien, Dr. F., rector, San José College (Ecclesiastical Department) Manila
Seun, O., clerk (Xavier & Co.) Yokohama
Seurat, sub-inspector, municipality, Saigon
Sevilla, L. M., secretary, San José College (Ecclesiastical Department) Manila
Seward, G. F., consul general (U. S. Consulate) Shanghai
Sewell, Thomas, clerk (McEwen, Frickel & Co.)
Sewjee,—., proprietor, Shanghai Dairy, Shanghai
Shadwell, Chas. F. A., C.B., F.R.S., vice-admiral, commander in chief (Naval Dept.)
Shaik Ahmed, S. D., merchant, Gage Street & Macao
Shand, A. A. (Jap. Govt.) Yedo
Shand, W. J. S., (Wilkin & Robison) Yokohama
Shanegan, H. (Germania Hotel) Nagasaki
Shann, T., asst. engineer (Govt. Railroad) Yokohama
Sharp, A., examiner, Customs, Ningpo
Sharp, C. S., clerk (Gibb, Livingston & Co.) Shanghai
Sharp, D.,Jr., merchant (H. Church & Co.) Yokohama
Sharp, Ed., attorney (Crown Solicitor) Supreme Court House and Robinson Road
Sharp, G., broker (Sharp & Co.) Bank Buildings, and Robinson Road
Sharp, J., broker (Lowe & Co.) Shanghai
Sharp, S. W., "Whampoa Hotel," W'poa

Sharp, W. F., clerk (Turner & Co.) H'kow
Shaw, Capt. S. L., marine surveyor, Foochow (Anchorage)
Shaw, J. Y. V., clerk (D. Lapraik & Co.) D'Aguilar Street
Shaw, M., resident, Yedo
Shaw, Miss H. J., (American Pres. Miss.) Canton
Shaw, Rev. Mr., missionary, Yedo
Shaw, T. K., Jr., merchant (Shaw & Co.) Yokohama (absent)
Shaw, W., foreman mechanic (Japan Railway Works) Yokohama
Shaw, W. H., clerk (Francis & Co.) Shanghai and Kewkeang
Shaw, W. J., storekeeper (Municipal Store) Shanghai
Shawcross, J. J., silk inspector (Vogel, Hagedorn & Co.) Canton
Shea, J., gunner, R.N. (*Thetis*)
Sheard, H., die engraver (Mint) Kawasaki
Shearer, G., M.D., Kewkeang
Shearer, J. H., constable (Anglo-Chinese Police) Pagoda Anchorage, Foochow
Shearer, J. H. (Taylor & Co.) Foochow
Sheargold, A., clerk (Hall and Holtz) S'hai
Shee, M. A, assistant, Customs, Amoy
Sheffield, Rev. D. Z. missionary (Am. B. Com. For. Mission) Tungchow
Shellim, S. E., merchant (E. D. Sassoon & Co.) Queen's Road
Shelton, E. M. (Government Agricultural Dept.) Yedo
Shepard, Col. C. O., consul (Amer. Consulate) Yokohama (absent)
Shepard, E. M., lieut. commander, U.S.N. (*Hartford*)
Shepherd, J. W, assist. (Taylor and Bennett) Shanghai
Sheppard, C., ass. engineer (Govt. Railroad) Yokohama
Sheppard, E., tea-taster (Russell & Co.) Foochow
Sheppard, Eli T., U. S consul, Tientsin
Sherkoonoff, L, clerk (Okooloff & Tokmakoff) Hankow
Sherrard, J. O., lieut., H.M 's 80th Regt.
Sherwinton, T. D., (Govt. Railroad) Y'hama
Sheveleff, M, clerk (Okooloff & Tokmakoff) Hankow
Shieras, G, assistant (A. Jaffray) Y'hama
Shillibeer, E., assistant (receiving ship *Emily Jane*) Shanghai
Shillingford, A. N., architect (Jap. Govt.) Yedo
Shinagawa, E., Japanese Consul, Shanghai
Shomaker, G., engineer (National S. S. Co. of Nipon) Yokohama
Short, W. H., storekeeper (Hall & Höltz) Shanghai
Shröm, G. B., telegraphist (Great Northern Ext. Tel. Co.)
Shuniau; C., writer, Sarawak

Shütt, Mrs, Beach Hotel, Chefoo
Shütt, N. P., manager, Beach Hotel, Chefoo
Siber, H., merchant (Siber & Brennwald) Yokohama (absent)
Sichel, J. P, merchant (Reiss & Co.) Yokohama
Siddall, B., M.D., Yokohama
Sidford, H. Æ., 1st assistant, (Customs) Chinkeang
Siebke, H, clerk (Müller & Co) Shanghai
Siebold, Henry von, interpreter (Austro-Hungarian Legation) Yedo
Siebs, N. A., clerk (Siemssen & Co.) Queen's Road
Siegas, P., "Café Oriental" Saigon
Siegfried, C. W., merchant (Pustau & Co.) (absent)
Siemssen, G. T., merchant (Siemssen & Co.) (absent)
Sienkiewicz, Adam, Consul for France
Sigg, H., assistant (Malherbe, Jullien & Co.) Bangkok
Sigrist, A., storekeeper (Sigrist & Pradier) Yokohama
Sillem, H., storekeeper (Vrard & Co.) Shanghai
Silva, A. A. da, clerk (Hedge & Co.) F'chow
Silva, A. M., da, clerk (Wm. Pustau & Co.) Bridges Street
Silva, A. S. G. da, ensign (Timor Corps) Macao
Silva, C. da, clerk (J. da Silva) Macao
Silva, C. F. da, public works Department, Macao
Silva, C. L da, lieutenant (National Guard) Macao
Silva, C. J. P. da, lieut, Military Department, Macao
Silva, D. A., clerk (Wheelock & Co.) S'hai
Silva, E. E., clerk (China Sugar Refinery) East Point
Silva, E. J. da, major (National Guard) Macao
Silva, E. M. da, clerk (Oriental Bank)
Silva, F. M. da, advocate, Macao
Silva, F., clerk (Mestern,& Hulse) Canton
Silva, F. A. da, capt. (National Guard) Macao
Silva, F. A. da, commission agent (Tribunal of Commerce) Macao
Silva, F. A. F. da, captain (Macao Battalion)
Silva, F. F., clerk (Hotel d'Europe)
Silva, G. A. da, merchant (J. P. da Silva & Co.) Macao
Silva, G. S. S. dá, clerk (British Post Office) Shanghai
Silva, H. H., compositor (*Saigon Advertiser*) Saigon
Silva, J. da, commission agent, Macao
Silva, J. M A. da, audit clerk (Auditor General's Department)

Silva, J M. E. da, emigration office, M'cao
Silva, J. P. da, member (Junta do Lançamento das Decimas) Macao
Silva, Joaquim, P. da, merchant (J. P. da Silva & Có.) Macao
Silva, L. da, clerk (B. S. Fernandes) Macao
Silva, L. A. da, colonial surgeon (Military Hospital) Macao
Silva, L. C. da, clerk (R. S. Walker & Co)
Silva, L. J. da, captain (National Guard) Macao
Silva, M. A. da, clerk (Chartered Mercantile Bank)
Silva, M. F. da, merchant, Macao
Silva, M. J. M. G. da, professor of elementary Portuguese (St. Joseph's College) Macao
Silva, M. S. da, ensign (Timor Corps) Macao
Silva, P. da, compositor (A. M. de Carvalho) Shanghai
Silva, P. F. da, clerk (Butterfield & Swire)
Silva, P. N. da, merchant, Macao
Silva, P. N. da, Jr., interpreter (Procurador's Department) Macao
Silva, T., chief clerk (Colonial Government) Macao
Silva, T. da, C.e, officer (*Tejo*) Macao
Silva, V. do., assistant (China Dispensary) Praya
Silva e Souza, J. M. da, teacher of portuguese (St. Saviour's College)
Silveira, A de, clerk (Union Insurance Society) Shanghai
Silveira, H. C. P, deputy com. of stores (Control Department) Queen's Road East
Silveira, J. J. da, clerk (Victoria Photographic Gallery) Shelley Street
Silveira, Maciel, V. de, commander (*Principe Dom Carlos*) Macao
Silverlock, John, merchant (J. Silverlock & Co) Foochow (absent)
Silverthorne, A., propr., "Little Astor," Shanghai
Silverthorne, A., general agent (Silverthorne & Co.) Shanghai
Silvester, J. W., clerk (Mourilyan, Heimann & Co.) Hiogo
Silvin, F. commis. (French Consulate) Yokohama
Silvin, M., assistant (Pequignot & Co.'s livery stable) Yokohama
Sim, Alex., clerk (Brand, Bros. & Co.) S'hai
Sim, A. C., dispenser (Llewellyn & Co.) Kobe
Simmonds, C. M., assistant (China Fire Insce. Co.)
Simmonds, L. A., clerk (Gibb, Livingston & Co.) Shanghai
Simmons, Chas E., master (str. *Plymouth Rock*) Shanghai
Simmons, Dr B., surgeon, Yokohama

Simmons, Rev. E. Z. (South Bap. con. U.S.A.) Canton
Simmons, Dr. (Jap. Govt. Hospital) Nagasaki
Simms, J., Surgeon, R. N. (*Midge*)
Simoens, C. P., clerk (British Consulate) Amoy
Simoens, J. dos R., clerk (M. Ribeiro & Co.) Saigon
Simões, B. P., bailiff (Procurador's Department) Macao
Simões, M. P., retired secretary, exchequer, Macao
Simões, N., clerk (B. S. Fernandes) Macao
Simões, S., clerk (Steam Rice Mills) B'kok
Simon, T , merchant (Simon, Evers & Co.) Yokohama (Hamburg)
Simoni, P. M , assistant (Bavier & Co) sec. Danish Consulate and agent Gt. N. Tel & Co. Yokohama
Simonis, II., clerk (Wm. Pustau & Co) Pottinger Street
Simonsen, E D., pilot, Foochow
Simpkins, Wm., superintendent of works (Public Works Dept) Yokohama
Simpsen, J pilot (Black Ball Pilot Co.) Shanghai
Simpson, C. L., Dep. Commis. (Customs) Shanghai (absent)
Simpson, C. R , freight clerk (P. M. S. S. Co) Yokohama
Simpson, J., act. collector of stamp revenue (General Post Office) Seymour Terrace
Simpson, J., shipwright (Farnham & Co.) Shanghai
Simpson, Miss (Wes. Meth. Miss.) Canton
Sinclair, C. A , consul (British Consulate) Foochow
Sinclair, E , resident, Bintulu outstation, Sarawak
Sinclair, W., supt. (Naconchaisee Sugar Factory) Bangkok
Sinclair, Wm., Pilot (Pilot Company) Newchwang
Sinclair, W. H , chief clerk, post office. Sarawak
Sinety, Cte. de, Attaché (French Legation) Yedo
Singleton, T. A., merchant (Cocking & Singleton) Yokohama
Sinnott, P. W., Examiner, Customs, Hankow
Sinson-Sainville, —., commis. de marine, Saigon
Sinzininex, Rev. E. (Wes. Meth. Miss.) Canton
Sites, Rev. N., missionary (American Meth. Epis. Miss.) Foochow
Sitwell, I. A., merchant (Sitwell, Schoyer & Co.) Yokohama
Sivat, J. T., clerk (Russell & Sturgis) Manila
Skeels, H. J., draper (Watson & Co.) S'hai

Skeggs, C. J., public silk inspector (Skeggs & Co.) Shanghai
Skelly, T. D., act. acct (Agra Bank) S'hai
Skey, Russell, teacher (Arsenal) Foochow
Skinner, E. G., Assistant Commissary, Control Depart.
Skinner, F., clerk (Russell & Sturgis) Cebu
Skipwith, Wm., Lieut. R.N ((Cadmu*.*)
Skipworth, W. G., (Skipworth, Hammond & Co.) Hiogo
Slade, G., clerk (Gilman & Co) Praya
Slaghek, E. H., merchant (Maclean & Co.) consul for Netherlands, Shanghai
Slaghek, F. H., clerk (Holmes, Wadman & Co.) Chefoo
Slaney, H. C. K., sub lieut., R.N. (*Ringdove*)
Slater, H. G., assistant (Sayle & Co.) Alex Terrace
Sloan, J., clerk (Findlay, Richardson & Co.) Manila
Sloane, J., 2nd officer (rec.-ship *Emily Jane*) Shanghai
Sloos, J. H. M. (Eureka Billiard Saloon) Hiogo
Sloys, P. J., physician (Jap. Govt.) Yedo
Smale, Sir John, chief justice (Supreme Court) Caine Road
Smart, G. F., resident, Shanghai
Smeaton, W., messenger (Oriental Bank Corporation) Yokohama
Smedley, J., architect &c, Yokohama
Smerdley, N., Kintoan light keeper, Customs, Shanghai
Smith, A., teacher (Gaim 'sho) Yedo
Smith, A., watchmaker (G. Falconer & Co.) Queen's Road
Smith, A., clerk (Hall & Holtz) Shanghai
Smith, A., pilot (P. & O. Co.) Shanghai
Smith, Arthur, merchant (Birley & Co.) (absent)
Smith, A. F., storekeeper (MacEwen, Frickel & Co.) Queen's Road
Smith, A.J., assist. act. (H'K and S. Bank) Yokohama
Smith, A. L. R., pilot (Newchwang Pilot Company) Newchwang
Smith, Charles, godown-keeper (Russell & Co.) Hankow
Smith, C. D., clerk (Gilman & Co.) Foochow
Smith, C. V., clerk (Russell, & Co.) Praya
Smith, D. Adam, merchant (Smith, Bell Co.) Manila
Smith, D. Wares, accountant (*North China Herald* Office) Shanghai
Smith, E. C., tailor (Cabeldu & Co.) Osaka
Smith, E. C., merchant (Turner & Co.) Shanghai
Smith, E.J., accountant (Borneo Company) Sarawak
Smith, E. J., chief examiner, Customs, Shanghai
Smith, E. M., land proprietor, Shanghai

Smith, E. R., merchant (Smith, Baker & Co) Yokohama
Smith, E. U., clerk (Olyphant & Co.) S'hai
Smith, F. H., tea inspector (Olyphant & Co.) Canton
Smith, F. dos S., captain (Timor Corps) Macao
Smith, F. H, shoemaker, Yokohama
Smith, F. M., clerk (Skeggs & Co) S'hai
Smith, Geo., merchant (Geo. Smith & Co.) Shanghai
Smith, George, master mechanic (Govt. Railroad) Yokohama
Smith, G. M., tea inspector (Jardine, Matheson & Co.) Canton
Smith, Herbert, clerk (Jardine, Matheson & Co) Yokohama
Smith, H, accountant (Hongkong and S'hai Banking Corporation) Albany Rd.
Smith, H., gunner, Chinese gun-boat *Anlan*
Smith, H., storeman (Naval Yard)
Smith, H. C., lieut. Col. commanding, H. M. 80th Regt.
Smith, H. R., tea inspector (Butterfield & Swire) Foochow
Smith, Hon. C. C., registrar general (Albany)
Smith, J, inspector (Government Telegraphs) Yedo and Yokohama
Smith, J., Dep. commr. (Customs) Canton
Smith, J, pilot, Bangkok
Smith, J., storekeeper (Smith & Co.) Chefoo
Smith, J, pilot, Ningpo
Smith, James, merchant (Loney & Co.) British vice consul, Cebu
Smith, J. B., clerk (Olyphant & Co) Praya
Smith, J. C., merchant (Holme, Ringer & Co.) Nagasaki
Smith, J. D, tidewaiter, Customs, Amoy
Smith, J. Gordon, captain's clerk, U.S.N. (*Palos*)
Smith, John G., storekeeper (MacEwen Frickel & Co.)
Smith, J. H., (Smith, & Co) Yedo
Smith J. L, coach-builder (Garchoritoreua & Smith) Manila
Smith, J. Mackrill, merchant (Walsh, Hall & Co) Yokohama
Smith, J. R., assistant accountant (Japan Railway)
Smith, J. U., proprietor (Commercial Hotel) Nagasaki
Smith, Capt. J. U., marine surveyor, Nagasaki
Smith, M. L., tide-surveyor, (Customs) Tamsui
Smith, Mrs., assistant (Hall & Holtz) Shanghai
Smith, Mrs. T. (Mrs. E. A. Vincent) Yokohama
Smith, Noel, merchant (Major & Smith) Hankow
Smith, O., pilot, Nagasaki

Smith, P., boarding-house keeper, Queen's Road West
Smith, Pat. Rose, sub-editor (*North China Herald* Office) Shanghai
Smith, R., pilot (Independence Pilot Co.) Shanghai
Smith, R. B., pilot, Foochow (Anchorage)
Smith, R. C., clerk (Ker & Co.) Manila (Leyte.)
Smith, Rev. G., missionary (Eng. Presby.) Swatow (absent)
Smith, Rev. Sam J. (Siamese Mission) editor, *Siam Weekly Advertiser*, Bangkok
Smith, Thomas, merchant (Geo. Smith & Co.) Shanghai (absent)
Smith, Thos., clerk (Cheshire & Marshall) Yokohama
Smith, T., clerk (Borneo Co.) Sarawak
Smith, T., merchant (J. Silverlock & Co.) Foochow (absent)
Smith, T., (Naval College) Yedo
Smith, T. G., chief clerk (Supreme Court Shanghai
Smith, T. J., clerk (Cheshire & Co.) Yokohama
Smith, Wm., weigher, (Mint) Osaka
Smith, W. H., manager (Yokohama Club)
Smith, W., McG. (China Sugar Refinery) East Point
Smith, —., engineer (steamer *Vulcan*) Yedo (kaitikushi)
Smith, W. E., act. acct. (Chartered Mercantile Bank)
Smith, W. F., chief engineer (Hongkong Canton and Macao Steamboat Co.)
Smithers, J., clerk (M. J. D. Stephens) Alexandra Terrace
Smyth, A. C., lieut., R.M., Yokohama
Smyth, W. A., lightkeeper, (Public Works Department) Yokohama
Smythies, P. R., lieut. R.N. (H. M. S. *Teazer*)
Snethlage, H., clerk (Reis, von der Heyde & Co.) Yokohama
Snow, E. B., capt. R.M., Yokohama
Snowden, J., pilot (Black Ball Pilot Company) Shanghai
Soab, A., clerk (A. Soab) Wellington St.
Soares, A. F., clerk (H.K. and S. Banking Corp.)
Soares, D., clerk (J. M. da Fonseca) Macao
Soares, Franco, F., officer (*Tejo*) Macao
Soares, F. P., druggist (Oriental Dispensary) Wellington Street
Soares, J. A., bailiff, Macao
Soares, M., clerk (P. & O. S. N. Company) Queen's Road West
Söderström, —., master mariner (B'kok)
Sodervist, G., proprietor (Albion Tavern) Nagasaki
Solbé, E., interpreter and postal agent (British Consulate) Ningpo (absent)

Soledade, J. da, padre (Retired Chaplain) Macao
Soler, Pedro, clerk (Y. Rocha & Co.) M'la
Solomiac, Marie Louise, sister (Maison de Jesus Enfant) Ningpo
Solomon, E. A., agent (D. Sassoon, Sons & Co.) and chairman mun. council, Tientsin
Solomon, J. A., merchant, 17, Cochrane Street
Solomon, M., clerk (D. Sassoon, Sons & Co.) Shanghai
Solomon, Reuben, Broker, Elgin Street
Solomon, R. J., clerk (D. Sassoon, Sons & Co.) Praya
Solomon, S. A., clerk (D. Sassoon, Sons & Co.) Hankow
Solstanoff, A. A., clerk (Haminoff Rodionoff) Hankow
Sombreuil, Vicompte V. de, assistant (Customs) Ningpo
Somerville, I., agent (Chartered Bank) Manila
Somerville, J. R., M D. (Customs) Pagoda anchorage) Foochow
Somes, M. F., clerk (Russell & Sturgis) Manila
Somjee, J. M., clerk (S. Visram) Gage St.
Sonne, C. C. Electrician (G. N. Teleg Co.) Amoy
Soonderam, I. M., indian interpret. (Harbour Master's Dept.)
Soper, Rev. J., missionary, Yedo
Sörensen, P. F., supt. (Great Northern Ex. Tel. Co.) Burd Lane
Sorensen, S., master mariner, Bangkok
Sörnsen, F., merchant (W. G. Hale & Co.) Saigon
Soto, J. de, attaché (Spanish Legation) Peking (absent)
Souper, E. B., assistant secty. (Municipal Council) Shanghai
Southan, J., issuer of stores (P. & O. Co.'s Office)
Southwell, R. E., clerk (Turner & Co.) Shanghai
Souza, —., bailiff, administraçao do concelho, Macao
Souza, A. de, apothecary, Lock Hospital
Souza, A. J. du S. e, foreman (De Souza & Co.) Hollywood Road
Souza, A. S. de, book keeper (*China Mail* Office) Bridges Street
Souza, B. de, clerk (Reid, Evans & Co.) Shanghai
Souza, B. de, clerk (Meller & Co.) S'hai
Souza, C. L. de, vice-consul for Hawaii, merchant, Macao
Souza, D. M., clerk (Wheelock & Co.) Shanghai
Souza, D P. de, clerk (Spanish Consulate)
Souza, E. de, clerk (J. das Neves e Souza & Co.) Macao

Souza, E. F. de, chancellor, Spanish Consulate, Bonham Road
Souza, F. A. de, commission agent, Gage Street
Souza, F S. de, clerk (F. A. Souza)
Souza, F. W. R. de, clerk (Peoló, Hubbell & Co.) Manila
Sousa, J. das Neves e (Lisbon Dispensary) Macao
Souza, J. de, printer (Dr. Souza & Co.) Hollywood Read
Souza, J. de junr. printer (De Souza & Co.)
Souza, J A de (member of the Junta do Lançamento das Decimas) Macao
Souza, J. M. de C., ensign, (Police Dept.) Macao
Souza, J. N. e, ensign (National Guard) Macao
Souza, J P. S. C. P. de, lieutenant (Military Depart.) Macao
Souza, M. de, book-keepe. (Hongkong & Whampoa Dock Co.'s Offic.)
Souza, M. de., clerk (Union Insurance Society)
Souza, M. J. M. de, ensign (Timor Corps) Macao
Souza, Major J. A. de, retired major, Macao
Souza, M. S. de, clerk (Frazar & Co.) S'hai
Souza, N. L., clerk (Hk. & S. Banking Corp.)
Souza, P. Z de lieut., Police Department, Macao
Souza, R. de, postmaster (Post-office) Macao
Spahn, J. H., merch. (Spahn & Co.) Osaka
Spain, G., assist. paymr. in charge, R.N. (*Ringdove*)
Spalding, L. G., master. U.S.N. (*Yantic*)
Spanier, J., merchant (Labhart & Co.) and consul for Austro-Hungary, Manila
Spears, W., engineer (P. & O. Service)
Specht, Dr. E., assist, (Customs) Amoy
Speechley, J., boarding officer (Harbour Master's Department)
Speiller, L., assist. (Greenburgh & Co.) Yokohama
Spence, W. D., assist. (British Consulate) Shanghai
Spencer, A. W., merchant, Chinkeang
Spencer, S. B., merchant, Chinkeang
Spencer, S. B., assist. (A. W. Spencer) Chinkeang
Spencer. W. A., marshall, U. S. consulate, Canton
Spinks, J., engineer, R.N. (*Frolic*)
Spitz, E., clerk (Pustau & Co.) Shanghai
Spooner, F. C., shipchandler (J. D. Carroll & Co.) Yokohama
Spooner, G. P., clerk (J. D. Carroll & Co.) Yokohama
Sprague, J. P., chief engr. U.S.N. (*Iroquois*)
Sprague, Rev. —., Missionary, Kalgan

Spratt, W. B., shipwright (Spratt & Co.) Praya East
Sprecher, Ch. clerk (Lutz & Co) Manila
Spring, C. A , draper (Spring & Co.) Manila
Spring, E. H., manager (Sayle & Co.) Shanghai
Spring, Miss, assist. (Spring & Co.) Manila
Sprowel, A., plumber (P. & O. S. N. Co.) Queen's Road, West
Sprungli, C., assist. (Lutz & Co.) Manila
Squires, James, gunner (Chinese gun-boat *Anlan*)
Stadeli, L., assist. (J. J. Bisch ff & Co.) Yloilo
Stael, L. merchant (Hesse & Co.)
Stafford, T. M., Chief Officer (*Ariel*) S'hai
Stainfield, G., overseer of works (Surveyor General's Depart.)
Stammann, O., merchant, Tientsin
Stanfield, G., overseer of waterworks (Fire Brigade)
Stanford, B. R , shipwright, Praya East
Stanford, Geo. A , assist. (Lane, Crawford & Co.) Queen's Road
Stanley, Rev. C. A., missionary, Tientsin
Stanton, O. F., commdr., U.S.N. (*Yantic*)
Staples, J. J., clerk (Smith, Baker & Co.) Hiogo
Stappen, J. van, student (Customs) Peking
Starick, Paul, publican, Chefoo
Starkey, E., clerk (J. M. Canny & Co.) Chinkeang
Starkey, E. P., clerk (Tait & Co.) Amoy
Starkey, R. D., act. agent (North China In. Co)
Startseff, A. D., merchant, Tientsin
St. Croix, G. C. de, clerk (H. K. & S'hai Banking Corp.) Queen's Road
St. Croix, W. de, clerk (Gilman & Co.) Shanghai
Steadman, J., chief officer (National S. S. Co. of Nipon) Yokohama
Stebbins, W , assistant examiner (Customs) Newchwang
Ste. Croix, C. W. de, assistant (Customs) Newchwang
Steele, H., asst. acct. (Char. Merc. Bank) Queen's Road
Steele, Joseph, Jr., master (str. *Shanse*) Shanghai
Steele, W. D., eng. (P. & O. Service)
Steffens, J., shipwright (Amoy Dock Co.) Amoy
Stoglich, O., assistant (Gt. Nor. Telegraph Co.) Shanghai
Steil, R , shipbroker (Hoinemann & Co.) 37 Wyndham Street
Stein, A., clerk (Schmidt, Westphal & Co.) Hiogo
Stein, F., clerk (Kirchnor, Böger & Co.) Shanghai
Stein, G A , clerk (Beazley, Paget & Co.) Hankow

Stella, Maria, superioress (The Convent) Caine Road
Stent, G. C., clerk (Customs) Shanghai
Stephen, J., shipwright (Stephen & Stewart) Yokohama
Stephens, J., engineer (P. & O. Service)
Stephens, M. J. D., solicitor, D'Aguilar St.
Stephenson, W. E., auctioneer (Stephenson & Co.) Shanghai
Steuart, C. S., act. agent (Oriental Bank) Osaka
Stevens, D. W., secretary of U. S. Legation, Yedo
Stevens, E., 2nd officer (Chinese gun-boat, Chen-to)
Stevens, H., teacher, (Jap. Govt.) Yedo
Stevens, J., foreman boilermaker (Hongkong and W'poa Dock Co.) K'loong
Stevens, R., assistant (Nachonchaisée Sugar Factory) Bangkok
Stevens, T., constable (British Consulate) Hankow
Stevens, W. J. (Kirby & Co.) Hiogo
Stevenson, Rev. J. W. and fam., missionary, Ningpo
Stevenson, W., auctioneer (Merriman & Stevenson) Yokohama
Steveson, J. H., paym. U. S N. (Lackawanna)
Steward, J., boarding-house keeper, Queen's Road West
Steward, R., assistant (Public Works Department) Yedo
Steward, W. F., midshipman, R.N. (Cadmus)
Stewart, C. C., assist. accountant (Oriental Bank) Osaka
Stewart, Edwin, fleet paymaster, U.S.N. (Hartford)
Stewart, F., head master (Central School) Gough Street
Stewart, G., engineer (H. K. & Wham. Dock Co.) Kowloong
Stewart, J., engineer (Imperial Arsenal) Tientsin
Stewart, J., cartridge maker, Kiangnan Arsenal, Shanghai
Stewart, J., shipwright (Stephen & Stewart) Yokohama
Stewart, J., boatswain, R.N. (Thistle)
Stewart, James, captain, Chinese gun-boat Sui-tsing
Stewart, J. A., assistant (Watson & Co.) Shanghai
Stewart, J. A., M.D. (Foochow Native Hospital) Foochow
Stewart, Mrs. J. A., assist. (Watson & Co.) Shanghai
Stewart, W., commander, R.N. (Growler) Shanghai
Stewart, W. J. E., bill and share broker, St. Florent, —., (Yokoska Arsenal) Yokohama
Stickler, F. M., assistant (J. Llewellyn & Co.) Shanghai

Stiebe, R., sergeant, police force (Customs) Pagoda Anchorage, Foochow
Stiller, Ernst, clerk (Paseday & Co.) Amoy
St. John, Chas., acting boatswain, R.N. (Curlew)
St. John, E., (Naval College) Yedo
St. John, J. A., surveyor (Survey Department) and supt. of coal mines, Sarawak
St. John, Oliver, C., assist. resident, Paku, Upper Sarawak
St. John, St. A., lieut., R M., Yokohama
Stockes, J., gun barrel borer (Kiangnan Arsenal) Shanghai
Stok, W., clerk (Bovet, Brothers & Co.) act. chancelier (Netherlands' Consulate) Shanghai
Stokes, C. S., assist. (Victoria Dispensary) Peidar's Wharf
Stokes, F., clerk (Dickinson & Co.) S'hai
Stollery, T. (P. & O. Hulk Tiptree) Y'hama
Stolterfoh:, H., clerk (Hesse & Co.)
Stone, Captn. R. W., H.M. 80th Regt.
Stone, F., steward (Nagasaki Club) N'saki
Stone, N. J., merchant (Chipman, Stone & Co.) Yokohama
Stone, W., master (loroba Relief) Shanghai
Stone, W. H., secretary (Govt. Telegraph) Yokohama
Storror, E. M., M.D., Saigon
Stott, Rev. G. & Mrs., missionaries, Ningpo (Hangchow)
Stout, M., D D S., Alexandra Terrace
Stout, Revd. H., missionary, Nagasaki
Stoves, F., overseer of works (Surveyor General's Department)
St. Pern, B. de, écrivain de marine, Saigon
St. Quentin, A. de, secretary (French Legation) Yedo
Strachan, R., assist. (Hongkong Dispensary)
Strachan, W. M., merchant (Strachan & Thomas) Yokohama
Strack, Ad., merchant (Deetjen & Co.) Praya
Strandberg, J., fitter (Japan Railway)
Strandt, H., compradore (Schlüter and Strandt) Hakodadi
Strauge, C. V., Lieut. R.N. (Cadmus)
Stransome, J., clerk (Sitwell, Schoyer & Co.) Yokohama
Strauss, L., consul (Belgian Legation) Yedo
Stretch, W., 2nd engineer (Chinese gun-boat Ling Feng)
Stretten, R. T., clerk (Gibb, Livingston & Co.) Canton
Stripling, A., police inspector (Hongkew Station) Shanghai
Stritmatter, Revd. A.; missionary, Kewkeang
Stroem, P., assist. (Domoney & Co.) Yokohama
Stronach, Rev. John, missionary (London Missionary Society) Amoy

Stronach, W. G., act. vice consul (British Consulate) Shanghai
Stroud, H., inspector (Police Dept) Police Hulk
Stuart, C. W., nav. sub-lieut., R.N. (Curlew)
Stuart, F. H., wharfinger (Canton Steamer Co.) Praya West
Stube, R., clothier, Nagasaki
Stuben, J. F., clerk (Smith, Bell & Co.) Cebu
Stucken, E., (T. Lenz) Hiogo
Studd, J., architect (Rawling, Medlen & Co.) Wyndham Street
Stuhlmann, C. C, assist (Customs) Swatow
Stünzi, H, clerk (Bower, Hanbury & Co.) Shanghai
Styles, Geo., mil. foreman of. works (R. Engineer Dept)
Such, A., chief officer (M. M. S. S. *Amazone*)
Suenson, A., assist. (G. N. Telcg. Co.) Nagasaki
Sulivan, J. Y. F., lieutenant, R.N. (*H.M.S. Avon*)
Summers, Rev. J., M.A. (Imp. College) Yedo
Sury, A., resident, Yedo
Sutherland, J. W., livery keeper (Cobb & Co.) Yokohama
Suttor, L'abbé Louis, R. C. missionary, Yedo
Sutton, F. W., (Naval College) Yedo
Sutton, G., clerk (M. C. Adams & Co.) Nagasaki
Sutton, M (L. Candrelior) Yedo (Shiba)
Sutton, W. D., assistant (Hongkong Dispensary) Queen's Road
Swaby, L, assistant book-keeper (Osaka Mint)
Swaby, W. S., sub-accountant (Comptoir d'Escompte de Paris) Yokohama
Swainson, G., tidewaiter (Customs) Kewkeang
Swan, G., gunner, U S N. (*Idaho*)
Swan, J., lieut., R.N (*Hornet*)
Swanberg, A., proprietor (Hotel) Ningpo
Swanson, Rev. W. S., missionary (English Pres. Mission) Amoy
Swany, A. F., clerk (Fogg & Co.) S'hai
Sweet, Albert, tidewaiter (Customs) Chefoo
Swendsen, P., master mariner, Bangkok
Swift, T. C., clerk (Japan Railway)
Swinhoe, R., consul (British Consulate) consul for Austria-Hungary, and Denmark, Ningpo
Sykes, Adam, clerk (Bower, Hanbury & Co.) Shanghai
Syle, Rev. E. W., acting chaplain, Yokohama
Symes, F. A., nav. sub. Lieut. R.N. (*Frolic*)
Symonds, J. W., assistant (Hongkong and Shanghai Bank) Queen's Road
Symondson, Ed., teacher (Jap. Govt.) Yedo

Symons, H., clerk (Hall & Holtz) S'hai
Symons, J., pilot (Independence Pilot Co.) Shanghai
Symons, John, clerk (F. and C. Walsh) Shanghai

T

Tabor, H. W., compradore (Tabor & Co.) Hiogo
Taintor, E. C, statistical secretary (Customs) Peking (Shanghai)
Talbot, F. R., clerk (Olyphant & Co.) C'ton
Talbot, G. W., merchant (Olyphant & Co.) (absent)
Talbot, W. H., public accountant, Y'hama
Talcott, Miss, missionary, Hiogo
Talmage, Rev. J. V. N., D.D., missionary (Reformed Church) Amoy (absent)
Talty, M. M., merchant, Cantou
Tams, E. C., master mariner, Bangkok
Tandberg, L. J., pilot, Newchwang
Tang, T. T., clerk (Engwat, Bro. & Co.) Amoy
Tapp, W. H., shipping clerk (British Consulate) Shanghai (absent)
Taraktemberk, —, (School of Foreign Languages) Yedo
Tardy, Rev. C. E., missionary, Swatow
Target, A. T., sub. lieut., R N. (*Thetis*)
Turney, —., Teacher (Jap. Govt.) Yedo
Tarver Geo, boatswain, R.N. (*Thalia*)
Tassara, A. B., captain commanding ('Taipa Fort) Macao
Tata, D. C., merchant, Hollywood Road
Tate, J. P., merchant (Tate & Hawos) Shanghai
Tatham, C. G., clerk (Holliday, Wise & Co.) Foochow
Tathin, Thos. S., clerk (U. S. Consulate) Canton
Tattersell, N.; tidewaiter (Customs) N'po
Tanfer, E., engineer (H.K. Fire Inco. Co.'s engine) Praya
Tanfer, Geo. (Hongkong Fire Insurance Co.'s Engine) Praya
Taumeyer, E., clerk (Bourjau & Co.) S'hai
Tavares, J., clerk (Messageries Maritimes) Hollywood Road
Tavares, L. A., clerk (Dent & Co.) chancelier (Portuguese Consulate) Shanghai
Tavares, S. A. (Tribunal of Commerce) Macao
Tavarez, P. J., foreman (Ching Foong Printing Office) Shanghai
Tavernier, —., chief of battalion, engineer corps, Saigon
Taveira, L. A. P. de M., sub. lieut., (*Principe Dom Carlos*) Macao
Tayeux, A., head steward (Grand Hotel) Yokohama
Taylor, A., foreman mechanic (Govt. Railway) Yokohama

Taylor, C., clerk (J. B. Lehmann) Saigon
Taylor, C., foreman (Morris, Barlow & Co.) Manila
Taylor, C. S., clerk (Jardine, Matheson & Co.)
Taylor, G., merchant (Hughes & Co.) Hiogo
Taylor, G. (Whitfield & Dowson) Y'hama
Taylor, G. W., engineer (Hongkong Times)
Taylor, H., missionary, Nankin
Taylor, J., coal hewer (Tanjore Kubong Mines) Labuan
Taylor, J., consulting engineer, (Nat. S. S. Co. of Nipon) Yokohama
Taylor, J., merchant (Hughes & Co.) H'go
Taylor, J. A. H., Student interpreter (British Legation) Peking
Taylor, J. K. (Chas. J. Strome & Co.) Hiogo
Taylor, J. M., commission agent (Taylor & Bennett) Shanghai
Taylor, J. R., storekeeper (Taylor & Co.) Foochow
Taylor, J. T., pilot Black Ball Pilot Co.) Shanghai
Taylor, R. (Old House at Home) Queen's Road
Taylor, Rev. J. H., and Mrs. missionaries, Chinkiang
Taylor, T. M. (Govt. Agricultural Dept.) Yedo
Taylor, Wm., boatswain, R.N. (Princess Charlotte)
Taylor, W. H., clerk (Elles & Co.) Amoy (Taiwanfoo)
Taylor, W. H., merchant (Cornes & Co.) Yokohama
Teale, W., assistant superintendent (Government Telegraph) Yedo
Tebbutt, J. L., assistant (G. Ludewig) Manila
Tecken, Von der, Mineralogist (Jap. Govt.) Yedo
Teillot, A., clerk (E. Millot & Co.) S'hai
Teixeira, M. A., Captain (Timor Corps) Macao
Tejada, Fermin Saenz de, vice-consul (Spanish Consulate) Amoy (Acting Consul at Hongkong)
Telford, James, gun forger, Kiangnan Arsenal, Shanghai
Telge, B., merchant (Telge, Nölting & Co.) Shanghai (absent)
Telles, J. C. da S., vice-president (Military Hospital) Macao
Telles, J. S. da S., druggist (National Dispensary) Macao
Temple, Francis, actg. agent (Oriental Bank) Foochow
Templemore, F. W., tidewaiter (Customs) Shanghai
Teohaeff, M., clerk (Dircks & Krüger) Swatow

Tennant, P., agent (Gibb, Livingston & Co.) Foochew
Tennant, T. W., tea taster (Gibb, Livingston & Co.) Foochow
Ternisien, —., subs. procureur, Saigon
Terp, C. I. F., assistant (Gt. N. Telegraph Co.) Shanghai
Terry, J. W., teacher (St. Saviour's College) Pottinger Street
Testera, Sister G. (The Convent) Caine Road
Testevuide, l'abbé L. G., Miss. Apost. Yokohama
Teuchert, A., 2nd engineer (German str. China)
Teus, V., merchant (Aguirre & Co.) Manila
Thabor, C. H., teacher, Osaka College
Thibaudier, sub-director (Yokoska Arsenal) Yokohama
Thiemer, G. (Cigar Depot) Yokohama
Thierry, —, Mission Catholique, Peking
Thimoteo, A., bailiff, Macao
Thistaed, T., locksmith (Thistaed & Co.) Yokohama
Thomas, C. (Boulangerie Française) N'saki
Thomas, Rev. J., pastor (Union Chapel) Shanghai
Thomas, J., pilot to Holt's Line, Shanghai
Thomas, J., shipchandler, Yokohama
Thomas, M., copyist (Trib. 1st instance) Saigon
Thomas, T., merchant (Strachan & Thomas) Yokohama (absent)
Thomas, Th., public tea inspector (Thomas & Mercer) Canton and Macao (absent)
Thomas, —., mariner (Japanese Government) Yedo
Thompson, A., paymaster, R.N. (Iron Duke)
Thompson, A. F., clerk (Smith, Archer & Co.) Shanghai
Thompson, A. G. (School of Foreign Languages) Yedo
Thompson, C., foreman mechanic (Government Railways) Yokohama
Thompson, Rev. D., missionary, Yedo
Thompson, D. J., assistant paymaster, R.N. (Princess Charlotte)
Thompson, G. M., U. S. consul and clerk (Boyd & Co.) Amoy (Takow)
Thompson, G. W., assistant accountant (Oriental Bank) Yokohama
Thompson, J., boatswain, R.N. (Thetis)
Thompson, J. (Thompson & Co.) Y'hama
Thompson, J. R., shipwright (Thompson & Bewick) Hakodadi
Thompson, J. V., engineer, R.N. (Hornet)
Thompson, M. E., storekeeper (Thompson & Co.) Foochow
Thompson, Rev. T. W., missionary, Kalgan
Thompson, W., draper (Thompson & Hind) Queen's Road
Thompson, W. A., livery stable keeper, Hiogo

Thompson, W. E., chief officer (P. & O. service)
Thompson, W. H. (Yedo Hotel) Yedo
Thompson, W. T., navig. sub-lieut., R.N. (*Thalia*)
Thomsen, J. C., master mariner, Bangkok
Thomsen, S., stevedore, (Thomsen & Worck) Hiogo
Thomsen, T., clerk (M. J. B. Hegt) Y'hama
Thomsett, H. G., R.N., harbour master (Harbour Master's Department) Seymour Terrace
Thomson, A., barkeeper (Hamburgh Tavern)
Thomson, C. E., acting accountant (National Bank) Queen's Road
Thomson, C. H., assistant paymaster, U.S.N. (*Palos*)
Thomson, Geo. W., act. account. (Oriental Bank) Yokohama
Thomson, Rev. E. H., missionary, Shanghai (West Gate)
Thorburn, Henry, acting agent (Chartered Bank) Hankow
Thorburn, R. F., merchant, Shanghai
Thorburn, T. D., clerk (Russell & Co.) Shanghai
Thorel, C., merchant (Thorel & Co.) Yokohama
Thorndike, J. K., godown proprietor, S'hai
Thorne, O. W., assist. eng., R.N. (*Cadmus*)
Thorne, J., merchant (Thorne Brothers & Co.) Shanghai (absent)
Thorne, Joh—, commission agent (Thorne, Rice & Co.) Shanghai
Thornicraft, T. C., M.R.C.S.E., Hiogo
Thornton, A. H., clerk (Tait & Co.) Takow
Thorp, C. H., clerk (Hudson, Malcolm & Co.) Yokohama
Thorp, R. W., clerk (Japan Railway)
Thurburn, A., broker, Shanghai
Thurburn, D., act. acct. (Chartered Mercantile Bank) Shanghai
Tibayan, A., assist. (Roxas' Soap Factory) Manila
Tiefenbacher, M., clerk (Siemssen & Co.) Shanghai
Tileston, H. N., clerk (P. M. S. S. Co.) Hiogo
Tilghman, W. C., clerk (Purdon & Co.) Shanghai
Tilman, W. P., agent (P. M. S. S. Co.) Nagasaki
Tippinge, L. F. G., mid., R.N. (*Iron Duke*)
Titgen, H., clerk (Carroll & Co.) Hiogo
Titoushkin, N., assist. (Customs) Keelung
Tobin, E., clerk (Gilman & Co.) Shanghai
Tokmakoff, T., merchant (Okooloff & Tomakoff) Hankow
Tolatee, B. F., merchant (F. M. Tolatee) Gage Street
Tolatee, D. E., merchant (F. M. Tolatee) Gage Street

Toller, W. W., solicitor (E. Sharp & Toller) Supreme Court House (absent)
Tolliday, Thos., examiner (Customs) Amoy
Tombrink, S. P. (Takasima Colliery) T'sima
Tomlin, Geo. L., clerk (Surveyor General's Department)
Tommugsen, J., assistant (Douglas & Co.) Yokohama
Tonnochy, M. S., interpreter (Col., Govt)
Tootal, J. B., manager (*North China Herald* Office) Shanghai
Tornoe, H., clerk (Siemssen & Co.) S'hai
Torp, von, clerk (Valmale, Schœne, and Milsom) Yokohama
Torre, F. M. de la, foreman (Mint) Manila
Torres, J., constable (Brit. Cons.) Ningpo
Torrey, J. W., agent (Parker & Co.)
Toselowsky, F. (School of Foreign Languages) Yedo
Toull, W. J., gunner, R.N. (*Cadmus*)
Towell, M. E., assistant (Customs) Foochow
Townend, Ed., merchant (Townend & Co.) Hankow (absent)
Townend, F. J., clerk (Townend & Co.) Hankow
Townley, F., storekeeper (Lane, Crawford & Co.) Yokohama
Townsend, A. M., agent (Hongkong and Shanghai Bank) Hankow
Tracey, O., lieut., R.N. (*Cadmus*)
Tracey, R. E., com., R.N., prof. of navigation (Arsenal) Foochow
Tracey, S. C., nav. lieut. R.N. (*Iron Duke*)
Trail, W., master mariner, Bangkok
Traineau, Rev. Th. (R. C. Church) Nagasaki
Tranchevent, —., sous com. de la marine, Saigon (absent)
Trannack, R., examiner (Customs) Takow
Treacher, Hon J. G., J.P., Labuan
Treat, A. O., M.D., missionary, Peking
Trebing, W., master, (light-ship *Newchwang*) Newchwang
Tremaine, H. E., lieut., U.S.N (*Hartford*)
Tremlett, C. F., clerk (W. G. Hale & Co.) Saigon
Treserra, Fr. D., rector, St. Thomas' College (Ecclesiastical Dept.) Manila
Tricot, —., pilot, Saigon
Trigg, W. H., clerk (China Sub. Tel. Co.) Burd's Lane
Triggs, A.S., clerk (Lane, Crawford & Co.) Shanghai
Triggs, T. R., mid., R.N. (*Thalia*)
Tripp, H. J. H., bill broker (C. S. Bland) Yokohama
Troing, J. B., clerk (Jardine, Matheson & Co.)
Trolho, A. P., major, Military Depart., Macao
Trotter, D. A., clerk (Tait & Co.) Amoy
Trotter, J. L., fitter (Japan Railway)
Trotzig, supt. (Municipal Council) Hiogo

Tswansia, Carlos, clerk (Danver & Co.) Amoy
Tuason, E., clerk (Macleod, Pickford & Co.) Cebu
Tuason, T., auctioneer (Genato & Co.) Manila
Tubel, H., teacher (Jap Govt.) Yedo
Tucker, J. J., Lloyd's registrar, Shanghai
Tucker, R. D., merchant (Peele, Hubbell & Co.) Manila (absent)
Tulloch, —., commander (steamer *Nanzing*) Shanghai
Tumboly, S. F., clerk (H. M. Padsha) Gage Street
Turnbull, W. A., merchant (Birley, Worthington & Co.) Shanghai
Turner, A. L., agent (Hongkong and Shanghai Banking Corporation) Foochow
Turner D., consul for United States, Hiogo
Turner, Isaac, master mariner, Bangkok
Turner, J., 2nd engineer (Sassoon's steamer *China*)
Turner, J., gunner (Chinese steamer *Peng Chao Hai*)
Turner, J. J., clerk (Butterfield & Swire) Queen's Road
Turner, W. H., master, U.S.N. (*Ashuelot*)
Turner, W. M., tidewaiter (Customs) Newchwang
Turney, Harry, clerk (Surveyor's Department) Labuan
Turpin, J. (Naval College) Yedo
Tutein, F., "Mariner's Hotel," Chefoo
Tuton F., merchant (Tuton & Sons) Macao
Tuton, J. A., merchant (Tuton & Sons) Macao
Tuton, T., merchant (Tuton & Sons) Macao
Twigg, Mrs P. O'B., undertaker, Shanghai
Twombly, J. F., merchant (H. Fogg & Co.) Shanghai
Tyler, J., constable (British Consular Gaol) Shanghai
Tyler, John C., clerk (Russell & Sturgis) Yloilo
Tyree, A. F., merchant, Ningpo

U

Ucola, M., shipchandler (Reyes & Co.) Manila
Uhlmann, H., colporteur (Brit. & Foreign Bible Society) Canton
Ulbrich, J. G., chief engineer (Gas Company) Yokohama
Ulderup, A. P., pilot, Taku
Ullmann, E., importer of jewelry, Manila
Ullmann, F., importer of jewelry, Manila
Ullmann, M., storekeeper, Hollywood Road
Ulrich, G., master mariner, Bangkok
Ulrichs, J. F., assistant (Ladage, Oelke & Co.) Shanghai
Umland, J. M., proprietor "Germania Hotel" Nagasaki

Underwood, Thos. (Occidental Hotel) Nagasaki
Unwin, F. S., assistant (Customs) Swatow
Upham, J. B., assistant engineer, U. S. N. (*Hartford*)
Ure, John, foreman moulder (Kiangnan Arsenal) Shanghai
Ureta, Don Candido, secretary (Ecclesiastical Department) Manila
Uriu, H., supt. (Customs) Hiogo
Urquhart, A., clerk (Public Works Depart.) Yokohama
Urquiola, J., judge, Manila
Usill, H. S. B., clerk (Turner & Co.) Shanghai

V

Vachell, H. G., clerk (Adamson, Bell & Co.) Shanghai
Vail, A. H., lieut., U.S.N. (*Hartford*)
Vail, John H., manager (Hunt's Wharf) Shanghai
Vaissiere, Père J., missionary (R. C. Mission) Ningpo (Tinghai)
Valdenebro y Olloqui, Jose, judge, Manila
Valentine, B. A., (Kirby & Co.) Hiogo
Valentine, Rev. J. D., missionary (Ch. Eng. Miss. Society) Ningpo (Shaouhying)
Valiant, —, captain (str. *Statesman*)
Valleut, Mlle, (Govt. Silk Reeling Factory) Yedo
Valls, José, Governor's secretary, Manila
Valmale, C., merchant (Valmale, Schwno & Milsom, Yokohama (absent)
Valny, R., merchant (V. Comi) Yokohama
Van Delden, M. C., merchant (Van Delden & Co.) Nagasaki
Van der Brock, T. H. W., secretary (Netherlands Legation) Yedo
Van der Vlies, G., proprietor (Oriental Hotel) Hiogo
Van Dyke, Rev. J. W., missionary (Amer. Pres. Miss.) Bangkok (Petchaburee)
Van Ectvelde, E., merchant (Groth & Co.) Ningpo
Van Es, J. C., pilot, Bangkok
Van Es, P. A., clerk (Holmes, Wadman & Co.) Chefoo
Van Ewyck, D. J., clerk (Netherlands Trading Society) Hiogo
Vanez, J. M., lieut. (Timor Corps) Macao
Van Lier, E. A., M.D., Saigon
Van Lissa, A. M., optical instrument maker (Van Lissa Bros) Yokohama
Van Lissa, J., optical instrument maker (Van Lissa Bros) Yokohama
Vannes, F., assistant (C. & J. Favre Brandt) Yokohama
Vaño, J., clerk (Smith, Bell & Co.) Leyte
Van Oordt, W. C., merchant (Van Oordt & Co.) Yokohama

Van Reed, E. M., merchant (Yokohama)
Van Reypen, W. K., surgeon, u. s. n. (*Iroquois*)
Vapereau, C., professor of French (Peking College)
Vaquinhas, J. dos S., lieut. (Timor Corps) Macao
Varang.t, J., commander (M.M.S. *Hoogly*)
Varnum, R. M., clerk (Walsh, Hall & Co.) Yokohama
Vassonjee, Dwarkadass, merchant (D. Vassonjee & Co.) (absent)
Vastel, —., boilermaker (Arsenal) Foochow
Vaucher, A. E., broker, Arbuthnot Road
Vaud, F., secretary (Municipality) Saigon
Vaughan, H., lieut., i.w.s., firemaster (Royal Artillery) Pedder's Hill
Vaughan, J., pilot (Black Ball Pilot Co.) Shanghai
Vedigal, V., matron (Lock Hospital)
Veeder, P. V., a.m., d.d., professor of Physics (Jap. Govt.) Yedo
Veitch, Andrew, assistant (H. & S. Banking Corporation) Shanghai
Veitch, J. L., nav. sub-lieutenant (H.M.S. *Hornet*)
Veloso, G., vice-consul for Portugal, Manila (Cebu)
Verbeck, Rev. G. F., missionary, Yedo
Vermitre, A. L., tidewaiter (Customs) Chinkeang
Vernede, A., resident, Yokohama
Vernet, E., assistant (George Polite) S'hai
Verny, M, secretary (Yokoska Arsenal) Yokohama
Verny, —., director (Yokohama Arsenal)
Verril, Edward, manager (French Hotel) Manila
Versoz, V., clerk (Peele, Hubbell & Co.) Manila
Vey, Rev. T. L., R. C. missionary, Bangkok
Viademonte, R. M., clerk (Jackson, French & Co.) Manila
Vianna, E. H., clerk (Administração do Conselho) Macao
Vichi, A. L., assist. harbour master, Macao
Vickers, A. J., clerk (Monro & Co.) S'hai
Vickers, J. M., merchant (Gibb, Livingston & Co.) Shanghai
Vidal, I., m.d., Yokohama
Vidlou, —., finisher (Arsenal) Foochow
Vieira, A. J, clerk (Holliday, Wise & Co.)
Vieira, I., dispenser (Oriental Dispensary) Wellington Street
Vieira, P., compositor (Noronha & Sons)
Vielfaure, Mlle. Clorinde (Govt. Silk Reeling Factory) Yedo
Vierow, H., assist. tide-surveyor, Customs, Amoy
Viesse, chief artificer (Jap. Govt.) Yedo
Vigano, B., missionary (Roman Catholic Church) Pottinger Street

Vignale, M. le Chev. Laurent, consul gen. (Italian Consulate) Shanghai
Vigroux, l'Abbé J. P., R. C. missionary, Yedo
Viguier, S. A., divisional inspector and harbour master, (Customs) Shanghai
Villanueva, M., vice-consul (Spanish Consulate) Canton
Villanueva, R., assistant (Loyzaga & Co.) Manila
Villanova, C., signalman (Customs) Shanghai (Pootung)
Villaralbo, A. de, secretary (Civil Govt.) Manila
Villard, —., aide com., Saigon (absent)
Villevielle, chief officer (M. M. S. S. *Menzaleh*)
Villiou, l'Abbé A. (R. C. Mission) Hiogo
Vimeux, C., Mdme., dressmaker, Saigon
Vina, Diego, assistant (Louey & Co.) Cebu
Vincenot, F., baker (Boulangerie d'Europe) Peel Street
Vincent, E., commission agent (Vincent & Co) and Lloyd's surveyor, Swatow
Vincent, E. A. (Mrs E. A. Vincent) Y'hama
Vincent, H., gaoler (British Consulate) Yokohama
Vincent, J., godown-keeper (P. & O. Co.) Shanghai
Vincent, Mrs E. A., milliner and draper, Yokohama
Vine, E. R., assist. engineer, r.n. (*Curlew*)
Viney, J., foreman (*Japan Herald*) Y'hama
Vinson, C., lawyer, Saigon
Vinton, Wm., clerk (P. & O. S. N. Co.) Shelley Street
Visscher, A., clerk (Van Delden & Co.) Nagasaki
Visram, S., merchant, Gage Street
Vitrac, Lieut. —., French Marines, Y'hama
Vlangely, H. E. General A., minister (Russian Legation) Peking
Vock, Arnold, clerk (Dell Oro & Co.) Yokohama
Vogel, C , merchant (Vogel, Hagedorn & Co.) Canton
Vogel, E., merchant (Vogel, Hagedorn & Co.) Praya
Vogel, E , clerk (Vogel, Hagedorn & Co.) Shanghai
Voight, E., assistant (Gaupp & Co.)
Voight, —., master mariner, Bangkok
Voight, O. (Faber & Voight) Hiogo (absent)
Voilkel, S., manager (Pharmacie de l'Union) Shanghai
Voisin, A., clerk (Russell & Co.) Shanghai
Volkmann, C. L., Hollywood Road
Vollhardt, A., steward (Club Germania) Yokohama
Von Bergen, Baron Werner, consul for Germany, Bangkok
Von der Heyde, E., merchant (Schultze, Reis & Co.) Hiogo (absent)

Von der Heyde, E., merchant (Reis, Von der Heyde & Co.) Yokohama
Von Doorn, J., Resident, Yedo
Von Glehn, W. A., clerk (N. A. Ivanoff & Co.) Hankow
Von Hemert, J. Ph., merchant, Yokohama
Von Moellendorff, P. G., assistant (Customs) Kewkeang
Vorobieff, A. S., clerk (N. A. Nefedieff) Tientsin
Vorrath, —., Master Mariner, Bangkok
Vosteen, H., Pilot (Takow)
Vouillemont, E. G., manager (Comptoir d'Escompte) Yokohama
Voyron, J., assistant (Oriental Hotel) Yokohama
Voyron, P., Hotel keeper (Oriental Hotel) Yokohama
Voysey, M., compradore (Domoney & Co.) Hiogo
Vrard, L., jeweller, &c. (Vrard & Co.) Shanghai
Vrooman, Rev. D., missionary, Canton
Vuillermoz, A., watchmaker, Saigon

W

Wachtels, P. H. M., merchant (Wachtels, & Co.) Hiogo
Wada, Y., student interpreter (Japanese Consulate) Shanghai
Wade, H. T., merchant (Findlay, Wade & Co.) Shanghai
Wade, Thomas, F., C.B, minister plenipotentiary and envoy extraordinary (British Legation) Peking
Wadleigh, E. C., merchant (Wadleigh & Emery) Chinkeang
Wadman, E., merchant (Wadman & Co.) Ningpo
Wadman, W. S., merchant (Holmes, Wadman & Co.) and vice consul for Denmark, Chefoo
Waeber, C., acting consul for Germany and actg. consul general for Russia, T'sin
Waggott, W., clerk (Lane Crawford & Co.) Yokohama
Waghorn, G., clerk (China Sub. Tel. Co.) Burd's Lane
Wagner, A., engineer (Novelty Iron-works)
Wagner, C., professor of music, Yokohama
Wagner, C., Jr., clerk (Control Department)
Wagner, L. G., 3rd engineer (Novelty-Iron-works)
Wagner, T., clerk (Pickenpack, Thies & Co.) Bangkok
Wagner, —., engineer (Whitfield & Dowson) Yokohama Iron Works
Wainewright, R. E., solicitor (Harwood & Wainewright) Shanghai
Waite, J. S., inspector (Govt. Telegraph) Gifu
Wake, Geo. E., supt. of cemetery, Y'hama

Wake, H., overseer (Takasima Colliery) Takasima
Wakfer, J., diver (Customs) Shanghai (Pootung)
Walcot, Jno. C. P., Sub. Lieutenant, R.N. (Hornet)
Walker, A., 2nd officer (Chinese gunboat Peng-chao hai)
Walker, A. L., chief officer (M. M. S. S. Meikong)
Walker, Capt. A., brigade major, Mosque Terrace
Walker, F., clerk (Shaw & Co.) Yokohama
Walker, F. D., ship-broker (F. D. Walker & Co.) Yokohama
Walker, F. ., sub-lieut., R.N. (Iron Duke)
Walker, H. B., assist accountant (Oriental Bank) Yokohama (absent)
Walker, H. B., nav. lieut., R.N. (Thetis)
Walker, R., 2nd engineer (Ti'kong C'ton & Macao steamboat Co.)
Walker R., merchant, Gough Street
Walker, Rev. J. E., missionary, Foochow
Walker, R. S., merchant (R. S. Walker & Co.) Gough Street
Walker, S., clerk (Blain & Co.) Shanghai
Walker, T., foreman mechanic (Govt. Railways) Yokohama
Walker, W., assist. eng., R.N. (Frolic)
Walker, W. F., commission agent, Chinkeang
Walker, W. H., clerk (Blain & Co.) S'hai
Walkinshaw, A. W., merchant (Turner & Co.) Foochow
Walkinshaw, Wm., merchant (Turner & Co.) (absent)
Wallace, J., engineer (Borneo Co.) Sarawak
Wallace, J. F., resident, Shanghai
Wallace, Thomas, storekeeper, (Lane, Crawford & Co.) Yokohama
Waller, C. H., assistant (Hongkew Wharf) Shanghai
Wa'ler, J. E., secretary (The Club) S'hai
Wallis, W., proprietor (Shanghai Dispensary) Shanghai
Walmisley, W. H., Lieut. H.M. 80th Regt.
Walsh, A., printer (F. & C. Walsh) Shanghai
Walsh, A. H. H, captain, R.M., Yokohama
Walsh, C. F., editor (Hiogo News) Hiogo
Walsh, F., (Hiogo News Office) Hiogo
Walsh, F. G., printer (F. & C. Walsh) S'hai
Walsh, J. G., merchant (Walsh, Hall & Co.) Yokohama
Walsh, J. J., gunner, U.S.N. (Iroquois)
Walsh, Rob. C., clerk (Walsh, Hall & Co.) Nagasaki
Walsh, Thomas, merchant (Walsh, Hall & Co.) Yokohama (absent)
Walsham, —., secretary (British Legation) Peking
Walter, J., sub. manager (Hongkong and Shanghai Banking Corporation)

Walter, J., clerk (Siber & Brennwald) Yokohama
Walter, W., clerk (Evans, Pugh & Co.) Hankow
Walter, W. B., clerk (Jardine, Matheson & Co.) Yokohama
Walters, H. E., lieut., R.N. (*Thetis*)
Walters, J. M., sub-accountant (Oriental Bank) Foochow (absent)
Walters, W. (Sarawak Trading Co.) S'wak
Walton, H. F., assist. eng., R.N. (*Kestrel*)
Waples, J., assist. (Sayle & Co.) Shanghai
Warburton, Wm., clerk (Browne & Co.) Hiogo
Ward, E., clerk (Jardine, Matheson & Co.) Shanghai
Ward, F., clerk (Govt. Tel.) Shimonoseki
Ward, R., fitter (Japan Railway)
Ward, Thos. C. H., captain, R.N., (*Thetis*)
Ward, W., foreman carpenter (P. & O. S. N. Co.)
Wardlaw, J. C., merchant (Tait & Co.) consul for Portugal, Amoy (absent)
Warfield, Maj. A. G. (Jap. Govt.) Yedo (Kaitikushi)
Waring, H. S., mid., U.S.N. (*Hartford*)
Warren, C., sergeant major, Sarawak
Warren, C. H., merchant (Russell & Sturgis) Manila
Warren, P. L., assistant (Brit. Consulato) Foochow
Warrick, A., clerk (Butterfield & Swire) Hankow
Warrick, W. M., assist. (North Ch. Ins. Co.) (absent)
Warte, —., artisan (Jap. Govt.) Yedo
Warrington, J. B. E., R.N., engineer (Naval Yard)
Washington, T. B. (First College, Jap. Govt.) Yedo
Wasserfall, A., clerk (Siemssen & Co.) Queen's Road
Wasson, James R. (Jap. Govt.) Yedo (Kaitikushi)
Waters, A. (Jap. Govt.) Yedo
Waters, D. W., commission agent, S'hai
Waters, E. J., Resident, Yedo
Waters, J., commission agent (Lucas & Waters) Hiogo
Waters, T., engineer in chief (Jap. Gov.) Yedo
Waterson, Captain, surveyor to insurance companies, Saigon
Watson, A., coal, hewer (Tanjong Kubong mines) Labuan
Watson, A. T., assistant (Yokohama Dispensary) Yokohama
Watson, H. A., clerk (McGregor & Co.) Burd's Lane
Watson, H., clerk (Butterfield & Swire) Shanghai
Watson, J., assistant (Stephen & Stewart) Yokohama
Watson, J., blacksmith (Watson & Co.) Yokohama
Watson, J. C., major (Anglo-Chinese Force) Ningpo
Watson, J., M. D., medical officer (Customs) Newchwang
Watson, J., tidewaiter, Customs, O'keang
Watson, J. W., eng., R.N. (*Thetis*)
Watson, Thos., clerk (Okoolof & Tokmakoff) Hankow
Watson, W., assistant tide-surveyor, (Customs) Swatow
Watson, Wm., bill collector, Shanghai
Watters, T., interpreter (British Consulate) Tientsin
Watt, W., foreman mechanic (Govt. Railways) Yokohoma & Osaka
Watt, W., fitter (Govt. Railways) Y'hama
Watts, A. C., merchant (rec. ship *Express*) and clerk of U. S. Court, Chinkiang
Watts, James, pilot, Taku
Watts, J. W., turnkey (Victoria Gaol)
Way, J. L., Commander, R.N. (*Iron Duke*)
Wauchope, George, accountant, lighthouse service (Japanese Government) Y'hama
Weatherstone, Th., in charge of Hulks *Tchapou* and *Kinsan*, Hankow
Webb, E., clerk (Russell & Co.)
Webb, G. A. C., nav. sub-lieut., R.N. (*Avon*)
Webb, S. D., merchant (Fogg & Co.) S'hai
Webb, W., clerk (Government Telegraph) Yokohama
Webb, W. H., lieut. U.S.N. (*Lackawanna*)
Webb, W. J., barkeeper (Welcome Tavern)
Webber, H. B., fitter (Govt. Railways) Yokohama
Weber, Carl, clerk (Bourjau & Co.) Praya
Webster, J. R., assistant (Holme, Ringer & Co.) Nagasaki
Webster, R., captain of Powder Hulk (Harbour Master's Department)
Webster, T. D., catechist, Sarawak
Webster, T. W., Lieutenant, R.N. (*Princess Charlotte*)
Webster, W., Constable, British Consulate, Chefoo
Weckherlin, W. F. H. van (Diplomatic representative for Denmark) and Minister for Sweden and Norway, Yedo
Weeks, C. D., clerk (Gibb, Livingston & Co.) Aberdeen Street
Weeks, C. O., engineer, R.N. (*Elk*)
Wefer, J. D., pilot, Bangkok
Wegener, F., tidewaiter, (Customs) Ningpo (absent)
Weigert, P., truck and drayman, Yokohama
Weill, J. G., secretary (General Hospital) Shanghai
Weiller, A., (School of Foreign languages) Yedo
Weiller, P., correspondent of *New York Herald*, Yokohama

Weiters, E. B., merchant (Moffat, Weiters & Co.) Shanghai
Welch, J., clerk (Adamson, Bell & Co.) Hankow
Weld, D., clerk (Russell & Co.) Shanghai
Weld, E. D, clerk (Russell & Co.) Kewkeang
Wellings, T., constable (Customs River Police) Shanghai
Wellis, Wm., physician (Jap. Govt.) Yedo
Wells, J., soda water manufacturer, Newchwang
Wells, J., tidewaiter (Customs) Newchwang
Welsh, D, collector (*Japan Gazette* Office) Yokohama
Welsh, D., merchant (McGregor & Co) Burd's Lane
Wennmohs, E., tailor, (Ladage, Oelke & Co.) Shanghai
Wertheimber, L, appraiser (Japanese Customs) Yokohama
Wertheimer, L., teacher (Gaim'sho) Yedo
West, S., (Naval College) Yedo
Wesser, R., assist. (B. Richio) Yedo
West, J., clerk (Hall and Holtz) Shanghai
West, W. A., captain (steamer *Hungchow*) Shanghai
Westall A. C., merchant (Westall, Brand & Co.) Shanghai
Westall, R. R., public tea insp. (Westall, Galton & Co.) Foochow
Westerfield —., band-master, Bangkok
Westoby, T., captn. (str. *Namoa*)
Weston, J. G., public tea inspector (Weston & Co.) Shanghai
Westphal, G., merchant (Schmidt, Westphal & Co.) Nagasaki
Wetmore, F. R., clerk (Chipman, Stone & Co.) Yokohama
Wetmore, W. S., merchant (Frazar & Co.) Shanghai
Wetton, H., engineer, Osaka
Wevezer, —., master mariner, Bangkok
Weys, Wm., employé (U. S. Naval Hospital) Yokohama
Wharry, C. J., M.D., &c., superintendent, Civil Hospital
Wheeler, E., M.D. (Japan Railway) Y'hama
Wheeler, Edwin, M.D., R.N., and Brit.
Wheeler, F., assist. (Watson & Co.) S'hai Legation, Yedo
Wheeler, G. H., clerk (Russell & Co.) Shanghai
Wheeler, H. W., director's secretary (Osaka Mint)
Wheeler, T., powder-maker (Imperial Arsenal) Tientsin
Wheeler, W., clerk (Olyphant & Co.) Praya
Wheeler, W., tidewaiter (Customs) Canton
Wheeler, W. A., officer (P. & O. service)
Wheeley, Ed., clerk (Dent & Co.) Shanghai
Wheelock, T. R., auctioneer (Wheelock & Co.) Shanghai

Wherry, Rev. John, miss., Peking
Whiffin, A., paymaster, R.N. (*Thalia*)
Whilden, Miss. L., (South Bap. Con. U. S. A.) Canton
White, A., broker (Miller, Mackenzie and White) Shanghai
White, C. H., surgeon, U.S.N. (*Idaho*)
White, F. E., constable (British Consulate) Yokohama
White, F. G., clerk (Gibb, Livingston & Co.) Shanghai
White, F. W., commissioner (Customs) Ningpo
White, F. W. A., clerk (Macpherson & Marshall) Yokohama
White, G., resident, Yokohama
White, G. H., assist. eng., U.S.N. (*Saco*)
White, J., pilot, Nagasaki
White, J. G., overseer of telegraphs and roads (Surveyor General's Dept.)
White, J. R., proprietor (Stag Hotel) Queen's Road
White, L. A, M.D., medical officer, Labuan
White, Rev. R. G. and Mrs., missionary, Chinkeang
White, W., clerk (Frazar & Co.) Shanghai
White, W. E. (P. & O. Hulk *Tiptree*) Yokohama
White, W. G., midshipman, R.N. (*Iron Duke*)
White, W. J., resident, Yedo
Whitehead, Rev. S., missionary (Wesleyan Meth. Miss. Soc.) Canton
Whitfeild, H. E., H. W., major general and lieut.-governor (Head-quarter House)
Whitfield, G., engineer (Whitfield & Dowson) Yokohama
Whiting, Rev. J. L., missionary, Peking
Whitkowski, —., (School of Foreign Languages) Yedo
Whitmore, G. F., nav. sub. lieut., R.N. (*Midge*)
Whittall, E., merchant (Jardine, Matheson & Co.) Yokohama
Whittall, James, merchant (Jardine, Matheson & Co.) acting consul for Hawaii, East Point
Whittall, P. G., clerk (Jardine Matheson & Co.) Yokohama
Whittom, Wm., engineer (Loney & Co.) Yloilo
Whymark, G., butcher (Domoney & Co.) Hiogo
Whyte, W. H., capt., R.N. (*Cadmus*)
Whyht, M., engineer, R.N. (*Ringdove*)
Wibmer, L. M., officer (P. & O. Service)
Wickham, B. R., clerk (Tait & Co.) Amoy
Wicking, H., clerk (Lane, Crawford & Co.) Hollywood Road
Wieler, G. A., merchant (Bourjou & Co.) Shanghai (absent)
Wieler, O., clerk (Bourjou & Co.) Shanghai
Wientraub, J. H., importer, Yokohama

Wiggins, C., ship-chandler (J. Carroll & Co.) Hiogo
Wight, J. M., mid., U.S.N. (Palos)
Wignall, J. H., shipwright (Hiogo Iron Works) Hiogo
Wignall, M., engineer (National S. S. Co. Nipon) Yokohama
Wijnhoven, —., Mission Catholique, Peking
Wild, C. A., merchant & consul for Denmark (Gilman & Co.) Foochow (absent)
Wildey, T., light-keeper (Woosung Lighthouse) Shanghai
Wiley, E. H., engineer, R.N. (Thalia)
Wilfrid, Sœur St., sister of charity, Yokohama
Wilgaard, A., tidewaiter (Customs) K'keang
Wilhelm, E., clerk (Muller & Co.) S'hai
Wilk, O., assistant (Ledage, Oelke & Co.) Shanghai
Wilkie, J., tidewaiter (Customs) Canton
Wilkie, J., 2nd engineer (S'r. Douglas)
Wilkin, A. J., merchant (Wilkin & Robison) Yokohama
Wilkins, J. H., shiphandler (Black & Co.) Yokohama
Wilkinson, H. S., 1st assistant (British consulate) Yokohama
Wilks, —., engineer (Wilks & Earnshaw) Manila
Willaume, John, bill broker, Aberdeen St.
Willcocks, E. J. R., second master (Central School) Gough Street
William, R. T., merchant, (reog. ship Express) Chinkeang
Williams, D., assist. (Vulcan Iron Works) Hiogo
Williams, F. T., assist. (The Club) S'hai
Williams, G. B. (Jap. Govt.) Yedo (absent)
Williams, H. D., tidewaiter (Customs) Bangkok
Williams, Joseph (Sacramento Tavern) Yokohama
Williams, P., pilot, Swatow
Williams, Rev. M., missionary (Am. B. Com. For. Missions) Kalgan
Williams, Rt. Rev. C. M., D.D. (Board of Missions U. S. A.) Osaka
Williams, Rev. N. B., missionary (South Bap. Con. U.S.A.) Canton
Williams, R., pilot (Black Ball Pilot Co.) Shanghai
Williams, R. B., clerk (Chapman, King & Co.) Shanghai
Williams, R. P., agent (D. Sassoon, Sons & Co.) Foochow
Williams, S. V., (Jap. Govt.) Yedo
Williams, S. W., L.L.D., secretary and Chinese interpreter (U. S. Legation) Peking
Williams, T. R., steward (The Club) S'hai
Williamson, G., commission agent (Williamson & Co.) Chinkeang

Williamson, Rev. Dr. (Scotch Bible Soc.) Chefoo
Williamson, Rev. J., missionary (Gankin) (absent)
Williamson, T., engineer (S. Easton & Co.) East Point
Williamson, T. G., clerk (Adamson, Bell & Co.) Shanghai
Williamson, W., engineer, R.N. (Curlew)
Willmann, H., clerk (Guichard & Fils) Manila
Willmann, W., assist. (Stilfried & Co.) Yokohama
Wills, G., interpreter (The Saibansho) Yokohama
Wills, W. J., clerk (Chas. Thorel & Co.) Yokohama
Willson, —., compradore (Woodruff & Co.) Yokohama
Wilson, A., police inspector (Lowza Station) Shanghai
Wilson, A., foreman mechanic (Japan Railway) Yokohama
Wilson, A. W., clerk (F. R. Gamwell) S'hai
Wilson, C., mate, U. S. N. (Idaho)
Wilson, F., engineer (Morris, Barlow & Co.) Manila
Wilson, H., (Imp. College) Yedo
Wilson, H., pilot (Independence Pilot Co.) Shanghai
Wilson, J. C., master U.S.N. (Iroquois)
Wilson, J., Tug engineer (P. M. S. S. Co.) Yokohama
Wilson, J. A., merchant (Howell & Co.) Hakodadi
Wilson, James, clerk (Lane, Crawford & Co.) Yokohama
Wilson, Jas., merchant (Wilson, Cornabe & Co.) Chefoo
Wilson, J., light-keeper (Gutzlaff lighthouse) Shanghai
Wilson, John, storekeeper, &c. (Lane, Crawford & Co.) Shanghai
Wilson, R., assist. (Public Works Depart.) Yedo
Wilson, R., clerk (Elles & Co.) Amoy
Wilson, Rev. Jonathan, miss., Bangkok
Wilson, W., architect (Wilson & Salway) Praya East (absent)
Wilson, W., shipchandler (Wilson, Nicholls & Co.) Amoy
Wilson, W. T., staff surgeon, R.N. (Iron Duke)
Wimmer, H., merchant (Wilkin & Robison) Hiogo
Windsor, D. T., merchant (Windsor, Redlich & Co.) Bangkok
Wingate, J. C. A., consul (U. S. Consulate) Swatow
Winkler, J., (H. Ahrens & Co.) Yedo
Winn, J. E., assist. (Walsh, Hall & Co.) Yokohama
Winn, H. H., D.D.S., dentist, Shanghai

Winser, Miss. E., barmaid (International Hotel) Yokohama
Winsor, A. Jr., captain (Str. *Shantung*)
Winstanley, A., assistant (Cornes & Co.) Yokohama
Winstanley, J., auctioneer (Bourne & Co) Yokohama
Winstanley, W., The Club, Shanghai
Wirgman, C. J., artist (*Japan Punch*) Yokohama
Wisner, J. H., clerk (Olyphant & Co.) Shanghai
Wit, J. J., master mariner, Bangkok
Withers, G., assistant (P. & O. S. N. Co.) Shanghai
Witkowsky, A., teacher (Gaim'sho) Yedo
Witkowsky, T., teacher (Gaim'sho) Yedo
Witte, A., clerk (Pustau & Co.) Pottinger St.
Witte, Julius, engr. (Witte & Co.) Manila
Wobbe, H., clerk (Carlowitz & Co.) Praya
Wodehouse, H. E., interpreter (Colonial Secretary's Department) and sheriff, Mosque Terrace
Wodehouse, H. J., sub-lieut., R.N. (*Rinaldo*)
Wohlters, A., proprietor (City of Hamburg Tavern) Queen's Road West
Wolf, L., merchant (Moore & Co.) Y'hama
Wolfe, A., chancellor (Swiss Consulate) Yokohama
Wolf, Rev. John R., missionary (Eng. Ch. Miss.) Foochow
Wolff, A., clerk (Siber and Brennwald) Yokohama
Wolff, Rev. C. H. H., missionary, Yokohama
Wolff, M., clerk (D. Sassoon Sons & Co.) Shanghai
Wolfs, J., clerk (Hecht, Lilienthal & Co.) Yokohama
Wolter, J., assistant (Ladage and Oelke) Yokohama
Wolthers, J. W., chief officer (Takasima Tug Boat) Nagasaki
Wong, F., M.D., medical officer (Customs) Canton
Wong, J. H., assistant (P. & O. S. N. Co.) Yokohama
Wood, A. G., merchant (Gibb, Livingston & Co.) Shanghai
Wood, B. F., asst. eng. U.S.N. (*Iroquois*)
Wood, Chas., clerk (Lane Crawford & Co.) Yokohama
Wood, James (What Cheer House) Hiogo
Wood, J. W., clerk (D. Sassoon, Sons & Co.) Foochow
Wood, R. H. R., clerk (Jardine, Matheson & Co.) Shanghai
Wood, R. P., merchant (Smith, Bell & Co.) Manila (absent)
Wood, Thos. clerk (Drysdale, Ringer & Co.) Hankow
Wood, T. T., master. U.S.N. (*Saco*)
Wood, W., trooper (Brit. Legation Guard) Yedo

Woodford, J. D., clerk (Hongkong and Shanghai Banking Corp.) Wyndham Street
Woodin, E. L., agent (Reuter's Telegram Co.) and storekeeper (P. & O. S. N. Co.) Staunton Street
Woodin, Rev. F. S., missionary, Foochow
Woodruff, F. E., Chinese secretary (Customs) Peking
Woodruff, F. G., compradore (F. G. Woodruff & Co.) Yokohama
Woods, A. G., mid., R.N. (*Iron Duke*)
Woodward, R. H. S., (C. and J. Marine Insurance Co.) Shanghai
Woodward, W. (Naval College) Yedo
Woollatt, G. H., tea inspector (Reiss & Co.)
Woollcombe, H. B., captain, R. N. (*Thalia*)
Woollett, H., asst. (F. Beato & Co.) Y'hama
Woolfe, H. D., tidewaiter, (Customs) T'sin
Woolgar, J., office gunner (P. & O. S. N. Co's. office)
Woolley, A S., nav. mid., R.N. (*Thalia*)
Woolley, W A., student interpreter (Brit. Legation) Yedo
Woolward, A., assist. paymaster in charge (*Hornet*)
Wooton, J., foreman mason (Jap. Govt.) Yedo
Worcester, W., officer (P. & O. service)
Worch, A., clerk (Bacherach & Oppenheimer) Saigon
Worch, Th., clerk (Behre & Co.) Saigon
Worck, T., stevedore (Thomsen & Worck Hiogo
Wortell, J., examiner (Customs) Tamsui
Worthington, G. A., gunner, R.N. (*Dwarf*)
Worthington, Thos., clerk (Ker & Co.) Manila
Wotton, W., solicitor (Caldwell and Brereton) Bonham Road
Wright, A., assistant (Alt & Co.) Nagasaki
Wright, D. M., clerk (Boyd & Co.) Amoy
Wright, F., reporter (*North China Herald* Office) Shanghai
Wright, F. E., commis. (Customs) Foochow
Wright, H. O. P., lieut., R.M., Yokohama
Wright, James H., comm. agent (Wright, Burkill & Co.) Shanghai (absent)
Wright, J. P., clerk (Bull Purdon & Co.) Canton
Wright, J. W., resident, Shanghai
Wright, R., assist. (Findlay, Richardson & Co.) Manila
Wright, Rev. Mr., missionary, Yedo
Wright, W. T., captain (Chinese gun-boat *Feiloong*)
Wringer, I. de, godown keeper (Netherlands Trading Society) Yokohama
Wulbrand, H., pilot, Takow
Wulfe, J., shipchandler (W. H. Hohuholtz & Co.) Yokohama
Wulff, T., proprietor, "Eureka Bowling Saloon," Yokohama

Wulff, W. L., assistant (Agra Bank) S'hai
Wunch, W. G., 3rd engineer (str. *Thales*)
Wusterhausen, E., assistant (Ledage, Oelke & Co.) Shanghai
Wyatt, O. M., clerk (Butterfield & Swire) Shanghai
Wychoff, M. N., teacher (Jap. Govt.) Yedo
Wylie, A., agent (British & Foreign Bible Society) Shanghai
Wylie, A., consulting engineer, Yokohama
Wylie, R. A., clerk (Cornes & Co) Y'hama
Wynesar, H., clerk (Smith, Baker & Co.) Hiogo
Wynn, capt. (Str. *Vu'can*) Yedo
Wyon, E., foreman, coin dept. (Osaka Mint)

X

Xavier, C. A., clerk (Olyphant & Co,) S'hai
Xavier, C. J., assist. (Novelty Iron Works) Praya West
Xavier, wardmaster (Civil Hospital)
Xavier, F., compositor (Noronha & Sons)
Xavier, F., member (Junta do Langamento das Decimas) Macao
Xavier, F. B., interpreter (Spanish Consulate) Canton
Xavier, F. M. D., writer (Naval Yard)
Xavier, J. A., clerk (R. H. Cairns)
Xavier, J. M., trader, Bangkok
Xavier, J. P., clerk (Comptoir d'Escompte) Shanghai
Xavier, L., trader, Bangkok
Xavier, L. A., clerk (McEwen, Frickel & Co.) Queen's Road
Xavier, L. J., shipping runner (Frisby & Co.)
Xavier, M. B., linguist (Procurador's Department) Macao
Xavier, M. F., assist. (Boyd & Co.) S'hai
Xavier, V. F., boiler maker (Novelty Iron Works)
Xitoo, A., clerk (Nachtrieb, Leroy & Co.) Shanghai

Y

Yague y Mateos vicar general (Ecclesiastical Department) Manila
Yaish, S. Y., clerk (E. D. Sassoon & Co.) Tientsin
Yangwell, —., manager (Yangtye Cargo Boat Co.) Shanghai
Yates, F., engineer (P. & O. Service)
Yates, M. T., vice-consul general and interpreter (U. S. Consulate) Shanghai
Yda, Y., Japanese consul general, S'hai
Yeck-chon, member (Junta do Langamento das Decimas) Macao
Yeend, D., assist. (Gribble & Co.) Nagasaki
Yeo, E. (Naval College) Yedo
Yeo, J. G., engineer and acting secretary (Shanghai Gas Co.) Shanghai

York, G. E., assist. (W. Watson & Co.) Shanghai
Yorke, L. A., assistant paymaster, U.S.N. (*Yantic*)
Yould, F. M., merchant (Adamson, Bell & Co.) Shanghai
Young, A., shipwright (Hongkong and Whampoa Dock Co.) Kowloong
Young, F., steward (Grand Hotel) Y'hama
Young, Geo. R., merchant (Smith, Bell & Co.) Manila (absent)
Young, J., pilot, Taku
Young, J., master mariner, Bangkok
Young, J. B., asst. engineer (Govt. Railroad) Yokohama
Young, J. G. K., lieut., H. M. 80th Regt.
Young, J. M., clerk (Rodewald, Schönfeld & Co.) Shanghai
Young, Laurence (London Inn) 126 Queen's Road
Young, M., Captn (str. *Thales*)
Young, R, Dr., L. R. C. P. Edin &c. Stanley St.
Young, S., Examiner (Customs) Chefoo
Young, W. S., merchant (Gilman & Co.) Foochow
Younger, W., 2nd engineer (str. *Namoa*)
Youngman, Miss K. M., Missionary, Y'hama
Yrisarry, J. M., clerk (Aguirre & Co.) Manila
Yuill, G. Skelton, clerk (Butterfield & Swire) Foochow
Yvanovitch, A., clerk (Jardine, Matheson & Co.) Shanghai
Yzquierdo, H. E. Don Rafael, governor and captain general, Manila

Z

Zachariæ, Dr. D. M., physician, German Consulate, Shanghai
Zappe, E., consul for Germany, Y'hama
Zappino, D. F., Collector General, Customs, Manila
Zea, Rev. F., miss. (R. C. Church, Kangboe) Amoy
Zedneizeck, W., proprietor (Marine Hotel) Bangkok
Zehnder, Rev. J. L., missionary, Sarawak
Zeigler, J., clerk (Lutz & Co.) Manila
Zembsch, J. P. A., clerk (Aymonin & Co.) Yokohama
Zetterlund, C. U., master mariner, B'kok
Ziegler, C., merchant (Ziegler & Co.) Yokohama
Zobel, J., apothecary (Zobel & Nohr) Manila
Zuanazzis, V., sister teacher (The Convent) Caine Road
Zudaire, Don Francisco, secretary (Ecclesiastical Department) Manila
Zuzarte, R., Compositor (*Saigon Advertiser*) Saigon

THE CHINA DIRECTORY.
1874.

香 HONGKONG. 港

Colonial Government.
總憲署 Tsung-hin-shü

Governor, Commander-in-Chief and Vice-Admiral—Kennedy, His Excellency Sir Arthur Edward, K.C.M.G., C.B.
Lieut. Governor—Whitfeild, His Excellency Major General H. W.
Private Secretary and Aide-de-Camp to the Governor—O'Callaghan, Captain C., 1st West India Regiment.
Aide-de-Camp to the Lieut.-Governor—Burn, D. B., Lieut 75th Regiment

EXECUTIVE COUNCIL.
議政總局 Ye-ching-tsung-kuk

President—His Excellency the Governor
Members—The Senior Military Officer; The Hon. the Colonial Secretary; The Hon. the Attorney General; Smith, the Hon. C. C.

LEGISLATIVE COUNCIL.
定例總局 Ting-lai-tsung-kuk

President—His Excellency the Governor
Official Members—The Hon. the Chief Justice; The Hon. the Colonial Secretary; The Hon. the Attorney General; The Hon. the Treasurer
Un-Official Members—Ryrie, Hon. Phineas; Rowett, Hon. Richard; Alexander, Hon. W. H.; Whittall, Hon. James
Clerk of Councils—D'Almada e Castro, L.

Government Departments.
(Alphabetically arranged.)

AUDITOR GENERAL'S DEPARTMENT.
Auditor General—Austin, Hon. J. G.
Audit Clerk—Silva, J. M. A. da
2nd Do.—Ribeiro, F. Vieira

CENTRAL SCHOOL.
大書院 Tai-shü-ün

Head Master and Inspector of Schools—Stewart, Frederick, M.A.
2nd Do.—Willcocks, E. J. R.
3rd Do.—Falconer, Alexander
Assistants—Chiu Chi Yeung
  Wong Yung Ching
  Chiu Chi Tsung
Chinese Masters—Chan U Ch'ün
  Ho Chuk Shan
  Ip Ut Lau

COLONIAL SECRETARY'S DEPARTMENT.
總督衙門 Tsung-took-nga-mun

Colonial Secretary—Austin, Hon. J. Gardiner
Chief Clerk—D'Almada e Castro, L.
1st do.—D'Almada e Castro, J. M.
2nd do.—Alves, J. M. S.
3rd do.—Guttierrez, S. C.
Temporay do.—Barretto, J. A.
Government Interpreters—Tonnochy, M. S.; Lister, A.; Wodehouse, H. E.

FIRE BRIGADE.

香港救火人員
Heung-kong-kau-fo-yan-yuen

Superintendent—May, Hon. Chas.
Assistant do.—Creagh, C. V.; Tonnochy, M. S.
Clerk—Seth, A.
Engineer—Bailie, H. C.
Overseer of Water Works—Stanfield, G.
Chinese Interpreters—Four
Foremen—Livingston, Jas.; O'Brien, Thos.; McClellan, Wm.
Assistant do.—Four
1st Class Engine Drivers—Kerr, G.; Power, E.
2nd do.—Two
European Firemen—Fourteen
Chinese Stokers—Four
Do. Firemen—Fifty Six
Do. Watchmen—Eight

GAOL.

監房 Kam-fong

Superintendent—Douglas, Francis
Warden—Grey, Alfred
Clerk and Interpreter—Lingmoi, Y.
Head Turnkey—Watts, J. W.
First Class European Turnkeys—Six
Second do. do.—Six
Debtor's Jail Turnkey—One
Matron—One
Chain Gang Guards—Sixteen

GENERAL POST OFFICE.

書信館 Shü-sun-koon

Postmaster General—Mitchell, F. W.
Assistant do.—Barff, S.
Accountant—Rocha, J. G. da
Sorters—Machado, J. M. E.; Costa, D. A. da; Leiria, A.; Simpson, John; Rodrigues, A. J.; Placo, A. M.; Barradas, Z. M.
Marine do.—Auila, A. L. Sanches del; Barradas, J. M.

AGENTS.

Canton—Hillier, Walter C.
Macao—Souza, R. de
Swatow—Ford, Colin M.
Amoy—Bristow, Henry B.
Foochow—Warren, P. L.
Ningpo—Giles, H. A.
Shanghae—Martin, J. P.
Clerk at Shanghai—Silva, G. S. S. da
Nagasaki—Quin, John. J.
Yokohama—Machado, F. G.
Hiogo—Miles, H. A.
Hankow—Parker, E. H. (absent); Fraser, J. P. Munro (acting)

GOVERNMENT GARDENS AND TREE PLANTING DEPARTMENT.

Superintendent—Ford, Charles

HARBOR MASTER'S DEPARTMENT.

船政廳 Shün-ching-t'ing

Harbor Master, Marine Magistrate, Emigration and Customs Officer—Thomsett, H. G., R.N.
Acting Assistant Harbor Master—Lister, Alfred
First Clerk—Lording, W. S.
Second do.—Machado, F.
Third do.—Alves, J. L. de S.
Fourth do.—Gutarres, A. P.
Fifth do.—Botelho, A. C.
Boarding Officers—Sampson, A. F.; Speechly, J.
Inspector of Cargo Boats and Junks—McClellan, W.; Collaço, J.; Curtin, John
Signalman at Victoria Peak—Mather, H., with one Chinese
Indian Interpreters—Soonderam, Idroos Moosdeen
Interpreters, Writer, Shroff—Chinese
Inspectors at Out-Stations—Burns, G. (Shaukiwan); McBeth—(Aberdeen); Duggan, C. (Stanley)
Officer in charge of Powder Hulk—Webster, R.
Gunner—Brown, C.
Health Officer and Medical Inspector of Emigrants—Adams, W. S., M.D.

MERCANTILE MARINE OFFICE.

At Sailor's Home

MARRIAGE REGISTRATION OFFICE.
(MAGISTRACY.)

婚姻事務司 Fan-yan-sz-mo-sz

Marriage Registrar—Collins, James

MEDICAL DEPARTMENT.

Colonial Surgeon and Inspector of Hospitals—Ayres, P. B. C., M.R.C.S.E., L.M., L.R.C.P.E.
Health Officer of the Port and Medical Inspector of Emigrants—Adams, W. S., M.D., C.M.
Inspectors of Nuisances—Hazlett, A.; and O'Brien, T.

CIVIL HOSPITAL.

Superintendent—Wharry, C. J., M.D., M.C., M.R.C.S.E., L.S.A.L (Assistant Surgeon, Royal Navy)
Apothecary—Botelho, Alberto
Ward-masters—Ryan, Thos.; Xavier, F.; Chun A Lok

HONGKONG. A 3

MEDICAL DEPARTMENT.
(*Continued.*)
LOCK HOSPITAL.

西營盤醫生館

Sai-ying-poon-i-shang-koon

Surgeon—Ayres. P. B. C., M.R.C.S.E., L.M., L.R.C.P.E.
Apothecary—Souza, A. de
Matrons—Assis, G.; Vedigal, V.
Inspector of Brothels—King, Wm.
Assistant do.—Horton, W.
Inspector in charge at Wanchai—Lee, J.

OFFICE OF THE COLLECTOR OF STAMP REVENUE.

印捐總局 Yan-kün-tsoor j-kook

Collector of Stamp Revenue—Mitchell, F. W.
Acting do.—Simpson, John
Clerks—Rodrigues, J. S.; Aquino, E. H. d'

POLICE DEPARTMENT.

大館 Tai-koon

Capt. Superintendent—Deane, W. M., M.A.
Deputy do.—Creagh, C. V.
Assistant do.—Vacant
Supt. of Chinese Contingent—Wodehouse, H. E.
First Clerk—Collago, M. A.
2nd do.—Blackwood, Hugh
Chinese do.—Choo-a-heem, Sung-a-sing, and Chung-a-wan

INSPECTORS.

Act. Chief Inspector—Horspool, G.
Central Barracks—Grimes, J.; Grey, T.; Gair, W. T.
Eastern District—Halloran, J. (absent); Craddock, J.
Western do.—Orley, G.
Water Police—Stroud, H.
Showkewan—Burns, J.
Aberdeen—McBeth, —. (acting)
Starley—Duggan, C.
Kowloong—Batten, W.

EUROPEAN FORCE.
Sergeants—11
Constables—89

INDIAN FORCE.
Jemadars—1
Interpreter—1
Sergeants—10
Constables—164

POLICE DEPARTMENT.
(*Continued.*)
CHINESE FORCE.
Interpreters—14
Sergeants—2
Constables—187

WATER POLICE.
European Inspector—1
Do. Sergeant—1 } included above
Do. Constables—24
Chinese Sergeants—11
Do. Constables (Boatmen)—140

POLICE MAGISTRATES' ESTABLISHMENT.

巡理廳 Tsun-li-t'eng

1st Police Magistrate—May, Charles
2nd do.—Russell, James (absent)
Acting do.—Mitchell, F. W.
Coroner—Lister, Alfred
1st Clerk—Collins, James
2nd do.—Seth, Arathoon
3rd do.—Chew A-kwan
4th do.—Ng Kwai Sang
1st Chinese Interpreter—Ng-a-Choy
2nd do.—Bedell Le Yun
3rd do.—Ho Atim
Chinese Clerk and Shroff—Ng Heung-Lun
European Usher and Process Server—Saunders, George
Assistant do—De Cruz Jose
Hindustani Interpreter, Acting—Abdool Kadir
Chinese Usher and Process Server—Le Ayum
Chinese Interpreter and Clerk to Coroner—Chun Tai-kwong
Coroner's Summoning Officer—Detailed from Police

REGISTRAR GENERAL'S DEPARTMENT.

華民政務司 Wa-man-ching-mo-sz

Registrar General—Smith, Hon. Cecil Clementi
Acting Registrar General—Tonnochy, Malcolm Struan
1st Clerk—Gerrard, John
2nd do.—Sanguter, C. F. A.
Registration Clerk—Osmund, C.
Chinese Clerk—Cheung Aleung; Im Among
Shroff—Yung-tso
Chinese Registration Clerks—U Lai-ün; Ch'an Atsau; Wong Ayau; Yung Ahung

HONGKONG.

SUPREME COURT.

案憲衙門 Nip-hin-nga-mun

Chief Justice—Smale, Hon. John
Puisne Judge—
Attorney General—Bramston, J.
Acting do.—Hayllar, Hon. T. C.
Registrar—Alexander, Hon. W. Hastings
Deputy Registrar—Huffam, F. S.
Crown Solicitor—Sharp, E.
Cle k of Court—Holmes, H. J.
Judge's Clerk—Amos, L. J. V.
Interpreter—Rozario, Rafael A. do
Chinese Clerk and Interpreter—Ch'un-tai-kwong
Clerk and Usher—Barrington, T. W.
Clerk and Shroff—Ng Mun Yu
Bailiff—McBean, Thos. R.
Appraisers—Huffam, F. S.; Willcocks, E. J. R.
Registrar of Companies—Huffam, F. S.

SHERIFF OF HONGKONG.

Wodehouse, H. E. (absent)
Lister, A.
Deputy Sheriffs—Stewart, F.; Willcocks, E. J. R.

SURVEYOR GENERAL'S DEPARTMENT.

量地官 Leung-ti-koon

Surveyor General—Price, John M., F.R.G.S., F.R.C.S.
Asst. Surveyor General—Vacant
Inspector of Buildings—Neate, S. R.
Clerks of Works—Danby, William; and Prestage, Ward
Overseers of Work—McLeod, E.; White, J. G.; Stoves, F.; Stainfield, G.
Watchman at Pokfulum—Lewis, E.
1st Clerk—Tomlin, Geo L.
2nd Do.—Chagas, F. Z. das
3rd Do—Gutierrez, M.
4th Do.—Chun A Fook
Interpreter—Ng A Tsün

TREASURY.

庫務司 Foo-mo-sz

Acting Treasurer—May, C.
1st Clerk and Cashier—Carvalho, J. A.
2nd do. and Accountant—Alves, A. F.
3rd Clerk—Madar, A. R.
4th do—Rangel, Q. A.
Valuators—Gerrard, John; Madar, A. R.
Notice Server—Lum Shu Tuk
1st Shroff—Cheong Aloy
2nd do.—Cheong Achow

VICE ADMIRALTY COURT.

按察司 On-tsat-sz

Judge and Commissary—Smale, Hon. John
Queen's Advocate—Hayllar, Hon. T. C.
Registrar—Alexander, Hon. W. H.
Queen's Proctor—Sharp, E.
Marshal—Tonnochy, M. S.
Surrogates—Huffam, F. S.; Holmes, H. J.

Justices of the Peace.

Alexander, Hon. William Hastings
Arthur, Edward (absent)
Belilios, Emanuel Raphael
Creagh, Charles Vandeleur
Deane, Walter Meredith
Douglas, Francis
Gower, Samuel John (absent)
Greig, James
Keswick, William (absent)
Lemann, Henry B.
Linstead, Theophilus Gee
Lister, Alfred
Lowcock, Henry
Magniac, Herbert St. Leger
May, Hon. Charles
McMurdo, Robert
Mitchell, Francis Williams
O'Brien, Richard Alfred, M.D.
Pyke, Thomas
Rowett, Hon. Richard
Russell, James (absent)
Ryrie, Hon. Phineas
Sassoon, Solomon David
Smith, Hon. Cecil Clementi
Stewart, Frederick
Thomsett, Henry G., R.N.
Tonnochy, Malcolm Struan
Whittall, Hon. James
Wilson, Wilberforce (absent)

Military Department, H. M.'s Army.

THE STAFF.

水師員弁 Sui-sz-yuen-pin

Commanding H. M. Forces in China and Straits Settlement—Whitfeild, Major General H. W.
Asst. Military Secretary—O'Shaughnessy, Brevet Major, 12th Regiment
Aide-de-Camp—Burn, Lieut. D. B. 75th Regiment
Brigade Major—Walker, Captain A., 99th Regiment
Fort Adjutant (Hongkong)—Blake, J. S. O. B., 1/10th Regiment

HONGKONG.

THE STAFF.
(Continued.)

Acting Military Chaplains—Baynes, Rev. W. H. (Church of England); Lamont, Rev. J. (Presbyterian); Longo, Rev. Father (Roman Catholic)
Brigade Department — Merritt, Charles, Garrison Sergeant Major

ROYAL ARTILLERY.
炮兵房 P'au-ping-fong

Colonel—Phillipps, P. W.
Lieut.—Hubback, H., W. J., acting adjutant and quarter-master
Lieut.—Vaughan, H., fire-master and inspector of warlike stores

ROYAL ENGINEERS.
烟赸尼也官 Yin-chin-ni-yah-koon

Lieut.-Colonel—Grain, E. M., commanding Royal Engineers
Captain—Jones, D. G.
Lieutenants—Gosset, F.; Rich, H. B.
Staff Serjeants—Marr, Thos.; Fireman, F.
Quarter-master Serjt.—Styles, Geo.
Staff Sergt.—Jarvis, David; Daniel, Robert
Chinese Draftsman—Wing Kee

H.M.'s 80TH REGIMENT.

Lieut. Colonel—Smith, H. C.
Major—Amiel, C. F.
Captains—Craufurd, F. B. N; Creagh, C. A.; Bradshaw, J. L.; Huskisson, S. G.; Stone, R. W.
Lieuts.—Brown, H. J.; Anderson, W. T.; Young, J. G. K; Prior, J. E. H.; Cole, C. C.; Sherrard, J. O.; Potts, L. C; O'Geran, E. H. B.; Walmisley, W. H.
Sub-Lieut.—Master, L. H.
Insp. of Musketry.—Young, J. G. K., Lt.
Adjut.—Saunders, A., St.
Quarter-master—Belt, J.
Surgeon Major—McFall, D. C.

ROYAL ENGINEER DEPARTMENT.
烟赸尼也署 Yin-chin-ni-yah-shu

Acting Surveyor—Vacant
Military Clerks—Marr, Staff-Sergt. Thomas; Firman, Staff-Sergt, Frederick
Do. Foremen of Works—Styles, Quartermaster Sergeant George; Jarvis, Staff-Sergt. David; Daniel, Staff-Sergt. Robert
Chinese Draftsman—Wing-kee

CONTROL DEPARTMENT.

Assistant Controller—Cleeve, C. K.
Clerk Controller's Office—Cruise, W.
Reserve Store Duties; Deputy Commissary—Silveira, H. C. P.
Do. Assistant Commissaries—Skinner, Edmund, G.; Arber, G.
Clerks, Store Offices—Garrett, W. R.; Wagner, C. J.
Issue of Stores—Dalgarno, A.
Foreman of Stores—Grimble, P.
Magazine Foreman—Coales, T.
Assist. Foreman—
Barrack, Transport, Supply and Hospital Duties; Deputy Commissary—Johnston, James
Do. Assistant Commissary—Gammell, W.
Barrack Clerk—Ferreira, F.
Clerk Supply & Transport Office—Manook, E.

PAY BRANCH.

Deputy Control Paymaster and Treasurer—Cooper, Thomas, W.
Assist. Control Paymaster—Mayers, E. G.

Army Medical Department.
品字行 Pan-taz-hong

Deputy Surgeon General and Principal Medical Officer in China and the Straits—Crocker, Alfred
Surgeon Major—McFall, D. C, 80th Regt.
Surgeons—Belcher, J. W., M.D.; Murray, J., M.B.; Cruickshank, B., M.D.
Apothecary to the Forces—Davies, John

CHAPLAINS DEPARTMENT.
CHURCH OF ENGLAND CHAPLAIN.
Baynes, Rev. W. H.
ROMAN CATHOLIC CHAPLAIN.
Longo, Rev. Father
PRESBYTERIAN CHAPLAIN.
Lamont, Rev. James

Naval Department.
H. M. Navy.
水師堤督 Shui-sz-tai-took

Vice-Admiral and Commander-in-Chief—Shadwell, Chas F. A., C B., F.R.S.
Flag Captain—Arthur, William
Secretary—Hutchison, William B.
Flag Lieut—Dicken, Frederick R.
Secretary's Clerk—Gifford, Chas. E. (asst. paymaster);

NAVAL YARD.

水師船政局 Shui-sz-shun-cheng-kuk

Commodore in charge of Naval Establishments H.M.'s Princess Charlotte—Pariah, John E.
Secretary to Commodore do.—Muir, George W., Paymaster, R N.
Master Attendant—Hewlett, W., R.N.
Naval and Victualling Storekeeper Cashier—Bremner, John, Paymaster, R.N.
Accountant—Hawke, R. F. (England)
Acting Inspector of Machinery—Bird, E. T. B.
Chief Clerks—Besant, E.; Rickard, George P.
Writers—Cunha, J. da; Danenberg, V.; Rocha, V. C., Jr.; Danenberg, H.; Poate, W. H.; Barradas, E. C.; Carvalho, L. F.; Xavier, F. M. D.; Pinna, J. de; Pereira, F. G.
Engineers—Bencke, G. A. C.; Harvey, J. R.; Warrington, J. B. E.; Cowpar, I. A.; Michell, G. N. H.; Goldsmith, H. C.
Boatswain—Melling, Robt., R.N.
Storemen—Randell, J.; Gilbie, W.; Martin, F.; Adnams, W. T.; Smith, H.; Afah, L.
Superintending Carpenter—Vacant
Assistant do.—Ellis, S. J., R.N.
Boilermaker—Hadley, A.
Smith—Grant, A. T.
Moulder—Gingell, J.

H. M. NAVAL HOSPITAL,
MOUNT SHADWELL, WANCHI.

Naval Officer in charge—Pariah, Commodore John E.
Deputy Inspector General—Loney, William, M.D.
Chaplain—Morton, Rev. Thomas F., M.A.
Surgeons—McDonald, Alex., M.D.; Burgess, Peter, M.A., M.S.
Clerk Civil Service—Coles, George
Assistant Dispenser—Cape, John S.

Vessels in Commission.

"AVON," (4), D. S. COMPOSITE GUN-VESSEL.
467 TONS, 120 H. P.

Commander—Patterson, John C.
Lieutenant—Sulivan, James Y. F.
Sub-Lieutenant—Nicholson, Charles S.
Nav. Sub-Lieut.—Webb, G. A. C.
Surgeon—Dunlop, James, M.D.
Assist. Paymaster in Charge—Lark, C. S.
Engineers—Robertson, Peter; Michell, G. N. H.; Adamson, James
Gunner—Lee, Jas. T.

"CADMUS," (17) S. CORVETTE.
1,466 TONS, 400 H.P.

Captain—Whyte, William H.
Lieutenants—McKechnie, Alexander G.; Skipwith, William; Pow, George L.; Strange, Charles, V.; Brenton, Reginald O. B. C.
Nav. Lieut.—Helby, Francis T.
Lieut. Mar.—Tracey, Osborn
Chaplain—Malet, Rev. A. S., B.A.
Staff Surgeon—Llyas, Jacob E.
Paymaster—Ceely, Charles H.
Chief Engineer—Martin, Charles F.
Sub-Lieuts.—Callwell, William H.; Brooke, Hans H. H.; Ash, Edward P.
Navigating Sub-Lieuts.—Roche, Henry C.; Greaves, Edmund E.; Newton, H. B.
Surgeon—Feltham, Charles
Assistant Paymasters—Ollard, Henry J.; Clarke, Richard H.
Engineer—Lavers, Robert H.
Gunner—Toill, William J.
Boatswain—Kent, John
Carpenter—Barr, John
Midshipmen—Stewart, William F.; Horsley Arthur J.; Knox, Hervey A.; Oswell, Thos. J.; Edwards, William R. H.; Jackson, Henry B; Pocock, John J.
Nav. Mid.—Marshall, John R. T.
Assit. Engineers—Haddy, George A.; Denny, J. S. H.; Thorne, C. W.
Clerk—Reed, William E. E.

"CURLEW," (3) DOUBLE S. GUN-VESSEL.
665 TONS, 160 H. P.

Commander—Church, Edmund J.
Lieutenant—Cotton, N.
Sub.-Lieut.—Ogle, Henry A.
Nav. Sub-Lieut.—Stuart, Charles W.
Surgeon—McClement, Fred., M.D.
Assist. Paymaster—Brown, Edwin R.
Engineers—Williamson, William; Bowman, James
Gunners 2nd Class—
Acting Boatswain 2nd Class—St. John, Charles
Assist. Engineer 1st Class—Vine, Ed. R.

"DWARF," (4), DOUBLE SCREW COMPOSITE GUN-VESSEL.
465 TONS, 120 H. P.

Commander—Bax, B. W.
Lieutenant—Foster, R. W.
Sub-Lieut.—Daniell, William H. M.
Nav. Sub-Lieut.—
Surgeon—Isaac, J. B.
Assist. Paymaster, in Charge—Meyer, B. F.
Engineers—Rowe, N.; Coombs, J. T.
Assit. Engineers—Broad, William
Gunner—Worthington, Geo. A.

HONGKONG.

"ELK," (4), DOUBLE SCREW COMPOSITE GUN-VESSEL.
485 TONS, 120 H. P.

Commander—Barnett, John B.
Lieut.—Davis, Edward H. M.
Sub-Lieut.—Primrose, Geo. A.
Nav. Sub-Lieut.—Lugden, William
Surgeon—Galloway, William, M.D.
Assist. Paymaster, in Charge—Jones, R. S.
Engineer—Grant, David
Assist. Engineers—Weeks, Courtenay O; North, Caleb J.

"FROLIC," (4), S. GUN-VESSEL, 462, TONS, 100 H. P.

Commander—Buckle, Clande E.
Lieut.—Bell, Charles E.
Sub-Lieut.—Bouverie, Charles W. P.
Nav. Sub-Lieut.—Symes, Francis A.
Surgeon—Brown, Richard G.
Assist. Paymaster, in Charge—Court, Archibald
Engineers—Spinks, John ; Allsop, Charles
Assist. Engineers—Walker, William
Boatswain—Bazill, Samuel

"GROWLER,"
(Same class as Teazer, Sister Ship.)
(Not yet arrived)
Commander—Stewar , Walter
Engineers—Bryan, William ; Craddock, George T.

"HORNET," (4) D. SCREW C. G. VESSEL.
464 TONS, 120 H. P.

Commander—Cameron, Oxford S.
Lieutenant—Swan, Joseph
Sub-Lieutenant—Walcot, John C. P.
Nav. Sub-Lieut.—Veitch, John L.
Surgeon—Colahan, William H., M.D.
Assist. Paymaster in charge—Woolward, A.
Engineer—Thompson, Joseph V.
Assist Engineers — Renfry, Arthur H. ; Egan, Oscar G.

"IRON DUKE," (14), DOUBLE S. IRON SHIP.

ARMOUR PLATED, 3,787 TONS, 600 H. P.
FLAG SHIP, CHINA.

Vice Admiral—Shadwell, Chas. F. A., C.B.
Flag Lieutenant—Dicken, Frederick R.
Secretary—Hutobison, William B.
Clerks to Secretary—Gifford, C. E. ; Herbert, Henry G., assistant paymaster
Captain—Arthur, William
Commander—Way, John L.
Lieutenants—Digby, Henry A. ; Drury, Charles C. ; Atkinson, George L. ; Carpenter, Alfred ; Norcock, Charles J. ; Russell, Gerard W.

"IRON DUKE," (4), DOUBLE S. IRON SHIP.
(Continued.)

Navigating Lieutenant—Tracey, Stopford C.
Chaplain and Naval Instructor—Edwards, Rev. John C., M.A.
Lieut. R. M. A.—Lambert, Walter M.
Staff Surgeons—Wilson, William T. ; Hill, George B. (for special service in connection with Lock Hospitals in China and Japan)
Staff Surgeons 2nd class—Caldwell, John (for service with Marine Battalion); Hilston, Duncan, M.D. (for sick quarters Yokohama)
Chief Engineer—Lamont, James
Paymasters—Thompson, Alex. ; Pittman, Frank (additional for service as Naval Accountant and Victualling Storekeeper at Yokohama)
Sub-Lieutenants—Kinder, Ernest; Jauncey, Henry H. ; Walker, Francis E. ; Clarke, Henry S. ; Rogers, Reginald W. S. ; Harrison, Gilbert K. ; Maturin, Wm. M.
Surgeons—Crawford, James; Irvine, Gerard J. ; Macdonnell, Henry (for sick quarters at Yokohama); Putsey, William H. (for service with Marine Battalion); Wheeler, Edwin, M.D. (for service at Legation, Yedo)
Assistant Paymaster—Malsher, Henry A.
Engineers—Ritchie, James; Rook, William B. ; Carte, Edward L. ; Scoble, James W. ; Davey, W. R.
Gunner 1st class—Eales, Ralph
Boatswain 1st class—Cooper, Henry V. C.
Carpenter 1st class—Kestell, John T.
Midshipmen— White, William G. ; Bone, Frank F. ; Miller, Thomas T. R. ; Edyvean, William H. ; Woods, Arthur G. ; Montresor, W. H. B. ; Bacon, A. C. A. ; Daberley, James G. ; Dillon, H. B. ; Tippinge, L. F. G.
Nav. Midshipman—Dockrell, Herbert J.
Assist. Engineer, 1st Class—Palmer, Alfred
Do. 2nd Class—Lock, Henry J.

OFFICERS OF MARINE BATTALION IN JAPAN.

Lieut. Col. Commanding—Richards, F. J.
Captain—Broughton, J. D., paymaster
2nd Captain—Hill, A., adjutant
Do. R. M. A.—Bridgford, S. T., control officer
Lieut.—Hungerford, T. E., quarter master; Captains—Snow, E. B., Walsh, A. H. H. ; Hill, Arthur ; Gray, E. O. B.
Lieuts.—St. John, St. A. ; Heseltine, G. A. ; Fagan, C. S. F. ; Drury, Fred R. B. ; Sandwith, J. H. ; Denny, B. St. L. ; Polkingborne, S. ; Smyth, A. C. ; Wright, H. O. P. ; Nepean, A. O.

"KESTREL," S. Gun-Vessel.
Commander—Boulton, William R.
Lieutenant—Gardner, Charles
Sub.-Lieut.—Muggeridge, James S.
Nav. Sub.-Lieut.—Grey, Henry
Surgeon—Davidson, Charles, M.B.
Assist. Paym. in Charge—Bolt, Charles J.
Engineer—Jones, Robert W. ; Pellew, Henry M. G.
Assist. Engineer—Walton, Horatio F.
Boatswain—Searle, James

"LAPWING," (8) S. Gun Vessel.
663 Tons, 160 H. P.
(Not yet arrived on the Station.)

"MIDGE," (4), Double Composite Gun-vessel.
484 Tons, 120 H. P.
Commander—Grant, John F. G.
Lieutenant—Cochran, Alexander
Sub-Lieut.—Lindesay, Abraham H.
Nav. Sub-Lieut.—Whitmore, George F.
Surgeon—Simms, James
Asst. Paym. in Charge—Corrie, Arthur Le B.
Engineer—Croome, Lambert J.
Asst. Eng.—Bascombe, George E.
Boatswain—Roberts, Joseph

"MOSQUITO," Gun-Boat.
295 Tons, 60 H. P.
Lieut. and Com.—Bond, William H.
Nav. Sub.-Lieut.—Buckner, William H. P.
Surgeon—Robertson, John A.
Engineer—Rice, John ; Bourke, Henry G.
Boatswain—Milton, Abraham

"OPOSSUM," Gun-Boat.
60 H. P.
(Tender to "Princess Charlotte.")
Lieut. and Com.—Fairlie, Henry J.
Engineer—Ball, George
Boatswain—Clarke, John
Assist. Engineer—Pellew, Henry W. R.

"PRINCESS CHARLOTTE," (12), Receiving Ship.
2,443 Tons.
Commodore—Pariah, John E.
Secretary—Muir, George W.
Lieutenants—Fairlie, Henry J. ; Ellis, Gerald A.
Nav. Lieut.—Webster, Thomas W.
Staff Com.—Hewlett, Wm. (for service in Dockyard at Hongkong)

"PRINCESS CHARLOTTE," (12), Receiving Ship.
(Continued.)
Chaplain—Morton, Rev. Thos. F. (for service in Naval Hospital)
Staff Surgeon 2nd class—Bennett, Will R., M.D.
Paymasters—Harvey, H. J. ; Derisley, Martin (for service at Shanghai) ; Bremner, John (for Hongkong Yard)
Inspector of Machinery—Bird, Edward T. (for service in China Station)
Surgeon—Atkinson, Robert
Assistant Paymaster—Ramsay, John S. ; Thompson, David J. (additional for Commodore office)
Engineers (for service in Hongkong Yard)—Benoke, G. A. C. ; Harvey, J. R. ; Warrington, J. B. E. ; Couper, J. A. ; Mitchell, G. N. H. ; Goldsmith, H. C.
Gunner—Callahan, James
Boatswains—Melling, Robert (for Hongkong Yard) ; Taylor, William
Carpenters—Elias, Samuel J. ; Roberts, W. E. (for Shanghai Yard)

"RINALDO," (7), S. Sloop.
951 Tons, 200 H. P.
Commander—Parsons, George
Lieutenants—Nuthall, Edward S. ; Dwarford, John
Nav. Lieut.—Lilburn, Selby
Staff Surgeon 2nd Class—Buckley, J.
Paymaster—Ashton, John
Chief Engineer—Sagar, Thos.
Sub.-Lieuts.—Wodehouse, Henry J. ; Alexander, Frederick
Surgeon—Low, G. W.
Engineer—Anderson, J.
Gunner—Large, George
Boatswain—Richard, P.
Carpenter—Berry, James T.
Clerk—Hume, Andrew
Assist. Engineer—Harris, Richard

"RINGDOVE," (8), Double Screw Gun-Vessel.
666 Tons, 160 H. P.
Commander—Pitman, Robert
Lieutenant—Bayley, Wentworth V.
Sub-Lieut.—Slaney, Harry C. Kenyon
Nav. Sub. Lieut.—Hughes, Valentine D.
Surgeon—Gorham, Anthony, M.D.
Asst. Paymaster in Charge—Spain, George
Engineers—Harrison, Holland ; Whyham, Maurice
Asst. Engineer—Morris, Thomas
Boatswain—Coombe, John

HONGKONG. A 9

"SALAMIS," (2), P. Despatch Vessel.
885 Tons, 250 H. P.

Lieut. and Com.—Littleton, Hon Algernon C.
Lieut—Browne, W. L. H.
Navig. Lieut—Hutton, Wilson
Surgeon—Powell, Scudamore K.
Chief Engineer—Harris, John T.
Nav. Sub. Lieut.—McFarlane, John W.
Asst. Paym. in Charge—Cannon, James T.
Engineers—Weeks, George J.; Weeks, Courtenay O.
Gunner—Cox, Philip
Boatswain—Miller, Alfred
Asst. Engineers—Rigler, George; Grieve, Wm. H.

"SWINGER," (4) S. Gun Vessel.
295 Tons, 60 H. P.
(Not yet arrived on the Station.)

"TEAZER," (4), Double S. Composite Gun-Vessel.
464 Tons, 120 H. P.

Commander—Fitzmaurice, Hon. James
Lieutenant—Smythies, Palmer R.
Sub-Lieut.—Logan, Francis H.
Nav. Sub-Lieut.—Scott, Alfred B.
Surgeon—Paton, William Y.; M.B.
Assist. Paymaster in Charge—Rae, W. H.
Engineer—Cape, Thomas
Assist. do.—Harding, George
Boatswain—Grant, F. G.

"THALIA," (6), Screw Corvette.
1,459 Tons, 400 H. P.

Captain—Woollcombe, Henry B.
Lieut.—Lewin, W. H.; Moysey, F. A.; Luscelles, Hon. F. C; Blackett, F. A.
Nav. Lieut.—Hackman, A.
Chaplain—
Staff Surgeon 2nd Class.—Head, Richard L. B.
Paymaster—Whiffin, Alfred.
Chief Engineer—Inness, William F.
Nav. Instr.—Healey, William L.
Sub Lieut.—Hungerford, Somerset A.; Creswell, William R.; Creswell, Philip, E.
Nav. Sub Lieut.—Thompson, William T.
Surgeon—Rallfborne, Charles A., M.D.
Assist. Paym.—Hall, Thomas W.
Engineers—Willey, Edward H.; Cole, William F.
Gunner—Ellis, Alexander
Boatswain—Tarver, George
Carpenter—Philips, Charles
Midshipmen—Triggs, Thomas B.; Raitt, Percy C.
Nav. Mid.—Woodley, Arthur S.
Asst. Engr.—McCarthy, John
Clerk—Belcher, Andrew

"THETIS," (13), S. Corvette.
1322 Tons, 350 H. P.

Captain—Ward, Thomas Le H.
Lieutenants—Walters, Henry E.; Lopez, James de B.; Og'e, Walter S. A.
Nav. Lieut.—Walker, Herbert D.
Chaplain and Nav. Instr.—Parry, Rev. William W.
Staff Surg. 2 Cl.—Magill, Marlin, M.D.
Paymaster—Moorman, Isaac B.
Chief Engineer—Davies, Owen A.
Sub-Lieut.—Target, Arthur T.; Henriques, William A. L.; Rosanquet, Seager S.
Surgeon—Nash, Herbert M.
Asst. Paym.—Mallard, Macleod G. O.
Engineers—Rigby, George; Watson, J. W.
Asst. Eng.—Rockett, Herbert S.
Gunner—Shea, John
Boatswain—Thompson, John
Carpenter—Griffiths, John H.

"THISTLE," (4), Double S. Composite Gun-Vessel.
465 Tons, 120 H. P.

Commander—Leet, Henry K.
Lieutenant—Boldero, Arthur A.
Sub-Lieut.—Roupell, Stuart B.
Nav. Sub-Lieut.—Donegan, Henry
Assist. Surgeon—Mulcahy, Edward
Assist. Paymaster—Scott, B C.
Engineers—Blackwell, George; Pringle, Thomas
Gunner—Hutchins, John
Boatswain—Stewart, James

Harbour Ships.

"FLAMER," Naval Hospital Tender

"MEANEE," Military Hospital

United States Navy.
ASIATIC STATION.

Rear Admiral—Parrott, E. G.
Chief of Staff—Colhoun, E. R.
Flag Lieut—Emory, W. H.
Secretary—
Fleet Surgeon—Bloodgood, D.
Fleet Paymaster—Stewart, E.
Fleet Engineer—Moore, J. W.
Fleet Marine Officer—Bartlett, H. A.

U. S. NAVAL DEPOT, HONGKONG.

Paymaster in Charge—Guild, Chas. F.
Paymaster's Clerk—Harder, Jacob

U. S. NAVAL HOSPITAL, YOKOHAMA.

Surgeon in Charge—King, William M.
Passed Assistant Surgeon—Dickinson Dwight

"ASHUELOT," U. S. S.
4TH RATE, 6 GUNS, 786 TONS.

Commander—
Lieut. do.—Cassel, Douglas
Lieutenant—Carmody, Rob E.
Masters—Turner, Wm. H.; Bolles, T. D.
Ensign—Nickels, J. A. H.
Surgeon—McMurtrie, D.
Assist. Paymaster—Addicks, J. T.
1st Assist. Engineer—Bumap, Geo. J.
2nd do.—Fulmer, D. M.

"HARTFORD," FLAG SHIP.
18 GUNS, 2900 TONS.

Captain—Colhoun, E. R.
Lieut. Commanders—Shepard, E. M.; Pigman, G. W.
Lieutenants—Vail, A. H.; Lisle, R. M.; Gill, C. B; Tremain, H. L.
Master—Rodgers, John A.
Midshipmen—Hunsicker, J. L.; Downes, Jno.; Marshall, Wm A.; Fox, Chas. E.; Waring, H. S.; Sawyer, F. E.; Baker, D. F.
Mate—Levin, Chas.
Paymaster—Stewart, Edwin
Surgeon—Bloodgood, D.
P. Assist. Surgeon—Babin, H. J.
Chief Engineer—Moore, Jn. W.
1st Assist. dos.—Upham, J. B.; Ford, J. D.
Chaplain—Lewis, J. K.
Captain Marines—Bartlett, H. A.
2nd Lieut. do.—Ela, F. P.
Boatswain—Miller, P. J.
Gunner—Cross, R. H.
Carpenter—Dixon, J. A.
Sailmaker—Bordsall, Jno. A.

"IDAHO," STORE-SHIP (YOKOHAMA.)

Lieut. Commander—Nelson, Thos.
Lieutenants—Nichols, H. E.; Marthon, Jos.
Mates—Wilson, Chas.; Callander, A. F.
Gunner—Swan, George
Surgeon—White, C. H.
Paymaster—Allen, Rob. W.

"IROQUOIS," SCREW.
6 GUNS, 1575 TONS.

Commander—Adams, H. A.
Lieut. do.—Glass, Henry
Lieutenant—Baker, H. R.

"IROQUOIS," SCREW.
(*Continued.*)

Masters—Ruschenberger, C. W.; Houston, N. T; Wilson, J. C; Hall, M. E.
Midshipman—Seabury, S.
Surgeon—Van Reypen, Wm. K.
Asst. Surgeon—Magruder, A. F.
Paymaster—McDaniel, Chas. A.
Chief Engineer—Sprague, J. P.
1st Asst. do.—Wood, B. F.
Boatswain—Butland, Francis
Gunner—Walsh, J. J.

"LACKAWANNA," U. S. S.
10 GUNS, 2220 TONS.

Captain—McCauley, E. Y.
Lieut. Commander—Crowninshield, A. S.; Nields, H. C.
Lieutenant—Webb, Wm. H.
Master—Colvocoresses, G. W. Potter, Wm. P.
Ensign—Bull, Jas. H.
Midshipmen—Elliott, W. P.; McIntosh, H. A.; Foster, Chas. A.
Surgeon—Schofield, W. K.
Assist. Surgeon—Black, C. E.
Paymaster—Stevenson, J. H.
Chief Engineer—Fitch, H. W.
1st Assist. do.—Brosnahan, J. G.
2nd do.—Mickley, J. P.
2nd Lieut. Marines—Schenck, W. S.
Boatswain—Hawkins, C. E.
Gunner—Hays, James
Carpenter—Junkin, N. H.
Sailmaker—Cuddy, Wm.

"MONOCACY," U. S. S.
4TH RATE, 6 GUNS, 747 TONS.

Lieut. Commander Comdg.—Phillip, Jno. W.
Lieut. Commander—Dickins, F. W.
Lieutenants—Grove, Thos. G.; Greenleaf, F. W.
Masters—Harber, G. B.; Prime, E. S.
Assist. Surgeon—Meyers, T. D.
Passed Assist. Paym.—Redfield, J. B.
1st Asst. Engineer—Adamson, A.
2nd Do.—Nagle, Chas. F.

"PALOS," SCREW.
4TH RATE, 806 TONS.

Lieut. Commander—Bridgman, W. R.
Master—House, J. B.
Midshipmen—Naber, F. W.; Hanus, G. C.; Wight, Jas. M.
Assist. Paymaster—Thomson, C. H.
Assist. Surgeon—Harvey, H. P.
2nd Assist. Engineer—Rowbotham, Wm.

HONGKONG.

"SACO," U. S. S.
8 Guns, 900 Tons.

Commander—McDougal, Chas. S.
Lieut. Commanders—Mullan, D. W.; Green, J G
Masters—Franklin, J.; Davenport, R. G.; Wood, T. T.
Ensign—Clark, Chas. A.
P. Assist. Surgeon—Ayers, J. G.
Assist. Paymaster—Breese, John
1st Assist. Engineer—White, Geo. H.

"YANTIC," U. S. S.
8 Guns, 900 Tons.

Commander—Stanton, O. F
Lieuts.—Edes, B. L.; Gillpatrick, W. W.
Masters—Spalding, L. G.; Bowman, C. G.; Breck, R. A.
Midshipmen—James, N. T.: Rhinehart, B. F.; Mertz, A.; Lusher, O. E
Passed Asst. Surgeon—Parker, J. B.
Asst. Paymr.—Yorke, L. A.
1st. Asst. Engr.—Hall, Geo. W.
2nd Do.—Galt, R. W.

Consulates.

AUSTRIA-HUNGARY.
雅爹厘啞領事官
A-ta-li-a-ling-sz-koon

Consul-General—Overbeck, G.

BELGIUM.
大卑之暗國領事官
Tai-pi-chi-am-kwok-ling-sz-koon

Consul—Nicaise, Hippolyte

DENMARK.
大顛辟國領事官
Tai-tin-mak-kwok-ling-sz-koon

Consul—Jensen, Rud.

FRANCE.
大法國領事官
Tai-fat-kwok-ling-sz-koon

Consul—Sienkiewicz, Adam
Chancelier & Vice-Consul—La Forest, Charles C. Lacathon de

IMPERIAL GERMAN CONSULATE.
28 Praya Central
大日耳曼國領事官
Tai-yat-i-man-kwok-ling-sz-koon

Consul—Cordes, J. F.
Secretary—Hauschild, L.
Physician—Clouth, C., M.D.
Shipping Master—Petersen, W.

HAWAIIAN ISLANDS.

Consul-General—Keswick, Hoabie William (absent)
Acting do.—Whittall, Hon. James

ITALY.
大意打厘國領事官
Tai-i-ta-li-kwok-ling-sz-koon

Acting Consul—Linstead, T. G.

NETHERLANDS.
大立化蘭國領事官
Tai-nap-fa-lan-kwok-ling-sz-koon

Consul—Beyer, Ludwig

PORTUGAL.
大西洋國領事官
Tai-sai-yeung-kwok-ling-sz-koon

Consul General—Remedios, J. J. dos
Vice-Consul—Romano, A. G.

RUSSIA.
大俄羅斯國領事官
Tai-ngo-lo-sz-kwok-ling-sz-koon

Consul—Heard, John (absent)
Acting Vice-Consul—Heard, George F.
Secretary—Pereira, J. P.
Chinese Writer—Mouy Kai

SIAM.
暹羅國領事官
Chim-lo-kwok-ling-sz-koon

Consul—Nicaise, Hippolyte

SPAIN
Arbuthnot Road.
大呂宋國領事官
Tai-lui-sung-kwok-ling-sz-koon

Consul—Lavalle, Don José Antonio de (absent)
Vice-Consul—Navarro, Don José de (absent)
Acting Consul—Tejada, Don Fermin Saenz de
Chancellor and Acting Collector—Souza, Don Eusebio Florentino de
Clerk—Souza, Don Donnolo P. de

SWEDEN AND NORWAY.
士威頓及那威國領事官
Sz-wei-tun-kap-noh-wei-kwok-ling-sz-koon

Consul—Jensen, Rud.

UNITED STATES.
大花旗國領事官
Tai-fa-ke-kwok-ling-sz-koon

Consul—Bailey, David H.
Vice-Consul—Loring, H. S.
Shipping Master—
Clerk and Interpreter—Ching Ah Chee
Usher—Chinese

Clubs, &c.

BIBLIOTHECA LUSITANA.
(Club Lusitano Building, Shelly St)

Committee—Lima, J. M. O.; Figueiredo, J. M. V. do; Costa, P. A. da

BIBLIOTHECA PORTUGUEZA.
GOUGH STREET.

Secretary—Carvalho, L. F.
Treasurer—Luz, J. A. da

CHAMBER OF COMMERCE.
ROOMS—CITY HALL.
香港通商總局
Hop-kong-toong-sheung-tsoong-kook

Chairman—Ryrie, Hon P.
Vice-Chairman—Greig, J.
Committee—Sassoon, S. D; Kaye, Wm.; André, A.; Heard, Geo. F.; Cordes, J. F.; Karberg, P.; Lemann, H. B.

CLUB GERMANIA.
大普國公司 Tai-poo-kwok-kung-sz

President—Behre, F.
Vice-President and Secretary—Erdmann, C.
Treasurer—Ruttmann, H.
Stewards—Stotterfoht, H.; Noodt, Emil
Librarian—Krebs, C.
Chinese Clerk—Lin Shuen Ting

CLUB LUSITANO.
新西洋公司 Sun-sai-yeung-kung-sz

Directors—Barretto, J. A. (chairman); Silveira, F. C. P. da (secretary); Alves, A. F. (treasurer); Machado, F. J., and Costa, P. A.
Clerk—Rodrigues, F. P.

HONGKONG CHORAL SOCIETY.
CITY HALL.
歌樂會 Ko-ngok-wui

President—Lemann, H. B.
Secretary—Starkey, R. D.
Treasurer—Lyall, R.
Conductor—Sangster, C. F. A.
Accompanyist—Lemann, H. B.
Members of Committee—Alford, R. G.; Falconer, G. B.; Coughtrie, J. B.

HONGKONG CITY HALL.
香港公院 Heong-kong-kung-yün

General Committee—Whittall, Hon. James (chairman); Ryrie, Hon. P. (vice-chairman); Rowett, Hon R.; Sassoon, S. D.; Overbeck, G.; Lemann, H. B.; Lowcock, H.; Jensen, R.; Cordes, J. F.; Ruttonjee, D.; Forbes, W. H.
Secretary, Librarian and Curator—Dennys, N. B.
Chinese Clerk—A-yow

HONGKONG CLUB.
新公司 Sun-kung-sz

Committee—Lowcock, H.; Whittall, Hon. Jas.; Dixwell, G B; Deacon, R.; Dods, G, M D.; Greig, Jas.; Coxon, A.; Pyke, T.; Lemann, H. B.; Coughtrie, J. B.; Kaye, W.
Secretary—Beart, Edward

HONGKONG.

HONGKONG CRICKET CLUB.
打地波會 Ta-ts-po-wui

President—Greig, James
Hon. Secretary—
Hon. Treasurer—Foss, H.
Additional Members of Committee—Darby, W. H. F.; Cole, C. C., 80th Regt.; Fairlie, H. J., R.N.

HONGKONG DEBATING SOCIETY.
香港敍事會 Hong-kong-pok-sz-wui

Committee—Ryrie, Hon. P. (President); Dulcken, A. C. (Hon. Secretary and Treasurer.)

HONGKONG RIFLE ASSOCIATION.
香港習洋鎗會
Heong-kong-tsap-yeong-tseong-wui

Patron—His Excellency the Governor
Committee—Coxon, Atwell
Hon. Sec. and Treasurer—Woodin, E. L.

HONGKONG YACHT CLUB.
Commodore—Heard, George F.
Vice-Commodore—Rowett, The Hon. R.
Hon. Sec. and Treasurer—Beart, Edward
Committee—Forbes, W. H; Nunn, C. F.; and the above-named officers

CLUB FLAGS.
The distinguishing Flags of the Club shall be as follows:—
Burgee—Red with a White Cross, and a Blue 5-pointed Star in the centre of the Cross
Commodore's Flag—A broad pendant with White Cross and Star as before, and one White Ball in the Upper left hand corner
Vice Commodore's Flag—The same as Commodore, with two White Balls
Ensign—Each Yacht shall be allowed to carry the Ensign of the Nation to which her owner belongs
Signals—The Commercial Code

YACHTS.
Wave—22 tons, cutter, Blue and White Triangles, W. H. Forbes
Cynthia—24 tons, cutter, White Flag, Blue St. Andrew's Cross and Red Diamond, F. W Coare
Loiterer—50 tons, schooner, Red, White Diamond, Swallow Tail, George F. Heard (Commodore)

HONGKONG YACHT CLUB.
YACHTS.
(Continued.)
Naiad—28 tons, cutter, Red, White, Red, Blue Maltese Cross, J. McLeod
Aura—26 tons, cutter, White, Red Maltese Cross, Blue border, Hon. R. Rowett (Vice-Commodore)
Daphne—20 tons, Red and Blue Swallow Tail, C. Vincent Smith
Marie—20 tons, cutter, Black, Red and White Squares, Theo. Schneider

PARSEE CLUB.
白頭會館 Pak-ts'u-oy-koon

Committee—Ruttonjee, D.; Horiwalla, M. S.; Tatta, D. C.
Hon. Secretary—Horiwalla, M. S.

PORTUGUESE CLUB.
GOUGH STREET.
西洋公司 Sai-yeung-kung-sz

President—Remedios, J. H. dos
Secretary—Carvalho, L. F.
Treasurer—Gutierrez, J. A.
Director—Remedios, D. A. dos

SAILOR'S HOME.
WEST POINT.
西管盤水手館
Sai-ying-p'oon-shui-shau-koon

Trustees—Whittall, Hon. Jas; Forbes, W. H; Dent, John; Thomsett, H. G., R.N.
Directors—Lowcock, H.; Heard, A. F.; McIver, A; Jensen, R; Lemann, H. B.; Sassoon, S. D.; Pyke, T.; Heaton, A. McG.
Chaplain—Baynes, Rev. W. H., M.A. (S. Peter's church)
Secretary—Thomsett, H. G., R.N.
Treasurers—Oriental Bank
Steward—Schuster, J. T.
Assistant—Keller, Jno.
Do.—Bleecker, A.

VICTORIA CLUB.
STAUNTON STREET.
Chairman—
Secretary and Treasurer—Agabeg, A. L., Jun.
Member of Committee—Chater, C. P.

VICTORIA RECREATION CLUB.

FOR BOATING, SWIMMING AND GYMNASTICS.
AT GOVERNMENT WHARF.

闘三板會 Tau-sam-pan-wui

President—Kennedy, H. E. Sir A.
Chairman—Greig, James
Secretary—Knowles, J. S.
Treasurer—Young, W. S.
Committee—(For Boat-house) Woodin, E. L.; McLeod, J.
Do.—(For Gymnasium) Straok, A.; Tonnochy, M. S.
Do.—(For Swimming Bath) Linstead, T. G.; Benecke, O.

Masonic Lodges.

DISTRICT GRAND LODGE OF FREE-MASONS IN CHINA.

(OFFICERS FOR 1878.)

雍仁會館 Yung-yan-ui-koon

Right Worshipful District Grand Master—Murray, Henry (absent)
Deputy D. G. M.—Linstead, T. G.
D. G. Senior Warden—
D. G. Junior Warden—Adams, W. S.
D. G. Chaplain—
D. G. Treasurer—Chater, C. P.
D. G. Registrar—Blakeman, A. N.
D G. Secretary—Remedios, A. F. dos
President, D. G. C. of G. Purposes—Caldwell, D. R.
D. G. Assistant do——
D. G. Senior Deacon—Levy, A.
D. G. Junior do.—Vincent, J.
D. G. Superintendent of Works—Salway, W.
D. G. Director of Ceremonies—Beaant, E.
D. G. Assistant do.—Dulcken, A. C.
D. G. Sword Bearer—James, H. G.
D. G. Organist—Sangster, C. F. A.
D G. Pursuivant—Fairbairn, J.
D. G. Assistant do.—Arthur, Wm. M. B.
D. G. Stewards—Manger, J. E.; Hodgkins, J. R.; Hassell, J. T. G.; Blackwell, R.
D. G. Tyler—Hogan, J.

DISTRICT GRAND CHAPTER.

D. G. Superintendent—Murray, H. (absent)
D. G. 2nd Principal—Gundry, R. S.
D. G. 3rd do.—Hart, J.

PERSEVERANCE LODGE, No. 1,165.

Worshipful Master—Caldwell, D. R.
Senior Warden—Hodgkins, J. R.
Junior do.—Dennys, N. B.
Treasurer—Symonds, J. W.
Secretary—Costa, P. A. da

PERSEVERANCE LODGE, No. 1,165.
(*Continued.*)

Organist—Arthur, W. M. B.
Senior Deacon—Pearson, T.
Junior do.—Chater, J. T.
Director of Ceremonies—Orley, G.
Steward—Driscoll, T. N.
Inner Guard—Dennys, H. L.
Tyler—Hogan, J

UNITED SERVICE LODGE, No. 1,341.

Worshipful Master—Cannon, S.
Senior Warden—Belt, J.
Junior do.—Adnams, W. T.
Treasurer—Brion, C. O.
Secretary—Merritt, C.
Senior Deacon—Watts, J. W.
Junior do.—Frayling, W. W.
Director of Ceremonies—Gillbee, W.
Inner Guard—Carline, J.
Steward—Smallwood, S.
Tyler—Hogan, John

VICTORIA CHAPTER, No. 525.

M. E. Z.—Kiær, H.
H.—Blakeman, A. N.
J.—Jameson, J. N.
Scribe E.—Hodgkins, J. R.
Scribe N.—Arthur, W. M. B.
P. S.—Chater, C. P.
1st Assist. S.—Manger, J. E.
Treasurer—
Janitor—Hogan, J.

VICTORIA ENCAMPMENT.

(OFFICERS FOR 1874.)

E. C.—Kiær, H.
Prelate—Blakeman, A. N.
1st Captain—Sangster, G. F. A.
2nd do.—
Registrar—Remedios, A. F. dos
Expert—Manger, J. E.
Captain of Lines—Arthur, W. M. B.
Treasurer—Chater, C. P.
1st Herald—
Equerry—Hogan, J.

VICTORIA LODGE, 1026, E.C.

W. M.—Jameson, J. N.
S. W.—Dulcken, A. C.
J. W.—Blackwell, R.
Treasurer—Legge, W.
Secretary—Hodgkins, J. R.
S. D.—Young, W. S.
J. D.—Hinckley, N. B.
D. of C.—
Steward—Matheson, W.
I. G.—Grey, A.
Tyler—Hogan, J.

HONGKONG.

ZETLAND LODGE, No. 525.
(OFFICERS OF 1874.)

Worshipful Master—Manger, J. E.
Senior Warden—Mallory, L.
Junior Warden—Sangster, C. F. A.
Treasurer—Maclehose, J.
Secretary—Arthur, W. M. B.
Senior Deacon—Humphreys, W. G.
Junior Deacon—Newitt, W. T.
Director of Ceremonies—Brook, W.
Inner Guard—Cox, J. S.
Steward—Ball, W.
Tyler—Hogan, J.

Missions, Churches, &c.

ASILE DE LA SAINTE ENFANCE FRANCAISE.
QUEEN'S ROAD EAST.

育嬰堂 Yuk-ying-t'ong

Superioress—Croix, Sœur Paul de la
Sisters—Gregorio, Sœur Marie; Sales, Sœur Françoise de; Joseph, Sœur Benoit; Benjamin, Sœur Maria

CHRISTADELPHIAN SYNAGOGUE.
No. 2 OVERBECK COURT.

基督兄弟會堂
Kee-tuk-hing-tai-wui-t'ong

Teacher and Expounder of Truth—Hart, Thomas

CHRISTADELPHIAN LIBRARY.
No. 2 OVERBECK COURT.

Librarian—Hart, Thomas

CHURCH MISSIONARY SOCIETY.
WEST POINT.

傳福音會 Chün-fuk-yam-wui
Hutchinson, Rev. A. B.

THE DIOCESAN HOME AND ORPHANAGE.

女書館 Nui-shü-koon

President—Kennedy, H. E. Sir Arthur, K.C.M.G. & C.B.
Vice-Presidents—Whitfeild, H. E. Major-General H. W.; Shadwell, H. E. Vice-Admiral Charles A., C.B.; Smale, Hon. Chief Justice; The Venerable the Archdeacon of Hongkong

THE DIOCESAN HOME AND ORPHANAGE.
(Continued.)

Hon. Treasurer—Whittall, Hon. James
Committee—Smith, Hon. C C.; Alexander, Hon. W. H.; Braddon, H. E.
Hon. Secretary—Kidd, R. Hayward
English Master—Arthur, W. M. B.
Matron—Arthur, Mrs

THE DOMINICAN MISSION,
CAINE ROAD.

呂宋巴禮行 Lui-soong-pa-lai-hong

Procurator—Heroe, Rev. F. B.
Vice-Procurator—Fernandez, Rev. V.

EVANGELICAL MISSIONARY SOCIETY OF BASEL, SWITZERLAND.

西營盤客家禮拜堂
Sai-ying-poon-hak-ka-lai-pai-tong

Lechler, Rev. R. (absent)
Piton, Rev. Ch. P.
Loercher. Rev. J. G.
Bellon, Rev. W. (Lilong)
Bender, Rev. H. (Chonglok)
Reusch, Rev. Ch. G. (Lilong)
Gussman, Rev. G. A. (Chonglok)
Ott, Rev. R. (Chonglok)
Chan, Rev. M. (Lilong)
Rong, Rev. A. (Chonglok)

FOUNDLING HOUSE, (GERMAN.)
WEST POINT.

西營盤育嬰堂
Sai-ying-poon-yuk-ying-t'ong

Superintendent—Klitzke, Pastor E.
Sisters—Brandt, Miss L.; Leesemann, Miss P.
Schoolmistress—Schroeder, Miss F.

FRENCH ROMAN CATHOLIC MISSION.
STAUNTON STREET.

天主教 (士丹頓街)
Tin-chü-kau (Sz-tan-tun-kai)

Procureur—Osouf, Rev. P. M.
Vice-Procureur—Coste, Rev. J.

POKEFOOLUM.

Directeur du Sanatorum—Patriat, Rev. Ch. E.

HONGKONG AUXILIARY ASSOCIATION OF THE BRITISH AND FOREIGN BIBLE SOCIETY.

Patron—His Excellency the Governor
President—The Right Revd. The Bishop of Victoria
Vice-President—The Hon. Chief Justice Smale
Lay Committee—Alford, Robert G.
Hon. Secretary—Hutchinson, Revd. A. B.

ITALIAN CONVENT.
羅瑪姑娘院 Lo-ma-koo-neung-ün

Superioress—Stella, Mother Maria
Sisters—Pietra, Adelaide; Bertelli, Matilde; Zuanazzis, Virginia; Compagnotti, Claudia; Manzoto, Giuditta; Barritto, Angelica; Frigerio, Luigia; Ferrario, Virginia; Luciano, Maria; Allocchio, Teresa; Bertolotti, Emilia; Allanson, Maria; Ricci, Tomasia; Barretto, Mathilda; Pereira, Anna
Chinese Sisters—Maddalena; and Ana

AZYLUM ST. JOSEPH, WANCHAI.
Italian Sisters—Testera, Giuseppina; and Ravioli, Angiolina
Chinese Sister—Agata

LONDON MISSIONARY SOCIETY.
倫敦傳教會 Lun-tun-chun-kau-ui

Legge, Rev. James, D.D., LL.D. (absent)
Eitel, Rev. E. J., M.A., PH.D.
Edge, Rev. Ch.

RELIGIOUS TRACT SOCIETY.
Treasurer—Davis, H. W.
Hon. Secretary—Hutchinson, Rev. A. B.

RHENISH MISSIONARY SOCIETY.
Louis, Rev. W. (Fukwing)
Faber, Rev. E. (Fumun)
Hubrig, Rev. F. (Canton)
Nacken, Rev. J.
Pritzsche, Rev. C. (Longheu)
Dilthey, Rev. W. (Fumun)

ROMAN CATHOLIC CHURCH.
WELLINGTON AND POTTINGER STREETS.
天主教堂 T'in-chü-kau-t'ong

Procurator of Propaganda and Prefect Apostolic—Raimondi, Very Rev. T.
Vice-Prefect—Burghignoli, Rer. G.
Missionaries—Vigano, B.; Longo, V.; Leang, M.
On the Mainland—Piazzoli, L.; Leang, M.; Leang, T.; Chu, S.

SEAMEN'S CHURCH.
Chaplain—Bayues, Rev. W. H., M.A.
Service at 6 p m in Summer, 5 p.m. in Winter. Morning Service and Communion at 11 a m. first Sunday in each Month. All seats free.

ST. JOHN'S CATHEDRAL.
大禮拜堂 Tai-lai-pai-t'ong

Lord Bishop of Victoria—Vacant
Archdeacon of Victoria—Gray, Venerable J. H., M.A. (Canto)
Canons of St John's Cathedral—McClatchie, Rev. T. (Hankow); Butcher, Rev. C. H. (Shanghai)
Registrar of Diocese—Sharp, Edmund
Colonial Chaplain—Kidd, Rev. R. Hayward, M.A.
Trustees—Colonial Chaplain (chairman); Smith, Lou. Cecil C.; Alexander, Hon. W. H.; Mitchell, F. W., Esq.; Pyke, T., Esq.; Lemann, H. B., Esq.
Treasurer—Mitchell, F. W
Auditors—May, Hon. C.; Smith, Henry Esq.
Organist—Sangster, C. F. A.
Verger and Sexton—Saunders, G.

ST. PAUL'S COLLEGE.
聖保羅書院 Shing-po-lo-shü-ün

Visitor—The Archbishop of Canterbury
Warden—The Bishop of Victoria

ST. SAVIOUR'S ENGLISH COLLEGE.
羅馬堂書院 Lo-ma-t'ong-shü-ün

Patron—Raimondi, Very Rev. T., P.A.
Directors—Vigano, Rev. B., for the Day Scholars; Longo, Rev. V., for the Boarders
Rector—Palmer, Rev. E. S., O.S.B.
Prefect—Macdonald, Rev. J. A.
Teachers—For English, Arithmetic, Bookkeeping and Geometry, Terry, J. W.; for Natural Philosophy, Longo, Rev. V.; for Portuguese, Silva e Souza, J. M. da; for Chinese, Chea-me-chu; for Music, Pinto, R.; for Drawing, Baptista, M. A.

ST. STEPHEN'S MISSION CHURCH.
聖士堤反禮拜堂 Shing-sz-tai-lan-lai-pai-t'ong

Native Clergyman—Lo Sam Ynen, Rev.
Church Missionary—Hutchinson, Rev. A. B.

HONGKONG.

TEMPERANCE HALL.
No. 2, OVERBECK COURT.
Manager—Hart, Thomas

UNION CHURCH.
大石柱禮拜堂
Tai-shek-ch'ü-lai-pai-t'ong
Minister—Lamont, Rev. James
Trustees—Legge, Rev. Dr James; Sharp, G.; Bailey, D. H.; Petrie, D.; and three others in England representing the London Missionary Society
Secretary of Committee of Management—Cox, J. S. (by application to whom sittings may be obtained)

WEST POINT REFORMATORY.
養正院 Yeung-tsing-un
Director—Raimondi, Very Rev. T., P.A
Vice-Rector—Vigano, Rev. B., M.A.
Resident Superintendent—Chu Sin-Sang
Chinese Teachers—Three

Coast Steamers, &c.

"AMAZONE," French Steamer.
MESSAGERIES MARITIMES.
亞美孫 A-me-sun
Captain—Champenois, Claude
Chief Officer—Such, Antoine
Chief Engineer—Meylan, —
Commissaire—Dumas, —

"AVA," French Steamer.
MESSAGERIES MARITIMES.
亞華 A-wah
Captain—Fleuriais, Hippolite
Chief Officer—Rival, Jules
Chief Engineer—Lauriol, Simon
Commissaire—Rastoul, Edouard

"CHINA," British Steamer.
D. SASSOON, SONS & Co.
猜拿 Chi-na
Captain—Gardner, T. S.
Chief Officer—Barker, W.
2nd do.—Macleod, A.
3rd do.—Barr, J.
Purser—Demetrius, G.
Chief Engineer—Leslie, J.
2nd do.—Turner, J.
3rd do.—Heaton, W.
4th do.—Graham, G.

"CHINA," German Steamer.
SIEMSSEN & Co.
千拿火船 Chin-na-fo-shun
Captain—Hennings, P. B.
Chief Officer—Schultz, G.
2nd do.—Ackermann, B.
3rd do.—Godt, O.
Chief Engineer—Lohr, G.
2nd do.—Teuchert, A.
3rd do.—

"CHINKIANG," British Steamer.
SIEMSSEN & Co.
鎭江 Chun-kong
Captain—Hogg, James
Chief Officer—Peat, John
2nd do. —
3rd do. —
Chief Engineer—
2nd do. —
3rd do. —

"DONNAI," French Steamer.
MESSAGERIES MARITIMES.
喃乃 Tun-nai
Captain—De Butler
Chief Officer—Carmac, Cyriele
Chief Engineer—Andrac
Commissaire—Jaudon, Adrien

"DOUGLAS," British Steamer
DOUGLAS LAPRAIK & Co.
德忌厘士 Tuk-ke-le-sz
Captain—Burnie, E.
Chief Officer—Pocock, J. G.
2nd do.—Hough, B. F.
3rd do.—Goddard, F. D.
Chief Engineer—Carnforth, J.
2nd do.—Wilkie, J.
3rd do.—Argo, J.
4th do.—Prophet, W. W.

"FAME," Steam-tug, 117 Tons, 110 H. P.
HONGKONG & WHAMPOA DOCK CO.
非暗 Fe-um
Captain—Richardson, S. V.

"FEI-WAN," Steamer (laid up in Canton)
H. C. & M. STEAM-BOAT CO.
飛云 Fei-wan
Captain—Graves, P. W.

"HAILOONG," British Steamer.
DOUGLAS LAPRAIK & Co.

海龍 Hai-loong

Captain—Punchard, J. E.
Chief Officer—Flemming, T. P.
2nd do.—Holland, C. J.
3rd do.—Dalgas, C.
Chief Engineer—Balfour, Wm.
2nd do.—Eason, B.
3rd do.—Scotland, J. J.

"HINDOSTAN," British Steamer.
D. SASSOON, SONS & Co.

軒都士丹 Hin-do-se-tan

Captain—Miller, J. A.
Chief Officer—Edwards, E. J.
2nd do.—Roy, H. L.
3rd do.—Morris, W. J.
Purser—Gregory, J.
Chief Engineer—Dunbar, W.
2nd do.—Fox, —
3rd do.—Dunbar, D.

"HOOGLY," French Steamer.
MESSAGERIES MARITIMES.

哭厘 Hook-lee

Captain—Varangot, Jules
Chief Officer—Catel, Louis
Chief Engineer—Guimard, Antoine
Commissaire—

"IRAOUADDY," French Steamer.
MESSAGERIES MARITIMES.

衣羅華地 E-lo-wah-te

Captain—Bourdon, Gustave
Chief Officer—Lequerre, Paul
Chief Engineer—Heemziger, Charles
Commissaire—Melizan, Édouard

"KIN-SHAN," British Steamer.
H. C. & M. STEAM-BOAT Co.

金山 Kum-shan

Captain—Cary, A. G.
Mate—Royland, J. P.
Purser—Hodgkins, W. R.
Chief Engineer—Lang, C. V.
2nd do.—Chesney, J.

"KIUKIANG," British Steamer.
H. C. & M. STEAM-BOAT Co.

九江 Kow-kong

Captain—Bunning, T. T.
Chief Officer—Gibson
Purser—Azevedo, A.
Chief Engineer—Harrold, F.
2nd do.—Reid, W.

"KWANGTUNG," British Steamer.
495 TONS. DOUGLAS LAPRAIK & Co.

廣東火船 Kwang-tung-fo-shun

Captain—Pitman, G. D.
Chief Officer—Ashton, F.
2nd do.—Goode, F. P.
3rd do.—Mackenzie, F. W.
Chief Engineer—Clarke, Senr. W.
2nd do.—Panton, W.
3rd do.—Jack, E.

"LEGISLATOR," British Steamer.
JARDINE, MATHESON & Co.

力之士厘多 Lek-che-ze-le-to

Captain—Craig

"MEIKONG," French Steamer.
MESSAGERIES MARITIMES.

美江 Mee-kong

Captain—Foûche, Gaston
Chief Officer—Walker, A. L.
Chief Engineer—Desgranges, François
Commissaire—Henri, Simon

"MENZALEH" French Steamer.
MESSAGERIES MARITIMES.

免思離 Min-sze-le

Captain—Mourrut, Phillippe
Chief Officer—Villevielle,—
Chief Engineer—Blanchet,—
Commissaire—Frager, Louis

"NAMOA," British Steamer.
DOUGLAS LAPRAIK & Co.

南澳 Nam-oa

Captain—Westoby, T.
Chief Officer—Brett, J. C.
2nd do.—Place, E. W.
3rd do.—Craig, W. G.
Chief Engineer—Clarke, W., Junr.
2nd do.—Younger, W.
3rd do.—Harvey, W. V.

"NIL," French Steamer.
MESSAGERIES MARITIMES.
你倪 Nei-ye
Captain—Samat, —.
Chief Officer—Foucanel, —.
Chief Engineer—Saynac, —.
Commissaire—Gauvain, —.

"NINGPO," British Steamer.
SIEMSSEN & Co.
寧波 Ning-po
Captain—Rayner, J. M.

"PEIHO," French Steamer.
MESSAGERIES MARITIMES.
北河 Pak-ho
Captain—Rigodit, Frederic
Chief Officer—Reynier, J. Baptiste
Chief Engineer—Gulou, —.
Commissaire—Daré, Albert

"POWAN," British Steamer.
H. M. & C. S. S. Co.
保安 Po-on
Captain—Benning, A. H.
Chief Officer—Reid, D.
Purser—Rocha, A. A.
Chief Engineer—Smith, W. F.
2nd do.—Walker, R.

"POYANG," British Steamer.
H. M. & C. S. S. Co.
鄱陽 Po-yeung
Captain—Carroll, R.
Chief Officer—Bennary, F. H.
Purser—Ribeiro, L. V.
Chief Engineer—Murphy, D.
2nd do —Buyers, W. B.

"PROVENCE," French Steamer.
MESSAGERIES MARITIMES.
布羅雲士 Po-lo-wan-sz
Captain—Brunet, Paulin
Chief Officer—Benoit, Honoré
Chief Engineer—Bonhomme, Louis
Commissaire—De Poli, —

"SINDH," French Steamer.
MESSAGERIES MARITIMES.
仙 Sin
Captain—Melizan, Gustave
Chief Officer—Pichat, Jules
Chief Engineer—
Commissaire—Magnan, Auguste

"SPARK," Steamer (laid up in H'kong.
H. M. & C. S. S. Co.
士迫火船 Sz-pak-fo-shun
Officer in Charge—McColen, F.

"STATESMAN," British Steamer.
JARDINE, MATHESON & Co.
士撻士文 Sz-tat-sz-mun
Captain—Valiant, —.

"TAKU" (late Peiho), British Steamer.
JARDINE, MATHESON & Co.
大沽火船 Tai-ku-fo-shun
Captain—Hooper, T. B.

"THALES," British Steamer.
DOUGLAS LAPRAIK & Co.
爹厘士 Te-le-sz
Captain—Young, M.
Chief Officer—Coles, C.
2nd do.—Groundwater, A.
3rd do.—Dowdney
Chief Engineer—Parlane, W.
2nd do.—McIntyre, A.
3rd do.—Wunch, W. G.

"TIGRE," French Steamer.
MESSAGERIES MARITIMES.
泰忌利 Tai-ke-loe
Captain—Lecointre, Ludovic
Chief Officer—Reynier, Amedée
Chief Engineer—Roussin, Louis
Commissaire—Boyé, Charles

"VOLGA," French Steamer.
MESSAGERIES MARITIMES.
和厘架 Woh-lee-ka
Captain—Flambeau
Chief Officer—Michel
Chief Engineer—Giraud
Commissaire—Faucon, de

"WHITE CLOUD," British Steamer.
H. M. & C. S. S. Co.

白雲火船 Pak-wan-fo-shun

Captain—Brady, George
Chief Officer—Mott, G. B.
Purser—Lopes, F. A.
Chief Engineer—Law, W.
2nd do.—Lanigan, S. W.

"YANGTSZE," British Steamer.
SIEMSSEN & Co.

洋子 Yang-tsze

Captain—Corner, A.
Chief Officer—Hooper, A.
2nd do.—Harris, W. H.
Chief Engineer—Eglin, J.
2nd do.—Bryan, T.
3rd do.—Lyons, E.

"YESSO," British Steamer.
DOUGLAS LAPRAIK & Co.

雅素火船 Nga-sho-fo-shun

Captain—Ashton, S.
Chief Officer—Abbott, J. C.
2nd do.—Hunter, W.
3rd do.—Naser, R H.
Chief Engineer—Bernard, Theodore
2nd do.—Scott, W.
3rd do.—Farron, S.

Public Companies, &c.

AMERICAN TRADING COMPANY OF BORNEO.

Organised under special concession from his Highness the Sultan of Borneo, and incorporated under the laws of the State of New York,

General Agents—Parker & Co.

CANTON INSURANCE OFFICE.

General Agents—Jardine, Matheson & Co

CHINA FIRE INSURANCE COMPANY, LIMITED.—See Advertisement.

48, QUEEN'S ROAD.

Directors—Lowcock, Henry (chairman); Heaton, A. McG.; Arthur, Edwd.; Ryrie, Hon., P.; Forbes, W. H.; Joost, A.; Huntington, S. E.
Secretary—Coughtrie, Jas. B.
Assistants—Lewis, A. J.; Simmonds, C. M.

CHINA SUBMARINE TELEGRAPHIC COMPANY, LIMITED.

(See Advertisement.)

Superintendent—Gavey, J. J. C.
Clerk in Charge—Newitt, W. T.
Assistant—Judd, W.
Brook, W.
Furze, J.
Trigg, W. H.
Waghorn, G.
Mortimer, H. W.
Hawkins, H.

CHINA TRADERS' INSURANCE CO., LIMITED.

48, QUEEN'S ROAD.

(See Advertisement)

Committee—Heaton, A. MacG.; Kaye, Wm.
General Agents—Heard & Co., Augustine

CHINA TRANS-PACIFIC STEAMSHIP COMPANY, LIMITED.

Agents—Russell & Co.

CHINESE INSURANCE COMPANY, LIMITED.

(PRAYA.)

(See Advertisement.)

Directors—Belilios, E. R.; Burrows, O. H.; André, Adolf; Seaman, J. F.
General Agents—Olyphant & Co. (H'kong)

COMPAGNIE RUSSE DE NAVIGATION A VAPEUR, DE COMMERCE ET DU CHEMIN DE FER D'ODESSA, ODESSA.

Agents—Pustau & Co., Wm.

EASTERN AND AUSTRALIAN MAIL STEAM COMPANY LIMITED.

Agents—Gibb, Livingston & Co.

GREAT NORTHERN EXTENSION TELEGRAPH COMPANY FOR CHINA AND JAPAN.

(Office and Residence, Burd's Lane.)

Superintendent—Sörensen, P. F.
Telegraphist—Lemcke, W.
Electrician—Bojesen, C.
Telegraphists—Poulsen, C. H. O.
Poulsen, E. A.
Shröm, G. B.

HONGKONG.   A 21

HONGKONG AND CHINA GAS COMPANY.
(See Advertisement)

煤氣公司 Mui-hi-kung-sz

OFFICE AND WORKS, West Point.

Manager—Newton, A.
Clerk—Alongo, V.
Do.—Parker, Thomas
Do.—Alongo, J. Jr.
Foreman of Works—Gill, John
Superintendent of Gas Fittings—Donald, Thomas

HONGKONG AND WHAMPOA DOCK COMPANY.
(See Advertisement.)

香港黃埔船澳公司
Heung-kong-wong-po-shun-kung-sz

Directors—Whittall, Hon. J., chairman
Heaton, A. McG., vice-chairman
Deacon, R.
Sassoon, S. D.
Joost, A.
Secretary—Duncan, R.
Sousa, M. de, book-keeper
Addyman, R. F., clerk

WHAMPOA.

Foreman in Charge—Mackay, G. S.
Clerk—Jesus, J. V. de
Storekeeper—Jesus, J. D.

KOWLOON.

Superintendent—Liddell, James G.
Engineer—Stewart, George
Shipwright—Young, A.
Foreman Boilermaker—Stevens, J.
Clerk—Rosario, M. J.
Storekeeper—Gomes, M.

ABERDEEN.

Superintendent—Brockat, John
Clerk—Paes, A. M.
Apprentice Engineers—Miranda, Antonio ; de Sá Caetano ; Candido, da Silva ; Lilienthall, John

HONGKONG, CANTON AND MACAO STEAM-BOAT COMPANY, LIMITED.
(See Advertisement.)

香港省城澳門火船公司
Heung-kong-shang-sheng-o-moon-fo-shun-kung-sz

General Agents—Heard & Co., Augustine (Hongkong and Canton)
Acting Agents—Mello & Co., De (Macao)

HONGKONG, CANTON AND MACAO STEAM-BOAT COMPANY, LIMITED.
(Continued.)

Directors—Heard, G. F. chairman
Deacon, Richard (Hongkong)
Heaton, A. McG.   (do.)
do Cercal, Baron   (do.)
Marine Superintendent—Sands, G. T.
Wharfingers—Stuart, F. H. (Hongkong)
Chop Dollar (Canton)
Nogueire, V. (Macao)

HONGKONG DISTILLERY COMPANY, LIMITED.

香港孖酒房 Heung-kong-tsing-tsau-fong

(IN LIQUIDATION.)

HONGKONG FIRE INSURANCE COMPANY, LIMITED.

Consulting Committee—Sassoon, S. D. ; Rowett, Hon R. ; Heard, G. F.
General Managers—Jardine, Matheson & Co.

HONGKONG FIRE INSURANCE COMPANY'S STEAM FIRE ENGINE.
Praya Central.
VOLUNTEER FIRE BRIGADE.
(Attached to H. K. F. I. Co.'s Engine.)

Foreman—Chambers, A, F.
Assistant Foreman—Cohen, C. C.
Blakeman, A. N.
Laddermen—Shaw, J. Y. V.
Bernhard, R.
Hughes, W. K.
Steele, H.
Moore, H.
Hughes, J. R.
Leading Hosemen—Glasse, G.
McEwen, A. P.
Baird, C. W.
James, H. G.
Hosemen—Nelson, T.
Ross, W.
Grant, J.
Blackwell, R.
Starkey, R. D.
Lewis, A. J.
Watson, H. M.
King, G.
Bovis, F de
Irving J. Bell
Foreman's A. D. C.—Manger, A. T.
In charge of Engine House—Taufer, G.
Engineer—Taufer, E.

HONGKONG.

HONGKONG HOTEL COMPANY, LIMITED.
香港酒店 Heung-kong-tsau-tim
Directors—Belilios, E. R. (chairman)
　Chater, C. P.
　Burrows, O. H.
　André, A.
Secretary—Baker, Ed.

HONGKONG PIER AND GODOWN COMPANY.
(IN LIQUIDATION.)

HONGKONG SINGAPORE & BORNEO TRADING COMPANY, LIMITED.
General Managers—Howard & Co., Thos.
Agent in Singapore—Moss, D.
Agent in Borneo—Moss, J.

HONGKONG SODA WATER MANUFACTURING COMPANY.
15, Graham Street.
香港荷蘭水館
Heung-kong-ho-lan-shui-koon
Costa, J. P. da
Ega, D. A. d'

INDO-CHINESE SUGAR COMPANY.
OFFICE—BANK BUILDINGS, QUEEN'S ROAD CENTRAL.
Directors—Overbeck, G. von; Geary, H. S.;
　Jensen, R.; Deacon, R.; Pollard, E. H.;
　Chomley, F.
Secretary—Blakeman, A. Noel
NACONCHAISEE FACTORY, NEAR BANGKOK.
Administrator—Sinclair, W.
Manager—Homan, J. A.
Engineer—Mountain, J. J.
Overseers—Stevens, R.; Schleming, C.

MESSAGERIES MARITIMES.
(SERVICES MARITIMES DES PAQUEBOTS POSTES FRANCAIS), PARIS.
佛蘭西火輪船公司
Fat-lan-sai-fo-shun-kung-sz
Principal Agent—Bertrand, C.
Assistants—Restalic, A. (absent)
　Guigné, A. de
　Tavarés, J.
　Kraal, F.
　Collago, H.
　Corveth, C.
　Lalande, C.

NORTH CHINA INSURANCE CO.
QUEEN'S ROAD
那千拿蕪梳館 No-tain-na-yin-sho-koon
Agent—Davis, J. Kennard (absent)
Acting Agent—Starkey, Reginald D.
Assistant—Church, T.
Clerk—Thomas Wong Aki

OCEAN STEM SHIP COMPANY.
Agents—Butterfield & Swire

ORIENTAL TELEGRAM COMPANY LIMITED.
Agent—Holmes, George

PACIFIC MAIL STEAM-SHIP CO.
PRAYA, WEST.
(*See Advertisement.*)
大美國火船公司
Tai-me-kwok-fo-shun-kung-sz
Agent—Harris, T. A.
Clerks—Emory, G. B.
　Baffey, G. W.
　Cromwell, J. H.
　Rozario, L. A.
　Pereira, A. M. Roza
　Favacho, V. A.
　Fung Far

PENINSULAR & ORIENTAL STEAM NAVIGATION COMPANY.
QUEEN'S ROAD & PRAYA.
鐵行火船公司
Tit-hong-fo-shun-kung-sz
Superintendent—McIver, A.
Clerks—Lind, A.
　King, G.
　Miller, A.
　Johnson, G F.
　De Rusett, W.
　Campos, E. P.
　Campos, L. P.
　Sapoorjee, E.
　Placé, J. L.
Superintendent Purser—Cowley, W. H.
Clerks—Vinton, William
　Greig, James
Storekeeper—Woodin, E. L.
Clerks—Armistead, A.; Guttierrez, A. O.;
　Britto, C. A. de
Issuers of Stores—Southan, J.
Office Gunner—Woolgar, J.

HONGKONG. A 23

PENISULAR & ORIENTAL STEAM NAVIGATION COMPANY.
(Continued.)
"FORT WILLIAM."
Commander—Purchase, J. W.
Chief Officer—Ahlmann, J. A.
2d do.—Encarnagao, A. L.

COAL DEPÔT.
Issuers—Duff, A.
Boatswain—Frost, r.

ENGINEER DEPARTMENT.
Superintendent—Green, Thos.
Foreman—Aitken, A. G.
Draughtsman—Findlayson, R.
Engineers—Jones, D. W.; Baines, R.
Plumber—Sprowel, A.
Moulder—Roper, H.
Boilermaker—Goodwin, A.
Foreman Carpenter—Ward, W.
Factory Clerks—Britto, J. de
  Soares, M.

COMMANDERS AND OFFICERS OF THE P. & O. SERVICE ON THE HONGKONG STATION.
Captains—Andrews, W. B.
  Davies, C. F.
  Edmond, E. M., R.N.R.
  Bernard, J.
  Pockley, W. N.
Officers—Thompson, W. E.
  Reeves, J.
  Harris, P.
  Patch, J. M.
  Cumberland, R.
  Worcester, W.
  Broadhead, C. A.
  Wheeler, W. A.
  Wibmer, L. M.
  Edwards, T. H.
Surgeons—Barrett, J.
  Barclay, T.
  Bolton, W.
  Clifford, J.
Chief Engineers—Brydon, J. H.
  Clarke, G.
  Kay, J. R.
  Gattrell, M.
  Bruce, R.
  Inglis, G.
Engineers—McIntyre, A.
  Duncan, J.
  Crossan, J.
  Sargent, T.
  Andrews, E.
  Fairburn, J. U.
  Mitchell, T.
  Boath, J.
  Stephens, J.
  Kerr, J.
  Mullis, J.

PENINSULAR & ORIENTAL STEAM NAVIGATION COMPANY.
(Continued.)
Barr, J.
McGregor, G.
Yates, F.
Spears, W.
Hogg, G. S.
Steele, W. B.
Ramsay, J.

UNION INSURANCE SOCIETY OF CANTON.
PEDDER'S WHARF.
(See Advertisement.)

於仁洋面保安行
U-yan-yeung-min-po-on-hong

Secretary—Ede, N. J.
Clerks—Barradas, Francisco
  Remedios, Filomeno dos
  Souza, Miguel de

UNION STEAM NAVIGATION COMPANY.
Agents—Olyphant & Co.

VICTORIA FIRE INSURANCE COMPANY OF HONGKONG, LIMITED.
QUEEN'S ROAD.
(See Advertisement.)
Board of Directors—Heard, George F.;
  Rowett, Hon. R.; Sassoon, S. D.;
  André, Adolphe; Kaye, Wm.
Secretaries—Heard & Co., A.

YANGTSZE INSURANCE ASSOCIATION.
(See Advertisement.)
Secretaries—Russell & Co. (Shanghai)
Agents at Hongkong—Russell & Co.

Banks.
渣打銀行 Cha-ta-ngan-hong

Chartered Bank of India, Australia and China, Queen's Road Central—*See Advertisement*
  Kaye, W., manager
    Boyd, M. W. (absent)
    Forrest, T., accountant
    Mein, P. W., sub-accountant
    Remedios, J. G., clerk
    Rozario, J. M. do.
    Carmichael, A. T., manager (S'hai)

Chartered Bank of India, Australia and China—(*Continued*)
    Pode, W. Y., accountant (S'hai)
    Banyard, M., sub-accountant (do.)
    Thorburn, H., act. agent (Hankow)

有利銀行 Yau-lee-ngag-hong

Chartered Mercantile Bank of India, London, and China, Queen's Road—*See Advertisement*

Draws on London Joint Stock Bank, London; and on Branches and Agencies at London, Bombay, Calcutta, Madras, Ceylon, Penang, Singapore, Shanghai, Yokohama, Hankow, Batavia and Mauritius. The Bank issues notes, which are received in payment of Government dues.

    Jackson, W., manager
    Smith, W. E, acting accountant
    Steele, Henry, assist. do.
    Hughes, J. R., do. do.
    Silva, M. A. da
    Nelson, H. H., acting agent (F'chow)
    Fergusson, Robt., manager (Shanghai)
    Thurburn, D., act. accountant (do.)
    Rowband, C. G., asst do. (do.)
    Baker, R. B., manager (Yokohama)
    Henderson, W. D., actg. acct. (do.)
    Robilliard, W., assistant do, (do.)
    Morrison, J., acting agent (Hankow)

佛蘭西銀行 Fat-lan-sai-ngan-hong

Comptoir d'Escompte de Paris, Bank Buildings, Queen's Road Central—*See Advertisement*
    Philippe, A., acting manager
        Dauré, L., chief accountant
        Placé, F. L.
        d'Almeida, T. M.
        Hardcastle. E. S., m'ager (S'hai.)
        Ewald, E. sub-manager (do.)
        Payne, Vh., chief accountant (do.)
        Felbel, A., accountant (do.)
        Fitz Henry, D., act. cashier (do.)
        Créty, de (do.)
        Vouillemont, E. G., manager (Yokohama)
        Cantelli, —., acct. (Yokohama)
        Roquerbe, H., manager (Saigon)
        Michelot, L., accountant (do.)

香港上海匯理銀行
Heung-kong-sheung-hoi-wui-li-ngan-hong

Hongkong and Shanghai Banking Corporation, Head Office, Hongkong, No. 1, Queen's Road.—*See Advertisement*
    Greig, James, chief manager
        Walter, John, sub-manager
        Smith. H.. accountant

Hongkong and Shanghai Banking Corporation—(*Continued*)
    Woodford, J. D.
    Pereira, A. A.
    Symonds, J. W.
    Morrison, J.
    St. Croix, G. C. de
    Bovis, F. de
    Moore, H.
    Gard'ner, J. P. W.
    Cope, A. E.
    Gonsalves, C. J.
    Luz, F. M.
    Soares, A. F.
    Souza, N. L.
    Cameron, E., manager (Shanghai)
    Greig, W. G., accountant (do.)
    Beveridge, C. H. (do.)
    Veitch, A. (do.)
    Grigor, J. M. (do.)
    Parnes, C. J. (do.)
    Haselwood, A. H. C. (do.)
    Johnston, G. R. (do.)
    Pereira, M. L. (do.)
    Barton, C. (do.)
    Carvalho, M. A. de (do.)
    Diniz, A. J. (do.)
    Guttarres, D. M. (do.)
    Rangel, S. G. (do.)
    Jackson, Thomas, manager, Yokohama (absent in Europe)
    Cope, H., act. manager (Yokohama)
    Hodgson, J. G., act. acct. (do.)
    Cook, R. H. (do.)
    McNab, J. (do.)
    Rickett, C. B. (do.)
    Smith, A. J. (do.)
    Turner, A. L., agent (Foochow)
    Harries, W. H., agent (Hiogo)
    Pereira, E. J. (do.)
    Townsend, A. M., agent (Hankow)
    Mitchell, F. W., Jr. (do.)
    Morriss, E., agent (Calcutta)
    Winton, J. J., accountant (do.)
    Stevenson, Robert, agent (Bombay) (absent in Europe)
    Noble, G. E., act. agent (Bombay)
    Leith, A., accountant (do.)
    Hardie, D., agent (Saigon)
    Abendroth, H., agent (Amoy)

那順那銀行 No-shun-no-ngan-hong

National Bank of India Limited, Queen's Road Central—*See Advertisement*
    Campbell, James, manager
    Thomson, C. E., act. accountant
    Pereira, A. L. G., clerk
    Turner & Co. (agents, Foochow)
    Turner & Co. (agents, Shanghai)
    Gilman & Co. (agents, Yokohama)
    Borneo Co. (Singapore)

HONGKONG.   A 25

舊銀行 Kau-ugan-hong

Oriental Bank Corporation, Queen's Road
————., manager
  Kerr, C. M., accountant (absent)
  Scott, G. O., act. accountant
  Prior, L., assist. acct. and cashier
  Innes, R., assistant accountant
  Barros, F. J., clerk
  Silva, E. M. da, do.
  Ferraz, J. A., do.
  Barretto, L. F., do.
  Temple, F., act. agent (Foochow)
  Walters, J. M. (absent)
  Micken, W. Mc., assist. acct. and cashier (Foochow)
  Paterson, A., act. manager (S'hai)
  Lethbridge, G., act. acct. (do.)
  Gardiner, T. J., asst. acct. and cashier (Shanghai)
  Johnston, Sir W., asst. acct. (do,)
  Carvalho, P. M., clerk (do.)
  Pereira, J. L., do. (do.)
  Robertson, J., agent (Yokohama)
  Russell, J., accountant (do.) (abs't)
  Walker, H.B., asst. acct. (do.)(do.)
  Thompson, G. W., asst. acct. and cashier (Yokohama)
  Elder, S. J., asst. acct. (do.)
  Reid, E J., assistant (do.)
  Burns, B. H., asst. acct. (do.)
  Peres, B. A., clerk (do.)
  Marques, E., (do.)
  Crombie, D. A. J., act. agt. (Hiogo)
  Stewart, C. S., asst. acct. (do.)
  Mackenzie, H., do. (do.)
  Carvalho, G. M., clerk (do.)

Insurance Agencies.

Arnhold, Karberg & Co.
  Java Sea and Fire Insurance Co.
  Lancashire Insurance Company, Fire and Life
  National Marine Insurance Company of South Australia
Borneo Co., Limited
  Commercial Union Fire Department
Butterfield & Swire
  British and Foreign Marine Insurance Company, Limited
  Royal Exchange Assurance of London
  China Navigation Co., Limited
Carlowitz & Co.
  Allgemeine Versicherungs Gesellschaft für See, Fluss und Landtransport in Dresden
  Deutscher Lloyds Transport Versicherungs-actien Gesellschaft, Berlin
China Fire Insurance Co.—*See Advt.*
  Secretary—Coughtrie, J. B.

Gibb, Livingston & Co.
  B'bay Insurance Company.—*See Advt.*
  Commercial Union Assurance C'pany, Life Department
  Eastern Marine Insurance Company of Bombay
  Forbes & Co.'s Constituents Ins. Co.
  Imperial Fire Insurance Company
  Reliance Marine Insurance Company
Gilman & Co.
  Liverpool Underwriters' Association
  Lloyds
  Merchant Shipping and Underwriters' Association of Melbourne
  Merchants' Marine Insurance Company, Limited
  North British and Mercantile Fire Ins. Company—*See Advt.*
  Underwriters' Union of Amsterdam
  Universal Marine Insurance Company, London, Limited
Heard & Co., Augustine—*See Advts.*
  Australasian Insurance Company
  China Traders' Insurance Co., Limited
  London and Provincial Marine Insurance Company
  Ocean Marine Insurance Company of London
  Victoria Fire Insurance Co., Limited
  Victoria Insurance C'pany of Bombay
Hogg & Co., A. G.
  Sun Fire Office—*See Advt.*
Holliday, Wise & Co.
  London and Bombay Traders' Insurance Company
  London Assurance Corporation, Fire, Marine and Life
  Manchester Fire Assurance Company
  Thames and Mersey Marine Insurance Company
Jardine, Matheson & Co.
  Alliance Fire Assurance Company
  Alliance Marine Assurance Company
  Bombay Insurance Society
  Canton Insurance Office
  Hongkong Fire Insurance Co., Limited
  Ocean Marine Insurance Co. of Bombay
  Triton Insurance Company
Lapraik & Co., Douglas
  Liverpool and London and Globe Fire Insurance Company
  Phœnix Fire Insurance Company—*See Advertisement.*
  " Triton " Marine Insur. Co.
McIver, A., P. & O. S. N. Co.
  Oriental and Steam Transit Ins. Office
Melchers & Co.
  The Austrian Insurance Co, "Donau"
  Deutsche National Bank at Bremen
  North German Fire Insurance Co. at Hamburg
Mody & Co., N.
  Bombay Mody Insurance Company

26 A   HONGKONG.

Morgan, Chas. H.
   Positive Government Security Life Assurance Company Limited
North China Insurance Co.
   Commercial Union Insurance Company (Marine)
Norton & Co., Edward
   The Queen Fire Insurance Company Liverpool
Olyphant & Co.—*See Advt.*
   Chinese Insurance Company, Limited
   Guardian Assurance Company, London
   New York Board of Underwriters
   San Francisco Board of Underwriters
Pustau & Co., W.—*See Advertisement*
   Austrian Lloyds Steam Navigation Company, Trieste
   Baseler Transport Versicherungs Gesellschaft uz Basel
   China and Japan Insurance Company
   Dusseldorfer Allgemeine Versicherungs Gesellschaft
   Hamburg and Bremen Fire Insurance Company
   Helvetia Allgemeine Versicherungs Gesellschaft, St. Gallen
   Rheinisch-Westphalischer Lloyd
   Transport Versicherungs Gesellschaft "Schweiz," in Zurich
   Frankfürter — Glass — Versicherungs Gesellschaft in Frankfurt a/m
   Compagnie Russe de Navigation á vapeur, de Commerce et du Chemin de fer d'Odessa, Odessa
   "Jakan" See Versicherungs Gesellschaft in Mallran
Russell & Co.—*See Advertisement*
   Yangtsze Ins. Association of Shanghai
   Batavia Sea and Fire Insurance Co.
   Compagnie Lyonnaise d'Assurance Maritime
Schellhass & Co., Eduard
   Bremen Underwriters
   Transatlantic Marine Insurance Company, Limited, Berlin
Siemssen & Co.
   Oosterling Sea & Fire Insurance Co., Batavia
   Samarang Sea and Fire Insurance Co., Samarang
   Swiss Lloyd's Transport Insurance Co., Winterthur
   Union of Hamburg Underwriters (for Hongkong, Canton and Macao)
   Globe Marine Insurance Company, Ld., London
   Transatlantic Fire Insurance Company of Hamburg
Turner & Co.
   Home and Colonial Ins. Co., Limited
   Netherlands India Marine Insurance Company, Limited
   Northern Assurance Co., Fire and Life

Union Insurance Society of Canton—*See Advertisement*
   Secretary—Ede, N. J.
Walker & Co., R. S.
   Amicable Insurance Office, Marine
   Jersey Mutual Insurance Society Shipping
   Royal Insurance Company. Fire and Life
   Topsham Western Clubs, Marine
   Universal Life Assurance Society

Merchants, &c.

Abdolkhaluk, Hajee John Mahomed, merchant, Wellington Street
   Abdolkhaluk, H. J. M. (Bombay)
   Ahmed, Moosa, manager

Abdool Star, Jan Mahomed, merchant
   Rehemtoola, Esmail

亞担士醫生 A-tam-sz-e-shang

Adams, W. S. M.D., C.M., Craigengower, health officer of the port and medical inspector of emigrants

埃架北 Ai-ka-pak

Agabeg, A. L., Jr., commission agent and opium broker, 12, Hollywood Road

Agabeg, G. L., broker, Wyndham Street

Alford, R. G., surveyor to the Hongkong Fire Insurance Company, 15, Stanley Street

Alladinbhoy, Rahimbhoy, merchants
   Alladinbhoy, Rahimbhoy (Bombay)
   Bogabhoy, Cassumbhoy Manager
   Rahimbhoy, Fazel Meherally
   Nuthoobhoy, Ebhrahimbhoy

Alli, boarding house keeper, Lower Lascar Row

不老顛押刀剌利
Put-lo-tin-ap-to-la-li

Amijibhoy, Futtabhoy, merchant, Cochrane Street, No. 25
   Casumji, Goolamhoossen, manager
   Abdoolali, Habiboolla
   Goolamhoossen, Abdoolaly (C'ton)

HONGKONG. A 27

Amos, L. J. V., solicitor and notary public

Anton & Middleton, brokers, Club Chambers
 Anton, J. Ross
 Middleton, W. N.

暗士蔫郎夜冷館
Om-sz-tong-long-yea-lang-koon

Armstrong, J. M., government auctioneer and general commission agent, No. 43, Queen's Road Central
 Armstrong, J. M.
  Marques, D. S.
  Remedios, V.

"Army and Navy," tavern, Queen's Road West
 Kock, Christian

瑞記洋行 Sui-kee-yeung-hong

Arnhold, Karberg & Co., merchants, Praya
 Arnhold, Jacob (London)
 Karberg, Peter
 Levysohn, Alexander C. (Canton)
 Mendel, L.
 Ruttmann, H.
 Kramer, J. (Canton)
 Poesnecker, L.
 Just, H. Z.
 Arnhold, P. (Canton)
 Schmidt, H.
 Cruz, E. da

Austrian Lloyds Steam Navigation Co.
 Agents—Pustau & Co., Wm.

碧架經紀 Pek-ka-king-ki

Baker, Edward M., public accountant, 7, Pedder's Hill

Baker & Co., drapers, milliners, dressmakers etc., Queen's Road
 Baker, J. H.
 Baker, Mrs
  Marques, A. G., Jr.

巴利 Pa-li

Barrelet, J. H., commission merchant, No. 5, Elgin street, agent for Leo Juvet

巴靈頓 Pa-ling-tun

Barrington & Algar, house and land agents 9, Hollywood Road.
 Barrington, T. W.
 Algar, Thos.

Battles & Co., commission merchants. Bank Buildings, Queen's Road
 Battles, William Ward

庇利剌士 Pé-li-la-sz

Belilios, E. R., merchant, Lyndhurst Terrace
 Belilios, E. R.
 Gomes, N. J.
 Sequeira, E. P.

Beltrao, Ignacio, boarding house keeper (15 Manila Seamen), Joao's Lane

Bendicht, W., & Co., merchants, No. 23, Wellington Street

福興行 Fook-hing-hong

Birley & Co., merchants, Queen's Road
 Smith, Arthur (England)
 Pyke, Thomas
  Roza, A. B. da
  Hassell, J. G. T.
  Foster, F. T. P.
  Roza, M. da
  Roza, J. F. da
  Dalrymple, H. L. (Foochow)
  Hales, G. (do.)
  Hardy, George (Canton)
  Dent, Herbert F. (do)
  Adams, K. D. (Macao)

Blackhead & Co., F., storekeepers, shipchandlers, auctioneers, Queen's Road
 Blackhead, F. B. (absent)
 Rapp, F.
  Reichert, T., book-keeper

撒鳥公司 Poon-niu-kung-sz

Borneo Company, Limited (London, Manchester, Calcutta, Singapore, Batavia, Sarawak, Siam and Hongkong), Queen's Road Central
 Nicaise, Hippolyte, manager
 Foss, Henry
 Rose, T. J.
 Ribeiro, A. F.

28 A HONGKONG.

巴泵厘 Pa-tam-li
Bottomley, C. D., broker and auctioneer, Gough Street
    Bottomley, C. D.

"Boulangerie D'Europe," 5, Wyndham Street
    Vincenot, F., proprietor

波素公司 Poo-so-kung-sz
Bourjau & Co., merchants, 7 Praya
    Bourjau, Adolph (absent)
    Behre, Ernst
    Wieler, G. A. (absent)
    Schultz, H. M.
    Cordes, C. D. H.
    Hagge, H.
    Rautenberg, T. H.
    Taumeyer, E. (Shanghai)
    Wieler, Oscar (do.)
    Bryner, J. A. (do.)
    Swensen, August (do.)
    Brunckhorst, Emil (do.)

巴令丁 Pa-ling-ting
Brandão & Co., merchants, Wellington St.
    Gomes, F. A.
    Gomes, J. B. Jr.
    Gomes, A. J.
    Alemão, D.

"British Crown" Tavern, 262, Queen's Road West
    Lobo, L. M.

"British Hotel," 2, Circular Buildings, Queen's Road West
    McNulty, John

"British Inn," Queen's Road Central
    Carr, Henry John H.

播羅庇晏多彌 Po-lo-pi-an-to-ni
Broadbear, Anthony & Co., storekeepers, and shipchandlers, 62, Praya
    Anthony, T. T.
    Seimund, C. H. E.

磅耶長生店 Pong-long-cheung-shang-tim
Brown, Jones & Co., undertakers and gravestone cutters, 9, Hollywood Road
    Algar, Thos.
    Considine, Dine

賛畢行 Jan-put-hong
Burd & Co., John, merchants, Praya
    Block, Frederick H. (absent)
    Jansen, Rud.
    Helland, A.
    Grant, J.
    Melbye, Emil

巴勞時 Pa-lo-shi
Burrows & Sons, S. E., merchants, St. John's Place
    Burrows, S. E., Jr.
    Burrows, C. H.
    Mallory, L.

太古洋行 Tai-koo-yeung-hong
Butterfield & Swire, merchants, Queen's Road
    Lang, W. (Shanghai)
    Scott, J. H. (absent)
    Harrison, W. D.
    Angus, J. Keith
    Hall, T.
    Turner, J. J.
    Blogg, J. A.
    Silva, P. F. da
    Remedios, Jan. A. dos
    Watson, Herbert (Shanghai)
    Mackintosh, E. (do.)
    Aubert, F. B. (do.)
    Kent, W. K. (do.)
    Bois, J. C. (do.)
    Warrick, A. (Hankow)
    Endicott, H. B. (Shanghai)
    Andrew, J. (do.)
    Hall, James (do.)
    Wyatt, O. M. (do.)
    Burrows, A. (do.)
    Gibson, T. (do.)
    Fonseca, J. B. (do.)
    Remedios, A. F. dos (do.)
    Remedios, S. A. (do.)
    Smith, H. R. (Foochow)
    Yuill, G. S. (do.)
    Robinson, W. J. (do.)
    Dodds, James (Yokohama)
    Joyes, H. O. (do.)

Byramjee, Bomonjee, broker, 26, Hollywood Road

Caderdina, R., merchant and agent, Gage Street
    Caderdina, Ramthola (absent)

云臣 Wan-shàn

Cairns, R. H., surveyor for Government and for Local Insurance Offices, Hamburg and Bremen Underwriters, Germanic Lloyds, and agent and surveyor for Bordeaux Lloyds; office, Club Chambers, d'Aguilar Street
  Cairns, R. H.
    Xavier, J. A., clerk

高露雲狀師 Ko-lo-wan-chong-az

Caldwell & Brereton, attorneys, solicitors, proctors and public notaries, 29, Queen's Road
  Caldwell, H. C.
  Brereton, W. H.
  Wotton, W., solicitor and manager
  Caldwell, D. E.
  Bowden, Frank
  Azavedo, M. d'
  Lopes, E. G.
  Chun Ayow, interpreter

三貴 Sam-kwai

Caldwell, D. R., Chinese interpreter, Aberdeen Street

鴨乎悲金廉 Ap-foo-pi-kum-ma

Cama, F. B., merchant, 13, Peel Street
Fatakia, D. B.
Polishwolla, M. B., broker

架剌威治 Ka-la-wei-chi

Carlowitz & Co., merchants, 15, Praya
  Carlowitz, R. von (absent)
  Hitzeroth, G. (Canton)
  Benecke, O.
  Buse, D.
  Reiff, R.
  Hirzel, F.
  Wobbe, H.
  Rost, W. (Canton)
  Ruff, J. (do.)
  Hertz, A. (do.)

Cassambhoy, Ebrahim, merchant, 2, Lyndhurst Terrace

Chater, C. P., bill and bullion broker, Bank Buildings, and 17, Caine Road
  Chater, J. T., share-broker

中國大藥房 Chung-kwok-tai-yeuk-fong

China Dispensary, Praya, Engholm & Co.
  Engholm, V.
  Ball, W.
  Silva, V. da
  Cruz, D. J. da
  Akim.

德臣印字館 Tuk-sun-yan-tsz-koon

China Mail Office, publishing, printing and book-binding establishment, 2, Wyndham Street. (Overland China Mail, fortnightly for the home mail; China Mail, every evening, except Sunday; Chinese Mail, three times a week, with daily supplement; China Review, once in two months.) —See Advertisement
  Bain, & Dennys, proprietors and publishers
  Bain, Geo. Murray (absent)
  Dennys, N. B., editor
  Chun Ayin, reporter
  Souza, A. S., book-keeper
  ————, marine reporter
  Rozario, J. J. do, overseer
  Sequeira, N., foreman
  Wong Chun, compositor
  Rozario, H. do.
  d'Assumpção, J. S. do.
  Tam Wing Kwai, book-binder

華字日報 Wa-tsz-yat-po

CHINESE DEPARTMENT — Chun Ayin, manager

糖局 Toong-kuk

China Sugar Refinery, East Point, Wahee, Smith & Co.
  Smith, Wm. McGregor
  Kresser, V. (Saigon)
  Sams, W. F. B.
  Dickie, H.
  Hyndman, H.
  Silva, E. E.
  Lapsley, W.
  Kyle, D.
  Purchase, E.
  Grencer, W.
  Hampshire, S.
  Lawrence, J.

"City of Hamburg," tavern, Queen's Road
  Wohlters, A., proprietor

其爐醫生 Ki-lu-i-shang

Clouth, Charles, M.D., 83, Wyndham Street

Cohen, H., merchant and commission agent, Burd's Lane

A HONGKONG.

高賢公司 Ko-yın-kung-sz
Cohen & Co., Chas. C., merchants, Burd's Lane
    Cohen, Chas. C.

哥倫時脫牙醫生 Ko-lun-shi-t'ut-nga-i-shang
Collins, Varnum D., dental surgeon, No. 7, Arbuthnot Road

今孖素印字館 Kum-ma-so-yan-tsz-koon
"Commercial Printing Office," Graham St.
    Luz, J. A. da

亞打些谷罷 Ah-ta-she-koo-pa
Cooper & Co., H. N., merchants, Stanley Street, No. 12
    Cooper, H. N.

"Crown and Anchor," tavern, Queen's Road West
    Bristow, Wm.
    Payne, Wm.

孖刺新聞紙館 Ma-la-san-mun-chi-koon
"Daily Press" Office, Wyndam Street, opposite St. Paul's College; *Daily Press* English edition, published every morning; *Chinese edition*, every alternate morning, with an extra every morning; *Overland Trade Report*, published fortnightly, on the mornings of the departure of the English Mail; *Daily Press*, edition of the *Straits Times Extra*, on the arrival of the inward mails
    Murrow, Y. J. (England)
    Bell, Wm. H., lessee and publisher
    Dulcken, Albert C., editor
    Hember, S., general manager
    Cumming, John, reporter
    Hart. Thomas, do.
    Ribeiro, Adelino A. V., foreman
    Santos, Amancio F. dos, compositor
    Almario, Francisco S., do.
    Leong A'kit, clerk
    Chinese Edition—Ng A'chan, general manager

Dantra, H. B., G.G.M.C., general practitioner, Parsee Villa, Robinson Road

Dantra, R. B., broker, Peel Street

Dantra, R. D., general broker, No. 24, Peel Street

D'Assis, Francisco, boarding house-keeper (12 Manila seamen), Tank Lane

燕刀馬吒近刀近 In-tiu-ma-moo-kan-tiu-kan
Davecurn, Balmoocurn, merchant, Hollywood Road
    Dowlutram, Shereeram (Bombay)
    Kissundass, Dowlutram (Calcutta)
    Davecurn, Balmoocurn
    Ramnaramjee, Sadmuljee, manager
    Kotwal, D. R.

悲爹別士 Po-te-pit-sz
Davies, B., Australian merchant and importer, 2 Peddar's Wharf

Deacon, Richard, bill and bullion broker, Club Chambers

亨泰行 Hang-tai-hong
Deetjen & Co., merchants, Praya
    Deetjen, Ed. (Hamburg)
    Strack, Ad.
    Koch, C.
    Boyes, Fredk.

爹件拿 Te-kin-na
Degenaer, Fred., merchant, D'Aguilar St.
    Degenaer, F.
    Mathisen, W.
    Gonsalves, R.
    Cappelen, D. von

的嬌厘啞 Te-kiu-li-a
Deguria & Co., R. N., merchants, Peel Street
    Deguria, Rustomjee Nowrojee
    Lungrana, Eduljee Dadabhoy (absent)

Dhunjeebhoy & Co., R., merchants and commission agents, Hollywood Road
    Mehta, D. B. (Calcutta)
    Mehta, R. Dhunjeebhoy
    Sagor, E. M., assistant

達士醫生 Tat-sz-e-shang
Dods, George, M.D., physician and surgeon, College Gardens, Upper Albert Road

第禮也公發洋行
Tai-lei-yah-kung-fat-yeung-hong

Dreyer & Co., merchants, 23, Queen's Road
 Dreyer, F.
 Budde, C. (absent)
 Schaar, B.

度波素行 To-po-so-hong

Dubost & Co., G., merchants, Queen's Road
 Dubost, G.
 Chastel, E.
  Senna, J. C. de
  Guédés, F. D.

Easton & Co., S., engineers, boiler-makers, brass and iron founders, &c.
 Easton, S., proprietor
  Williamson, Thos.
  Hitchcock, F., foreman

鴨都刺厘依把刺謙公司
Ap-to-la-li-i-pa-la-him-kung-sz

Ebrahim & Co., Abdoolally, merchants, Cochrane Street
 Ebrahim, Abdool Tyeb
  Abdool Kadar, M.
  Bhoymeea, E.
  Gulamally, S.
  Habiboolla, A.
  Abdoolrahim, Ebrahim (Canton)

謙信洋行 Him-sun-yeung-hong

Ehlers & Co., Paul, merchants, 20, Praya
 Ehlers, Paul (absent)
  Lembke, Justus
  Coch, Fr.

亞知亞厘行 A-chi-a-li-hong

Emamoodeen, S., general broker, 15, Gage Street

"Empire" tavern, Queen's Road West
 Humby, John

Fakeera, Mahomed, boarding house keeper, (86 Indians), Lower Lascar Row, No. 18

霍見拿鐘鏢行
Fok-kin-na-chung-piu-hong

Falconer & Co., G., watchmakers, jewellers, &c., Queen's Road—*See Advertisement*
 Falconer, Geo. B.
 Noble, J.
 Smith, A.
 McGregor, J:
 Ross, W.
 Rathbone, W.
 Baird, J. V.
 Cruz, A. A. da

Freerks, Rodatz & Co., shipchandlers and general storekeepers, 29, 30, 31, Praya
 Freerks, R.
 Rodatz, G. C. F.

French Bakery
 F. Vincenot, proprietor, 2, Peel St.

佛蘭西藥房 Fat-lan-sai-yeuk-fong

French Dispensary, 181A, Queen's Road
 Britto, J. L., proprietor, chemist and druggist
  Sanches, J. M., manager and druggist
  Liger, F. P., apothecary
  Pussos, J. M., do.

占士辨館 Chin-sz-pan-koon

Frisby & Co., James, butchers and compradors, Wellington Street and Central Market
 Rozario, S. R.
  Assis, A. R., clerk
  Burrows, Ed., book-keeper
  Ah Yik Lee, Chinese clerk
  A Peng Lee, shroff
  Xavier, L. J., shipping runner

Gardner, William, boarding house-keeper (20 European seamen), Queen's Rd. West

加律店 Ka-lut-t'im

Garrett, M., silk mercer, milliner and dressmaker, Queen's Road—*See Advt.*
 Garrett, M.
  Hams, Mrs
  Butler, Miss
  Marques, E.

32 **A** HONGKONG.

播威鐘表店 Po-wei-chung-piu-t'im

Gaupp & Co., Charles J., watchmakers and jewellers, Queen's Road
  Gaupp, Charles (absent)
  Gaupp, E. (do.)
  Gaupp, H. (do.)
  Keiser, J.
    Heermann, C.
    Voigt, E.
    Rech, M.

查勒醫生 Ga-lach-i-sang

Gerlach, C., M.D., 89, Wyndham Street

"German Tavern," 224, Queen's Road West
  Petersen, C. F. Wm.
    Gehlsen, H. J., barkeeper

澗地 Kan-ti

Ghandy & Co., M. D., merchants, Hollywood Road
  Ghandy, Dinshaw Dadabhoy (Bombay)
  Ghandy, Dadabhoy Dinshaw (do)
  Mehta, D. M.
  Mehta, M. M.

刼行 Kip-hong

Gibb, Livingston & Co., merchants, Aberdeen Street
  Gibb, H. B. (London)
  Lowcock, H.
  Vickers, J. M. (Shanghai)
  Wood, A. G. (do.)
  McLeod, A. (do.) (absent)
    White, F. G. (do.)
    Case, A. M. (do.)
    Simmonds, L. A. (do.)
    Daniel, H. W. (do.)
    Sharp, C. (do.)
    Caldbeck, E. J. (do.)
    Hancock, B. S. (Hankow)
    Tennant, H. P. (Foochow)
    Tennant, T. W. (do.)
    Morison, W. O. (do.)
    Gepp, A. M. (Canton)
    Stretten, R. T. (do.)
    McLeod, J. (Hongkong)
    Nunn, C. F. (do.)
    Darby, W. H. F. (do.)
    Weeks, C. D. (do.)
    Layton, B. (do.)

刼佛 Kip-fat

Gifford & Co., merchants
  Gifford, John (Liverpool)
  Gifford, Alex. (do.)
  Gifford, Geo. (do.)
  Gifford, Patrick (Canton)
    Gutierrez, L. J. (Hongkong)

太平行 Tai-ping-hong

Gilman & Co., merchants, 8, Praya
  Gilman, R. J. (England)
  Wild, C. A. (do.)
  Lemann, H. B. (Hongkong)
  Lemann, W. (do.)
  Lavers, E. R. (Shanghai)
  Ramsay, H. F. (Hankow)
  Gilman, F. (Shanghai)
  Young, W. S. (Foochow)
  Roberts, J. H. (Hongkong)
  Bernhard, R. (do.)
  Hiden, C. S. (do.)
  Slade, G. (do.)
  Costa, J. da (do.)
  Price, W. G. (Foochow)
  Harton, C. F. (do.)
  Smith, C. D. (do.)
  Tobin, E. (Shanghai)
  Green, F. J. (do.)
  Miller, W. (do.)
  St. Croix, W. de (do.)
  Clifford, J. (do.)
  Gouilloud, L. (do.)
  Howell, R. W. (do.)
  Harton, W. H. (do.)
  Fraser, L. (Hankow)
  Melhuish, C. J. (Yokohama)
  Glennie, A. W. (do.)
  Abbott, E. (do.)
  Barthe, C. (do.)

"Globe Hotel," 29, Praya Central
  O'Flaherty, T. H.

Goolamhoosein & Co., Dewjeebhoy Javair, N., manager
  Munjeebhoy, Ebhrahimbhoy

Guedes, J. M., Jr., auctioneer, Lyndhurst Terrace, No. 2, and residence Mosque Street, No. 1

葛爹厘氏印字舘 Kot-te-li-shi-yan-tsz-koon

Gutierrez, R. F., printer and stationer, 12, Wyndham Street

葛爹厘士 Kot-te-lo-sz

Gutierrez, Vernancio, merchant, Wyndham Street

HONGKONG.   **A** 33

Habibbhoy, A., merchant, 67, Wellington Street
  Habibbhoy, Ahmedbhoy (Bombay)
  Jairaz, Jamalbhoy, agent

亞知亞厘行 A-chi-a-li-hong

Hajee Ali Asger & Hajee Esmail, merchants and agents, 17, Gage Street
  Haager, M. E.
  Esmail, M. S. H.
    Namasy, H. A.

"Hamburg Tavern," 272, Queen's Road West
  Juster, John
    Thomson, Albert

惺厘 Han-li

Handley, Ed. Rich., plumber, coppersmith, brass-founder, and gasfitter; 39 and 40, Praya West
  Handley, E. R.
  Rose, E.
    Chagas, M. J.

Handley, P. A., barrister-at-law

Hawkins's Horse Repository, rear of Murray Barracks
  Hawkins, T. E.
    Fernandez, F. F.

夏剌大狀師 Ha-la-tai-chong-sz

Hayllar, T. C., barrister-at-law, acting attorney general, Supreme Court House, Queen's Road

曷公司 Hot-kung-sz

Heard & Co., Augustine, merchants
  Heard, John (absent)
  Heard, Augustine (do.)
  Heard, Albert F.
  Heard, George F.
  Dixwell, George Basil (absent)
  Fearon, Rob. I. (Shanghai)
    Parker, C. E.
    Costa, P. A. da
    Seabra, F. A.
    Ray, W. H.
    Heywood, H. C.
    Head, F. S.
    Hodgkins, J. R.
    Arnold, T.
    Cruz, O. A. da

Heard & Co., Augustine—*(continued)*
    Pereira, I. P.
    Baptista, L. M.
    Figueiredo, H. C. V. de
    Sedgewick, R.
    Cheshire, F. D. (Canton)
    Crace, E. L. H. (do.) (absent)
    Bennett, A. G. (do.)
    Daly, A. M. (Foochow)
    Gammon, E. (do.)
    Hunter, R. P. (do.)
    Oliver, Geo. (do.)
    Aquino, J. C. d' (Shanghai)
    Low, E. G. (do.)
    Endicott, Charles E. (do.)
    Redding, J. (do.)
    Jenkins, T. O. S. (do.)
    Fonseca, F. (do.)
    Pethick, W. A. (Peking)
    Pinel, John, Jr. (Yokohama)
    Farley, Gustavus, Jr. (do.)
    Fraser, J. A. (do.)
    James, F. S. (do.)
    Low, F. (Kobé)
    Livingston, H. W. (Kobé)

軒利文 Hin-li-man

Heinemann & Co., ship brokers, 16, Bank Buildings
  Heinemann, S. L.
  Kiner, H.
  Steil, R.

希士公司 He-sz-kung-sz

Hesse & Co., merchants, Queen's Road
  Staël, Leonhard
  Stolterfoht, H.
  Laackmann, J. C. N.
  Krauss, A. (Canton)

克公司 Hok-kung-sz

Hogg & Co., A. G., merchants, Aberdeen Street
  Hogg, A. G. (Saigon)
  Linstead, T. G.
  Johnston, H. B. (Saigon)
  Freire, F.

Holmes, Edmund R., coal and general broker, Peddar's Wharf

堪士 Hom-see

Holmes, George, ship and general broker, 2, Peddar's Hill

34 A   HONGKONG.

何羅爹威士公司
Ho-lo-te-wei-sz-kung-sz

Holliday, Wise & Co., merchants, Praya
  Holliday, John (Manchester)
  Farbridge, C. W. (do.)
  Holliday, J. F. (do.)
  Rowatt, R.
  Barnes, J. P. (Shanghai)
  Coller, R. L. (Manila)
  Hunter, D. L. (do.)
    George, E.
    MacEwen, A. P.
    Baird, C. W.
    Reddie, A. C.
    Lima, J. M. O.
    Vieira, A. J.
    Tatham, S. G. (Foochow)
    Beattie, J. G. (Shanghai)
    Barlow, H. J. E. (Shanghai)
    Reddie, J. (do.)
    Hogarth, J. B. (do.)
    Rozario, P. H. do (do.)
    McCulloch, J. B. (Manila)
    Grundy, A. (do.)
    Drummond, J. (do.)

香港及中國麵飽舖
Heung-kong-kap-chung-kwok-min-bow-poo

Hongkong & China Bakery Co. (Limited)
  Managers—MacEwen, Frickel & Co.

香港大藥房 Heung-kong-tai-yeuk-fong

Hongkong Dispensary, Queen's Road—*See Advertisement*
  Watson & Co., A. S.
  Humphreys, J. D.
    Engholm, V.
    Sutton, W. D.
    Noble, Charles J.
    Strachan, B.
    Anthony, J.
    Achoong
    Apoy

香港大酒店 Heung-kong-tai-tsau-tim

"Hongkong Hotel," 17, Queen's Road Central
  Dorabjue & Hing Kee, lessees
  Madar, Ismael P., clerk
  Cawasjee, S., clerk
  Fisher, E., barman
  Pang Achoou, clerk
  Brown, John J., bill collector

刺臣印字館 La-shun-yan-tsz-koon

"The Hongkong Times, Daily Advertiser and Shipping Gazette," morning newspaper, 5, Duddell Street—*See Advertisement*
  Curtis, William, proprietor and publisher
    Curtis, H. L., Court reporter
    Nazer, B. W., do.
    Nesbitt, C., harbour reporter
    Emanuel, B. E., book-keeper
    Dinnis, H. A. D., foreman (jobbing)
    Knight, R. H., foreman (machinery)
    Carion, F. D., foreman (compositors)
    Taylor, G. W., engineer
    Bothelho, M. M., compositor
    Machado, M. M., do.
    Flores, C., do.
    Beltrao, P. A., do.
    Roberts, C., do.
    Carion, L. J. F., do.
    Morone, S., do.
    6 Chinese do.

福公司 Fook-kung-sz

Hook, Son & Co., J. S., shipping and commission agents, and proprietors Hongkong Lighterage and Storage Company, 13, Queen's Road—*See Advertisement*
  Hook, J. S. (England)
  Hook, T. R. S.
  Ribeiro, J. S. V.
  Nunes, A. A.
  Collago, F. C.

Hormusjee & Co., Framjee, merchants, 7, Hollywood Road
  Dhunjeeshaw, Rustomjee (Bombay)
  Hormusjee, Framjee (Shanghai)
  Muncherjee, Dadabhoy, manager
  Mehta, M. M.

鈉那治乞臣治
Nau-lo-chi-hat-sun-chi

Hosungjee, Nowrojee, merchant, Hollywood Road

"Hotel d'Europe," 2 & 6 Hollywood Road
  Estarico & Co., E.
    Estarico, E.
    Silva, F. F.

"Hotel de l'Universe," Wyndham Street
  Favre, Virgil

HONGKONG. A 35

楛核公司 How-wae-kung-sz

Howard & Co., Thomas, merchants, West Point
 Howard, T.
 Petrie, D.
 Davis. H. W.
  Petrie, J. I.

Hughes, W. Kerfoot, general broker, Gough Street

Inglis & Co., J., shipbuilders, engineers, boilermakers and founders
 Inglis, J.
 Chart, A.
  Scott, W.
  Naser, J. S.

Ismael, boarding house keeper (45 seamen), Circular Pathway, No. 9

渣化杯 Cha-fa-pooy

Jafferbhoy & Co., Ameerodeen, merchants, 10, Stanley Street
 Abdoollatiff, Ameerodeen (Bombay)
 Giassoodin, Abdoolrahim
 Abdoolcader, Hajee Ebrahim

Jamaesjee, J., broker, 15, Gage Street

占未臣 Cheem-me-son

Jamieson and Barton, general brokers, inspectors of opium and commission agents, Hollywood Road
 Agabeg, A. L., Jr.

渣顛公司 Cha-teen-kung-sz

Jardine, Matheson & Co., merchants, East Point
 Jardine, Robert (England)
 Whittall, James
 Keswick, William
 Magniac, H. St. L.
 Whittall, Edward (Yokohama)
 Johnson, F. B. (Shanghai)
 Gower, S. J.
  Barretto, J. A.
  Maclean, H. C.
  Kirby, W.
  Chambers, A. F.
  James, H. G.
  Smith, Herbert
  Taylor, O. S.
  Cheyne, A.
  Troing, J. Bell
  Glover, T. G. (absent)
  Beckett, W.

Jardine, Matheson & Co.—(continued)
 Costa, J. P. da
 Azevedo, F. H.
 Remedios, G. dos
 Britto, A. de
 Ozorio, C. A. Jr.
 Ribeiro, A. V.
 Barretto, J. A. Jr.
 Smith, G. M. (Canton)
 Clarke, B. A. (Shanghai)
 Jaffray, W. (do.)
 Cheverton, J. H. (do.)
 Orme, Peter (do.)
 Ward, E. (do.)
 Gubbins, W. H. (do.)
 MacGregor, J. (do.)
 Alford, E. F. (do.)
 Wood, A. H. (do.)
 Keswick, J. J. (do.)
 Orme, Philip (do.)
 MacIvor, A. (do.)
 Glass, D. (do.)
 Couto, E. J. (do.)
 Yvanovich, A. (do)
 Sa, A. F. de (do.)
 Hill, G. B. (receiving ship *Berwick Walls*), (Shanghai)
 Laurie, P. G. (Foochow)
 Paterson, W. (do.)
 Angus, A. F. (do.)
 Noach, C. (do.)
 Nicholson, G. W. (do.)
 Beveridge, H. (Tientsin)
 Walter, W. B. (Yokohama)
 Reimers,— (do.)
 Montgomery, L. (do.)
 Whittall, P. (do.)

Jenkins, Andrew, boarding house keeper (15 West Indian Seamen), Lower Lascar Row

Jumsedjee, Pestonjee, broker, 10, Peel St.

Jumsetjee, Manuckjee, shopkeeper, No. 10, Peel Street
 Jumsetjee, M.
 Ruttonjee, B.

記修治公司 Kee-sow-chee-kung-sz

Kessowjee & Co., Nursey, merchants, &c. &c., Lyndhurst Terrace
 Kessowjee, Nursey (Bombay)
 Khetsey, Kassumbhoy (Bombay)
 Khetsey, Mahamedbhoy
 Khetsey, Jafferbhoy (Bombay)
 Bánájee, N. P.
 Kurumsey, M.

Khamise, boarding house keeper, Lower Lascar Row

顺利洋行 Sun-lee-yeung-hong

Kirchner, Böger & Co., merchants, 10, Queen's Road
  Grossmann, C. F.
  Böger, H. (Shanghai)
  Kirchner, A. (absent)
    Heimann, M.
    Noodt, O.
    Burchard, E. (Shanghai)
    Stein, F. (do.)

Kueebone, G. A., bill, stock and bullion Broker, 9, Seymour Terrace

辣打治 Lat-ta-chi

Koss & Co., tailors, clothiers and general outfitters, Queen's Road—*(See Advertisement)*
  Koss, F.
  Ladage, H.

架林文拿加 Ka-lum-mun-na-ka

Krummenacher & Co., merchants, Stanley Street
  Rüdecker, R.

古勞事公司 Koo-loo-az-kung-sz

Kruse & Co., jewellers, watchmakers, tobacconists and commission agents, sole agent for China and Japan of La Ferme cigarettes, and for Hongkong of Wilson's sewing machines, Queen's Road Central—*See Advertisement*
  Kruse, J. C.
  Kuhlmann, H.
    Krug, A., watchmaker

欖勿押件臣 Lam-mat-at-kin-sun

Lammert, Atkinson & Co., naval and general storekeepers, auctioneers and commission agents
  Lammert, G. R.
  Moore, W. H.
  Friedrich, Otto
    Fisher, S.
    Fonseca, E. F.
    Rogers, F. R.

蘭士田公司 Lan-sz-tin-kung-sz

Landstein & Co., merchants, Queen's Road
  Landstein, Wm. R. (absent)
  Erdmann, C.
  Levy, Alexander
  Caldwell, Ch. F.
  Pereira, A. F.
  Pearson, Thos. (Wanchai Timber Yard)

"Land We Live In," tavern, 294, Queen's Road Central
  Kirchmann, Louis
  Peterson, Peter

連卡剌佛行 Lin-ka-la-fat-hong

Lane, Crawford & Co., shipchandlers, wine and spirit merchants, general storekeepers, tailors, news agents, auctioneers, Queen's Road—*See Advt.*
  Crawford, David R. (absent)
  Cox, John S.
  Fairbairn, John
  Wilson, John (Shanghai)
  Harvie, J. A. (do.)
  Relph, Henry (do.)
  Townley, Fred. (Yokohama)
  Wallace, Thomas (do.)
  St., F. de
  Crawford, Henry
  Wicking, Harry
  Rogerson, W. J.
  Dunn, W. E. H.
  Boffey, Wm.
  McCallum, John
  Stanford, George A.
  Robertson, James
  Fonseca, A. Jr.
  Morton, Andrew (Shanghai)
  Harris, W. R. J. (do.)
  Hewett, W. (do.)
  Fairbairn, Thomas P. (do.)
  Allen, J. W. (do.)
  Annand, F. (do.)
  Cuthbertson, R. B. (do.)
  Cunningham, J. (do.)
  Purvis, J. (do.)
  Triggs, A. S. (do.)
  Braga, J. (do.)
  Wilson, James (Yokohama)
  Henderson, John Y. (do.)
  Owston, Allan (do.)
  Richmond, T. G. (do.)
  De Nully, R. (do.)
  Wood, Charles (do.)
  Booth, George (do.)
  Schonhardt, H. (do.)
  Waggott, W. (do.)

德忌厘士公司 Tak-ke-le-az-kung-sz

Lapraik & Co., Douglas, merchants, D'Aguilar Street
  Lapraik, John S.
  Heaton, A. MacG.
  Manger, Alfred T.
  Shaw, J. Y. V.
  Remedios, A. F.
  Remedios, A.
  Remedios, F. J.

HONGKONG. A 37

Lassen, H. P. C., broker, corner of Wyndham and Wellington Streets

"Liverpool Arms," tavern, 232, Queen's Road Central
  Mariano, Fernandez

洛乞醫生 Lock-hut-s-shang
Lockhead, John, H. M. D., No. 2 Elgin Street

倫敦烟 Lun-tun-in
"London Inn," 126, Queen's Road Central
  Young Laurence
  Greave, Vincent, manager

Lowndes, R. W., merchant, 109, Queen's Road East, office No. 87 Queen's Road, Central

馬嬌云啡叻架 Ma-kiu-wan-fee-lik-ka
MacEwen, Frickel & Co., ship chandlers and commission agents, 48, Queen's Road and 22, Praya—Agents for Dr. D. Jayne and Sons, Philadelphia, U. S. A.; Messrs Samuel Allsopp & Sons, Burton on Trent; *London & China Express*; and *N. C. Herald* and *Daily News*, Shanghai
  Smith, John G.
  Smith, A. F.
  Dolan, W.
    McConachie, Alexander
    Herbst, E.
    Sewell, T.
    Heurmann, F. W.
    Cruckshanks, W.
    Xavier, L. A.
    Meira, X.
    Chape, George

Maclean, G. F., merchant, Queen's Road Central (absent)

Mámá, H. P., broker, Peel Street

孖地 Ma-te
Marty, A. R., Japan and China ware commission agent, 92, and 24 Queen's Road
  Marty, A. R.
    Legar, Mdme. F.
    Marty, P.
    Nunes, A. Jr.

McDonald & Co., A., West Point
  McDonald, J., manager
  O'Ryan, J.
  Caldwell, R.

麥忌厘架公司 Ma-ke-le-ka-kung-sz
McGregor & Co., R., merchants, Burd's Lane
  Baldwin, J. C. (absent)
  Welsh, D.
  Watson, H. A.

墨馬道 Ma-ma-to
McMurdo, R., government and marine surveyor and surveyor for French Lloyds, Praya Central

憲仁藥房 Lai-yan-yeuk-fong
Medical Hall, 87, Queen's Road—*See Advt.*
  Roffer, Th.
  Niedhardt, E.

勿者士公司 Mut-che-sz-kung-sz
Melchers & Co., merchants, Praya Central
  Melchers, Hermann (Bremen)
  André, Adolf
  Reiners, Wm. (Europe)
  Krebs, C
  Mardfeldt, Joh. Fr.
  Goosmann, J.
  Grote, M.
  Rozario, C. do

Merwanjee, S., broker, Gage Street

咪也行 Mei-ya-hong
Meyer, Alabor & Co., merchants, 4, Stanley Street
  Meyer, A. E.
  Alabor, J.
  Meyerink, H F.
  Hauschild, R.
  Fischer, G.

磨地夜冷館 Mo-te-ye-lang-koon
Mody, H N., auctioneer, hill, bullion, share and general broker, Lyndhurst Terrace—*See Advertisement*

歷地司公 Mo-te-kung-sz

Mody & Co., N., merchants, 40, Queen's Road
 Mody, Nusserwanjee B. (Bombay)
 Mody, Ardashir, N. (do.)
 Mody, Jehangerjee N. (do.)
  Horewalla, Maneckjee S., manager
  Hakimna, H. R., assistant
  Mehta, B. M. do.
  Arjanee, F. H. do.

歷剪髪人 Mo-tzin-fat-yan

Moore, W. P., hair-dresser, Hongkong Hotel—*See Advertisement*
 Moore, W. P.
 Butt, N. F.
 Gusman, Saturnina
 Reyes, Mariana

歷件 Mo-kin

Morgan, Chas. Henry, broker, and auctioneer, Staunton Street

舊歷近 Kau-mo-kan

Morgan & Co., W. M., brokers, Bank Buildings
 Morgan, W. M.

歷厘時 Mo-lee-sz

Morris, A. G., ship broker, Pechili Terrace

"National Tavern," 292, Queen's Road Central
 Olsen, John

羅郎也印字館 Lo-long-yah-yun-tze-koon

Noronha & Sons, general printers and stationers, and printers to the Government of Hongkong and to H B M.'s Legation and Consulates in China; the "Hongkong Government Gazette" and Chinese issue of same published every Saturday; "Chinese Gazette" published every Monday, Wednesday, and Thursday, Oswald's Terrace, Wellington Street
 Noronha, Delfino, manager
 Noronha, Leonardo
  Campos, B. P., foreman
  Pinna, F. F. de, compositor
  Xavier, F., do.
  Vicira, P., do.
  Noronha, S. A., do.
  Pereira, A. S., do.

Norton, & Co. Edward, merchants, Praya
 Norton, Edward
 Lyall, Robert
 Bottado, R.

Novelty Iron Works, West Point
 Dumphy, William, manager
 Xavier, V. F., Boilermaker
 Croker, J. W., Engineer
 Xavier, C. J., clerk
 Barros, E. M., do.
 Allison, James, Engineer
 Mitchell, John, do.
 Games, Romas, do.
 Wagner, Arthur, do.
 Collago T., apprentice do.
 Demé, F., do. do.
 Beaudel, W., do. do.

多笠治 To-lap-chi

Nowrojee & Co., Dorabjee, merchants and bakers, Ground floor Hongkong Hotel, Queen's Road Central
 Nowrojee, Dorabjee
 Dorabjee, D., assistant
 Cowasjee, F.
 Rustomjee, F.
 Cowasjee, H.
 Muncherjee, E.
 Pereira, Paccoal.
 Pestonjee, J. manager (Yokohama)
 Sapourjee, E. do.

茹那治 Nau-lo-chi

Nowrojee & Co., merchants, Hollywood Road
 Guzder, B. N.
 Guzder C. B. (Calcutta)
 Guzder, A. R.
 Allymahomed, A. T.

阿巴懸仁醫生 O'Pa-lai-yan-e-shang

O'Brien, R. A., M.D., medical practitioner, Corner of Arbuthnot and Caine Roads

"Old House at Home," tavern, Queen's Road Central, 188
 Taylor, Richard

阿利芬 O-le-tun

Olyphant & Co., merchants, Praya Central
 Parkin, W. W. (New York)
 Talbot, George W. (do.)
 Hayes, A. A., Jr. (Shanghai)
 Geary, H. Seymour
 Olyphant, Talbot (Shanghai)
 Seaman, John F.
 Pim, Tobias (Foochow)

Olyphant & Co.—(continued)
　Smith, J. Bradlee
　Jameson, J. N.
　Moore, Edward
　Wheeler, William
　Nelson, Thomas
　Luz, J. A. da
　Botelho, A. A.
　Franco, F. M.
　Gutierrez, J. G.
　Wisner, J. H.　(Shanghai)
　Chrystall, W.　(do.)
　Smith, E. U.　(do.)
　Hollingworth, H. G.　(do.)
　Allen, J. C., Jr.　(do.)
　Fuller, J. O.　(do.)
　Campbell, A.　(do.)
　Reid, Frank　(do.)
　Abbott, G. W.　(do.)
　Xavier, C. A.　(do.)
　Gutterrez, E. B.　(do.)
　Barretto, J.　(do.)
　Carvalho, J.　(do.)
　Bathgate, John (Foochow)
　Rothwell, A. W.　(do.)
　Davis, Edward　(do.)
　Loring, R. F.　(do.)
　Talbot, F. R.　(Canton)
　Smith, F. B.　(do.)
　Hutchinson, St. John (do)
　Gourdin, A. O. D.　(do.)

梳厘藥房　Sho-le-yeuk-fong

Oriental Dispensary and Aerated Water Manufactory, Wellington St. No. 62
　Soares & Co., F. P.
　Soares, Francisco Paulo
　Vieira, Ignacio
　Rebello, Sebastião

"Oriental Hotel," Bowling Alleys and Billiard Rooms, 4, Wellington Street
　Francis & Duncan, proprietors
　Francis, F.
　Duncan, A.

柯花碧　O-fa-pig

Overbeck, G., merchant, Pedder's Hill
　Ozorio, C. J.

咽治奄八沙行
It-chi-yim-pat-sha-hon

Padsha, H. M., merchant, corner of Gage and Peel Streets and Canton
　Padsha, H. M.
　Tumboly, S. F.

加華冶巴倫冶　Ka-wa-chi-pa-lum-chi

Pallanjee & Co., Cowasjee, merchants, Lyndhurst Terrace
　Cooverjee, Rustomjee
　Cooverjee, Hormusjee (absent)
　Cursetjee, Vania R.
　Cooverjee, Maneckjee
　Rustomjee, Cooverjee　(Shanghai)
　Rustomjee, Pestonjee (absent) (do)
　　Metta, S. M.　(do.)
　　Bomanjee, Pustakia F.　(do.)
　　Cursetjee, S. Khan　(do.)

Paris Soda Water Manufactory, Dubost & Co., G.
　Senna, J. Da, manager

伯架公司　Pak-ka-kung-sz

Parker & Co., general commission merchants
　Torrey, J. W.

砵爹路　Pot-te-lo

Patell, P. N., broker, Wellington Street

查顛船澳　Cha-tin-shun-o

Patent Slip, East Point
　Jack, John (absent)

派利洋行　Pi-lee-yeung-hong

Peil, F., merchant, Peddar's Wharf
　Peil, F.
　Heyden, F. E. (Shanghai)
　Buse, J.
　Bosch, W.
　Schnell, Th.
　Goetz, W. (Shanghai)

收呂宋票館　Shau-lui-soong-pin-koon

Pereira, Francisco Porfirio, agent, Manila lottery tickets, Ladder Street Terrace

波律大狀師　Po-lut-tai-chong-sz

Pollard, Edward H., barrister at law, 1, Club Chambers, D'Aguilar Street
　Pollard, E. H., Q.C.
　Remedios, Florentino dos

伯頓行 Pak-tun-hong

Purdon & Co., merchants, West Point
    Purdon, John G. (Shanghai)
        Davis, H. W. (H'kong & Canton)
        Odell, John (Foochow)
        Tilghman, W. C. (Shanghai)

布士兜公司 Po-sz-tau-kung-sz

Pustau & Co, Wm., merchants, Pottinger Street
    Pustau, William (Hamburg).
    Behn, O. C. (Shanghai)
    Cordes, Joh. F.
    Lancken, F. (absent)
    Siegfried, C. W.
        Simonis, H.
        Lütkens, L.
        Beyer, F.
        Robers, W. von
        Behn, Chr.
        Denecke, C.
        Silva, A. M. da
        Witte, A.
        Donner, C. M. (Canton)
        Detmoring, H. (Shanghai)
        Burchardi, F.   (do)
        Beyfuss, C.   (do.)
        Spitz, E.   (do)
        Pandorf, F.   (do.)
        Maltean, Geo., tea-inspector S'hai
        Rehders, E. Shanghai
        Gonner, A. von (do.)

Quinn, J., tailor and outfitter Corner of Wellington and D'Aguilar Streets
    Allemao, A. E., clerk

Ramos, Joaquim, boarding house keeper, (15 Manila Seamen), Tank Lane

羅凌乜連 Lo-ling-mat-lean

Rawling, Medlen & Co., architects, civil engineers and surveyors, offices over the Hongkong Dispensary
    Medlen, G. A. (absent)
    Studd, J.

連拿公司 （如意洋行）
Lin-na-kung-sz (Yu-ee-yeung-hong)

Raynal & Co., merchants, 14 and 16, Stanley Street
    Raynal, Gustave
    Milisch, Carl (Macao)
    Noodt, Emil
    Meyn, M. C.

泰和行 Tai-wo-hong

Reiss, & Co., merchants, Praya
    Kahn, Leopold
    Crutch, S. J., tea-inspector
    Woollatt, G. H.,   do.
    Gray, R. M., silk-inspecto"
    Danenberg, C.

廉美地澳士公司
Lim-me-te-o-sz-kung-sz

Remedios, & Co., merchants, 18, Gough St.
    Remedios, José A. dos
    Remedios, José Candido dos
    Remedios, D. A. dos
    Remedios, Celidonio C. dos

老美者時公司 Lo-me-che-shi-kung-sz

Remedios & Co., J. J. dos, merchants, 16, Gough Street
    Remedios, João Joaquim dos
    Remedios, J. H. dos
    Remedios, A. A. dos (absent)
    Leiria, H. A.
    Gonsalves, B. F.
    Remedios, J. M. dos
    Rozario, R. do

鐵行 T'it-hong

Reuter's Telegram Company, Limited
    Agent—Woodin, E. L., P. & O. Office, Queen's Road

"Rising Sun," tavern, Queen's Road West
    Kirchmann, Henry
    Rickards, Ferdinand

Robinson, John, exchange and share broker, The Club

Rogers, G. O., D. D. s., dentist, No. 7, Arbuthnot Road

羅時 Lo-shi

Rose & Co., drapers, mercers and milliners, Queen's Road and Wellington Street
    Rose, Miss J. (absent)
    Rose, J. F.
    Robinson, J. S.
    Dunn, Miss S.
    Merredew, Miss M. A.

"Royal Oak," tavern, 208, Queen's Road Central
    Medina João de Castro
    Murphy, J. J.

HONGKONG. A 41

那沙剪髪店 Lo-sha-chin-fat-tim
Roza & Co.; João da, barbers and hairdressers, Wellington Street
  Roza, João da
    Chai-foon, assistant

素些厘公司 Soo-she-li-kung-sz
Rozario & Co., merchants, 8, Stanley St.
  Rozario, Marcos C. do
    Gonsalves, Francisco M.
    Leong, Francisco

旗昌行 Kee-cheong-hong
Russell & Co., merchants, Praya
  Forbes, Paul S. (absent)
  Cunningham, E. (do.)
  Forbes, William H.
  Forbes, F. B. (Shanghai)
  Gitz, W. Scott (Hankow)
  Forbes, John M., Jr.
  Pomeroy, S. W., Jr. (Foochow)
  Hitch, F. D. (Shanghai)
  Forbes, H. de C. (do.)
    Anthony, E. D.
    Blackwell, R.
    Bush, L. L.
    Cunningham, T. B. (Canton)
    Cordeiro, A. (do.)
    Dubost, J. (do.)
    D'Almeida, J.
    Gutierrez, Q. A.
    Gutierrez, Q. O.
    Gutierrez, J. A.
    Henderson, F.
    Hurlburt, S. M.
    Jones, T., (Foochow)
    Jorge, F.
    MacClymont, A.
    Pereira, B. (Foochow)
    Ray, E. C.
    Sheppard, E. (Foochow)
    Smith, C. V.
    Almeida, E. F. (Shanghai)
    Beebe, Chas. G. (Kewkeang)
    Broadbent, J. W. (Shanghai)
    Bush, F. D. (do.)
    Cordier, H. (do.)
    Cunningham, H. M. (Hankow)
    Hinckley, N. B. (Shanghai)
    Du Jardin, F. (do.)
    Dumaresq, P. K. (do.)
    Eckfeldt, T. W. (do.)
    Gabain, P. (Ningpo)
    Gilbert, S. S. (Shanghai)
    Goodfellow, J. F. (do.)
    Heise, G. (Ningpo)
    Howard, J. J. (Hankow)
    Johanssen, F. (Shanghai)
    Lovett, W. W. (do.)
    Lösch, E. (Tientsin)

Russell & Co.—(continued)
  Moore, M. G. (Tientsin)
  Nash, J. (Shanghai)
  Nickels, M. C. (do.)
  Rohl, E. (do.)
  Rose, S. C. (Kewkeang)
  Senna, C. M. (Shanghai)
  Thorburn, J. D. (do.)
  Voisin, A. (do.)
  Webb, E. (do.)
  Wheeler, G. H. (do.)

律墩治公司 Lut-tun-cheo-kung-sz
Ruttunjee & Co., D., merchants, Lyndhurst Terrace
  Ruttunjee, D.

西治公司 Sai-chi-kung-sz
Sage, Edward J. (Estate of), Club Chambers, D'Aguilar Street
  Lopes, Lino J., clerk

山打公司 Shan-ta-kung-sz
Sander & Co., merchants and commission agents, Peel Street
  Sander, F. (absent)
  Grobien, F.
    Raven, E. A.
    Bröschen, W.
    Dittmer, F. C.

Sandilands, John A., general broker. Club Chambers

衣的沙宜公司 I-tee-sha-sun-kung-sz
Sassoon & Co., E. D., merchants, Queen's Road
  Shellim, S. E.
  David, S. J.
  Sassoon, Jacob E. (Shanghai)
    Obadaya, Isaac E.
    Sassoon, E. E.
    Ezekiel, M. D.
    Elias, E. J.
    Moses, J. S.
    Joseph J. S. (Shanghai)
    Elias, J. B. (do.)
    Joseph, D. (do.)
    Moses, S. E. (do.)
    Nathan, J. J. (do.)
    O'Hara, H. (do.)
    Ezra, Isaac (Chefoo)
    Nathan, S. J. (do.)
    Benjamin, B. D. (Tientsin)
    Yaish, S. Y. (do.)
    Nathan, E. E. (do.)
    Joseph, Isaac (Newchwang)
    Perry, J. S. (do.)

沙宜公司 Sha-sun-kung-sz

Sassoon, Sons & Co., David, merchants, Praya Central
  Sassoon, S. D.
  Sassoon, F. D.
  Gubbay, M. S. (Shanghai)
  Moses, S. M.   (do.)
    Saul, M. M.
    Ezra, N. S.
    Abraham, A. E.
    Solomon, R. J.
    Hardoon, S. A.
    Rhodes, Percival
    Rocha, V. F. da
    Brandão, A. J.
    Rozario, A. J., in charge of opium godown
    Costa, A. P. da
    Rozario, E. F. do
    Fonseca, A., in charge of cotton godown
    Williams, R. P. (Foochow)
    Wood, J. W.   (do.)
    Saul, J. S.   (Shanghai)
    Solomon, M.   (do.)
    Nathan, J. A.   (do.)
    Moses, D. E.   (do.)
    Meyer, J. E.   (do.)
    Wolff, M.   (do.)
    Hunt, W. E.   (do.)
    Clarke, Geo.   (do.)
    Dawbarn, A. H. (Hankow)
    Solomon, S. A.   (do.)
    Nathan, S. A. (Newchwang)
    Ezra, A.   (do.)
    Solomon, Ezekiel A. (Tientsin)
    Benjamin, D.   (do.)
    Abraham, J.   (Chefoo)
    Hardoon, E. A.   (do.)
    Gubbay, E. S.   (Ningpo)
    Barnard, A. (Yokohama)

些俚店 Sho-lee-teem

Sayle & Co., linen drapers, mercers, milliners, and merchant tailors, Victoria Exchange, Queen's Road and Stanley St. Residence, 5, 6, Alexandra Terrace
  Sayle, R. (England)
    Sayle, D.
    Black, J.
    Slater, H. G.
    Slater, Mrs.
    Downey, Miss
    Humphreys, W. G.
    Bains, J.
    Boustead, R. N.
    Munday, N.
    Loxley, W.
    Blake, J.
    Byrne, G.

Sayle & Co.—(continued)
    Spring, E. H., manager (S'hai)
    Sayle, T. H.   (do.)
    Eustace, G. O.   (do.)
    Johnson, R.   (do.)
    Richards, Mrs.   (do.)
    Lourtie, Miss.   (do.)
    Chalker, A. C.   (do.)
    Burton, W.   (do.)
    Cruz, A. da   (do.)
    Rider, H.   (do.)
    Waples, J.   (do.)

Scheffer, J. F., shipchandler, and general storekeeper, 54, Praya Central, near Scott Lane
  Scheffer, J. P.
  Collago, L. F. A.

些剌士公司 She-la-sz-kun-sz

Schellhass & Co., Eduard, merchants, Junction of Graham and Wellington Streets
  Schellhass, Eduard (Hamburg)
  Beyer, Ludwig
  Bade, C. Emil (Shanghai)
    Richter, Georg
    Buschmann, R.
    Dorrinck, J. J.
    Pereira, E.
    Claussen, F. E. (Shanghai)
    Schomburg, A.   (do.)
    Burmeister, E.   (do.)
    Bohlschau, P.   (do.)

士勿鎗店 Sz-mit-ch'eung-teem

Schmidt & Co., Wm., commission agents in arms, &c., &c., machinists and artists in general, scientific mechanics and inventors of spring mountain chairs, &c., 94, Queen's Road Central, corner of Peel and Wellington Streets
  Schmidt, Wm., M.A.
  Native workmen

士基剌修整洋琴 Sz-ke-la-sau-chang-yeung-kum

Sequeira, P. A., pianoforte tuner, repairer, &c., Hollywood Road, corner Aberdeen Street

舌 Sheet

Seth, S. A., trader and broker, 34, Hollywood Road

HONGKONG.

昔打活昔加蔑

Suek-ta-oot-shek-ka-mit

Shaik Ahmed, Shaik Dawood, merchant, Gage Street and Macao

雲多喇狀師公司

Shap-to-lah-chong-sz-koong-sz

Sharp & Toller, Edmund, attorneys, solicitors, proctors and notaries public, Supreme Court House
  Sharp, Edmund, Crown solicitor, Q.'s proctor, and actuary of the diocese of Victoria
  Toller, Wm. Wilkinson
    Johnson, Alfred B., solicitor and managing clerk
    Rozario, Lindoro
    Baptista, M. A., Jr.
    One Native

雲匯單銀兩輕紀

Shap-uy-tan-ngan-loung-king-kee

Sharp & Co., bill, bullion & share brokers, Bank Buildings and Bonham Road
  Sharp, Granville

禪臣公司 Shim-sun-kung-sz

Siemssen & Co., merchants, Queen's Road
  Siemssen, G. T. (Hamburg)
  Nissen, Woldemar (do.)
  Joost, A.
  Nissen, Ferd.
  Hoppius, H.
    Hübbe, P. G.
    Siebs, N. A.
    Hockmeyer, F.
    Meyer, H. Breithaupt
    Reimers, O.
    Georg, E.
    Wasserfall, A.
    Schriever, W.
    Peters, G. (Shanghai)
    Koch, W.   (do.)
    Tornoe, H.   (do.)
    Pinkvoss, J. H. (do.)
    Tiefenbacher, M. (do.)
    Paasch, C. W. (do.)
    Oelrichs, H.   (do.)
    Gültzow, A. (Foochow)
    Lübbes, H.   (do.)

隆盛行 Loong-shing-hong

Smith, Archer & Co., merchants, Praya Central
  Blydenburgh, W. J. (Shanghai)
  Hurlbut, Geo. (Yokohama)
  Huntington, S. E.
  Heitmann, J. O. (Canton)
  Low, C. Palmer
  Cruickshank, W. J. (Yokohama)
  Endicott, Samuel (do.)
  Thompson, A. F. (Shanghai)
  Robertson, P. (do.)
  Carlton, L Osgood (do.)

Smith, Peter, boarding house keeper (20 Seamen), Queen's Road West
  Rickards, Ferdinand, assistant

Soab, Ahmed, merchant, Wellington Street
  Hubib Hajee Esmail Hajee (Bombay)
  Jaffer Soomar (Calcutta)
  Soab, Ahmed
  Ooaman, Abha
  Aboobucker, Alleemahomed

Solomon, J. A., merchant, 17, Cochrane Street
  Elias, Ezekiel E. J.

沙羅文 Sha-lo-mun

Solomon, Reuben, general broker, 31, Elgin Street

非厘庇梳沙 Fe-le-pe-sho-sha

Souza, F. A. de, commission agent, 24, Gage Street
  Souza, F. S. de

梳沙印字館 So-sha-yan-tsz-koon

Souza & Co., De, printers, stationers and bookbinders, 38, Hollywood Road—See *Advertisement*
  Souza, J. de
  Souza, J. de, Jr.
    Lima, F. M., book-keeper
    Souza, A. J. da Silva e, foreman
    Rodrigues, Manoel, compositor
    Costa, F. Gomes, do.
    Costa, G.   do.
    Ten Chinese do.

Spratt & Co., W. B., shipwrights and carpenters, 9, Praya East
  Spratt, W. B.
  Emanuel, J. M.
  Edwards, W. Cochran

44 A HONGKONG.

Stag Hotel, Queen's Road Central—See Advt.
    White, J. R., proprietor

Stanford, B. R., shipwright

" Star Tavern," Queen's Road Central
    Hollowell, Thos.

士的芬狀師
Sz-teh-fun-choug-sz

Stephens, Matthew John Denman, attorney, solicitor, proctor, and notary public, 2, Club Chambers
    Stephens, M. J. D.
        Smithers, John
        Guttierrez, S. J.
        Chu Alok, interpreter

Steward, John, boarding house keeper (20 Seamen), Queen's Road West
    Otto, Joh. H., assistant

云醫生
Win-e-sang

Stout, M., D.D.S., Alexandra Terrace

Tata, D. C., merchant, Hollywood Road
    Tata, D. C.
        Burjorjee, C.
        Cotwal, H. R., cotton broker
        Burjorjee, D. (Shanghai)

Thompson & Hind, drapers and silkmercers, 33, Queen's Road
    Thompson, W.
    Hind, J. (England)
        Pearse, J. B.
        Pearse, Mrs.

都剌地
To-la-tee

Tolatee, Framjee Merwanjee, merchant, 15, Gage Street
    Tolatee, B. F.
    Tolatee, D. E.

冰廠
Ping-chong

Tudor Company, Ice House Street
    Agent—Holton, Charles F.

丹拿公司
Tan-na-kung-sz

Turner & Co., merchants, Queen's Road
    Walkinshaw, William (absent)
    Ryrie, Phineas
    Smith, E. C. (Shanghai)
    Walkinshaw, A. W. (Foochow)
        Hart, James (Shanghai)
        McCulloch, David
        Cox, J. H.
        Jesus, J. A. de
        Carvalho, M. de
        Dunne, H. (Foochow)
        Reynell, H. (Shanghai)
        Usill, H. S. B. (do.)
        Southwell, R. E. (do.)
        Sharp, W. F. (Hankow)
        Hickling, A. (Shanghai)

Ullmann, M., general dealer in jewelley and watches, fancy goods and Japan curios of all kinds, 15, Hollywood Road
    Ullmann, Maurice

華臣治
Wa-sun-chi

Vassonjee & Co., Dwarkadass, merchants, Stanley Street
    Vassonjee, Dwarkadass (Bombay)
    Gangjee, Mahomedbhoy
    Anwarally, Cassamally
    Abdool Raheem, Gayasoodin

富些
Foo-she

Vaucher, Albert Emile, general broker, silk inspector and commission agent, Bayview, 14, Arbuthnot Road

佛嚹西麵包舖
Fat-lan-sai-min-pau-p'o

Victoria Bakery, 28, Wellington Street
    Pereira, L., proprietor

卡剌士藥房
K'a-la-sz-yeuk-fong

Victoria Dispensary, Pedder's Wharf—See Advertisement
    Glasse, George
    Stokes, C. S.
    Poate, W. H., accountant
    Ah Yeem, Chinese interpreter

Victoria Hotel, 9, Gage Street
    May, Henry

Victoria Photographic Gallery, Wellington Street
  Floyd, W. P.
  Silveira, J. J. da

Victoria Soda Water Manufactory, 30, Hollywood Road
  Pereira, J. A., proprietor

心治杯 Sam-chi-pooy

Visram, Somjeebhoy, merchant, Gage St.
Somjee, John Mahomed
Limjee, Dossabhoy

科古蝦忌當公司
Fo-koo-ha-ki-tong-kung-sz

Vogel, Hagedorn & Co., merchants, Praya
  Vogel, Emile
  Hagedorn, F. W. (London)
  Kirchhoff, Heinrich (Shanghai)
  Schneider, Theodore
  Held, Richard
  Remedios, A. A. dos
  Remedios, J. dos
  Vogel, Charles (Canton)
  Shawoross, J. J., silk inspector (Canton)
  Vogel, Edward (Shanghai)
  Höhne, Arno   (do.)
  Hohn, Gustav   (do.)

亞或架洋行 A-wak-ka-yeung-hong
Walker, R., merchant, 12, Gough Street

或架罷刺爹公司
Wak-ka-pa-la-te-kung-sz

Walker & Co., Robert S., merchants, Queen's Road
  Walker, R. S.
  Notley, W. H.
  Maclehose, James
  Silva, L. C. da

"Welcome Tavern," 288, Queen's Road Central
  Gomes, Joaquim
  Webb, W. J.

威林 Wei-lum

Willaume, John, bill broker, Almack Place, Aberdeen Street

威林沙路圍畫跡
Wai-lum-sha-lo-wei-wak-chek

Wilson & Salway, architects, surveyors and civil engineers, 87, Queen's Road
  Wilson, Wilberforce, c.e.
  Salway, William
  Too Cheok, draughtsman

Young, Richard, L.R.C.P. Edin., F.R.C.S. Edin., 20, Stanley Street

LIST OF PRINCIPAL COMPRADORES, &c., IN HONGKONG.

List of Compradores.

Armstrong, J. M.—Cheong Sing
Arnhold, Karberg & Co.—Chun Kum
Belilios, E. R.—Wong Hew Chun
Birley & Co.—Pow Choong Hung
Borneo Company, Limited—Hr Yook Shau
Bourjau & Co.—Ng Tsz Yin
Brandão & Co.—Choy Chip
Burd & Co., John—Chu Pew
Butterfield & Swire—Ng Ahip
Carlowitz & Co.—Leong Wah ting
Chartered Bank of India, Australia and China—Yoong Leung
Chartered Mercantile Bank of India, London and China—Wai Akwong
Comptoir d'Escompte De Paris—Yip Ayuen
Commissariat—Pang Fong Poo
Deetjen & Von Bergen—Lum King Wan
Ehlers & Co., Paul—Tam Tse Nem
Gaupp & Co., C. J.—Chew Ting Yü
Ghandy & Co.—Tam Lok Chee
Gibb, Livingston & Co.—Leong On
Gilman & Co.—Chop Achip
Great Northern Telegraph Company—Chü Kum Tong
Grün & Co.—Foong Kew Sun
Heard & Co.—Mok Sz Yeung
Hesse & Co.—Chew Choong Ngam
Hogg & Co.—Foong Ming Shan
Holliday, Wise & Co.—Lai Alun
Hongkong and China Gas Company—Choy Hung
Hongkong Club—Cheong Sik Hin
Hongkong Fire Insurance—Choy Sing Nam
Hongkong and Shanghai Banking Corporation—Lo Yew Kee
Jardine, Matheson & Co.—Ng Kee
Kirchner, Boger—Lo Tsz Tsung
Lammert, Atkinson & Co.—Yip Sing
Landstein & Co.—Cho Tai
Lane, Crawford & Co.—Foong Cheong
Lapraik & Co.—Ng Sang
MacLean, G. F.—Ho Tsun Shan
McEwen & Co.—Chun Man Poo
McGregor & Co.—Wai Piu
Melchers & Co.—Wong Chew
Messageries Maritimes—Ng Fai
Meyer & Co.—Pow Kai Ming
Mody & Co.—Loo Pew
National Bank of India—Yoong Chew
Norton, Lyall & Co.—Foong Kam Chow
Olyphant & Co.—Pow Chow
Oriental Bank Corporation—Foong Awui
P. M. S. S. Company—Poon Chim Hing
P. & O. S. N. Company—Wong Sü Tong
Pustau & Co.—Wong Sun
Raynal & Co.—Kan Hing Wan
Reiss & Co.—Yip On
Remedios & Co., J. A. dos—Leong Choong Tsin
Remedios & Co., J. J. dos—Choy Aloy
Russell & Co.—Kwok Achun
Ruttunjee & Co., D.—Wong Seu Hing
Sander & Co.—Chow Chee Tin
Sassoon & Co., E. D.—Foong Hing Yin
Sassoon, Sons & Co., D.—Loo Yam Shing
Schellhass & Co.—Poon Yuet Low
Siemssen & Co.—Wong Ayew
Smith, Archer & Co.—Wong Yook Chune
Turner & Co.—Sung Pang
Vogel, Hagedorn & Co.—Poo Kat
Wahee, Smith & Co.—Choy Tsz Mee
Walker, R.—Yoong Sew Poo
Walker & Co., R. S.—Pow Yun

The Chinese Hospital.

東華醫院 Tung-wah-e-yuen

Board of Directors.—President—Chew Yu Tin. Members—Pang Fong Poo, Wong Yik Pun, Yuen Oi Yü, Yip Chook Kai, Wong Kwan Tong, Lee Chook Kai, Yü Yam Tong, Chea Oi Yan, Kan Hing Wan, Lee Yuet Chee, Kwok Ching Shan.

Assistant Directors.—Mok Sz Yeung, Chun Sui Sang, Hu Chat Sang, Lee Yat Low, Hoong Cheuk Wan, Foong Yin Ting, Wong Shu Tong, Ow Kim Hing, Ling Ho Woon, Foong Ming Shan, Shó Yü Man, Leong Ping Hew, (these were Ex-Directors); Mok Ting Sang, Chin Seung Nam, Lum King Nam, Chew King Ngam, Lee Lai Hing, O' Man Chai, Hu Yook Shan, and Ng Heung l ün.

Ordinary Committee.—Thirty-two members.

MAN-MOO JOSS-HOUSE COMMITTEE.

街坊公所 Kai-fong-kung-sho

For Chung Wan District.—Wai Sing, Hoong Sing, Luen Sing, Tai Sing, Kwong Loong, Chui Lee, Tun Hop, Choy San, Yuet Woh Loong, Toong Foong, Mow Sang, Sun Kwong Loong, Yoongkee, Yow Loong, and Tak Cheong.

For Taipingshan District.—Woh Foong, Tai Hing, Lai Cheong, Wan Kee, Woh Tai, Tang Yuen Cheong, Kee Cheong, Yow Tai, Sun Woh Cheong, On Tai, Tai Kat, and Ying Mow.

For Ha Wan District.—Kin Nam Chan, Sam Woh, Tak Hop, Sun Hing, Yün Cheong, Yee Yik, Yik Yuen and Wing Tai.

For Sheung Wan District.—Fook Hing Woh, Fook Chui Yuen, Fook Loong, Kwong Tai, Hang Lee, Ku Tai, Chün Cheong Loong, Kwong Cheong Loong, Yuet Hing Loong, Tung Mow, Sui Loong, Man Foong, Wing Hop, Shing Cheong, Wing Kat, Tai Hing, and Yuet Loong.

For Saiyingpoon District.—Tak Mee Hong, (principal member) Yuen On Tai, Yeong Tai Loi, Ching Loong, Wo Tai Hong, Yee Loong Lan, Him Yuen, Chui Chan, Tak Mee Hop, Chee Hing Loong, Koong Yuen Tai, Koong Woh, Fook Loong, Yee On Lan, Toong On Chan, and Kong On.

THE YU-LAN PROCESSION COMMITTEE.

盂蘭　值事

For the several districts, there are 78 members in all.

NATIVE HONG LIST.

The following List of the Native Hongs will prove useful to Merchants and Foreign Residents generally.

中西通貿易之香港華商人名錄

General Merchants.

志興隆
Chi Hing Loong, 71, Bonham Strand West

晉昌行
Chun Cheong Hong, 56, Bonham Strand West

俊昌榮
Chun Cheong Wing, 77, Bonham Strand West

振源行
Chun Yuen Hong, 12, Bonham Strand West

福隆行
Fook Loong Hong, 21, Bonham Strand West

福茂隆
Fook Mow Loong, 46, Bonham Strand West

福盛隆
Fook Shing Loong, 65, Praya

福榮隆
Fook Wing Loong, 81, Praya

福裕隆
Fook Yue Loong, 50 Bonham Strand

興泰棧
Hing Tai Chan, 44, Bonham Strand

合興行
Hop Hing Hong, 124, Bonham Strand

厚和行
How Wo Hong, 87, Praya West

建昌行
Kin Cheong Hong, 60, Bonham Strand West

乾豐行
Kin Foong Hong, 82, Bonham Strand West

建隆行
Kin Loong Hong, 98, Bonham Strand

建南行
Kin Nam Hong, 24, Wing Lok Street

乾泰隆
Kin Tai Loong, 68, Bonham Strand West

乾元興
Kin Yuen Hing, 75, Bonham Strand West

均昌隆
Kwan Cheong Loong, 78, Wing Lok Fong

廣昌隆
Kwong Cheong Loong, 46, Bonham Strand

廣福和
Kwong Fook Wo, 16, Praya West

廣興昌
Kwong Hing Cheong 58, Bonham Strand West

廣萬祥
Kwong Man Cheong, 18, Bonham Strand West

廣萬豐
Kwong Man Foong, 71, Praya

廣茂發
Kwong Mow Fat, 43, Bonham Strand West

廣茂泰
Kwong Mow Tai, 72, Praya

廣兆祥
Kwong Shew Cheung, 63, Praya

廣順隆
Kwong Shun Loong, 63, Bonham Strand

廣泰隆
Kwong Tai Loong, 67, Praya

廣永信
Kwong Wing Shun, 115, Praya

廣仁安
Kwong Yan On, 60, Wing Lok Street

萬福成
Man Fook Sing, 60, Bonham Strand

萬成隆
Man Sing Loong, 58, Bonham Strand

寶泰行
Po Tai Hong, 5, Wing Lok Street

新振成
Sun Chun Sing, 85, Bonham Strand

泰豐順
Tai Fung Shun, 71, Bonham Strand

泰利
Tai Li, 19, Bonham Strand West

德美合記
Tak Mee Hop Ke, 11, Bonham Strand West

得美行
Tak Mi Hong, 18, Praya West

同大盛
Tung Tai Shing, 14, Bonham Strand West

同德棧
Tung Tak Chan, 97, Wing Lok Street

同和昌
Tung Woh Cheong, 16, Bonham Strand

永祥吉
Wing Cheong Kut, 42, Bonham Strand

怡泰行
Yee Tai Hong 28, Bonham Strand West

永安行
Wing On Hong, 39, Wing Lok Street

永誠信
Wing Shing Shun, 57, Bonham Strand West

和德興
Wo Tak Hing 53, Praya

怡豐
Yee Foong, 22, Bonham Strand West

怡記
Yee Kee, 81, Bonham Strand West

儀安行
Yee On Hong, 189, Wing Lok Street

怡順行
Yee Shun Hong, 42, Bonham Strand

義順泰
Yee Shun Tai, 67, Bonham Strand

義和昌
Yee Wo Cheong, 109, Praya

和泰行
Wo Tai Hong, 88, Bonham Strand

元發行
Yuen Fat Hong, 10 Bonham Strand West

源安泰
Yuen On Tai, 20, Bonham Strand West

粤興隆
Yuet Hing Loong, 54, Bonham Strand

Bakers.

意隆
E'Loong, 85, Endicott Lane

吉盛
Kut Shing, 13, Wing On Lane

安和
On Wo, 12, Wing On Lane

Bird's-nest Merchants.

洪茂
Hung Mow, 7, Hillier Street

義合隆
Yee Hop Loong, 111, Jervois Street

裕源
Yue Yuen, 96, Jervois Street

Bookbinders.

祥盛
Cheong Shing, 62, Queen's Road Central

致盛
Chi Shing, 82, Queen's Road Central—*See Advertisement*

祺盛
Kee Shing, 46, Wellington Street—*See Advertisement*

來盛
Loi Shing, 80, Queen's Road Central

南生
Nam Sang, 66, Queen's Road Central

泰昇
Tai Sing, 75, Queen's Road Central

天成
Tien Shing, 77, Queen's Road

宏昇
Wang Sing, 65, Queen's Road Central

Carpenters.

逢勝
Fung Shing, 9, Lyndhurst Terrace

協勝
Hip Shing Aho, 19, D'Aguilar Street—*See Advertisement*

廣成
Kwong Shing, 9, Wellington Street

廣悅隆
Kwong Yuet Loong, 6, D'Aguilar Street

茂發
Mow Fat, 11, Lyndhurst Terrace

HONGKONG.

新美南
San Mi Nam, 39, Wellington Street

勝和
Sing Wo, 14, D'Aguilar Street

泰益
Tai Yik, 48, Stanley Street—*See Advertisement*

德昌
Tak Cheong, 11, Webster Row

德茂
Tak Mow, 55, Wellington Street—*See Advertisement*

同興
Tung Hing, 20, D'Aguilar Street

和隆
Wo Loong, 7, Lyndhurst Street

匯隆
Wui Loong, 12, D'Aguilar Street

Chair-makers.

義祥
Yee Cheong, 14, Wellington Street

義和
Yee Wo, 18, Wellington Street

悅和隆
Yuet Wo Loong, 16, Wellington Street

Charterers.

俊德榮
Chun Tak Wing, 85, Praya West

恒安泰
Hung On Tai, 70, Praya

金祥泰
Kum Cheong Tai, 41, Bonham Strand

廣利源
Kwong Lee Yuen, 48, Bonham Strand

廣和盛
Kwong Woh Shing, 19, Praya West

廣義昌
Kwong Yee Cheong, 64, Queen's Street

禮興
Lai Hang, 89, Queen's Road Central

凌雲
Ling Wan, 16, Queen Street

聯和棧
Luen Woh Chan, 72, Wing Lok Street

萬安隆
Man On Loong, 95, Bonham Strand

普源公棧
Po Yuen Koong Chan, 75, Wing Lok Street

新昌棧
Sun Cheong Chan, 18, Queen Street

東順和
Tung Shun Woh, 84, Praya West

維盛
Wai Shing, 129, Queen's Road Central

永興祥
Wing Hing Cheong, 45, Bonham Street

永源來
Wing Yuen Loi, 82, Praya West

和棧
Wo Chan, 20, Queen's Street

和祥發
Wo Cheong Fat, 68, Wing Lok Street

China-ware Dealers.

福興
Fook Hing, 96, Bonham Strand

廣福昌
Kwong Fook Cheong, 175, Queen's Road West

廣盛隆
Kwong Shing Loong, 124, Queen's Road Central

隆源
Loong Yuen, 182, Bonham Strand West

聯彰
Luen Cheong, 72, Queen's Road Central

義茂
Yee Mow, 118, Bonham Strand

Cigar Dealers.

洪源
Hung Yuen, 73, Hollywood Road

廣磬和
Kwong Hing Wo, 183, Queen's Road Central

廣元磬
Kwong Yuen Hing, 61, Queen's Road Central

Clothiers and Drapers.

怡德
Atick, 1, Wellington Street—*See Advertisement*

三興
Sam Hing (Stultz), 88, Queen's Road Central—*See Advertisement*

同昌
Tung Cheong, 95, Queen's Road Central

Coal Merchants.

成利
Shing Lee, 87, Tung Man Lane—*See Advertisement*

榮記
Wing Kee, 15, Endicott Lane

和記
Wo Kee, 88, Wing On Lane

Contractors.

昌利
Cheong Lee, 208, Queen's Road

廣勝
Kwong Sing, 64, First Street

廣德
Kwong Tuk, 66, First Street

德源
Tuk Yüen, 70, Queen's Road East

同合
Tung Hop, A-Sau, 20, Queen's Road West

同德
Tung Tuk, 27, Wanchai

裕隆
Yue Loong, 10, Gage Street

Cotton Merchants.

俊昌泰
Chun Cheong Tai, 14, Wing Lok Street

阜昌
Fow Cheong, 45, Bonham Strand

建興祥
Kin Hing Cheong, 80, Wellington Street

萬興
Man Hing, 12, Wing Lok Street

德安
Tak On, 80, Wing Lok Street

永和生
Wing Wo Sang, 11, Wing Lok Street

瑤記
Yew Kee, 80, Wing Lok Street

悅和隆
Yuet Woh Loong, 88, Wellington Street

Dyers.

中和
Chung Wo, 186, Hollywood Road

信孚
Shun Foo, 176, Queen's Road West

Fancy Goods Stores.

祥和
Cheong Wo, 28, Queen's Road

恒安泰
Hang Oh Tai, 71, Queen's Road Central

浩生
Ho Sang, 56, Queen's Road

洪昇
Hung Sing, 106, Queen's Road

公泰和
Koong Tai Who, 65, Queen's Road Central

公昌
Kung Cheong, 83, Queen's Road

均泰
Kwan Tai, 104, Queen's Road

廣興
Kwong Hing, 176, Queen's Road

廣南生
Kwong Nam Sang, 85, Queen's Road

廣泰亨
Kwong Tai Hang, 83, Queen's Road

廣和
Kwong Wo, 100, Queen's Road

南興隆
Nam Hing Loong, 81, Queen's Road

南昇隆
Nam Sing Loong, 77, Queen's Road

安盛
On Shing, 86, Queen's Road

新盛
Sun shing, 64, Queen's Road—*See Advertisement*

泰盛
Tai Shing, 78, Queen's Road

陶盛
To Shing, 59, Queen's Road

德彰
Tuk Cheong, 107, Queen's Road

華隆
Wah Loong, 60, Queen's Road—*See Advertisement*

榮隆
Wing Loong, 26, Queen's Road Central

和利
Wo Li, 60, Queen's Road

裕盛
Yue Shing, 82, Queen's Road—*See Advertisement*

Gold Dealers.

昌 盛
Cheong Shing, 71, Bonham Strand

昌 源
Cheong Yuen, 64, Wing Lok Street

祥 盛
Cheung Shing, 88, Bonham Strand

全 盛
Chuen Sing, 81, Bonham Strand

鉅 隆
Ku Loong, 28, Bonham Strand

麗 興
Lai Hing, 71. Bonham Strand

麗 隆
Lai Loong, 89, Bonham Strand

麗 生
Lai Sang, 25, Bonham Strand

南 生
Nam Sang, 58, Bonham Strand

生 昌
Sang Cheong, 25, Bonham Strand

永 盛 隆
Wing Shing Loong, 24, Bonham Strand

匯 源
Wui Yuen, 60, Wing Lok Street

日 隆
Yat Loong, 27, Bonham Strand

怡 隆
Yee Loong, 109, Queen's Road Central

源 隆
Yuen Loong, 75, Bonham Strand

源 源
Yuen Yuen, 55, Bonham Strand

Gold and Silver Smiths.

利 昌
Lee Cheong, 143, Queen's Road

利 貞
Lee Ching, 118, Queen's Road

利 昇
Lee Sing, 10, Queen's Road—*See Advertisement*

榮 珍
Wing Chun, 25, Stanley Street

Gun Makers.

聚 隆
Chui Loong, 45, Stanley Street

毅 隆
Chun Loong, 8, Tung Mun Lane

全 勝
Chuen Sing, 126, Queen's Road West

公 和
Kung Wo, 5, Kwong Yuen Lane West

瑞 生
Soey Sang, 168, Queen's Road West

耀 隆
Yew Loong, 76, Queen's Load

Iron Dealers.

安 記
On Kee, 16, Hillier Street

福 利
Fook Lee, 14, Hillier Street

恒 安
Hang On, 18, Hillier Street

泰 棧
Tai Chan, 11, Burd Street

昌 隆
Cheong Loong, 87, Endicott Lane

怡 興
Yee Hing, 14, Kwong Yuen East Street

英 昌
Ying Cheong, 228, Queen's Road Central

Iron and Copper Smiths.

廣 聚
Kwong Chui, 286, Queen's Road Central

利 隆
Lee Loong, 19, Gilman Street

利 南
Lee Nam, 8, Endicott Lane

怡 昌
Yee Cheung, 83, Queen's Road East

怡 和
Yee Wo, 18, Queen's Road Central

Mat and Bag Sellers.

昌 隆
Cheung Loong, 80, Bonham Strand

昌 和
Cheung Wo, 187, Queen's Road

恒 發
Hang Fat, 99, Bonham Strand

廣 昌
Kwong Cheung, 63, Bonham Strand

隆 昌
Loong Cheung, 107, Bonham Strand

隆 發
Loong Fat, 74, Bonham Strand

成 發
Sing Fat, 51, Bonham Strand

肇 來
Siu Loi, 180, Bonham Strand

大 昌
Tai Cheung, 69, Bonham Strand

泰 昌
Tai Cheung, 127, Queen's Road Central

德 記
Tuk Kee, 4, Endicott Lane

同 發
Tung Fat, 56, Bonham Strand

Money Changers.

關 記
Kwan Kee, 128, Queen's Road Central

紹 亨
Shiu Hang, 119, Queen's Road Central

順 昌
Shun Cheung, 107, Bonham Strand

錫 記
Sik Kee, 107, Queen's Road Central

紹 祥
Siu Tseung, 181, Queen's Road Central

端 記
Tun Kee, 95 a, Queen's Road Central

同 吉
Tung Kut, 67, Queen's Road Central

NATIVE HONG LIST.

元 昌
Yuen Cheung, 22, Bonham Strand

惠 和
Wai Wo, 55, Queen's Road Central

Opium Dealers.

祥 順 利
Cheung Chun Lee, 117, Jervois Street

全 貞
Chuen Ching, 181, Jervois Street

全 聚
Chuen Choi, 82, Bonham Strand

全 興
Chuen Hing, 125, Jervois Street

阜 亨
Fau Hang, 145, Queen's Road Central

阜 生
Fau Sang, 98c, Bonham Strand

謙 信
Him Shun, 118, Jervois Street

經 和
King Wo, 85, Jervois Street

鉅 源
Kü Yuen, 87, Jervois Street

萬 全
Man Chuen, 109, Jervois Street

生 泰 隆
Sang Tai Loong, 8, Praya

生 源
Sang Yuen, 74, Jervois Street

時 和
Shee Wo, 71, Jervois Street

定 安 昌
Ting On Cheung, 19, Queen's Road West

同 昌 發
Tung Cheung Fat, 49, Bonham Strand

會 興
Wui Hing, 6, Queen's Road West

粵 興
Yuet Hing, 75, Jervois Street

雍 和
Yung Wo, 62, Wellington Street

Opium (Prepared) Dealers.

春 源
Chūn Yuen, 86, B, Bonham Strand

福 隆
Fook Loong, 77, Jervois Street

麗 源
Lai Yuen, 105, Jervois Street

炳 記
Ping Kee, 25, Jervois Street

兆 隆
Shew Loong, 57, Bonham Strand

集 成 公 司
Tsap Sing Company, 29, Bonham Strand

裕 順
Yue Shun, 81, Jervois Street

Photographers.

華 芳
A Fong, 54, Queen's Road Central—*See Advertisment*

興 昌
Hing Cheung, 66, Queen's Road Central

文 典
Mun Hing, 82, Queen's Road Central

南 楨
Nam Ching 26, Queen's Road Central

璸 綸
Pun Lun, 56, Queen's Road Central

日 成
Yat Shing, 28, Praya Central

宜 昌
Yee Cheung, 58, Queen's Road Central

Piece Goods Merchants.

長 隆
Cheung Loong, 51, Jervois Street

貞 綸
Ching Lun, 135, Queen's Road Central

晉 昌 隆
Chun Cheung Loong, 49, Jervois Street

福 記
Fook Kee, 79, Jervois Street

福 泰
Fook Tai, 189, Queen's Road Central

逢 源 隆
Fung Yuen Loong, 53, Jervois Street

謙 吉
Him Kat, 3, Bonham Strand

合 昌 隆
Hop Cheung Loong, 86, Jervois Street

輕 綸
King Lun, 21, Jervois Street

輕 泰
King Tai, 60, Jervois Street

高 隆 泰
Ko Loong Tai, 23, Jervois Street

廣 福 隆
Kwong Fook Loong, 41, Jervois Street

廣 隆 源
Kwong Loong Yuen, 19, Jervois Street

廣 紹 隆
Kwong Shew Loong, 39, Jervois Street

美 璋 隆
Mee Cheong Loong, 84, Jervois Street

美 南
Mee Nam, 45, Jervois Street

瑞 祥
Soey Cheong, 57, Bonham Strand

瑞 隆
Soey Loong, 15, Jervois Street

瑞 源
Soey Yuen, 17, Jervois Street

新 安 隆
Sun On Loong, 76, Jervois Street

新 泰 隆
Sun Tai Loong, 46, Jervois Street

德 隆
Tak Loong, 141, Queen's Road

德 泰
Tak Tai, 87, Jervois Street

達 昌
Tat Cheong, 17, Bonham Strand

永 盛 隆
Wing Shing Loong, 78, Jervois Street

永 泰 祥
Wing Tai Cheong, 29, Jervois Street

和綸
Wo Lun, 85, Jervios Street

會隆
Wui Loong, 27, Jervois Street

仁隆
Yan Loong, 28, Jervois Street

溢隆安
Yat Loong On, 11, Bonham Strand

Portrait Painters.

浩生
Ho Sang, 55, Queen's Road Central

麗生
Lai Sang, 106, Queen's Road Central

文興
Mun Hing, 82, Queen's Road Central

成昌
Shing Cheong, 66, Queen's Road Central

同興
Tung Hing, 123, Queen's Road Central

怡興
Yee Hing, 98, Queen's Road

Rattan Dealers.

福興昌
Fook Hing Cheong, 16, Sai Woo Lane

謙和益
Him Wo Yik, 84, Queen's Road West

遂和
Shuey Wo, 68, Queen's Road West

遂和泰
Shuey Wo Tai, 48, Queen's Road West

和記
Wo Kee, 48, Battery Road

匯興昌
Wui Hing Cheong, 1, Sai Woo Lane

Rattan Chair Makers.

德利
Tuk Lee, 180, Queen's Road Central

Rice Merchants.

聚棧
Choy Chan, 26, Bonham Strand West

聚盛
Choy Shing, 30, Wing Lok Street

行利
Hang Lee, 89, Bonham Strand

合棧
Hop Chan, 148, Wing Lok Street

公泰
Kung Tai, 82, Praya West

公和
Kung Woh, 183, Wing Lok Street

公益棧
Kung Yik Chan, 180, Wing Lok Street

公源
Kung Yuen, 10, Praya West.

廣聚
Kwong Choy, 20, Bonham Strand West

廣來
Kwong Loi, 150, Wing Lok Street

廣茂
Kwong Mow, 104, Praya West

HONGKONG.

廣安隆
Kwong On Loong, 105, Wing Lok Street

廣生
Kwong Sang, 6, Bonham Strand West

廣盛
Kwong Shing, 89, Bonham Strand West

茂生
Mow Sang, 27, Bonham Strand West

茂源
Mow Yuen, 20, Praya West

三棧
Sam Chan, 87, Wing Lok Street

時豐
Shee Foong, 42, Wing Lok Street

成信
Shing Shun, 18, West Street, West Point

新同和
Sun Tung Wo, 4, Bonham Street West

新永興
Sun Wing Hing, 118, Bonham Strand

泰益
Tai Yik, 20, Praya West

德茂
Tak Mow, 8, Praya West

同豐
Tung Foong, 114, Praya West

同勝棧
Tung Shing Chan, 84, Bonham Strand W.

永興棧
Wing Hing Chan, 49, Bonham Strand W.

永裕隆
Wing Yü Loong, 127, Queen's Road West

義棧
Yee Chan, 22, Praya West

宜豐
Yee Foong, 86, Wing Lok Street

義興
Yee Hing, 116, Bonham Strand

悅盛
Yuet Shing, 42, Bonham Strand West

Saltpetre and Sulphur Dealers.

昌記
Cheong Kee, 14, Hillier Street

正和
Ching Wo, 216, Queen's Road, West

阜隆
Fow Loong, 76, Praya West

廣阜生
Kwong Fow Sang, 12, Kwong Yuen Lane

廣盛利
Kwong Shing Lee, 4, Wing Lok Street

新合隆
Sun Hop Loong, 103, Praya

Ship Compradors and Chandlers.

昌記
Cheong Kee, 40, Endicott Lane

忠和
Choong Woh, 80, Endicott Lane

發興
Fat Hing, 4, Queen's Road West

NATIVE HONG LIST.

福隆
Fook Loong, 10, Central Market

恒昇
Hang Sung, 47, Central Market

興記
Hing Kee, 12, Central Market

興隆
Hing Loong, 23, Scott Lane

浩泰隆
Ho Tai Loong, 43, Praya Central—*See Advertisement*

金記
Kam Kee, 31, Endicott Lane

其昌
Kee Cheong, 50, Central Market

廣記
Kwong Kee, 39, Endicott Lane

廣生
Kwong Sang, 38, Central Market

廣順
Kwong Shun, 11, Endicott Lane

運昌
Lin Cheong, 69, Praya Central

萬興泰
Man Hing Tai, 33, Gilman Street

茂生
Mow Sang, 27, Endicott Lane

生利
Sang Lee, 52, Central Market

生泰
Sang Tai, 48, Central Market

紹元
Shew Yuen, 4, Central Market

成興
Shing Hing, 1, Webster's Bazaar

盛記
Shing Kee, 4, Scott Lane

成記
Shing Kee, 12, Webster's Bazaar

成利
Shing Lee, 6, Wing Lok Street

順合
Shun Hop, 40, Endicott Lane

遂利
Soey Lee, 29, Endicott Lane

帶記
Tai Kee, 23, Edicott Lane

泰生
Tai Sang, 25, Endicott Lane

泰源
Tai Yune, 2, Central Market—*See Advertisement*

德興
Lak Hing, 35, Pray Central

德利
Tuck Lee, 58, Praya Central—*See Advertisement*

同記
Tung Kee, 6, Webster's Bazaar

永椿
Wing Chan, 8, Central Market

永興隆
Wing Hing Loong, 14, Central Market

永隆泰
Wing Loong Tai, 18, Central Market

永生
Wing Sang, 20, Central Market

永盛
Wing Shing, 24, Central Market

永裕泰
Wing Yue Tai, 25, Endicott Lane

仁興
Yan Hing, 41, Endicott Lane

溢記
Yat Kee, 69, Wing Lok Street

容記
Yoong Kee, 51, Praya Central

有合
Yow Hop, 39, Endicott Lane

裕記
Yue Kee, 21, Endicott Lane

Shoe Makers.

松盛
Chung Shing, 8, Gage Street

興陞
Hing Sing, 24, Wellington Street—*See Advertisement*

開盛
Hoi Shing, 18, Wellington Street

廣盛
Kwong Shing, 23, Scott Lane

順盛
Shun Shing, 17, Endicott Lane

成合
Sing Hop, 70, Queen's Road Central

義昌
Yee Cheong, 7, Scott Street

Sugar Dealers.

合泰和
Hop Tai Wo, 93, Praya

天益
Tien Yek, 44, Bonham Strand West

Sweet Meat Dealers.

萬和祥
Mau Woh Cheong, 236, Queen's Road Central

廣昌泰
Kwong Cheong Tai, 324, Queen's Road Central

Tailors.

開利
Hoi Lee, 112, Queen's Road Central

洪昌
Hoong Cheong, 9, Scott Lane

南昌
Nam Cheong, 23, Scott Lane

南盛
Nam Shing, 127, Queen's Road Central

成昌
Sing Cheong, 8, Webster's Bazaar

和 昌
Wo Cheong, 18, Webster's Bazaar

Tea Merchants.

瑞 昌 隆
Soey Cheong Loong, 69, Queen's Road West

達 盛
Tat Shing, 8, Bonham Strand

定 泰 興
Ting Tai Hing, 811, Queen's Road Central

裕 章
Yue Cheong, 120, Queen's Road Central—
See Advertisement

Watch Makers.

何 凌 記
Ho Ling Kee, 123, Queen's Road

何 廷 記
Ho Ting Kee, 125, Queen's Road Central

利 昌
Lee Cheong, 145, Queen's Road Central

利 貞
Lee Ching, 118, Queen's Road Central

勝 記
Shing Kee, 75, Queen's Road

榮 珍
Wing Chun, 25, Stanley Street

澳 MACAO. 門

Colonial Government.
總督衙門 Tsung-t‑ok-nga-mun
The Governor—Sam Januario, H. E. Viscount de
Colonial Secretary—Castro, Dr Henrique de
Private do.—Mesnier, Pedro G.
Aide-de-Camp—Carvalho, Alberto Carlos Moraes de
Officer at Order—Sampaio, Julio Eleabão Pereira
Chief Clerk—Silva, Tercio da
1st do.—Franco, J. F.
2nd do.—Lemos, José Correa
3rd do.—Lacerda, Antonio F. C.
4th do.—Costa, H. A. Fidellis da
Porter—Marques, José Gomes

COUNCIL OF GOVERNMENT.
議政總局 I-ching-tsung-kuk
President—Sam Januario, H. E. Viscount de
Members—
Castro, Dr. Henrique de (Colonial Secretary)
Brandão, Antonio Carlos (Acting Judge and President of Tribunal of Commerce)
Assumpção, João Correa Paes de (Acting Chief Clerk of Exchequer)
Caldeira Junior, Francisco Antonio Marques (Attorney General)
Leite, Lieut.-Colonel Jeronimo Pereira (Commanding the Police Corps)
Mesquita, Lieut.-Colonel Vicente Nicolao de (Commanding the Monte Fort)
Silva, Dr. Lucio Augusto da (Colonial Surgeon)
Marques, Lourenço (President of Municipal Chamber)
Carvalho, Antonio Luis de (Governor of the bishopric)

COUNCIL OF TECHNICAL SERVICE OF PUBLIC WORKS.
President—Sam Januario, H.E. Viscount de
Director of Public Works—Luna, Lieut.-Colonel Francisco Jeronimo

COUNCIL OF TECHNICAL SERVICE OF PUBLIC WORKS.
(*Continued.*)
Members—Assumpção, João Correa Paes de ; Caldeira Junior, Francisco Antonio Marques ; Cercal, Baron do
Secretary—Ferreira, Antonio Augusto

COUNCIL FOR INSPECTION OF PUBLIC INSTRUCTION.
President—Sam Januario, H. E. Viscount de
Members—Carvalho, Rev. Antonio L. de ; Basto, Dr Julio Ferreira Pinto ; Leite, Luiz Pereira
Secretary—Cabral, João Albino Ribeiro (Delegado inspector de instrucção publica)

COUNCIL OF THE PROVINCE.
President—Sam Januario, H. E. Viscount de
Secretary—Castro, Dr Henrique de
Members—Caldeira Junior, Francisco Antonio Marques ; Viscount do Cercal ; Bastos Junior, Antonio Joaquim
Substitutes—Pitter, Vicente de Paula Salatwich ; Pacheco, Albino Antonio

JUNTA DA JUSTICA MILITAR.
President—Sam Januario, H. E. Visc. de
Members—
Brandão, Antonio Carlos (Act. Judge)
Cabral, Lieut. Fernando Augusto da Costa
Leite, Lieut.-Colonel Jeronimo Pereira
Barbosa, Lieut.-Colonel Domingos José d'Almeida
Scarnichia, Captain João Eduardo

JUNTA DA JUSTICA CIVIL.
President—Sam Januario, H. E. Viscount de
Members—
Brandão, Antonio Carlos (Act. Judge)
Viscount do Cercal
Bastos Junior, Antonio Joaquim
President of Municipal Chamber—Marques, Lourenço
Procurador for the Chinese—Basto, Dr Julio Ferreira Pinto

MACAO.

JUDICIAL DEPARTMENT.

Judge—Brandão, Antonio Carlos (acting)
Substitute—Hyndman, João
Attorney General—Caldeira Junior, F. A. Marques
Advocates—Pacheco, Albino Antonio; Lobo, Felicissimo da Cruz; Pereira, Vicente Saturnino; Bastos, Antonio Joaquim, Jr.; Ferreira, Leoncio Alfredo; Lourenço, Caetano Jose; Mendes, Antonio Nogueira; Silva, Ephraim Manassés da; Sequeira, Faguardes Patrocinio
Clerks and Notaries Public—Costa, José Maria da; Leite, Luiz Pereira (Escrivães do Juiz de Direito, do Tribunal Commercial, da Policia Correccional, da Junta de Justiça e Tabelliães de Notas)
Judge's Clerk and Clerk of Orphan's Fund—Lemos, José de
Account. and Distributor—Rangel, Antonio
Bailiffs—Placé, Antonio Felix; Soares, J. Antonio; Thimoteo, Amenio

CONSERVATORIA.

Conservador—Caldeira, Jr., F. A. Marques
Private Adjutant of Conservatoria—Gordo, Faustino Joaquim Ferreira (acting)
Amanuensis—Perpetuo, José Eulalio

JUNTA DO LANÇAMENTO DAS DECIMAS, &c.

President—d'Assumpção, João Correa Paes
Secretary—Ribeiro, Francisco Vieira
Fiscal—Caldeira Jr., Francisco A. Marques
Members—Souza, Joaquim Antonio de; Silva, Joaquim Peres da; Luz, Demetrio Francisco da; Xavier, Francisco; Yeckchong

TRIBUNAL OF COMMERCE.

President—Brandão, Antonio C. (Acting Judge)
Secretary—Caldeira, Junior, Francisco [A. Marques (Attorney General)
Jurors—Tavares, Simplicio Antonio; Silva, Francisco Antonio da; Luz, Demetrio Francisco da
Substitute—Lopez, Evaristo

CHINESE EMIGRATION OFFICE.

招工所 Tsin-kung-sho

Superintendent—Scarnichia, João Eduardo (acting)
Assistant do.—Roza, Simão Vicente
Clerks—Rozario, Maximo das Nevas; Pereira, Joaquim O. da Costa; Hyndman, João A.; Silva, João Maria Ega da

CHINESE EMIGRATION OFFICE.

(*Continued.*)

Interpreter—Marques, Augusto Oscar
Chinese do.—Three
Watchmen—Ten Europeans
Chinese do.—Five
Porter—One European

TREASURY.

Treasurer—Rocha, Carlos Vicente da
Chief Clerk—Nogueira, Francisco D. G. de
Clerk—Marçal, Edmundo M.

ADMINISTRACAO DO CONCELHO.

Administrador do Concelho—Baracho, Francisco de Mello
Chief Clerk—Francisco de Paula
Clerk—Vianna, Euclides Honor
Bailiff—Souza

PROCURADOR'S DEPARTMENT.

議事亭街華政衙門

I-az-ting-kai-wa-tsing-nga-mun

Procurador—Bastos, Julio Ferreira Pinto
1st Class Interpreters—Silva Jr., Pedro Nolasco da; Marques, Eduardo; Marçal, João de C.; Jorge, Cancio
2nd do. do.—Marques, Ignacio Martinho; Roza, Evaristo da
Clerks—Carvalho, Pio M. de; Goularte, José B.; Placé, Cornelio
Linguists—Xavier, Mauricio E.; Robarts, José T.; Luz, Vicente E. da
Bailiffs—Simoës, Benjamin P.; Carvalho, Januario L. de; Luz, Felippe da; Carvalho, José G. de; Carvalho, Alfredo de

REVENUE DEPARTMENT.

Secretary—d'Assumpção, João Correa Paes (acting)
Accountant—
Book-keeper—d'Azevedo, José Joaquim (acting)
1st Clerk—
Assistant Book-keeper—Marçal, Francisco de Paula (acting)
2nd Clerk—Nunes, Lino (acting)
Porter—Oliveira, Vedasto dos Santos e
Messenger—Correia, João Luiz
Inspector Intendant of Troops—d'Assumpção, João Correa Paes
Assistant do.—d'Azevedo, José Joaquim

MACAO.

ADMINISTRATIVE COMMISSION OF THE ESTATE OF THE PORTUGUESE MISSION OF THE S. JOSEPH COLLEGE IN CHINA.

President—Carvalho, Rev. Antonio L. de
Members—Pinto, Rev. Joaquim Frederico (absent); Santos, Rev. Maximo A. dos; d'Assumpção, João Correa Paes
Secretary—Roza, João Miguel da (acting)

COMMISSION OF THE MILITARY HOSPITAL OF MACAO.

President—Silva, Dr Lucio Augusto da
Vice-President—Telles, J. C. da Silva
Secretary—d'Azevedo, José Joaquim
Chief Ward-Master—Never, Camillo L. das
1st do.—Louzada, José do R.
2nd do.—Lemos, Vicente de P. da C.
3rd do.—Pedro, Joaquim; Perreque, José de Freitas

RECEBEDORIA DAS DECIMAS.

Chief Clerk—Ribeiro, Francisco A. V.
1st do.—Rocha, Francisco Paula da
2nd do.—Rodrigues, Joaquim

INSPECÇÃO DOS INCENDIOS.

Inspector—Corte-Real, F. G. Freire
Substitute—Cunha Jr., Antonio de Azevedo e

HARBOUR MASTER'S OFFICE.

船頭官 Shün-t'au-koon

Harbor Master—Scarnichia, João Eduardo
Assistant do.—Vichi, Augusto Ludgero
Clerk—Gomez, Francisco N. H.

POLICE DEPARTMENT.

Lieut-Colonel—Leite, Jeronimo Pereira
Lieut. and Adjutant—Reis, João Severino da Silva
Surgeon—Roza, Bernardo Maria das Neves Araujo
Captain-Fiscal—Corte-Real, Frederico Guilherme Freire
Captain—Baracho, Francisco de Mello
Lieuts.—Guimarães, José da Silva; Arrobas, Antonio M. Barreiros; Souza, Porphyrio Z. de; Sardinha, F. P.
Paymaster—
Ensigns—Souza, José M. de Carvalho e; Ferreira, José Augusto

PUBLIC WORKS DEPARTMENT.

Lieut.-Colonel—Luna, Francisco Jeronimo
Ensign—Cunha Jr., Antonio d'Azevedo e
Conducting do.—Lobo, Antonio Felippe; Silva, Carlos Freitas da
Secretary—Ferreira, Antonio Augusto
Painter, &c.—Brito, José Maria de Souza

MUNICIPAL COUNCIL.

President of the Chamber—Marques, Lourenço A.
Vice-President do.—Baron do Cercal
Members—Carvalho, J. H. de; Baptista, L. J.; Portaria, V. P.; Pacheco, D. A.
Secretary—Marques, Pedro
Treasurer—Nogueira, Francisco D. G. de
Assistant—Roza, Francisco Henrique da
Messenger—Rozario, Luis Maria do
Bailiffs—Fernandes, Miguel de Souza; Rozario, Antonio Elleuterio do

Military Department.

Lieut.-Colonel Commanding—Barbosa, Domingos J. d'Almeida
Major—Trolho, André Pires
Adjutant—Ferreira, Antonio Augusto
Chief Surgeon—Telles, J. C. da Silva
Assistant do.—Alvares, João J. F.
Lieut. Quarter-Master—d'Oliveira, José F.
Captains—Coutinho, M. d'Azevedo; Silva, Francisco A. Ferreira da; Luz, Francisco de Paula da; Garcia, Antonio Joaquim; Sampaio, M. de Castro; Tassara, Antonio Baptista
Lieutenants—Silva, Carlos J. P. da; Souza, J. P. S. C. Pinto de: Barros, Vicente de Paula
Ensigns—Azedo, C. M. Dias; Antunes, João; Maher, J. J.; Rego, Adriano Augusto
Officer in Charge of Monte Fort—Mesquita, Lieut.-Colonel V. N. de
Officer in charge of Barra Fort—
Officer in charge of Bomparto Fort—Ferreira, Ensign A. Augusto
Officer in charge of Taipa Fort—Tassara, Graduated Captain A. B.

INSPECTION OF WAR MATERIAL.

Inspector—Miranda, Major Miguel C. G. d'Oliveira

RETIRED MILITARY OFFICERS.

Lieut.-Colonels—Roza, B. M. A.; Almeida, Januario Agostinho de
Majors—Gonsalves, Joaquim Manoel; Collaço, Francisco Xavier; Souza, Joaquim A. de
Chaplain—Soledade, Pe. José da

RETIRED GOVERNMENT OFFICERS.

Secretary of the Revenue Department—Simoes, Miguel Pereira
Clerk and Notary Public—Migueis, Thomaz d'Aquino

MACAO.

OFFICERS OF TIMOR CORPS.

Governor—Castello-Branco, Major Hugo Goodair de Lacerda
Captains—Teixeira, Manoel Antonio; Smith, Francisco dos Santos
Lieutenants—Vanez, J. Manoel; Vaquinhas, José dos Santos; Dores, Rafael das; Costa, João Alves da
Ensigns—Baptista, João; Pereira, Rebello J.; Fernando, Antonio; Souza, Malaquias J. M. de; Ribeiro, J. da Silva; Ruas, A. J.; Silva, Alarico Sarmento Gomes da; Silva, M. Soares da; Miranda, Francisco Ferreira de

RETIRED OFFICER.

Major—Cabreira, Duarte Leão

NATIONAL GUARD.

Commandant—Cercal, Baron do
Major—Silva, Elias J. da
Adjutant—Maher, Josino
Lieut. Quarter-Master—Peres Jr., Miguel
Chief Surgeon—Pitter, Dr V. S.
Captains—d'Azevedo, J. J.; Silva, Luiz João da; Silva, F. A. da
Lieutenant—Silva, Claudio I. da
Ensigns—Marques, L. J. Martinho; Barretto, Luiz; Lopes, Clementino Vicente; Bastos, A., Jr.; Rosa, M. d'Araujo; Souza, J. Neves e

Naval Department.

CAMOENS, GUNBOAT.

Commander—Guimarães, José M. Teixeira
2nd do.—Leite, A. Mendes
Sub-Lieut.—Ghira, A. A.

PRINCIPE DOM CARLOS, MAN-OF-WAR.

IN MACAO.

Commander—Silveira Maciel, Vicente da
2nd do—d'Avila, José Almeida
Sub-Lieuts.—Caminha, Caetano Rodrigues; Taveira, L. A. P. de Moura

TEJO, GUNBOAT.

Commandant—Cabral, Fernando Augusto da Costa
2nd do.—Capello, Hermygido Carlos de Brito
Lieuts.—Rio, Ernesto Alves de; Pereira, Carlos d'Avellar
Officers—Cinatti, Diometrio; Soares Franco, Francisco; Silva, Theodorico da Costa e
Paymaster—Pereira, M. Cezario
Surgeon—Lima, M. C. da Silva
Engineer—Araujo, C. A. P. Faria

Educational.

ST. JOSEPH'S COLLEGE.

Rector—Carvalho, Rev. A. Luiz de
Vice-Rector—Santos, Rev. Maximo Antonio dos
Do. Mathematics and Navigation—Marques, Francisco J.
Do. Philosophy—Rodrigues, Theodozio J.
Do. Latin—Cabral, João Albino Ribeiro
Do. Theology and Portuguese—Carvalho, Rev. A. Luiz de
Do. Chinese—Lyra, Rev. Lucas
Do. Mandarin Dialect—Silva, Jr., Pedro Nolasco da
Do. Portuguese Elementary—Medeiros, Rev. Antonio Joaquim de; Silva, Manoel J. M. Gonsalves da
Do. English do.—Hyndman, Francisco
Do. Music—Medeiros, Rev. Antonio Joaquim de
Do. English—Alvares, Mariano F.
1st Prefect of the Orphans—Costa, José da
2nd do.—Fernandes, Francisco
3rd do.—Dias, Luiz Philippe
Steward—Lopes, Antonio Conceição
1st Clerk—Roza, João Miguel da
2nd do.—Roza, Jr., João Miguel da
Compositor—Roza, Severiano da
Advocate—Bastos, Jr., Antonio J.

Post Office.

AT "NATIONAL DISPENSARY," 81, PRAYA GRANDE.

Postmaster—Souza, Ricardo de, 1, Rua do Campo

Theatro de Dom Pedro V.

President—Baron do Cercal
Secretary—Bastos, Antonio, Jr.
Treasurer—Rocha, Carlos V. da
Members—Souza, J. Neves e; Pacheco A.

Consulates.

AUSTRO-HUNGARIAN MONARCHY.

雅爹簾啞領事官

A-to-li-a-ling-sz-koon

Consul-General—Overbeck, Gustav von (residing in Hongkong)
Vice-Consul—Milisch, Carl

BELGIUM.

卑之暗領事官 Pi-che-um-ling-sz-koon

Consul—Cercal, Baron do
Chancellor—Pereira, B. A.

BRAZIL.

巴剌斯領事官 Pa-la-sz-ling-sz-koon

Consul—Cercal, Viscount do
Vice-Consul—Cercal, Baron do

FRANCE.

佛蘭西國領事官

Fat-lan-sai-kwok-ling-sz-koon

Vice-Consul—Cercal, Baron do

GERMAN EMPIRE.

波羅斯國領事官

Po-lo-sz-kwok-ling-sz-koon

Vice-Consul—Ebell, H.

HAWAII.

Vice-Consul—Souza, C. L. de

ITALY.

意打厘領事官 I-ta-li-ling-sz-koon

Consul—Cercal, Baron do
Vice-Consul—

NETHERLANDS.

荷蘭國領事官

Ho-lan-kwok-ling-sz-koon

Acting Consul—Ebell, H.

PERU.

Consul-General—Delboy, Captain Ulises, P. N.
Clerk—Beltran, Pedro

SIAM.

Consul—Fernandes, B. de Senna
Vice-Consul—Pacheco, D. C.

SPAIN.

呂朱國領事官

Lui-soong-kwok-ling-sz-koon

Consul—Caño, J. A. Muñus del
Vice-Consul in Charge—Priego, D. Juan Ortiz y
Acting Chancellor—Lopez, José J.

Insurances.

Deacon & Co.
  Union Insurance Society
Margesson & Co.
  North China Insurance Co.
Mello & Co., A. A. de
  China Traders' Insurance Company, Limited
Raynal & Co.
  Samarang Sea and Fire Insurance Company of Samarang
  China and Japan Marine Insurance Company, Shanghai

Steamers.

HONGKONG, CANTON AND MACAO STEAMBOAT COMPANY, LIMITED.

咩路公司 Mè-lo-kung-sz

Agents—Mello & Co., A. A. de, Praya Grande

STEAMER "WHITE CLOUD"
CANTON AND MACAO.

Captain—Brady, G.
Engineer—Low, W.
Purser—Lopez, F.

Merchants, &c.

Alvares, João Jacques Floriano, M.D., 3, Rua do Campo Velho

Astorquia, Antonio, merchant
  Ribeiro, J. Vieira

Bastos, Antonio Joaquim, Jr., advocate, Praya Grande

"Boletim da Provincia de Macao e Timor," Typographia Mercantil, Praça de Ponte e Horta, No. 14
  Fernandes, N. T., proprietor
  Costa, L. da, foreman
  Mendonça, L. M. de, compositor
  Marçal, Sabino A.   (do.)
  Perpetuo, Alfredo V.   (do.)
  Rozario, Anselmo F. do   (do.)
  Pereira, Alfredo E.   (do.)
  Diniz, Adolpho J.   (do.)
  Cordeiro, Loreno M. G.   (do.)

Brandão & Co., merchants, 14, Travessa do Trunco Velho

MACAO.

的件公司 Ti-kin-kung-sz

Deacon & Co., public tea and silk inspectors and commission agents, Praya Grande
 Hutchison, Alfred
 Deacon, Ernest
 Deacon, Sidney
  Howie, Robert, silk inspector
 d'Azevedo, F.

荷蘭行 Ho-lan-hong

Ebell & Co., merchants
 Ebell, H.
  Senna, V. P. de

Fernandes, B. de Senna, 33, Praya Grande
 Fernandes, B. de S.
 Pacheco, D. C.
 Simoes, N.
 Silva, Luiz da
 Barros, José E. F.

Ferreira, Leoncio A., advocate, Praya Grande

Fonseca, A. J. de, merchant, Ponta de Rede

佐士科西架 Cho-sz-fo-sai-ka

Fonseca, José Maria da, shipchandler, sail-maker, wine and spirit merchant, Ponta de Rede
 Fonseca, José Maria da
 Soares, D.

Garcia y Garcia, N., merchant
 Allanson, Wm., clerk

Graça, L. A. de, shipchandler and general storekeeper, wine and spirit merchant, auctioneer, commission agent, — ships supplied with water
 Graça, L. A. de
 Jorge, E. A.
 Jesus, J. G. de

Graça, V. A. de, merchant, Rua de Prata

"Lisbon Dispensary and Soda Water Manufactory"
 Souza & Co., J. das Neves e
 Souza, J. das Neves e
  Cruz, Theotonio da
  Souza, Egydio de
  Senna, Antonio P. da

Lobo, Felicissimo da Cruz, advocate, Rua Formosa

Lourenço, Caetano José, advocate, Praya Grande

孖治臣公司 Ma-che-shun-kung-sz

Margesson & Co., merchants
 Schutze, F. S. (absent)
 Murray, Mortimer E.
 Coles, F. W., tea-inspector
 Senna, F. P.
 Mendes, A. N., Jr.

白鴿巢 Pak-kop-chau

Marques, L., merchant, Praça de Luis de Camoës, No. 4
 Marques, L
 Marques, Eduardo Pio

咩路公司 Me-lo-kung-sz

Mello & Co., A. A. de, merchants, Praya Grande
 Mello, A. A. de (Viscount do Cercal)
 Mello, Antonio de (Baron do Cercal)
 Cruz, F. A. da
 Pereira, R. N.
 Cruz, S. da
 Campos, J. P.

Mendes, Antonio Nogueira, advocate, Rua de S. Antonio

大藥房 Tai-yuek-fong

"National Dispensary," 81, Praya Grande
 Telles, José Severo da Silva, 15, do.

Olano, A., merchant, Praya Grande
 Lionel, Gutterres

Pacheco, Albino Antonio, advocate, Praya Grande

Pearce, E. W., emigration agent

庇厘剌 Pé-lé-la

Pereira, B. A., merchant, 18, Rua de Sé
 Pereira, L. A. I.

Pereira, Vicente Saturnino, advocate, Rua Formosa

Portaria, Vicente de P., merchant, Chunambeiro

Raynal & Co., merchants and commission agents, 12, Rua de Sé
 Milisch, C.

MACAO.

羅美耆士 Lo-mʏ-che-az
Remedios, M. A., merchant, Rua do Barão
  Remedios, M. A. dos
  Remedios, A. dos
  Maher, Miguel M.
  Remedios, M. A. dos, Jr.
  Rozario, Florencio J. do

南灣酒店 Nam-wan-tsau-tim
"Royal Hotel," Praya Grande
  Graça, L. A. de, proprietor
  Jorge, E. A.
  Kraal, G. F.

Silva, F. A. da, commission agent, Praya Grande

這思厘化 Ché-sz-li-fa
Silva, J. da, commission agent, printer and auctioneer
  Silva, J. da
    Silva, C. da

厭鴨扶思厘化 Im-ap-fo-sz-li-fa
Silva, M. F. da, Fonte de Lilao

思厘化 Sz-li-fa
Silva, P. N. da, merchant, 1, Rua de Santo Agostinho

若京思厘化公司 Yeuk-king-sz-li-fa-kung-sz
Silva & Co., Joaquim Peres da, merchants and general commission agents, 15, Praya Grande
  Silva, Joaquim Peres da
  Silva, Genuino Augusto da
    Hyndman, João

Souza, Camillo L., merchant, 59, Praya Grande

Thomas & Mercer, public tea inspectors (also at Canton)
  Thomas, T.
  Mercer, T.
    Mann, J. A.

Tuton & Sons, José A., merchants
  Tuton, J. A.
  Tuton, F.
  Tuton, T.
    Graça, F. M. de
    Gutterres, R. A.

黃 WHAMPOA. 埔

Consulates.
GREAT BRITAIN.
大英國領事官
Tai-ying-kwok-ling-sz-koon

Vice-Consul—Hance, H. F., PH.D.
Constable—Jones, J. H.

Imperial Maritime Customs.
黃埔海關 Wong-po-hoi-kwan

Tide-surveyor—Dawson, Frederick
Tidewaiters—Duncan, Andrew; Johnstone, Wm.; Liedcke, L.; Molloy, E.; Fan Chen Hing; Chen Ah Loong
Watcher—Chuey Che Cheong

Docks, &c.
香港黃埔船澳公司
Heong-kong-wong-po-shün-o-kung-sz

Hongkong and Whampoa Dock Company
  McKay, Geo. S.
  Jesus, J. Victor de, clerk

Franklyn L. H., L.R.C.P., M.R.C.S., L.S.A. London

"Union Tavern," Bamboo Town
  Camran, Charles

"Whampoa Hotel," New Town, billiard and bowling alleys
  Sharp, S. W.

省 CANTON. 城

Consulates.

AUSTRO-HUNGARIAN MONARCHY.
奧 期 馬 叻 國 領 事 官
Ao-sze-ma-ka-kwok-ling-sze-koon
Consul—Robertson, Sir Brooke, C.B.

DENMARK.
大 丹 國 領 事 官
Tai-tan-kwok-ling-sze-koon
Consul—Magniac, H. St. L., Shameen (non-resident)

FRANCE.
大 法 國 領 事 署
Tai-fat-kwok-ling-sze-shu
Consul—Dabry de Thiersant, P.
Chancelier Interprete—Sales, V. A.

GERMAN EMPIRE.
大 德 國 領 事 府
Tai-tak-kwok-ling-sze-foo
Consul—Lueder, C. (absent)
Acting Consul & Interpreter—Freusberg, C.
Writer—Liu-Tung-fu

GREAT BRITAIN.
大 英 國 領 事 官
Tai-ying-kwok-ling-sze-koon
Consul—Robertson, Sir Brooke, C.B.
Interpreter and Acting Vice-Consul—Gardner, Christopher T., F.R.G.S., F.A.S.
Assistant—Hillier, W. C.
Acting do.—Mansfield, R. W.
Linguist—Mun ching
Constable—Marquand, P. Le
Head Writer—Lu tung tsu
2nd Do.—Li meng hiang

POSTAL AGENCY.
Agent—Hillier, W. C.

NETHERLANDS.
大 荷 蘭 國 領 事 官
Tai-ho-lan-kwok-ling-sze-koon
Consul—Hulse, Wm.

SPAIN.
大 呂 宋 國 領 事 官
Tai-lui-soong-kwok-ling-sze-koon
Vice-Consul—Villanueva, M.
Interpreter—Xavier, F. B.

SWEDEN AND NORWAY.
大 瑞 威 頓 國 領 事 官
Tai-sui-wai-tun-kwok-ling-sze-koon
Vice-Consul—Cunningham, T. B. (Old Factory Site)

UNITED STATES.
大 美 國 領 事 官
Tai-mei-kwok-ling-sze-koon
Consul—Jewell, R. G. W.
Vice-Consul—Vacant
Interpreter—Wai Ng Wun
Clerk—Tat-hin, Thos. S.
Chinese Clerk—Tsai Ashing
Marshal—Spencer, Wm. A.

Imperial Maritime Customs.
粵 海 關 Yüt-hoi-kwan

Commissioner of Customs—Kleinwächter, F.
Duty Commissioner—Smith, Jas.
Assistants—Morgan, F. A.; Morehouse, W. Noyes; Carrall, J. W.; Hirth, F.; de Segonzac, E. D.
Medical Attendant—Wong Fun, M.D.
Tide-surveyors—Parkhill, S.; Eldridge, H.
Examiners—Ewer. F. H.; Jones, G.; Burrows, T. D.
Tidewaiters — Wheeler, W.; Mahon, J.; Bryant, C. J.; Habgood, T. E.; Ruthven, J.; Wilkie, J.; Chapman, T.; Moore,

Imperial Maritime Customs.
(Continued.)

F; Logan, J. H.;—Chinese: Lam Soo; Wong Shek Hing
Linguists—Lim Chinguan; Lew Soey Seng; Chun Tsung; Ho Chee Chuen; Sung Ying Chun; Au kai Ying; Chun Mun; Lee Wing Shang; Wong Kam Ming; Chun A Ku; Li Shü Wing; Ip A Hon; Chun A Fu

WHAMPOA CUSTOMS.
Tide-surveyor—Dawson, F.
Tidewaiters— Poynter, J.; Duncan, A.; Johnstone, W.; Liedcke, L.; Molloy, E.; Chinese: Chuey Chee Tseong; Fung Chun Hang; Chun A Lung
Medical Attendant—Franklyn, L. H.

Chinese Armed Steamers.

"AN-LAN," H.I.C.M. GUN-VESSEL
7 GUNS.
安瀾 An-lan
Captain—Godsil, John
Chief Engineer—Cuthill, W.
Chief Officer—Murray, J. B.
2nd Engineer—Bruce, G.
2nd Officer—Harvey, J.
Gunners—Smith, H.; Squires, James

"CHEN-TO," H.I.C.M. GUN-VESSEL.
7 GUNS.
鎮濤 Chen-to
Captain—Robertson, George
1st Lieut.—Langelier, F. B.
2nd do.—Stevens, E.
1st Engineer—Hudson, A. J.
2nd do.—Corder, G.
Gunners—Cunniffy, Patrick; Lord. F.

"CHING-TSING," H.I.C.M. GUN-BOAT.
4 GUNS.
澄清 Chin-tsing
Captain—Bessard, François
1st Lieut.—Le Roux, Jean François
2nd do.—
1st Engineer—Costard, Gabriel
2nd do.—Auzet, Amédée

"CHUN-HOI," H I.C.M. GUN-BOAT.
6 GUNS.
鎮海 Chun-hoi
Captain—Domée, François
1st Lieut.—Legrand, Andre
2nd do.—Fabre, André
1st Engineer—Bernard, Charles
2nd do.—Berger, Laurent

"FEI-HOO." H.I.M. REVENUE S.S.
飛虎 Fei-hoo
Captain—Clayson, W. H.
1st Officer—Brenan, E. V.
2nd do.—Goulding, T.
Chief Engineer—Gardiner, C.
2nd do.—Kirkwood, J.

"FEILOONG," H.I.C.M. GUN-BOAT.
5 GUNS.
飛龍 Fei-loong
Captain—Wright, Wm. Tregerant
Lieut.—Brown, D.
Chief Engineer—Brisbane, E.
Gunner—Onslow, G. R.

"LING-FENG," H I.M. REVENUE S.S.
凌風 Ling-fung
Captain—Cooker, T. E.
1st Officer—Ring, A. R.
2nd do.—Maitland, James
Chief Engineer—Fettes, D.
2nd do.—Stretch, Wm.

"PENG-CHAO-HAI," H.I.C.M. STR.
5 GUNS.
平洲海 Peng-chao-hai
Captain—Palmer, C. H.
Chief Officer—Lane, H.
2nd do.—Walker, A.
Chief Engineer—Crawford, J.
2nd do.—Dinnen,—.
Gunner—Turner, J.
Carpenter—Rye, J.

"SUI-TSING," H.I.C.M. GUN-BOAT.
5 GUNS.
綏靖 Sui-tsing
Captain—Stewart, Jas.
Chief Officer—Calder, J.
1st Engineer—Pender, Jno.
2nd do.—Ralston, W.

"TIEN-PO," H.I.C.M. GUN-BOAT.
6 GUNS.
恬波 Tien-po
Captain—De Longueville, Charles
1st Lieut.—Sérié, Jean
2nd do.—Paltenweek, Gabriel
1st Engineer—Faure, Jules
2nd do.—

Chinese Government School.
同文館 Tung-man-koon

Head Master—
*Acting do.—*Sampson, Theo.
*Assistant do.—*Sit Him Kuk
*Teachers—*Three Natives

British West Indian Emigration Office.
大英招工公所
Tai-ying-taiu-kung-kung-sho

Government Emigration Agent— Sampson, Theo.
*Overseer—*Marshall, W. D.

Canton Club.
SHAMEEN.

*Committee of Management—*Hirth, F., PH.D.; Cunningham, T. B.
Hon. Librarian— Gray, Venerable Archdeacon, M.A.
*Hon. Curator of Billiard Room—*Howie, R.
*Hon. Sec. and Treasurer—*Sampson, Theo.

Canton Garden Trustees.
Sampson, Theo.
Smith, G. M.

Municipal Council.
*Chairman—*Hutchison, A.
*Treasurer—*Mercer, T.
*Secretary—*Smith, G. M.
Gepp, H. M.
Deacon, E.

Missions.

AMERICAN PRESBYTERIAN BOARD.
Happer, Rev. A. P., D.D., and family
Preston, Rev. C. F., and family
Kerr, J. G., M.D., and family
Noyes, Rev. H. V.
Henry, Rev. B. C., and family
Noyes, Miss H.
Shaw, Miss H. J.
Happer, Miss Lillie B.
Noyes, Miss M.
Crouch, Miss L. H.

BOARD OF UNITED PRESBYTERIAN CHURCH, U. S. A.
Nevin, Rev. J. C.

BRITISH EPISCOPAL CHURCH SOCIETY.
沙面英國禮拜堂
Sha-min-ying-kwok-lai-pai-t'ong

*Chaplain—*Gray, Ven. Archdeacon, M.A.

BRITISH AND FOREIGN BIBLE SOCIETY.
*Colporteur—*Uhlmann, H.

CHINESE EVANGELIZATION SOCIETY OF BERLIN.
巴淩書室 Pa-ling-shü-shat
Hubrig, Rev. F.
Prietzsche, Rev. O. (Longheu)

FRENCH MISSION.
天主教堂 T'ien-chü-kau-t'ong
Guillemin, Right Rev. Z., bishop of Canton (absent)
Jolly, L., pro-prefect apostolique
Goutagny, —., supérieur de l'orphelinat
Barrois, —., supérieur de l'orphelinat
Houery, —., procureur

LONDON MISSIONARY SOCIETY.
倫敦教會 Lun-tun-kau-ui
Chalmers, Rev. John, M.A.
Roach, Rev. N. A.

MEDICAL MISSIONARY SOCIETY.
*President—*Colledge, T.R., M.D. F.R.S. ED. (England)
*Vice Presidents—*Williams, S. Wells, LL.D.; Robertson, Sir Brooke, C.B.; Gray, Ven. Archdeacon, M.A.; Keswick, Hon. W.; Heard, G. F.; Forbes, W. H.; Nye, G., Jr.; Menke, J.; Pyke, Thos.; Lowcock, H.; Ryrie, Hon. P.; Rowett, Hon. R.; Dent, J.; Chalmers, Rev. J., M.A.; Glover, G. B.; Bowra, E. C.; Jewell, Hon. R. G. W.; Helland, G. J.; Talbot, F. R.; Happer, Rev. A. P., D.D.; Preston, Rev. C. F.; Parker, Hon. P., M.D. (U. S.); Delano, W., Jr. (U. S.); Purdon, J. (U. S.)—(In Europe.) Carlowitz, R. von; Legge, Rev. J., D.D., LL.D.; (In U. S.) Hitchcock, E. A.; Bulkley, A. B.
*Corresponding & Recording Secretary—*Kerr, J. G., M.D.
*Treasurers—*Russell & Co.
*Acting Auditor—*The Commissioner of Customs.

CANTON.

SOUTHERN BAPTIST CONVENTION, U. S. A.

Graves, Rev. R. H.
Williams, Rev. N. B.
Simmons, Rev. E. Z.
Whilden, Miss L.

WESLEYAN METHODIST MISSIONARY SOCIETY.

Preston, Rev. J.
Parkes, Rev. H.
Gibson, Rev. J.
Whitehead, Rev. S.
Selby, Rev. T. G.
Sinsininex, Rev. E.
Simpson, Miss
Rowe, Miss

Insurance.

Arnhold, Karberg & Co.
    Java Sea and Fire Insurance Company
    Lancashire Insurance Company
Deacon & Co.
    Union Insurance Society
Heard & Co., Augustine
    China Traders' Insurance Co., Limited
    Victoria Fire Insurance Co., Limited
Mestern and Hulse
    The Globe Marine Insurance Company, Limited, London
    The Samarang Sea and Fire Insurance Company of Samarang
    K. K. Priv. Oestereich Versicherungs Gesellschaft " Donau "
    North-German Fire Insurance Company, at Hamburg
Olyphant & Co.
    Chinese Insurance Company, Limited
Pustau & Co. Wm.
    Actien Bank in Vienna
    Allgemeine Versicherungs Gesellschaft fur See, Fluss und Land Transport, Dresden
    Basler Transport Virsicherungs Gesellschaft in Basel
    Dusseldorfer Allgemaine Vesicherungs Gesselschaft fur See, Fluss und Land Transport in Duseldorf
    Elementar Veraicherungs
    Rheinisch Westfalischer Lloyd in N. Gladbach
Russell & Co.
    Batavia Sea and Fire Insurance Co.
    Yangtsze Insurance Association
Thomas and Mercer
    North China Insurance Company

Merchants, &c.

Ahmed, Moosa, merchant, Honam and Hongkong

Aladin, Rahim, merchant, Honam and Hongkong

剌刀甲顛剌刀八 Li-la-to-kap-tin-la-to-pat
Ameijeebhoy, F., merchant, Honam and Hongkong

惡士佛公司 Ok-sz-fat-kung-sz
Arnhold, Karberg & Co., merchants, Honam
    Levysohn, A. C.
    Kramer, J., silk inspector
    Arnhold, P.

巴厘公司 Pa-li-kung-sz
Birley & Co., merchants
    Hardy, George, tea inspector
    Dent, H. F., silk inspector

伯頓公司 Pak-tun-kung-sz
Bull, Purdon & Co., merchants, Honam
    Wright, J. P

Canton Dispensary, Canal Road
    Muffitt, Joseph

廣東酒店 Kwang-tung-tsau-tim
"Canton Hotel," Honam
    Rosario, A. F. do, manager, and auctioneer

Canton Printing and Bookbinding Establishment, and Canton Daily Shipping News Office
    Parker, James, proprietor
    5 Chinese Assistants

加路渭冶公司 Ka-lo-wut-tsz-kung-sz
Carlowitz & Co., merchants, Honam
    Carlowitz, R. von
    Hitzeroth, G
    Benecke, O.
    Rost, W.
    Hertz, A.
    Ruff, T., silk inspector

哥牙 Ko-a
Coare, Lind & Co., public silk inspectors, Shameen
    Coare, F. W.
    Lind, A. A.
    Rennell, E., silk inspector
    Roberts, A. S., silk inspector

CANTON.

Cooper, H. N., merchant, Honam and Hongkong

的件公司 Ti-kin-kung-sz
Deacon & Co., public tea inspectors and general commission agents
  Hutchison, Alfred
  Deacon, Ernest
  Deacon, Sidney
  Howie, Robert
  Azevedo, F. d'

南記行 Nam-kee-hong
Deguria & Co., R. N., merchants, Honam and Hongkong
  Deguria, R. N.
  Fatakia, D. B.

鴨都剌厘衣布剌謙公司 Ap-to-la-li-l-po-la-him-kung-sz
Ebrahim & Co., Abdoolaly, merchants. Honam and Hongkong

謙信洋行 Him-sun-yeung-hong
Ehlers & Co., Paul, merchants, Honam
  Ehlers, Paul (absent)
  Meuser, Otto

南記行 Nam-kee-hong
Futtakia, Dadabhoy Sorabjee, merchant, Honam
  Byramjee, M.

Gibb, Livingston & Co., merchants
  Gepp, A. M.
  Stretten, R. T.

拈毛批亞卑杯 Nim-moo-pie-a-pi-pooi
Habibhoy, Ahmedbhoy, merchant, Honam and Hongkong

Habibhoy, Ramoobhoy, merchant, Honam and Hongkong

曷公司 Hot-kung-sz
Heard & Co., Augustine, merchants, Honam
  Cheshire, F. D.
  Bennett, A. G.

希士 Heh-sz
Hesse & Co., merchants, Honam
  Krause, Alfred

"International Hotel," Billiards and Bowling Alleys, Honam
  Brown, Edward

亞之亞泵衣素乃 A-chi-a-tum-i-soo-nai
Ismael, Hajee Adam, merchant, Honam and Hongkong
  Hajee Fazul Absitar

亞麼老顛渣化杯 A-mo-lo-tin-cha-fa-pooy
Jafferbhoy and Ameeroodin, merchants, Honam and Hongkong

Jan Mohamed, Absitar, merchant, Honam

渣顛公司 Cha-tin-kung-sz
Jardine, Matheson, & Co., merchants, Shameen
  Smith, G. Mackrill, tea inspector

佐曼公司 Cha-an-kung-sz
Johannes, S. P., commission merchant, Honam and Hongkong

Manookjee, Merwanjee & Co., merchants, Honam

禪臣 Sim-shun
Mestern and Hulse, public tea and silk inspectors and commission agents
  Mestern, C. J.
  Hulse, Wm.
    Cozon, J., silk inspector
    Ottomeier, P. A. W.
    Silva, F.

中利行 Chung-lee-hong
Metta, E. N., merchant, Honam
  Metta, E. N., manager
  Metta, Shapoorjee F., assistant

Nursey Kessewjee & Co., merchants, Honam and Hongkong

欄公司 Nei-kung-sz
Nye & Co., merchants
  Nye, Gideon, Jr.

同孚行 Toong-foo-hong
Olyphant & Co., merchants
  Talbot, F. R.
  Smith, F. B., tea inspector
  Hutchinson, St. John, silk inspector
  Gourdin, A. O'D.

CANTON.

Oomar, Mohamed, merchant, Honam and Hongkong

昌利棧 Cheung-li-tsan

Padsha, H. M., merchant, Honam and Hongkong

Peerbhoy, Jairazbhoy, merchant, Honam and Hongkong

Pebany, Ebrahim, merchant, Honam and Hongkong

布士兜公司 Po-sz-tau-kung-sz

Pustau & Co., Wm. merchants, Shameen
    Rehders, Emil
    Devens, Rich.

剌士利公司 La-sz-li-kung-sz

Russell & Co., merchants, Old Factory Site
    Cunningham, T. B.
    Dubost, J., silk inspector
    Cordeiro, A. A.

隆盛 Loong-shing

Smith, Archer & Co., merchants
    Heitmann, J. C.

Talty, M. M., Honam

建興 Kin-hing

Thomas and Mercer, public tea and silk inspectors, and general commission agents
    Thomas, Thomas (absent)
    Mercer, Thomas
    Rowe, Alfred
    Mann, J. Ayton
    Pascoal, J. P.

Union Steam Navigation Co.
    Agents—Olyphant & Co.

科古行 Fo-koo-hong

Vogel, Hagedorn & Co., merchants, Shameen
    Vogel, Charles
    Shawcross, J. J., silk inspector

富文先生 Foo-man-sin-saug

Vrooman, Rev. D. (self-sustaining missionary)

黃寬醫生 Wong-fun-i-sang

Wong, F., M.D., L.R.C.S.ED., Honam

汕 SWATOW. 頭

Consulates.

AUSTRO-HUNGARIAN EMPIRE.
Acting Consul—Forrest, R. J.

DENMARK.
大顛摩國領事官
Tai-tin-mak-kwok-ling-sz-koon
Consul—Dircks, H. A.

FRANCE.
大法國領事官
Ta-fat-kwok-ling-sz-koon
Vice-Consul—Forrest, R. J.

GERMAN EMPIRE.
大日耳曼國領事官
Tai-yih-yeh-man-kwok-ling-sz-koon
Vice-Consul—Krüger, C. (absent)
Act. Vice-Consul—Forrest, R. J.

GREAT BRITAIN.
大英國領事官
Tai-ying-kwok-ling-sz-koon
Acting Consul—Forrest, R. J.
Assistant and Acting Interpreter — Ford, Colin M.
Constable— Sage, H.

POSTAL AGENCY.
Agent—Ford, Colin M.

NETHERLANDS.
大荷蘭國領事官
Tai-ho-lan-kwok-ling-sz-koon
Consul—Richardson, Thos. W.

SWEDEN AND NORWAY.
大瑞威頓國領事官
Ta-sui-wei-tun-kwok-ling-sz-koon
Vice-Consul—Dircks, H. A.

UNITED STATES.
大美國領事官
Ta-mei-kwok-ling-sz-koon
Consul—Wingate, J. C. A.
Vice-Consul and Interpreter—Ashmore, W.
Constable—Devlin, Henry

Imperial Maritime Customs.
潮海關 Chao-hai-kwan

Commissioner—
Assistant-in-Charge—Moorhead, R. B.
Assistants—Imbert, A.; Urwin, F. S.; Stuhlmann, C. O.
Tide-surveyor and Harbour master—Gunther, C.
Boarding Officer—Folsom, W. A.
Examiners—Harman, G.; Allcot, G.
Tide-waiters—Schaumlöffel, H.; Olsen, A.; Carr, J. H.; McGiffie, J. D.; Bond, G; Forsaith, G. A.; Allcot, J. H; Paterson, J. W.
Medical Attendants—Scott and Scott

DOUBLE ISLAND STATION.
Assistant Tide-surveyor—Watson, W.

Pilots.
帶水人 Tai-sui-yan

Johnson, H.
Piersdorff, A. L.
Focken, F. W.
Williams, P.
Nissen, A.
Quedous, H. G.

SWATOW.

Missions.

AMERICAN BAPTIST MISSION.
Ashmore, Rev. William
Partridge, Rev. S. B.
Johnson, Mrs. L. W
Fielde, Miss A. M.

ENGLISH PRESBYTERIAN CHURCH
Smith, Rev. George (absent)
Mackenzie, Rev. H. L.
Duffus, Rev. William
Gauld, William, M.D.

FRENCH MISSION.
Bernom, Rev. A. (Kya-in)
Jacquemin, Rev. J. B. C. (Chow-chow-foo)
Tardy, Rev. C. E.

Insurance.

Bradley & Co.
    Amicable Marine Insurance Office
    China Fire Insurance Co.
    China Traders' Marine Insurance Co., Limited
    Imperial Fire Insurance Co.
    Lloyd's
    London and Oriental Steam Transit Insurance Co.
    North British and Mercantile Ins. Co.
    North China Marine Insurance Co.
    Royal Insurance Co.
    Union Insurance Society of Canton
Dircks & Krüger
    Chinese Insurance Company, Limited
    Batavia Sea and Fire Insurance Co. of Batavia
    Colonial Sea and Fire Insurance Co. of Batavia
    Samarang Sea and Fire Insurance Co. of Samarang
    De Oosterling Sea and Fire Insurance Co. of Batavia
    Victoria Fire Insurance Co., Limited
    Hamburg and Bremen Underwriters
    Germanic Lloyds
Frewin & Co.
    Hongkong Insurance Company
    China and Japan Marine Insurance Company
    Austrian Insurance Company "Donau"
Vincent & Co.
    Canton Insurance Office
    Hongkong Fire Insurance Company
    Triton Insurance Company
    Yangtsze Insurance Association.

Merchants, &c.

德記行 Tuk-kee-hong
Bradley & Co., merchants
    Richardson, Thos. Wm.
    Grant, Cardross
    Hill, Robert H.
    Monro, J. D.
    Fergusson, W. S.
    Horne, T. W., godown-keeper

China Coast Steam Navigation Company
    Agents—Vincent & Co.

Dircks & Krüger, commission merchants
    Dircks, Hinrich Andreas
    Krüger, Cäsar
    Tenhaeff, M.
    Branth, A.
    Feyerabend, R.

Douglas Lapraik & Co.'s Steamers
    Agents—Vincent & Co.

Frewin & Co., commission merchants
    Frewin, Henry
    Chung Shun

蝦唎士公司 Hah-li-se-kung-sz
Harris & Co., shipwrights and blacksmiths
    Harris, William

Hongkong and Shanghai Banking Corporation
    Agents—Bradley & Co.

Meyer & Fehrs, shipwrights and blacksmiths
    Meyer, J. D.
    Fehrs, Henry

Peninsular and Oriental Steam Navigation Company
    Agents—Bradley & Co.

Quelch & Campbell, shipchandlers, auctioneers, compradores and general commission agents
    Quelch, C. B.
    Campbell, P.

Scott & Scott, physicians, surgeons and accoucheurs
    Scott, C. M., M.D., L.R.C.S.S., &c., &c.
    Scott, E. J., M.D., L.R.C.S.S., L M., M.P.S.L., &c., &c.

Vincent, E., surveyor for Lloyd's Agents and Local Offices

福源行 Fok-yuen-hong
Vincent & Co., E., commission merchants
    Vincent, E.
    Drown, T. Pickering
    Grunauer, L.

夏 AMOY. 門

Consulates.

AUSTRO-HUNGARIAN MONARCHY.
奧斯馬叻國領事官
Ao-sz-ma-lik-kwok-ling-sz-koon

Consul—Pedder, W. H.

DENMARK.
黃旗國領事官
Wong-ki-kwok-ling-sz-koon

Consul—Petersen, H. A.

FRANCE.
大法國領事官
Tai-fat-kwok-ling-sz-koon

Vice-Consul—Pye, Edmund

GERMAN EMPIRE.
大日耳曼國領事官
Tai-yat-ye-man-kwok-ling-sz-koon

Acting Consul—Pedder, William Henry

GREAT BRITAIN.
大英國領事官
Tai-ying-kwok-ling-sz-koon

Consul—Pedder, William Henry
Acting Interpreter and Post Office Agent—Bristow, H. B.
Clerk—Simoens, C. P.
Constable—Balzano, Michele

NETHERLANDS.
大荷蘭國領事官
Tai-ho-lan-kwok-ling-sz-koon

Vice-Consul—Paterson, J.

PORTUGAL.
大西洋國領事官
Tai-sai-yeung-kwok-ling-sz-koon

Consul—Wardlaw, J. C.

SPAIN.
大呂宋國領事官
Tai-lui-soong-kwok-ling-sz-koon

Consul—Morejon, Senor Don C. de Ortega
Vice-Consul—Tejada, Don Fermin Saenz de (absent)
First Chinese Interpreter—Cosiang, José
Constable—Espina, Mariano

SWEDEN AND NORWAY.
大瑞威國領事官
Tai-sui-wai-tun-kwok-ling-sz-koon

Vice-Consul—Craig, Robert

UNITED STATES.
大美國領事官
Tai-me-kwok-ling-sz-koon

Consul—Henderson, J. J.
Clerk—Edwards, St. J. H.
Interpreter—Lin Kien Chin
Gaoler—Celestin, Francis

Imperial Maritime Customs.
海關 Hai-kwan

Commissioner—Hughes, George
Assistants—Lord, Charles A.; Archer-Shee, M.; d'Arnoux, Vte. G.; Specht, Dr. E.
Assistant Tide-surveyor—Vierow, H.
Examiners—Moran, R. (absent); Tolliday, T.; Lark, D. J. (absent); Price, C. J.
Tide-waiters—Penrose, J. H.; Poffin, J.; Smith, J. D.; Lant, T. J.; Davidson, G. R.; Loam, W. B.; Calver, E. V.

CHAPEL ISLAND LIGHTHOUSE.
Lightkeeper—Daniels, G. R.
Assist. Lightkeeper—Naudin, V.; Botello, D.

AMOY.

Pilots.
HARBOUR PILOTS.
Hauenstein, Gustav
Bushmann, John
Paterson, D.

SEA PILOTS.
19 Chinese Licensed Pilots

Seamen's Hospital.
水手醫館 Shui-shau-i-koon
Management—Drs. Jones, Müller & Manson

NATIVE HOSPITAL.
济世醫館 Tsai-shai-i-koon
Management—Manson, Patrick, M.D.

Missions.
ENGLISH PRESBYTERIAN MISSION.
Douglas, Rev. Carstairs, LL.D.
Swanson, Rev. W. S.
Cowie, Rev. Hugh (absent)
McGregor, Rev. William (absent)
Gordon, Rev. Robert

LONDON MISSIONARY SOCIETY.
Stronach, Rev. John
Macgowan, Rev. John
Sadler, Rev. James

REFORMED CHURCH, U.S.A.
Talmage, Rev. J. V. N , D.D. (absent)
Rapalje, Rev. D.
Kip, Rev. L. W.

ROMAN CATHOLIC MISSION IN CHINA.
Chian-chiu-'to, Province of Fokien.
CHURCH OF THE "HOLY ROSARY," AMOY.
Burno, Rev. Guillermo

CHURCH OF THE "CONCEPTION," KANGBOE.
Zea, Rev. Francisco
One Native Priest

CHURCH OF "SANTO DOMINGO," AN-POA.
Dutras, Rev. José
One Native Priest

CHURCH OF "SANTO DOMINGO," LAM-PI-LAU.
Guixa, Rev. Nicolas

Insurances.
Andersen, L. A.
  Surveyor to German Lloyds and Local Offices
Boyd & Co.
  Lloyds
  China Traders' Insurance Co. (Limited)
  China and Japan Marine Insurance Co
  Royal Insurance Co., Fire and Life
  Sun Fire Office
  Netherlands India Marine Ins. Co.
  Bremen Marine Insurance Companies
  Jersey Mutual Insurance Society for Shipping
  Joint Underwriters' Union of Amsterdam
Brown & Co.
  Yangtze Insurance Association
  Victoria Fire Insurance Co., Limited
Dodd & Co.
  British and Foreign Marine Ins. Co.
Elles & Co.
  Alliance Fire Assurance Co.
  Bengal Insurance Society
  Bombay Insurance Society
  Canton Insurance Office
  China Fire Insurance Co., Limited
  Hongkong Fire Insurance Co., Limited
  Imperial Fire Insurance Co.
  Ocean Marine Insurance Co.
  Triton Insurance Co.
  Union of Hamburg Underwriters
Pasedag & Co.
  Batavia Sea and Fire Insurance Co.
  Colonial Sea and Fire Insurance Co.
  German Lloyd's
  Oosterling Sea and Fire Insurance Co.
  Samarang Sea and Fire Insurance Co.
  Second Colonial Sea and Fire Ins. Co.
Petersen & Co., H. A.
  Chinese Insurance Company, Limited
  K. K. Privil. Osterr. Versicherung Gesellschaft "Donnau"
Tait & Co.
  Java Sea and Fire Insurance Co.
  London and Oriental Steam Transit Insurance Co.
  North British and Mercantile Fire Insurance Co.
  North China Insurance Co.
  Northern Assurance Co.
  Union Insurance Society of Canton

Merchants, &c.
Andersen, L. A., marine surveyor

裕順行 Yu-sun-hong
Anderson, Jno. L., public tea inspector and commission merchant

AMOY.

船澳 Shun-o

Amoy Dock Company
    Farrow, John, manager and secretary
    Gordon, Wm., accountant
    Fielding, Charles, machinist
    Steffens, John, master shipwright

和記 Wo-kee

Boyd & Co., merchants, agents for Lloyds
    Boyd, T. D. (absent)
    Craig, Robert
        Rose, Edwards N.
        Fenton, Robert B.
        Thompson, George M (Takow)
        Laidlaw, Walter (Tamsui)
        Orr, William S.
        Budd, U. A.
        Covil, Thomas, tea inspector
        Harkness, T. G.
        Wright, D. Moncrieff
        Mackenzie, Wm.

布郎公司 Po-long-kung-sz

Brown & Co., merchants
    Brown, D. G. (England)
    Chomley, F.
    Davidson, Duncan
        Darling, D. A.
        Boyol, H. V.

China Coast S. S. Co.
    Agents—Elles & Co.

China & Straits Steam Navigation Company Limited
    Agents—Brown & Co.

China Trans-Pacific S. S. Co.
    Agents—Elles & Co.

裕記 Yu-kee

Danver & Co., merchants
    Danver, H. R.
        Sanger, P. M.
        Gwauhe, T.
        Tawansia, Carlos
        Beng, Victor Sheaw
        Khesoojee, Tew
        Po Gaglo
        Tew Kassay
        Tea Acheng
        Lim Song Kha
        Lim Konggee

寶順行 Paou-shun-hong

Dodd & Co., merchants
    Dodd, John
    Kerr, Crawford D.
    Bird, S. G.

怡記行 Ee-kee-hong

Elles & Co., merchants, agents for Douglas Lapraik & Co.'s steamers
    Elles, Jamieson (England)
    Pye, Edmund
    Pye, Randall H.
    Wilson, R.
    Bain, A. W.
    Allan, H. T.
    Graham, J. W.
    Cass, J. G. (Tamsui)
    Taylor, W. H (Taiwanfoo)
    Christy, W.
    McMinnies, H. H.
    Elles, James
    Cass, Frank

錦興洋行 Kam-hing-yeung-hong

Engwat Brother & Co., merchants and general commission agents
    Engwat, S.
        Lay, U. S.
        Choon, C. K.
        Sake, N. K.
        Eng, C. S.
        Loo, C. G.
        Chwe, T. K.
        Tang, T. T.
        Chwe, T. T.

天裕 Tian-yu

Forster & Co., John, merchants
    Chambers, H. J. J., tea inspector
    Bandinel, J. J. F.

Gerard & Co., C., shipchandlers and sailmakers
    Jacobsen, P.
    Kopp, C. O.

齋路公司 Chai-lo-kung-sz

Giles & Co., shipchandlers, auctioneers, general dealers and compradores
    Giles, John
    Ayres, C. A. S.

電線行 Tien-sin-hong
Great Northern Telegraph Company, Office
K'ulangsew
    Nielsen, C. P., superintendent
    Henningsen, J.
    Sonne, C. C., electrician
    Kragh, C. H.
    Mühlensteth, J. A.
    Christiansen, F. C.
    Green, S. A. A.
    Ronnenkamp, W. H.

Heard & Co., Augustine, merchants
    Murton, N., tea inspector

匯豐銀行 Oi-foong-ngan-hong
Hongkong and Shanghai Banking Corporation
    Agent—Abendroth, H.

震記洋行 Chan-kee-yeung-hong
Hosungjee & Co., D., merchants
    Hosungjee, D. (absent)
    Hosungjee, N. (Hongkong)
    Dorabjee, P.
    Nowrojee, C.

Ice Manufactory
    Jok Lin, manager

奸厘恩醫生 Kan-li-ke-i-sang
Jones, Müller and Manson, physicians and surgeons
    Jones, Charles M., F.R.C.S., L.R.C.P. (at home)
    Müller, Augustus, M.D., &c., &c. (at home)
    Manson, Patrick, M.D.
    Manson, David, M.D.

李馬達 Lee-ma-tat
Lomattro, Ernest, watchmaker, and importer of foreign goods

Munro, D., merchant and commission agent

安記 On-kee
Ollia, N., merchant and commission agent
    Ollia, Nusserwanjee Dadabhoy Framjee, Cursetjee

慶記 Kheng-kee
Ollia & Co., D.D., merchants and commission agents
    Ollia, D. D.
    Bomonjee, P.
    Mehta, B. S.

Pacific Mail S. S. Co.
    Agents—Elles & Co.

寶記 Po-kee
Pasedag & Co., merchants
    Pasedag, C. J.
    Stiller, Ernst
    Driahaus, O.

德記 Tak-kee
Peninsular & Oriental Steam Navigation Company
    Agents—Tait & Co.

成記行 Shing-kee-hong
Petersen & Co., H. A., merchants
    Petersen, H. A.
    Danielsen, J. W.
    Michelsen, L.

和明 Wo-ming
Reuter's Telegram Company, Limited
    Henningsen, J., agent

鍾毓麟 Chung-yook-lun
Soda Water Manufactory
    Jok Lin, manager

德記 Tak-kee
Tait & Co., merchants, agents for P. & O. S. N. Co.
    Wardlaw, James C. (absent)
    Paterson, John
    Johnston, W. C.
    Bruce, James
    Alexander, J. T. A.
    Bruce, R. H., tea inspector (Tamsui)
    Wickham, B. R.
    Hardie, J. D. (Takow)
    Masson, Jas. (Tamsui)
    Starkey, E. P.
    Lopez, C. J.
    Ludlam, T. E.
    Trotter, D. A.
    Thornton, A. H. (Takow)

廣順 Kwong-shun
Wilson, Nicholls & Co., shipchandlers, sailmakers and commission agents
    Wilson, W.
    Nicholls, B.
    Brown, F. C.

臺 FORMOSA. 灣

TAKOW & TAIWAN.

Consulates.

AUSTRO-HUNGARIAN MONARCHY.
(*Also for Taiwan.*)
Consul—Alabaster, Chaloner
Officiating Consul—Gregory, Wm.

DENMARK.
(*Also for Taiwan.*)
Consul—Alabaster, Chaloner
Officiating Consul—Gregory, William

FRANCE.
(*Also for Taiwan.*)
Consul—Alabaster, Chaloner
Officiating Consul—Gregory, Wm.

GERMAN EMPIRE.
(*Also for Taiwan.*)
Consul—Alabaster, Chaloner
Officiating Consul—Gregory, Wm.

GREAT BRITAIN.
大英國領事官
Tai-ying-kwok-ling-sz-koon
(*Also for Taiwan.*)
Consul—Alabaster, Chaloner
Acting Consul—Gregory, William
Assistant—Bullock, T. L.
Constable—Alborado, Antonio

UNITED STATES.
AMOY AND DEPENDENCIES.
大英國領事官
Tai-mei-kwok-ling-sz-koon
Consul—Henderson, J. J.
Consul at Takao & Taiwanfoo—Thompson, Geo. M.
Clerks—Edwards, G.; Julien, Hugh
Interpreter—Lin Kien-chin
Gaoler—Choa Yeng

Imperial Maritime Customs.

TAKOW AND TAIWANFOO.
Commissioner—Hart, James H.
Assistants—Lent, R. J.; Segar, H.
Tide-surveyor—Gue, G.
Examiner—Trannack, R.
Tidewaiters—Hastings, R.; Breton, Leonard Le; Bayley, G. J.

Pilots.
Wulbrand, H.
Vosteen, H.

Missions.

ENGLISH PRESBYTERIAN MISSION.
Ritchie, Rev. Hugh (Takow)
Maxwell, Jas. L., M.D. (absent) (Taiwanfoo)
Dickson, M., M.D. (do.)
Campbell, Rev. W. (do.)

CANADIAN PRESBYTERIAN MISSION.
Mackay, Rev. Geo. (Tamsui)

ROMAN CATHOLIC MISSION IN FORMOSA.
天主教堂 Tien-chü-kau-tong
Chinchon, Rev. Andrés
Colomer, Rev. Miguel
Gimenez, Rev. Federico
Farazona, Rev. Manuel
Gomar, Rev. Vicente

Insurances.
Boyd & Co.
  Lloyds
  China and Japan Marine Insurance Co., Limited
Brown & Co.
  The Yangtsze Insurance Association
Tait & Co.
  North China Insurance Company

Merchants, &c.

Boyd & Co., merchants
    Thompson, Geo. M., agent

Brown & Co., merchants
    Darling, D. A. (Tamsui)
    Santos, E. dos (Taiwanfoo)
    Mannich, J. (Takow) agent

Elles & Co., merchants
    Taylor, W. H. (Takow)
    Eckhouse, H. (Taiwanfoo)
    Kraal, P. C. (do.)
    Assai, Mahomed, gunner (do.)

Manson, David C. M., M.D. (Takow)

Tait & Co., merchants (Formosa)
    Hardie, James D., agent (Takow)
    Kavanagh, M. R.
    Lopes, C. J. (Takow)

TAIWAN.

Insurances.

Boyd & Co.
    China and Japan Marine Ins. Co.
    Lloyds
Brown & Co. (Taiwan)
    Yangtaze Insurance Association

Merchants, &c.

Boyd & Co., merchants
    Thompson, Geo. M., agent

Brown & Co., merchants
    Mannich, Julius, agent
    Santos, E. O. dos

Elles & Co., merchants
    Eckhouse, H.
    Kraal, P. C.
    Assai, Mahomed, gunner

TAMSUI.

Consulates.

AUSTRO-HUNGARIAN MONARCHY.
Acting Consul—Baber, E. Colborne

GERMAN EMPIRE.
Acting Consul—Baber, E. Colborne

GREAT BRITAIN.
大英國副領事府.
Tai-ying-kwok-foo-ling-sz-foo
Acting Vice-Consul—Baber, E. Colborne.

TAMSUI AND KEELUNG.
Netherlands Consulate.
Vice-Consul—Dodd, John

UNITED STATES.
TAMSUI AND KEELUNG.
大美國領事官
Tai-mei-kwok-ling-sz-koon
Consul—Le Gendre, Chas. W. (absent)
Vice-Consul—Pye, Edmund
Consular Agent—

Imperial Maritime Customs.

TAMSUI OFFICE.
Commissioner—Hobson, H. E.
Assistant—Leslie, S.
Tidesurveyor—Smith, M. L.
Examiner—Wortell, J.
Tidewaiter—Baudain, S.
Linguist—Lok Kwong Sung

Insurances.

Dodd & Co.
    Lloyds
    North China Insurance Company
Elles & Co.
    Union Insurance Society of Canton

Merchants.

Boyd & Co., merchants
    Laidlaw, Walter R., tea-inspector

Brown & Co., merchants
    Darling, D. A.

Dodd & Co., merchants
    Dodd, John
    Larken, M. tea inspector
    Greig, J. assistant
        Moss, John, godown-keeper
        Hammersley, W. do.

Elles & Co., merchants
  Cass, J. Gratton, agent
    Goty, William, in charge of receiving ship *Caesar*

KEELUNG.

Imperial Maritime Customs.
Assistant—Titoushkin, N.
Examiner—Land, J. M.
Tidewaiter—Hall, J. H.
Linguist—Cheong Kwang-sung

Insurances.

Dodd & Co.
  Lloyds
  North China Insurance Company
Elles & Co.
  Union Insurance Society of Canton

Merchants.

Dodd & Co.
  Maher, J., coal agent

Elles & Co., merchants
  Cass, J. Gratton, agent

福 FOOCHOW. 州

Consulates.

DENMARK.
大丹國領事官
Ta-tan-kwoh-ling-shih-kwan

Consul—Wild, Chas. A.
Acting Vice-Consul—Price, William G.

FRANCE.
法國公館 Whatt-kwo-koong-kuan

Consul—Lemaire, Gabriel (absent)
Chancelier Substitue—Estienne, M.

GERMAN EMPIRE.
大德國公館 Toy-tek-kwo-koong-kuang

Acting Consul—De Lano, M. M.
Interpreter—Lee, K. B.
Chinese Writer—Ho-tsz-ho

GREAT BRITAIN.
英國公館 Yun-kwo-koong-kuan

Consul—Sinclair, C. A.
Assist. & Acting Interpreter—Warren, P. L.

AT PAGODA ANCHORAGE.
Vice-Consul—Carroll, Charles (absent)
Acting Vice-Consul—Philips, George
Constable—Kennedy, Francis

ANGLO-CHINESE POLICE.
Sergeant—Gallagher, James
Constables—Shearer, J. H.; Pitman, W. J.

POSTAL AGENT.
Agent—Warren, P. L.

NETHERLANDS.
大荷蘭國領事官
Tai-ho-lan-kwoh-ling-shih-kwan

Acting Consul—Pim, T.

RUSSIA.
大俄羅斯國領事官
Tai-ngo-lo-sze-kwok-ling-shih-kwan

Vice-Consul—Bennett, M. E.

SWEDEN AND NORWAY.
大瑞威顧及那威國領事官
Tai-sui-wei-tan-kih-no-wei-kwok-ling-shih-kwan

Vice-Consul—Pomeroy, S. W., Jun.

UNITED STATES.
美國公館 Mee-kwo-koong-kuan

Consul—De Lano, M. M.
Marshal—Lyman, B. G. (absent)
Interpreter—Lee, K. B.
Chinese Writer—Ho-tsz-ho
Constable—Rodrigues, S. M.

Imperial Maritime Customs.
閩海關 Min-hai-kwan

Commissioner—Wright, F. E.
Deputy Commissioner—
Assistants—Lay, W. T.; Towell, M. E.; Krey, W.; Fisher, H. J. (on leave)
Medical Officers—Beaumont, Dr. J. M., at Nantai; Dr. Somerville, at Pagoda Anchorage

OUT-DOOR STAFF AT NANTAI.
Acting Tide-surveyor—Lowe, Rob.
Examiners—Luther, W. H.
Tide-waiters—Burrel, E. D.; Johnson, B. R.; Cordeiro, M.
Linguists—Lum Kok-cheng; Ong Keat-seng; Loke Chew-leong; Cheak Quan-leok

AT PAGODA ANCHORAGE.
Div. Inspector and Harbour-Master—Bisbee, A. M.
Assistant Tide-surveyor—Saunderson, J. P.

Imperial Maritime Customs

(Continued.)

Examiners—Jenkins, W. (on leave); Goodridge, R.; Busch, C.
Tidewaiters—Delestre, E.; Dubarry, P. R.; Campbell, D

POLICE FORCE.

Sergeant—Stiebe, R.; Bartolini, L.; Green, —.; Jansen, M.; Blacklock, F.
Constable—Mullins, D.

WHITE DOG LIGHT HOUSE.

Lightkeepers—Ross, J.; Freeth, G.; Petersen, —.

Pilots.

帶水人 Tai-shui-yan

PAGODA ANCHORAGE.

Porter, C. E.
Smith, R. B.
Randal, T.
Mitchell, W.
Petersen, P. L.
Oeltze, C.
Head, A.
Johnson, F.
Simonsen, E. D.

Missions.

AMERICAN BOARD OF COMMISSIONERS FOR FOREIGN MISSIONS.

Baldwin, Rev. C. C.
Walker, Rev. J. E.
Hartwell, Rev. Chas.
Woodin, Rev. F. S.
Osgood, D. W., M.D.
Payson, Miss Adelia M.

AMERICAN METHODIST EPISCOPAL MISSION.

Maclay, Rev. Robt. S., D.D. (absent)
Baldwin, Rev. S. L.
Sites, Rev. Nathan
Ohlinger, Franklin
Plumb, Nathan J.

ENGLISH CHURCH MISSION.

Wolfe, Rev. John R.
Mahood, Rev. John E.

Steam-Tugs.

吳淞 Wu-sung

"WOOSUNG," tug-boat, Pagoda Anchorage
Allen, Geo., master
Deas, J., mate

Imperial Foochow Arsenal.

船政局 Soon-chin-ke

Chief Director—Giquel, P.
Sub-Director—Segonzac, L. D. de
Chaplain—Allier, R. P.
Civil Engineer—Jouvet, E.
Physician—Poujade, A.
Secretary Interpreter—Giquel, J.
Accountant—Borel, A.
Clerks—Piry, T.; Estienne, M.
Sto. ekeeper—
Clerk—Rey, J.
Head Master Naval School—Carroll, J.
Teacher—Skey, Russell
Professor of Practical Navigation—Tracey, Richard E.
Professor of Chemistry—Rousset, L.
Professor of Mathematics—Médard, L.
Teacher—Roberdeau
Professor of Practical Engineering—Allan, W., Jun.
Chronometer Shop—Puthon
Optician—Le Marchaud
Carpenters—Robin, Marzin, Peter, Raffeneau, Latouche, Guiraud, Quénaon, Boulineau
Founders—Robeson, W.; Rivasseau; Decauchuis
Finishers—Dessant, Scheidecker, Vidlou, Piron, Cabouret
Forgers—Brossement, Cerle, Pailler, Rabillié, A. Serreau, C. Serreau, Besangon
Patternmakers—Guérin, Müller, Pons
Boilermakers and Coppersmiths—Gosselin, Vastal
Draughtsmen—Louis; Kerdraon
Instructor Gunner—Harwood, J.
Instructor Boatswain—Johnson, H.
Overlooker—Beloin

SAIL MAKING AND RIGGING DEPARTMENT.
Saunders, Capt. J. C.

Insurances.

Adamson, Bell & Co.
    Commerical Union Assurance Company, London
    South Australian Insurance Company
Butterfield & Swire
    British and Foreign Marine Insurance Company
    The Royal Exchange Assurance Corporation
Foster & Co., John
    China and Japan Marine Insurance Co.
    North British and Mercantile Insurance Company
Gilman & Co.
    Association of Underwriters, Glasgow
    Imperial Fire Insurance Co.
    Liverpool Underwriters' Association

Gilman & Co.—(continued.)
   Lloyd's
   London Fire Assurance Corporation
   North China Insurance Co.
   Universal Marine Ins. Co., Limited
   Ocean Marine Insurance Co.
   Merchants Marine Ins. Co., Limited
   London & Lancashire Fire Insurance Company, Limited
Heard & Co., Augustine
   China Traders' Insurance Co., Ld.
   Victoria Fire Insurance Co., Limited
Holliday, Wise & Co.
   Manchester Fire Assurance Company
   London Assurance Corporation, Marine and Life departments
Jardine, Matheson & Co.
   Alliance Fire Insurance Co.
   Alliance Marine Insurance Co.
   Bengal Insurance Society
   Bombay Insurance Society
   Canton Insurance Office
   Hongkong Fire Insurance Co., Limited
   Ocean Marine Ins. Co. of Bombay
   Triton Insurance Co.
Odell, John
   Royal Insurance Company
Olyphant & Co.
   Guardian Fire Assurance Company
   China Fire Insurance Co., Limited
   New York Board of Underwriters
   Chinese Insurance Company
Phipps, Hickling & Co.
   Liverpool and London and Globe Fire Insurance Company
Russell & Co.
   Yangtze Insurance Association
Silverlock & Co., John
   Queen Insurance Co. (Fire)
Tennant, H P.
   Union Insurance Society of Canton
   Commercial Union Assurance Company (Life department)
Turner & Co.
   Home and Colonial Marine Insurance Company, Limited
   Netherlands India Marine Ins. Co.
   Northern Fire and Life Insurance Co.
Westall, Galton & Co.
   Phœnix Fire Insurance Company

Merchants, etc.

天祥 Tien-Cheong

Adamson, Bell & Co., merchants
   Hunter, W. L.
   Dermer, T. M.

Agra Bank Limited
   Agents—Gilman & Co.

秀嚴醫生 Son-ngam-i-sang

Beaumont, J. M., M.D. physician & surgeon

福興 Hok-hing

Birley & Co., merchants
   Dalrymple, H. L.
   Hales, G.

太古 Tai-koo

Butterfield & Swire, merchants, agents Ocean Steamship Company of Liverpool
   Smith, H. R., tea-inspector
   Yuill, G. Skelton
   Robinson, W. J.

則文 Cha-wan

Chapman, Thomas H., public tea inspector

有利 Yew-lee

Chartered Mercantile Bank of India, London and China
   Nelson, H. H., agent

祥茂 Cheong-mow

Cheong Mow & Co., butlers for Foochow Foreign Hongs

道車 To-pee

Dobie & Co., shipchandlers and coal dealers, Pagoda Anchorage, agents for Foochow Pilot Company
   Bunker, C. G., in charge
   Kraal, S. A.

閩船澳 Min-shün-o

Foochow Dock, Pagoda Anchorage
   Bryant, N. E., clerk

萬文印書館 Wan-wan

Foochow Herald Office
   MacMaLon, J. P., proprietor
   Mello, P., compositor
   Ozorio, F. A., do.

施濟醫館 Si-chae-e-kuán

Foochow Native Hospital
   Beaumont, Dr.
   Stewart, Dr.
   Ho Min San, assistant apothecary

FOOCHOW.

天裕 Tin-yu
Forster & Co., John, merchants.
  Forster, John
  Greig, M. W.
  Kitching, F. W.
  Mitford, B. A.
  Devenny, B. M.
  Powell, C. S.

乾記 Kien-kee
Gibb, Livingston & Co., merchants
  Tennant, H. P., agent and tea inspector
  Morison, W. O.
  Tannant, T. W., tea-taster

太平 Tai-ping
Gilman & C., merchants
  Young, W. S.
  Price, W. G.
  Harton, C. F.
  Smith, C. D.

Great Northern Telegraph China and Japan Extension Company, Limited
  Agent—The Consul for Denmark

隆順 Loong-shun
Heard & Co., Augustine, merchants
  Bennett, M. E., tea inspector
  Pinel, John, Jr.
  Oliver, George
  Sedgwick, Robt.
  Hunter, R. P.

義利 Gee-lee
Hedge & Co., merchants, and agents Shanghai Local Post
  Dunn, Thos.
  Hedge, T. B.
  Silva, A. A. da

復利 Hok-lee
Hok Lee & Co., general storekeepers and commission agents

義記 Gee-kee
Holliday, Wise & Co., merchants
  Tatham, C. G., agent

匯豐 Huey-hoong
Hongkong and Shanghai Banking Corporation
  Turner, A. L., agent

阜通 Fow-woong
Ivanoff & Co., N. A., merchants

義和 Gee-ho
Jardine, Matheson & Co., merchants
  Laurie, Peter G.
  Angus, A. Forbes, tea inspector
  Noack, Charles
  Nicholson, C. W.

怡興 E-hing
Kaw Hong Take & Co., ships' brokers and commission agents

廣成泰 Kwong-seng-tai
Kwong Seng Tai & Co., ships' compradores, Pagoda Anchorage

廣盛隆 Kwong-sing-loong
Kwong Sing Loong & Co., butlers for Foochow Foreign Hongs

平行 Ping-hong
Kyle & Co., ice house, ice and aerated water manufacturers
  Kyle, Thomas Douglas

隆泰 Loong-tai
Lalor, J. P., broker

和記 Ho-kee
Latham, Oliver, exchange broker (absent)

同記 Toong-kee
Lee Kipby, broker

順和 San-woh
Long Legs & Co., ships' compradores, Pagoda Anchorage

協昌 Hip-cheong
Morris & Co., B. J., merchants

隆文 Loong-wan
Newman & Co., public tea inspectors and commission merchants
  Newman, Walter
  Gittins, John

FOOCHOW.

Ocean Steam Ship Company
 Agents—Butterfield & Swire

同孚 Tong-hoo

Olyphant & Co., merchants
 Pim, T.
  Rothwell, A. W., tea inspector
  Bathgate, John
  Loring, R. F.

麗如 Lai-yu

Oriental Bank Corporation
 Temple, Francis, agent
 McMicken, Wm., accountant

Peninsular and Oriental Steam Navigation Company
 Agents—Turner & Co.,

公裕 Kung-yu

Phipps, Hickling & Co., merchants
 Phipps, A. L.
 Hickling, H.
  Phipps, H. G.
  Sayce, J. N.

同珍 Tong-tin

Purdon & Co., merchants
 Odell, John
 Odell, W. L.

羅弼臣 Lo-pi-suu

Robertson & Co., commission agents, general storekeepers and auctioneers, Customs Road, Foochow; shipchandlers and sailmakers, Mamoi Point, Pagoda Anchorage
 Robertson, H. G. (Foochow)
  Brockett, Thos. (Pagoda Anchorage)
  Drewer, A. (Pagoda Anchorage)

裕豐 Yu-hoong

Rodewald, Schonfeld & Co., merchants
 Schonfeld, F.
 Rodewald (Shanghai)

正方 Chin-fong

Rusden, A. W. G., public tea inspector and commission agent (absent)

旗昌 Kee-cheong

Russell & Co., merchants
 Pomeroy, S. W., Jun.
 Sheppard, E., tea-taster
 Jones, Thos.
 Pereira, B.

泰來 Tai-lai

Ruttonjee & Co., R., opium hong

沙孫 Sha-soon

Sassoon Sons & Co., D., merchants
 Williams. R. P.
 Rhodes, Percival

Saunders, Capt. J. C., Chop *Min*, marine surveyor for Lloyds agents, and other Local Insurance offices, Pagoda Anchorage

生記 Seng-kee

Schoenke, F., watchmaker & photographer

Shaw, Capt. S. L., marine surveyor for the Germanic Lloyds, and the local insurance offices, Pagoda Anchorage

釋臣 Siem-sin

Siemssen & Co., merchants
 Gültzow, A.
 Lübbes, H.

中和 Teong-ho

Silverlock & Co., merchants
 Silverlock, John (England)
 Fry, John G.   (do.)
 Smith, Thomas (do.)
 Haslam, Robert H.
 Fry, F. W.

所美富醫生 So-may-foo-e-sang

Somerville, J. R., M.D., F.R.C.S.ED., physician and surgeon, Pagoda Anchorage

司徒醫生 Sze-to-i-seng

Stewart, J. A., M.D., L.R.C.P.E.

FOOCHOW.

天犂 Teen-lee
Taylor & Co., general storekeepers and ship compradores, Pagoda Anchorage
    Taylor, John R.
    Shearer, John H.

泰成 Tay-sing
Tay Sing, bookbinders and stationers

Thompson & Co., shipchandlers, Pagoda Anchorage
    Thompson, M. E.
    Reilly, F. E.

西胆 Sa-tan
Teng Seong, T., ships' broker and commission agent

同昌 Toong-cheong
Toong Cheong & Co., ships' compradores, Pagoda Anchorage

華記 Wa-kee
Turner & Co., merchants
    Walkinshaw, A. W.
    Dunne, H.

公易 Kung-yak
Westall, Galton & Co., public tea inspectors and commission agents
    Westall, R. R.
    Galton, W. P.
    Reeves, W. M.
    Drought, J. A. H.
    Kinnear, H. R.

宁 NINGPO. 波

Consulates.

AUSTRO-HUNGARIAN MONARCHY.
雅爹厘亞領事官
Yah-teh-lih-ah-ling-sz-kwan

Consul—Alabaster, C.

DENMARK.
顛麥領事官
Tien-mak-ling-sz-kwan

Consul—Alabaster, C.

FRANCE.
法國領事官
Fuh-kwoh-ling-sz-kwan

Consul General—(Consul at Shanghai)

GERMAN EMPIRE.
德意志國領事官
Tak-yee-che-kwoh-ling-sz-kwan

Vice Consul—Gabain, P. (absent)
Acting Vice-Consul—Alabaster, Chaloner

GREAT BRITAIN.
大英領事官
Ta-ying-ling-sz-kwan

Consul—Alabaster, C.
Interpreter—Giles, Herbert A.
Constable—Torres, J.

POSTAL AGENCY.
Agent—Giles, Herbert A.

NETHERLANDS.
荷蘭國領事官
Ho-lan-kwoh-ling-sz-kwan

Acting Consul—Huchting, F.

SWEDEN AND NORWAY.
士威顱及那威國領事官
Sz-wei-tan-kih-noh-wei-kwoh-ling-sz-kwan

Acting Vice-Consul—Beebe, C. G.

UNITED STATES.
大美國領事官
Tah-mi-kwoh-ling-sz-kwan

Consul—Lord, E. C.

Anglo-Chinese Force.
Col. and Commandant—Cooke, J. E.
Major—Watson, J. C.

Imperial Maritime Customs.
新海關 Tsit-hai-kwan

Commissioner—White, F. W.
Assistants—Mackey, Jas.; Budler, H.; Sombreuil, Vicomte V. de; Martin, P.
Tide-surveyor & Har. Master—Kliene, A.
Examiners—Sharp, A.; Reeves, Geo.
Tidewaiters—Wegener, F. (absent); Tattersell, N.; Demetts, T.; Elahout, J. M.; Henry, J. P.
Chinhai Station, Assistant Tide-surveyor—Brennan, Wm.
Light-house keeper, Square Island—José, F.
Do.   Tiger Island—Antonio, L.

Pilots.
Cutter "Alarm"—Hoar, J.
Cutter "Dido"—Brun, J.; Petersen, P. M.
Cutter "Naomi"—Smith, J.; Meldrum, A.

Police Force.
Controller—Cooke, J. E.
Superintendent—Golding, T. B.
Constables—Barr, Geo.; Roberts, H.; Bailey, C.; and 16 Natives

Missions.

AMERICAN BAPTIST MISSION
大美浸禮公會
Knowlton, Rev. M. J., D.D.
Goddard, Rev. J. R.
Jenkins, Rev. H. (absent)

AMERICAN PRESBYTERIAN MISSION.
大美國長老公會
Leyenberger, Rev. J. A., and family
Butler, Rev. Jno.
Dodd, Rev. S., and family (Hangchow),
Lyon, Rev. D. N., and family (do)

CHINA INLAND MISSION.
大英內地會
Stott, G., and Mrs. (Hunchow)
Jackson, J. (do.)
Rudland, W. D., and Mrs. (T'ai-chow)
Crombie, Rev. G., and Mrs. (Funghwa)
Stevenson, J. W., and Mrs. (Shaochow)
McCarthy, Rev. J., and Mrs. (Hangchow)
Fishe, Edward (T'ai-chow)

CHURCH OF ENGLAND MISSIONARY SOCIETY.
大英公會
Russell, Right Rev. W. A. D.D., bishop
Gough, Rev. F. F.
Moule, Rev. A. E.
Bates, Rev J.
Laurence, Miss M., superintendent of C. M. S. boarding school
Moule, Rev. G. E. (Hangchow)
Elwin, Rev. A. (do)
Galt, James, L.R.C.P., medical missionary (do.)
Valentine, Rev. J. D. (Shaou-hying)
Palmer, Rev. R. (do.) (absent)

ENGLISH AND CONTINENTAL BAPTIST MISSION.
Bäschlin, Conrad

ENGLISH BAPTIST MISSION.
胡德邁大英浸會
Hudson, Rev. Thos. H.

ENGLISH METHODIST FREE CHURCH.
偕我堂
Galpin, Rev. F.

HOPITAL ST JOSEPH.
Superieure—(absent)
Sisters—Célard, Madeleine ; Luscan, Angélique ; Ridez, Jeanne

INDEPENDENT BAPTIST MISSION.
福音浸禮會
Lord, Rev. E. C.
Lord, Mrs. E. C.
Barchet, S. P.
Barchet, Mrs. S. P.

MAISON DE JESUS ENFANT.
Superieure—Pasquier, Catherine
Sisters— Solomiac, Marie Louise ; Louy, Louise; Mervé, Stephanie; Frontil, Félicité ; Houles, Joseph ; Geffroy, Elizabeth ; Carrère, Françoise ; Parada, Eugénie ; Dauverchain, Germaine ; Andreu, Vincent

MAISON DE LA PRESENTATION.
TINGHAI, CHUSAN.
Superieure—Leclercq, Flore Josephine
Sisters—Perboyre, Gabriel; Cacqueray, Catherine; Lacôte, Vincent; Duparc, Josephine

MAISON DE ST. VINCENT.
HANGCHOW.
Superieure—Dutrouilh, Madelaine
Sisters—Faure, Vincent ; Roddier, Louise ; Lethimonnier, Marie

ROMAN CATHOLIC.
Monseigneur—Guierry, E. F., vicaire apostolique
Missionaries — Montagneux, P. ; Bret, J. B. (Tinghae, Chusan) ; Vaissiere, J. (Tinghae, Chushan); Rizzi, J. (Taichow); Barbier, J. B. (Hangchow); Guillot, A. (Kiashing)

Insurances.
Coit & Co.
    China and Japan Marine Insurance Co.
    Chinese Insurance Co., Limited

NINGPO.

Davidson & Co.
  Canton Insurance Office
  China Fire Insurance Company
  Hongkong Fire Insurance Company
  North China Insurance Company
  Commercial Union Assurance Company (of London), Life Department
Rees & Co.
  China Traders' Insurance Co., Limited
  Victoria Fire Insurance Company of Hongkong, Limited
Russell & Co.
  Yangtsze Insurance Association
Wadman & Co.
  Imperial Fire Insurance Co. of London
  Union Insurance Society of Canton

Merchants, &c.

甯順 Ning-shing
Coit & Co., merchants
  Coit, F.

廣源 Kwong-yuen
Davidson & Co., merchants
  Davidson, Wm.
  Davidson, W. R.
  Davidson, R. M.
  Davidson, P.

Great Northern Telegraph China and Japan Extension Company
  Hudson & Co., J. S., agents

裕順 Yue-shun
Groth & Co., J., merchants
  Groth, Johannes
  Van Ectvelde, Edmond

Hamburg Coffee House
  Knäpel, M. F. G., proprietor and manager

Hart & Co., Wm., merchants
  Hart, William

Hongkong and Shanghai Banking Corporation, Limited
  Agents—Davidson & Co.

遇昌 Sun-chong
Hudson & Co., J. S., merchants
  Hudson, J. S.

Mackenzie, J. H., M.D.,

North China Herald and S. C. & C. Gazette and *North China Daily News*
  Agents—Rees & Co.

P. & O. Steam Navigation Company
  Agents—Davidson & Co.

Parker, John, M.D., surgeon

Rees & Co., merchants
  Rees, Wm. (absent)
  Bowers, S.
  Hunt, J. H.

Rossich, Antonio, keeper of the Bridge of Boats

旗昌 Kee-chong
Russell & Co., merchants
  Beebe, C. G.
  Huchting, Fr.

利生 Lee-sung
Sassoon, Sons & Co., D., merchants
  Gubbay, E. S.

Shanghai Steam Navigation Company
  Agents—Russell & Co.

遇昌棧 Sun-chong-chan
Sun Chong Chan, merchants and commission agents
  Wong Chin Tuan
  Wong Kow Sia

Swanberg, Hotel
  Swanberg, A., proprietor

復勝 Fok-shing
Tyree, A. F., merchant and commission agent

Union Steam Navigation Co.
  Agent—Coit & Co.

華順 Wha-shing
Wadman & Co., merchants
  Wadman, E.

上 SHANGHAI. 海

Names of Streets in the English Settlement.

NORTH AND SOUTH ROADS.

ORIGINAL NAME.	SECOND NAME.	PRESENT NAME.	CHINESE NAME.
Bund	Yangtsze	Yangtsze	洋于路
None	Yuen Ming Yuen	Yuen Ming Yuen Upper	圓明園上路
None	Gnaomen	Yuen Ming Yuen Lower	圓明園下路
Bridge Street	Keangsoo	Szechuen	四川路
Church Street	Keanse	Keangse	江西路
Barrier Street	Honan	Honan	江南路
Temple Street	Shantung	Shangtung	山東路
Lowsar	Shanse	Shanse	山西路
None	Chlii	Chili	直隸路
Shackloo	Fukien	Fuhkien	福建路
Soochow	Soochow	North of Nanking Rd. Chinkiang	浙江路
		South of Nanking Road Hoopeh	湖北路
Sikh	Quangse	Quangse	廣西路
None	Yunan	Yunnan	雲南路
None	None	Thibet	西藏路

EAST AND WEST ROADS.

ORIGINAL NAME.	SECOND NAME.	PRESENT NAME.	CHINESE NAME.
Bund on the Soochow Creek	Soochow	Soochow	蘇州路
None	Hongkong	Hongkong	香港路
Consulate	Peking	Peking	北京路
None	None	Amoy	厦門路
None	None	Woosis	無錫路
Kirk's Avenue	Ningpo	Ningpo	寧波路
None	Taiwan	Taiwan	臺灣路
Fives' Court Lane	Tientsin	Tientsin	天津路
Park Lane and Maloo	Nanking	Nanking	南京路
Rope Walk Road	Kanking	Kiukiang	九江路
Custom House Road	Hankow	Hankow	漢口路
Mission Road	Foochow	Foochow	福州路
North Gate Street	Canton	Canton	廣東路
None!	None	Woohoo	無湖路
Bund on Yung-king-pang	Sungkiang	Sunkiang	松江路

Consulates.

AUSTRO-HUNGARY.
布林晏國公館
Poo-lin-yen-kwoh-kung-kwan

Consul—Schlick, Rudolph
Linguist—Hsia-I-ni

BELGIUM.
大比利時國領事葛館
Ta-pe-le-sz-kwoh-ling-shih-ko-kwan

(81, Keangse Road.)
Consul—Morel, E.

DENMARK.
大丹國公館 Ta-tan-kwoh-kung-kwan

(18, Yang-tsze Road.)
Acting Consul—Johnson, F. B.

FRANCE.
大法蘭西國總領事衙門
Ta-fa-lan-seh-kwoh-tsung-ling-shih-ya-men

Consul Général—Godeaux, E.
Chancelier—Rouhaud, H.
Interpréte—Blancheton, E.
Élève Interpréte—Arène, J.
Commis de Chancellerie—Collin, J.
1er. lettré chinois—Young
2de. do.—Tchang

GERMAN EMPIRE.
德意志國領事衙門
Ta-i-chih-kwoh-ling-shih-ya-men

Consul—Annecke, W. (absent)
Acting Consul—Lueder, C.
Interpreter—Himly, K.
Secretary—Ruprecht, W.
Physician—Zachariæ, D. M.
Linguist—Tschön
Constable——Kock, M.

GREAT BRITAIN.
大英國領事官
Ta-ying-kwoh-ling-shih-kwan

Consul—Medhurst, W. H.
Vice-Consul Act. and British Assessor at Mixed Court—Stronach, W. G.
Acting Interpreter—Jamieson, Geo.
Chaplain—Butcher, Rev. C. H.

GREAT BRITAIN.
(Continued.)
Assistant in charge Shipping Office—Spence, W. D.
Do. in charge of Records—Ayrton, W. S.
Do. in charge of Accounts—Crawford, J. D.
1st Linguist—Yang-he-ding
2nd do.—Leong C. Wing

BRITISH CONSULAR GAOL.
Visiting Medical Officer—Johnston, J., M.D.
Head Constable—Cox, W.
2nd do.—Clifton, C.
3rd do.—Hodges, H.
4th do.—Tyler, J.

ITALY.
大意大利國總領事衙門
Ta-i-ta-li-kwoh-tsung-ling-shih-ya-men

Consul General—Vignale, M. le Chevalier Laurent

JAPANESE CONSULATE GENERAL.
大日本總領事衙門
Ta-jih-pen-tsung-ling-shih-ya-men

Consul General—Yda, Y.
Consul—Shinagawa, E.
Chinese Interpreter—Kumashiro, T.
Student Interpreters—Wada, Y. ; Ban, S.

NETHERLANDS.
大荷蘭國領事官
Ta-ho-lan-kwoh-ling-shih-kwan

Consul for Shanghai and the Ports of the river Yangtsze—Slaghek, E. Heukensfeldt
Acting Chancelier—Stok, W.

NETHERLANDS CONSULAR COURT FOR CHINA AT SHANGHAI.

Acting President—Slaghek E. Heukensfeldt
Assessors { Heyden, F. E.
          { Haas, J.
Acting Chancelier—Stok, W.
Usher—Rhein, H. H. G.

CHINKIANG.
Vice-Consul—Salter, Albert O.

KIUKIANG.
Vice-Consul—Rose, Stephen C.

HANKOW.
Vice-Consul—Fitz, W. Scott

PORTUGAL
大西洋國領事官
Ta-si-yang-kwoh-ling-shih-kwan

Acting Consul General—Hanssen, H. P.
Chancelier—Tavares, L. A.

RUSSIA.
大俄羅斯國公館
Ta-o-lo-sze-kwoh-kung-kwan

Consul—Reding, —.

SPAIN.
日斯巴呢亞國公館
Yih-zee-pah-nee-ah-kwok-kung-kwan

Consul—Emperanza, J. J. de
Chinese Secretary—Yü Chia-tung

SWEDEN AND NORWAY.
Consul General—Forbes, F. B.

UNITED STATES.
大美國總領事官
Ta-mei-kwoh-tsung-ling-shih-kwan

Consul General—Seward, George F.
Vice-Consul General and Chinese Interpreter—Yates, Matthew, T.
Deputy Consul General—Bradford, Oliver B.
Clerk—Coryell, John R.
Marshal—Phœnix, Richard
Medical Attendant—Macgowan, D. J., M.D.
Jailer—Hendricks, W. H.

H. B. M.'s Supreme Court for China and Japan.
大英總理中華日本按察衙門
Ta-ying-tsung-li-chung-hua-jih-pun-an-cha-ya-mên

Chief Judge—Hornby, Sir Ed.
Assistant Judges—Goodwin, C. W.; Hannen, N. J. (acting)
Law Secretary and Registrar—Mowat, R. A.
Private Secretary and Chief Clerk...Smith, T. G.
Clerk Civil Department—Bishop, R.
Clerk, Summary Civil, and Criminal Department—(Vacant)
Chief Usher—Hore, T.

H. B. M. OFFICE OF WORKS.
FOR CHINA AND JAPAN.
(Yuen-ming-yuen Road)

Surveyor—Boyce, Robt. H., C.E.
Assistant—Assiter, Wm.
Clerk—Donaldson, C. P. M.
Clerks of Works—Bennett, C. R.; Hooper, John; Power, W.

H. B. M.'s Naval and Victualing Yard.
Paymaster in charge and Accountant—Martin, Derisley
Store Issuers—Oliver, J. W.; Cottle, Thos.

Municipal Departments, &c.
MUNICIPAL COUNCIL.
佛公部 Fa-kung-poo

(15, Honan Road, between Foochow and Hankow Roads.)

Chairman—Fearon, R I.
Vice Chairman—Wetmore, W. S.
Members—Seligmann, E.
 Purdon, A. G.
 Barnes, F. D.
 Moses, S. M.
 Wilson, J.
 Little, R. W.
 Kalb, M.
Asst. Secretary—Souper, E.

MUNICIPAL COUNCIL OFFICES.
(15, Honan Road.)
工部 Kung-poo

Asst. Secretary—Souper, E. B.
Assistants—Pond, J. A.; Jones, A. E.; Barton, Geo.; Fabris, J.; Hart, G. M.; Reynell, S.
Foreign Tax Collector—Roggers, Geo.
Assistant do.—Gale, S. R.
Linguist—Z. Chang Sang

SANITARY DEPARTMENT.
Health Officer—Henderson, E., M D.
Inspector of Markets—Keele, O. R. (absent)
Acting do.—Kennedy Sergt.
Inspector of Nuisances—Howes, J.

ENGINEER'S OFFICE.
(No. 14 Honan Road.)

Engineer—Oliver, E. H.
Clerk of Works—Clark, C. B.
Overseer of Roads—Beckhoff, J.
Drainage Foreman—Pigeon, J.
Linguist—Keeshaw, Z.

LOCAL POST OFFICE.
(14, Nankin Road.)

工部信館 Kung-poo-sin-kwan

Local Postmaster—McMillan, John

MUNICIPAL GENERAL STORE.
(16, Honan Road.)

工部棧房 Kung-poo-taan-fang

Storekeeper—Shaw, W. J.

MUNICIPAL POLICE HEAD QUARTERS.
(14, Honan Road.)

巡捕廳房 Chun-poo-ting-fang

Superintendent—Penfold, C.
Foreign Officers—Eleven
Do. Constables—Twenty One
Native Sergeants and Constables—89

HONGKEW STATION.
Inspector—Stripling, A.

CENTRAL STATION.
Inspector—Fowler, W.

LOWZA STATION.
Inspector—Wilson, A.

RIVER POLICE.
Sergeant—Harris, Uriah William
Corporal—Farthing, James
Constables—Ferguson, John; Howell, Jas.

French Municipal Council.

President—Voisin, A.
Vice-President—Aymeri, A.
Members—Galle, P.; Leroy, E.; Mackintosh, E.; Maignan, H.; Wheelock, T. R.
Secretary—Sayn, H.

FRENCH POLICE.

大法國巡捕廳房
Ta-fah-kwoh-ts'ung-foo-t.ng-fang

(Post Central a l'Hotel Municipal.
Rue du Consulat.)

Chef de la Garde Municipale—Barbe, J.

FRENCH SECRETARY'S OFFICE.

大法國公部局
Ta-fah-kwoh-kung-poo-koh

Secretary—Sayn, H.
Accountant—Renucoli, J.
Tax-Collectors—Giudicelli, T.; Binos, L.; Legraud, L.; Sauné, B.
Copying Clerk—Jamaux, E.

PUBLIC WORKS.
Overseer—Percebois, C.

FRENCH NAVAL YARD.
(Woosung.)

Chief Commissaire de Marine—Meesemaecker (Woosung)
Agents—Hall & Holtz

Post Offices.

FRANCE.

大法國書信館
Ta-fa-kwoh-shoo-sin-kwan

(Near French Bund.)

Postal Director—Maignan, H. Champromain
Assistants—Laborde, O.; Fournier, J.

GREAT BRITAIN.

大英書信館 Ta-ying-shoo-sin-kwan

(15, Nanking Road.)

Postmaster—Martin, J. P.
Clerk—Silva, G. S. S. da
Shroff—Chung-mow-yeong

LOCAL.

工部書信館 Kung-poh-shoo-sin-kwan

(14, Nankin Road.)

Local Postmaster—McMillan, John

UNITED STATES.

大英國衙門書信局
Ta-mei-kwoh-ya-mên-shoo-sin-koh

The Consulate General

SHANGHAI.

Imperial Maritime Customs.

CUSTOM HOUSE.

江南海關 Kiang-nan-hai-kwan

Commissioner—Glover, G. B.
Deputy Commissioner and Chief Clerk—
 Simpson, C. L. (absent)
Clerks First Class—
 Piry, P.
 Jones, J.
 Schenck, W. S.
 Markwick, R.
 Brown J. McL.
 Jamieson, C.
 Hughes, T. F. (absent)
 Jaques, J.
Clerks Second Class—
 Lowder, G. G. (absent)
 Hollins, H. H. (do.)
 Daae, J. M.
 O'Brien, M. J.
 Blackmore, J. L.
 Hippisley, A. E.
Clerks Third Class—
 Holwill, E. T.
 Murray, D. G.
 Mouillesaux, A.
 Hillier, H. M.
Clerks Fourth Class—
 Müller, G. F.
 Campbell, S.
 Stent, G. C.
 Paul, S.
Statistical Department—Taintor, E. C., Commis. of Customs and Statistical Secretary
Printing Office—Palamountain, B., manager
Consulting Physician, &c.—Jamieson, R. A.
Medical Attendant—Pichon, L.
Chief Tide-surveyor in Charge of Local Lights
 —Meade, H. J.
Tide-Surveyors—
 Halsey, J. S.
 Bake, H.
Chief Examiner—Smith, E. J.
Examiner—Fenning, W.
Assist. Examiners—Sanders, W.
 Möller, L. P.
 Edwards, J.
 Ritchie, J.
Tidewaiters 1st Class—
 Dredge, G. H.
 Ross, J.
 Pollock, W.
 Morgan, J.
 Godwin, A. A.
 Foster, W.
 Newbury, J.
 Boyol, J.
Tidewaiters 2nd Class—
 Chartin, T.
 Nielsen, J.
 Hoskings, F. J.

Imperial Maritime Customs.

(Continued.)

Tidewaiters 2nd Class—
 Cobb, C. E
 Bono, C. V.
 Jacobsen, F.
 Lovett, H. F.
Tidewaiters 3rd Class—
 Templemore, F. W.
 Holstius, O.
 Mackay, J.
 Pearson, J.
 Kenrick, H. E.
 Clodd, W. E.
 Courtenay, F.
 Rylander, G.
 Castle, W. C.
 Cavendish, J.
 Osterholen, L.
 Lee, E. W.
 Elliott, G. J.
Harbour Master's Office—
 Viguier, S. A., divisional inspector and
  harbour master
 Croad, A., assist. harbour master
 Deighton Braysher, C., do.
 Dudfield, J. B., clerk
River Police—
 Harris, U. W., sergeant
 Howell, J., corporal
 Fergusen, J., do.
 Wellings, T., constable
 Macphail, T., do.
Engineer's Department—
 Henderson, D. M., engineer-in-chief
 Bryson, R., asst. engineer (Foochow)
 Hare, H. T., do.
Pootung Yard—
 Fawcett, T. mechanic
 Malcolm, J., do.
 Green, A., diver
 Wakfer, J., do.
 Krager, H., godown keeper
 Sangster, T., signalman
 Villanova, C., do.
S. S. "Kwa Hsing"—
 Anderson, N. P., officer commanding
 Passmore, J. H., chief officer
 Grandon, J., 2nd officer
 Houstoun, W., engineer
Woosung Inner Bar Station—
 Carlson, W., light-keeper in charge
Langshan Light-vessel—
 Crighton, R. T., master
 Eckhold, M., mate
Kintoan Light-house—
 Smerdley, N., light-keeper
 Mazziole, A., asst. do.
Tungsha Light-vessel—
 Kraul, W., master
 Devine, J. G., 1st mate
 Müller, J., 2nd do.

Imperial Maritime Customs
(Continued.)

Sha-wei-shan Light-house
　McIntosh, J., light-keeper
　Amy, C., asst do.
　Anderson, J, 3rd class light-keeper
North Saddle Light-house
　Miller, J., light-keeper in charge
　Coffin, J. M, assistant light-keeper
　Poynton, H., do.
　Becker, A. W, do.
Gutzlaff Light-house—
　Hayden, G. W., light-keeper
　Wilson, J., assist. do.
West Volcano Light-house—
　Boehncke, A. W., acting light-keeper
Woosung Light-house
　Wildey, T.; light-keeper
Spare Light-vessel—Rebbeck, J. G.

Kiangnan Arsenal.
高昌廟 Kau-t'sang-meau
江南製造總局
MARINE DEPARTMENT.
Superintendent Engineer—Rolls, John
Naval Architect—Lambert, A. J.
　Do.—Christie, W.
Engineer—Allan, J. M.
Draughtsman—Rey, C.
Foreman Moulder—Ure, John
Master Shipwright—Mainland, F.
Small Arms Department—Bayly, Alfred
Foreman Machine Shop—Reid, G. G.
　Do.—Brimley, Thomas
Draughtsmen—Gilles, G. H.; Price, Samuel
Gun Barrel Borer—Stockes, John
Cartridge Factory—Stewart, J.
Gun Forger—Telford, James

TRANSLATION DEPARTMENT.
KIANGNAN ARSENAL.
傅蘭雅 Foo-lan-ya
Fryer, John

Pilots.
福利 Foo-lee
BLACK BALL PILOT COMPANY.
(Corner of Foochow and Szechuen Roads)
　Agents—Hall & Holtz
Members—
　Williams, R.　　Snowden, J.
　Campbell, D. C.　Jurgenson, J.
　Mooney, Jno. K.　Simpsen, J.
　Vaughan, J.　　Taylor, J. T.

晉隆 Chun-lung
INDEPENDENCE PILOT COMPANY.
Cutters "G. F. Seward" and "S. C. Farnham."
Agent—Bennett, C. C. 4, Canton Road
Members—
　Symons, J.　　Cunningham, J. W.
　Andersen, R.　Hendrick, C. E.
　Smith, R.　　Wilson, H.
　Bain, W. B.　Dobbyn, W. A.
　Dalrymple, L. D.　Corbach, W. van

MERCANTILE PILOT COMPANY.
Sloops "Syren" and "Susan."
　Agent—Kelly & Co.
Members (Hongkew Pilots)—
　Burr, W. A.
　McCaslin, R. J.

EUROPEAN LICENSED PILOTS.
　Smith, A. to P. & O.
　Coates, J. E. (to do.)
　Brand, E.
　Knott, R., to P. M. S. S. Co.
　Thomas, J., to Holt's Line
　Kofoed, E. C.

Clubs, Companies, &c.

AUSTRIAN LLOYDS STEAM NAVIGATION COMPANY.
Agents—Pustau & Co.

CHAMBER OF COMMERCE.
Officiating Secretary—Corner Geo. N.

CHINA COAST STEAM NAVIGATION COMPANY.
Directors—
General Agents—Jardine, Matheson & Co, Shanghai
Outport Agents—Beveridge, H., Tientsin; Holmes, Wadman & Co., Chefoo; Bush Brothers & Co., Newchwang; Jardine, Matheson & Co., Foochow; Elles & Co., Amoy; Vincent & Co., E., Swatow; Jardine, Matheson & Co., Hongkong

CHINA AND JAPAN MARINE INSURANCE COMPANY.
Secretary—Schmidt, W.
　Woodward, R. H. S.
　Robertson, A. L.

SHANGHAI.

CHINA MERCHANTS' STEAM NAVIGATION COMPANY.

召商公司局 Chü-shang-kung-ssu-chü

Manager—Tong King Sing

CHINA NAVIGATION COMPANY.
(French Bund.)

太古輪船公司

Agents—Butterfield & Swire

THE CHINA TELEGRAM COMPANY.

Agents for the ORIENTAL TELEGRAM AGENCY, LONDON.

源順洋行 Yuen-chuan-yang-hong

Agent in Shanghai—Rivington, Charles.

CLUB CONCORDIA.

四馬路彈子房

Sz-ma-loo-dan-tsz-vong

Baffy, G. T., 22, Foochow Road

COMPAGNIE DU GAS.
(Yang-king-pang—French Concession.)
Agents—Nachtrieb, Leroy & Co.

EASTERN EXTENSION AUSTRALASIAN & CHINA TEL. CO., LIMITED.

電線行 Deen-seen-hong

Agent—Oxlade, George
Rozario, R. M.

GREAT NORTHERN TELEGRAPH CHINA AND JAPAN EXTENSION COMPANY.
(Nankin Road.)

電線行 Deen-seen-hong

General Agent in China and Japan—Dreyer, H., D.B.N.
Chief Engineer—Nielsen, J.
Accountant—Lepper, H. F. G.
Electricians—Hoffmeyer, V.; Terp, C. I. F.; Schultz, C. A.; Lauritzen, S.; Steglich, O.; Orsted, A. S.; Kolwig, F.; Schmidt, N. C.; Irminger, F. C. G.; Poulsen, O.

HAN YANG STEAMER CO.

Agents—Morris, Lewis & Co., French Bund

KOONG TSING WHARVES AND GODOWNS.

公正 Koong-tsing

Agents—Olyphant & Co., French Bund
Wharfinger—Gibson, T.

MESSAGERIES MARITIMES,
FRENCH MAIL COMPANY.
(Bund, French Concession.)

大法國火輪船公司

Ta-fah-kwoh-hwo-lun-chuan-koong-ss

Agent—Hennequin, A.
Assistants—Bonebean, J.; Beer, H. A.; Campos, F. N. P. de; Poo-chi

NORTH-CHINA INSURANCE CO.
21, (Keangse Road.)

保家行 Pau-ka-hong

Secretary—Morris, Herbert S., (absent)
Acting Secretaries—Davis, J. K; Starkey, Reginald D. (Hongkong Branch)
Bayne, W. G., (Yokohama Branch)
Leitch, R. M.
Percival, W. H.
Church, Thos (Hongkong)
Warrick, W. M. (absent)
Clifton, A. S. T.
Foosung, Z.
Tucker, Joseph J. (Marine Surveyor)

NORTH CHINA STEAMER COMPANY

Agents—Jardine, Matheson & Co.

OCEAN STEAMSHIP COMPANY.
(Szechuen Road.)

Agents—Butterfield & Swire

OLD DOCK FOUNDRY, AND SHIPYARD.

老船廠 Law-chuan-tsang

Farnham & Co., S. C.

PACIFIC MAIL STEAM-SHIP COMPANY.
(Hongkew.)

Agent—Bowman, Geo. F.
Bookkeeper—Langhorne, M. B.
Freight Clerk—Luce, A. E.
Asst. do.—Clark, W. T.

PENINSULAR & ORIENTAL STEAM NAVIGATION COMPANY'S OFFICE.
(15, Yangtaze Road)

火輪船公司行

Hwo-lun-chuan-kung-sze-hong

Agent—Barnes, F. D.
Chief Assistant—Withers, G.
Assistant—Joseph, H. H.
Do.—Vincent, J.
Gunner—Cooper, H. (Pootung)
Do.—Fryer, H.   (do.)

POOTUNG DOCK SHIP-YARD.

浦東董家渡船戶

Poo-tung-tong-ka-doo-chuan-ao

Farnham & Co., S. C.

POOTUNG LUMBER YARD.

浦東旗旌木行

Poo-toong-gee-ts'ang-moo-houg

Manager—Law, W. C.
Schmidt, C. W.

SAILOR'S HOME.
(27, Hongkew Road.)

豐順 Foong-züng

Superintendent—Bowen, E.
Steward—Reeve, R.
1st Constable—Bailey, Geo.
2nd do.—Reeve, J.

SEAMEN'S LIBRARY AND MUSEUM.
(Adjoining the Seamen's Church, Pootung.)
Acting Chaplain and Librarian—Butcher, Rev. Canon

SHANGHAI CLUB.
(2, Yang-tsze Road.)

總會 Tsoong-way

Secretary—Waller, J. E.
Assistant—Williams, F. T.
Steward—Williams, T. R.

SHANGHAI DOCK COMPANY.
Secretary—Cowie, G. J. W.

SHANGHAI FIRE DEPARTMENT.
No. 1 *Company Engine House*, 1C, Honan Road
No. 2 do.—17, Whangpoo Road, American Settlement
No. 3. do.—Kin Le Yuen Godown, French Settlement
No. 4 do.—Steam Engine *Deluge*, Company House, Central Police Station, Honan Road
No. 5 do.—French Municipal Hall
No. 6 do.—French Gas Works
No. 7 do.—Steam Engine, Gibb, Livingston & Co's Compound, Bund
No. 1 *Hook and Ladder Truck House*—Central Police Station, Honan Road
No. 2 do.—French Municipal Hall
Chief Engineer—Mackenzie, Robt. (acting)
Engineer for District No. 1, Hongkew Settlement—Ashley, C. J.
Do. for No. 2, English Settlement—Mackenzie, Robt.
Do. for No. 8, French Settlement—Charrier, A.
Surgeon—Henderson, E., M.D.

SHANGHAI GAS COMPANY.
Chairman—Purdon, John G.
Engineer and Acting Secretary—Yeo, J. G.
Assist. Engineer—
Chief Clerk—Seabrook, Wm.
Assistant—Bellbin, Ed.

SHANGHAI AND HONGKEW WHARF COMPANY.

公和祥 Koong-hwo-ts'iang

Manager—Mayne, G. G.
Clerk—Henderson, G.
1st Assistant—Batten, H.
2nd do.—Waller, C. H.
Customs Officer—Pollock, Wm.
Do.—Edwards, J.

SHANGHAI LIBRARY.
(Upper Yuen Ming Yuen Road.)

洋文書館 Yang-vung-sü-kwan

Hon. Secretary—Maclellan, J.
Hon. Treasurer—Payn, T.
Librarian—Menzies, A.
Open from—9 to 11 A.M. 4 to 7.30 P.M.

SHANGHAI PILOT COMPANY.
Agents—Silverthorne, & Co., A.

SHANGHAI.

SHANGHAI & POOTUNG FOUNDRY AND ENGINEERING CO.

浦東鐵廠 Poo-toong-tih-tsang

Manager—Muirhead, D.
Secretary—Mackenzie, J.
  Prentice, John
  Dick, James
  Middleton, Wm.
  Cranston, D.
  Mackenzie, M.
  Mitchell, Wm.
  Hill, John

SHANGHAI RACQUET CLUB.
(Maloo.)

抛球場 P'au-gew-zean

Hon. Secretary—Cooper, John
Hon. Treasurer—Scott, James L.

SHANGHAI STEAM NAVIGATION COMPANY.
(5, Yangtsze Road)

旗昌 Kee-chang

Agents—Russell & Co.
Marine Superintendent—Coryell, Myers

KIN-LEE-YUEN WHARF.

Superintendent of Godowns—Butler, G. A.
Wharf Clerk—Kendall, C. C.
Clerk—Dormer, O. F.
Assistant—Fritz, J.

KIN-FONG-TOONG WHARF.
Wharf Clerk—Ellis, E. W.

KIN-WING-SING WHARF.
Godown-keeper—Boswell, J. B.

S. S. N. COMPANY'S DOCK,

Manager—Lambert, A. G.
Foreman—Black, D.

SHANGHAI TUG AND LIGHTER COMPANY.
(5, Yang-tsze Road.)

駁船公司行 Poh-chuan-kung-sz-hong

Managers—Thorne, Rice & Co.
  Pemberton, T.

UNION INSURANCE SOCIETY OF CANTON.
(19, Keangse Road, corner of Kewkeang Road.)

保安 Pau-an

Agent—Brown, Saml.
  Silveira, A. da

UNION STEAM NAVIGATION COMPANY.
(French Bund.)

公正 Koong-tsing

General Agents—Olyphant & Co.
  Smith, E. U.

YANG-TYE CARGO BOAT COMPANY.
(Szechuen Road, four doors from Messrs Little & Co.)

榮泰駁船行 Yoong-t'a-poh-chuan-hong

Manager—Yangwell

Hospitals.

AMERICAN EPISCOPAL MISSION HOSPITAL.
(Hongkew.)

同仁醫館 Tung-jin-e-kwan

Medical Officer—Henderson, E., M.D.
Native Physician—Ng-Hung-Yuh
Rector—Nelson, Rev. R.

CHINESE HOSPITAL.
(3, Shantung Road).

仁濟醫館 Jin-tse-e-kwan

Medical Officer—Johnston, James, M.D.

GUTZLAFF HOSPITAL.
(N. side of Ningpo Road, close to Lowza.)

體人醫院 Ti-jin-e-yuan

Surgeon—Jamieson, R. A.

HONGKEW HOSPITAL.
(Rear of Hongkew Police Station.)

同仁醫館 Toong-jin-e-kwan

Surgeon—Henderson, Dr.

MUNICIPAL VACCINATION DEPOT.
Public Vaccinator—Henderson, Dr. E.
Do.—Jamieson, Dr. R. A.

INSTITUTION FOR THE CHINESE BLIND POOR.
Trustee—Thomson, Rev. E. H. (West Gate)

SHANGHAI GENERAL HOSPITAL.
(French Bund.)
上海公病院 Sheung-hai-kung-ping-yuen
Physician—Little, Dr. L. S.
Secretary—Weill, J. G.

Masonic Lodges.
OFFICERS FOR 1874.
CELESTIAL ENCAMPMENT.
E. C.—Miller, J. I.
Prelate—Clarke, B. A.
1st Captain—Gundry, R. S.
2nd do.—Orme, P.
Expert—Eastlack, W. C.

COSMOPOLITAN LODGE.
Worshipful Master—Clarke, B. A.
Senior Warden—Pollock, W.
Junior Warden—Morgan, J.
Senior Deacon—Griffiths, D.
Junior Deacon—Williams, J.
Inner Guard—Kleine, A.
Secretary—Scheppelmann, C.
Treasurer—Howes, J.
Senior Steward—Houstoun, W.
Junior Steward—Hirsbrunner, J.
Tyler—Hore, T.

ROYAL SUSSEX LODGE, No. 501.
Worshipful Master—Parker, J. H.
Past Master—Evans, H.
Senior Warden—Stent, G.
Junior Warden—Gale, R.
Senior Deacon—Johnsford, A.
Junior Deacon—Camajee, —.
Treasurer and Secretary—Pappa, Wm.
Inner Guard—Passmore, J.
Tyler—Hore, T.

TUSCAN LODGE, No. 1027.
Worshipful Master—Miller, J. I.
Past Master—Holdsworth, Ed.
Senior Warden—Orme, P.
Junior Warden—Gombert, C.
Secretary—Schutze, C. H. F.

ZION CHAPTER, No. 570.
M. E. Z.—Maitland, J. A.
H.—Miller, J. I.
J.—Orme, P.
Scribe E.—Smith, F. M.
Scribe N.—Hardy, H. W.
P. S.—Kingsmill, T. W.
Treasurer—Rodewaldt, J. F.

Missions, Churches, &c.

BOARD OF FOREIGN MISSIONS OF THE PRESBYTERIAN CHURCH, U. S. A.

范先生 Van-sien-san.
(Outside Little South Gate.)
Farnham, Rev. J. M. W. (absent)
Fitch, Rev. Geo. F. (Soochow.)
Schmidt, Chas.   do.

BOARD OF MISSIONS OF THE PROTESTANT EPISCOPAL CHURCH, U. S. A.
Williams, Right Rev. C. M., D.D. (Osaka, Japan)
Nelson, Rev. R. (Hongkew)
Thomson, Rev. E. H. (West Gate)
Fay, Miss L. M. (Hongkew)
Schereschewsky, Rev. S. I. J. (Peking)
Hohing, Rev. A. C. (Hankow)
Hoyt, Rev. S. I. J. R. (Wu-chang)
Boone, Rev. W. J.   (do.)
Morris, Rev. A. R. (Osaka, Japan)

BRITISH AND FOREIGN BIBLE SOCIETY.
(5 Shantung Road.)
Agent—Wylie, A.

THE CHAPLAINCY.
(19, Keangse Road).
禮記 Le-ke.
Butcher, Rev. Canon

EURASIAN SCHOOL.
Head Master of the Anglo-Chinese School—Gill, Henry S. (Hongkew)
Mistress of the Eurasian School—Gill, Mrs. H. S.

LONDON MISSIONARY SOCIETY.
麥家圈 Mah-ka-k'euen
Muirhead, Rev. W. (Shantung Road)
Barrett, Rev. E. R., B.A.

SHANGHAI.

METHODIST MISSION.
藍先生 Lan-sien-sang
鄭家木橋 Tsang-kia-mooh-jau
Lambuth, J. W. and family (French Concession)

NORTH CHINA BRANCH R. ASIATIC SOCIETY.
(Gnaomen Road.)

PROCURE DES LAZARISTES.
(Rue Laguerre)
Aymeri, A.
Salvan, H.

SEAMAN'S CHURCH.
浦東禮拜堂 Poo-tung-li-pai-t'ang
Acting Chaplain—Butcher, Rev. C. H.

SOUTHERN METHODIST MISSION, U. S. A.
林牧師 Lien-keng-sz
Allen, Rev. Young J.

SHANGHAI FEMALE SCHOOL SOCIETY.
(Outside West Gate).
禪文堂西門外湯先生
Pi-men-taug-hsi-men-wai-tang-hsien-sheng
Secretary—Thomson, Rev. Elliot H.

UNION CHAPEL.
(Shantung Road.)
Minister—Thomas, Rev. James (London Mission)

Steamers, Tugs, &c.

"APPIN,"
BRITISH STEAMER.
Jardine, Matheson & Co.
Captain—Russell, H. V.
Chief Officer—Hamlin, Thos.
2nd do.—Melvin, Wm.
Chief Engineer—Lang, Archibald
2nd do.—Maxwell, John
3rd do.—Connell, Robert

"ARIEL,"
BRITISH SHIP.
順記 Shun-kee
Commander—Croal, R.
Chief Officer—Stafford, T. M.
Purser—Azevedo, P. de

"BERWICH WALLS,"
RECEIVING SHIP
Commander—Hill, B. G.
Knox, J.

"BUNKER HILL,"
STEAM-TUG.
Captain—Kirby

"CHILI,"
Captain—Patterson, W. F.

"CHUSAN,"
AMERICAN STEAMER, 847 TONS.
Shanghai Steam Navigation Company.
Russell & Co., agents.
Captain—.

"DRAGON,"
BRITISH STEAMER, 461 TONS.
Jardine, Matheson & Co.
Captain—Paynter—.

"EMILY JANE,"
RECEIVING-SHIP.
Captain—Dealandes, E. J.
Chief Officer—Lindsay, Geo.
Clerk—Castillo, S. P.
2nd Officer—Sloane, J.
Assistant—Shillibeer, E.

"FIRE QUEEN,"
AMERICAN STEAMER, 1,172 TONS.
Shanghai Steam Navigation Company,
Russell & Co., agents.
Captain—Andrews, G. W.

"FO-KE-LIN,"
STEAM-TUG.
Captain—Murray, —.

"FUSI-YAMA,"
AMERICAN STEAMER, 1,113 TONS.
Shanghai Steam Navigation Company.
Russell & Co., agents.
Captain—Harmon, J.

"GLENGYLE,"
BRITISH STEAMER, 1,265 TONS.
Union Steam Navigation Company.
Captain—McQueen, —.

"HANGCHOW,"
AMERICAN STEAMER, 955 TONS.
Shanghai Steam Navigation Company.
Russell & Co., agents
Captain—West, W. A.

"HIRADO,"
AMERICAN STEAMER, 1,084 TONS.
Shanghai Steam Navigation Company.
Russell & Co., agents.
Captain—Gray, H. N.

"HONAN,"
Captain—Friend, A. F.

"HUPEH," (late Moning)
AMERICAN STEAMER.
Shanghai Steam Navigation Company.
Russell & Co., agents.
Captain—Johnson, Geo. C.

"KIANGSE,"
AMERICAN STEAMER, 574 TONS.
Shanghai Steam Navigation Company.
Russell & Co., agents.
Captain—Pratt, N.

"MAGGIE LAUDER,"
BRITISH STEAM-TUG, 130 TONS.
Mackenzie & Co.
Captain—Ryder, F. H.
Engineer—Carmichael, James

"MILLET,"
AMERICAN STEAMER, 181 TONS.
Shanghai Steam Navigation Company.
Russell & Co., agents
Captain—Crowell, J.

"NANKING."
Captain—Morse, A. H.

"NANZING,"
BRITISH STEAMER, 419 TONS.
Jardine, Matheson & Co.
Captain—Tulloch, —.

"NGAPUHI,"
HULK.
Harbour Master's Department.
1st Asst. Harbour Master—Croad, A.
2nd do.—Deighton-Braysher, C.

"ORPHAN,"
STEAM-TUG.
Farnham & Co., S. C., agents
Captain—McCaslin, C. H.

"PLYMOUTH ROCK,"
AMERICAN STEAMER, 768 TONS.
Shanghai Steam Navigation Company.
Russell & Co., agents
Captain—Simmons, Chas. E.

"ROCKET,"
STEAM-TUG.
Farnham & Co., S. C., agents
Captain—Hadler, —.

"SAMSON," STEAM-TUG.
Frazar & Co., agents
Captain—Pike, John
Engineer—Kirk, James

"SHANSE,"
AMERICAN STEAMER, 561 TONS.
Shanghai Steam Navigation Company.
Russell & Co., agents
Captain—Steele, Jos., Jr.

"SHANTUNG,"
AMERICAN STEAMER, 724 TONS.
Shanghai Steam Navigation Company.
Russell & Co., agents
Captain—Winsor, A., Jr.

"SHINGKING,"
Captain—Howes, C. P.

"SZECHUEN,"
AMERICAN STEAMER, 553 TONS.
Shanghai Steam Navigation Company.
Russell & Co., agents
Captain—

SHANGHAI.

"TSATLEE,"
AMERICAN STEAMER, 56 TONS.
Shanghai Steam Navigation Company.
Russell & Co., agents
Captain—(Chinese)

"TUNG CHE,"
CHINESE STEAMER.
Chinese Government.
Captain—Chinese

"TUN SIN,"
BRITISH STEAMER.
Union Steam Navigation Company.
Captain—Howlett, —.

"WATER WITCH,"
RECEIVING-SHIP.
Lewes and Benton "Surveyors for Lloyds Agents," "Germanischer Lloyds Register Internationales," Union and other Local Insurance Offices.
Marine Surveyors—
  Lewes, W. F. (absent)
  Benton, L.
  Elphick, F.
  Roman, G.
  Pereira, E.

"WELLINGTON,"
開源 Kae-yuen
RECEIVING SHIP
David Sassoon, Sons & Co.
Captain—Bennett, G. W.
Chief Officer—Parker, J. H. P.
2nd do.—Sedgewick, E. W.
Purser—Fonseca, V. P.
Assistant do.—Oliveira, A. S.

Banks.

亞架剌銀行 A-ka-la-ngan-hong
Agra Bank, Limited, 3, Kewkeang Road
  Lemarchand, F. W., manager
  Skelly, Thomas D., act. accountant
  Wulff, W. L., assistant

有利 Yew-le
Chartered Mercantile Bank of India, London and China, 2, Kewkeang Road
  Fergusson, Robt., manager
  Thurbur, John, accountant
  Rowband, O. F., assistant do.
  Rozario, J. E.
  Sanches, V. F. D.

法蘭西銀行 Fa-lan-ani-yin-hong
Comptoir d'Escompte de Paris, Yangtsze Road
  Hardcastle, E. J., manager
  Ewald, L.
  Payn, Th., accountant
  Feibel, Th.
  Fitz Henry, D.
  De Crety, C.
  Jorge, H.
  Xavier, J. P.

德意志銀行 Tăh-i-chi-ngan-hong
Deutsche Bank, 22, Kiangse Road
  Seligmann, E., manager
  Krug, E., accountant
  Hartmann, G. W.

匯豐銀行 Way-foong-yin-hong
Hongkong and Shanghai Banking Corporation, 12, Yangtsze Road
  Cameron, Ewen, manager
  Greig, W. Geo., acting accountant
  Beveridge, C. H.
  Veitch, A.
  Grigo., J. M.
  Haselwood, A. H. C.
  Barnes, C. J.
  Pereira, M. L. (absent)
  Barton, C.
  Johnston, G. R.
  Carvalho, M. A. de
  Diniz, A. J.
  Gutterres, D. M.
  Rangel, S. J.
  Townsend, A. M., acting agent (Hankow)
  Mitchell, F. W., Jr. (Hankow)
National Bank of India, Limited
Agents—Borneo Company

麗如 Lai-ju
Oriental Bank Corporation, The Bund
  Paterson, A., acting manager
  Lethbridge, G., acting accountant
  Gardiner, T. J., assistant accountant and cashier
  Johnston, W., assistant accountant
  Carvalho, P. M. de
  Pereira, J. L.
  Gutterres, A. N.

Insurances.

Adamson, Bell & Co.
  Lancashire Insurance Company of Manchester

14 J   SHANGHAI.

Barnes, F. D.
  London and Oriental Steam Transit Insurance Company
  Marine and General Mutual Life Assurance Society
Barnet & Co., Geo.
  Scottish Imperial Fire and Life Insurance Co.
Birley, Worthington & Co.
  Liverpool and London and Globe Insurance Company
Butterfield & Swire
  British and Foreign Marine Insurance Company, Limited
  Royal Exchange Assurance of London
Chapman, King & Co.
  Sun Fire Office
Drysdale, Ringer & Co.
  China Traders' Insurance Co., Limited (Marine)
  Hongkong Marine Insurance Company for 1868
  Queen Insurance Company (Fire)
  Sun Fire Office
  Canton Insurance Office (Marine)
  Hongkong Fire Ins. Co., Limited
Frazar & Co.
  American Shipmasters' Association Boston (U.S.A.) Underwriters
  Java Sea and Fire Insurance Company, Batavia
  National Marine Insurance Company, South Australia
  New York Underwriters
  Queen Fire Insurance Company, Liverpool and London
  Trident Marine Insurance Co., Limited
Gibb, Livingston & Co.
  Bombay Insurance Company
  China Fire Insurance Company, Limited, Shanghai and Hankow.
  Forbes' Constituents Insurance Co.
  Imperial Fire Insurance Company, Shanghai and Hankow
  Lloyds
  Merchant Shipping and Underwriters Association of Melbourne
Gilman & Co.
  North British & Mercantile Ins. Co.
  Ocean Marine Insurance Company
  Royal Exchange Assurance Company of London, Limited
  Merchants' Marine Insurance Company
  London and Lancashire Fire Insurance Co.
Heard & Co.
  China Traders' Insurance Company, Limited
  London & Provincial Marine Insurance Company
  Victoria Fire Insurance Co., Limited
  Australasian Insurance Company
  Victoria Insurance Company

Holliday, Wise & Co.
  Liverpool and Bombay Traders Insurance Company
  London Assurance Corporation, Fire and Marine
  Manchester Fire Insurance Company
  Thames and Mersey Marine Insurance Company Limited
Jardine, Matheson & Co.
  Canton Insurance Office
  Triton Insurance Company
  Bombay Insurance Society
  Ocean and Marine Insurance Company of Bombay
  Hongkong Fire Insurance Company Limited
  Alliance Fire Insurance Company
Jarvie & Co., J.
  City of Glasgow Life Assurance Company
Maclean, Wallace & Co.
  Joint Underwriters Union Association. Amsterdam
Holdsworth, Edw.
  Standard Life Assurance Company in China & Japan
Olyphant & Co.
  Union Steam Navigation Co. (office French Bund)
  Chinese Insurance Company, Limited
  Compagnie Russe de Navigation a Vapeur
  Guardian Assurance Co., London
  San Francisco Board of Underwriters
Pustau & Co.
  Hamburg & Bremen Fire Insurance Company
  Rheinisch Westphälischer Lloyds
  Verein Hamburger Assecuradeure
  Bremische See Assecuranz Company
  Düssedorfer Allgemeine Versicherungs Gesellschaft
  Basler Transport Versicherungs Gesellschaft
  Allgemeine Versicherungs Gesellschaft (Helvetia)
  Transport Versicherungs Gesellschaft (Schweiz)
  Dresdener feuer Verscherungs Gesellschaft
  Niederländisch Allgemeine Versicherungs Gesellschaft in Tiel
  Deutsche Transport Versicherungs Gesellschaft in Berlin
  Rhenaria Versicherungs Actien Gesellschaft in Köln
  Vaterländische Transport Versicherungs Actien Gesellschaft in Elberfeld
Russell & Co.
  Compagnie Lyonnaise d'Assurances Maritimes
  Yangtsze Insurance Association

SHANGHAI.

Siemssen & Co.
  De Oosterling Sea and Fire Insurance Company of Batavia
  Samarang Sea and Fire Insurance Company of Samarang
  Globe Marine Insurance Company, Limited, London
  North German Fire Insurance Company of Hamburg
  Trans-Atlantic Fire Insurance Company, Limited, of Hamburg
Schellhass & Co., Eduard
  Deutsche Feuer Versicherungs Actien Gesellschaft, Berlin
  Transatlantische Güter Versicherungs Gesellschaft, Berlin
Shaw, Brothers & Co.
  Union Marine Insurance Company, Limited, of Liverpool and London
Thorne Bros.
  Alliance Marine Assurance Company
Turner & Co.
  Northern Assurance Company, Fire & Life
Westall, Brand & Co.
  Phoenix Fire Insurance Company
Union Insurance Society of Canton
  Brown, Saml., agent
    Silveira, A. da

Merchants, &c.

天長 Tien-chang

Adamson, Bell & Co., merchants, The Bund
  Bell, F. H.
  Grant, C. Lyall
  Youd, F. M.
    Mylne, H. A.
    Vachell, H. G.
    Welch, Joseph
    Anderson, Arthur
    Williamson, T. G.
    Quekett, J. F.
    Lewis, F. E.
    Hunter, W. L. (Foochow)
    Dermer, T. M. do.
    Dodwell, G. B. do.
    D'Iffanger, F. (Yokohama)
    Pryer, H. do.

新永發 Sien-yoong-fah

Ashley, C. J., sail-maker, Old Dock, Hongkew

禮查 Lee-zo

"Astor House," 8, Whampoa Road, Hongkew
  Jansen, De Witt C., manager
  Garraway, C.

晉原 Tsing-yuen

Balfour, Butler & Co., 14, Peking Road
  Balfour, Frederic H.
  Butler, George

悖信 Tun-sin

Barnet & Co., Geo., merchants
  Batt, E. W.
  Ellis, Elias (absent)
  Glover, W.
  Newbigging, W. C.

得利 Tuh-le

Baron, J. S., ship and general agent
  Baron, J. S.
  Seabrook. W.

圓明園巴敦醫生 Yuen-ming-yuen-po-toong-e-sung

Barton, George Kingston, M.D., F.R.C.S., 4 Yuen-ming-yuen (absent)

碧斯畢 Bee-sz-bee

Bigsby, W. E. D., bill and bullion broker

梅博閣 Mai-poh-koh

Bird, R. W. M., (absent) 1 Yuen-ming-yuen Buildings
  Myburgh, Alex barrister-at-law
  Hore, Thos., clerk

祥太 Chang-tai

Birley, Worthington & Co., merchants Keangse Road
  Turnbull, W. A.
  Howie, W.
  Harding, J. W.
  Macvicar, C. Y.
  Scott, J. L.
  Ogle, R. G.

平和 Ping-hwo

Birt & Co., W., silk inspectors and commission merchants
  Birt, W.

電氣機造者 Tien-ho-ke-tsau-che

Bishop, J. D., telegraph engineer and contractor, 4, Nanzing Road, Hongkew

Bisset & Co., J. P., share brokers, and land agents, No. 28, Szechuen Road
  Bisset, J. P.
  Mitchell, Wm.
    Buchanan, James
    Hock, L. C.
    Pereira, E. F.

公道 Koong-tau

Blain & Co., 21 Nankin Road
  Blain, John
    Lucas, Clement (absent)
    Walker, Samuel
    Walker, W. H.

Blair, John H., piece goods and general broker

恰順 Yee-shun

Bonney, & Co., N. B., ship and freight brokers, Yang-king-pang, French Concession
  Bonney, N. B.

華惇 Tung-woo

Borntraeger & Co. 26 Foochow Road
  Borntraeger, F.
  Borntraeger, J. M., (absent)

Bottomley, C. D., broker and auctioneer

廣豐 Kwang-fung

Bourjau, & Co., merchants, 2, Hongkong Road
  Bourjau, A. (absent)
  Behre, Ernst (Hongkong)
  Wieler, G. A. (absent)
    Taumeyer, E.
    Wieler, Oscar
    Bryner, J. A.
    Iversen, A.
    Brunckhorst, E. G.

播威 Poo-way

Bovet, Brothers & Co., 9, Pekin Road
  Bovet, A.
  Bovet, G.
  Stok, W.

公平 Kung-ping

Bower, Hanbury & Co., 8, Nankin Road
  Hanbury, Thomas (absent)
  Iveson, Egbert
  Ranken, A. A. (absent)
    Stunzi, H.
    Sykes, Adam
    Artindale, Robt, H.
    Char, Gnokee

內各生 Noi-ka-sang

Boyd & Co., engineers and shipbuilders
  Grant, P. V.
  Robertson, Wm. (Nagasaki)
  Riach, John
  Fail, Chas. C.
  Johnston, James
  Ridings, G. E.
  Paterson, G.
  Berwick, Wm.
  McCallum, A.
  Xavier, M. F.

義源 E-yuen

Brand, Brothers & Co., 6, Yangtsze Road
  Brand, J. T.
  Brand, Robt. (absent)
  Brand, David (absent)
  Sim, Alexander
  Cullen, J. P.
  Brand, John
  Herdman, W. G.

字來泰 Ba-lai-tah

Brandt, O., bill, bullion, and general broker and accountant, Bubbling Well Road, opposite Grand Stand address " Shanghai Club."

British Dispensary, 9, Nanking Road
  Churton & Co., C. S., chemists, &c.
  Churton, C. Stanley

Broom, Augustus, broker, Ningpo Road

寶隆 Paw-loong

Brown, Richd C., 23, Szechuen Road

載生 Tsai-sang

Buchheister, J. J., 4, Rue Colbert, French Concession
  Buchheister, J. J.
  Bidwell, H. S.
    Fabris, Frank

SHANGHAI.

太古行 Tai-koo-hong
Butterfield & Swire, merchants, and agents Ocean Steam-ship Company, Szechuen Road
  Lang, William
    Watson, Herbert
    Mackintosh, Edwin
    Aubert, F. B.
    Kent, W. K.
    Bois, J. C.
    Warrick, A. (Hankow)
    Endicott, H. B.
    Andrew, J.
    Hall, James
    Wyatt, O. M.
    Burrows, A.
    Gibson, T.
    Fonseca, J. B.
    Remedios, A. F. dos
    Remedios, S. A.

廣南 Kwang-nan
Camajee, D. N., & Co., 24, Keangse Road
  Camajee, D. N.
    Hormusjee, C.

金布 Kin-poo
Campbell, Archibald & Co., 80, Szechuen Road
  Campbell, Arch.

Cann, J. J., commission agent

亨利 Hang-le
Canny, J. M. & Co., 14a Pekin Road
  Canny, J. M. (absent)
  Carnie, F.
  Mackillop, John

Carlton House Refreshment Rooms, Foochow Road
  Hanlon, M., proprietor
  Barker, C. B., manager

中和 Chung-hwo
Carter & Co., W. H., 10, Honan Road
  Carter, W. H.
  Rees, C. A.
    Dalgliesh, W. H.
    Cummins, F. (absent)
    Crawford, Wm.
    Mackersie, W.

望益紙館 Wang-yuh-tz-kwan
Carvalho, A. H. de, printer and stationer, 37, Keangse Road
  Pereira, H.
  Silva, P. da
  Aquino, J. F. de
  Pereira, T. S.

廣昌 Kwang-ts'ang
Cawasjee Pallanjee & Co., merchants, No. 4 Keangse Road
  Pestonjee, Rustomjee (absent)
  Cooverjee, Rustomjee
  Sorabjee, Maneckjee Metta
  Framjee, Bomanjee
  Sorabjee, Cursetjee

豐興 Foong-hing
Chalmers & Co., J. C., painters, carpenters, paper-hangers, and upholsterers, 17 Nankin Road
  Chalmers, J. C.
  Binglane, T.

復昇 Fu-shing
Chapman, King & Co., merchants, 5, Peking Road
  Chapman, Fredk. (absent)
  King, Chas. J. (absent)
  Michie, A.
    Williams, R. B.
    Pollock, A. J.

法馬醫生 Fah-mo-e-sâng
Charrier, A., proprietor, French Livery Stables, French concession, veterinary surgeon

豐裕 Foong-yu
China & Japan Trading Company, importers of and dealers in general merchandise, commission agents and auctioneers, 1, Bund, Head Office
  Fogg & Co., H., general agents
  Haskell, F. E., local agent
  Rogers, Edward
  Brandão, J. G.
  Dickman, Geo.
  Gordon, H. L.
  Nail, Chas., H.

正豐印字館 Tsing-foong-yin-tse-kwan

Ching Foong Printing Office, 25, Szechuen Road
  Da Costa & Co., agents for the proprietors
  Loureiro, P. general manager
    Tavarez, P. J., foreman

康頤馬車行 Hong-tun-ma-ch'ai-hong

Compton & Co., Hongkew Livery Stables, 858 Woosung Road, Hongkew

密四可克 Mei-sz-ko-kah

Cook, M. H., sail-maker and rigger, Old Masonic Hall, Canton Road

和成 Woo-sing

Cooper, D., 12 Pekin Road

可栢 Ko-pah

Cooper, W., general commission agent, Ningpo Road

和明 Ho-ming

Corner, George R., accountant, 15 Szechuen Road
  Officiating Secretary Shanghai General Chamber of Commerce
  Acting Agent Reuter's Telegram Co., Limited

豐茂 Foong-mow

Coutts & Co., 15 Foochow Road
  Coutts, J. C. (absent)
  Coutts, G. W.
    Hague, F. M.

高易 Kow-yih

Cowie, G. J. W., solicitor, 21 Foochow Road
  Cowie, Geo. J. W.
    Tong, L. Q.
    Chubing, L.

Cromie, Charles, public silk-inspector, 4 Nanking Road

錦名 King-meng

Cumine & Co., merchants, 6, Kiangse Road
  Cumine, Chas. (absent)
  Cumine, A. G. T.
  Cooper, John

Cussum, K., trader

正豐 Chin-foong

Da Costa & Co., Public Accountants, 25 Szechuen Road

復泰 Fooh-t'uy

Dadabhoy, Burjorjee, Shantung Road

Dallas, Barnes, bill and bullion broker, Bubbling-well Road

日昇 Yeh-shing

Daly, S., 26, Keangse Road, Thorne's Building

寶順 Pao-shun

Dent & Co., merchants
  Dent, John
    Wheeley, E.
    Tavares, L. A.

Dent & Co., Alfred, merchants, 4, Yangtsze Road
  Dent, Alfred
  Hanssen, H. P.
  Lawson, J.
  Russell, R. P.
  Johnsford, A.

廣興 Kwang-hing

Dhurumsey Poonjabhoy, 2, Szechuen Road
  Allybhoy, Khatow, (absent)

Dickinson & Co., merchants, 8, Peking Rd.
  FitzGerald, M. O.
  Stokes, F.

道盆 To-pun

Dobbyn, W. A., 20, Nanzing Road, Hongkew

聚盛 Chü-shing

Donaldson, & Co., 19, Wangpoo Road, Hongkew
  Donaldson, C. M.

和記 Hwo-ke

Dow, James, bill and bullion broker, 17, Peking Road

Drysdale, Ringer & Co.
  Drysdale, T. M.
  Ringer, J. M.
  Hawtrey, M.
  Danenberg, J.

敦和 Tun-wo

Dunn, C. A. L., 28, Szechuen Road
Gore-Booth, E. H.

愛密 Ai-mei

Eames, I. B., counsellor-at-law, 13, Yuen-ming-yuen Road
Enevinovo, A.

電線行 Teen-seen-hong

Eastern Extension Australasia and China Telegraph Co., Limited, 5, Nanking Road
  Ozlade, George, agent
  Rozario, R M.

八巴利 Pah-pa-le

Ebrahimbhoy Pabaney, 10, Sunkiang Road
  Fukir, M., manager

蘇州僑押卜祿 Nie-pa-doo-mo-wong

Edbrook & Co., carriage-builders and livery stable-keepers, Kiangse Road and Soochow Creek
  Edbrook, O.
  Mawhood. F.

合記冰廠 Hoh-ke-ping-ts'ang

E-kee Ice Houses, Soochow Creek, Hongkew
  Mustard & Co., agents

Empire Brewery & Aerated Mineral Water Works
  Evans, H., proprietor
  Knott, T.
  Josephs, L.
  Jims, T.

有立客 Yu-le-kah

Eureka Hotel, Hongkew Road
  Anderson, Mrs, manager

埃凡饅首店 Yae-fan-man-sae-teen

Evans & Co., shipchandlers, brewers, bakers, and Aerated Mineral Water Manufacturers; Manufactory, Hongkew Town Depot, Szechuen Road.
  Evans, H.
  Knott, J.

福盛 Foob-sung

Fabris, E. A., Corner of Peking and Keangse Roads

順昌洋行 Sun-chang-yang-hong

Fajard, Eugene & Co., public silk inspectors and general commission agents, Rue Montauban

Farnham, & Co., S. C., shipwrights, Hongkew
  Farnham. S. C.
  Blethen, C. P.
  Röhl, E.
  Blethen, C.
  Galles, F. W.
  Bruse, A.
  Simpson, J.
  Carmichael, A.
  Armstrong, O.
  Allan, J.
  Adams, G.
  Ivey, H.
  Giles, J.

末士法 Mih-sz-fah

Farr, E., Aerated Water Manufacturer 11 Foochow Road

恒安斐記

Fay, Miss, L. M., (Hongkew Road.)

德利琴行 Tub-le-jin-hong

Fentum, Geo. B., professor of music, piano tuner & repairer 8, Soochow Road

承和 Yoong-ho

Findlay, Wade & Co., merchants and commission agents, 6, Hankow Road
  Findlay, J. (absent
  Wade, H. T.
  Altum, W. E.
  Findlay, Jno.

理地會 Lee-tee-ni
Fisler, L. F., photographer

豐裕 Foong-yu
Fogg & Co., H. merchants, The Bund
    Twombly, J. F.
    Webb, S. D.
        Lines, A. J.
        Swany, A. F.

順章 Zung-tsang
Framjae Hormusjee & Co., 7 Keangse Road
    Hormusjee, Framjee (absent)
    Pestonjee, D
        Ruttonjee Maneckjee
        Framjee Cowasjee

英茂 Ying-mow
Francis & Co., R., merchants
    Francis, R.
    Shaw, W. H.

豐泰 Foong-tae
Frazar & Co., merchants, corner Foochow and Szechuen Roads
    Frazar, Everett (absent)
    Wetmore, W. S.
    Lindsley, John
        Eastlack, R. F.
        White, W.
        De Souza, M. S.
        Marques, J. M.
        Botelho, A. G.

法病房 Fah-bing-vong
Galle, P. E., ex-médecin de la marine, 3, Hongkong Road
    Pichon, L., D.M.P., Do.

太豐 Tai-foong
Gamwell, F. R., silk broker. 8, Hankow Road
    Gamwell, F. R.
    Hearn, H. R.
    Wilson, A. W.

Gervais, L., gunsmith, and practical engineer, Rue de Consulat, French Concession

慎生洋行 Zung-sung-yang-hong
Ghandy & Co., M. L., 7, Keangse Road
    Framjee Hormusjee and Co., agents

仁記 Jǎn-kee
Gibb, Livingston & Co., 14, Yangtsze Road
    Vickers, J. M.
    Wood, A C.
        White, F. G.
        Case, A. M.
        Simmonds, L. A.
        Daniel, H. W.
        Caldbeck, E. J.
        Sharp, C. S.
        Housman, O. V.
        Kerr, R. J.
        Hancock, H. S. (Hankow)

近看 Zung-ke
Gibb's Wharf
    Manthei, J.

英華書院 Ying-wa-shu-yuan
Gill, H. Scott, 18, Nanzing Road, Hongkew

太平 Tai-ping
Gilman & Co., merchants, 44, Kiukiang Road
    Lavers, E. H.
    Ramsay, H. F. (Hankow)
    Gilman, F.
        Green, F. J.
        Miller, W.
        Tobin, E.
        St. Croix, W. de
        Marsh, S.
        Gouillond, L.
        Harton, C. F.
        Fraser, Lewis (Hankow)
        Howell, R. W.

興隆 Shin-loong
Gipperich, E., merchant, corner of Canton and Honan Roads

萬利麵包舖 Van-le-mien-pau-poo
Godenrath & Co., H., bread and biscuit bakers and confectioners, 2 Ming-ong Road, Hongkew

福茂 Fooh-mow
Gombert, C., chronometer, watch, and clock maker, 3 Foochow Road
    Rietschler, R., assistant
    Gundorph, F.   do.

總會 Tsoong-way
Gore-Booth, R. H., 2, Yangtsze Road,

SHANGHAI.

郭部醫生 Go-bu-e-sang
Gottburg, W., M.D., 1 Foochow Road

克勒餒洋行 Kuh-luh-noo-yang-hong
Grenot, A., store-keeper, 50 Rue du Consulat, French Concession

Groom, Francis A., share broker, 15, Peking Road

老恆豐 Laou-hêng-foong
Habibhoy, Ahmedbhoy, Sungkiang Road
Habibhoy, A.
Khakeebhoy, C.

恆豐洋行 Hêng-foong-yang-hong
Habibhoy, R., merchant, Sungkiang Road
Khakeebhoy, C., manager

德泰 Teh-ta
Hague, W. A., public tea inspector, 4, Foochow Road

萊歌厲 Lay-koo-le
Haille, Ch. de la, ingénieur civil, No. 308, Rue de Consulat

褔利 Fuh-ie
Hall & Holtz, ship chandlers, general storekeepers, bakers, tailors, milliners, &c.
  Everall, H.
  Short, W. H.
  Dyer, H.
    Symons, H.
    Cowderoy, W.
    Seel, A. B.
    Sheargold, A.
    Cowderoy, J.
    Kahler, W. R.
    Kilner, W. outfitting department
    West, J. tailoring department
    Handel, H. do.
    Smith, A. millinery department
    Smith, Mrs. A. do.

哈華托 Hah-wa-t'oh
Harwood & Wainewright, 2 Balfour Buildings
  Harwood, W., solicitor (absent)
  Wainewright, R. E., solicitor
    Martin, M., clerk

Haslam, W. H., public tea inspector, Hankow Road (absent)

瓊記 K'ing-kee
Heard & Co., Augustine, merchants
  Fearon, R. I.
  Low, E. G
  Reding, J. E.
  Endicott, U. E.
  Jenkins, T. O. J. S.
  Hopkins, G. G.
  Fearon, J. S.
  D'Aquino, J. C.
  Kleczkowski, A.
  Fonseca, R. R.

Heard's Wharf
  Rohl, Gustav
  Allen, R.

Heinemann, Fritz, merchant

天茂 Tien-mow
Helbling & Co., J. C., 4 Nanking Road
  Hyslop, Walter

栢醫生 Pa-e-sang
Henderson, Edward, M.D., L.R.C.P., L.R.C.S. Edin., Municipal Surgeon and Health Officer, 22, Foochow Road

Hill, Charles E., care of J. H. Vail, Hunt's Wharf

永昌 Yung-chang
Hirsbrunner & Co., watchmakers, jewellers and general importers, 14, Foochow Rd.
  Hirsbrunner, J.
  Munz, J.

海利外國賬部 Hai-le-wai-kwok-cheung-poo
Hoilee & Enam, Nos. 1 to 5, Canton Road
  Hoilee, Y. manager
  Hock, L. C., assistant

老和記 Laou-ho-kee
Holdsworth, Edward, Hankow Road, public silk inspector

兆豐 Tsau-foong
Hogg Brothers, 13, Nanking Road
  Hogg, James (absent)
  Hogg, E. J.
  Burman, Andrew

Hogquist & Co., auctioneers and general commission agents, Rue Montauban
  Hogquist, Max.
  Nysten, G.

義記 Yi-kee

Holliday, Wise & Co., merchants, Keangse and Foochow Roads
  Barnes, J. P.
    Barlow, H. J. E.
    Beattie, Joseph
    Reddie, J. R.
    Hogarth, J. B.
    Rozario, P. do

清美 Tsing-mei

Holmes, & Co., M. G., shipping and commission agents, French Concession, corner of Montauban and Consulat Rds.
  Holmes, M. G.

天和 Tien-hwo

Hooper, E. A., upholsterer and cabinet-maker, 20, Foochow Road

德順羊牛肉庄 Tah-shun-yang-niew-yuh-tsang

Hopkins, W., butcher, 2, Tientsin Road

宵肉 Shau-yuh

Hotel Des Messageries Maritimes, 12, Rue du Consulate
  Chagneau, R., & Cie.

密采里 Mih-ts'ay-le

Hotel et Restaurant des Colonies, No. 66 Rue Montauban
  Brossard, J.
  Seisson, A.

華利洋行 Hwah-le-yang-hong

How, A. J., 2, Yuen-Ming-Yuen

Howie, Robt., general broker and commission agent

Hunt's Wharf, Hongkew Road
  Vail, John H., manager
  Rühl, Gustav
  Allen, R.
  Croal, J. P. (Pootung)
  Dredge, G. H., cust.-house officer

和興 Hwo-hing

Hutchings & Co., C. H., general brokers, shipping and commission agents

公茂 Koong-mow

Ilbert & Co., 22, Nankin Road
  Ilbert, A.

Imperial Hotel, French Bund
  Mills, H., proprietor
  Bernthal, H.
  Maloney, H.

利記 Le-ke

Jairazbhoy, Peerbhoy, merchant, 80, French Bund
  Mowjeebhoy, G., manager

廣利 Kwang-le

Jamieson & Co., merchants and commission agents, French Bund
  Jamieson, W. B.

哲醫生 Chi-i-sang

Jamieson, R. Alex., M.D.; M.R.C.S. Lond.; M.A.; F.R.G.S.

怡和 E-hwo

Jardine, Matheson & Co., merchants
  Agent — Russian Bank for Foreign Trade St. Petersburg, in China
  Johnson, F. B.
    Clarke, B. A.
    Jaffray, W.
    Orme, Peter
    Alford, E. P.
    Cheverton. J. H.
    Macgregor, J.
    McIvor, A.
    Glass, D.
    Yvanovich, A.
    Couto, F. J. de
    Ward, E.
    Gubbins, W. H.
    Sa, A. F. de
    Wood, R. H. R.
    Keswick, James, J.
    Orme, Philip

盈記 Ying-ke

Jenke & Co., C., milliners and drapers and general outfitters, 15, Szechuen Road
  Jenke, C.
  Lippe, J. F.

稟源 Way-yuen

Jenkins, F. H. B., 3, Honan Road.

SHANGHAI.

錫張醫生 Sheh-tsang-e-sang
Johnston, James, M D., Medical Officer, Judicial department, H.B.M. Consulate 8. Shantung Road

保德 Pao-tah
Jurgens and Borchardt, general brokers, commission agents and auctioneers, 12, Canton Road
  Jürgens, H. J.
  Borchardt, F.

有威 Yu-wai
Juvet, Leo., manufactory of soda water syphons, agent for Juvet's watches and general importers, 47 Rue Montauban, French Concession
  Juvet, Leo.

大英牛棚 Ta-ying-niew-p'ang
Keele, O. R. (the British Dairy), Maloo and Defence Creek, opposite the Racket Court

Kelly, & Co., booksellers, stationers, news and commission agents, Canton Road
  Kelly, J. M.
  Kelly, J. F.

同和 Toong-hwo
Kidner, Wm., architect, 14, Pekin Road

有恒 Yew-hŭng
Kingsmill, Thos. W., civil engineer and architect, 20, Keangse Road

順利 Zung-li
Kirchner, Böger & Co., 7, Hankow Road
  Böger, H.
  Grossmann, C. F. (absent)
  Burchard, E.
  Stein, F.

生源 Shang-yuen
Knights, A. E., French Concession, 3, Yang-king-bang

隆泰 Loong-tae
Knoop & Co., ship chandlers, storekeepers navy contractors, Szechuen Road, corner of Yang-king-bang Creek
  Knoop, H. A.
  Peters, H. (absent)

Knoop & Co.—(continued:)
  Pfaff, L.
  Hey, E.
  Remedios, S. B.
  Clans, Joh.

金先生 Kin-sin-sĕng
Kreyer, Carl T., Kiangnan Arsenal, translating department

法昌 Fuh-tsang
Lacroix, Cousins & Co., Yang-king-pang, French Concession
  Louvier, M.
  David, C.

怡豐 E-foong
Ladage, Oelke & Co., tailors and general outfitters, 6, Canton Road
  Oelke, D.
  Wennmohs, E.
  Wusterhausen, E
  Ulrichs, J. F.
  Wilk, C.

利記 Lee-kee
Lalcaca, E. P., general broker, 60, French Bund

陸家嘴角 Loh-kea-tsz-kohio
Lambert, A. G., ship builder, S. S. N. Co.'s Dock, Pootung, 44, Broadway, Hongque

泰興 Tae-shing
Lane, Crawford & Co., storekeepers, ship chandlers and auctioneers, Nanking Road
  Wilson, John
  Harvie, J. Alex.
  Relph, Henry
  Crawford, D. R. (Hongkong) absent
  Morton, J.
  Harris, W R. J.
  Hewett, W. H.
  Fairbairn, T. P.
  Allen, J. W.
  Annand, F.
  Cunningham, J.
  Purvis, J.
  Cuthbertson, R. B. (piano tuner)
  AUCTION DEPARTMENT.
  Triggs, A. S., auctioneer
  Braga, J.

羅林士 Loo-ling-sz
Laurence, H. A., account and estate agent, Thorne's Buildings, Kiangse Road

源源 Yuen-yuen
Lent, Wm., 19, Foochow Road

德和 Teh-oo
Lester, H., architect and contractor, surveyor Hongkong Fire Insurance Company, Yuen-ming-yuen Road

Limby & Co., H. J., accountants and brokers, wine and spirit importers and merchants 24, Nanking Road
    Limby, H. J.
    Papps, W.

景昌 King-ts'ang
Lindsay & Head, 3, Pekin Road
    Lindsay, G. A.
    Head, R. G.

小禮查 Seau-le-zo
Little Astor, 9, Wang-poo Road, Hongkew
    Silverthorne, A., proprietor

Little & Co., merchants, 22, Szechuen Road
    Little, Archd. J.
    Little, Robert W.
        Cance, W.
        Harvey, C. J.
        Dillon, J. G. B.

拜加醫生 Pa-ka-e-sung
Little, L. S., M.D., F.R.C.S.E., 10, Keangse Road

老德記 Lou-tih-ke
Llewellyn & Co., J., chemists, 1, Nanking Road
    Bradfield, J.
    Brewer, T.
    Coate, T. A.
    Stickler, F. M.

保家行 Pau-ka-hong
Lloyd's Register of British and Foreign Shipping, 21, Keangse Road
    Tucker, Joseph J., surveyor

美記 Mei-ke
Lowe & Co., W., next door to Messrs Telge, Nolting &c., French Bund
    Lowe, W.
    Sharp, J.

生昌 Sung-chang
MacBean, John 24, Nanking Road

裕盛 Yu-shing
Maclean & Co., P., 10, Canton Road
    Maclean, Peter
    Slaghek, E. H.

順信 Sing-zung
Maclean, Wm. S., public tea inspector, &c.

瑪高溫醫生在虹口五十三號 Mo-kau-wüng-e-sing
Macgowan, D. J., M.D., 85, Hongkew Road
    Carrigan, A. C.

大豐 Ta-foong
Mackay, G. & Co., upholsterers and cabinet makers, importers of furniture, and contractors, 11, Nanking Road
    Mackay, James
    Mackay, G.

隆茂 Loong-mow
Mackenzie & Co., 10, Canton Road
    Mackenzie, James (absent)
    Mackenzie, Robt.
    Powrie, James
    Richards, C. W.

Mackie, J. H., French Bund

崇雲 Zoong-yun
Mackintosh, L., bill and bullion broker

Macomber, Wm. H., (At Adamson, Bell & Co.)

Maertens, A. H., public silk inspector, 9, Keangse Road
    Maertens, A. H., (absent)
    Lessmann, G. W.

美查洋傢 Mei-cha-yang-chan
Major, Ernest, office, 197 Shantung Road, residence,—on the Bubbling Well Road

英商公生洋行
Malcolmson, W. L., coal merchant 10, Peking Road

麥利南傳而米大洋行
Mah-le-nan-boo-urh-u-me-da-yung-hoon
Marinelli, & Co., storekeepers 26, and 28, Rue du Consulat, French concession
　Marinelli, E.
　Parlati, A.

Mariner's Home 5, Hongkew Road
　Murphy, M. W., proprietor
　　Reardon, J. H., assistant

規矩堂 Kway-chü-dong
Masonic Hall, 21, Yangtsze Road
　Hore, T.

McLoughlin, Eugene, share broker, Balfour Buildings

第福來 Dee-fuh-ta
Meilhan, A. & Co., Boulangerie Provençale, Rue Montauban, next door to the Hotel des Colonies
　Meilhan, A.

義泰洋行 Ee-t'a-yang-hong
Meller, & Co., auctioneers of real estate, shares and damaged goods, 15, Szechuen Road
　Meller, Hy.
　　Souza, B. de

同治印書館 T'ung-che-yin-shoo-kwan
Mercantile Printing Office
　Rozario, C. E. do
　Rozario, Arnaldo A. do

彌納 Me-nah
Meynard, Cousins & Cie.
　Meynard, Henri (absent)
　　Pelegrin, Henri (Yokohama)

中庸 Chung-yung
Miller, McKenzie & White, bill and bullion brokers, 18a, Nankin Road
　Miller, Rowley
　McKenzie, R. (absent)
　White, Aug.
　Miller, J. J.
　　Kum Allum

長源裡面和明 Chang-yuen-le-meen-ho-ming
Miller, W., 13, Szechuen Road
　Green, F. J.

Millot & Co., E., merchants, Yang-king-pang
　Millot, E.
　Teillot, A.

恒豐 Hüng-foong
Mody, P. C., general broker, 11, Sungkiang Road

寶昌 Pau-t'sang
Moffat, Weiters & Co., 9, Kiangse Road
　Moffat, Robt. C. D. (absent)
　Weiters, E. B.
　Bean, Alfred

稟源 Wai-nuen
Möller, Maitland & Co., temporary address 8, Honan Road
　Möller, J. C. Julius
　Maitland, John
　　Hübler, Ad.

資賜 Lay-zu
Möller, Nils, ship, freight and general broker, commission agent and auctioneer, 4, Foochow Road
　Möller, Nils
　Möller, Rehr

安成 Oan-zhing
Monro & Co., G. A., tea inspectors and general commission agents, Canton Road
　Monro, G. A.
　McAllister, D.
　Vickers, A. J.

魯意師摩 Loo-e-sz-mo
Moore, L., broker and commission agent, 13, Kiangse Road

莫汝 Moh-zü
Morel, E., bill, bullion and stock broker 81, Kiangse Road

Morphew, John S. Newspaper agent

浦東 P'o-toong
Morrice, Behncke & Co., shipwrights and blacksmiths
　Morrice, Thomas
　Behncke, Henry

馬立師 Mo-le-sz

Morris, Lewis & Co., commission and ship agents, French Bund
  Morris, John (absent)
  Lewis, George
  Brown, A. N.
  Yungkee, T., agents tug steam "Foheen"

Morriss, Henry, bill and bullion brokers, Mohawk Lodge, Race Course, Office 18, Szechuen Road

美記 May-ke

Muller, & Co., H., watchmakers Canton Rd.
  Pfaff, I.
  Pfaff, L.
  Pfaff, R.
  Wilhelm, E.

天和 Tien-oo

Muller & Fisher, general contractors for house-work, house and sign painters, 20, Foochow Road
  Fisher, A. A.

地亞士 Di-a-sze

Muller & Co., J. W., merchants 12, Szechuen Road
  Muller, J. W.
  Siebke, H.
  Muller, O.
  Jansen, J. E.
  Ricke, Th.

Mustard & Co., California store and general agency, commission agents, 4, Canton Road
  Mustard, R. W.
  Bennett, C. C.

梅博閣 May-pho-koh

Myburgh, Alex., barrister-at-Law, 1 Yuen-ming-yuen buildings
  Hore, Thos. clerk

泰昌 Tae-chang

Nachtrieb, Leroy & Co., merchants, and agents of French Gas Co., 6, Kiangse Road
  Nachtrieb, A.
  Leroy, E.
  Schönhard, G.
  Baconnier, A.
  Xitco, A.

南登洋行 Nam-tang-yang-hong

Nathan, Maurice J., merchant, 7, Foochow Road

字林洋行 Tze-lin-yang-hong

North-China Herald and *Supreme Court & Consular Gazette*, and *North China Daily News* Office, 10, Hankow Road
  Tootal, J. Broadhurst (absent)
  Gundry, R. S., editor
  Smith, Pat, Rose, sub-editor
  Smith, D. Wares, accountant
  Brown, John, clerk
  Wright, F., reporter
  Merrilées, A. G., foreman printer

"Nucleus, The," Billiard and Luncheon Rooms, 2, Canton Road
  Ocker, John J.

萬福 Man-fook

Nysten & Co., auctioneers, Szechuen Road
  Nysten, G.

通源 T'oong-neuen

Oliveira & Co., general brokers and commission agents 17, Rue de Consulat
  Oliveira, A. M. d'

阿力弗 Ah-lih-feh

Oliver, E. H., civil and mining engineer and surveyor, lower Yuen-ming-yuen Road

同孚 Tung-foo

Olyphant & Co., merchants, Nanking Road
  Hayes, A. A., Jr.
  Olyphant, Talbot
  Wisner, J. H.
  Chrystall, W.
  Hollingworth, H. G.
  Smith, E. U.
  Allen, J. C., Jr.
  Fuller, J. O.
  Campbell, A.
  Reid, F.
  Xavier, C. A.
  Gutierrez, E. B.
  Barretto, L.
  Carvalho, J.

順發 Zung-fah

Overbeck, & Co., merchants, Macao Buildings, Yuen-ming-yuen
  Overbeck, Hermann
  Scheeffer, G.

SHANGHAI. J 27

Oxley, E. G., 11, Foochow Road

永泰 Yung-tah

Papps, Wm., wine and spirit merchant, and importer, French Bund

裕記 Yu-ke

Paul, R., compradore, French Concession

深利 Pae-lee

Peil, F., Szechuen Road
  Peil, F. (absent)
  Heyden, F. E.
  Goetz, A.

Penrose, J. H., broker, Soochow Road

高花藥房 Ko-fa-yeuk-foug

Pharmacie de l'Union, Corner of Canton and Keangse Roads.—*See Advt.*
  Koffer, Th. (Hongkong)
  Voilkel, S., manager
  Grimm, B.

筆刺 Pe-la

Pila, Ulysse, & Co., 9, Pekin Road
  Pila, Ulysse (absent)
  Geller, R.

波利 Poo-la

Polite, George, hairdresser (opposite the British Post Office), Nanking Road
  Vernet, Edouard
  Pearse, Henry

Pootung Wharf
  Croal, J. P.
  Dredge, G. H., Customs Officer

昇寶 Sing-pau

Primrose & Co., commission merchants, Canton Road, Corner of Honan Road
  Primrose, J. A.

惠麟 Way-ling

Primrose, W. M., 21, Canton Road

萬隆 Wan-loong

Provand & Co., A., 8, Pekin Road
  Provand, A.
  Monat, A. R. Dundas (absent)
  Farrar, A. A. E.
  Diniz, S. J.

同珍 Tung-chin

Purdon & Co., 12 Nankin Road
  Purdon, J. G.
  Tilghman, Jr., W. C.

Pustau & Co., Wm., merchants, The Bund
  Behn, O. C.
  Detmering, H.
  Burchardi, F.
  Beyfuss, Ch.
  Spitz, E.
  Pandorf, G.
  Malteau, G., tea inspector
  Rehders, E.
  Gönner, A, von

利華 Lee-wah

Rainbow, B., broker and commission agent

履泰 Lo-tae

Reid, Evans & Co., merchants, Peking Rd.
  Reid, David
  Evans, M. P.
    Manson, J. B.
    Robertson, Thos.
    Cordova, J. de
    Arbuthnot, E. O.
    Macdonald, T. J.
    Souza, B. de

泰和 Tae-wo

Reiss & Co., merchants, corner of Hankow and Szechuen Roads
  Kalb, Moritz
  Bromley, J. R.
  Percival, M. H.
  Marçal, F. P. S.

Remé & Co., William, merchants, Hankow Road
  Remé, W.
  Schutze, C. H. F.

利名 Le-ming

Remi de Montigny, merchant, Yang-king-pang, French Concession
  Montigny, Rémi de (absent)
  Agents—Millot & Co.

Remusat, Mons., 80, Kiangse Road, Corner of Pekin Road.

連厘狀師 Lian-le-chong-sz
Rennie & Drummond, Barristers at Law, 2 Yuen-ming-yuen buildings
 Rennie, R. T.
 Drummond, W. V.
  Aroozoo, J. J., clerk

Reuter's Telegram Company, Limited, 18, Szechuen Road
 Corner, Geo. R., acting agent

利南查 Le-nay-zo
Reynolds, E. A., Pootung Point

源順 Yuen-zung
Rivington, Charles, stock and share broker and commission agent, 23, Szechuen Road & Bubbling Well Road, general agent for China Telegram Co.

Roberts, John P., surveyor, office with Messrs. John Thorne & Co.

源利 Yuen-le
Robins & Co., furniture dealers, 48, Rue Montauban

樂皮生 Loh-be-sung
Robinson, A., solicitor, 4, Balfour Buildings
 Bailey, John

復隆 Vooh-loong
Robison, J. S., public silk inspector 16, Yangtsze Road
 Gillett, B.

阿化威 Ah-hwo-way
Rodewald, Schönfeld & Co., 4, Hongkong Road
 Rodewald, J. F.
 Schönfeld, F. (Foochow)
 Young, J. M.
 Götze, W.

昇泰 Sing-tae
Rothwell, Love & Co., merchants, Canton Road
 Rothwell, Thomas
 Love, J., Jr.
 Love, S. C.

羅生藥房 Loo-sung-yah-fong
Rozario & Co., F., chemists, No. 27, Broadway, Hongkew
 Rozario, F.

旗昌 Kee-chang
Russell & Co., merchants, Yangtsze Road
 Forbes, F. B.
 Fitz, W. Scott (Hankow)
 Hitch, F. D.
 Forbes, H. De C.
  Dalmeida, E. F.
  Beebe, Chas. G. (Ningpo)
  Broadbent, J. W.
  Bush, F D.
  Cordier, H.
  Cunningham, H. M. (Hankow)
  Du Jardin, F.
  Dumaresq, P. K.
  Eckfeldt, T. W.
  Gilbert, S. S.
  Goodfellow, J. F.
  Hüchting, F. (Ningpo)
  Howard, J. J. (Hankow)
  Johanssen, F.
  Lovet, W. W,
  Losch, E. (Tientsin)
  Moore, M. G. do.
  Maclay, R. H. do.
  Nash, Herbert
  Nickels, M. C.
  Röhl, E.
  Rose, S. C. (Kewkiang)
  Thorburn, J. D.
  Voisin, A.
  Webb, E.
  Weld, J. D.
  Wheeler, G. H.

永順泰 Yoong-zung-t'a
Russell, Roa & Co., brokers, 6, Sunkiang Road

新沙遜 Sin-so-sung
Sassoon & Co., E. D., merchants, 14, Foochow Road
 Sassoon, Jacob E.
  Elias, J. B.
  Joseph, D.
  Nathan, J. J.
  Muslieh, M. H.
  O'Hara, H.
  Ezra, J. (Chefoo)
  Nathan, S. J.
  Benjamin, B. D. (Tientsin)
  Yaish, S. Y. (do)
  Nathan, E. E. (do.)
  Joseph, J. (Newchwang)
  Ferry, J. S. do.

SHANGHAI.

沙宜 Sa-suen

Sassoon, Sons & Co., David, merchants, The Bund (temporarily removed to Hankow Road)
  Gubbay, M. S.
  Moses, S. M.
  Saul, J.
  Solomon, M.
  Nathan, J. A.
  Moses, D. E.
  Meyer, J.
  Wolff, Marcus
  Hunt, W. E.
  Clarke, George

森泰像館 Sǔng-t'a-zeung-kwan

Saunders' Photographic Studio, 8, Wangpoo Road, Hongkew
  Saunders, W.
  Griffith, D. K.
  Carani, F.
  Saunders, H. C.

些厘公司 Sa-lee-kung-sz

Sayle & Co., linen drapers, silk mercers, tailors and outfitters, Nanking and Szechuen Roads, and Victoria Exchange, Hongkong
  Sayle, Robt. (England)
  Spring, E. H.
  Sayle, T. H
  Eustace, F. O.
  Johnson, R.
  Chalker, A.
  Waples, H.
  Cruz, A. da
  Richards, Mrs.

杏利生 Aug-le-sung

Sayn, Henri, Rue Consulat, Municipal Hall

元亨 Yuen-hang

Schellhass, E. & Co., French Bund
  Schellhass, Eduard (absent)
  Beyer, Ludwig (Hongkong)
  Bade, C. Emil
    Claussen, Franz E.
    Schomburg, Aug.
    Burmeister, Emil
    Bohlschau, P.

Scheppleman, Chr., accountant and Bookkeeper

Schmidt, J. Meinhard, public accountant, bill collector, &c., 16, Rue du Consulat

裕豐洋行 Hiew-foong-yang-hang

Schofield, R., Rue de Colbert, French concession

大來 Da-lai

Schrader, H. L., watch and chronometer maker, 18, Keangse Road

公記西棧 Kung-chi-see-bah

Scott, Thomas, 11, Rue Colbert, French Concession

上海牛乳房龍飛對門 Shan-hai-new-lu-vong-loong-fei-tuy-mun

Shanghai Dairy, opposite the Shanghai Horse Bazaar, New Race Course
  Sewjee, proprietor

補醫生 Poo-e-sung

Shanghai Dispensary, 1, Canton Road
  Wallis Wm.

通聞館 Toong-vung-kwan

Shanghai *Evening Courier*, 8, Honan Road
  Lang, H., editor and proprietor
  Marshall, T., accountant
  Rooke, A. J., general assistant
  Milley, W., foreman

龍飛 Loong-fe

Shanghai Horse Bazaar, New Race Course commission agents, auctioneers, &c.
  Crofts, J.
  Sewjee,

老上海 Laou-shang-hai

Shanghai Hotel, 10 and 11, Foochow Road
  Searle and Kermath, proprietors
  Searle, J.
  Kermath, J. S.

老德記 Lao-toh-kee

Shanghai Medical Hall
  Llewellyn & Co., J.
  Bradfield, J.
  Bremer, T.
  Coate, T. A.
  Stickler, F. M.

Shanghai News-Letter, monthly newspaper, office, 8, Canton Road
 Thorne & Co., Jno., proprietors

李百里 Le-pah-le
Shaw, Brothers & Co., 10, Yangtsze Road
 Krauss, Alfred A.
 Nicholson, C.
 Buckley, H. P.

申報館 Shun-pau-koon
"Shun-pau" Daily News, 197, Shantung Road
 Major, Ernest, General manager
 Tsiang Tsz siang, Editor
 Ou Tsz-kiang,   do.
 Liu Hoh-peh,   do.
 Pau Yan-yun,   do.

禪臣 Sim-zŭng
Siemssen & Co., merchants, 19, Yangtsze Road
 Nissen, F.
 Peters, G.
 Koch, W. L. jr.
 Tornöe, H.
 Pinckvoss, J. H.
 Paasch, C. W.
 Oelrichs, H.
 Tiefenbacher, Max.

Silverthorne & Co., A., coal and general agents, 8, Wangpoo Road, Hongkew
 Silverthorne, A.

義昌 Yie-chang
Skeggs & Co., C. J., public silk inspectors and commission agents, 1, Kewkeang Rd.
 Skeggs, C. J.
 Gilmour, D. (absent)
 Smith, F. M.

成昌 Zŭng-ts'ang
Smart. Geo. F., 20, Kiangse Road

隆盛 Loong-zŭng
Smith, Archer & Co., 7, Hankow Road
 Blydenburgh, W. J.
 Thompson, A. F.
 Robertson, P.
 Carlton, I. Osgood

麗泉 Le-zien
Smith, E. M., 1, Honan Road

廣和 Kwang-wo
Smith, George & Co., wine, spirit and beer merchants, Foochow Road
 Smith, George
 Smith, Thomas (absent)
 Pallister, Edmund
 Morphew, J. S.

裕生 Yue-sung
Stephenson & Co., general auctioneers, Canton Road, adjoining Messrs. Mackenzie & Co.'s
 Stephenson, W. E.
 Senna, C. M.

老元方 Lau-yuen-fong
Stewart & Ellis, bill, bullion, share and general brokers
 Stewart, W. J. E.
 Ellis, G. J.

庚興 Kang-hsing
Tata, D. C., 9, Rue Montauban, Concession
 Tata, D. Burjorjee
 Pestonjee, R.

公立 Koong-lih
Tate & Hawes, Masonic Hall, on the Bund
 Tate, J. Priestley
 Hawes, J. A.
 Duval, A. T.

安泰 An-t's
Taylor & Bennett, 24, Szechuen Road
 Taylor, Joseph M.
 Keir, W.
 Shepherd, J. W.

泰來 T'a-lai
Telge, Nölting & Co., French Bund
 Telge, B., (absent)
 Nölting, J.
 Dietrich, O.
 Meincke, G.

英茂 Ying-mow
Thorburn, R. F., 7, Peking Road

SHANGHAI.

廣達 Kwong-deh

Thorndike, & Co., J. K., 1, Whangpoo Road, Soochow Creek Godowns and Lumber Yard
  Thorndike, J. K.

元芳 Yuen-fong

Thorne, Brothers & Co., merchants 9a, Yangtsze Road
  Thorne, J. (absent)
  Maitland, J. A.
    Pryer, W. B. (absent)
    Hague, E. P.
    Bradley, W. M.
    Rasch, J. M.

同茂 Toong-mow

Thorne, Rice & Co., merchants, Yangtsze Road
  Thorne, John
  Rice, E. W.
    Hagelstange, G. E.

義茂洋行 Ee-mow-yang-hang

Thurburn, A., 22, Nankin Road

華記 Wah-kee

Turner & Co., 7, Yangtsze Road
  Smith, E. C.
    Sharp, W. Forbes (*Hankow*)
    Reynell, H.
    Uaill, H. S. B.
    Southwell, R. Elliot

松茂 Soong-mow

Twigg, Mrs., P. O'B., undertaker and municipal sexton, Rue de Montauban

富碩 Foo-zah

Vaucher Freres, Yang-king-pan Creek
  Millot & Co., agents

天源洋行 Tien-yuen-yang-hong

Vogel, Hagedorn & Co., merchants, 9, Honan Road
  Kirchhoff, Heinrich
    Vogel, Edward
    Höhne, Arno
    Hohn, Gustav

威公館 Wei-koong-kwan

Viguier, S. A., divisional inspector and harbour master, 1, Whangpoo Road, Hongkew

亨達利 Hang-dah-le

Vrard, & Co., L., storekeepers, and watch and clock makers, 2, Keangse Road
  Vrard, L.
  Laidrich, F. (Tientsin)
  Sillem, H.
    Borel, L. (Tientsin)
    Martinot, G. (do.)
    Ribert, F.
    Loup, P. (Tientsin)
    Hirsbrunner, J.

華立師 Wa-lap-sz

Wallace, James F., 6, Yuen-Ming-Yuen Buildings

華而師 Wha-erh-szu

Walsh, F. & C., printers publishers and stationers, 3, Canton Road
  Walsh, F. G.
  Walsh, A.
    Symons, J.
    Blanchard, Capt. ("Puck" office)

南順泰 Nam-sun-tai

Waters, D. W., & Co., commission agents and general merchants, Bund, French Concession

公咸 Kung-zing

Watson, Will, Rue Colbert, French Concession

Watson & Co., W., milliners and outfitters Nankin Road
  Peacock, T. (London)
  Byrne, E.
  Skeels, H. J.
    Stewart, J. A.
    York, G. E.
    Dunnill, J.
    Rawlinson, C. J.
    Hull, W. M.
    Wheeler, F.
    Goodwin, W.
    Osborne, J. H.
    Allen, Mrs J. W.
    Garrette, Miss M. D.
    Stewart, Mrs J. A.

大藥房 Tai-yeuk-iong
Watson, Cleave & Co., English & Foreign Chemists, 2, Nankin Road, "Shanghai Pharmacy"
 Cleave, S. W.
  Bateman, T. H.
  Clarke, W. L.

公易 Kung-yih
Westall, Brand & Co., Public Silk Inspectors, 23, Nankin Road
 Westall, Alfred C.
 Brand, William
  Dyce, C. M.
  Phillips, S. T. L.

大成洋行 Da-zung-yang-hong
Weston & Co., public tea inspectors, 3, Peking Road
 Weston, J. G.

Wheelock & Co., commission merchants, &c
 Wheelock, T. R.
 Silva, D. A.
 Souza, D. M.
 Matthews, W. G.

Winn, H. H., D.D.S., dental surgeon, 33, Szechuen Road

祥茂 Tsiang-meaou
Wright, Burkill & Co., commission agents and public silk inspectors, 11, Szechuen Road
 Wright, James H. (absent)
 Burkill, A. R.

天陞 Tien-sung
Wright, J. W., 6, Honan Road
 Birt, W., agent

鎭 CHINKEANG. 江

Consulates.

AUSTRO-HUNGARY.
大奧國領事官
Ta-ngao-kwoh-ling-shih-kwan

Consul (residing at Shanghai)—Schlick, Rudolf

DENMARK.
大丹國領事官
Ta-tan-kwoh-ling-shih-kwan

Acting Consul—Allen, C. F. R.

GREAT BRITAIN.
大英國領事官
Ta-ying-kwoh-ling-shih-kwan

Interpreter in Charge—Allen, C. F. R.
Constable—Nunn, Charles

UNITED STATES.
大美國領事官
Ta-mei-kwoh-ling-shih-kwan

Consul—Flint, Weston
Vice-Consul and Deputy Consul—Emery, David A.
Interpreter—Emery, David A.
Marshal—
Clerk of Court—Watts, Andrew C.
Chinese Secretary—Li-Jeu-chai

Imperial Maritime Customs.
鎭海關 Chun-hai-kwan

Commissioner—Detring, G. (absent)
Acting Commissioner—Novion, A.
1st Assistant—Sidford, H. Æ.
2nd do.—Courtan, A.

Imperial Maritime Customs.
(Continued.)

3rd do.—Abbott, R. J.
Tide Surveyor—Goldspink, R. J.
Examiners—Lowe, J., Menzies, A. B.; Dubois, J.
Tidewaiters—Watson, J.; Gray, W.; Crouch, J.; Eggert, J.; Maitland, T. W.; Vermaitre, A. L.
1st Linguin—Wang Kum Ping
2nd do.—Lam Tat Hing
3rd do.—Wang

DORIC LODGE, 1,488, E.C.

Worshipful Master—Sidford, H. Æ.
Senior Warden—Gearing, J. G. W.
Junior do.—Abbott, R. J.
Secretary and Treasurer—Williamson, Geo.
Senior Deacon—Menzies, A. B.
Junior do.—Deslandes, F.
Inner Guard—Goldspink, R. J.
Tyler—Nunn, C.
Meets: Second Tuesday in each month at 9 P.M.

Missionaries.

CHINA INLAND MISSION.
大英內地會
Ta-yin-nai-ti-hwui

Judd, C. H., and Mrs. (absent)
Desgraz, Miss (Girls' School)
Bowyer, Miss (do.) (absent)
Taylor, Rev. J. H., and Mrs (Yangchow)
Williamson, Rev. J. (Nankin)
Fishe, E., and Mrs (Yangchow)
Fishe, C. T.

UNCONNECTED.

White, R. G., and Mrs
Bagnall, B.

Insurance.

Canny & Co., J. M.
    Hongkong Fire Insurance Co. Limited
    Chinese Insurance Company Limited
    Hongkong Insurance Co. 1871-74
    China Traders' Insurance Co. Limited
Salter, A. E.
    Pacific Life Company
    Yangtsze Insurance Association, S'hai
Spencer, A. W.
    Scottish Imperial Insurance Company

Merchants, &c.

有源行 Yu-yün-hong
Bean, William, merchant and commission agent

亨利行 Hêng-li-hang
Canny & Co., J. M., merchants
    Canny, J. M. (absent)
    Carnie, F.
        Starkey, E.

萬和行 Man-ho-hong
Chee Yeong, C., merchant and commission agent

China Navigation Company
    Agents—Canny & Co., J. M.

順章行 Shun-chang-hong
David, D. W., merchant and commission agent

德隆行 Tê-lung-hong
Deslandes & Co., F., freight broker and commission agent

Express, Shanghai Steam Navigation Co.'s Receiving Ship
    Agent—Salter, A. E.
        Watts, A. C.
        William, R. T.

新德和行 Hsin-tê-ho-hong
Gearing, J. G., merchant and commission agent

徐來泰行 Hsü-lai-t'ai-hong
Giolitti, —., merchant and commission agent

中和行 Chung-ho-hong
Jerdein, M. S., merchant and commission agent

萬順 Man-shun
Middleton & Co., O., storekeepers and compradores

旗昌行 Ch'i-ch'ang-hong
Salter, A. E., merchant and commission agent

怡和行 I-ho-hong
Spencer, A. W., merchant and commission agent
    Spencer, S. B., assistant

泰昌行 Tai-ch'ang-hong
Wadleigh & Emery, general and commission merchants
    Wadleigh, E. C. (New York City)
    Emery, David H.

裕順行 Yü-shun-hong
Walker, W. F., commission agent

永祥行 Yung-hsiang-hong
Williamson & Co., general commission and freight agents
    Williamson, Geo.

祥興行 Hsiang-hsing-hong
Spencer, S. B., merchant and commission agent

九 KEWKEANG. 江

Consulates.

AUSTRO-HUNGARIAN MONARCHY.
Consul—King, W. E.

DENMARK.

大丹國領事官
Ta-tan-kwoh-ling-shih-kwan

Consul—King, W. E.

FRANCE.

大法國領事官
Ta-fa-kwoh-ling-shih-kwan

Acting Consul and Chancellor Interpreter—Blancheton, Ernest (resident at Hankow)

GREAT BRITAIN.

大英國副領事官
Ta-ying-kwoh-fu-ling-shih-kwan

Vice-Consul—King, W. E. (absent on leave)
Acting Interpreter in Charge—Parker, E. H.
Constable—Adams, M. J.

UNITED STATES.

大美國領事官
Ta-mei-kwoh-ling-shih-kwan

Consular Agent—Rose, S. C.

Municipal Council.

工部 Kung-po

Chairmen—King, W. E.
Secretary—Shaw, W. H.
Treasurer—Anderson, J. H.
Constables—Adams, M.; and 4 Chinese policemen

Imperial Maritime Customs.

九江海關 Kew-keang-hai-kwan

Commissioner—Kopsch, H.
Assistants—May, F. Nevill; Von Moellendorff, P. G.
Tide Surveyor—Lovatt, W. N.
Examiners—Porter, J. C.; Moore, C. F.
  Ballantine, G.
Tide Waiters—Harrison, W. G.; Wilgaard, A.; Brown, R.; Castro, A.; Swainson, G.; Reeks, A. J.

Missions.

AMERICAN METHODIST EPISCOPAL.

福音堂 Fooh-yin-tang

Hart, V. C., and Wife
Ing, John, and Wife
Hall, Henry H. (absent)
Stritmatter, A.
Houy, Miss Lucy H.
Howe, Miss Gertrude

CHINA INLAND MISSION.

大英內地會 Tai-yin-nai-ti-hwui

Cardwell, Rev. J. E., and Mrs
Groombridge, F.
Donovan, J. (Gan-k'ing)

FRENCH.

Bishop—Bray, Monseigneur
Priests—Rouger, Rev. F.; Portes, Rev. A.; Anot, Rev. P.; Sassi, Rev. P.

Insurances.

Francis & Co., R.
  Hongkong Insurance Co., 1871-74
  North China Insurance Company
  China Traders' Insurance Company
  Chinese Insurance Co., Limited
  China and Japan Marine Ins. Co.
  China Fire Insurance Company
  Imperial Fire Insurance Company

Jardine, Matheson & Co.
    Canton Insurance Office
    Hongkong Fire Insurance Company
Russell & Co.
    Yangtsze Insurance Association
    Victoria Fire Insurance Co. of Hongkong, Limited

Merchants, &c.

英茂 Ying-mow

China Navigation Company
    Agents—Francis & Co., R.

Francis & Co., R., merchants
    Francis, R.
    Shaw, W. H.

Hulk *Sultan*
    Hulk Keeper—Beangie, John

怡和 E-wo

Jardine, Matheson & Co., merchants
    Anderson, R. (Hankow)
    Anderson, J. H.

同利 Toong-li

Lethbridge, Tyndall, M.D.

Receiving Hulks, Russell & Co., *Ganges* and *Sterling*
    In charge—Alsing, Auguste H.

旗昌 Chee-chang

Russell & Co., merchants
    Rose, S. E.
    Weld, E. D.
    Buffam, C. H.

Shanghai Steam Navigation Company
    Agents—Russell & Co.

Shearer, George, M.D., physician

漢 HANKOW. 口

Consulates.

AUSTRO-HUNGARIAN MONARCHY.
Consul—Hughes, Patrick J.

DENMARK.
大丹國領事官
Ta-tan-kwoh-ling-shih-kwan
Consul—Hughes, Patrick J.

FRANCE.
大法國領事官
Ta-fa-kwoh-ling-shih-kwan
Acting Consul—Blancheton, Ernest

GREAT BRITAIN.
大英國領事官
Ta-ying-kwoh-ling-shih-kwan
Consul—Hughes, Patrick J.
Interpreter—McClatchie, H. P.
Senior Assistant—Fraser, J. P. M.
Constable—Stevens, T.

PORTUGAL.
Consul—Evans, J. H.

RUSSIA.
大俄羅斯國領事官
Ta-ngo-lo-sze-kwoh-ling-shih-kwan
Vice-Consul—Ivanoff, N.

UNITED STATES.
大美國領事官
Ta-mei-kwoh-ling-shih-kwan
Consul for Hankow & Kewkiang—Johnson, R. M.
Acting Vice-Consul—Jenkins, M. A.
Interpreter—Jenkins, M. A.
Acting Marshal—Corter, John

Municipal Council.
工部 Kung-po
Anderson, R.
Dawbarn, A. H.
Falconer, J.
Ramsay, H. F.
Mackellar, M. R., secretary

Police.
Sergeant—Blackert, Hermann Johann
10 Chinese Constables

Imperial Maritime Customs.
江漢關 Kiang-han-kwan
Commissioner—Macpherson, A.
Deputy do.—Noetzli, G. H.
1st Assistant—Brett, A. L.
2nd do.—Lay, A.
3rd do.—Lépissier, E. L.
Tide-surveyor—May, J. H.
Examiners—Dix, W.; Eldredge, C. J; (on leave) Burnett, J. H.; Pike, C. H.; Sayle, W. J.; Sinnott, P. W.; Mesney, J.
Tidewaiters—Purcell, P. U.; Bayley, O. E.; Kindblad, A.; Gika, N. D.; Keymer, W. J.; Borrodaile, J. F.

MEDICAL OFFICER.
Reid, A. G., M.D.

Missions.

AMERICAN PROTESTANT EPISCOPAL MISSION.
Höhing, Rev. A. C.
Hoyt, Rev. S R J. (Wuchang)
Boone, Rev. W. S. (do.)

LONDON MISSIONARY SOCIETY.
倫敦會 Lun-don-wui
John, Rev. Griffith
Bryson, Rev. Thomas (Wuchang)
Foster, Rev. Arnold, B.A. (Hanyang)

WESLEYAN MISSIONARY SOCIETY.

Scarborough, Rev. Wm.
Hardey, E. P., medical missionary, L.R.C.P.
 London, M R C S. England
Cox, Rev Josiah (Wu-chang)
Brewer, Rev. J. W. (do.)
Hill, Rev. David (Wusueh)
Race, Rev. Joseph (do.)

Insurances.

Ballance & Co.
 Scottish Imperial Insurance Company
Drysdale, Ringer & Co.
 Canton Insurance Office (Marine)
 China Traders' Insurance Co., Limited (Marine)
 Hongkong Fire Insurance Company, Limited
 Queen Insurance Co. (Fire)
Evans Pugh & Co.,
 Phœnix Fire Insurance Co.
 Chinese Insurance Co., Limited
 Merchants' Mutual Marine Insurance Co. of San Francisco
Gibb, Livingston & Co.
 Imperial Fire Insurance Co (London)
 Union Insurance Society of Canton
 China Fire Insurance Co., Limited
Gilman & Co.
 North British and Mercantile Insurance Company (Fire)
 Universal Marine Insurance Company of London
 Ocean Marine
 Merchants' Marine, Limited
 London and Lancashire Fire Insurance Company
Gordon Bros.
 Swiss Lloyds Marine Insurance Co.
Ivanoff, N. A.
 "Jakor" Insurance Co.
Major & Smith
 Guardian Assurance Office
 China and Japan Marine Insurance Company
Russell & Co
 Yangtsze Insurance Association
 Victoria Fire Insurance Company of Hongkong
Shaw, Ripley & Co.
 Royal Insurance Company of Liverpool
 The Union Marine Insurance Company, Limited
 Lloyds
Turner & Co.
 North China Insurance Company
 Northern Assurance Company

Merchants, etc.

名利 Ming-lee

Ballance & Co., merchants
 Ballance, T. F.

Beazley, Paget & Co., merchants
 Beazley, Henry
 Paget, Thomas Guy (absent)
 Stein, G. A.

原大 Yün-ta

Bell, Captain G. E., hotel proprietor

廣豐 Kwang-fung

Bröndsted, R., merchant

密架釐 Ma-ka-lee

Chartered Bank of India, Australia and China
 Thorburn, Henry, agent

Chartered Mercantile Bank of India, London and China
 Morrison, John, acting agent

德興 Tuck-hing

China Navigation Company
 Agents—Drysdale, Ringer & Co.
Hulks "Tchapou," and "Kinsan"
 In charge—Weatherstone, Thos.

德興 Tuck-hing

Drysdale, Ringer & Co., merchants
 Drysdale, T. M.
 Ringer, J. M. (Shanghai)
 Wood, Thos.
 King J. D.
 Miller, D. A.

普義 Po-yee

Dupuis, J., merchant

寶順 Po-shun

Evans, Pugh & Co., merchants
 Evans, J. H. (absent)
 Pugh, W.
 Fonseca, F. V. da
 Walter, W.

HANKOW.

和昌 Ho-ch'ang
Falconer, J., M.R.C.S.

仁記 Yun-kee
Gibb, Livingston & Co., merchants
  Hancock, H. S., agent and tea inspector

太平 Tai-ping
Gilman & Co., merchants
  Ramsay, H. F.
  Fraser, L.

Glasgow Art Union
  Agent—Mackellar, M. R.

隆太 Lung-t'ai
Gordon Bros., commission agents
  Gordon, W. G.
  Gordon, C. W.

永豐 Yung-fung
Grosclaude, E. & U., watchmakers
  Grosclaude, Ed.
  Grosclaude, U. (Hiogo)

恒順 Hung-sun
Haminoff, Rodionoff & Co., merchants
  Haminoff, J. S. (Irkutsk)
  Rodionoff, A. L.
  Rodionoff, N. L.
    Remiannikoff, S. J.
    Krasnopolsky, J. A.
    Pegemsky, J. P.
    Solstanoff, A. A.
    Charnieh, J. N.

Hankow Printing Office
  King, J. D.
  Jenkins, M. A.

Han-Yang Steamer Company
  Agents—Major & Smith

播威 Po-wai
Hirsbrunner & Co., watchmakers
  Hirsbrunner, John

匯豐 Hwei-fung
Hongkong and Shanghai Banking Corporation
  Townsend, A. M., agent
  Mitchell, F. W., Jr.

阜通 Fou-t'ung
Ivanoff & Co., N. A., merchants
  Ivanoff, N. A.
  Piatkoff, M T. (Foochow)
  Moltchanoff, J. M.
  Von Glehn, W. A.
  Lebedeff, J. R.
  Lebedeff. N. R.
  Nemtchinoff, W. J.
  Nemtchinoff, M. J.
  Nemtchinoff, F. J.
  Koseshin, J. A.

Mackellar, M. R., bill and general broker

信和 Sin-ho
Major & Smith, merchants
  Major, F.
  Smith, Noel

德昌 Teh-tsang
Matthews & Co., storekeepers, auctioneers and general agents
  Matthews, A. E.

順豐 Seun-fung
Okooloff & Tomakoff, merchants
  Tomakoff, T.
  Sheveleff, M.
  Sherkoonoff, L.
  Cherepanoff, T.
  Watson, Thos.
  Gribooshin, G.

Price, Alexander, bill broker, Club

立德 Leih-tih
Reid, A. G., M.D., F.R.C.S.E.

旗昌 Kee-chang
Russell & Co., merchants
  Fitz, W. Scott
  Howard, J. J.
  Cunningham, H. M.
  Smith, Chas., godown-keeper
  Brown, J.,   do.

Russian Steam Navigation, Trading and
  Odessa Railway Company
    Agent—Ivanoff, N. A

沙宣 Sha-sun

Sassoon, Sons & Co., D., merchants
  Dawbarn, A. H.
  Solomon, S. A.

旗昌 Kee-chang

Shanghai Steam Navigation Company
  Agents—Russell & Co.

李百里 Le-pih-le

Shaw, Ripley & Co., merchants
  King, W. W.

Townend & Co., Edward
  Townend, Ed. (absent)
  Bourke, R.
  Townend, F. J.
  Fisher, E.

華記 Wha-kee

Turner & Co., merchants
  Sharp W. F.
  Hickling, A.

治 CHEFOO. 府

Consulates, etc.

AUSTRO-HUNGARIAN MONARCHY.
大奧國領事官
Ta-ngao-kwoh-ling-shih-kwan

Consul—Lay, W. H. (absent)
Acting Consul—Cooper W. M.

DENMARK.
大丹國領事官
Ta-tan-kwoh-ling-shih-kwan

Vice-Consul—Wadman, W. S.

FRANCE.
大法國領事官
Ta-fa-kwoh-ling-shih-kwan

Vice-Consul—Merlaude, F.

GERMAN EMPIRE.
大布國領事官
Ta-pu-kwoh-ling-shih-kwan

Vice-Consul—Hagen, C.

GREAT BRITAIN.
大英國領事官
Ta-ying-kwoh-ling-shih-kwan

Consul—Lay, W. H. (absent)
Acting do.—Cooper, W. M.
Assistant and Acting Interpreter—Marjary, A. R.
Constable—Webster, W.

NETHERLANDS.
大荷蘭國領事官
Ta-ho-lau-kwoh-ling-shih-kwan

Consul—Cornabé, W. A.

SWEDEN AND NORWAY.
瑞國領事官
Shwui-kwoh-ling-shih-kwan

Vice-Consul—Cornabé, W. A.

UNITED-STATES.
大美國領事官
Ta-mei-kwoh-ling-shih-kwan

Vice-Consul—Cornabé, W. A.

Imperial Maritime Customs.

Acting Commissioner—Brown, H. O.
Assistants—Palm, J. L. E.; Hobson, R. M.; Fauvel, A.
Tide surveyor and Harbour Master—Howard, W. C.
Examiners—Rae, W.; Young S.
Tidewaiters—Hulse, R.; Iffland, A.; Hamilton, E.; Ottaway, E. F.; Sweet, A.

LUSON LIGHT HOUSE.
Light House keeper—Campbell, T.

French Government Marine Department.

COMMISSARIAT.
糧房 Leong-fang

Merlaude, F., chef du service administratif de la marine

Taoutai's Constable.
巡丁 Sün-ting

Housden, J.

Missionaries.

大英美國耶穌教人
Ta-ying-mei-kwoh-ye-su-chiao-jen

AMERICAN PRESBYTERIAN MISSION.
Corbett, Rev. Hunter
Nevius, Rev. John L., D.D.
Eckard, Rev. Leighton W.
Downing, Miss C. B.

AMERICAN PRESBYTERIAN MISSION, TUNGCHOW.
Mills, Rev. C. R.
Mateer, Rev. C. W.
Capp, Rev. E. P. (absent)
Crossette, Rev. J. F.
Dickie, Miss

AMERICAN SOUTHERN BAPTIST MISSION, TUNGCHOW.
Hartwell, Rev. J. B. (Chefoo)
Crawford, Rev. T. P.
Holmes, Mrs.
Moon, Miss E.
Moon, Miss L

ENGLISH BAPTIST MISSION.
Brown, Wm., M.B., C.M.
Richard, Rev. T.

ROMAN CATHOLIC CHURCH.
Marchi, Rev. Pere

SCOTTISH NATIONAL BIBLE SOCIETY.
Williamson, Rev. A., LL.D.

U. P. CHURCH OF SCOTLAND.
Henderson, W. A., L.R.C.S. & P.ED.
Williamson, Rev. A., LL.D.
MacIntyre, Rev. J.

Insurances.

Crasemann & Hagen
  Colonial Sea and Fire Insurance Co. of Batavia
  Oosterling Sea and Fire Insurance Co.
  Second Colonial Sea and Fire Ins. Co. of Batavia
  China and Japan Marine Insurance Co.
  Bremen Underwriters

Fergusson & Co.
  Lloyds
  North British and Mercantile Ins. Co.
  North China Insurance Company
  China Fire Insurance Company
  Merchant Shipping and Underwriters' Association of Melbourne, N.S.W.
  Chinese Insurance Company Limited
Holmes, Wadman & Co.
  China Traders' Insurance Co. Limited
  Hongkong Fire Insurance Company
Wilson, Cornabé & Co.,
  Canton Insurance Office
  Germanic and International Lloyds
  Imperial Fire Insurance Co.
  Royal Fire and Life Insurance Co. of Liverpool
  Samarang Sea and Fire Insurance Co.
  Union Insurance Society
  Victoria Fire Insurance Co.
  Yangtsze Ins. Association of Shanghai

Merchants, etc.

"Beach Hotel"
  Shütt, N. P., manager and proprietor
  Shütt, Mrs.

加寶架醫生 Ka-mai-kia-i-sheng
Carmichael & Myers, physicians and surgeons
  Carmichael, J. R., M.D., M.R.C.S.
  Myers, W. Wykeham, M.B., C.M., &c.

"Chefoo Family Hotel"
  Newman, E., manager and proprietor
  Newman, Mrs.

Consterdine, H., Naval contractor
  Consterdine, H.
  Killeen, C.

"Corean Snake," sloop
  Brown, W.

"Cosmopolitan Hotel"
  Campbell, Thos. M.

Coutris & Co., contractors for the French Navy
  Coutris, A.
  Myres, C.

寶興 Paou-hing
Crasemann & Hagen, merchants
  Crasemann, E.
  Hagen, C.
    Bauermeister, H., clerk

滋大 Tax-tai
Fergusson & Co., merchants
 Fergusson, T. T.
 Clarke, W. J.
 Head, R. L.
 Cousins, E.
 Brown, W., godown-keeper

Forssblad, Bernhard, M.C., proprietor of Chefoo Medical Hall, Broadway

架拿 Kia-na
Gardner & Co., provisioners and bakers
 Gardner, Mrs. F. E.

"German Hotel"
 Behrens, H.

"Glenvue House"
 Damström, O. P.
 Brown, P.

Great Northern Telegraph China and Japan Extension Company, Limited
 Agent—Wadman, W. S.

架厘酒店 Ka-leh-chiu-tien
Grey, E.; baker

慳心酒店 Han-sin-chiu-tien
Hanssen, Peter, publican

華泰 Hwa-tai
Holmes, Wadman & Co., commission agents, merchants and agents for Messrs. Jardine, Matheson & Co.'s Steamers
 Holmes, M. G.
 Wadman, W. S.
 Van Es, P. A.
 Slaghek, F. H.

Hoyrup, Mrs. J. C., hotel-keeper

機路酒店 Ki-loo-chiu-tien
Ling A King & Co., butchers, contractors and general brokers
 De Greeuw, N., manager

禮也驗船人 Li-yeh-yen-chuan-jer
Lyell, Thomas, marine surveyor

"Mariner's Hotel"
 Tutein, Francis

邊丫爹厘 Pin-a-toh-li
Pignatel, J., general trader

P. & O. Steam Navigation Co.
 Agents—Fergusson & Co.

Rosenbaum, Jos., merchant

老沙宣 Lo-sha-sun
Sassoon, Sons & Co., David, merchants
 Abraham, J.
 Hardoon, E. A.

新沙宣 Sun-sha-sun
Sassoon & Co., E. D., merchants
 Ezra, Isaac, agent
 Nathan, S. J.

Scott, Thos., shipwright and blacksmith

Shanghai Steam Navigation Company
 Agents—Wilson, Cornabé & Co.

蝦厘 Ha-li
Sietas & Co., H., storekeepers
 Kirschstein, J. C.
 Schröder, E.
 Saurs, Charles

士米 Sze-mi
Smith & Co., storekeepers, bakers and compradores
 Smith, J.

士迪力酒店 Sz-ta-lui-chiu-tien
Starick, Paul, publican

和記 Wo-kee
Wilson, Cornabé & Co., merchants
 Wilson, Jas.
 Cornabé, W. A.
 Eckford, A. M.
 Farmer, Jas. M.
 Seth, A. P.
 Allin, L.

Yentai Butchery, Broadway
 Knight, W.

大 TAKU. 沽

Consulates.

GREAT BRITAIN.

大英國領事官
Ta-yeng-kwoh-ling-shih-kwan

Vice-Consul—
Acting Vice-Consul—Middleton, J. T.
Constable—Mackay, G. G.
Writer—Tang-hsi-woo

Imperial Maritime Customs.

海關 Hai-kwan

Examiner in Charge—Moorehead, T.
Tidewaiter—Moulls, J.
Signalman—French, W.

Merchants, etc.

Collins & Co., G. W., storekeepers, ship-chandlers, wine and spirit merchants
  Collins, G. W.
    Anderson, Wm. C. C.

Pilots.

TAKU & TIENTSIN.

帶水 Tai-shui

Folser, Jno.   Baxter, A. G. (absent)
Mitchell, Geo. (ab't) Ulderup, A. P.
Hill, Jno. C.   Hicks, G. W.
Young, J.   Collins, G. W.
Lüders, J. (tug-boat) Livingston, T.
Boad, Wm.   Watts, James

Tug Boats.

ALGERINE.

Master—Boad, William
Engineer—Schmidt, —.

PATHFINDER.

Master—Lüders, J.
Engineer—Eckman, C.

天 TIENTSIN. 津

Consulates.

AUSTO-HUNGARIAN MONARCHY.
Consul—Mongan, James

DENMARK.
大丹國領事官
Ta-tan-kwoh-ling-shih-kwan
Consul—Meadows, John A. T.
Interpreter—Kieruliff, P.

FRANCE.
大法國領事官
Ta-fa-kwoh-ling-shih-kwan
Consul—Dillon, C. (absent)
Acting Consul—Ristelhuber, —.

GERMAN EMPIRE.
大布國領事官
Ta-puh-kwoh-ling-shih-kwan
Acting Consul—Waeber, C.

GREAT BRITAIN.
大英國領事官
Ta-ying-kwoh-ling-shih-kwan
Consul—Mongan, James
Interpreter—Watters, T.
Acting 3rd Assistant—Crawford, J. D.
Constable—Featherstone, T.

NETHERLANDS.
大荷蘭國領事官
Ta-ho-lan-kwoh-ling-shih-kwan
Consul—Meadows, John A. T.

PORTUGAL.
大西洋國領事官
Ta-sai-yang-kwoh-ling-shih-kwan
Consul—

RUSSIA.
大俄羅斯國總領事官
Ta-ngo-lo-sz-kwoh-tsung-ling-shih-kwan
Acting Consul General—Waeber, C.
Secretary—Ouspensky, V.

SWEDEN AND NORWAY.
大瑞威頓國領事官
Ta-sui-wei-tun-kwoh-ling-shih-kwan
Vice-Consul—Moore, M. G.

UNITED STATES.
大美國領事官
Ta-mai-kwoh-ling-shih-kwan
U. S. Consul—Sheppard, Eli T.
Vice-Consul & Interpreter—Pethick, Wm. N.

Imperial Maritime Customs.
天津海關 Tien-tsin-hai-kwan

Commissioner—Huber, A.
Assistants—Dillon, A.; Schoenicke, J. F.; Chalmers, J. L.
Tide-surveyor and Harbour Master—Callagher, F.
Examiners—Moorehead, T. (Taku)
Assistant Examiners—Brackenridge, J.; Diercks, F.
Tidewaiters—McDonald, J.; Castro, C. C. de; Moulls, J. (Taku); Manners, T. N.; Woolfe, H. D.; Collins, J.
Signal-man, Taku—French, W.

Imperial Arsenal.
天津軍器廠 Tien-tsin-kwan-chi-chwang

Superintendent—McIlwraith, Robert
Pattern-maker—Bracegirdle, George
Engineer—Keeton, Alexander
Powder-maker—Wheeler, Thomas
Engineer—Stewart, James

TIENTSIN

Municipal Council.

Chairman—Solomen, Ezekiel A.
Hon. Secretary—Beveridge, Henry
Hon. Treasurer—Livingston, John
Members—Moore, M. G.; Hatch, John J.
Superintendent of Roads and Police—Mostyn, R. B.

Missions.

AMERICAN BOARD OF COMMISSIONERS FOR FOREIGN MISSIONS.

Stanley, Rev. C. A.
Smith, Rev. Arthur H.
Porter, Rev. Henry D.

AMERICAN METHODIST EPISCOPAL MISSIONS.

Davis, Rev. George R.

CHAPELLE DE TIENTSIN ET PROCURE DE LA MISSION ST. LAZARE.

天主堂 Tien-chu-tang

Delemasure, l'Abbé

HOPITAL DES SŒURS DE ST. VINCENT DE PAUL.

仁慈堂 Jen-chi-tang

Superioress—

LONDON MISSIONARY SOCIETY.

Lees, Rev. J. (absent)
Byrant, Rev. Evan
Barradale, Rev. J. S.

METHODIST MISSIONARY SOCIETY.

Innocent, Rev. J. and family
Hodge, Rev. W. B.
Hall, Rev. W. N. (absent)

Insurances.

Cordes & Co., A.
  North China Insurance Company
  China & Japan Marine Ins. Co.
  Germanic Lloyds.
Hanna, John
  China Fire Insurance Company
  Liverpool and London Fire Insurance Company
  Union Insurance Society
  Chinese Insurance Company
Henderson, James
  Sun Fire Office

Jardine, Matheson & Co.
  Canton Insurance Office
  Hongkong Fire Insurance Co.
Russell & Co.
  Yangtaze Insurance Association
Stammann, Oscar
  Samarang Sea and Fire Insurance Co.

Merchants, &c.

Amoor Steam Navigation Company
  Agent—Startseff, A. D.

寶通 Pao-toong

Boordacheff, P. S., merchant

Canton Insurance Office
  Agents—Jardine, Matheson & Co.

China Coast Steam Navigation Co.
  Agents—Jardine, Matheson & Co.

China Navigation Company
  Agents—Jardine, Matheson & Co.

Collins & Co., G. W., storekeepers, shipchandlers, wine and spirit merchants
  Collins, G. W.
  Anderson, Wm. C. C.

信遠洋行 Sin-yuen-yang-hong

Cordes & Co., A., merchants
  Cordes, Aug. C. (absent)
  Cordes, Ad. S.
  Dreusche, H. Von

Frazer, Jno., L.R.C.P., L.M., M.R.C.S., medical officer

貴平 Kwai-ping

Goohkine & Koosnetzoff, merchants
  Startseff, A. D., agent

恒順 Hen-shun

Haminoff Rodionoff & Co., merchants
  Nefedieff, N. A., agent

保順 Pau-shun

Hanna, John, commission agent (absent)
Hatch, John J.

廣隆 Kwang-loong

Henderson, James, merchant

TIENTSIN.

Hongkong Fire Insurance Company
  Agents—Jardine, Matheson & Co.

阜通 Foo-toong

Ivanoff & Co., N. A., merchants
  Belogolovy, A. A.
  Pejemaky, J. P.

Jardine, Matheson & Co., merchants
  Beveridge, H., agent

Kieruliff, P., merchant and commission agent

Laen & Co., P. L., storekeepers and auctioneers.
  Laen, P. L.
  Blow, H. MoC.

隆順 Loong-shun

Nefedieff, N. A., merchant
  Nefedieff, A. A.
  Lichagoff, K. F.
  Bohdanoff, I. N.
  Vorobiaff, A. S.

North China Steam Co.
  Agents—Jardine, Matheson & Co.

Ocean Steam Ship Company
  Agents—Jardine, Matheson & Co.

順豐 Shun-fuug

Okooloff & Tokmakoff, merchants
  Startseff, A. D, agent

旗昌 Kee-chang

Russell & Co., merchants
  Moore, M. G.
  Lösch, E.

Sassoon & Co., E. D., merchants
  Benjamin B. D.
  Yaish, S. Y.
  Nathan, E. J.

沙宣 Sha-sun

Sassoon, Sons & Co., D., merchants
  Solomon, Ezekiel, A.
  Benjamin, D.

世昌 Shih-chaug

Stammann, Oscar, merchant
  Meyer, E.
    Grabe, O.
    Clasen, H. G.

薩寶寶 Sa-pao-shi

Startseff, A D., merchant
  Startseff, A. D.
  Maligen, A. P.
  Bartasheff, J. A.
  Sedneff, N. N.

Union Steam Navigation Co.
  Agents—Jardine, Matheson & Co.

亨達利 Han-ta-li

Vrard & Co., L., merchants
  Gaidrich, F.
  Goup, P.
  Borel, L.

Chang-Kia-Kau or (Kalgan)
張家口

MISSIONS.

AMERICAN BOARD OF COMMISSIONERS FOR FOREIGN MISSIONS.

Gulick, Rev. John T., and family
Williams, Rev Mark, and family
Thompson, Rev. Thos W.
Diament, Miss Naomi

MERCHANTS

寶通 Paou-toong

Andreevsky & Avramoff, merchants
  Andreevsky, J. S.
  Avramoff, P. G
  Pejemsky, J. P

義利 E-li

Botkin & Sons, P., merchants
  Agent—Molchanoff, J. M.

雷恒 Lay-hang

Gromoff, K. S., merchant

德利 De-li

Matreninsky & Kasantzoff, merchants
  Matreninsky, V. J.
  Kasantzoff, P. J. (absent)
    Jooniff, A. L
    Plotnikoff, K.
    Koloboff, J. A.
    Bikoff, P. M.
    Bartasheff, N. A.

牛 NEWCHWANG. 庄

Consulates.

AUSTRO-HUNGARIAN MONARCHY.
Vice-Consul—Adkins, Thomas (absent)
Acting Vice-Consul—Harvey, Alex. S.

DENMARK.
大丹國領事官
Ta-tan-kwoh-ling-shih-kwan

Vice-Consul—Adkins, Thomas (absent)
Acting Vice-Consul—Harvey, Alex. S.

FRANCE.
大法國領事官
Ta-fa-kwoh-ling-shih-kwan

Vice-Consul—Knight, F. P.

GERMANY.
大布老士國領事官
Ta-po-lo-sz-kwoh-ling-shih-kwan

Vice-Consul—Knight, F. P.

GREAT BRITAIN.
大英國領事官
Ta-ying-kwoh-ling-shih-kwan

Consul—Adkins, Thomas (absent)
Acting Consul—Harvey, Alex. S.
Constable—Lister, Wm.

NETHERLANDS.
大荷蘭國領事官
Ta-ho-lan-kwoh-ling-shih-kwan

Consul—Knight, F. P.

SWEDEN AND NORWAY.
大瑞威頓國領事官
Ta-suy-wei-tun-kwoh-ling-shih-kwan

Vice-Consul—Knight, F. P.

UNITED STATES.
大美國領事官
Ta-mei-kwoh-ling-shih-kwan

Consul—Knight, F. P.
Vice-Consul—Knight, A. M. (absent)

Imperial Maritime Customs.
牛莊海關 Niu-chwang-hai-kwan

Commissioner—Man, Alexander J.
Assists.—Ste. Croix, C. W. de; Schjöth, F.
Medical Officer—Watson, J., M.D.
Harbour Master and Tide Surveyor—Rennell, T. B.
Examiner—Clarke, G.
Assistant Examiner—Stebbins, W.
Tidewaiter—Hamlyn, J.; Carr, R. P.; Lovett, H. F.; Turner, W. M.; Wells, J.

LIGHT-SHIP "NEWCHWANG."
Master—Trebing, W.
Mate—Dillon, O.

LORCHA "RELIEF."
Master—Stone, W.

Insurance.

Bush Bros.
  Canton Insurance Office
  China and Japan Marine Insurance Co.
  Lloyds, London
  North China Insurance Company
  Germanischer Lloyd
  Hongkong Fire Insurance Company
Knight & Co.
  China Traders' Insurance Company
  Imperial Fire Insurance Company
  Yangtsze Insurance Association
  Chinese Insurance Co. Limited

Merchants, &c.

遠來 Yuan-lae

Bush Bros., merchants
  Bush, H. E.
  Bielfeld, Alex.

China Coast Steam Navigation Company
  Agents—Bush Bros.

克來洋行 Hak-lae-yang-hong

Clyatt & Co., shipchandlers and storekeepers
  Clyatt, W. B.

Haliday & Co., storekeepers and shipchandlers
  Haliday, D. J.
  Tandberg, L. J.
  Davies, T.

Hunter, J., M.D.

旗昌 K'i-ch'ang

Knight & Co., merchants
  Knight, F. P.
  Knight, A. M. (absent)
  Milisch, J.

Newchwang Lightship
  Kraul, W., master (absent)
  Trebing, W., acting master
  Dillon, O., mate

North China Steam Company
  Agents—Bush Bros.

Ross, Rev. J., United Presbyterian missionary

沙遜 Sa-un

Sassoon, Sons & Co., D., merchants and commission agents
  Nathan, S. A., agent
  Ezra, A.

新沙宜 Sun-sha-sun

Sassoon & Co., E. D., merchants and commission agents
  Joseph, J., agent
  Perry, J. S.

Schultze & Co., F. A., shipchandlers and storekeepers
  Schultze, F. A.
  Luhrs, C.
  Ha-li-yang-hai

瓦醫生 Ya-ee-sheng

Watson, J., M.D., L.R.C.S.E.

Wells, J., soda-water manufacturer

Pilots.

NEWCHWANG PILOT COMPANY.

Sinclair, Wm.
Smith, A. L. R.
Richard, G. C.
Blachfood, B. F.
Plunket, J.
McThorne, H.
Haliday, D. J.
O'Malley, A. B.
Pulsipher, C. H.
Friedrichsen, A.
Tandberg, L. J.
Carlos, B.

比 PEKING. 京

Legations.

AUSTRO-HUNGARY.
Minister Resident and Consul General for China—Calice, Henry de (resident at Shanghai)
Interpreter—Haas, Joseph (absent)

FRANCE.
大法國府 Ta-fa-kwok-fu
Ministre Plénip.—Geofroy, M. Louis de
Premier Secrétaire—Rochechouart, Comte Julien de (en mission)
2me. do.—Rouquette, Guillaume de
3me. do.—Balloy, René de
Attaché Libre—Kergariou, Comte Philibert de (en mission spécial)
Attaché Militaire—Contenson, Comte Guy de (le Capitaine d'etat Major)
Premier Interprète—Devéria, Gabriel
Chancelier Interprète—Scherzer, Fernand
Elèves Interprètes—Gaston, Vicomte de Saint Servan de Bezaure
Médécin—Estublier, Dr. Anatole Dugat

GERMAN EMPIRE.
大德國府 Ta-teh-kwoh-fu
Minister Plenipotentiary—Rehfues, M. de (absent)
Chargé d'Affaires—Holleben, Baron von
Secretary and Interpreter—Bismarck, Carl von (absent)
Student—Möllendorff, Otto von
Interpreter—Arndt, C.
Constable—Hinz, E.

GREAT BRITAIN.
大英國府 Ta-ying-kwoh-fu
Envoy Extraordinary, Minister Plenipotentiary and Chief Superintendent—Wade, T. F., C.B.
Secretary of Legation—Walsham, —.

GREAT BRITAIN.
(Continued.)
Second Secretaries—Sandford, W. Graham; Grosvenor, Hon. T. G.
Chinese Secretary—Mayers, W. F.
Assistant do.—Hewlett, A. R.
Accountant—Pirkis, A. E.
Physician—Bushell, S. W., M.D. (absent); Du Year, J., M.D (acting)
Chaplain—Collins, Rev. W. H.
3rd Assist. and Private Secretary—Carles, W. R.
Student Interpreters—Brown, G.; Playfair, G. M. H.; Holland, W.; Fraser, M. F. A.; Johnson, O; Allen, G. L B.; Hurst, R. W.; Taylor, J. A. H; and Scott, J.

ITALIAN.
Minister Plenipotentiary to China and Japan—Ostiani, Conte Fe d' (non-resident)

NETHERLANDS.
Diplomatic Agent and Consul General for China—Ferguson, J. H.
Secretary Interpreter—Groeneveldt, W. P.
Student Interpreter—Roelofs, J. J.
Assistant—Rhein, J.

RUSSIA.
大俄國國府 Ta-ngo-kwoh-fu
Envoy Extraordinary and Minister Plenipotentiary—Vlangaly, His Excellency General A.
Secretary of Legation—Koyander, A.
Attaché—Bakhméteff, G.
Interpreter—Lenzy, A.
Students—Ouspensky, V.; Popoff, P.
Physician—Bretschneider, Dr. E.
Postmaster—Vacant
Cossacks Guard—Five

RUSSIAN OBSERVATORY.
Director—Fritsche, Dr. H. (absent)

PEKING.

SPAIN.
大呂宋國府 Ta-lu-su..kwoh-fu

Envoy Extraordinary and Minister Plenipotentiary—Pereira, H. E. Juan Manuel (absent)
Chargé d'Affaires—Otin y Mesias, F.
Attaché—Soto, José de (absent)

UNITED STATES.
大美國府 Ta-mei-kwoh-fu

Envoy Extraordinary and Minister Plenipotentiary—Low, H. E. Hon. Frederick F. (absent)
Secretary of Legation and Chinese Interpreter—Williams, S. Wells, LL.D.

COLLEGE OF PEKING.
President—Martin, W. A. P., LL.D.
Proctors—Chinese
Professor of English—McKean, Edw.
Professor of French—Vapereau, C.
Professor of Russian and German—Hayan, W.
Professors of Chinese—Chinese
Professor of Natural Philosophy—Martin, W. A. P., LL.D.
Professor of Mathematics—Ji-shen-lan (Chinese)
Professor of Natural History and Chemistry—Billequin, A.
Professor of Anatomy and Physiology—Dudgeon, J., M.D.
Professor of Astronomy—Vacant

Inspectorate General of Imperial Maritime Customs.
總稅務司公署
Tsung-shwui-wu-sz-kung-shu

Inspector General—Hart, Robert
Chief Secretary—Bredon, Robert E.
Chinese do.—Woodruff, F. E.
Statistical do.—Taintor, E. C.
Accountant—Gibbs, J. H.
Clerks—Rocher, L.; Ohlmer, E.
Students—Russell, W. B.; Grimani, E. H.; Stappen, J. Van; Estvelde, E. Van
Medical Officer—Dudgeon, J., M.D.
Gas Engineer—Child, Thos.

Missions.

AMERICAN BOARD OF COMMISSIONERS FOR FOREIGN MISSIONS.
Blodget, Rev. H., D.D., and family
Holcombe, Rev. Chester, and family

AMERICAN BOARD OF COMMISSIONERS FOR FOREIGN MISSIONS.
(*Continued.*)
Hunt, Phineas R., and family, superintendent of the press
Porter, Miss Mary H., in charge of girls' school
Chapin, Miss Jane E.
Hunt, Rev. Myron W., and family

AMERICAN METHODIST EPISCOPAL MISSION.
Lowry, Rev. H. H., and family
Davis, Rev. G. R., (Tientsin)
Pilcher, Rev. L. V.
Porter, Miss Mary Q.
Browne, Miss Maria
Harris, Rev. S. D. and family
Combs, Miss L. L., M.D.

CHURCH MISSIONARY SOCIETY.
Collins, Rev. W. H. and family
Gretton, Rev. H., and family

AMERICAN EPISCOPAL MISSION.
Schereschwesky, Rev. S. J. J., D.D., and family

GREEK CHURCH MISSION.
Archimandrite—Palladius
Missionaries—Rahinsky, Johannes; Levitski, Gerontius

LONDON MISSIONARY SOCIETY.
Edkins, Rev. Joseph, B.A., and family (absent)
Dudgeon, John, M.D., and family (in charge of Chinese hospital)
Gilmour, Rev. J., M.A. (Mongol Mission)
Meech, Rev. S. E., and family

MISSION CATHOLIQUE DE PEKING ET DU TCHE-LY NORD.
CONGRÉGATION DE LA MISSION DITE DU LAZARISTES.

Vicaire Apostolique—Delaplace, Monseigneur L. G.
M.M.—Favie   Humblot
D'Addosio   Chevrier
Provost

DANS LA MISSION.
M.M.—Thierry   Delemasure
Saupivius   Fioritti
Sarthou   Wijnhoven
Garrigue

PEKING.

PRESBYTERIAN BOARD (U.S.) OF MISSIONS.
McIlvaine, Rev. Jasper S.
McCoy, Rev. D. C., and family
Whiting, Rev. J. L., and family
Wherry, Rev. J., and family

SŒURS DE CHARITE' DE ST. VINCENT DE PAUL.
Supérieure—Jaurias, Sœur

ETABLISSEMENT DU JEN-SZE-TANG.
Sisters—Seven

HOPITAL DE PEKING.
Sisters—Four

WOMEN'S UNION MISSIONARY SOCIETY, U.S.
Douw, Miss D. M. (absent)
North, Miss M. B.

Pau-ting-fu.

AMERICAM BOARD OF COMMISSIONERS FOR FOREIGN MISSIONS.
Pierson, Rev. Isaac
Treat. Alfred O., M.D.

Tungchow.

AMERICAN BOARD OF COMMISSIONERS FOR FOREIGN MISSIONS.
Chapin, Rev. Lyman D., and family
Sheffield, Rev. D. Z., and family
Andrews, Miss Mary E.
Evans, Miss J.
Goodrich, Rev. C., and family

KALGAN.
Gulick, Rev. J. T., and family
Williams, Rev. Mark, and family
Thompson, Rev. W.
Diamant, Miss
Spraque, Rev., and family

JAPAN.

YEDO.

Yedo Legations.

AUSTRO-HUNGARY.
Minister Resident and Consul General for Japan—Calice, Baron Henry de
Interpreter—Siebold, Henry von

BELGIUM.
Minister Resident—Groote, Ch. de (nommé)

DENMARK.
Diplomatic Representative for Denmark—Weckherlin, Monsieur van

FRANCE.
Ministre Plénipotentiaire—Berthemy, J.
Sécretaire de première classe—St. Quentin, A. de
Attaché—Sinety, Cte. de
Secrétaire Interprète—Klotz, Francis
Interprète Auxiliaire—Kouroda

GERMANY.
Minister—Brandt, M. von
Secretary—Kempermann, S.
    Knoblock, A. von (1)
    Knoblock, A. von (2)
    Krien, T.

GREAT BRITAIN.
Envoy Extraordinary, Minister Plenipotentiary and Consul-General—Parkes, Sir Harry, S., K.C.B.
Secretary of Legation—
Second Secretary—Lawrence, C. W.
Japanese Secretary—Satow, Ernest M.
Interpreter and Translator—Aston, W. G.
Student Interpreters—Woolley, W. A.
    do.   Gubbins, J. H.
    do.   Paul, Edward B.
Medical Officer—Wheeler, Edwin

GREAT BRITAIN.
(Continued.)
MOUNTED ESCORT.
Inspector—Peacock, P.
Sergeant—Aberdain, A.
Constables—Dillon, E. ; Davies, T. ; Wood, W.; Reeve, H.

H. B. M.'s CONSULATE.
Acting Consul—Dohmen, M.
Constable—Bye, J.

HAWAII.
Envoy Extraordinary and Minister Plenipotentiary—

ITALY.
Envoy Extraordinary and Minister Plenipotentiary—Fé d'Ostiani, Conte Allcessandro
Secretary—N. N.

NETHERLANDS.
Minister Resident—Weckherlin, W. F. H. Von
Secretary—Van der Brock, T. H. W.

PERU.
Envoy Extraordinary and Minister Plenipotentiary—Captain Aurelio Garcia-y-Garcia (absent)
Secretary of Legation—Elmore, J. F. Dr.
Attaché—Lieut. Freyro, O. ; Garland, G.
Acting Consul—Heeren, O.

PORTUGAL.
Consul General—Loureiro, E.

YEDO

SPAIN.

Chargé d'Affaires—Fibureio, Rodriguez y Munoz (absent)
Sécretaire — Emilio de Ojeda, Chargé d'Affaires ad interim
Troisième Secretaire—Enrique, M.
Chargé du Consulat a Yokohama—Dupuy de Lôrne

SWEDEN AND NORWAY.

Minister Resident—Weekherlin, W. F. H. von

U. S. OF AMERICA.

Envoy Extraordinary and Minister Plenipotentiary—Bingham, Hon. John A.
Secretary of Legation—Stevens, D. W.
Interpreter—Rice, N. E.

Missions.

AMERICAN EPISCOPAL MISSION.
Newman, Rev. J.

AMERICAN PRESBYTERIAN.
Thompson, Rev. David
Carrothers, Rev. C.
Parke, Miss M.

ENGLISH CHURCH SOCIETY—PROPAGATION OF THE GOSPEL.
Wright, Rev. Mr.
Shaw, Rev. Mr.

REFORMED CHURCH IN AMERICA.
Verbeck, Rev. Guido F.
Soper, Rev. J.

ROMAN CATHOLIC.
Missionaires Apostoliques—Marin, L'Abbé Jean Marie
Midou, L'Abbé F.
Armbruster, L'Abbé Henri
Vigroux, L'Abbé Francois Paulin
Allen, Rev. M.
Sutter, L'Abbé Louis
Testevuide, L'Abbé Leger German
Drouart, L'Abbé de Lezey, Lucien
Brotelande, L'Abbé Charles Alex.

TEPPOZU.
Metzner, W.

Masonic Lodges.

NIPPON LODGE, YEDO,
No. 1844, E. C.

Worshipful Master—Freame, W. H.
Senior Warden—Wheeler, Dr. E.
Junior Warden—Weiller, A.
Secretary—Boulet, J. H.
Treasurer—Mitchell, Geo. N.
Senior Deacon—
Junior Deacon—
Inner Guard—Mc Donald, —.

Government Service.

GAIM' SHO.
Teachers—Jaudon, F
Witkowsky, A.
Wertheimer, L.
Smith, A.
Schmid, P.
Legendre, —.
Jaudon, P.
Witkowsky, T.
Frachtenberg, S. T.

HIO-BU-SHO.
Gunnery Instructor—Brinkley, F., Lt. R. A.
Gunnery do.—Hawes, Lt. R., M. A.
Band Master—Fenton, J. W.
Pilkington, J.

OFFICIERS.
Lieut. Colonel—Marquerie, —.
Capitaine—Descharmes, —.
Do.—Jourdan, —.
Do.—Lebon, —.
Do.—Echemann, —.
Do.—Orcel, —.
Lieut.—Ohl, —.

SOUS-OFFICIERS.
Adjutant—François, —.
Do.—Cros, —.
Do.—Cartier, —.
Do.—Jocquel, —.
Chef Armourer—Moulins, —.
Chef Artificier—Laurie, —.
Do.—Lassere, —.
Jocquil,—
Phillippi,—
Barberot,-
Dagron,—
Viesse,—
Legardeur,—
Schilles,—
Amade,—
Fortant,
Bouffier,—
Engel,—
Jauris,—

YEDO.

HIO-BU-SHO.
(*Continued.*)

KAITIKUSHI.

Capron, Gen. H.
Antisell, Dr. Thomas
Warfield, Maj. A. G.
Wasson, James R.
Munroe, Henry Smith
Eldridge, Dr. Stuart.
Holt, N. W.
Boehmer, Louis
Clark, Sanford
Baumann, Miss
De Reuter, Miss

Vulcan, steamer—Wynn, Capt.
  Engineer—Smith, —.
Sadkia—Frome, Capt.

Farmer for Kentokushi—Shelton, E. M.
  Do.—Taylor, T. M.
  Do.—Boehmer, Louis
Supt of Govt. Tailors—Brandt, P.
Oges Tannery—Henninger, —.

O'KURASHO.

Williams, G. B., (absent)
Williams, S. V.
Shand, A. Allan
Engineer in Chief to Government—Waters, T.
Architects—Shillingford, A. N.; Dorn, C. J. von; Lindo, T.

KOBU-SHO.
(PUBLIC WORKS DEPARTMENT.)

Section of Surveys.

Surveyor General—Colin, A. McVean, C.E.
Chief Assistant—Joyner, H. B., C.E.
Assistant—Hardy, J. T., C.E.
Do.—Klasen, A. J., C.E.
Do.—Arthur, A. M., C.E.
Do.—Cheesman, W. E.
Do.—Wilson, R.
Do.—Steward, R.

TEACHERS.

Mathematical Surveying—Jones, Rhymer, R. O.
Do.—Eaton, G.
Architect and Assist. Surveyor—Boinville, Alfred Chasel de
Foreman Mason—Wooton, J.
Foreman Carpenter—Anderson, J.

FIRST COLLEGE OF THE FIRST SCHOOL DISTRICT OF JAPAN.
(Late KAI SEI JO, or NAN KO.)

Foreign Superintendent—Verbeck, G. F.

ENGLISH DEPARTMENT.

Professor of Chemistry—Griffis, Wm. F., A.M.
Do. Physics—Veeder, P. V. A.M., D.D.
Do. Literature—House, E. E.
McCartee, D. B., A.M., M.D.
Gray, G. H., A.M., M.D.
Cressy, E. P.
Washington, T. B.

FRENCH DEPARTMENT.

Prof. of Chemistry and Physics—Maillot, X.
Mathematics Do.—Lepissier, E.
Literature Do.—Fontaine, H. G.
Pigeon, F.
Brun, F.

GERMAN DEPARTMENT.

Knipping, E.
Schenk, C.
Greeven, G. A.
Seger, P.
Scott, M. M., (English Normal school.)
Holz, —. (Special German school.)

IN THE INTERIOR.

ASHIWA (FUKUI.)

Teacher—Wyckoff, M. N.
Do.—Mudgett, E.

HIKONE.

Mariner—Allert, H.

IMARI.

Teacher—Hiato, C.
Artisan—Moset, —.
Physician—Junghanns, Dr.

IWAKUNI.

Teacher—Stevens, H.

KIOTO.

Teacher—Freeman, Reuter
Do.—Handoin, Chas.
Evans, Mr. & Mrs. Hornby

KANAZAWA.

Machinist—Heiss, Wm.
Mineralogist—Tecken, Von der
Teacher—Symondson, Ed.
Physician—Sloys, P. J.

KAGOSHIMA.

Teacher—Tubel, H.
Ship Master—Kerriman, E.
Physician—Wellis, Wm.
Do.—Peynet, H.

YEDO.

IN THE INTERIOR.
(Continued.)

KUMAMOTO.
Physician—Mansfeldt, J. von
Military Instructor—James, Capt.

KOCHI.
Artisan—Remerchiad, —.
Teacher—Ateriana, F.
Military Instructor—Anton, —.
Teacher—Hall, S. T.
Physician—Massey, Dr.
Teacher—Heria, T.
Do.—Riener, —.

KOSHUI.
Mineralogist—Morris, —.

KOCHI.
Mariners—Raynor, —.
Benson, —.
Jackson, —.
Thomas, —.
Edwards, —.
Macroin, —.
Japp, —.
MacKenzie, —.
Drummond, —.
Engineer—Matthews, —.
Emerson, —.
Roberts, —.

NAGOYA.
Teacher—English, A.
Do.—Murly, —.

NAMBU, (AWORI.)
English Instructor.—Lucy, Alfred
Farmer—McKinnon, A.

OKAYAMA.
Teacher—Horne, P.

SADO.
Gower, Erasmus.
Engineer—Scott, Jas.

SHIDZUOKA.
Instructor in English and French—Clark, E. W., A.M.

TOKUSHIMA.
Teacher—Kurchis, D.
Do.—Curtis, H.
Machinist—Hardee, —.

TOTOTSU.
Teacher—Hancaster, —.

TAKANABI.
Machinist—Caswell, —.

IN THE INTERIOR.
(Continued.)

WAKAYAMA.
Artisan—Bratmuller, —.
Do.—Kaffen, —.
Do.—Warte, —.

YAMAGUCHI.
Physician—Behring, —.
Military Instructor—Croset, —.
Teacher—Tarney, —.

YONEZAWA.
Teacher—Dallas, C. H.

TOMI-OKA SILK REELING FACTORY.
Director—Brunat, Paul
Mailher, M. le docteur
Bellen, Justin, *Foreman*
Prat, Paul,
Vielfaure, Mlle. Clorinde
Monier, Mlle. Louise
Vallent, Mlle. Alexandrine
Charay, Mlle. Marie
Chatron, Jules
Bourguignon, Louis
Cherami, Jules
Chaberisner, Victoire

OKURASHO.
Williams, G. B.
Williams, S. V.
Waters, T.
Shillingford, A. N.
Waters, A.

DAI SAN BAN CHUGAKKO, WASEDA.
Reiche, Th. M.
Broek, V. A. van den

IMPERIAL ACADEMY OF MEDICINE AND SURGERY.
Mueller, Dr L.
Hoffmann, Dr Ph.
Doenitz, Dr W.
Cochins, Dr H.
Hilgendorff, Dr F.
Funk, Dr H.
Holz, V.
Niewerth, R.
Prann, W.

YEDO.

TELEGRAPH DEPT.
Dunk, T.
Morris, J.
Teale, W.
Schaeffer, L.
Smith, J.
Malcolm, G. W.
Prowse, F.
Stone, W. H.

Imperial College Of Engineering.
KOGAKURIGO.
OFFICERS OF THE COLLEGE.

Principal—Dyer, Henry, C.E., M.A., B.SC., University of Glasgow

PROFESSORS FOR THE GENERAL AND SCIENTIFIC COURSE.

Natural Philosophy—Ayrton, W.E., University College. London; Honorary Secretary for Japan of the Society of Telegraph Engineers, London
Mathematics—Marshall, David H., M.A., University of Edinburgh
Chemistry—Divers, Edward, M.D., F.C.S., Queen's University, Ireland
Drawing—Mondy, Edmund F., A.R.S.M., Royal School of Mines, London
English Language & Literature—Craigie, William, M.A., University of Aberdeen
Secretary—Craigie, William, M.A.
Modeller—King, Archibald
General Assistants—Cawley, George; Clark, Robert

NAVAL COLLEGE.
Douglas, Archibald L.
Jones, Charles P.
Baillie, Charles W.
Sutton, Frederick W.
Gissing, Thomas S.
Harding, William J.
Austin, John W.
Higgins, Joseph
James, Willonghby
St. John, Edwin
Bryant, Charles
Yeo, Emmanuel
Nichols, C. W.
Collins, Cornelius
Donaldson, Donald
Christison, John
Libson, William
Chipp, William
Hammond Fredk.
Baillie, Alexander
Bennett, Henry

NAVAL COLLEGE.
(*Continued.*)
Grant, Reuben
Smith, Thomas
Gribble, Timothy
Woodward, William
Collins, John
Crocker, James
West, Samuel
Glanville, Roger
Turpin, James
Pepperill, Geo.
Hopton, Halbert
Quick, W. H.
Abbs, Mark

Imperial College.
(KAI SEI GAKKO.)

ENGLISH DEPARTMENT.
Griffis, W. E., A.M.
Veeder, P. V., A.M., D.D.
McCartee, D. P., A.M., M.D.
Wilson, Horace
Summers, The Revd. James. M.A.

FRENCH DEPARTMENT.
Maillot, X.,
Fontaine, G.,
Foque, P.,

GERMAN DEPARTMENT.
Ritter, H., PH. D.
Knipping, E.
Schenck, C.
Seger, P.

School of Foreign Languages.
(GAI KOKU GO GAKKU.)

ENGLISH DEPARTMENT.
Weiller, A.
Johnston, T.
Bevill, F. W.
Lagden, C. W.
Phillipps, R.
Thompson, A. G.
Davies, T.

FRENCH.
Lepissier, E.
Pigeon, M.
Bran, M.
Freudenthaler, M.

GERMAN.
Toselowaky, F.
Hensen, —.
Whitkowski, —.

RUSSIAN.
Taraktemberk, —.

Merchants, &c.

Ahrens & Co., H.
    Winkler, J.
    Scott, J. K.
        Hake, Th.

Allen, M.

Ayrton, Dr.

Batchelder, Capt. J. M.,

Bair, M. M.

Bevitt, F.

Butcher, Geo. Marshall

Candrelier, Louis, Storekeeper, Tekidji
    Dunnon, T. W., Tekidji.
    Brooks, C. W.   ,,
    More, M.   ,,
    Elliott, M.   ,,
    Sutton, M., Shiba.
    Harding, M.   ,,

Canse, R. M. C. Restaurant keeper

Christy, F. C.

Clark, R.

Clatand, M., store-keeper

Cobb, & Co.

Conard, A., teacher

Du Bousquet, Albert, Captaine d'Infanterie, attaché au Consul d'État de S. M. Le Tenno

Dunn, Col.

Evans, Hornby

Ewart, W.

Fahrer, M., teacher

Favre, Brandt, C. & J., Watchmakers and Importers

Feafield, G.

Fream, C. resident

Galy, A.

Gardner, L.

George, Edgar

Gilbert, G. M.

Greeven, Seger & Co
    Greeven, G. A.
    Seger, P.

Gregoire, —.

Grimmen, L. architect,

Grinsen, H.

Hall, C. F.

Hare & Co.,
    Hare, D. J.
    Hare, A. J.

Hartley & Co.
    Hartley, H.
    Hartley, J.

Heeren, O.

Holt, Victor

Hooper, J.

Hotel des Colonies
    Ruel, J.

Isaacs, Abraham, wine and spirit merchant

Lamber, E. B., school master

King, H. E.

Kunaring, T.

YEDO.

Lindo, F.

Nishin Shin-ji-shi—Newspaper
   Black, J. R., proprietor
   Rosa, F. da

Perregeaux, F.

Perry, M., carpenter

Pfounds, C.,

Poate, T. P.

Richie, B.
   Wesser, R.

Rosenstand, A.

Shaw, M.,

Siber & Brennwald,
   Müller, C.

Smith & Co.
   Smith, J. H.
      Campbell, A.
      Thompson, A. G.

Sury, A.

Vondoorn, J.

Walsh, Hall & Co.,

Waters, E. J.

White, W. J.

Yedo Hotel
   Thompson, W. H.

YOKOHAMA.

Consulates.

BELGIUM.
Consul for Yedo—Strauss, L.
Vice-Consul for Yokohama—Moulron, E.

DENMARK.
Consul-General—Bavier, E. de
Secretary—Simoni, P. M.

FRANCE.
Consul—Colleau, Oscar
Eleve Consul—Plichon, H.
Chancelier—Kraetzer, Emile
Premier Commis.—Silvin, F.
Second Commis.—Groupiere, F.
Interprète Auxiliare—Oueda, C.
Interprete pour les langues Anglais et Espagnole prèssle tribunal Consulaire—Dousdebes, A.

GERMAN EMPIRE.
Consul—Zappe, Ed.
Secretary—Gebaner, R.
Assistant—Kritsch, K.
Interpreter—Inada

GREAT BRITAIN.
Consul—Robertson, Russell
1st Assistant—Wilkinson, Hiram Shaw
2nd do.—Longford, J. H.
Gaoler—Vincent, H.
Constable—White, F. E.
Clerks of Works—Hooper, John; Bennett, Charles

HAWAII.
Consul General—Brown, Robert M.

ITALY.
Consul—Nobile, N. Barrilis
Vice-Consul—Brunl, F.

NETHERLANDS.
Acting Consul—Bauduin, A. J.

PORTUGAL.
Consul—Loureiro, E.

SWEDEN AND NORWAY.
Acting Consul—Bauduin, A. J.

SWITZERLAND.
Consul General—Brennwald, C.
Chancellor—Wolf, A.

U. S. OF AMERICA.
Consul and Postal Agent—Shepard, O. O. (absent)
Vice-Consul—Mitchell, Geo. N.
Deputy Consul—Denison, H. W.
Deputy Marshal—Elmer, W.
Post Office Clerk—Lamb, John A.
Messenger—Yaski

Postal Agencies.

BRITISH POST OFFICE.
Postmaster—Machado, F. G.
Shroff—Foong Achan

U. S. POST OFFICE.
Postal Agent—Shepard, O. O. (absent)
Clerk—Lamb, John A.
Messenger—Yaski

FRENCH POST OFFICE.
Director—Degron, H.
*Ouchen, Chas.
Compradore—Footey

H. M.'s PROVINCIAL COURT.
Acting Assistant Judge—Hannen, N. J.
Acting Registrar and Interpreter—Hall, J. C.
Court Usher—White, F. E.

YOKOHAMA.

Imperial Government Railways.

Director—Cargill, W. W., F R G S.
Consulting Engineer—Pole, Wm , F R S.
London Agents—Malcolm, Brunker & Co.

Principal Japanese Officials.

Acting Chief Commissioner—Obota, S.
Acting Chief Assistant do—Sabata Kanaki
Assistant do.—Yeguwa, K.

Principal Foreign Officials.

CONSTRUCTION & MAINTENANCE.

Engineer-in Chief—Boyle, R. Vicars, C.S.I. & M.I.C E.
Assistant Engineers—Blundel, A. W.; Day, Jas. E.; Dewing, J. A.; Diack, J.; England, J. (chief assist. engineer); Gray, T.; Hardy, C.; Holtham, E. G.; Jones, T. M. R.; Kinder, O. W.; Newcombe, Edward; Nordenstadt, N. N.; Rogers, W.; Shann, T.; Sheppard, C.; Sherwinton, T. D.; Young, J. B.
Secy. to the Engineer-in Chief—Pole, G. H.
Foremen Mechanics—Balaam, G.; Colomb, J.; Conwell, T.; Cooper, J. E; Denny, J.; Edwards, W.; Halsey, W.; Impey, G.; King, G; Livick, E.; Matthews, N.; Mightom, G.; Newton, C.; Phillips, O.; Rasmussen, N. C.; Shaw, W.; Smith, G.; Taylor, A.; Thompson, C.; Walker, Thos; Watt, W.; Wilson, A.

TRAFFIC.

Traffic Manager, etc., etc.—Galwey, W.
Police Inspectors—Blockley, A.; Cole, T.; Dillon, W.; Doel, P.; Harding, H.
Yardsman—Hellenloal, P. J.

LOCOMOTIVE DEPARTMENT.

Locomotive Superintendent—Christy, F. C.
Clerk—Charlesworth, G.
Head Foreman—Aunand, J.
Foremen—Houghton, Henry
Engine Drivers, Fitters, Smiths & Boiler Makers—Allan, A.; Bristow, H.; Carroll, A.; Caswell, S.; Cook, L.; Cripps, G.; Cross, T.; Davidson, J.; Doherty, F.; Eager, R.; Ellis, G.; Fennell, H. J.; Gray, D.; Gray, J.; Hall, J.; Hartman, H. A.; Henderson, P.; Hurt, T.; King, R.; Lilley, J. S.; Mackenzie, J.; Martin, E.; Pritchard, J.; Ramsay, R.; Roberts, E.; Roberts, H.; Robertson, J.; Senior, T.; Strandberg, J.; Trotter, J. L.; Ward, R.; Watt, W.; Webber, H. B.

GENERAL.

Chief Accountant—Aldrich, A. S.
Assistant Accountant—Smith, J. R.
Clerks—Andrew, W. P.; Board, W. K.; Brooks, J. M.; Child, F. A.; Elliott, G; Ribiero, F. C. C.; Swift, T. C.; Thorp, R. W.

MEDICAL.

Principal Medical Officer—Purcell, T. A.
Harris, J., M.D.; Wheeler, E., M.D.

Imperial Government Telegraphs.

STAFF.

Director—Cargill, W. W., F R G S.
Engineer-in-Chief—Boyle, R. Vicars, C.B., C S I.

JAPANESE OFFICIALS.

Chief Commissioner—Ishimai, T.
Vice-do.—Ishie, T.
Assist. do.—Ikuda, T.
Vice Assist. do.—Okumura, M.

PRINCIPAL OFFICERS.

Chief Superintendent—George, E. (Yedo) (absent)
Electrician and Mechanician—Schaefer, L. (Yedo)
Correspondent—Stone, W. H.
Asst. Supt.—Morris, J. (Yedo & Y'hama)
    Teale, W. (Yedo)
    Hallifax, T. E. (Toyobasi)
    Larkin, T. J. (Kobe)
    Foster, J. T. (Shimonosaki)
    Fry, J. O. (Nagasaki)
Inspectors—Dunk, T. (Yedo & Yokohama); Smith, J. (Yedo and Yokohama); Waite, J. S. (Gifu); Fisk, F. (Himeji and Onomidu)
Storekeeper—Prowse, F. (Yedo)
English Teacher at the Telegraph School—Malcolm, J. W. (Yedo)
Clerks—Webb, W. (Yokohama); Driver, A. J (Yokohama); O'Brien, W. F. (Kobé); Mayhew, J. (Kobé); Ward, F. (Shimonoseki); Pyne, F. C. (Nagasaki); Kennedy, W. (Nagasaki)

HARBOUR MASTER'S OFFICE.

Harbour Master—Purvis, Capt. J. R., R.N.

MUNICIPALITY.

Municipal Director—Benson, E. S.
Chinese Interpreter—Leong Cheu Shing

YOKOHAMA.

MUNICIPALITY.
(Continued.)

MUNICIPAL POLICE.

English Sergeant—Chester, F.
Do. Constables—Clow, R. H.; Braund, J.; Connor, J.; Plunkett, J.; Carter, W.
French Corporal—Lafitte, Benjn.
Do. Constables—Montant, G.; Erevegniac, G. L.
2 Chinese

Public Works Department.

LIGHTHOUSE SECTIO', **BENTEN.**

1st Commissioner—Satow Yozo
2nd do.—Hara Takayoshi
Assistant do.—Nishimuda Toyoiyasu; Hasingawaya Yoshinushi
Chief Engineer—Brunton, Henry R., M.I. C.E., F.R.G.S., F.G.S.
Assistant Chief Engineer—Fisher, Sterling; McRitchie, J.
Secretary & Acct.—Wauchope, George
Clerk—Urquhart, A.
Teacher of Engineering—Farman, C.
Do English—Sandeman, F.
Superintendents of Works—Pearce, J.; Oastler, J; Simpkins, W.; Herdman, J.
Lighthkeepers—Charleson, G.; Dick, J.; Bowers, W.; Harris, C.; Egart, H.; Forrest, T.; Hurdle, W.; Legg, H.; Figgins, A. F.; Smyth, W. A.; Reddock, G.; Seitz, O.; Budge, James

LIGHTHOUSE TENDER S.S. "THABOR."

Captain—Brown, A. R.
Chief Officer—Pendred, J.
Second do.—
Chief Engineer—McNab, A. F.
Second do.—Jones, F.
Boatswain—
Chief Steward—Gray, J.
Second do.—

THE SAIBANSHO.

JUDICIAL COURT OF KANAGAWA.

Interpreters—Motz, Robert; Wills, George
Legal Adviser—Hill, G. W.

THE KENCHO.

Foreign Secretary—Percival Osborn

JAPANESE IMPERIAL CUSTOMS.

Legal Adviser—Lowder, F.
Appraisers—Miller, H. M.; Wertheimer, L.

Arsenal d'Yokoska.

EMPLOYÉS FRANÇA.-.

Ingénieur de la Marine, Directeur—Verny
Do. do. Sous-Directeur—Thibaudier
Médecin de la Marine—Savatier
Chef des Travaux Hydrauliques—St. Florent
Chef de la Comptabilité—de Montgolfier
Sous Ingr. des Constructions Navales—François
Secretaire—Verny, Maurice
Charpentiers—David; Provost
Charpentier calfat—Quillien
Modeliste—Michel
Forgeron serrurier—Le Troter
Mécanicien—Dubois; Mange; Capitaine; Bretonnière
Fondeur—Girard
Chaudronniers—Berger; Join
Maitre de Manœuvres—Liccionni
Chef-dessinateur—Fautrat
Maitre Maçon—Caill
Cordier—Le Hérisson
Capitaine d'Armes—Bonville
Professeurs—Sarda; Laurent

ATELIERS DE CONSTRUCTIONS MECANIQUES DU GOUVERNEMENT A YOKOHAMA.

EMPLOYÉS FRANÇAIS.

Ingénieur—Barbier
Mécaniciens—Barbançon, Le; Barelle
Fondeur—Even
Chaudronnier—Deninud

Naval and Military.

BATTALION OF ROYAL MARINE LIGHT INFANTRY.

Lieutenant Colonel Commanding—Richards, Fleetwood J, Colonel
Captains—Snow, Edmund, B. (Bt. Major); Walsh, Arthur H. H.; Hill, Arthur; Gray, E. O. B.
Lieutenants—St. John, St. Andrew; Heseltine, Gerald A.; Fagan, Christopher S. F.; Drury, F. B.; Denny, Barry St L; Polkinghorne, Stewart; Smyth, Arthur C; Wright, H. O. Percival; Nepean, O.
Paymaster—Broughton, Capt. J D.
Lie t. and Adjt.—Sandwith, John H.
Control Officer and Superintending Civil Engineer—Bridgford, Capt. Sidney T. R.M.A.
Acting Quartermaster—Hungerford, Lieut. T E.
Staff-Surgeon—Caldwell, John
Surgeon—Putsey, William H.

4EME. REGIMENT D'INFANTERIE DE MARINE.

Capitaine 6th Compe.—Desconnet
Lieutenant do.—Vitrac
Sous-Lieut. do.—Meunier
Capitaine 24th Comp.—Corion
Lieutenant do.—Adam
Sous-Lieutenant do.—Coiffier

THE ROYAL NAVAL VICTUALLING DEPOT.

Naval Accountant and Storekeeper—Pittman, Frank, R.N.
Chief Quartermaster—Calloway, H.
Ship's Steward—Bremner, Charles

Hospitals.

L'HOPITAL JAURES.

Surgeon in Charge—Forné, M., medicin de 1ére classe, Chargé du service de sante
Martin, M., aide commissaire, chef du service administratif

ROYAL NAVAL HOSPITAL.

Medical Officers—Hilston, Duncan, M. D.; MacDonnell, Henry
Steward &c.—Lawless, W. J.

YOKOHAMA GENERAL HOSPITAL.

Committee—Robertson, Russell; Shepard, C. O.; Zappe, E.; Wilkin, A. J.; Lane, Geo. E.; Fraser, J. A.; Allen, H., Jr.; Jackson, T.
Hon. Sec. and Treasurer—Kirby, E. C.
Physician—Dalliston, J. J. R., M.D.
Steward in Charge—Nicolayson, N. O.
Assistant Stewards—Miller, J.; Sami, V.

U. S. NAVAL HOSPITAL.
99, BLUFF.

Surgeon in Charge—King, Wm. M.
Assistant Surgeon—Dickinson, Dwight
Employés—Pirie, H R.; Eagling, Ephraim; Kauppe, Silvester; Weys, William

Clubs, &c.

CEMETERY.

COMMITTEE.—Hill, Capt. A., R.M.
Geisenheimer, F.
Piquet, E.
Pearson, J. C.
Allen, Jr., H.
Supt. of Cemetery—Wake, Geo. E.

CHAMBER OF COMMERCE.
COMMITTEE.

Chairman—Wilkin, A. J.
Vice-Chairman—Winstanley, A.
Johnstone, Robert
Thomas, Thos.
Fraser, J. A.
Pistorius, P. E.
Brent, A.
Dodds, J.
Evers, A.
Secretary—Dare, J. Julius
Auditors—Baker, R. B.
Jackson, Thos.

CRICKET CLUB.

Secretary—Abbott, E.

AMERICAN FIRE BRIGADE.

Foreman—Hurlbut, Geo.
Asst. do.—Haskell, H B.
Foreman Hose Carriage—Endicott, J.
Hon. Secretary and Treasurer—Allen, H., Jr.

PRIVATE FIRE "HOOK AND LADDER" BRIGADE.

Foreman—Hohnholz, H. W.
Asst. Foreman—Mills, H.
Leading Hose—Watson, J.
Asst. do.—Kubick, Y.
Suction Hose—Clausen, P.
Asst. do.—Rogers, H.
1st Officer of Hook and Ladder—Stibolt, N.
2nd do.—Laufenberg, J.
3rd do.—McKenzie, D.
Secretary and Treasurer—Liebermann, J.

FOOTE'S CLUB.

Manager—Foote, C.

CLUB GERMANIA.

President—Ohl, H.
Vice-President—Ziegler, O.
Secretary—Kempermann, T.
Steward—Vollhardt, A.

NATIONAL STEAM SHIP COMPANY OF NIPON.

Director—Pfoundes, C.
Consulting Engineer—Taylor, J.
Chief Engineers—Ellis, J.; Carlisle, E.; Bell, T.
Masters—Drummond, J.; Eckstrand, J.
Chief Officer—Steadman, J.
Boilermaker—Kasby, J.

YOKOHAMA. S 5

NATIONAL STEAM SHIP COMPANY
OF NIPON.
(Continued.)
Engineers—Mathews, E.; Shomaker, G.;
Mercer, T.; Mercer, J.; Cahill, D.;
Kirkham, J.; Wignall, M.
Blacksmith—Anderson, J.
Engineer in Charge—Jenkins, W.
Navigating Officer—Bonger, E.

PHILHARMONIC SOCIETY
Secretary—Michel, L.

PUBLIC HALL COMMITTEE.
Smith, W. H.
Bridgford, Capt., R.M.A.
Townley, F.
Mitchell, A., Hon. Sec.

RACE CLUB.
Stewards—Baker, R. B.; Sandwith, J. H.
(Royal Marines); Davison, J.; Lane,
Capt. Geo. E.; Fraser, J. A.

RACQUET CLUB.
Secretary—Tripp, H. J. H.

SWISS RIFLE CLUB.
President—Mottu, A.
Secretary—Hormann, S.
Assessor—Favre Brandt, J.

ROYAL ASIATIC SOCIETY.
President—Hepburn, J. C., M.D.
Vice-Presidents—Brown, Rev. S. R., D.D.;
Parkes, Sir Harry S., K C.B.
Treasurer—Baker, R. B.
Recording Secretary—Bellamy, A.
Correspondent Secretary—Syle, Rev. E. W.
Curator and Librarian—Pryer, H.
Council—Satow, E.; Wilkin, A. J.; Howell,
W. G.; Brunton, R. H.

YOKOHAMA RIFLE ASSOCIATION.
Secretary—Barnard, A.

YOKOHAMA ROWING CLUB.
Secretary—Hamilton, G.

YOKOHAMA UNITED CLUB.
Manager—Smith, W. H.
Steward—Lipsett, W.
Cook—Pauline, J.

THE YOKOHAMA GAS COMPANY.
WOARS AT NONGE.
Japanese Director—Takashima Kayemon
Chief Engineer—Ulbrich, J. G.
Assistant Engineers—Berlingard, L.; Sarda,
G.
Interpreter—Fleury, J. A.

Masonic Lodges.

YOKOHAMA LODGE, No. 1092, E.C.
Worshipful Master—Bourne, Wm. (acting)
Senior Warden in Charge—Bourne, R. M.
Junior Warden—Shaw, T. K.
Secretary—Geoghegan, E. J.
Treasurer—Fletcher, C. A.
Senior Deacon—Pistorius, A. A.
Junior Deacon—Urqnhart, A.
Inner Guard—Sandeman
Tyler—Miller, W. A.

OTENTOSAMA LODGE, No. 1263, E.C.
Worshipful Master—Black, J. R.
Senior Warden—Crane, W. A.
Junior Warden—Langfeldt, A.
Secretary—Crane, W. A. (acting)
Treasurer—Liebermann, J. L.
Senior Deacon—Moss, H.
Junior Deacon—Laufenberg, J.
Inner Guard—Dutt, H.
Tyler—Miller, W. A.

Religious Institutions.

AMERICAN BAPTIST MISSIONARY
UNION.
Brown, Rev. N., D.D., No. 75B., Bluff.
Goble, Rev. J.   do. 75A., do.
Arthur, Rev. J. H.
Doyen, Rev. J. T.

AMERICAN METHODIST EPISCOPAL
CHURCH MISSION.
Maclay, Rev. R. S., No. 60, Bluff
Cornell, Rev. I. H., No. 57. do.

AMERICAN PRESBYTERIAN MISSION.
Hepburn, J. C., M D., LL.D., No. 89
Loomis, Rev. H., No. 89
Miller, Rev. E. R., No. 89
Youngman, Miss Kate M., No. 89

THE REFORMED CHURCH IN
AMERICA.
Brown, Rev. S. R., D.D., No. 211, Bluff
Ballagh, Rev. J. H., Mission House, No.
167

YOKOHAMA.

THE REFORMED CHURCH IN AMERICA.
(Continued.)

Wolff, Rev. C. H. H.
Miller, Mrs. E. R.
Hequembourg, Miss S. K. M., No. 211, Bluff

CANADIAN WESLEYAN MISSION.

Cochrane, Rev. George, No. 143, Bluff
McDonald, Rev. M., M.D.   ,,

CHRIST CHURCH.

Act Consular Chaplain—Syle, Revd. E. W.
Trustees—Murray, E. D.; James, F. S.
Treasurer—Jackson, T.

ROMAN CATHOLIC.

Bishop of Myrfiti, and Apostolic Vicar of Japan—Petitjean, Mgr. B. T ,
Mis Apost. — Chamaison, L'Abbe Jean Baptiste,
Missionaires Apost.—Evrard L'Abbe Felix Pettier, L'Abbe Alfred Eugene Midon L'Abbe Felix, Testevuide, L'Abbe Leger, Germain Langlais, L'Abbe Albert, Julien

SISTERS OF CHARITY.

PENSIONNAT DU ST. ENFANT JESUS.

Superieure—Norbert, Sœur St.
  Grégoire, Sœur St.
  Wilfrid,   Do.
  Gélase,   Do.
  Marthe,   Do.
  Ephrem,   Do.

WOMAN'S UNION MISSIONARY SOCIETY OF AMERICA.

Pruyn, Mrs. Mary, No. 212, Bluff
Pierson, Mrs. L. H.   Do.
Crosby, Miss Julia   Do.
Guthrie, Miss L. M.   Do.
Benton, Mrs. L. E.   Do.

Insurances.

Adamson, Bell & Co.
  Globe Marine Insurance Co., Limited
Butterfield & Swire
  Royal Exchange Fire Assurance
  British and Foreign Assurance
Clark, W. A.
  General Agent for Japan of the New England Mutual Life Ins. Co.
Cornes & Co.
  Lloyd's London
Findlay, Richardson & Co.
  North British and Mercantile Ins. Co.
  Scottish Commercial Insurance Co.
Fletcher, C. A.
  San Francisco Board of Underwriters
Fraser & Co , J. C.
  Thames and Mersey Marine Insurance Company
Gilman & Co.
  Commercial Union Assurance Co., Fire and Marine
  Union Insurance Society of Canton
  Universal Marine Insurance Co.
  Queen Insurance Co. of Liverpool
  London and Lancashire Fire Ins. Co.
  Merchants' Marine Insurance Co.
Gutschow & Co.
  London Assurance Corporation
Heard & Co , Augustine
  China Traders' Insurance Co., Ld.
  Victoria Fire Insurance Company, of Hongkong, Limited
  London and Provincial Marine Insurance Company
Hecht, Lilienthal & Co.
  La Compagnie Lyonnaise d'Assurance Maritimes
Hudson, Malcolm & Co.
  Lancashire Fire Insurance Company
  Batavia Sea and Fire Insurance Co.
Jardine, Matheson & Co.
  Canton Marine Insurance Company
  Hongkong Fire Insurance Co., Limited
Kingdon, Schwabe & Co.
  Phœnix Fire Assurance, London
  Manchester Fire Insurance Company
Kniffler & Co.
  Trans-Atlantische Feuer Versicherungs Actien Gesellschaft in Hamburg
Macpherson & Marshall
  Imperial Fire Insurance Company
  Transatlantic Marine Insurance Co.
McDonald, Wm.
  Surveyor for Lloyds' Agents and Local Offices
North China Insurance Company
  Agent—Bayne, W. G.
Reis, Von der Heyde & Co.
  Hamburg—Bremen Fire Ins Co.
  Colonial Sea and Fire Insurance Co. of Batavia
  North-German Fire Insurance Company in Hamburg
  Vaterländsche Transport — Versicherungs-Actien-Gesellschaft, Elberfeld
Rickett, J.
  London and Oriental Steam Transit Insurance Co.
Siber & Brennwald
  Helvetia Marine Insurance Co.
Smith, Baker & Co.
  Guardian Fire and Life Assurance Co., London

YOKOHAMA.

Strachan & Thomas
  Northern Assurance Company, Fire and Life
  China and Japan Marine Insurance Co.
Van Oordt & Co.
  Netherlands India Sea and Fire Insurance Company
  Samarang India Sea and Fire Ins. Co.
Von Hemert, J. Ph.
  The Oosterling Sea and Fire Insurance Company of Batavia
  Second Colonial Insurance Company of Batavia
  Java Sea and Fire Insurance Co.
Walsh, Hall & Co.
  Yangtsze Ins. Association, Marine
Wilkin & Robison
  Sun Fire Office
Ziegler & Co
  Swiss Lloyd's Marine Insurance Company, Winterthur
  German Fire Insurance in Berlin

Merchants, &c.

Abegg, Borel & Co., merchants, No. 10 (jiu-ban)
  Abegg, F.
  Borel, L.
    Becker, H.
    Jaquemot, J., Jr.

Abel, K., resident, 137

Adamson, Bell & Co., 72
  D'Iffanger, F. (absent)
  Pryer, H.

Adds, C., coal merchant and aerated water manufacturer, 16 (jiu-roku-ban)
  Adds, C.
  Roach, H.

Ahrens & Co., H.
  Ahrens, H. (absent)
  Bair, M. M.   (do.)
  Schmid, E.   (do.)
  Hake, T. H.

Alexandre, Dr., dentist, 89 (ku-jiu-san-ban)

Allard, & Co., G., importer, 80 (san-jiu-ban)

Allen, H., Junior, commission agent, 32 (san-jiu-ni-ban)

Aymonin & Co., V., merchants, 28, (ni-jiu-hachi-ban)
  Aymonin, V.
  Deveze, A.
    Giussani, C., silk inspector
    Zembsch, J. P. A.

Baker, R. B., resident, 78

Barnard, W., resident, 120 (hy'aku-ni-jiu-ban)

Barucco, P., watchmaker, 166

Bavier & Co., 75 (shichi-jiu-roku-ban)
  Bavier, Ed.
  Bavier, Ant. (absent)
  Bavier, Ernest
    Anderson, H.
    Simoni, P. M.
    Noyer, G.
    Ludwig, H.
    Senn, O.
    Colombo, L.
    Takaki, interpreter
    Kam-ki, L., compradore

Bayne, W. G., agent, N. China Ins. Co.

Beato & Co., F., photographers
  Beato, F.
    Woollett, H., assistant

"Bee Hive," The, 81
  Dutton, G., proprietor
    Human, W. H.

Benjamin & Co., express agents, 59 and 50
  Isaacs, E. M.
  Benjamin, A.

Bennett & Brent, bill-brokers, 98
  Bennett, W. R.
  Brent, W.

Berger, E., Bank Buildings, 61 (roku-jiu-ichi-ban)

Berrick Bros., stationers, &c., 60
  Berrick, G. B.
  Berrick, L.

Bertrand & Co., Ch., importers and commission agents
  Bertrand, Ch.

Black & Co., Wm., general storekeepers and shipchandlers
  Black, Wm.
  Wilkins, J. H.

Black, Batavus & Co.
  Batavus, Edward

Bland, C. S., bill and bullion broker
  Bland, C. S. (absent)
  Tripp, H. J. H.

Bland, C., resident, 104 (hy'aku-yo-ban)

Bohn, P., undertaker and furnisher, 114 (hy'aku-jiu-yo-ban)

Bolmida, G., merchant, 154 (nyaku-go-jiu-yo-ban)
   Bolmida, G.
   Crinlsi, G.

Bonand, Emile, watchmaker and store-keeper

Borneo Company, Limited
   Agents--Findlay Richardson & Co.

Boulangerie Française, 166 (hyaku-roku-jiu-ro-ku-ban)
   Giovanni, E.

Boulangerie Française, 184
   Centurioni, C.

Bourne & Co.
   Bourne, W.
   Winstanley, James
   Marsh, G.

Brett, W. R., chemist, 70 (shichi-jiu-ban)

Bridgens, R. P., architect, 124 (hy'aku-ni-jiu-go-ban)

"British Queen," tavern
   Livingston, R. F., proprietor
   Greensward, E.

Brodhurst, R. C., merchant
   Brodhurst, R C.
   Brown, W. T.
   Herrring, T.

Brook, —., resident, 141

"Brooklyn Hotel," 40 (shi-jiu-ban), Crittenden & Scott, proprietors
   Crittenden, F.
   Scott, M.

Brower, T. L., chemist

Brun, —., resident, 187

Brundell, Bryan, commission and general agent, 178 (hyaku-shichi-jiu-san-ban)

Buckle, W. T., M.B., L.R.C.P.L., 67

Burgess & Co., butchers and compradores, 42 (shi-jiu-ni-ban)
   Hovenburg, G. W. Van
   Clark, W. E.
   Reuter, H.

Busch, Schraub & Co., shipchandlers, 55 (go-jiu-go-ban)
   Busch, H.
   Schraub, E.

Bush and Blass, 72 (shichi-jiu-ni-ban)
   Bush, Isaac
   Blass, Meyer (absent)
   Blass, Morris
   Bush, Siegfried

Butterfield & Swire, merchants
   Dodds, Thomas
   Jeyes, H. O.

"Café du Japon," 169 (hy'aku-roku-ku-ban)
   Arnoux, F., proprietor

Caillens & Co., J., saddlers
   Caillens, J.

Campbell, Mrs, private resident, 129

Carroll & Co., J. D., store-keepers, shipchandlers and general commission agents, 16 (jiu-roku-ban)
   Carroll, J. D.
   Spoonor, F. C.
   Wiggins, Chas., (Hiogo)
   Spooner, G. P.
   Titgen, H., (Hiogo)
   Roberts, H. M.

Casembrost, L. G. de, resident

Chartered Mercantile Bank, 78 (sh'chi-jiu-hachi-ban)
   Baker, R. B., manager
   Henderson, W. D., acting account.
   Robilliard, W. S.
   Abell, H. J.
   Gordo, W. F.

Cheshire & Co., average adjusters, public accountants, &c., 115
   Cheshire, W.
   Hall, J. W.
   Smith, Thos. J.
   Merriman, W.

China and Japan Trading Company
   Brunier, J., agent
   Beauchamp, T. W.

Chipman, Stone & Co., 28 (ni-jiu-hachi-ban)
    Chipman, H. S.
    Stone, N. J.
    Wetmore, F. R.

Christien, —., resident, 187

Church & Co., Howard, 176
    Church, Howard
    Sharp, Daniel, Jr.
    Brush, Stephen, Jr.

"City of Hamburg," 170 (hy'aku-sh'chi-jiu-ban)
    Goldsmith, Mrs

Clark, Wm. L., commission and general agent, Ice House, 48 (shi-jiu-sam-ban)
    Clark, Wm.

Cobb & Co., 61 (roku-jiu-ichi-ban)
    Farmer, J.
    Sutherland, J. W.
    Francis, M. H.

Cocking & Singleton, 171 (hy'aku-sh'chi-jiu-ichi-ban)
    Cocking, S. Jr.
    Singleton, T. A.

Colomb, & Co., J.
    Colomb, Jules
    Colomb, P.

Comi, Vincent, merchant, 10 (jiu-ban)
    Comi, V.
    Valny, R.
    Ponti, F. De

Commercial Auction Sales Room, 55 (go-jiu-go-ban)
    Crane, H. A.

Comptoir d'Escompte de Paris, 57 (go-jiu-sh'chi-ban)
    Vouillemont, E. G., manager
    Cantelli, V., cashier
    Swaby, W. S., sub-accountant
    Glénat, L., do.

Cook, H., carpenter and shipwright, 115 (hy'aku-jiu-go-ban)
    Cook, H.
    Cook, W.

Cook, H. L., importer, news agent and commission agent 81.(hachi-jiu-go-ban)

Cook, Mrs. D., millinery and fancy goods store

Cornes & Co., 55 (san-jiu-go-ban)
    Cornes, Frederick (absent)
    Taylor, William Henry
    Winstanley, Arthur
    Le Mare, J.
    Wylie, R. A.
    Jamieson, W.

Crane, W. A., piano tuner, 117 (hy'aku-jiu-roku-ban)

Crown and Anchor
    Ehman, S.

Culty, A., hairdresser, 51 (go-jiu-ichi-ban)

Curnow & Co., J., storekeepers, 83
    Russell, M.
    Mitchell, A.

Dalliston, Dr. J. J. R., physician, 85

Davis, D., resident, 45 (shi-jiu-go-ban)

Davis, Mrs. E., dressmaker

Davis, L., general trader, 87

Davis, T., government road and drain inspector, 16

Davison & Co., merchants and silk inspectors, 28 (ni-jiu-hachi-ban)
    Davison, Jas.
    Engelhardt, —.

Degron, H., 184 (hy'aku-san-jiu-yo-ban)

De Jong, Dr. C. G., 179a

Dell'Oro & Co., J., 156 (hy'aku-go-jiu-roku-ban)
    Dell'Oro, Isidore
    Dell'Oro, J., (absent)
    Bartesaghi, Carlo
    Vock, Arnold

Deutsche Bank, 79 (sh'chi-jiu-ku-ban)
    Mammelsdorff, J., manager
    Hübner, M., cashier
    Da Ponseca, J. A., clerk
    Mühlenfeld, H., clerk

Dickins, F. V., barrister-at-law, 57 (go-jiu-ah'chi-ban)

Domoney & Co., G , butchers, ship. compradores, and general storekeepers
  Domoney, G.
  Plummer, A.
    Noble, A. K.
    Hardwick, W. O.
    Morris, S.
    Stroem, P.
    Ah Yeong

Douglas & Co., F., butchers and compradores
  Douglas, F.
    Collyn, J. E.
    Tommugsen, J.
    Ah Tuck

Driscoll & Co., tailors, hosiers and outfitters, 61 (roku-jiu-ichi-ban)
  Driscoll, W. F. (Kobé)
  Frischling, C. J.
  Powys, Edward
    Groves, F. J. (Kobé)

Druse, R., baker, 81 (hachi-jiu-ichi-ban)

Dymstan, —., resident, 187

Echo du Japon, newspaper, 188 (hy'aku-hachi-jiu-san-ban)
  Levy, C.

Edwards, James, storekeeper, 89 (hachi-jiu-ku-ban)
  Edwards, J.
  Hearne, A.

Elliott, W. St. G., M.D., D.D.S., dentist, 75 (ah'chi-jiu go-ban)

Esdale, James, tailor, 81 (san-jiu-ichi-ban)

"Eureka" Bowling Saloon, 81
  Wulff, T.
  Schmidt, T. P.

Ewart, W., accountant, 170 (hy'aku-ah'chi-jiu-ban)

Fabre & Co., A., 81
  Fabre, A.
    Hormann, J.
    Baader, W.
    Estienne, G.
    Ah Wang

"Far East" and Sailor's Home, The, 186 (hyaku-sah-jiu-roku-ban)
  Lewis, Evan, proprietor

Farfara & Grenet, 90
  Farfara, G. (absent)
  Grenet, J.

Favre Brandt, O. & J., watchmakers, 175 (hyaku-ah'chi-jiu-go-ban)
  Favre Brandt, O. (Osaka)
  Favre Brandt, J.
  Huot, Ch.
  Vannes, P.

Findlay, Richardson & Co., merchants
  Richardson, Francis (London)
  Findlay, Chas. B. (Glasgow)
  Caw, Thomas (Manila)
  Brown, M. (Glasgow)
  Johnstone, Robt.
  Dunlop, Charles G.
  Brown, M., Jnr.

Fourgade, J. J., storekeeper, 10c (jiu-ban)

Fraser & Co., J. C., merchants, 48 (shi-jiu-hachi-ban)
  Fraser, J. C. (absent)
  Mollison, J. P.
  Fraser, E. J.
  Murray, E. D.
  Hamilton, Geo.

"Fulton Market House" Tavern, 40a (shi-jiu-ban)
  Pierce, T.

Gallstell, —., resident, 169

Geffeney, C. H., hair dresser

Gérard, A., navy water works office, 169 (hyaku-roku-jiu-ku-ban)
  Gérard, A.
  Hoffman, G.

Gilman & Co., 74 (ah'chi-jiu-shi-ban)
  Gilman, R. S. (England)
  Wild, C. A.   "
  Ramsay, H. F.   "
  Gilman, F.   "
  Lemann, H. B. (Hongkong)
  Lemann, W. (Foochow)
  Lavers, E. H. (Shanghai)
    Melhuish, C. J.
    Abbott, E.
    Barthe, C.
    Glennie, A. W., (absent)

YOKOHAMA. S 11

Ginsburgh & Co., S. L., general merchants and commission agents, 45
  Ginsburgh, S. L.
  Speiller, L.
  Greenberg, M.

Glackmeyer, G., 107 (hy'aku-sh'ochi-ban)

Grand Hotel
  Smith, W. H., managing director
  Lyons, J., manager
    Davieson, Joseph, clerk
    Furumatz, S., do.
    Tayeux, Alfred, head steward
    Caylor, Alfred, steward
    Young, Fredrick, do.
    Ford, Mrs., stewardess
    Béguex, Louis, chief cook

Grauert, H., 179 (hyaky-shichi-jiu-ku-ban)
  Grauert, H.

Great Northern Telegraph Co.
  Simoni, P. M., agent

Grosser & Co., merchants, 180 (hyaku-hachi-jiu-ban)
  Grosser, E.
  Hagens, E.
  Grosser, F.

Guirrini, N., resident, 80

Gutschow & Co., merchants, 92 (ku-jiu-ni-ban)
  Gutschow, P.
  Gutschow, O.
    Kempermann, T. H.
    Machenhauer, B.
    Gill, Eug H.
    Hudoffsky, H.

Haber, L.
  Haber, L.
  Finke, H.
  Rochkugel, A.

Hahn, A., piano-tuner, 121 (hy'aku-ni-jiu-ichi-ban)

Harley, —., resident, 137

Hartley & Co., J., 24 (ni-jiu-shi-ban)
  Hartley, John
  Henson, John

Hatton, Mrs., laundress, 132 (hy'aku-san-jiu-ni-ban)

Havana Cigar Co.
  Jonas, F.
  Heymanson, B.

Heard & Co., Augustine
  Farley, Gustavus, Jr.
  Fraser, John A.
  James, F. S.
  Pinel, J.

Hecht, Lilienthal & Co., 8 (hatchi-ban)
  Geisenheimer, F.
  Wolfs, J.
  Broeschen, H.
  Schaal, F.
  Douille, P.
  Schaeffer, Fr.
  Fischer, F. von (Hiogo)
  Fleischer, H. M. (do.)

Hegt, M. J. B. Noordhoek, 68 (roku-jiu-hatchi-ban)
  Hegt, M. J. B. Noordhoek
  Eyton, J. L. O.
  Harrymann, F.
  Prisbee, C.
  Thomsen, T.
  Boutkes, P.

Heinemann & Co., 189 (hy'aku-hachi-jiu-ku-ban)
  Heinemann, Paul
  Camp, H. de la
  Hawkins, H. J.

Hertzog & Roth, 179 (hy'aku-sh'chi-jiu-ku-ban)
  Hertzog, —.
  Roth, T.
  Blass, M.

Hill, G. W., barrister-at-law

Hohnholz & Co., W. H., shipchandlers and general storekeepers, 82
  Hohnholz, H. W.
  Wulff, J.

Hongkong & Shanghai Bank, 62 (roku-jiu-ban)
  Jackson, T., manager
  Hodgson, J. G., accountant
  Cook, R. H., assistant accountant
  Rickett, C. B., do.
  Macnab, John, do.
  Smith, A. J., do.
  Harries, W. H., agent (Hiogo)
  Pereira, E. J., assistant (do.)
  Van Delden & Co., agents (Nagasaki)

12 S YOKOHAMA.

Hooper Brothers, merchants, 22 (ni-jiu-ni-ban)
   Hooper, H. J.
   Hooper, C. F.

Hotel de la Marine, 41 (shi-jiu-ichi-ban)
   Giaretto, J.
   Cristian, —.

Hudson, Malcolm & Co., merchants, 78 (ah'chi-jiu-san-ban)
   Hudson, John
   Malcolm, W. A. (absent)
   Brent, Arthur
   Hyde, E. L.
      Hardman, C. R.
      MacArthur, H.
      Bellamy, A
      Jones, E. B.
      Kilby, E. F.
      Thorp, C. H.

Ice Company of Yokohama, The, 88 (hy-aku-go-jiu-hachi-ban)

International Hotel & Sweatmeat Castle, 18 (jiu-hachi-ban)
   Curtis, W., proprietor
   Winser, Miss E., barmaid
   Curtis, A. W., Jr.
   Hearns, H., steward

Isaacs, Brothers, general merchants, 42 (shi-jiu-ni-ban)
   Isaacs, Israel
   Isaacs, R.
      Isaacs. Marcus

Jacobs, F. S., 57

Jaffray, A., livery and veterinary stable, 123 (hyaku-ni-jiu-san-ban)
   Jaffray, A.
   Shieras, G.
   Jaffray, R.

James & Wilson, draymen and milkmen, 98
   Broadhurst, R. C.
   Brown, W. J.
   Herring, F.
   Reid, G.

Japan Butchery and Bakery Company, 60 (roku-jiu-ban)
   Hassell, J., manager
   Blundell, B.
   Reed, W.

"Japan Gazette" Office, printing and publishing establishment, 85 (hachi-jiu-go-ban)
   Black, J. R., editor
   Moss, E. J., manager
   Moss, C. D., bookkeeper
   Welsh, D., collector
   Miller, A., foreman
   Joole, P.
   Anstin, J. H.
   Klyne, L.

"Japan Herald" Office
   Brooke, J. H., proprietor
   Pim, J. F., manager
   Harding, T., reporter
   Viney, J., foreman
   O'Toole, P., compositor
   Long, B.   do

"Japan Hotel," 44 (shi-jiu-ban)
   Moss, H., proprietor

"Japan Mail" office, 32 (son-jiu-ni-ban)
   Howell, W, G., proprietor
   Howell, G. H., sub-editor
   Collins, H., foreman
   Santos, J. M., compositor
   Rozario, J. P. de do
   Ah Ching   do
   Ah Leong   do
   Four Japanese do
   Ah Kow, machinist
   Kimbei, comprador

Jaquemot, J. M., 82
Jaquemot, J.
Jaquemot, C. P.

Jardine, Matheson & Co., 1 (ichi-ban)
   Whittall, Edward
   Walter, W. B.
   Montgomery, G. L.
   Reiuers, C. F.
   Whittall, P. G.

Kent, W. P., 29 (Bluff)

Kiley, J. D., sailmaker, 120 (hy'aku-ni-jiu-ban)

Kingdon, Schwabe & Co., merchants, 89a (hachi-jiu-ku-ban)
   Kingdon, N. P., 16 & 17 Bluff
   Schwabe, R. S., 144 Bluff

Kirby & Co., E. C., merchants, 100
   Kirby, E. C.
   Hunter, E. H.

YOKOHAMA.

Kniffler & Co., L., 54 (go-jiu-yo-ban)
  Kniffler, L. (absent)
  Reddelien, G.
  Illies, C. (Hiogo)
  Pardun, Wrr.
  Oestmann, A.
  Kniffler, Alex.
  Bollenhagen, E.
  Elfen, H.
  Francke, O. (Hiogo)
  Naudin, N.   (do.)
  Berga, J., godown-man (Hiogo)
  Raspe, M. (Osaka)
  Leesen, F. von   (Nagasaki)
  Kniffler, H.   (do.)
  Röhr, W.   (do.)
  Falck, O. godown-man (do.)

Krause, O., private resident, 125 (hy'aku-ni-jin-go-ban)

Kubik & Co., J., shoemakers, 132 (hy'aku-san-jiu-ui-ban)
  Kubik, J.
  Brown, J.

Kuhn, M. M., China and Japan importer and exporter, 51

Ladage, and Oelke, tailors and outfitters, 58 (go-jiu-san-ban)
  Oelke, J. D. W. (absent)
  Hager, Richard
  Bauer, A. T.
  Wolter, J.
  Mielanhausen, E.

Laiyon, Jacob, storekeeper, 51 (go-jiu-ichi-ban)

Lane, Crawford & Co., general store-keepers, tailors and outfitters, commission agents and auctioneers
  Townley, Frederic
  Wallace, Thos.
  Crawford, David R. (Hongkong)
  Cox, John S.   (do.)
  Fairbairn, John   (do.)
  Wilson, James
  Henderson, John Y.
  Owston, Alan
  Roy, John A.
  Richmond, T. G.
  Nully, R. de
  Wood, Charles
  Waggott, W.
  Schonhardt, H.
  Booth, G., manager, tailoring and outfitting department

Landeshut, S. S., accountant and commission agent, 61c, Main St.

Langfeldt & Mayers, storekeepers, &c., 52 (go-jiu-ni-ban)
  Langfeldt, A.
  Mayers, S.
  Mayers, J. L.
  Deidenbach, J

Lescasse, J., civil engineer and architect, 183 (hy'aku-hachi-jiu-san-ban)

Lichtenstein, L., importer, 57a (go-jiu-sh'chi-ban)

Liebermann J. L., furniture depot, 83 (hachi-jiu-san-ban)
  Liebermann, J. L.
  Francis, M. H.

Lohmann, Kuchmeister & Co., tailors and general outfitters, 70
  Peltzer, Tul.
  Lohmann, H.
  Kuchmeister, A.
  Molin, O.
  Goltze, W.

Machefer, F., apothecary, U. S. A., 137 (hy'aku-san-jiu-sh'chi-ban)

Macpherson & Marshall, merchants
  Macpherson, A. J.
  White, F. W. A.
  Smith, Thos.
  Dinsdell, G. K.

Macrae, K., commission agent, &c.

Mangue, A., blacksmith, 119 (hy'aku-jiu-ku-ban)

Marcus & Co., S., general importers, 56 (go-jiu-roku-ban)
  Marcus, S.
  Marcus, A.
  Marcus, E.

"Marine Hotel," 41 (shi-jiu-ichi-ban)
  Giaretto, T.

Marou & Co., merchants
  Maron, J. H.
  Reynaud, J.
    Freudenthaler, —.
    Hébé, —.
    Yamamoura

Martin & Co., coal merchants
  Martin, Jas.
  Martin, Jas., Jr.
  Burrell, Thomas

Marzaudin, —., resident, 137

McDonald, Wm., Lloyd's surveyor
  McDonald, W.
  Scott, D.

McDonald & Dare, bill, bullion, and ship brokers
  McDonald, W.
  Dare, G. M.

Meier & Co., A., 70
  Meier, A.
  Maier, L.

Mendelson Bros., merchants, 71 (sh'chi-jiu-ichi ban)
  Mendelson, S.
  Mendelson, J.

"Mercantile Printing" Office, 81 (san-jiu-ichi-ban)
  Gordo, A. F.

Merriman and Stevenson, auctioneers and forwarding agents
  Merriman, J.
  Stevenson, W.

Messageries Maritimes Co.
  Conil, A., agent
  Chapsal, J.
  Revest, Ch.
  Juery, H.
  Jourdan, P., coal depot
  Tai Hip Sam

Meyers, A., importer of European merchandise, 70 (sh'chi-jiu-ban)

Michel, Louis, 71 (sh'chi-jiu-ichi-ban)

Miller, W. A., ballast master. 114

Millinery, and Drapery Establishment
  Lockyer, Mrs. E.
  Ellis, Miss

Moore & Co., merchants, 89 (san jiu-ku-ban)
  Moore, L. P.
  Wolf, L.

Morf & Co., H. C., 176
  Morf, H. C.
  Grunwald, F.

Moritz, G., storekeeper, 81 (san-jiu-ichi-ban)
  Moritz, G.
  Marmelstein, J.

Myers, Mrs., resident, 20b

Ness, G. P. barrister at law, 80

Netherlands Trading Society
  Bauduin, A. J., chief agent
  Pistorius, P. E., agent
  Mees, R. A.
  Dames, M.
  Wringer, I. de, godown keeper

"New York House"
  Bank, J.

Noronha & Co., D., agents for Manila Lottery, 70
  Noronha, D. L.
  Kingsalle, F.

North German Hotel, 12b-7-8 (hy'aku-ni-jiu-roku-ban, sh'chi-ban, hachi-ban)
  Lotz, H.

Nowrojee & Co., D., bakers, general storekeepers and commission agents, 87b (hachi-jiu-sh'chi-ban)
  Nowrojee, Dorabjee (absent)
  Pestonjee, Jehangurjee
  Sapoorjee, E.

Ocean Steam Ship Co.
  Agents—Butterfield & Swire

"Old Brown Jug," The, 186 (hy'aku-san-jiu-roku-ban)
  Harley, J.

Oriental Bank Corporation, 11 (jiu-ichi-ban)
  Robertson, John, agent
  Thomson, Geo. W., acting accountant
  Reid, E. J., asst. account. and cashier
  Elder, Sam. J.   do.
  Burns, Benjamin H., asst. accountant
  Peres, B. A., clerk
  Marques, E. J., clerk
  Smeaton, Wm., messenger
  Crombie, D. A. J., act. agent (Hiogo)
  Mackenzie, H., asst. account. (do.)
  Carvalho, G. M., clerk   (do.)
  Claude, C. S., asst. account. (Osaka)

"Oriental Hotel," 84 (hachi-jiu-yo-ban)
  Bonnat, L.
  Licavo, P.
  Voyron, P.
  Boulle, E.
  Voyron, J.

Orny, V., storekeeper, 80 (hachi-jiu-ban)

YOKOHAMA.   S 15

Pacific Mail Steam Ship Company, 4a
  Lane, Geo. E., agent
    Simpson, C. R.
    Lillibridge, H. P.
    Blanchard, H. M.
    Hayne, R. B.
    McLane, L.
    Bellows, Jno.
    Olmsted, F. H.
    Hance, E. W.
    Harris, Geo. L., supt. engineer
    Brown, J. W., supt. coal yards
    Wilson, J., tug engineer
    Conners, Jno. R., supt. carpenter
    Jansyan, P., foreman
    Ropke, C. K., stevedore
    Miller, N., stevedore
    Cook, Harry

Pagden & Co., H., sailmakers and riggers, 88 (san-jiu-hachi-ban)
  Pagden, H

Paterson, T., resident, 118 (hy'aku-jiu-ban)

Patow, W., commission agent, 132 (hy'aku-san-jiu-ni-ban)

Paulin, M. M., cook, 187

Pearson & Laurence, 99 (ku-jiu-ku-ban)
  Pearson, G. C.
  Laurence, S. A.
  Bazing, Z.

Peninsular and Oriental Steam Navigation Company, 15 (jiu-go-ban)
  Rickett, J., agent
    Henley, H. B.
    Davidson, F. G.
    Wong, J. H.
      COAL DEPÔT.
    Hood, W.
    "TIPTREE," HULK.
    Stollery, T.
    White, W. E.

Pequignot & Co., French livery stable, 187 (hy'aku-san-jiu-sh'chi-ban)
  Pequignot, —., proprietor
  Silvin, M.

Perrin, E., hair dresser and perfumer, 81 a (san-jiu-ichi-ban)

Pillon & Co., 174 (hy'aku-sh'chi-jiu-yo-ban)
  Pillon, A.
  Carrier, E.

Pinto, A., hair dresser

Pitman & Co., agents Japanese Government Railway Department, 82 a
  Pitman, John
    Cargill, William

Ply, F., resident, 169

Pohl Freres & Co., 67 (roku-jiu-sh'chi-ban)
  Pohl, John
  Pohl, Hermann
  Pohl, S.

Poitevin, L., confectioner, 58

Pradier & Co., storekeepers, 175 (hy'aku roku-jiu-yo-ban)
  Pradier, A.

Rand & Co.
  Rand, J.
    Nègre, A. F.
    Fraissinet, J.
  Rand, A.

Rangan, W., 122 (hy'aku-ni-jiu-no-ban)
Rappeport, J. M., Chinese Exchange

Regenberg, Julius, importer, 60

Reiss & Co., merchants, 96 (ku-jiu-roku-bah)
  Sichel, J. P.
  Marques, C. V. M.
  Hüllimann, G.

Reis, Von der Heyde & Co., 23 (ni-jiu-san ban)
  Reis, Adolph, (absent)
  Von der Heyde, Eug.
  Behncke, Ernst (Hiogo)
  Rohde, C
  Gargin, A.
  Schaeffer, A.
  Snethlage, H.

Roe, Pratt & Co., haberdashers, &c.
  Pratt, B. H.
  Bird, E. A.

Rosenthal, J. W., 166

Roule, —., resident, 137

Sassoon, Sons & Co., David, merchants, 75 (sh'chi-jiu-go-han)
  Barnard, A.

Schinne, Otto, general agent and commission merchant, 158 (hy'aku-go-jiu-ichi-ban)

16 S   YOKOHAMA.

Schmidt, Edouard, 187

Schmidt & Co., C. H., stevedores and ballast-masters, 68
   Schmidt, C. H.
   Devine, R.

Schner, S., furniture depot, 166

Schwartz & Co., E., watchmakers and jewellers, 80 (hachi-jiu-ban)
   Schwartz, E.
   Retz, F.

Scoti, Scoto, resident, 164

Scott, Capt. David, 119 (hyaku-jiu-ku-ban)

Searle, Mrs. J., millinery and drapery establishment, 82 (hatchi-jiu-ni-ban)
   Searle, Mrs. J.
      Cottam, J. P.
      Barnett, B. S.

Shaw, & Co., merchants, 94 (ku-jiu-yo-ban)
   Barlow, H.
   Shaw, T. K., Jr. (absent)
      F. Walker, clerk

Siber and Brennwald, 90 (ku-jiu-ban)
   Siber, H., (absent)
   Brennwald, C.
      Wolff, A.
      Walter, James
      Haenni, C.
      Lary, J. (cook)

Siddall, B., M.D., 67 (roku-jiu-sh'chi-ban)

Sigrist et Pradier, general importers and storekeepers
   Sigrist, A.
      Aussenac, Eugene

Simmons, Dr. B., physician and surgeon, 109 (hy'aku-ku-ban)

Simon, Evers & Co.,
   Simon, Tul. (Hamburg)
   Evers, Aug.
   Burchard, Martin
      Lienhardt, C. E.
      Assung, shipping clerk
      Afax, compradore

Sitwell, Schoyer & Co., merchants, 70 (sh'chi-jiu-ban)
   Sitwell, I. A.
   Schoyer, E. A.
      Stransome, J.

Smedley, J., architect and civil engineer

Smith, Archer & Co., 18 (jiu-san-ban)
   Hurlburt, George
   Cruickshank, W. J.
   Endicott, Saml.

Smith, Baker & Co., 178 (hyaku-sh'chi-jiu-hachi-ban)
   Baker, Colgate
   Morse, W. H. (Hiogo)
   Atkinson, Hoffman
   Smith, Elliott R.
   Ramee, P. A.
   Staples, John J. (Hiogo)
   Drake, C.

Smith, F. H., 108 (hy'aku-hachi-ban)
   Smith, F. H.
   Carlmann, T.

Snug Saloon, 41 A (shi-jiu-ichi-ban)
   Gibbs, J. B.

Snug Tavern, 102 (hy'aku-ni-ban)
   McKenzie, D.

Société, Anonyme Franco Japonaise, agents for Ch. Bracss, 91 (ku-jiu-ichi-ban)
   Blakeway, G.
   Jubin, E. (absent)
   Jubin, C.
   Biagioni, F.
   Dorel, C.

Stephen, & Stewart, shipwrights, house carpenters, blacksmiths and farriers &c.
   Stephen, James
   Stewart, John
   Watson, J.
   Barry, Wm.
   Oastler, Wm.
   Anderson, Wm.

Stentz, Harvey & Co., butchers and compradores, army and navy contractors, 179
   Harvey, John
   Clark, Alex.

Stilfried & Co., (Yokohama Library) photographers, 59 (go-jiu-ku-ban)
   Rateniz, Baron R. Stilfried
   Willmann, W.

Strachan and Thomas, 68 (roku-jiu-san-ban)
   Strachan, W. M.
   Thomas, T.
   Bissett, J.
   Pollard, F. L.
   Lynill, C. S. S.
   Dare, A. H.

YOKOHAMA.   S 17

Syle, Rev. E. W., H. M. acting consular chaplain, 101 (hy'aku-ichi-ban)

Talbot, W. H., average adjuster and public-accountant, 89 (hachi-jiu-ku-ban)

Thiemer. G., cigar depot

Thistaed & Co., gunsmiths, 106 (hy'aku-roku-ban)
   Thistaed, T.

Thomas, J., storekeeper, 81

Thompson & Co., J., 60 (roku-jiu-ban)
   Broadfield, J.
   Thompson, J.
   Kimber, J.

Thorel & Co., Chas., merchants, 50 (go-ju-ban)
   Thorel, Charles
   Wills, W. J.
   Sadewaeser, O.

"Union Saloon," 133 (hy'aku-san-jiu-san-ban)
   Claussen, P.
   Coleman, J.

United Service Sailors' Home, 138 (hy'aku-san-jiu-san-ban)
   Hodges, G., proprietor

United States Naval Yard, 111-112 (hy'aku-jiu-ichi-ban)
   Brown, W.

Valmale, Schœne & Milsom, 177 (hy'aku-sh'chi-jiu-sh'chi-ban)
   Valmale, Chas. (absent)
   Schoeme, F.
   Milsom, A.
   Torp, von

Van Lissa Brothers, instrument makers & armourers, 10 (jiu-ban)
   Van Lissa, J.
   Van Lissa, A. M.

Van Oordt & Co., 12 (jiu-ni-ban)
   Van Oordt, W. C.
   Rernvaan, J. M.
   Pistorius, A. A.
   Bernheim, A.

Van Reed & Co., 93 (ku-jiu-san-ban)
   Van Reed, E. M.

Vernede, A., 14 (Bluff)

Vidal, Dr. 1, 20c (ni-jiu-ban)

Vincent, Mrs E, A., 85
   Vincent, E. A.
   Vincent, Mrs E. A.
   Smith, M. s T.

Von Hemert, J. Ph., merchant

Walker & Co., F. D., ship brokers, 71 (sh' chi-jiu-ichi-ban)
   Walker, F. D.

Walsh, Hall & Co., merchants, 2 (ni-ban)
   Walsh, John G.
   Walsh, Th. (absent)
   Gay, A. O. (Kobe)
   Smith, J. Mackrill
   Lowtrop, S K
   Irwin, R. W.
   Henderson, J. W. (Kobe)
   Howe, E. A., Jr. (Nagasaki)
   Walsh, Robert G. (do.)
   Piquet, E
   Bryner, Julius (Nagasaki)
   Goodison, F. S.
   Cramer, Francis
   Sa, L. J. de
   Winn, J. E.
   Monat, J.
   Milne, A.
   Heemskerk, C. (Kobe)
   Hall, C. P.
   Remedios, G. M. dos
   Haskell, H. B.
   Varnum, R. M.

Watson & Co., blacksmiths and carpenters, 107 (hy'aku-sh'chi-ban)
   Watson, J.
   Laufenberg, L.

Weigert, P., truck & drayman, 126 (hy'aku-ni-jiu-go-ban)

White, G., resident, 137

Whitfield & Dowson, Yokohama Iron works, engineers, agents for Jno. Penn & Sons, London, and Robey & Co., Perseverance Iron Works, Lincoln, 69 (roku-jiu-ku-ban)
   Whitfield, G.
   Dowson, P. S.
      Higginbotham, J.
      Rose. G.
      Esdale, C.
      Morrison, John
      Taylor, G.
      Edwards, R.
      Ross, G.
      Wagner, —.

Wientraub, Jacob Hersche, importer, 145 (hyaku-shi-jiu-goban)

Williams, Joseph, Sacremento Restaurant and Tavern, the Lone Star of Chile

Wilkin & Robison, 8 (san-ban)
  Wilkin, A. J.
  Robison, R. D. (absent)
  Polley, E. S. (do)
  Leckie, J
  Shand, W. J. S.
  Remedios, F. T. dos
  Esdale, James T.
    2 Chinese Boys

Woodruff & Co., F. G., ships compradores, and general storekeepers, 26 (ni-jiu-roku-ban)
  Woodruff, F. G.
  Hyde, W.
  Willson, —.
  Boulet, J. H.

Wylie, A., consulting engineer, iron merchant, surveyor to Lloyds agent, 159 (hy'aku-go-jiu-ku-ban)

Yokohama Aerated water manufactory
  Nethersole, H.
  Nethersole, H., Jnr.
  Ah Cheong

Yokohama Bakery
  Clarke, R., proprietor

Yokohama Butchery
  Sin-san and Kit-san

Yokohama Dispensary
  North, J.
  Watson, A. T,

Ziegler & Co., 47 (shi-jiu-hichi-ban)
  Ziegler Chas
  Dumelin, A.
  Da Silva, F. R.

OSAKA.

Consulates.
GREAT BRITAIN.
Vice-Consul—Annesley, A.
Acting Vice-Consul—Enslie, J. J.

Municipal Council.
The Governor
The Consular Body
Herrmann, F.
Lepper, T.
Samson, D., Inspector

Japanese Government Mint.
Director—Kinder, T. W.
Assayer—Dillon, B. E.
Assayer of Silver Bullion—Hunter, G. W.
Supt. Gold and Silver Melting Department— Atkins, E.
Metallurgist & Supt. Copper Melting Department—Gowland, W.
Director's Secretary—Wheeler, H. W.
Die Engraver—Sheard, H.
Supt. of Balances and Weighing—Smith, W.
Foreman Coin Department—Wyon, E.
Foreman Sulphuric Works—Finch, R., F.C.S.
Assistant Engineer—Hackett, T.
Do.—Maclagan, R.
Assistant, Rolling Room—Mancini, N.
Do.—Howlett, T.

COMMISSIONERS OF THE MINT.
BULLION DEPARTMENT.
Accountant—Braga, V. E.
Assist. Bookkeepers—Swaby, L.; Braga, C.

Missions.
AMERICAN BOARD MISSION
Gulick, Rev. C H.
Gordon, Rev. M. L., M.D.
Dexter, Rev. G. M.

AMERICAN EPISCOPAL MISSION.
Williams, Right Rev. C. M., D.D.
Quinby, Rev. G. H.
Morris, Rev. A. R.
Lanning, H., M.D.
Harr, Miss L. H.

ROMAN CATHOLIC MISSION.
Cousin, L'Abbé Jules
Noël, L'Abbé André Léonard

Osaka College.
GOVERNMENT SCHOOL.
Teachers—Eaton, J.
Thabor, C. H.
Price, R. E.

Osaka Hospital.
Armarins, Dr.

Imperial Railway Department
Rogers, W.
Kinder, C.
Riddle, O.
Impey, G.
Watt, W.

Merchants, &c.
Batteke, Geo.

Bavier & Co.
Bon, H.

Blackwell & Co.
Blackwell, A. H.
Masefield, W. J.

Bogel, F. L. W. N.

OSAKA.

China and Japan Trading Company
   Drummond, A., agent
   Fitzgerald, M.

Colomb, F.

Favre-Brandt, C. & J.
   Favre-Brandt, C. (absent)
   Favre-Brandt, J.

Fischer & Co., A.
   Fischer, A.
   Lepper, T.

Friebe, H.

Gordes, A.
   Gordes, A.
   Gordes, H.

Grover, W.

Hartley & Co., J.
   Hartley, John (Yokohama)
   Henson, John

Hecht, Lilienthal & Co.

Herhaussen, O.

Hongkong and Shanghai Banking Corporation
   Fischer & Co., E., agents

Huggan, J. G.

Hughes & Co.
   Hughes, R.

Kirby & Co., E. C.

Klein, J. C.

Kniffler, & Co., L.

Krebs, Frederick

Lehmann, Hartmann & Co.

McLeod, N.

Mourilyan, Heimann & Co.
   Mourilyan, W.
   May, J. C.

Netherlands Trading Society
   Rappard, C. H. A.

Oriental Bank Corporation
   Steuart, C. S., acting agent

Oriental Club
   Hay, D., hon. secretary

Osaka Billiard and Bowling Saloon
   Guieu, —., manager

"Osaka Hotel"
   Raymond, B.

Real & Co., A.
   Dubief, L.

Spahn & Co., J. H.
   Spahn, J. H.
   Mahns, H.

Walsh, Hall & Co.

Wetton, H., engineer

KOBÉ—HIOGO.

Consulates.
BELGIUM.
Act. Consul—Low, F.

BRITISH AND AUSTRO-HUNGARIAN.
British and Austro-Hungarian Consul and Act. Consul for France, Spain and Italy—Gower, Abel A. J.
Act. Vice-Consul—Annesley, A.
Assistant—Enslie, J. J.
2nd do.—McLatchie, T. R. H.
Constable and Post Office Agent—Miles, H. A.

DENMARK.
Consul—Palano, L.

GERMAN EMPIRE.
Act. Consul—Foche, Dr. J. H.
Clerk—Gutbrod, —.

NETHERLANDS.
Consul—Korthals, W. C.

SWITZERLAND.
Consular Agent—Fricke, P. H.

UNITED STATES.
Consul—Turner, D.
Marshal—Cothrall, L. W.

Imperial Departments.
CUSTOMS.
Superintendent—Uriu, H.

IMPERIAL RAILWAY WORKS.
England, J.
Diack, J.
Blundell, A. W.
Gray, J.
Rogers, W.
Harris, J. M. D.
Nordenstedt, N.

IMPERIAL RAILWAY WORKS.
(Continued.)
Brookes, J. M.
Andrew, W. P.
Doel, P.
Board, W. J.
Caswred, S.
Dewing, J. A.
Hardy, C.
Houghton, H.
Shand, T.
Swift, T.

TELEGRAPH DEPARTMENT.
Asst. Supt.—Larkin, Thos.
Clerk in Charge—O'Brien, W. F.; Mayo, J.

Municipal Council.
The Governor of Hiogo
The Consular Body
Byrne, Ed.
Crombie, D. A. G.
Illies, C.
Superintendent—Trotzig, H.

POLICE FORCE.
Sergeant—Peterson, G.
De Beer, G.
Green, J.
Millar, C.
DeVos, H.

HARBOUR MASTER'S OFFICE,
WESTERN CUSTOM HOUSE.
Harbour Master—Marshall, J.

Chamber of Commerce.
(HIOGO AND OSAKA.)
General Committee—Gray, A. O.
Goldsmith, L. R.
Korthals, W. C.
Westphal, G.
Mourilyan, W.
Secretary—Abell, J. C.

Missions

AMERICAN BOARD.
Greene, Rev. D. C. (Kobé)
Davis, Rev.
Atkinson, Rev.
Berry, Rev. J. C., M.D.
Talcott, Miss
Dudley, Miss
Doane, Mrs.

ROMAN CATHOLIC.
Arrivat, l'Abbe J.
Villion l'Abbe A.
Faurie, l'Abbe Urbain (Niigata)
Pélu, l'Abbe Albert (Kobé)

UNION PROTESTANT CHURCH.
Trustees—Gower, A. A. J.; Waters, J.; Fobes, A. S.

INTERNATIONAL HOSPITAL OF HIOGO.
Trustees—Fobes, A. S., chairman; Morse, W. H.; Lunau, C.; Fisher, E.; Gillingham, J.
Medical Director—Thornicraft, J. C.

Insurances.

Aspinall, Cornes & Co.
    Northern Fire and Life Insurance Co.
Browne & Co.
    British and Foreign Marine Insurance Company, Limited
    China Fire Insurance Company
    London and Oriental Steam Transit Insurance Company
    Phœnix Fire Assurance Company, London
    Union Insurance Society of Canton
Cornes & Co.
    Northern Assurance Company
Fischer & Co., E.
    Canton Insurance Office (Marine)
    Hongkong Fire Insurance Company
    Scottish Imperial Insurance Company
Gutschow & Co.
    London Assurance Corporation
Hartmans & Besier
    North British and Mercantile Fire Insurance Company
Heard & Co., Augustine
    China Traders' Insurance Co., Limited
    Victoria Fire Insurance Company of Hongkong, Limited
Hecht, Lilienthal & Co.
    Compagnie Lyonaisse d'Assurances Maritimes
Holme, Ringer & Co.
    China and Japan Marine Insurance Co.
Hughes & Co.
    Commercial Union Fire Insurance Co.
    Queen's Fire Insurance of London and Liverpool
    Commercial Union Marine Insurance Company
Joseph & Co., L.
    Ocean Railway and General Traveller's Assurance Company Limited
Kniffler & Co., L.
    De Oosterling Sea and Fire Insurance Company of Batavia
Langgaard & Co.
    Globe Marine Insurance Co., Limited
Lenz, T.
    Swiss Lloyd's Insurance Company
Lunau & Polano
    Netherlands India Sea and Fire Insurance Company of Batavia
    Samarang Sea and Fire Insurance Co.
    Second Netherlands-India Sea and Fire Insurance Company of Batavia
Mourilyan, Heimann & Co.
    Imperial Fire Insurance Co. (sub-agents)
    North China Insurance Company
Reis, Von der Heyde & Co.
    Colonial Sea and Fire Insurance Co. of Batavia
Schmidt, Westphal & Co.
    German Fire Insurance Company
Schut, Schenten & Co.
    Union Board of Underwriters at Amsterdam
Smith, Baker & Co.
    Chinese Insurance Company, Limited
    Guardian Fire and Life Assurance Company
Walsh, Hall & Co.
    Yangtsze Insurance Association of Shanghai
Wilkin & Robison
    Lloyds
    Sun Fire Office

Merchants, &c.

Abell, J. C.

Aspinall, Cornes & Co., merchants (in liquidation)

Avril, P.

Badge, G.

Bergen, Mrs. G.
    Harrisson, Miss E.

Board & Co., W. K.
   Board, W. K.

Bogel, Nering F. W.

Bonger Brothers
   Bonger, M. C.
   Bonger, W. C.

Brissonnet, Ferd.

Browne & Co., merchants
   Browne, H. St. J.
   Goldsmith, L. R.
      Macpherson, M. T. B.
      Kimpton, B. T.
      Warburton, Wm.

Buchannan, J. R.

Byrne, Ed.

Cabeldu & Co.
   Cabeldu, P. S.
   Smith, E. (Osaka)

Carroll & Co.,
   Wiggins, Chas.
   Titjen, H.

China and Japan Trading Company
   Fobes, A. S., agent
      Beauchamp, J. W.
      Pasch, W.

City of Hamburg tavern
   Muller, J.

Cohn, B.

Compagnie des Messageries Maritimes
   Fricke, P. H., agent

Crown and Anchor tavern
   Grinberg, Mrs.
      Corbett, J. W.

Cunha, F. da

De Ath & Co., A.
   De Ath, A.

De Ath, W. H., 4 Bellevue Buildings

Domoney & Co.
   Domoney, G.
   Whymark, G.
      Voyey, M.
      Henderson, C.

Driscoll & Co., tailors and clothiers, &c.
   Driscoll, W.
   Groves, T. J.

Eureka Saloon
   Sloos, J. H. M.
      Collins, J.

European Laundry
   Guitard, Madame L.

Euziere, Jules
   Cunha, J. de

Faber & Voight
   Faber, H.
   Voight, O. (absent)
   Kuhhardt, A. M.

Fischer & Co., E.
   Fischer, Ed.
   Leppar, Thos.
   Cobden, C. H.
   Abel, Geo.

Fisher, Frank
   Morris, A.

Goldman, S.

Gordes & Co.
   Gordes, A.
   Gordes, H.

Göttlinger, L.

Great Northern Telegraph Company
   Polano, L.

Grosclaude, E. & U.

Gütschow & Co.
   Gütschow, P. (absent)
   Gütschow, O.
      Hudofsky, H.
      Gill, E. H.

Hagart & Co.
   Hagart, H. W.

Harris, J., M.D.

Hartman & Besier
   Besier, J. N.

Heard & Co., Augustine
  Low, F.
    Gillingham, J.
    Livingstone, H. W.

Hecht, Lilienthal & Co.
  Fischer, F. von
  Keischer, H. M.

Hiogo Hotel
  Green, Mrs. M. E., manager
  Ravallo, F.

Hiogo Iron Works
  Wignall, J. H.
  Rose, W.

Hiogo Gas Co.
  Directors—Korthal, W. C.; Morse, W. H.; Byrne, E.; Goldsmith, L. K.; Illies, C.
  Browne & Co., general agents and secretaries,

"Hiogo News" Office
  Walsh, F.
  Johnson, W. G.
    Walsh, C. F., editor
    Oxley, C.
    Riberiro, J. M. V.

"Hiogo and Osaka Herld
  Crouchley, F.
    Collaço, R. S.
    Holttum, W. W.

Holme, Ringer & Co.
  Holme, Ryle
  Evans, J. R.

Hongkong & Shanghai Banking Corporation
  Harries, W. H., agent
    Pereira, E. J., cashier

Hooper Brothers, No. 53

Hughes & Co.
  Hughes, R. (Osaka)
  Sands, W. G.
  Hutton, M. L.
  Taylor, J.
  Owens, J.
  Taylor, G.

Imperial Copper Works
  Roeser, P. A.

Isaacs, & Co.
  Isaacs, S.
  Marians, J.

Jack, Young, ship's compradore

Johnson & Co.
  Johnson, W. G.

Joseph & Co., L.
  Joseph, M.
  Braga, J.

Kaga Foundry
  Hase, W., manager

Kennelly, T. F., resident

Kirby & Co., E. C.
  Kirby, E. C. (Yokohama)
  Valentine, B. A.
  Stevens, W. J.
  Benney, C.
  Kirby, R. (Osaka)
  Esdale, O.

Kobe Iron Works
  Huggan, R., manager

Kniffler & Co.
  Kniffler, L. (absent)
  Reddelien, G. (Yokohama)
  Illies, C.
  Francke, O.
  Naudin, J.
  Bergan, J., godown-keeper
  Raspe, H.

Kobe Club
  Marshall, Jno., hon. sec.
  Van der Vlies, G. & Co., stewards

K. R. & A. Club
  Groom, A. H.
  McKenzie, A., hon. sec. and treas.

Langgaard, Kleinwort, & Co.
  Kleinwort C.
  Iwersan, C.

Lehmann, Hartmann & Co.
  Lehmann, C. (Osaka)
  Hubener, F. W.
  Herrmann, F. (absent).

Lenz, T.
  Stucken, Edm.

Lentz, A., 49 (Native town)

Llewellyn & Co., J., druggists, &c.
  Sim, A. O.
  Rae, W.

Lucas & Waters, merchants, &c.
  Lucas, H.
  Waters, J.
  Benjamin, R. J. K.

Lunau & Polano
  Lunau, C.
  Polano, L.

Marmelstein, E.
  Hart, W.

Mourilyan, Heimann & Co.
  Mourilyan, W. (Osaka)
  Heimann, C. A. (absent)
    Groom, A. H.
    Gillingham, A. W.
    Allcock, G. H.
    Exton, T.
    Silvester, J. W.

Nachtigal & Co., G.
  Nachtigal, G.
  Olse..., J.
    Gorman, H. J.
    Brown, H.

Netherlands Trading Society
  Korthals, W. C., agent
  Mertens, J.
  Bosma, H.
  Van Ewyck, D. J.

Ocean Steam Ship Co.
  Heard & Co., Augustine, agents

Oriental Banking Corporation
  Crombie, D. A. J., acting agent
    Mackenzie, H., asst. acct. and cashier
    Carvalho, G., clerk

Pacific Mail S. S. Co.
  Center, A., agent
    Tileston, H. N.
    Graham, W. J., barge master
    Howard, F.

Peninsular & Oriental Steam Navigation Company
  Mourilyan, Heimann & Co., agents

Price, R. E.

Ravetta & Co.
  Ravetta, F.

Real & Co., A.
  Real, A. (Osaka)
  Dubief, L.
    Duplaquet, G.

Reis, Von der Heyde & Co.
  Behncke, A.
  Gurlitt, H.
  Schöning, H.

Reimers, Bechr & Co.
  Reimers, O.
  Bechr, H.

Renard & Co., E.
  Renard, Ed. (Paris)
  Fricke, P. H.
    Genth, Ad. S.
    Plate, F.

Reuter's Telegram Company
  Piotranski, K. do

Richter, R.
  Richter, G.

Schmidt, Westphal & Co.
  Westphal, G. (Nagasaki)
  Militzer, Max., do.
  Krümmel, Carl (Hamburg)
    Stein, A.
    Reiyter, J. S.
    Dolling, R.
    Luther, H.

Schokker Hunnink, Dr. J. A. C.

Schultze, Reis & Co.
  Schultye, Ad. (absent)
  Reis, Ad. (do.)
  Von der Heyde, E. (do.)
  Angart, M.

Schut, Scheuten & Co.
  Schut, J.
  Groenewout, J. A. A. (absent)
  Scheuten, H. A.

Scott & Co.
  Scott, J. Marshall
  Guterres, F.

Scott & Frost
  Scott, J.
  Frost, A.

Skipworth, Hammond & Co.
  Skipworth, W. G.
  Hammond, W. H.

Smith, Baker & Co.
  Morse, W. H.
  Wynesar, H.
  Yamamoto, S.

Steam Aerated Water Works
  Kleinmann, J.
  Collomb, F., manager

Strome & Co., Chas. J.
  Taylor, I. K.

Tabor & Co.
  Tabor, H. W.
  Foot, M.
  Jones, B.

"The Snug," tavern
  Jennings, B.

Thomsen & Worck
  Thomsen, S.
  Worck, T.

Hiogo Livery stables
  Thompson, W. A.

Thornicraft, Thos. C., M.R.C.S.E.

Tillson & Co.
  Bennett, P.
  Henriques, W.
    Hansen, L.

Union Club
  Kleinwort, P. A., hon. sec. and treas.

Van der Vlies & Co., G.
  Van der Vlies, G.

Vulcan Iron Works
  Huggan, R., manager
  Keetch, J. R.
    Ross, Douglass
    Owens, J.
    Williams, D.
    Melville, M.

Wachtels & Co.
  Watchels, P. H. M.
  Crtmans, H. A. (absent)

Walsh, Hall & Co.
  Arthur, O. Gay
    Henderson, J. W.
  Brynar, J.
  Pritchard, A. T.

"What Cheer House," Tavern
  Wood, James

Wilkin & Robison, merchants, 81
  Wimmer, H.

NAGASAKI.

Consulates.

AUSTRO-HUNGARY.
Acting Consul—Flowers, Marcus, O.,

BELGIUM.
Consul—Dalden, M. C. van

DENMARK.
Acting Consul—Dalden, M. C. van

FRANCE.
Acting Consul—Flowers, Marcus O., (in charge)

GREAT BRITAIN.
Consul—Flowers, Marcus O.
Interpreter—Quin, J. J.
Constable—Brown, John

POSTAL AGENCY.
Packet Agent—Longford, J. H.

HAWAII.
Consul—Fisher, Chas. L. M.D.,

ITALY.
Consular Agent—Pot, J. J. van der

NETHERLANDS.
Acting Consul—Pot, J. J. van der
Secretary—Keg, J. J.

NORTH GERMANY.
Acting Consul—Hermann, Iwersen

PORTUGAL.
Acting Consul—Mangum, W. P.
Chancellor—Figuerredo, J. A.

RUSSIA.
Acting Consul—Hermann, Iwersen

SPAIN.
Acting Consul—Flowers, Marcus O.,

SWEDEN AND NORWAY.
Acting Consul—Pot, Van der

SWITZERLAND.
Acting Consul—Hermann, Iwersen

UNITED STATES.
Consul—Mangum, Willie P.
Vice-Consul—Fisher, Chas. L.
Marshal—Powers, Rodney H.

POSTAL AGENCY.
Postal Agent—Fisher, Chas. L.

Municipal Council.

Chairman—Inglis, D. D.
Hellyer, F.
Hay, C. W.
Howe, H. A. Jr.
Secretary—Jalland, Wm.
Constables—Harris, Wm.
Nickle, Andrew

Japanese Government Hospital.

Duivenenbode, Dr. W. K. M. van Lenween van
Geertz, Dr. A. J.
Simmons, Dr.

Japanese Government Patent Slip.

Acting Supdt.—Douglas, William

Japanese Government School.

Instructors—Bonnell, S. R.; Arnold, A. S.; Perpigna, Arthur de

Japanese Government Telegraph.

Superintendent—Fry, O. James
Clerk in charge—Pyne, Fredk.
Clerk—Kennedy, W.

Pilots.

Anderson, George
Johnson, C.
Smith, O.
White, J.

Nagasaki Club.

Secretary—Smith, J. C.
Steward and Librarian—Stone, F.

PROTESTANT MISSIONARIES.
Burnside, Rev. H.
Stout, Rev. Henry
Davison, Rev. J. C.

Roman Catholic Church.

Petitjean, Right, Rev. Bernard, bishop of Japan
Laucaigne, Rev. J.
Poirier, Rev. B.
Salmon, Rev. A.
Marechal, Rev. J. L.
Jamault, Rev. D.
Chatron, Rev. D.
Traineau, Rev. Th.

Insurances.

Alt & Co.,
  Lloyds
  North China Insurance Co.
  China Fire Ins. Company
  Commercial Union Assurance Co.
Gribble & Co., Henry
  Canton Insurance Office
  Hongkong Fire Insurance Co., Limited
  Northern Fire Insurance Company of London
Hartmans & Besier,
  North Brit. & Mercantile Fire Insurance Company
  Union of Underwriters of Amsterdam
Holme, Ringer & Co.
  China & Japan Marine Insurance Co.
  Chinese Insurance Company, Limited

Kniffler & Co., L.
  London Assurance Corporation
  Imperial Fire Insurance Company
  De Oosterling Sea and Fire Insurance Company of Batavia
Reddelien & Co. A.
  Oosterling Sea & Fire Insurance Company of Batavia (Fire Branch)
Schmidt, Westphal & Co.
  German Fire Insurance Co., Limited, Berlin
  North German Fire Insurance Company, Hamburg
  Bremen Board of Underwriters
  Hamburg Board of Underwriters
Van Delden & Co.
  China Traders' Insurance Co., Limited
  Netherlands India Sea & Fire Insurance Company
  Colonial Sea and Fire Insurance Co. of Batavia
  Second Colonial Sea & Fire Insurance Company of Batavia
  Samarang Sea and Fire Insurance Co.
  Netherlands India Sea and Fire Ins. Company of Batavia
  Victoria Fire Insurance Company of Hongkong, Limited
Walsh, Hall & Co.
  Pacific Insurance Company
  Yangtsze Insurance Association of Shanghai

Merchants, &c.

Adams & Co., M. C., ship chandlers, compradores and H. B. M.'s Navy Contractors
  Adams, M. C.
  Sutton, Geo.
  Peter, —

"Albion Tavern"
  Soderviat, G., proprietor

Alt & Co., merchants
  Hunt, H. I.
  Hellyer, F.
  Wright, Alex.
  Figueiredo, J. A.
  Elliott, J. R.

Barge "Shamrock"
  Furber, E. G., barge master
  Moore, J., freight clerk

Boeddinghaus, Dittmer & Co., merchants
  Boeddinghaus, C. E.
  Dittmer, F.
  Busch, Hermann

Boulangerie, Française
  Thomas, C.

Boyd & Co., iron founders and engineers
  Robertson, Wm.
  Hay, Chas. W.
  Calder, J. F.
  Robertson, A.
  Hunter, H.

Breen, John, fresh water supplier

Caldwell, Dr. R., physician and surgeon

China Merchants Steam Ship Company
  Agents—Amook & Co.
  Begier, Geo.

China & Japan Trading Co., shipchandlers, &c.
  Agent—Inglis, D. D.
  Fontayne, J.

"Commercial Hotel," billiard and bowling saloon
  Smith, J. U., proprietor

"Eureka Hotel"
  Sambuck, J., proprietor

"Falcon Hotel," bowling saloon
  Nickel, Mrs Carl J., proprietress

Ford & Co., A. R., stevedores and ballast suppliers
  Ford, A. R.
  Linch, J. H.

"Fulton Market Butchery," coffee and oyster saloon
  Bremer, Kamp & Co.
  Bremer, L J.,

"Germania Hotel," bowling saloon
  Umland, J. M.
  Shanegan, H.

Glover & Co. (In Liquidation)
  Trustee—Pot, Van der J. J.
          Glover, Thos. Blake
  Accountant—Burmeister, E.
  Committee of Inspectors—Robertson, Wm.; Maltby, J.; Hunt, H. J.; and Gribble, Henry

Goldenberg, —., storekeeper

Grange, Alexander, marine surveyor

Great Northern Telegraph Company
  Russell, Thos., superintendent
  Petersen, J.
  Suenson, A.
  Homblad, J.
  Nielsen, F. C. C.
  Czarnewaky, C.

Gribble & Co., Henry, merchants
  Gribble, Henry
  Yeend, Duer

Hartmann & Besier, merchants
  Hartmann, W. L.

Holme, Ringer & Co., merchants
  Holme, E. (absent)
  Ringer, F.
  Smith, J. C.
  Holme, Ryle (Hiogo)
    Webster, James R.
    Almeida, A. T. d'
    Brown, C., godown keeper

Hongkong and Shanghai Banking Corporation
  Agents—Van Delden & Co.

Hyver, J. P., general store-keeper
  Hyver, J. P.

"International Hotel"
  Massie, John S., Proprietor

"Nagasaki Medical Hall"
  Jalland, Wm., Proprietor

Kassburg & Co., A., compradores, provisioners and naval contractors
  Kassburg, A.
  Powers, Rodney H.

Kniffler, & Co., L., merchants
  Kniffler, Louis, (absent)
  Reddelien, G. (Yokohama)
  Pardun, W. (do.)
  Illies, C. (Hiogo)
    Leesen, Emil von
  Kniffler, H.
  Röhr, V.
  Falk, C., godown-keeper

Rake & Co., Geo. W., ship chandlers, storekeepers and provisioners
  Lake, Geo. W. (absent)
  Lake, Edward
  Davis, John

"London Tavern"
  Bezer, Thos., proprietor

Maltby & Co., merchants
  Maltby, John
  Maltby, Samuel
    Colthrup, Geo. J.
    Repenn, J. A., godown-keeper

"Nagasaki Express" Office
  Braga, F.
  Senna, F.
  Cardoza, A. L.
  Ford, R. A., reporter

"Nagasaki Gazette" Office
  De Souza & Co., S. R.
  Louroiro, Antonio, proprietor
  De Souza, S. R.   do.
  Ford, R. A., reporter
  Rodrigues, B. V., compositor

Netherlands Trading Society
  Pot, J. J., Van der
  Keg, J. C.
  Casteren van Cattenburch, H. W.

"Occidental Hotel"
  Underwood, Thos.

"Ocean Tavern"
  Fielder, J. W.

Pacific Mail Steam Ship Company
  Agent—Tilman, W. P.
  Shipping Clerk—Ferreira, C. J.,

P. & O. S. N. Co.
  Gribble, Henry
  Yeend Duer

Petersen, Hans, boot and shoe maker

Pignatel & Co., storekeepers, &c.
  Pignatel, V. L.
  Pignatel, C. (Saga)
    Couder, J.

Pol, L. van de, importer

Rasch, Carl, agent for Textor & Co.

Reddelien, & Co., A.
  Reddelien, A.

Ross, W. M., hair dresser

Russell, T. O., auctioneer and commission agent

Schmidt, Westphal & Co.
  Westphal, George (Hiogo)
  Kummel, Carl (Hamburg)
  Hermann, Iwersen
  Ruyter, L.

Smith, Captain J. U., marine surveyor
  Smith, J. U.
  Bernhardt, R., godown keeper

"Sung Hotel & Bowling Saloon"
  Johnson, J. H., Proprietor
  Ryle, —.

"St. Petersburg Hotel"
  Anderson, John, Proprietor

Stube & Co., R., tailors and clothiers
  Stube, R.

Takasima Colliery, Nagasaki Office
  Pot, J. J., Van der, manager
  Burmeister, E., accountant
  Glover, Alfred B.
  Hall, Alex., engineer   (Takasima)
  Glover, Alex. B.   (do.)
  Tombrink, S. P.   (do.)
  Wake, H., overseer   (do.)
  Beresford, J. S., do.   (do.)
  Mulershíp, S.   (do.)
  Brown, W., godown keeper (Sagaritnatz)

Takasima Tug Boat, S. S. "Argus"
  Captain—Cheetham, John C.
  Engineer—Chisholm, Eugene A.
  Chief Officer—Wolthers, J. W.,

Van Delden, & Co., merchants
  Van Delden, M. C.
  Visscher, A.

Walsh, Hall & Co., merchants
  Howe, H. A., jr.
  Walsh, Robt. G.

HAKODADI.

Consulates.

AUSTRO HUNGARY.
Acting Consul—Eusden, R.

DENMARK.
Consul—Duus, J. H.

FRANCE.
Acting Consul—Eusden, R.

GERMAN EMPIRE.
Consul— —.

GREAT BRITAIN.
Consul—Eusden, R.
Constable—Lawrence, S. F.

UNITED STATES.
Consul— Hawes, —.

Missions.

MISSION APOSTOLIQUE.
Plessis, L'Abbé Marien Justinien
Leblanc, L'Abbé René

Insurances.

Howell & Co., Agents for—
  North China Insurance Company
  Chinese Insurance Co., Limited

Merchants, &c.

Blakiston, Marr & Co., merchants
  Blakiston, Thomas

Duus, Jno. H., merchant

Howell & Co., merchants
  Albinson, J.
  Wilson, J. A.

Porter, A. P., marine surveyor

Russian Hotel
  Alexieff, Mrs. P.
    Paranchin, G. P.

Sarloff, V.

Schluter & Strandt, compradores, &c.
  Schluter, P.
  Strandt, H.

Scott, J., engineer (Sado Island)

Thompson & Bewick, shipbuilders, naval contractors and commission merchants
  Thompson, J. R.
  Bewick, Geo.

THE PHILIPPINES.

MANILA.

Colonial Government.
Governor and Captain General—Yzquierdo, H. E. Don Rafael
Lieut. Governor—
Secretary—Valls, José

SUPREME COURT OF APPEAL.
Chief Justice—Echevarria, Prudencio H. E.
Attorney General—Escalera, José
Judge and President of the 1st Chamber—Valdenebro y Olloqui, José
Judge and President of 2nd Chamber—Urquiola, Julian
Judges—Elio, Rovira, Cañete, Davila, Cortey, Carmona, Arguedas
Secretary—Barrosa, Mateo

FINANCIAL DEPARTMENT.
Intendant—Agius, Don J. Jimeno
Accountant General—Beruete, José
Treasurer General—Codevilla, José

CIVIL GOVERNMENT OF THE PROVINCE OF MANILA.
Governor—Diaz, José Maria
Secretary—Villaralbo, A. de

DISTRICT MAGISTRATES.
1st—Junquitu, Manuel Gonzales (acting)
2nd—Alvarez Guerra, Juan (do.)
3rd—
4th—Espinosa de los Monteros, Narciso (do.)

WAR DEPARTMENT.
Judge—H. E. the Captain General
Councellor—Asensi, Manuel

NAVAL DEPARTMENT.
Rear-Admiral and Commander of the Station—Antequera, Juan
Captain—Carvanza, José
Harbour Master—Montojo, Vicente
Do. at Cavite—Espin, Francisco
Commander of Arsenal (Act.)—Martinez, Pedro
Lieut. Colonel of Marine Artillery—Sallardo, Augusto
Commander of Engineers of Arsenal—Ginart, Manuel
Paymaster General—Aranda, Joaquin
Captain of the Flag Ship—Maymo, José

OFFICE OF COLLECTOR GENERAL OF CUSTOMS.
Collector General of Customs—Zappino, D. Felipe
Accountant—Echevania, D. F.
1st Officer—Hidalgo, Diaz Diego D.
Valuators—1st—Peray, D. Victor
2d—Añino, Manuel
3d—Andnaga, D. Arturo

POSTAL DEPARTMENT.
Administrator General—Guerrero, Scarnichia Eduardo D.
Officials—Plazuelos, D. Casto
Clemente, D. Enrique
Ganohe, D. Federico
Mompeon, D. Juan
Morero, D. José

MINT.
Administrative Director—Alvarez, Manuel
Director and 1st Assayer—Fafont, Francisco C. E.
Accountant—(absent)
Treasurer—Rios, Manuel R. de los
2nd Assayer—Alonzo, Teodoro
1st Engraver—Sancho, José
2nd do.—Estruch, Alberto
Foreman—Torre, Francisco M. de la

THE PHILIPPINES.—MANILA.

MUNICIPALITY.

President—H. E. the Captain General
Vice President—The Civil Governor
Magistrate of 1st Election—Franco, Don Antonio
Aldermen—Twelve
Secretary—Villaralbo, Adelardo de

ECCLESIASTICAL DEPARTMENT.

Royal Vice Patron—H. E. the Captain General
Archbishop Metropolitan of the Philippines—Martinez, H. E. Sr. Don Gregorio Meliton
Provisor and Vicar General—Yagüe, y Mateos
Dean—Peralta, Manuel
Commissary of the Holy Crusade—Yagüe, y Mateos
Secretaries—Ureta, Candido; Zudaire, Don Francisco
Counsellor—Ramiez, Don Simon
Notaries General—Cuyugan, D. Vicente; Perez, D. Mariano

BISHOPRIC OF NUEVA CARCERES.

Bishop—Gainza, H. E. Friar Francisco Amente
Provisor and Vicar General—Garcia, Dr. Vicente

BISHOPRIC OF CEBU.

Bishop—Gimeno, H. E. Friar Romnaldo
Provisor—Aquilar, Leon E.

BISHOPRIC OF YLOILO (JARO).

Bishop—Cuartero, H. E. Friar Mariano
Secretary—Bonifacio, V.
Counsellor—Ramirez, D. R.

BISHOPRIC OF NUEVA SEGOVIA.

Bishop—Arngones, H. E. Friar Juan José
Provisor—Osset, Don Juan
Secretary—Paloma, Lorenzo

STO. TOMAS COLLEGE.

Rector—Treserra, Fr. Domingo
Vice do.—Fonseca, Fr. Joaquim

SAN JOSE' COLLEGE.

Rector—Sotien, Dr. Felipe
Secretary—Sevilla, L. Mariano

SAN JUAN DE LETRAN.

President—Corominas, Fr. Benito

ATENEO MUNICIPAL.
(JESUITS' COLLEGE.)

Superior—Bertran, Pedro

Steamer Agencies.

Aguirre & Co.
  P. & O. S. N. Company

Macleod, Pickford & Co.
  Spanish Steamers *Visayas, Cebu, Dagupan, Tutuan*

Rocha & Co., Y.
  Cagayan Line (Str. *Sud Oeste*)

Russell & Sturgis
  Pacific Mail Steam Ship Company
  Compagnie Messageries Maritimes
  Spanish Steamer *Leonor*
  Coasting Steamers *Albay, Corregidor, Felisa, Lingayen*

Consulates.

AUSTRO-HUNGARY.

Consul—Spanier, Julius

BELGIUM.

Consul—Ross, John (absent)
In charge—Hens, J. P.

DENMARK.

Consul—Edwards, O. E. (absent)
In charge—Pierce, G. H.

FRANCE.

Consul—Méchain, E.
Chancellor—Hébrard, Scipion

GERMAN EMPIRE.

Consul—Herrmann, M. A. (absent)
Acting Consul—Parr, R. B.
Secretary—Sackermau, E.

GREAT BRITAIN.

Consul—Ricketts, George Thorne (absent)
Surgeon—Burke, John, M.D.

NETHERLANDS.

Consul—Petel, G. van Polanen

PORTUGAL.

Consul—Hidalgo, A.
Vice-Consul—Veloso, G. (Cebú)

SWEDEN & NORWAY

Acting Consul—Russell, J.
Secretary—Austen, J. G.
Surgeon—Burke, J. M.D.

SWITZERLAND.

Consul—Germann, Charles
Vice-Consul—Meily, J. U.

UNITED STATES.

Vice-Consul—Russell, J.
Secretary—Austen, J. G.
Surgeon—Burke, J., M.D.

Insurances.

Baer & Co.
   Java Sea and Fire Insurance Company
Barretto & Co., B. A.
   Canton Insurance Office
Blanco, Domingo & Co.
   Tutelar y de la Soc. Esp. de Credito Commercial de Madrid
Findlay, Richardson & Co.
   Northern Insurance Company
   Scottish Commercial Insurance Co.
   Chinese Insurance Co., Limited
Guichard & Fils
   Société Française de Prets à la Grosse de Paris
Holliday, Wise & Co.
   The Liverpool, London and Globe Insurance Company
   North China Insurance Company
Jenny & Co.
   Austrian Lloyds S. N. Ins. Trieste
   "Baloise" Trans. Insurance Co., Basel
   Board of Hamburg Underwriters
   Bremen Sea Insurance Company
   Deutscher Lloyd in Berlin
   Deutsche Transport Versicherungs Gesellschaft in Berlin
   Francfort Transport and Glass Ins. Co.
   General Ins. Co., "Helvetia," St. Gall
   General Netherlands Trans. Insurance Company, at Thiel
   General Trans. Ins. Co., at Vienna
   General Trans. Ins. Co., at Dresden
   General Trans. Ins. Co., Dusseldorf
   "La Neuchateloise" Transp. Ins. Co., at Neuchatel
   "Merkur," Transport Insurance Company, at Vienna
   Swiss Lloyd's Trans. Insurance Co., at Winterthur
   Veterländische Versicherungs Gesellschaft in Elberfeld

Ker & Co.
   British and Foreign Marine Insurance Co., Limited
   Liverpool Underwriters Association
   Lloyds
   Sun Fire Office
   Merchant Shipping and Underwriters' Association of Melbourne
   Union Marine Insurance Co., Limited and Reduced
   Lloyd Andalus
Labhart & Co.
   Germanic Lloyds
   The Transatlantic Fire Insurance Coy. of Hamburg, Limited
Lutz & Co., C.
   Rhein Westphalia Lloyds, at Gladbach
   Nord-Deutsche Feuer Versicherungs Gesellschaft, Hamburg
   Schweiz Transport Versicherungs Gesellschaft, Zurich
   Rhenania Verricherungs Artien Gesellschaft Cologne
Martin, Dyce & Co.
   Merchants, Marine Ins. Co., Limited
Peele, Hubbell & Co.
   Queen Insurance Co. of Liverpool and London (Fire)
   Union Ins. Society of Canton (Marine)
   Yangtsze Ins. Association of Shanghai (Marine)
Petel & Co., G. van Polanen
   Oosterling Sea and Fire Ins. Company
Russell & Sturgis,
   American Lloyds
   Batavia Sea & Fire Ins. Company
   Colonial Sea & Fire Ins. Company
   China Traders Ins. Co., (Limited)
   London Assurance Corporation
   North British & Mercantile Ins. Co.
   Victoria Fire Insurance Company of Hongkong (Limited)
Smith, Bell & Co.
   Commercial Union Assurance Co.
   Imperial Fire Office
   Netherlands India Sea and Fire Ins. Company
   Standard Marine Insurance Company
Tillson, Herrmann & Co.
   Guardian Fire and Life Ins. Office
   Phœnix Fire Insurance Office
   Royal Insurance Co. (Fire and Life)
   Samarang Sea and Fire Insurance Co.

Merchants, &c.

Aguirre & Co., merchants
Aguirre, F. (Spain)
Teus, Valentine
Hidalgo, Antonio
Yrisarry, J. M.

4 W   THE PHILIPPINES.—MANILA.

Andrews & Co., H. J., merchants
   Andrews, H. J.
   Rotschke, C. A. (Manchester)
   Ede, J. M.
   Ogden, J.
   Carlos, S. A.

Baer & Co., S., merchants
   Baer, S.
   Heymann, J.
   Prieto, L.

Barretto & Co., B. A., merchants
   Barretto, B. A.
   Matias, Francisco

Bischoff & Co., J. J., watch and clockmakers
   Bischoff, J. J.
   Bischoff, J. S. (Yloilo)
   Stadeli, L. (do.)
   Preciado, T.

Blanco, Domingo & Co., merchants
   Blanco, Joaquim
   Domingo, Francisco
   Quintana, P. P
   Gruet, José
   Nales, José
   Leon, Lucas de
   Alvarez, José

Bordenave, D., marine surveyor to Lloyd's agents and local offices

Borries, W. v., apothecary and druggist, pharmaceutical and chemical laboratory, contractor of the medicines for the Royal Armada 14, Binondo, Escolta

Botica de San Gabriel
   Leon, M. P. de

Casal Brothers, timber merchants
   Casal, A. P.
   Casal, José de
   Llopez, A.
   Base, G.
   Guzman, G.
   Anacleto, C.
   Gregorio, Capitan

Chartered Bank of India, Australia and China
   Somarville, J., agent
   Meily, J. U.

Cucullu & Co., merchants
   Cucullu, José de
   Alegre, Juan

Diario de Manila, newspaper
   Ramirez y Giraudia, printers and publishers

Dudley, Dr. David E., Surgeon, Oculist

Eugster & Co., merchants
   Eugster, J.
   Eugster, E.
   Muns, J.
   Eugster, R.
   Eugster, Ph.
   Claro, S.
   Feliciano, M.

Findlay, Richardson & Co., merchants and commission agents
   Caw, Thomas
   Beech, Walter E. (absent)
   Sloan, James
   Brown, John
   Barretto, L. A.
   Curballo, E.
   Wright, Robert
   McGavin, J. P.

French Hotel
   Ari, Lala, proprietor (*See Advert.*)
   Verril, Edward, manager

Garchitorena & Smith, coach-builders (30, Escolta)
   Garchitorena, A. M.
   Smith, J. L.
   Garchitorena, V. M.
   Leyva, J.
   Aquino, P.

Genato & Co., Government auctioneers
   Genato, Manuel
   Tuason, Thomas
   Queri, Mariano

Germann, Chs., merchant
   Germann, Arnold
   Rappolt, Chr.

Guichard & Fils, merchants
   Guichard, J. A.   (Paris)
   Guichard, Auguste (do.)
   Guignard, Fr.   (do.)
   Guichard, Eug.   (do.)
   Cherest, Victor
   Willmann, H.
   Guevarra, B.
   Alouaz, C. S. de
   Alouaz, José de

Heinszen & Co., C., merchants
  Heinszen, Conrad (absent)
  Heinszen, J. N.
    Krause, Adolph
    Klopfer, Emil
    Groth, Adolph
    Aloya, Felix

Holliday, Wise & Co., merchants
  Coller, R. L.
    Hunter, D. L.
    McCulloch, J. B.
    Grundy, A.
    Drummond, J.
    Martines, R. Javier

Honiss & Co., merchants, Manila and Batangas
  Honiss, Albert

Hughes, P., clock and watchmaker, jeweller, &c.

Icaza, Ygnacio, rope maker

Jackson, French & Co., merchants
  French, Hugh Smith
  Jackson, Edward
    Viademonte, Ramor Martinerde

Ker & Co., merchants
  Ross, John (absent)
  Coates, Albert
  Forbes, D. M.
    Worthington, Thos.
    Roberton, R. C.
    Porteous, H. L.
    Cassels, J. T.
    Bolton, Fred
    Cembrano, J.
    McMicking, T.
    Ogilvie, J.
    Crescini, D.
    Arcé, J.
    Munn, Dugald (Yloilo)
    Carballo, J. (Yloilo)
    Saul, G. M. (Yloilo)
    Holding, Joseph (Leyte)
    Smith, R. Calder (Leyte)

Labhart & Co., merchants
  Labhart, J. C.
  Spanier, Julius
    Ruttmann, Theodore
    Ruppaner, J.

Loney & Co., merchants (See *Yloilo*)

Loyzaga & Co., J. de, printers; proprietors of *Mercantile Review* and *El Comercio*, afternoon paper, Vivac, 8
  Loyzaga, J. de
  Puertas, F. Diaz y
    Ibañez P. Bautista
    Sar Buenaventura, A.
    Villanueva, R.
    Ibañez, F. Bautista

Ludewig, George, chemist and druggist, Plaza de Binondo, No 24
  Tebbutt, James Louis

Lutz & Co., C. merchants
  Lutz, C.
  Keller, E.
  Sprecher, Ch.
  Sprungli, C.
  Ziegler, J.

Macleod, Pickford & Co., merchants
  Macleod, N. (Cebú)
  Pickford C. R. B (absent)
    Macleod, A. Y.
    Blyth, P. L. (absent)
    Birchal, E. F.
    Savacho, D.
    Hepper, F. H. (Cebú)
    Pike, O. O. (do.)
    Colquhoun, W. (do.)
    Tuason, F (do.)
    Martinez, V. (do.)
    Carrion, M. (do.)

Martin, Dyce & Co., merchants
  Mackie, J. B.
    Johnston, W.
    Hay, O. E.
    Rogers, J.
    Ogilvie. T.
    Fabie, F. R.
    Fuentes, M. de la
    Hernandes, J.

Mestres, B., y Hermano; auctioneer and commission agent
  Mestres, Benito
  Mestres, Tayme

Morris, Barlow & Co., (engineers, to the Manila Aerated Bread Company)
  Morris, Sam. J.
  Barlow, J. Simeon, c.e., m.s.e.
    Aguirre, Segundo
    Roldan, J. C., draftsman
    Wilson, F., travelling engineer
    Taylor, Chas., shop foreman

O. S. S. Co, Holt's Line
  Tillson, Herman & Co., agents

Owens & Co., L. merchants and shipchandlers
    Owens, L.

Pan & Co., J. F. del, merchants and commission agents
    Pan, J. F. del
    Praysler Guilermo
    Par, Estanislao del

Peele, Hubbell & Co., merchants
    Palmer, Horatio Nelson (absent)
    Edwards, Ogden Ellery (absent)
    Tucker, Richard Dalton (absent)
    Pierce, George Herry
    Foster, Frederick Emery
        Endicott, J. B. (Albay)
        Deblois, J. E.
        Downs, V. B.
        Lane, R. A.
        Marvin, A. T. (Albay)
        Eaton, F. C. (Leyte)
        Bibby, H. K.
        Heuschell, J. H.
        Greenough, H., Jr.
        Jorge, Pompilio
        Souza, F. W. R. de
        Otadiu, F. de
        Versoza, V.
        Genton, F.
        Arlegui, R. (Leyte)

Petel & Co., G. van Polanen, merchants
    Petel, G. van Polanen
    Petel, G. van Polanen, Jr
    Carbollo, José

Prehn & Co., merchants
    Prehn, Luis Otto
    Liebich. R.

Reyes & Co., shipchandlers
    Reyes, Francisco
    Ucela, Manuel
    Reyes, José

Rocha & Co., Y., merchants
    Rocha, Ygnacio
    Soler, Pedro
    Reyes, A.
    Modesto, F.
    Escalante, A.

Roxas, J. B., proprietor, "San Miguel" Soap Factory
    Roxas, J. B.
        Fernandez, Ysidoro
        Fernandez, Joaquin V.
        Roxas, Pedro P.
        Granados, Gregorio
        Francisco, Pedro A.
        Tibayan, Aguedo

Russell & Sturgis, merchants
    Russell, J.
    Jeffries, H. U. (absent)
    Heron, F. G.
    Ernst, J. E.
    Warren, C. H. (Yloilo.)
    Methvin, J.
    Oakey, F.
    Henry, M.
    Somes, M. F.
    Ray, J. J.
    Austen, J. G.
    Haffenden, J.
    Bunker, A. W. (Albay.)
    Sivart, J. T.
    Ryan, W. S.
    Gaskell, J. M.
    Lapuente, A.
    Lerma, M. L.
    Bordenave, D. Marine Surveyor

Santa Mesa Rope-factory
    Russell & Sturgis, agents
    Klinck, C., engineer
    Aylett, A., assistant

Sartorius, Pablo, pharmaceutist and chemist, Escolta
    Sartorius, Pablo (absent)
    Moerike, Gustav
    Friedrich, Rudolph

Secker & Co., M., hatters
    Secker, Engelbert
    Moritz, Carl
    Böche, Julius (Cebú)

Smith, Bell & Co., merchants
    Wood, R. P. (Liverpool)
    Young, Geo. R. (London)
    Cadell, Geo. B. (Liverpool)
    Mackenzie, Geo.
    Smith, D. Adam
    Honey, G. A. K.
    Fleming, J. M.
    Armstrong, Geo.
    Glehn, E. von
    Marshall, R.
    Marcaida, A. de
    Reyes, G.
    Reyes, F.
    Eguares, R.
    Stüben, J. F. (Cebu)
    Cundall, C. H. (do.)
    Galian, M. (do.)
    Vaño, J. (Leyte)
    Collingwood, Geo. (Camiguin)

Spring & Co., drapers, mercers, milliners and general outfitters, 1, St. Gabriel
 Spring, C. A.
 Spring, Miss
 Cutting, James
 George, W. D.

Tilson, Herrmann & Co., merchants
 Parr, Edward (London)
 Hermann, Moritz A. (absent)
 Boustead, Edward, Jr.
 Parr, Richard E.
  Sackerman, E.
  Ortega, Manuel
  Javier, Juan
  Blakeley, Charles
  Antonio, Olona
  Lanuza, J.

Tutuban Rope Factory
 Eugster & Co., L., agents
 Feliciano, M., manager
 Feliciano, B., assistant

Ullmann, Felix, importer of Jewellery &c.

Ullmann, Emanuel, Do.

Wilks & Earnshaw, engineers

Witte & Co., Julius, Baraca, No. 21
 Witte, Julius
  Cooper, Charles, supt. engineer
  Falcon, Ysidoro, clerk
  Gomara, Fernando, assistant engineer

Zobel & Nohr, apothecaries
 Zobel, J.
 Nohr, J.
  Plitt, C.
  Grupe, G.
  Eydner, A.
  Le Sage, E.

YLOILO.

Consulates.

GREAT BRITAIN.
Vice-Consul—Higgin, John

UNITED STATES.
Acting Consular Agent—Warren, C. H.

Insurances.

Fyfe, James S.
 Netherlands India Sea and Fire Insurance Co.
Loney & Co.
 Royal Insurance, Fire and Life
 The Netherlands India Sea and Fire Insurance
 The Samarang Sea and Fire Insurance
 Lloyds

Merchants, &c.

Aguado, A., shipchandler, merchant, &c.

Bischoff & Co., watchmakers
 Bischoff, J. S.
 Stadeli, L.

Diaz, Filipi, timber merchant, ship owner, &c.

Fyfe, James S., merchant

Higgin, John, merchant

Ker & Co., merchants
 Munn, D.
 Carballo, J.
 Saul, G. M.

Loney & Co., merchants
 Loney, Robert (Negros)
 Ker, William G.
 Smith, James (Surigao)
 MacGibbon, Thomas
 Innes, Thomas (Leyte)
  Hoskyn, R. F.
  Llorenti, Juan
  Pearce, Alfred (Negros)
  Whittom, Wm., engineer
  Herreva, José de (Surigao)
  Viña, Diego (Hijo, Cebú)

Luchcinger, F., merchant
 Luchcinger, F.
 Haxty, R.

Mascañana, Ricardo, merchant

Russell & Sturgis, merchants
 Warren, C. H.
 Bush, E. D.
 Tyler, J. C.

CEBU.

Consulates.

GERMAN EMPIRE.
Consul—Stüben, J. F.

GREAT BRITAIN.
Vice-Consul—Smith, James

PORTUGAL.
Vice-Consul—Veloso, C.

UNITED STATES.
Acting Consular Agent—Austen, G.

Insurances.

Loney & Co.
  Royal Insurance, Fire and Life
  Lloyds
  Samarang Sea and Fire Insurance Co.

Merchants.

Loney & Co., merchants
  Smith, James
    Gardiner, Wm. A.
    Lagueras, G.
    Ruiz, V.

Macleod, Pickford & Co., merchants
  Macleod, N.
    Hepper, F. H.
    Pike, O. O.
    Colquhoun, W.
    Tuason, E.
    Martinez, V.
    Carrion, M.

Russell & Sturgis, merchants
  Warren, C. H.
  Austen, G.
  Skinner, F.
  Elio, J. (Camiguin)
  Carlotta, C. (Surigao)

Secker & Co., Hatters
  Büche, J.

Smith, Bell & Co., merchants
  Stüben, J. F.
    Cundall, C. H.
    Galien, M.
    Collingwood, Geo. (Camiguin)
    Vaño, J. (Leyte)

SUAL.

Consulates.

GREAT BRITAIN.
Vice-Consul—Bosch, José de

Merchants.

Frank, Heald

SAIGON.

Government.

Governor, Rear Admiral and Commander-in-Chief—Dupré, Jules Marie
Acting Secretary—Chomereau-Lamotte

ETAT MAJOR OF THE GOVERNOR.

Chief of the Staff—Hardy
Aide-de-Camp—De Montesquiou-Fezensac
Officiers d'Ordonnance—Guyon; Goudard

PRIVY COUNCIL.

President—The Governor
Members—The Commander of the Troops; The Chief of the Administrative Service; The Director of the Interior; The Chief of the Judicial Service; The Colonial Comptroller
Secretary—Chomereau-Lamotte

DIRECTION DE L'INTERIEUR.

Directeur—Montjon, A de
Secrétaire Générale—Guiraud, L.

1ER. BUREAU.

Chef—Morin, L.
Sous Chef—Moisy, L.

2EME. BUREAU.

Chef—Béliard, E.
Sous Chef—Marey, A. de Lanneau de

3EME. BUREAU.

Chef—d'Audigier, F.
Sous Chef—Pernay, E. Daniel de

4EME. BUREAU.

Chef—Richaud, F., détaché comme fondé de pouvoirs du Trésorier Payeur
Sous Chef—Didier, F., chef p. i.

JUSTICE.

Procureur Général—Guillet des Grois
Substitut—Esquer (annoucé)

COUR.

Président—Laude (attendu)
Conseiller—Bulan (en congé)
Roumain de la Touche (en congé)
Conseiller p. i.—Jouslin
  do.   Postel
Conseiller-auditeur—Ducroux

TRIBUNAL DE PREMIERE INSTANCE.

Juge de première instance—Bahunot du Liscoët (attendu)
Juge de première instance p. i.—Augier
Juge-suppléant; Conseiller p. i. à la cour—Postel
Juge-suppléant—Le Jemble

PARQUET.

Procureur de la République, Conseiller p. i. à la cour—Jouslain
Substitut faisant fonctions de Procureur de la République p. i.—Ternisien

GREFFE DE LA COUR D'APPEL, DU TRIBUNAL DE 1RE INSTANCE ET DE LA JUSTICE DE PAIX.

Greffier-en-chef—Coudroy de Laureal
Commis-greffiers—Le Garnisson, De Mérendol, Cléonie, Hubert-Delisle
Expéditionnaires—Canal, Filatriau, Thomas Mién

PARQUET DU PROCUREUR GENERAL.

Chef du Secrétairat—Pott
Secrétaire-redacteur—Marsau
Expéditionnaire—Justinien

PARQUET DU PROCUREUR DE LA REPUBLIQUE

Secrétaire—Buchard

SAIGON.

THE DIFFERENT POSTS
THE FRENCH ARE OCCUPYING.

Cholon
Cangioc
Gocong
Tan An
Tay ninh
Trambang
Mytho
Canlo
Bienhoa
Baria
Thúdaumot
Long Thanh
Vinh Long
Travinh
Bentré
Mocai
Bactrang
Chaudoc
Sadec
Soctrang
Longxuyen
Cantho
Hatien
Rachgia

INSPECTION DES AFFAIRES INDIGENES.

Inspector—Henry, Alexandre-Antoine

MISCELLANEOUS OFFICES.

Commandant des Troupes, p. i.—De Trentenian
Directeur de l'Arsenal Maritime—Caselles
Docteur en Chef—D'Ornay
Artillerie, Chef d'Escadron, Directeur—Brinster
Génie, Chef de Bataillon, Directeur p. i.—Tavernier
Service Télégraphique, Directeur—Demars
Ponts et Chaussées et Travaux Hydrauliques p. i.—Chariot
Bâtiments Civils Architecte, Chef du Service p. i.—Callinaud
Finances, Trésorier Payeur—Philidor, Danican
Poste—Sée
Curate—De Kerlan

DIVISION NAVALE DE COCHINCHINE.

"FLEURUS," Admiral's Flagship

Commander—Sauze, capitaine de vaisseau

COMMISSARIAT DE LA MARINE.

Commissaire—Lacouture
Sous Commissaires—Berteau (Chef du Bureau Central du Contrôle); de Gaillande (Chef du Détail des Revues et der Hôpitaux); Frasque (Chef du Détail des Armements et Inscription Maritime); Féraud (Chef du Détail des Subsistances); Chatelain (Chef du Détail des Approvisionnements); Gibort Des Vallous (Chef du Détail des Travaux); Bayet; Galerié; Tranchevent (en congé); de Tersannes (do.); Lestang (do.); Dutouquet (attendu); Guyomar (do.); Delafon (do.); Bruere (do.)

COMMISSARIAT DE LA MARINE.
(Continued.)

Aides Commissaires—Des Vallons (Chef du Détail des Fonds et Chef du Secrétariat de l'Ordonnateur); de St. Pern (Chargé du Service Administratif à Vinhlong); Baudry (do. do. do. à Mytho); Badaire (do. do. do. à Chaudoc); Ciret (do. do. do. à Baria); Huard, Lanoiraix (Garde Magasin Général); Badaire Garde Magasin des Subsistances; Aphalo; Le Pontois (en congé); Sabourean (do.); Rand (do.); Deshouliéres
Commis. de Marine—Jacque; Bourlet (Commis aux entrées à l'hôpital); Le Petit de Sauques; Broni; Maleschal; Damas-Ribeiro (en congé); Coridon (attendu); Le Boucher (do.); Courtier (do.); Greffrier (do.); Léonce (do.); Sinson-Sainville (do.); Dublanc Laborde (do.); Roberdeau (do.); Pacquetot (do.); Granier de Cassagnac (do.)
Ecrivains de Marine—Lamour; Pellicot; St. Pern, B. de; Gleizes; Gabrié; Sandred; Dufresne (en congé)

OFFICIERS ET EMPLOYES DU COMMISSARIAT PLACES HORS CADRE.

Commissaire Adjoint—De Montjon (Directeur de l'Intérieur)
Sous Commissaires—Bonnissent (Chef du 1er Bureau à la Direction de l'Intérieur); D'Engente, Du Mesgnil (Inspecteur des Affaires Indigénes à Hatien)
Aides Commissaires—Gouin (Inspecteur des Affaires Indigénes à Thúdaumót); Richaud (Chef du 4eme Bureau à la Direction de l'Intérieur); Desmazes (Directeur de l'Hôpital de Choquan); Le Peltier, (Inspecteur des Affaires Indigénes à Soctrang); Villard (Inspecteur des Affaires Indigénes à Longxuyen); Gest (Directeur de l'Imprimerie Nationale)
Commis. de Marine—Campana (Directeur de Prison Centrale)

Government Departments.

HARBOUR MASTER'S DEPARTMENT.

Harbour Master—Bertrand, G.
Clerk—Dubois

GAOL.

Gaoler—Campana

SAIGON.

POLICE.

Chief Commissioner—Girard, P. C. E.
Second do.—Launuy-Céphas, E. G.
Third do.—Larrieu-Manan
Do.—Laval, in charge of the Police at Cholon
Commissioner in charge of the Municipal Police at Saigon—Lannes, C. B.
Brigadiers—Six
European Constables—Twenty
Asiatic do.—Sixty-seven
Interpreters—Two

ECOLE NORMALE.

Directeur—Robert, J.

Municipal Departments.

MUNICIPALITY.

Maire—Lourdeault.
Chef du Secrétariat—Semanne, H.
Sous Chef—Sère, Ch.
Secrétaires—Vaud, Finet; Morando; Lallemand; Lamour
Inspecteur—Picault
Sous Inspecteurs—Roché, Seurat
Chefs Cantonniers—Chenenaille, Lorestcaré
Cantonniers—40

CONSEIL MUNICIPAL.

Lourdeault (Président)
Sandner
Blancsubé
Chaignon
Hamonic
Mayer, A.
Schroeder
Hubert
Leroy
Burté
Macaire
Callinaud
Lacaze, A.
Morice ainé
Mauras Fernand

POLICE MUNICIPALE.

Commissaire en chef—Lannes, C. B.
  1 Inspecteur de Police
  3 Sous-Inspecteurs
  8 Agents européens
  4 Agents asiatiques
  2 Interpretes asiatiques

PARC DE LA VILLE.

Chef Gardien—Moreau
Gardien de 1er classe—Harlet
Natives—Two

ENTRETIEN DES ARBRES DE LA VILLE.

Chargé—Mougeol
Cantonniers—10

MUNICIPAL EDUCATIONAL INSTITUTION.

Directeur provisoire—Lallemand, (détaché)
Professeurs—Blaise; Bao; Paul

GREFFE DU TRIBUNAL DE COMMERCE.

Greffier—Ellie
Commis-expeditionnaire—Ayavoussamy

MEMBRES DU TRIBUNAL.

Président—Denis, G.
Juges—Dierx, Ed.; Sandner, E.; Roquerbe; Macaire

Chamber of Commerce.

Honorary President—de Montjon, Directeur of the Interior
President—Dierx, Ed.
Secretary—Denis, G.
Members—Lourdeault; Williaume; Hubert, J.; Catoire, A.; Macaire, J.; Lehmann, J. B.; Samuel; Roquerbe; Mauras, C.
Secretary Archiviste—Belliet, John

Consulates.

AUSTRIA.
Consul—Sornsen, F.

BELGIUM.
Acting Consul—Sandner, E.

DENMARK.
Consul—Schroeder, K.

GREAT BRITAIN.
Consul—Caswell, J. G.

GERMAN EMPIRE.
Consul—Niederberger, G. (Europe)
Acting Consul—Saltzkorn, E.

ITALY.
Consul—Schroeder, K.

PORTUGAL.
Consul—Ribeiro, M.

SPAIN.
Consul—Ruiz, Don Juan

River Pilots.

Alessn, (affecté aux Messag. Marit.)
Granger, (commande dans la Co. Larrien)
Arduser
Duzac
Marin
Michel (en congé en France)
Lescandron
Pioch, aîné (en congé en France)
Gonineau (en congé en France)
Brunet (commande dans la Co. Larrien)
Marquant
Pallas
Legludic
Orieux
Roux
Prockter
Luperne
Gavini
Merlu
Pioch, jeune
Castera

Masonic Lodge.

LOGE REVEIL DE L'ORIE

Worshipful Master—Doublet
Senior Warden—Sandner, E.
Junior Warden—Semanne, H.
Deacon—Lequerré
Secretary—Schroeder

Insurances.

Behre & Co.
   North China Insurance Co.
   Canton Insurance Office
   Samarang Sea & Fire Insurance Co.
   Deutsche Transport Versicherungs Gesellschaft
   Verein Hamburger Assecuradeure
   Germanic Lloyd
   Hongkong Fire Insurance Co. (Limited.)
   Transatlantic Fire Insurance Co. of Hamburg (Limited)
Denis Freres
   Des Compagnies d'Assurances de Bordeaux, Paris, Marseilles et Havre
Dierx, Ed.
   Compagnie Lyonnaises d'Assurances Maritimes
Hale & Co., Wm. G.
   Lloyds
   Western Clubs, Topsham
   China Traders' Insurance Co., Limited
   Union Insurance Society of Canton
   Batavia Sea and Fire Insurance Company
   Colonial Sea and Fire Insurance Company
   North British Mercantile Ins. Company
   Victoria Fire Insurance Co., Limited
   China Fire Insurance Co., Limited
   Java Sea and Fire Insurance Company

Hogg & Co., A. G.
   Chinese Insurance Company Limited
   Sun Fire Office
Kaltenbach, Engler & Co.
   China and Japan Marine Insurance Company
Renard & Co., Ed.
   Zutphen and Nederlanden Fire Insurance Company
   Oosterling Sea Insurance Company

Merchants, &c.

Andrieu, —., contractor for light-fittings, Rue Catinat

Antolini, —., soda-water manufacturer, Rue Catinat

Bacharach Oppenheimer & Co., merchants and commission agents. Rue Rigault de Genouilly
   Bacharach, N. (absent)
   Oppenheimer, C (Europe)
   Worch, A., signs p. pro.
   Russel, —.

Bareil et Fils Freres, storekeepers, Rue Catinat

Barthelemy, Madame, storekeeper, Rue Catinat

Baudran & Fargeot, Mme., ladies' and children's dresses, Rue Catinat

Bazière, P., contractor, Rue Nationale

Beauregard, Mdlle., "Débit Lefèbvre," Rue Nationale

Behre & Co., merchants
   Niederberger, G. (Europe)
   Saltzkorn, E.
   Nisale, G.
   Gehmeyer, A.
   Röver, B.
   Worch, Th.
   Miller, R.

Bénaguet, P., contractor and timber merchant, Rue MacMahon

Bénézech, Antoine, tavern keeper, Rue de Batavia

Berthelier, F., public auctioneer and general commission agent, Rue Catinat

SAIGON

Blancsubé, Jules, lawyer, Rue Catinat Citrate, —.

"Botanical Gardens"
Pierre, J. B., director

Burté, contractor, Rue d'Espagne

Café de Paris, Quai du Commerce
Martin, Madame Veuve

Caraman, Frédéric Thomas de, newspaper correspondent, and wine merchant

Cardi, J., Senior, M.D., ice manufacturer, Rue Catinat

Cardi, J., apothecary and druggist, Rue Catinat

Catoire, A., shipwright and timber merchant

Cazeaux & Salvaire, tinmen, Rue Catinat

Chaalons, Mdlle., institution for educating young ladies, Rue Rigault de Genouilly

Chaignon, notary public, Rue Vannier

Champon, Michel, butcher, Rue de l'eglise

Charpentier, E., farmer to the slaughter house of the town

Chartered Bank of India, Australia and China
Agents—Behre & Co.

Chartered Mercantile Bank of India, London and China
Agents—Hale & Co., Wm. G.

Clément, contractor and boarding house, Route de Cholon

Clément, Madame, store-keeper, Rue Catinat

Codry, E. (surveyor general), architect and contractor (absent)
Calinaud, 2nd architect, manager

Commélerant, C., "Débit de la plaine de Jones," Rue Chasseloup-Laubat

Comptoir d'Escompte de Paris, Quai du Commerce
Roquerbe, H., manager
Michelot, L., accountant

Cosmopolitan Hotel
Austin, proprietor (Wang Tai's buildings)

Courrier de Saigon, Government Gazette fortnightly newspaper
Gest, —., director

Denis Frères, merchants and commission agents
Denis, Emile
Denis, Gustave
Denis, Alphonse
Bézian, Edouard
Jourde, Alphonse

Dierx, Ed., merchant and commission agent
Dierx, Loricourt

Dimitri, "Café de la Petite Californie" Rue de Batavia

Donnet, pastry-cook, Rue Catinat

Drell, contractor, Rue MacMahon

Duo, Ferdinand, manager "Hotel & Café de l'Univers," Rue Vannier

Dufourg, C., watch-maker, Rue Catinat

Dussutour, A., auctioneer, 50, Rue Charner

Eastern Extension Australasian & China Telegraph Company, Limited
Agents—Hale & Co., Wm. G.

Fabre, Hair dresser and dealer in perfumery, Rue Rigault de Genouilly

Farinole, J. B., "Bureau d'Encaissements et Recouvrements," Rue Rigault de Genouilly

Ferrand & Co., bakers, Rue de l'église

Ferrier, Madame, proprietor "Café de France," Quai du Commerce

Firmin-Marrot, Madame Veuve, store-keeper, Rue Catinat

SAIGON.

Freund, " Café de Marseille," Rue Amiral Roze

Fricot & Co., A., storekeepers, Rue Charner

Géraud, baker and wine merchant, Rue Catinat

Girard, Watch-maker, Rue Catinat

Goldstein, " Café de London," Rue Charner

Grandpré, Madame de, storekeeper, Rue Charner

Gsell, E., photographer, Rue Rigault de Genouilly

Hale & Co., Wm. G., merchants
 Hale, Wm. G.
 Caswell, James
 Sörnsen, F.
 Detmering, W.
 Tremlett, C. F.
 Kufahl, C. T.

Hainard, watch-maker, Rue Catinat

Hamonic Frères, engineers, machinists and coach builders, Rue Rigault de Genouilly
 Hamonic, J.
 Hamonic, H.

Hogg & Co., A. G. merchants
 Hogg, A. G.
 Linstead, T. G. (Hongkong)
 Johnston, H.
 David, A.
 Agents—Tug Steamer " Little Orphan"

Hongkong and Shanghai Banking Corporation, Limited
 Agent—Hardie, D.
  Perrin, A., clerk
  Apack, do.

" Hotel-Café de l'Univers," Rue Vannier
 Lacaze, A., proprietor

Hubert, —., storekeeper, Rue Catinat

Imprimerie Commerciale Indépendant de Saigon, fortnightly newspaper
 Semanne, H., editor

" Imprimerie Commerciale "—*Saigon Advertiser & Shipping Gazette* Office, weekly newspaper, *L'Indépendant*, a fortnightly newspaper
 Bloom, J. H., general manager
 Mello, A., compositor
 Silva, H. H., do.
 Luz, C. S., do.
 Cruz, J. M., do.
 Zuzarte, Ricardo do.
 2 Chinese and 8 Annamites
Bookbinding Establishment
 2 Chinese bookbinders
 1 Kling do.

Jame, F., merchant, Rue Rigault de Genouilly
 Coutel, J. B. (signs pe" pro.)

Jouvet, A., commission agent and public accountant, Rue d'Espagne

Kaltenbach, Engler & Co., merchants
 Kaltenbach, Gustav (absent)
 Engler, Frédéric (do.)
 Grün, Ernst
 Opstelten, J. C.
 Fünfgeld, E.
 Lugo, Carl
 Engler, A.
 Cauchefert, E.

Lacant, boarding house, Rue Catinat

Lacaze, A., storekeeper, Rue Catinat

Larrieu & Roque, merchants and commission agents, and contractors to Government for river steamship navigation to different provinces in Cochin-china Messageries a Vapeur de Cochin-chine
 Larrieu, Marcolin (Saigon)
 Roque, Victor (Europe)
  H. Roque (in the interior)
 Branzell, A., agent in the Provinces
 Roze, T., capitaine d'armement
 Candau, V., assistant
 Prémont, M., do.
 Brécard, T., do.
 Cowie, F., do.
  Fleet :
Saltee—Master, E. Sampson
Attalo— do. M. Kelvie
Vaico— do. Piton
Powerful—do. Brunet
Sadec— do. N........
Mongom—do. N........
  Pilot, A. Granger

SAIGON.

Laurent, supplier to the Messageries Maritimes steamers, Rue Nationale

Lautier & Guérin, hair-dressers and dealers in perfumery, Rue Catinat

Legros, "Café de la Marine," Rue Nationale

Lehmann, J. B., agent for Alphonse Cahuzac of Bordeaux, and Steam service between Saigon and Cholon
    Bonnefond, B.
    Taylor, C.
    Grandpré, C.

Lemaire, farmer to Saigon market, Rue de l'hopital

Léopold Perrichon & Baud, contractors and light-fittings, Rue Catinat

Leroy, E., general drapers, stationary and library, Rue Catinat

Lourdeault, apothecary and druggist, Rue Catinat

Marx, L , Government supplier
    Schroeder, Karl

Martin, plumber and tinman, Rue Catinat

Mas, C., tinman, Rue Vannier

Mauras, Fernand, lawyer, Rue de l'Eglise

Mauras, Vve. A., denrées and liquides
    Mauras, Camille
    Aledor
    Crémazy

Mayer, Alb., contractor and timber merchant, Rue MacMahon

Messageries Maritimes, Saigon Agency
    Macaire, Jules, inspector, in charge
    Henriot, Charles, 1st assistant
    Rieutord, N., 2nd do.
    Desbois, Antoine, storekeeper
    Rouet, watchman

Michel, J., tavern-keeper, Rue de l'hopital

Monnier, "Café de la Marine," Quai du Commerce

Montfalconnet, Regina, Madame, "Café de la Régence," Quai du Commerce

Morice Frères & Bailly, general drapers and outfitters, Rue Catinat

Mulaton, —., contractor, Rue Rigault de Genouilly
    Mulaton
    Loiseleur

Niobey, lawyer, Rue d'Espagne

Opium Farm
    Tan Keng Hoon, manager

Pellisser, V., contractor and timber merchant, Rue MacMahon

Perrimond, "Café Restaurant," Rue de l'hopital

Perrin, A., Madame, restaurateur, Rue Rigault de Genouilly

Pun Lun, photographer, Rue Charner

Ravel, contractor for public works, Rue MacMahon

Renard & Co., Ed., merchants, agents Rice Mill at Cholon
    Renard, Ed. (Paris)
    Pilliet, A. (do.)
    Cornu, Ed.
        Cornu, Albert
        Ricou, W.
        Saillant

Reuchlin, "Café Militaire," Rue Nationale

Ribeiro & Co., M., merchants and commission agents
    Ribeiro, M. J. V.
    Bloom, J.
    Simoens, José dos Reis
    Appassamy

Richard, Madame, dressmaker & milliner, Rue Rigault de Genouilly

Rollet, Madame Veuve, storekeeper, Rue Catinat

Roglin, engineering and coppersmith, Rue de l'église

Rondard, saddle and collar-maker, Rue de l'église

"Salon Louis XV.," Rue Vannier
　Bertrand, hair dresser and dealer in perfumery

Saigon Rice Mill
　Renard & Co., Ed., proprietors

Schroeder, Karl, merchant and commission agent
　Schroeder, Albert

Semanne, Paul, lawyer, Rue Catinat

Siegas, Pierre, "Café Oriental," Quai du Commerce

Spirit Farm
　Tan Keng Hoon, manager

Storror, E. M., M.D., Rue de Canton

Van Lier, E. A., M.D., Rue Vannier

Vimeux—Colmache, Madame, dress-maker and milliner, Rue Catinat

Vinson, lawyer, Rue Charner

Vuillermoz, A., watchmaker, Rue Catinat

Waterson, Captain, surveyor to Insurance Companies, Rue Rigault de Genouilly

BANGKOK.

Legations and Consulates.

AUSTRO-HUNGARY.
Minister Resident and Consul General for Siam (residing at Yedo)—Calice, Chevalier Henry de
Consul—Masius, Wihelm

DENMARK.
Consul—Köbke, F. C. C.

FRANCE.
Consul and Commissioner—Garnier, Benoit
Chancelier—Knecht, Emile
1st Interpreter—Vacant
2nd do.—Khruminh, Jacques
Clerks—Chin
Constable—Dieu, Pedro

GERMAN EMPIRE.
Consul—Von Bergen, Baron Werner
Secretary—Hausmann, Capt. T.
1st Interpreter—Hendricks, R.
2nd do.—Bua
Messenger—Cheng

GREAT BRITAIN.
Consul General—Knox, Thom. George
Interpreter—Newman, W. H.
1st Assistant—Edwardes, D. J.
2nd do.—Gould, E. B.
Studen Interpreter—Bickmore, H. F.
Medical Attendant—Campbell, W., M.D., F.R.C.S.E. &c.
Constable—Ourdner, H. A.

NETHERLANDS.
Consul—Pickenpack, V. (absent)
Acting Consul—Muller, Wm.

PORTUGAL.
Consul General—
Secretary in Charge—D'Almeida, Joaquim Vicente
Interpreter—Sh, Honorato de
Clerk—Luz, Antonio Joaquim Franco da

SWEDEN AND NORWAY.
Consul—Pickenpack, V. (absent)
Acting Consul—Muller, Wm.

UNITED STATES.
Consul—Partridge, Gen. F. W.
Interpreter—Bush, Henry
Marshal—Partridge, F. P.

Customs' Department.
Commissioner of Customs—Bateman, S.
Inspector—Da Costa, J. M. F.
Tidewaiters—Chivers, J.; Williams, H. D.; Sowchong

Harbour Master's Department.
Harbour Master and Master Attentant and Registrar of Shipping—Bush, Capt. John
Clerk—Hendrinks, N. F.
Interpreter—Yam
Ghaut Serang—Sulayman

Bangkok Branch Pilots.
Aastrome, O.
Berkeley, G. A.
Christians, J. H.
Dyer, A.
Ecclestone, G.
Lampe, L.
Peterson, F.
Reynolls, W. H.
Smith, J.
Van Es, J. O.
Wefer, J. D.

PILOT SCHOONERS.
"Kestrel" and "Menam."

Docks.
BANGKOK DRY DOCK COMPANY.
Manager—Bush, Captain John
Assistant—Apcar, M. T.
Foreman—Apow

BANGKOK.

Master Mariners.

Andersen, S. P.
Andreason, J.
Andresen
Aurojo, F. D.
Benedictsen, T.
Bentzen, E. W.
Bjugreen
Bloom, Henry
Boutefol, P. H. T.
Buchholtz, L.
Buur, A. H.
Christiansen, C.
Christiansen, K. L.
Clohn
Colberg, M. T.
Davis, J. M. C.
Davis, J. W. C.
Dethlefsen
Euxiere
Every, J.
Fredriksen, F.
Freudenberg
Garnier, L.
Gedes, J.
Hansen, A. C. W.
Hansen, H. A. D.
Hansen, N. P.
Hansen, J. G. R. C.
Hansen, O. S.
Hanssen, H. H.
Heimsoht
Henningsen, S. H.
Higgins, W. J.
Hochreuter
Hoffman
Hunt
Jessen, C.
Jessen, J. P.
Jorgensen, C. L.
Jorgensen, J.
Jorgensen, E.

Kent, J.
Klint, H.
Kobke, F. C. C.
Kofoed, P. J.
Kramer, W. A. T.
Kross, J.
Kruse
Lange, H.
Lauritzen
Leiser
Minden, P.
Moller, S. H.
Munchan
Nisted, F.
Olsen, M. P.
Orton, G.
Paulsen, C.
Petersen, F. C.
Plettner
Raonkilde, W.
Rademaker
Razario, C.
Resident, James
Reynolds, W. H. H.
Sass
Saxtorph, W.
Söderström
Sörensen, S.
Swendsen, P.
Tams, E. C.
Thomsen, J. C.
Trail, W.
Turner, Isaac
Ulrich, G.
Voight
Vorrath
Wevezer
Wit, J. J.
Young, J.
Zetterlund, C. U.

Europeans in Government Employ.

Affourtit, F. C., steward to the first King
Ames, S. J. B., commissioner of police
Bateman, S., commissioner of Customs
Burke, P. W., drill-master
Bush, Captain John, harbour master and master attendant (absent)
Chandler, J. H., interpreter
Clunis, J., civil architect
Costa, J. M. F. da, inspector of Customs
Court, S. V., interpreter to International Court
Hewetson, C., band master of 2nd King
Westerfield, —., band master

Engineers.

Black, A.
Cook, J. H.
Crawley, —.
Gartner, H.
Hauschild, H.
Hottinger, J.
Howarth, Chas.
Jaffrey, W.
Lewis, H.
Lyon, J. M.

Missions.

AMERICAN BAPTIST MISS. UNION.
CHINESE MISSION.
Dean, Rev. Wm., D.D.
Partridge, Rev. S. B.

AMERICAN MISSIONARY ASSOCIATION.
Bradley, Mrs. Sarah B.
Bradley, Rev. C. B.
Bradley, Mrs. Mary C.
Bradley, Miss M. A., assistant
Bradley, Dan F., do.

AMERICAN PRESBYTERIAN MISSION.
House, Rev. Samuel R., M.D.
McDonald, Revd. Noah A.
Culbertson, Rev. J. N.
PRINTING PRESS ATTACHED.
Manager—Macdonald, N. A.
STATIONED AT PETCHABUREE.
McFarland, Rev. Samuel G. (absent)
Van Dyke, Rev. Jas. W.
STATIONED AT CHIENGMAI (ZIMME) N. LAOS.
McGilvary, Rev. Daniel (absent)
Wilson, Rev. Jonathan
STATIONED AT AYUTHIA.
Carrington, Rev. J.

FRENCH ROMAN CATHOLIC MISSION.
Dupond, Right Rev. F. A. A., Bishop of Azoth
Daniel, Rev. S., provicaire
Ranfaing, Rev. R. (Chantaboon)
Larnaudie, Rev. F. L.
Gibarta, Rev. S. F.
Martin, Rev. T. P.
Martin, Rev. T.
Rabardelle, Rev. (Ban Chang)
Kieffer, Rev. F. H.
Schmitt, Rev. (Petrin)
Vey, Rev. T. L.
Perraux, Rev. (Packpret)
Fanque, Rev. (Petrin)
Guego, Rev. (Bang Plasoi)
D'Hont, Rev. (Chantaboon)
Chevillard, Rev. (Thakhien)
Barbier, Rev. (Petrin)

BANGKOK.

FRENCH ROMAN CATHOLIC MISSION.
(Continued.)
Rousseau, Rev. P. L.
Saladin, Rev. S.
Chaumet, Rev. B. M.
Colombet, Rev. E. A.

SIAM MISSION (SELF-SUSTAINING.)
Smith, Rev. Samuel J.

Insurances.

Borneo Company, Limited
Lloyds
North China Insurance Co.
Northern Insurance Co.
Markwald & Co., A.
   Canton Insurance Co.
   Hamburg, Dresden and Bremen Underwriters
   Westphalia Lloyds
Pickenpack, Thies & Co.
   China Traders' Insurance Co., Limited
   Colonial Sea and Fire Insurance Co.
   Oosterling Sea and Fire Insurance Co.
   Victoria Fire Insurance Co. of Hongkong, Limited
   Transatlantic Fire Insurance Co. of Hamburg, Limited
Windsor, Redlich & Co
   Batavia Sea and Fire Insurance Co.
   Chinese Insurance Company Limited
   Samarang Sea and Fire Insurance Co.
   Union Insurance Society of Canton

Merchants, &c.

Ah Paie, tailor

Alloin & Co., merchants
   Alloin, J. M.
   Lamache, E.
      Möller, Julius
      Herb, Francis
      Burros, G. A. de
      Four Natives

American Steam Rice Mill
   Pickenpack, Thies & Co.
      Moore, Alonzo
      Lewis, Henry

Bangkok Advertiser
   Graham, Geo. G., ed. and proprietor

Bangkok Dry Dock Company (established 1864)
   Bush, Capt. John, manager
   Apcar, M. T., assistant
   Apow, foreman
   Ayang, assistant
   Pha, engineer

"Berns' Hotel"
   Berns, H. L., proprietor

Borneo Company, Limited, merchants
   Blyth, John, manager (absent)
   Hay, R. M., acting do.
   Clarke, F. S., assistant
   Lee Boon Geoh
   Lee Ching Tiew
   Tan Teh Hoo
   Low Leang Ann

Borneo Company Steam Rice Mill
   Lyon, J. M., superintendent
   Black, A., assistant
   Cocke, J. H., do.
   Lee Boon Hin, clerk

Bouret, H A., compradore, butcher and baker, New Road, rear of the French Consulate

Brown, W., watch repairer

Campbell, William, M.D., F.R.C.S.E., &c., surgeon to H.B.M. Consulate

"Carter's Hotel"
   Carter, P.

Chartered Bank of India, Australia and China
   Markwald & Co., agents

Chartered Mercantile Bank of India, London and China
   Pickenpack, Thies & Co., agents

Clyde Dock & Ship Building Yard
   Maclean & Co. D., proprietors

Clyde Steam Saw Mills and Timber Yard
   Maclean & Co., D., proprietors
   Syrangyan and native engineers

Da Costa, J. M. F., merchant
   Braga, G. M., assistant
   Ah Thay

De Bay, Götte & Co., merchants
   De Bay, H. A.
   Götte, R.
   Klopp, H.
   Beck, M.
   Jean Gam
   Several natives

Dupont, George, auctioneer and commission agent

Dyer, Atkins, pilot, back of French Consulate

BANGKOK.

Elye & Kesam, tailors

Falck Hotel, Bowling Alley and Billiard Rooms
  Falck & Richten, proprietors
    Falck, C.
    Richten, A.

"Falck Hotel," Paknam
  Falck & Richten, proprietors
    Falck, C.
    Richten, A.

Gowan, Peter, M.B., C.M.B. Sc.

Hongkong and Shanghai Banking Corporation
  Pickenpack, Thies & Co., agents

Hutchinson, Wm L., M.D., opposite the English Consulate

Indo Chinese Sugar Co.
  Agents—Borneo Co. Limited

Maclean & Co., D., merchants
  Maclean, Daniel
  Maclean, John
    Hanssen, H. H., assistant
    Boon, Chim clerk
    Nin, Poo clerk

Malherbe, Jullien & Co.
  Malherbe, L. (absent)
  Jullien, St. Cyr do.
  Jucker, A., manager, signs p. pro
  Sigg, H.
  Demianoff, A.
  Yew Eng Chouan
  Swee Beng

BRANCH HOUSE—(East side of the River)
  Bjurling, A., manager
  Tan King Kee

"Macgregor" Steam Line between Bangkok and Hongkong
  Windsor, Redlich & Co., agents

Manyn & Ammin, compradores and butchers

"Marine Hotel"
  Zedneizeck, W.

Markwald & Co., A., merchants
  Lessler, P.
  Masius, Wm.
    Richmann, J.
    Kurtzhalss, A.

Markwald & Co., A.—(continued)
  STEAM RICE MILL.
  Hauschildt, O., miller
  Simões, S., clerk

Menam Roads, Paknam and Bangkok Mail Steam Boat Post
  Falck & Richten, proprietors
  [The steamer Post runs daily from Bangkok and returns from outside the Bar the same day.]

Model Rice Mill
  Nakoda Ismail Soloomanjee, proprietor

Möller & Meisner, shipchandlers and aerated water manufacturers
  Möller, H. A.
  Meisner, C. F.

Moor, A. F., trader

Novelty Press, New Road, rear of the Custom House
  Graham, Geo. G., proprietor

Oriental Bank Corporation
  Borneo Company Limited, agents

Pickenpack, Thies & Co., merchants
  Pickenpack, V. (Europe)
  Müller, W.
    Schaab, W.
    Müller, F.

Printing office and Book-Bindery
  Bradley, D. F., manager

"Reina's Hotel"
  Reina, F. S., proprietor

Siam Repository and Siam Weekly Advertiser
  Smith, S. J., editor and proprietor

Windsor, Redlich & Co., merchants
  Windsor, D. T.
  Redlich, Alexis
    Wagner, Th.
    Jesus, F. M. de
    Wee Chin Heng
    Koon Sew

Windsor, Redlich & Co's Steam-Rice Mill
  Hottinger, J., engineer
  Scherzinger, L. S., assistant

Xavier, J. M., trader

Xavier, L., trader

Zedneizeck, W., book-binder

STRAITS SETTLEMENTS.

SINGAPORE.

Colonial Government.

Governor, Vice-Admiral and Commander-in-Chief—Clark, His Excellency Sir Andrew
Colonial Secretary—Birch, Hon. J. W. W.
Acting Colonial Secretary—Irving, E. A.
Lieut.-Governor of Penang—Anson, Hon. Lieut.-Col. Archibald Edward Harbord
Lieut.-Governor of Malacca—Shaw, Hon. Commander Edward Wingfield, R.N.
Chief Justice, and Commissary of Vice-Admiralty Court—Sidgreaves, His Honor Thomas
Attorney General—Braddell, Hon. Thomas
Solicitor General—Logan, Daniel
Treasurer, Commissioner of Stamps and Accountant General Supreme Court—Willans, Hon. William Willans
Assistant Colonial Treasurer—Isemonger, Edwin Empson
Auditor General—Irving, Hon. Charles John
Colonial Engineer and Comptroller of Convicts—McNair, Hon. Major John F. A., (Madras) Royal Artillery
Deputy Colonial Engineer and Deputy Comptroller of Convicts—Sheppard, Frederick Augustus, C.E.
Inspector General of Police, Straits Settlements—Plunkett, Hon. C. B.
Superintendent of Police—Waller, Charles Brown (Europe); Dunlop, Captain S. B.A. (acting)
Colonial Post Master—Trotter, H.
Colonial Surgeon—Randell, Henry Lloyd
Assistant Surgeon—Anderson, Andrew Ferguson
Sheriff—Skinner, Alan M.; Velge, Charles E. (acting)

Foreign Consulates.

AUSTRIA.
Consul.—Conighi, A. G.

BELGIUM.
Consul.—Hinnekindt, Henri

BRAZIL.
Consul.—d'Almeida, José

DENMARK.
Consul.—Padday, R.

FRANCE.
Consul.—Hartung, Victor (Straits' Settlements)

ITALY.
Consul.—Remé, G. H.

NETHERLANDS.
Consul.—Read, W. H., K.N.L.
Vice-Consul.—Maier, S.

OTTOMAN EMPIRE.
Consul.—Junied, Said Junied bin Omar Al, in charge

PORTUGAL.
Consul.—d'Almeida, Joaquim

RUSSIA.
Vice-Consul.—Whampoa, Hon'ble H. A. K.

SIAM.
Consul.—Ching, Tan Kim

SPAIN.
Consul.—Mencarini, A.

SWEDEN AND NORWAY.
Consul.—Read, W. H.
Vice-Consul.—Read, R. B.

UNITED STATES OF AMERICA.
Consul.—Studer, Major A. G.

Merchants, &c.

"Adelphi Hotel," Bonham Street and Battery Road
  Pullman, C., proprietor

Aitken, A. M., & Rodyk, B., advocates, attorneys, proctors and notaries public, 12 Collyer Quay
  Aitken, Alexander Muirhead
  Donaldson, J.
    Mitchell, James Charles ; Sheriff, Benjamin Manuel

Allen, Whitworth, merchant

Almeida & Co., Ed., water purveyors, Bonham Street, Tug and Water boat *Enterprise*

Almeida, Joaquim, merchant, Collyer Quay

Almeida, José, commission agent and broker, Collyer Quay

Angus, Gilbert, auctioneer and commission agent, Battery Road

Ann Lock & Co., storekeepers, Battery Road

Asmus, H., auctioneer and commission agent, De Souza Street

Atchison, John Simons, attorney, advocate, proctor and notary public, Princes Street
  Atchison, John Simons
    Cork, F. T., managing clerk
    Hendriks, C. L., articled clerk

Barreto, M. A., Organist St. Jose's Church, music teacher, pianoforte tuner and repairer, Victoria Street

Baxter & Kirby, marine surveyors, Battery Road
  Baxter, John
  Brown, A. E.

Behn, Meyer & Co., merchants, established 1840—Malacca Street
  Meyer, Arnold Otto (Europe)
  Glinz, Caspar
  Brussel, J. ; Kobler, Friederich ; Lütjens, Johannes; Heyde, Eduard von der ; Kirchhoffer, Oscar; Doral, John P.; Varella, Antonio

Bernard, Alfred, bill, bullion and stock broker

Bing, A. C., marine surveyor and pilot

Borneo Company, Limited
  Mulholland, William, manager
  Currie, Andrew ; Neubronner, A. W.; Neubronner, J. L. ; Palmer, H. ; Beins, M.

Bosustow, G., marine surveyor and pilot

Boustead & Co., merchants
  Boustead, Edward (London)
  Shaw, Wm. Wardrop (do.)
  Young, Jasper   (do.)
  Young, John Stow (Penang)
    Armstrong, Farleigh ; Henderson, Isaac ; Cuthbertson, Thomas ; Aitken, A. M., Jr. ; Anderson, John, Jr.; Donough, Wm. ; Jansen, Anthony; Leicester, James; Leicester, James K.; Minjoot, Fred. ; McIntyre, Anthony

Brennand & Co., merchants
  Brennand, Richard (Europe)
  Brennand, James
  Banner, Thomas George

Brinkmann, Kumpers & Co., merchants
  Brinkmann, John G.
  Kumpers, Ernest N. (Europe)
  Krohn, Wilhelm ; Gildemeister, B.; Freusberg, Max.; De Cruz, Zechariah ; Angus, J. W.

British India Extension Telegraph Company, Limited—British Australian Telegraph Company, Limited, and China Submarine Telegraph Company, Limited
  Fuller, J. W., manager
  Fisher, H. T., electrician
  Alston, W. H.
  Mance, R. H.
  Lloyd, F.; Driver, A.; Revening, W.; Hawes, J. E.; Topping, T.; Collier, A. J.; Hambling, T.; Mayhew, J.; Blewett, J.; Blanchard, W. E.; Godding, G.; Brook, A.; Blanchard, W.; Asmus, L. H.

STRAITS SETTLEMENTS.—SINGAPORE. Z 3

Brown & Co., merchants and agents
  Brown, George Henry
    Brown, G W.; Cassein, M.

Burjorjee Khodadad & Co., merchants
  Eranee, B. K.
  Rutnagur, D. C. (Bombay)
  Peerozshaw, Pestonjee (do.)
    Eranee, F. J.; Pestonjee, Rustomjee

Burrows, W., licensed pilot

Buyers & Robb, shipwrights
  Buyers, John Craig
  Robb, Daniel

Byramjee Pestonjee, merchant
  Pochajee, Pestonjee, signs per pro.

Cameron, John & Co., merchants
  Cameron, John (London)
  Rozario, D. F.; Eber, S.

Campion, William Gilbert, attorney at law and notary public
  Mynssen, H. J. G.

Carapiet, M. J., merchant
  Moses, M. J.

Cazalas, J., iron and brass founder, engineer and machinist

Chartered Bank of India, Australia and China
  Carmichael, A T., manager (absent)
  Harper, Robert I., acting manager
  Wilkinson, C. F., acting accountant
  Neave, Thos., sub-accountant
    Zechariah, Gregory I.; Rozario, G.

Chartered Mercantile Bank of India, London and China,—established 1855
  Bishop, F. C., manager
    Angus, James M.; Matthews, James Daniel; Scheerder, J. Leonard; Bateman, F. G.

Cheng Tee & Seng Poh,—proprietors Alexandra Magazine
  Mayo, W.,—in charge

Co Ah Chong, shipwright
  Waller, William, foreman; Stubbs, Samuel; De Souza, A.

Colonial Press,—Zuzarte, D., proprietor

Commercial Press,—Hansen, J. F., proprietor
  Vass, J., printer

Coulson, R. & Co., storekeepers

Crane Bros., auctioneers and parcel agents
  Crane, Thomas Henry
  Crane, Charles Edwin

De Cotta, Joze L., pianoforte tuner and repairer, Victoria Street

Dennis, G. M.
  Wakefield, Cyrus

Desker, H. F., butcher

De Souza, A. D., sign painter and paper hanger

Emmerson, C., veterinary surgeon

Emmerson, C., proprietor, Emmerson's tiffin & billiard rooms

Frederick, A., painter and paper hanger

Frederick, S., painter and paper hanger

Gilfillan, Wood & Co., merchants
  Gilfillan, Samuel (Europe)
  Adamson, William
  Wood, Henry William
    Mosley, A.; Miller, James; Donough, John; Lazaroo, V. W.; Hansen, J. A.; Strugnell, W.

Guthrie & Co., merchants
  Guthrie, James (London)
  Scott, Thomas
    Glass, Louis J. R., signs per pro.; McKerrow, William; Salmon, Rowland Montague; Glass, C. C. N.; Arozoo, S. J.; Wee Lim Guan; Blankenhein, F.

Hamilton, Gray & Co., merchants
  Padday, Reginald
  Wilsone, C. H. H. (Glasgow)
    MacArthur, James R. (Europe); Quadling, Alfred E., signs per pro.; Stiven, Robert G.; Marcus, F. H.; Elvin, N.; Marcus, Walter; Ann Jan

4 Z   STRAITS SETTLEMENTS.—SINGAPORE.

Harrison, C., merchant

Harrison, G. L., licensed pilot

Hartwig, F. von, ship chandler, sailmaker and auctioneer

Hieber, G. & Co., commission agents and storekeepers
   Hieber, G.
      Frank, H.; Hieber, Julius; Rodriguez, T. E.

Hinnekindt, E. & H., merchants
   Hinnekindt, Henri
      Collinet, Edmond; Leisk, William Robert; Joaquim, Narcis P.

Hooglandt, & Co., merchants
   Hooglandt, Jan Daniel (Europe)
   Riedtmann, Johann Rudolph
      Hooglandt, Daniel; Diethelm, Henry; Wastenecker, M. E.; Rappa, Jacob Adam

"Hotel D'Europe"
   Becker, Albert, proprietor
      Affourtite, F. C., chief waiter; Streiff, E. T., barkeeper; Oliveiro, B. H. de, bookkeeper

"Hotel Hamburg"
   Neumann, F., proprietor

"Hotel de la Paix"
   Voss, C. de, proprietor

Iburg, C., music teacher, pianoforte tuner and repairer

Jacob, James, butcher

Jamie & Wynd, shipchandlers, sailmakers and auctioneers
   Basagoiti, J. P. de
   Wynd, Alex.
      Schelkis, L. V.

John, M. H., licensed pilot

Johnston, A. L., & Co., merchants
   Read, William Henry Macleod
   Read, Robert Barclay
      Buckley, Charles B.; Maier, Sebastian J.; Kenn, Alfred Ferdinand

Johore Steam Saw Mills Company, New Johore
   Meldrum, James, managing director
      Read, R. R., assistant; Rankine, James, engineer; Jaffrey, William, asst. engineer; Croley, James, asst. engineer; McLean, James, carpenter; Grant, John, carpenter; Kelly, James, apothecary; Joseph, T., clerk; Lowe, G. W., time-keeper

Joshua Brothers, merchants
   Joshua, Joseph
   Joshua, Raphael
      Joshua, A. R.; Elias, J. B.; Joshua, B. R.

Kaltenbach, Engler & Co., merchants
   Kaltenbach, Gustav (Paris)
   Engler, Friederich (Europe)
   Rutishauser, John George (Europe)
   Zeltmann, Theodor
      Fischer, Heinrich; Huber, Heinrich

Katz Brothers, storekeepers and commission agents
   Katz, H. (Europe)
   Katz, A.
      Waldstein, Oscar; Mackertoom, J. G.; Behr, A.

Keiser, M., M.A.O. CH.D.

Koek, Edwin, advocate, attorney, proctor and notary public
   Koek, Edwin
      Hendriks, Charles Edward; Hendriks, Daniel Jacob; Fernandis, L. A.

Kugelmann, Gustav, farrier and horsebreaker

Lambert Brothers, coach builders
   Lambert, R. I.
   Lambert, E.
   Longue, M. E.

Leisk, J. S. & Co., watchmakers
   Leisk, J. S.
   Moses, J.

Lemercier, E., wine merchant and soda-water manufacturer

Liddelow & Martin, tailors, drapers and outfitters
   Liddelow, R.; Martin, A.

STRAITS SETTLEMENTS —SINGAPORE.   Z 5

Little, John & Co., storekeepers and commission agents
  Little, J. M. (London).
  Little, M.
  Martin, A. M.
    Hill, E.; Anderson, J.; Adams, A. P.; Banister, C. J. F.; Davidson, T.; Velge, A. C.; Leicester, S. N.

Maclaine, Fraser & Co., merchants
  Fraser, James (Europe)
  Dunlop, Charles (do.)
  Fraser, Lewis James
  Fraser, George John (London)
    Watson, Andrew Muir; Dunlop, W. G. K.; Augns, Thomas; Reutens, Patrick A.; Minjoot, J. J M.; Simons, J. G.; Jambu, J. A.; Reutens, F. G.

Mansfield, W. & Co., merchants
  Mansfield, Walter (Europe)
  Mansfield, Geo. J.
    Mansfield, J. Burgess; Bogaardt, T. C.; Tessensohn. J. E. R.; B. Aaron Pillay

Marshall, William, licensed pilot

Martin, Dyce & Co., merchants
  Martin, George (Glasgow)
  Campbell, Thomas H. (do.)
  Martin, John M. (do.)
  Hannay, W. Cathcart
  Steel, John (Java)
  Wenley, Robert M. (Java)
  MacVicar, Neil (Java)
  Maccoll, Archd. (Java)
  Mackie, James B. (Manila)
    Campbell, Robert; Wilson, John Tolson, R. H.

McAlister & Co., shipchandlers, sailmakers and general merchants
  McAlister, Alex.
  Niven, J. P.
    McAlister, Ebenezer; Story, J.; Cornelius, J. M. L.; Rozario, Antonio; G. Whye Teit

Mercantile Press
  Especkerman, B. H., proprietor

Meritt, John, licensed pilot

Messageries Maritimes
  Brazier, Paul, agent
    Guigne, A. de; Anchant. C.; Elie Maunier

Mission Press
  Keasberry, B. P., proprietor
    Scott, Theo. A.; Danker, G., printer; Rodrigues, L. S.; De Souza, J. B.

Motion, James, watchmaker
  Motion, James
    Graham, J.

Moses, M. J., merchant and commission agent

Netherlands Trading Society, established 1858—Collyer Quay
  Wyngaarden, P. A. C. van, agent
    Fol. J. H.; Norris, R. O.

New Dispensary
  Woodford, J. I.
  Scheerder, L. J.
    Woodford, H. B.

Niven, James Parker, butcher

Oriental Bank Corporation, established 1846—Raffles Place
  Harrison, George
    Matson, John Melville (Europe); George, John C. H., act acct.; Ogilvy, James L., act. sub-acct.; Bateman, Frank; Vierra, Anthony J.

Oriental Dispensary
  Lloyd, Henry

Patent Slip and Dock Company
  Cloughton, Wm., managing director
    Wishart, C., sup. shipwright; Hosking, T., chief engineer; Richardson, W. S., Forrest, W., asst. engineers; Glass, Thos., chief clerk; Mauricio, Ignacio; Pereira, Em.

Paterson, Simons & Co., merchants
  Ker, William Wemyss (London)
  Paterson, William (do.)
  Simons, Henry Minchin (do.)
  Shelford, Thomas
  Gulland, William Giuseppi
    Neave, John (Europe); Watkins, Charles H. K.; Ker T. R.; Eber, Alberto; De Souza, E. L. M.; Jeremiah, J.; Hendriks, Geo.

STRAITS SETTLEMENTS.—SINGAPORE.

Peninsular and Oriental Steam Navigation Compan
  Caldbeck, J. B., agent
    Geiger, H. W., chief assistant ; Rodrigues, Jose M. ; Lazar, Philip R. ; Massang, P. N. ; Veirra, J. H.
  Marshall, W., pilot

Perreau, D. C., undertaker and tomb sculptor

Poisson, C. & Co., merchants
  Poisson, C. ; Valtriny, V. C.

Powell & Co., auctioneers
  Powell, Hector T.
  Marshall, John

Purvis, J. M., bill, bullion and stock broker

Puttfarcken, Rheiner & Co.
  Puttfarcken, Otto (Hamburg)
  Ritter, Eugen
  Sohst, Th.
    Busch, H. ; Muhlinghaus, H. ; Trachsler, J. H. ; Seth, Philip Joseph ; Hendricks, Samuel Edward

Rautenberg, Schmidt & Co., merchants
  Schmidt, Adolph Emil (Hamburg)
  Küstermann, Franz   (do.)
  Hasche, A.   (do.)
  Sturzenegger, Conrad
  Suhl, Martin (Penang)
    Herwig, Heinrich ; Klünder, Rütger ; Brenner, Rudolph ; Cramer, Johannes ; Koll, Wilhelm ; Behncke, Albert ; Menzies, Bras de ; Cruz, Almeiro da ; Hawkshaw, Charles Bernette

Remé Brothers, merchants
  Remé, George Adolph (Europe)
  Remé, George Hermann
  Maack, Hermann Friedrich
    Crasemann, Richard ; Berndt, Charles ; Camp, W. de la ; Palmer, Horatio Benjamin

Renard, ed. & Co., merchants
  Renard, Edouard (Paris)
  Pillirt, Arthur   (do.)
  Cornu, Edouard (Saigon)
    Tuller, Peter Willem ; Ricou, William

Riley, Hargreaves & Co., civil and mechanical engineers, &c.
  Riley, Richard
  Hargreaves, William
    Cater, J. J. ; Erskine, S. ; Warberg, C. ; Haworth, J. ; Rozario, L. A.

Robinson & Co., milliners and dressmakers
  Robinson, P. ; Robinson, Mrs.

Robertson, John & Co., shipwrights
  Robertson, John
  De Souza, A. E.

Sachtler, A., photographer
Sarkies & Moses, merchants
  Moses, Catchick
  Moses, Aristarchus C. , Moses, Narses C

Schuster & Engel, merchants
  Schuster, Heinrich
  Engel, Eduard
    Kwast, A. P. van der ; Hartig, Gustav ; Becker, Julius

Schomburgk, C. & Co., merchants
  Schomburgk, Carl
  Hollmann, Gustav
    Alder, Otto ; Morren, Rodolphe ; De Souza, F.

Seth, P. A., auctioneer, Malacca Street

Singapore Dispensary
  Little, Robert, M.D., F.R.C.S.E.
  Robertson, J. H., M.D
  Jamie, R., dispensing chemist

Singapore Ice Manufactory
  Riley, Robert
  Hargreaves, Wm.
  Ochlers, H., engineer

Singapore Gas Company
  Wells, Ed. J., manager and secy.
  Coveney, W. ; Buckley, J., asst. working managers

Solomon, Abraham & Co., merchants
  Solomon, Abraham ; Solomon, Ezekial

Spottiswoode, Wm. & Co., merchants
  Spottiswoode, Archibald J. (Europe)
  Weir, James
  McClelland, Charles Grey (Europe)
    Bryce, Robert O., signs per pro. ; Bruce, Robert R. ; Cargill, Wm

STRAITS SETTLEMENTS.—SINGAPORE.

Straits Dispensary
  Rowell, Thomas I., M. D.; Miles, Richard A., dispensing chemist

Straits Times Press
  Cameron, John, editor
  Duff, Alex., manager
    Westlake, C., sub-editor; Augustin, S. W., foreman; Morbergen, B., clerk

Syme & Co., merchants
  Bolton, Joseph Cheney (Glasgow)
  McMicking, Gilbert (Liverpool)
  Jardine, Robert (do.)
  Murray, James (Glasgow)
  Ross, John (Manila)
  Paton, Jas. Richmond (Batavia)
    Johnston, Alex., signs per pro.; Bolton, William; Nicholson, John Francis; Porteous, Hugh L.; Place, Lorenzo

Staehelin & Stalknecht, merchants
  Staehelin, Georg Emil
  Stalknecht, Carlos German
    Hagedorn, Egmont, signs per pro. (Europe); Wirth, Otto; Stalknecht, Detmar; Leicester, W. B.; Brandt, P.

Tanjong Pagar Dock Company, limited
  Smith, Edward Maher, manager
    Marples, Edward M., accountant; Nail, Chas. H.; Lazaroo, P.; Desker, A.; Tan Keng Goek, clerk; Smith, Reginald H., engineer; Fulton, Peter, turner and fitter; Wells, Graham, wharfinger; Daniels, D., asst. wharfinger; Hughes, G., shipwright; Green, C. J., Blankenhein, L., storekeepers

Telegraph (Local)
  Fisher, John; proprietor

Union Hotel
  Lowell, J., proprietor

United Service Hotel
  Kugelmann, G., proprietor

Vaughan, J. D., barrister at law, attorney, advocate, and proctor
  Vaughan, J. D.
    Cassin, Joseph; De Rosario, Cordiano

Veevers & Co., merchants
  Alexander, Alex. Henry (Europe)
  Veevers, Holden (do.)
  Veevers, Sagar

Velge, Bros. & Co., merchants
  Velge, Abraham
  Velge, Christian Jacob
    Leicester, H. E.; Antonio d' Almeida

Whampoa & Co., commission agents and warehousemen
  Ho Ah Kay (Whampoa)
  Chunfook; Peng Kian

Woods & Davidson, advocates, attornies, proctors and notaries public
  Woods, Robert Carr
  Davidson, James Guthrie

Yosouf & Esmail Mansoors, merchants
  Yoosouf Hasim Mansoor; Muhammed Sayaly

BORNEO.

SARAWAK.

Government.

Rajah—Brooke, His Highness Charles

SUPREME COUNCIL.

President—H. H. The Rajah
Members—Rodway, Capt. W. H.; Hassan, Datu Bandar Haji Bua; Karrim, Datu Emaum Haji Abdul; Hassan, Tumonggong Abang Mohamed; Kassim, Tuan Khatib Haji Abdul; Aim, Tuan Haji Mohamed; Kassim, Abang Mohamed
Clerk to the Council—Innes, J.
Malay Writer—Boyoung, Inchi

RESIDENCY OF SARAWAK.

Acting Resident—Rodway, Capt. W. H.
Assist. Resident, Paku, Upper Sarawak—St. John, O. C.
Writer do. do—Hugh, A.
Resident, Lundu—Nelson, J. H.
Writer do.—Shunian, C.
Resident, Sadong—Houghton, A. R.
Writer do.—Eng Kue, M.
Do. Simatau—Soon An, L.

Government Departments.

TREASURY.

Treasurer—Innes, J.
Accountant—McKenzie, R. M.
Clerk—Lewis, J. N.

POST OFFICE.

Postmaster—Denison, N.
Chief Clerk—Sinclair, W. H.
2nd do.—Leicester, H.
Bill Collector—Kin Chong, H.

SHIPPING OFFICE.

Registrar—Denison, N.
Chief Clerk—Sinclair, W. H.
2nd do.—Leicester, H.
Bill Collector—Kin Chong, H.
[Buoy and Light dues at 3 cents per ton on vessels of 5 tons and over.

IMPORT AND EXPORT OFFICE.

Registrar—Denison, N.
Chief Clerk—Sinclair, W. H.
2nd do.—Lange, A. E.
3rd do.—Leicester, H.
Assistant do.—Kin Chong, H.

GOVERNMENT PRINTING OFFICE.

Printer—Sam Jew, P.
Assistant do.—Foo On, P.

CUSTOMS.

Superintendent—
Collector—Boyoung, Inchi
Assistant—Bakor, Inchi Abu
Writer—Usman, Inchi

MEDICAL DEPARTMENT.

DISPENSARY.

Medical Officer—Houghton, E. P., M.D., L.R.C.P.
Assistant—Keun, R. M.
Dresser—Tye, J. Kay
Mandor—What, Y. Kee

HOSPITAL.

In Charge—Medical Officer
Dresser—Tye, J. Kay
Assistant—Keun, R. M.
Mandor—What, Y. Kee

CORONER.

Denison, Noel

COURT ESTABLISHMENT.

Judges of Supreme Court—The Rajah; Rodway, Capt. W. H.
Members—Bandar, The Datu; Emaum, The Datu; Tumonggong, The Datu; Khatib, The Tuan; The Treasurer; The Commandant
Clerk—Leicester, E. C.
Malay Interpreter and Writer—Boyoung, Inchi
Chinese Interpreter and Writer—Choon, Nye
Executioner—

POLICE AND GENERAL COURT.

Magistrate—The Acting Resident of Sarawak
Members—Bandar, The Datu; Emaum, The Datu; Tumonggong, The Datu; Khatib, The Tuan; Kassim, Abang Mohamed
Clerk—Leicester, E. C.
Inspector—Goodenough, R. B.
[Writers and Interpreters same as Supreme Court]

COURT OF REQUESTS.

Magistrate—Denison, N.
Members—Emaum, Datu; Tumonggong, Datu; Khatib, Tuan; Kassim, Abang Mohamed
[Clerk, Inspector, Writers, and Interpreters same as Police and General Court]

DATU'S COURT.

Bandor, The Datu
Emaum, The Datu
Tumonggang, The Datu
Khatib, The Tuan
Belal, The Tuan
Hakim, The Juan
Aim, Haji Mohamed
Kassim, Abang Mohamed

SURVEY DEPARTMENT.

Surveyor—

Public Works.

Superintendent—Anderson, T. C.

CONVICT DEPARTMENT.

Superintendent—Anderson, T. C.

MILITARY DEPARTMENT.

Commandant—Rodway, Capt. W. H.
Sergeant Major—Warren, C.
Corporal—Awang
Sergeant—Luboh, Awang Bin

STORE DEPARTMENT.

Storekeeper—Linge, A. E.
Writer—Lani

Naval Department.

"HEARTSEASE,"
SCREW GUN-BOAT, 75 TONS, 40 H. P.
Commander—Helyer, G.
Chief Engineer—Cropley, J. P. P.
1st Engine Driver—Marali
2nd do.—Sudin
Gunner—Leman, Inchi
Sirang—Salleh, Inchi

"ROYALIST,"
SCREW STEAMER, 151 TONS, 40 H. P.
Commander—Kirk, W.
Chief Officer—Lincoln, R.
Chief Engineer—Macallan, A.

"MATA SIBU."
SCREW STEAM YACHT, 7 TONS, 10 H. P. Stationed at Simanggang.
Owner—Sarawak Govt.
Engine Driver—Salleh
Sirang—Kadir

Outstations.

BATANG LUPAR, AND SAREBUS.
FORT "ALICE."
Acting Resident—Guerits, G.
Asst. do.—Maxwell, F.
Clerk—Middleton, P.
Malay Writer—Ismail, S.
Writer at Lingga—Ading, Abang

KALUKA.
FORT "CHARLES."
Resident—Chapman, T. S.
Writer—Ki Chin, K.

EEJANG, SIBU.
FORT "BROOKE."
Resident—Cruickshank, The Hon. J. B.
Asst. do.—Everett, A. H.
Cadet—Low, H. B.
Writer—Mowe, S.
Writer at Matu—Anderson, W.
Do. Kanowit—Rozario, F. De

MUKA AND OYA.
FORT "BURDETT."
Resident—Crespigny, C. C. De

BORNEO.—SARAWAK.

BINTULU.
Fort "Keppel."
Resident—Sinclair, E.
Writer—Rozario, J. De

See of Borneo.
(Founded on 6th of August, 1855.)

The Lord Bishop of Labuan and Sarawak—Chambers, The Right Rev. Walter [Consecrated in London on June 29, 1869.

MISSIONARIES (S. P. G.)
Lundu and Sudamac—Zehnder, Rev. J. L.
Quop and Murdang—
Banting—Mesney, Rev. W.; Bubb, Rev. S. C.
Undup—Crossland, Rev. W.
Krian—Perham, Rev. J.
Kuching—Rev. Foo Ngoon Khoon

Churches and Chapels.

ST. THOMAS' CHURCH.
Chaplain—
Missionary—Rev. Foo Ngoon Khoon
Organist—Poucelet, H.

ST. JAMES' CHURCH.
Quop.
Missionary—Abe, Rev. F. W. (absent)
Catechist—Webster, T. D.

MURDANG.
Missionary—Abe, Rev. F. W. (absent)
Catechist—Webster, T. D.

CHRIST'S CHURCH.
Lundu.
Opened 9th August, 1855.
Missionary—Zehnder, Rev. J. L.

SUDAMAC.
Missionary—Zehnder, Rev. J. L.

ST. PAUL'S CHURCH.
Banting.
Missionary—Mesney, Rev. W. R.

Undup Chapel.
Missionary—Crossland, Rev. W.

Kaluka, Krian.
Missionary—Perham, Rev. J.

MISSION SCHOOL.
Warden—The Bishop
Sub-Warden—
Head Master—Bristow, H. W.
Monitor—Howal, W.
Chinese Master—Rev. F. Ngoon Khoon

MISSION PRESS.
Superintendent—The Bishop
Printer—Mortley, J.

FORT SCHOOL.
Teacher—What, Y-Kee

Sarawak Reading Room.
Hon. Secretary—McKenzie, R. M.
Librarian—Mun Si

Borneo Company Limited.
Manager—Helms, L. V. (absent)
Act. do. at Kuching—Brodie, W. G.
Do. at Muka—Hardie, J.
Accountant—Smith, E. J.
Clerk—Smith, T.
Cashier—Keng Chew, K.
Abdullah, T.
Supt. of Antimony-Mines at Busan—Everett, H. H.
Supt. of Cinnabar Mines at Tegora—Fenwick, J. M.
Dispenser at Jambusan—Henry, P.
Clerk—Nail, W. H.
Engineer—Wallace, J.
Metallurgist and Assayist—Blake, J.
Miner—Johns, P.
Overseer—Pereira, J.
Overseer at Muka—Pereira, R.

"SRI SARAWAK,"
Screw Steamer, 97 Tons, 40 H. P.
Commander—Hewat, W.
Chief Officer—
Do. Engineer—
2nd. do.—
Owners—Borneo Company, Limited

The Sarawak Trading Company.
Established 1870.
Walters, Crocker & Co.
Partners—Walters, W.; Crocker, W. M.; Lew Ah Chick
Writer—Haslem, J.
Agents Singapore—Maclaine, Fraser & Co.

BORNEO.—SARAWAK.

"BERTHA,"
SCRE STEAMER, 40 TONS, 5 H. P
Commander—Crocker, W.
Engineer—Haslem, W.
Owners—Walters, Crocker & Co.

BILLIARD ROOM.
Proprietor—Lewis, J. N., "Rajah's Arms" Hotel
Proprietor—Lew Ah Chick, Tavern

BEEF CLUB.
Manager—Lewis, J. N.
Butcher—Ah Lick

HOTEL "RAJAH'S ARMS."
Manager—Lewis, J. N.
Writer—Moshergen, W.

WATCH MAKER & REPAIRER.
Rifkens, Charles

MUSIC TEACHER AND REPAIRER.
Poucelet, H. I.

LITHOGRAPHIC PRESS.
Owner—Majid, Inchi Abdue
Superintendent—Bakar, Inchi Abu
Writer—Ziu, Said
Bookbinder—Ali, Inchi

WHARVES.
Kuching—Sarawak Government
Do.—Borneo Company Limited
Pinding—Do.   Do.
Do.—   Do.   Do.   Coal Depot

LINGGA COAL MINES.
Superintendent—Walters, W.

SADONG COAL MINES.
Superintendent—St. John, J. A.

ESTATES.
Satang, Cocoanuts (Oil Manufacture)—The Rajah, H. H.
Salak, Cocoanuts—The Rajah, H. H.
Peninjauh and Matang, Coffee—Government. Supt.—Anderson, T. C.
Seramboo, Coffee—
Quop, Pepper and Gambier—Ken What & Co.
Tanah Puteh, Pepper and Gambier—Ken What & Co.
Sampadian, Cocoanuts (Oil Manufacture)—Crookshank, A. C.
Grissik, Fruits—Crookshank, A. C.

SAGO FACTORIES.
Kuching and Muka—Borneo Company Limited; Oya—Walters, Crocker & Co.; Kuching—Ong Ewe Hai; Eh Soon; Tong Bee; Ghee Han; Swee Ghee

GENERAL STORE DEALERS.
Tambi Abdullah & Co.
Syed Mohamed & Co.
Tambi Mustan & Co.
Tambi Molass & Co.
Abdul Kadir & Co.
Mohamed Usop & Co.
Tambi Kadidsah & Co.

SPIRIT SELLERS.
Ghee Soon & Co.   Lew Ah Chick
"Rajah's Arms" Hotel

BRICKS, TILES, POTTERY.
SARAWAK.
Ong Ewe Hai   Swee Eh
Chin An

CHINESE MERCHANTS.
Gnee Soon & Co.	Kia Lee
Ewe Hai & Co.	Ngee Lee
Eng Bee	Seng Lee
Chie Heng	Chap Sin
Kong Chong Hin	Soon Liong
Gnee Hong	Hong Liong
Ti Hin	Guan Mong
Eng Hn	Yam Heng
Jo Bee	Joo Seng
Yap Hong	Eng What
Seng Huck	Seng Wat
Tad Ha	Tiang Soon Lee
Eh Swee	Wha What
Chiu Ann	Kiang Hak
Joo Hin	Kiang Wan
Weng Seng	Yap What
Chuan Hap	Hok Hin
Chup Seng	Seng Heng
Chin Hin	Ho Hin
Hong Hak	Soon Why

SCHOONER "PIONEER,"
50 TONS.
Owners—Borneo Company Limited
Nacoda—Ah Ku

SCHOONER "VENUS,"
48 TONS.
Owner—Kassan, Haji
Nacoda—Hussin, Haji

BORNEO.—SARAWAK.

SCHOONER "ZULEIHA,"
142 Tons.
Owner—Taha, Haji Mohamed
Nacoda—Mohamed Said

SCHOONER "SULTANA,"
118 Tons.
Owner—Razak, Haji Abdul
Nacoda—Mah Sait

SCHNR. "BINTANG SILANGGOR,"
54 Tons.
Owner—Aim, Haji
Nacoda—Kassim

SCHOONER "RAJAH ISKANDAR,"
80 Tons.
Owner—Razak, Haji Hbdul
Nacoda—Aim, Haji

SCHOONER "MAS NONA,"
Owner—Aim, Haji
Nacoda—

SCHOONER "KADRI,"
50 Tons.
Owner—Matan, Abdul
Nacoda—

SCHOONER "JULIA,"
56 Tons.
Owner—Kadir, Haji
Nacoda—

AGENTS FOR THE GOVERNMENT OF SARAWAK.
London—Borneo Company, Limited, 28, Fenchurch Street, E.C.
Singapore—Johnston & Co., A. L., Johnston's Pier

LABUAN.

Government.

Governor, Commander-in-Chief and Vice-Admiral and Consul General in Borneo—Bulwer, His Excellency S. H. A., F.R.G.S., and F.R.S.A.
Private Secretary—Bulwer, —.
Aid-de-Camp—

LEGISLATIVE COUNCIL.

President—His Excellency The Governor
Members—Low, The Honorable Hugh; Howard, The Honorable John Raw
Clerk of Council—The Colonial Secretary

COLONIAL SECRETARY'S OFFICE.

Colonial Secretary—Clark, James Stephen
Clerk—
Malay Writer—Muka

LAND OFFICE.

Registrar—Howard, The Honorable John Raw

SURVEY DEPARTMENT.

Colonial Surveyor—Howard, The Honorable John Raw
Clerk—Turney, Harry
Draftsman—Laut
Apprentice—Booyong

POLICE COURT.

Magistrate—Low, The Honorable Hugh
Malay Interpreter—Muka
Chinese do.—Ah Tek

REGISTRAR OF BIRTHS, DEATHS, AND MARRIAGES.

The Colonial Secretary

POLICE.

Superintendent—Hennessy, William Popo

CORONER.

Cody, L. A.

GENERAL COURT OF LABUAN.

Judges—His Excellency The Governor, President, and 2 Justices
Registrar—Clark, James Stephen
Malay Interpreter—Rajah, Moonshee
Chinese do.—Ah Tek

JUSTICES OF THE PEACE.

Low, The Honorable Hugh
Cha Bok Tong
Howard, The Honorable J. Raw
Treacher, John Gavaron

VICE ADMIRALTY AND PRIZE JURISDICTION ABROAD.

Vice-Admiral—His Excellency The Governor
Judge—
Registrar—
Marshal—

CONVICT DEPARTMENT.

Superintendent—Howard, The Honorable John Raw
Gaoler—
Medical Officer—The Colonial Surgeon

TREASURY.

Colonial Treasurer—Cody, Brayan Archdekan
Clerk—McDermott, R. H.

AUDITOR.

Clark, James Stephen

SUPERINTENDENT OF FARMS.

Howard, The Honorable J. R.

MEDICAL DEPARTMENT.

Colonial Surgeon—McClosky, James Hugh

LABUAN CIVIL HOSPITAL.
Medical Officer—White, L. A., M.D.
Apothecary—

VICTORIA CORPORATION.
4 *Members to be appointed by the Governor and* 7 *Members to be elected.*
Hony. Treasurer—
  Do. Engineer—Howard, The Hon'ble J. R.
  Do. Secretary—Clark, J. S.

REGISTRAR OF SHIPPING.
Acting—Low, The Honorable Hugh

HARBOUR MASTER.
Acting—Low, The Honorable Hugh

POST MASTER.
Acting—Low, The Honorable Hugh

Ecclesiastical Department.
BISHOP OF LABUAN.
Chambers, Walter, The Right Rev.

CHURCH OF ST. SAVIOUR.
Foundation Stone Laid on the 17th November 1865. Opened for Service July 1866. Consecrated by the 1st Bishop of Labuan on 18th December 1866.
Colonial Chaplain—Beard, Rev. William Day, B.A.

Labuan Reading Club.
Secretary and Treasurer—

CONTROL DEPARTMENT.
Deputy Commissary—Baker, R. C.

THE ORIENTAL COAL COMPANY, LIMITED.
Head Office, 55 Bernard Street, Leith, N.B.
Managing Director—MacGregor, Donald R.
Secretary—

TANJONG KUBONG MINES.
Manager—Lumsden, Alexander
Accountant—
Clerk—Shaban, Bakar bin
Engineer—Flemming, Mathew
Blacksmith—Galshore, Neal
Scotch Coal Hewers—Taylor, J.; Watson, Alexander; Gillies, J.; Baird, Jas.; Baird, Alexander; Maxwell, R.; Maxwell, J.; Gillespie, J.; Jones, Edward

"VINE,"
STEAMER, 441 TONS, 90 H. P.
Master—Mann, J.

"WILLIAM MILLER,"
STEAMER, 680 TONS, 120 H. P.
Master—Nyberg, W.

JOHN POPE HENNESSY,
STEAMER.
Master—

CROWN AGENTS.
Singapore—The Borneo Company Limited
London—Julyan, P. G., C.B.; Sergeaunt, W. C.

GENERAL STORE-DEALERS.
Lee Cheng Ho

SAGO MANUFACTURERS.
Choa Mah Soo & Co., Lee Cheng Ho, Lim Tye Seng

COCOANUT PLANTATIONS.
"Pulo Daat," proprietor—Treacher, The Honorable J. G. Manager—Treacher, W. H.
"Orange," proprietor—Low, The Honorable Hugh
"Lemon," proprietor—Howard, The Honorable John Raw

APPENDIX.

APPENDIX

(A 1)

General Post-Office. Hongkong.

REVISED AND CORRECTED BY THE POSTMASTER GENERAL
ON THE NOVEMBER, 1879.

POST-OFFICE NOTIFICATION.

Colonial Postage Stamps may be purchased at the General Post-Office, and all the British Postal Agencies in China and Japan. The Stamps represent the following amounts in value:—

Two cents	One Penny.	Eighteen cents	Nine Pence.
Four cents	Two Pence.	Twenty-four cents	One Shilling.
Six cents	Three Pence.	Thirty cents	Fifteen Pence.
Eight cents	Four Pence.	Forth-eight cents	Two Shillings.
Twelve cents	Six Pence.	Ninety-six cents	Four Shillings.

It must be understood that the Postage Labels of this Colony are alone available for the payment of postage on correspondence posted at the General Post-Office in Hongkong, or the Agencies thereof at Canton, Macao, Swatow, Amoy, Foochow-foo, Shanghai, Ningpo, Hankow, Hiogo, Nagasaki, and Yokohama.

They may be used on correspondence to places to which the prepayment of postage is either compulsory or optional; no credit will be given to these Stamps on correspondence addressed to places to which the postage cannot be prepaid in Hongkong.

All correspondence for places to which prepayment is compulsory must be prepaid in Hongkong Postage Stamps.

The latest time for posting letters by the *English* Mail Packet is 11 A.M. ; by the *French* 11 A.M., and by the *American*, 2.30 P.M. on the day of sailing.

All letters posted by the English Mail Packet between 10 and 11 A.M. on the day of sailing are chargeable in addition to the usual postage with a *late fee* of 18 cents.

Late Letters (but Letters only) addressed to the United Kingdom, *via Brindisi*, or to Singapore, may be posted on board the English Packet from 11.80 A.M. to the time of sailing, on payment of a *Late Fee* of 48 cents each in addition to the postage.

Letters, &c., are received for registration up to 10 A.M. on the day of departure of each Packet with homeward Mails.

Letters can be posted on board the American Packet from 2.30 to 2.50 P.M. on payment of a Late Fee of 12 cents in addition to the Postage.

The Prepayment of the Postage to all places by the American route is compulsory. Correspondence insufficiently prepaid will be forwarded by the English Packets.

Correspondence addressed to Yokohama, and the United States by American Packet, must be superscribed per "————," and that addressed to the United Kingdom must be superscribed "*via San Francisco.*"

Sealed Boxes containing the correspondence of Box Holders will be received at the window set apart for the purpose on the East side of the Building.

Insufficiently Stamped Letters addressed to the United Kingdom will be sent on, charged with a fine of One Shilling in addition to the Postage.

Letters posted after 10 A.M. on the day of the sailing of the English Packet will not be forwarded unless the *Late Fee* as well as the postage is prepaid.

Postage Stamps should be placed on the upper right hand corner of the correspondence, except in cases where they may be used in payment of *Late Fees*, when the Stamp or Stamps representing *Late Fee* or *Registration Fees* should be placed on the lower left hand corner.

All transactions in fractional parts of a Dollar will be conducted in the Coins prescribed by Ordinance No. 1, 1864, and the Proclamation of the 22nd January, 1864, and no other Coins but those therein specified will either be received or given in change as fractional parts of a Dollar.

Payment for Postage Stamps must be made in the Current Dollars of the Colony or Bank Notes.

Money Orders on any of the Money Order Offices in the United Kingdom are granted until 5 P.M. on the day prior to the departure of each packet.

Money orders between Hongkong and the United Kingdom and between Hongkong and Shanghai, and Hongkong and Yokohama, are granted and paid daily between 10 A.M. and 4 P.M. (Sundays and authorized holidays excepted).

Rates of Postage.

Chargeable in Hongkong, upon Letters, Newspapers, Prices Current, Books and Patterns, forwarded to the undermentioned Countries and Places.

* Denotes that prepayment is Compulsory, it being in all other cases voluntary.
† Denotes that if Sent Unpaid, the Letter will be liable to an extra charge on delivery.

COUNTRIES, &c.	LETTERS. Under ½ oz.	LETTERS. Under 1 oz.	LETTERS. Every Additional ½ oz.	*Newspaper or †Price Current.	*BOOK PACKET. Under 8 oz.	*BOOK PACKET. Under 4 oz.	*BOOK PACKET. Every Additional oz.	*PACKET OF PATTERNS	*REGISTRATION FEE.
	cts.	cts.	cts.	cents.	cts.	cts.	oz. cts.		cents.
*Aden,...... per British Packet,	...	...	8	2	...	8	... 6	Book Rate.	12
" French Packet,	...	14	14	2	8	8	4 6	Do.	12
*Africa, West Coast of,... via Southampton,	...	34	34	6	12	12	4 12	Do.	None.
" Brindisi or Marseilles.	...	40	40	8	18	18	4 18	Do.	Do.
*Africa, East Coast of,... " Aden,	...	20	20	8	...	6	4 8	Do.	12
Alexandria,...... *per British Packet,	12	12	12	2	8	6	4 4	Do.	8
" French Packet,	...	24	24	8	6	6	4 6	Do.	12 cts. per ¼ oz.
*Amoy,...... via Aden,......	...	8	8	2	...	6	4 6	Do.	8
*Ascension,...... " Ceylon,......	...	20	20	2	...	8	4 8	Do.	12
*Australia,...... " Southampton,...	...	24	24	3	2 4	16	2 8	Do.	12
Austria,...... †" B'disi, per Brit. Pkt.	...	34	34	8	8	8	4 8	Do.	16
" per French Packet,	24	48	24	4	Cannot be paid.			Can't be sent.	24 cts. per ¼ oz.
*Batavia,...... " Br. Pkt pd. to S'pore,	...	8	8	2	...	6	4 4	Book Rate.	24 " ¼ "
" Fr. do. do.,	...	18	18	2	6	6	4 5	Do.	None.
" †Fr. pd. to destination,	...	30	30	4	Letter Rate.			......	Do.
Belgium,...... †via Southampton,...	...	30	30	4	4	8	2 8	Book Rate.	18 cts. per ¼ oz.
" B'disi, per Brit. Pkt.	...	24	24	4	...	12	4 12	Do.	16
" per French Packet,	20	40	20	...	Cannot be paid.			Can't be sent.	24 cts. per ¼ oz. 20 " ¼ "

RATES OF POSTAGE.

Country	Route									
Bermuda,	via Southampton,............	34	34	6		12	4	12	Book Rate.	16
*Bolivia,	" Brindisi or M'seilles,	40	40	8		18	4	18	Do.	16
	" Southampton,.............	58	58	6		14	4	14	Do.	None.
*Brazil,	" Brindisi or M'seilles,	64	64	8		20	4	20	Do.	Do.
	" Southampton,.............	46	46	6		12	4	12	Do.	Do.
	" Brindisi or M'seilles,	52	52	8		18	4	18	Do.	16
Brunswick, (Germany),...	† " Southampton,............	34	34	8		10	2	8	Do.	24 cts. per ½ oz.
	" B'disi, per Brit. Pkt.	24	24	4	8	16	2	8	Do.	24 " " ¼ "
	per French Packet,...	24	24	Can't be pd.		Cannot be paid.			Can't be sent.	None.
*Buenos Ayres,	via Southampton,............	46	46	6		12	4	12	Book Rate.	Do.
	" Brindisi or M'seilles,	52	52	8		18	4	18	Do.	12
Calcutta,	(*per British Packet,......	8	8	2		6	4	6	Do.	12
	* " French Packet,........	14	14	2		6	4	6	Do.	12
	" Indian Packet,........	8	8	2		6	4	6	Do.	8
*Canton,	via Aden,....................		8	2		8	4	8	Do.	12
*Cape of Good Hope,	" Southampton,.............	20	20	6		12	4	12	Do.	18
*Canada, and Vancouver's Island,	" Brindisi or M'seilles,	28	28	8		18	4	18	Do.	16
	" Southampton,.............	34	34	2		16	9	8	Do.	None.
*Canary Islands,	" Brindisi or M'seilles,	46	46	Book Rate.		22	4	22	Do.	Do.
	" Southampton,.............	52	52	Do.	8	12	4	6	Do.	16
Cape de Verde Island,	" Brindisi or M'seilles,	34	34	Do.	6	18	4	10	Do.	18
	" British Packet,........	40	40	2		8	4	6	Do.	13
*Ceylon,	" French Packet,.........	8	8	2	2	6	4	6	Du.	12
*Chili,	via Southampton,............	14	14	6		14	4	14	Do.	Norc
	" Brindisi or M'seilles,	58	58	8		20	4	20	Lo.	Do.
*Columbia, U.S. of,.........	" Southampton,.............	64	64	6		12	4	12	Can't be sent	16
	" Brindisi or M'seilles,	46	46	8	8	18	4	18	Book Rate.	16
*Costa Rica,	" Southampton,.............	52	52	6		12	4	12	Do.	None.
	" Brindisi or M'seilles,	46	46	8		18	4	18	Do.	8
*Constantinople, Smyrna, and Beyrout,	per British Packet,...	53	52	8		18	4	18	Do.	8
	French Packet,.........	20	20	4	2	4	2	2	Do.	
*Curaçoa,	via Southampton,............	12	24	12		Cannot be paid.			Can't be sent.	12 cts. per ¼ oz.
	" Brindisi or M'seilles,	46	46	6		12	4	12	Book Rate.	16
	" Southampton,.............		52	8		18	4	18	Do.	16
Denmark,	† " B'disi, per Brit. Pkt.	28	28	8		16	2	8	Do.	16
	per French Packet,...	62	32	4	8	12	4	12	Do.	
*Ecuador,	via Southampton,............	26	26	Can't be pd.		Canno't be paid.			Can't be sent.	82 cts. per ½ oz.
	" Brindisi or M'seilles,	58	58	6		14	4	14	Book Rate.	26 " " ¼ "
			64	8		20	4	20	Do.	Dc

RATES OF POSTAGE.

COUNTRIES, &c.		LETTERS. Under ½ oz.	LETTERS. Under 1 oz.	LETTERS. Every Additional ½ oz.	*Newspaper or *Price Current.	*BOOK P'CKET. Under 2 oz.	*BOOK P'CKET. Under 4 oz.	*BOOK P'CKET. Every Additional 2 oz. (oz. | cts.)	*PACKET OF PATTERNS	*REGISTRATION FEE.
		cts.	cts.	cts.	cents.	cts.	cts.			cents.
*Falkland Islands,	via Southampton,	...	34	34	6	...	12	4 | 12	Book Rate.	16
	" Brindisi or M'seilles,	...	40	40	8	...	18	4 | 18	Do.	16
*Foochow,		...	8	8	2	...	6	4 | 6	Do.	8
France,	per Brit. Pkt., via B'disi,	18	36	18	Can't be pd.	Cannot be paid.			Can't be paid.	18 cts. per ½ oz.
	Do., via M'seilles,	12	24	12	Do.	Do.			Do.	12 " " " "
	" French Packet,	12	24	12	Do.	Do.			Lo.	12 " " " "
Gambia,	via Southampton,	...	34	34	6	...	12	4 | 12	Book Rate.	16
	" Brindisi or M'seilles,	...	40	40	8	...	18	4 | 18	Do.	16
German States:— Baden, Saxe Altenburg, Bavaria, Saxe Coburg Gotha, Hesse, Hohenzollern, Saxe Weimar, Nassau, Schwarzburg, Reuss, Wurtemburg,	†via Southampton,	...	34	34	8	8	16	2 | 8	Do.	16
	" B'disi, per Brit. Pkt	...	24	24	4	8	...	...	Do.	24 cts. per ½ oz.
	" per French Packet,	20	40	20	Can't be sent.	Cannot be sent.			Can't be sent.	20 " " ¼ "
Gibraltar,	" British Packet,	...	24	24	2	...	8	4 | 8	Book Rate.	8
	* " French Packet,	18	36	18	Can't be st.	Cannot be sent.			Can't be sent.	None.
Gold Coast and Liberia,	via Southampton,	...	34	34	6	...	12	4 | 12	Book Rate.	16
	" Brindisi or M'seilles,	...	40	40	8	...	18	4 | 18	Do.	16
*Greece, and Ionian Islands,	" Alexandria,	12	24	12	Can't be pd.	Cannot be paid.			Can't be sent	None.
*Guadaloupe, *Guatemala, and *Grey Town,	" Southampton,	...	46	46	6	...	12	4 | 12	Book Rate.	Do.
	" Brindisi or M'seilles,	...	52	52	8	...	18	4 | 18	Do.	Do.
Hanover,	" Southampton,	...	34	34	4	8	16	2 | 8	Do.	13
	" B'disi, per Brit. Pkt.	24	48	24	4	8	...	...	Do.	24 cts. per ½ oz.
	" M'seilles, per Fr. Pkt.	...	46	46	Can't be pd.	Cannot be sent.			Can't be sent.	24 " None.
*Hayti,	" Southampton,	...	52	52	6	...	12	4 | 12	Book Rate.	Do.
	† " Brindisi or M'seilles,	...	88	88	8	...	18	4 | 18	Ivo.	16
	" Southampton,	...	82	82	4	8	16	2 | 8	Do.	16
Heligoland,	" Brindisi,	26	52	26	Can't be pd.	Cannot be paid.			Can't be sent.	82 cts. per ½ oz.
	" per French Packet,									26 " " ¼ "

RATES OF POSTAGE.

*Hiogo,	per British Packet,	8	8	2	...	6	4	6	Book Rate.	8
	" French Packet,	14	14	2	...	6	4	6	Do.	8
Holland,	†via Southampton,	28	28	6	...	8	2	4	Do.	18
	" B'disi, per Brit. Pkt.	24	24	4	4	12	4	12	Do.	24 cts. per ½ oz.
	per French Packet,	20	20							20 " " ¼ "
Honduras,	via Southampton,	46	46	Can't be pd.	Cannot be paid.				Can't be sent.	16
	" Brindisi or M'seilles,	52	52	6		14	4	14	Book Rate.	16
India,	*per British Packet,	8	8	2		20	4	20	Do.	12
	" French Packet,	14	14	2		6	4	6	Do.	12
	" Indian Packet,	8	8	2		6	4	3	Do.	12
Italy,	" British Packet,	16	16	6		6	4	6	Do.	12
	" French Packet,	20	20	8		6	4	6	Do.	16 cts. per ½ oz.
La Guayra,	via Southampton,	46	46	Can't be pd.	Cannot be paid.				Can't be sent.	20 " " ¼ "
	" Brindisi or M'seilles,	52	52	6		12	4	12	Do.	None.
Lagos,	" Southampton,	34	34	8		18	4	18	Do.	Do.
	" Brindisi or M'seilles,	40	40	8		18	4	18	Book Rate.	18
*Macao,	via Southampton,	8	8	2		6	4	6	Do.	16
*Madeira,	" Brindisi or M'seilles,	34	34	6		12	4	12	Do.	8
*Manila,	" British Packet,	40	40	8		18	4	18	Do.	None.
Malta,	via Aden,	8	8	2		6	4	6	Do.	Do.
*Mauritius,	" Southampton,	22	22	2		8	2	6	Do.	6
	†" B'disi, per Brit. Pkt.	34	34	2	8	16	2	8	Do.	12
Mecklenburg,	per French Packet,	24	24	4		8	4	8	Do.	16
*Mexico,	via Southampton,	46	46	Can't be pd.	Cannot be paid.				Can't be sent.	24 cts. per ½ oz.
	" Brindisi or M'seilles,	52	52	6		12	4	12	Book Rate.	24 " " ¼ "
*Monte Video,	" Southampton,	46	46	8		18	4	18	Lo.	None.
	" Brindisi or M'seilles,	52	52	8		12	4	12	Do.	Do.
*Nagasaki,	per British Packet,	8	8	2		18	4	18	Do.	Do.
	" French Packet,	14	14	2		6	4	6	Do.	8
*Natal,	via Aden,	20	20	2		8	4	8	Do.	12
*New Granada,	" Southampton,	46	46	6		12	4	12	Can't be sent.	None.
	" Brindisi or M'seilles,	52	52	8		18	4	18	Do.	Do.
New Brunswick, Newfoundland, and Nova Scotia,	" Southampton,	28	28	6		18	4	18	Book Rate.	16
*New Caledonia,	" Brindisi or M'seilles,	34	34	8		12	4	12	Do.	16
	per French Packet,	36	36	2		18	4	18	Can't be sent.	None.
*New Zealand,	via Ceylon,	18	24	2		Letter Rate		2 4 8 4 8	Book Rate.	12

RATES OF POSTAGE.

COUNTRIES, &c.	LETTERS.			*Newspaper or *Price Current.	*BOOK PACKET.			*PACKET OF PATTERNS	*REGISTRATION FEE.
	Under ½ oz.	Under ½ oz.	Every Additional.		Under ½ oz.	Under 4 oz.	Every Additional.		
	cts.	cts.	cts.	cents.	cts.	cts.	cts. oz. cts.		cents
*Ningpo,............ †vaā Southampton,......	...	54.	8	2	8	6	4	8	Book Rate.	8
" B'disi, per Brit. Pkt.	...	46	34	8	16	2	8	Do.	16
Norway,........... per French Packet,....	38	76	46	4	12	4	12	Do.	46 cts. per ½ oz.
*vaā Southampton,......	...	46	38	Can't be pd.	Cannot be paid.	Can't be sent.	38 " " ½ "
*Panama,............ " Brindisi or M'seilles,	...	52	46	6	12	4	12	Do.	Do.
" Southampton,......	...	46	38	8	18	4	18	Do.	Do.
*Paraguay and Uruguay, " Brindisi or M'seilles,	...	52	46	6	12	4	12	Do.	Do.
*per British Packet,.....	...	8	8	8	18	4	18	Do.	12
Penang,............ " French Packet,.....	...	8	8	2	6	4	6	Book Rate.	12
" Indian Packet,......	...	8	8	2	6	4	6	Do.	12
*vaā Southampton,......	...	56	68	6	14	4	14	Do.	Do.
*Peru,.............. " Brindisi or M'seilles,	...	64	64	8	20	4	20	Do.	None.
per French Packet,....	...	14	14	2	6	4	6	Can't be sent.	14 cts. per ½ oz.
Pondicherry,........ " Southampton,......	...	46	46	6	8	4	8	Book Rate.	None.
*Porto Rico,........ " Brindisi or M'seilles,	...	52	52	8	12	4	12	Do.	Do.
" Gibraltar,............	...	24	24	4	18	4	18	Do.	16
" Southampton,......	...	46	46	Can't be st.	Letter Rate.	Can't be sent.	16
Portugal,........... * " Brindisi,..............	26	52	26	Can't be pd.	6 12 2 6	Do.	28 cts. per ½ oz.
per French Packet,....	20	40	20	6	Cannot be paid.	Do.	20 " " ½ "
Prince Edward Islandτάi Southampton,......	...	28	20	6	12	4	12	Book Rate.	16
" Brindisi or M'seilles,	...	34	34	8	18	2	8	Do.	16
" Southampton,......	...	34	34	4	8	4	8	Do.	12
Prussia,............ + " B'disi, per Brit. Pkt.	24	48	24	Can't be pd.	Cannot be paid.	Can't be sent.	24 cts. per ½ oz.
per French Packet,....	24	24	24	4	8 16 2 8	Book Rate.	24 " " ½ "
Do., Rhenish,...... †vaā Southampton,......	...	34	34	4	8	4	8	Do.	16
per French Packet,....	20	40	20	Can't be pd.	Cannot be paid.	Can't be sent.	24 cts. per ½ oz.
" B'disi, per Brit. Pkt.	...	40	40	8	8 16 2 8	Book Rate.	20 " " ½ "
Russia and Poland,.. †vaā Southampton,......	...	46	46	4	8	4	8	Do.	46 cts. per ½ oz.
per French Packet,....	38	76	38	Can't be pd	Cannot be paid.	Can't be sent	38 " " ½ "

RATES OF POSTAGE.

Destination	Route								
Saigon,	per French Packet,		14	14	2		6	4	6	Do.	14 cts. per ¼ oz.
Saxony, Schleswig and Holstein,	†viâ Southampton,		34	34	8	8	16	2	8	Book Rate.	16
	" B'disi, per Brit. Pkt.	24	24	24	4		8	4	8	Do.	24 cts. per ½ oz.
	per French Packet,		48	48	Can't be pd.	Cannot be paid.	Can't be sent.	24 " " ¼ "
*Shanghae,	" British Packet,		8	8	2		6	4	6	Book Rate.	8
	" French Packet,		14	14	2		6	4	6	Do.	16
*Sierra Leone,	viâ Southampton,		34	34	6	12	4	12	Do.	16
	" Brindisi or M'seilles,		40	40	8	18	4	18	Do.	12
Singapore,	*per British Packet,		8	8	2		6	4	6	Do.	12
	" French Packet,		8	8	2		6	4	6	Do.	12
	" Indian Packet,		8	8	2		6	4	6	Do.	12
*Smyrna and Beyrout,	" British Packet,	12	20	20	2	2	4	2	2	Do.	8
	" French Packet,		24	24	2	Cannot be paid.	Can't be sent.	12 cts. per ½ oz.
	viâ Gibraltar,		24	24	8	Letter Rate.	Do.	None.
Spain,	*" Southampton,		48	48		8	16	2	8	Book Rate.	Do.
	*" Brindisi,	24	36	36	Can't be st.	Cannot be sent.	Can't be sent.	Do.
	*per French Packet,	18	20	20	Can't be pd.	Do.	Do.	12
*St. Helena,	viâ Aden,		12	12	2		8	6	8	Book Rate.	12
*Suez,	per British Packet,		24	24	2		6	4	6	Do.	8
	" French Packet,	12	8	8	2		6	4	6	Can't be sent.	16
*Swatow,	†viâ Southampton,		34	34	8	8	16	2	8	Book Rate.	16
Sweden,	" B'disi, per Brit. Pkt.	88	46	46	4	12	4	12	Do.	46 cts. per ½ oz.
	per French Packet,		76	76	Can't be pd.	Cannot be paid.	Can't be sent.	88 " " ¼ "
Switzerland,	" British Packet,		24	24	4		8	4	6	Br.ok Rate.	24 " " ¼ "
	" French Packet,	20	40	40	Can't be pd.	Cannot be paid.	Can't be sent.	20 " " ¼ "
*Trieste, (and the Continent of Europe paid to Alexandria only),	" British Packet only,		12	12	2		6	4	2	3	Book Rate.	None.
*Turkey,	" British packet,	12	20	20	2		2	4	2	2	Do.	8
	" French packet,		24	24	2		Can't be paid	Can't be sent.	12 cts. per ¼ or.
*United Kingdom,	viâ Southampton,		24	24	4	24	8	14	8
	" Brindisi,		30	30	6	48	4	12	4	Book Rate.	8
	" Marseilles,		30	30	6	48	4	12	4	Do.	8
	" San Francisco,		24	24	4	24	8	4	8	Do.	8
	per Private Ship,		12	12	2	24	8	4	8	Do.	8
	" Do., viâ B'disi.		24	24	6	46	12	4	12	Do.	6

RATES OF POSTAGE.

COUNTRIES, &c.		LETTERS. Under 1 oz.	LETTERS. Under 2 oz.	LETTERS. Every Additional.	*Newspaper or *Price Current.	*BOOK PACKET. Under 2 oz.	*BOOK PACKET. Under 4 oz.	*BOOK PACKET. Every Additional.	*PACKET OF PATTERNS	*REGIS- TRATION FEE.
		cts.	cts.	cts.	cents	cts.	cts.	cts.		cents
*United States of America,	per U.S. Packet,	...	8	8	2	...	8	4	Book Rate.	None.
	via Southampton,	...	28	28	6	...	12	4	Do.	16
	" Brindisi or Marseilles,	...	34	34	8	...	18	4	Do.	16
*Venezuela,	" Southampton,	...	46	46	6	...	12	4	Do.	None.
	" Brindisi or Marseilles,	...	52	52	6	...	18	4	Do.	Do.
West Indies, (British)	" Southampton,	...	46	46	6	...	12	4	Do.	16
	" Brindisi or Marseilles,	...	52	52	8	...	18	4	Do.	16
*West Indies, (Foreign),	" Southampton,	...	46	46	6	...	12	4	Do.	None.
	" Brindisi or Marseilles,	...	52	52	8	...	18	4	Do.	Do.
*Yokohama,	per British Packet,	...	14	14	2	...	6	4	Do.	8
	" French Packet,	...	8	8	2	...	6	4	Do.	8
	" U.S. Packet,	...	8	8	2	...	6	4	Do.	None.
*Zanzibar,	via Aden,	...	20	20	2	...	8	4	Do.	12

Unpaid or insufficiently Prepaid Letters cannot be forwarded by United States' Packets.

Prepayment is compulsory on Letters sent by *Private Ship* to all other places (the United Kingdom excepted) at 8 cent. for every ½ ounce. Newspaper and Prices Current, 2 cents each.

F. W. MITCHELL, *Postmaster General.*

General Post Office, Hongkong, 24th November, 1878.

POST-OFFICE NOTIFICATIONS.

It is hereby notified for general information that henceforward Letters containing coin posted in the United Kingdom addressed to Hongkong, or posted in Hongkong addressed to the United Kingdom, on which the Fee for Registration has not been paid will be compulsorily registered and charged on delivery with a double Registration Fee, and further, any Letters having the word "Registered" written upon them which may be posted without Registration, will be forwarded, charged in like manner with a double Registration Fee.

In the event of a Letter being supposed to contain coin, and being consequently thus treated, and proof being afterwards afforded that the letter did not contain coin, the amount charged will be refunded.

F. W. MITCHELL, *Postmaster General*.

General Post Office, Hongkong, 24th October, 1867.

It is hereby notified for general information that henceforward Correspondence intended to be forwarded to the United Kingdom in the mails by the French Packets may be posted at the *British* Post Office at Shanghai and Yokohama, and that the same will be forwarded in closed Mails to London.

F. W. MITCHELL, *Postmaster General*.

General Post Office, Hongkong, 27th November, 1867.

Circular.

The Undersigned solicits the Bankers and Mercantile Community to post all Letters, &c., as early as practicable, especially when sent in large numbers, as facility is given to the Post-Office in discharge of its duties, and greater security afforded to the public by such a course; whereas great inconvenience, and frequently confusion, occurs through the whole of the correspondence from many of the large Firms being sent to the Post Office at the last moment, before closing the Mails for Europe, by both the English and French Packets.

F. W. MITCHELL, *Postmaster General*.

MONEY ORDER REGULATIONS.

1.—On the 1st of October next, and thenceforward, Money Orders will be issued at this Office and at the Agencies thereof at Shanghae and Yokohama on all the Money Order Offices in the United Kingdom of Great Britain and Ireland, for amounts not exceeding £10, at the rate of Exchange Current for each Mail and charged with Commission according to the following Scale, viz:—

For Sums not exceeding	£2	18 cents.
Above £2 and not exceeding	5	36 "
" 5 "	"	7	54 "
" 7 "	"	10	72 "

2.—No Money Order to include a fractional part of a Penny.

3.—Orders drawn in the United Kingdom upon Hongkong, Shanghae, and Yokohama, will be paid at the rate of Exchange of the day of the receipt of the advices of such Money Orders at the places named.

4.—Alphabetical List of over 3,700 Money Order Offices in the United Kingdom, shewing the Counties in which they are situated, are hung up for public reference at this Office, and also at Shanghae and Yokohama.

5.—Applicants for Money Orders must furnish, in full, the surname, and, at least, the initial of one Christian name, both of the Remitter and the Payee; if the Remitter or Payee be a Peer or a Bishop his ordinary title will be sufficient, if a firm, the usual designation of such firm, such as "Baring Brothers," will suffice. but the mere term Messrs., such as "Messrs. Rivington," or the name of a Company trading under a title which does not consist of the names of the persons composing it, such as "Caron Co.," is inadmissible.

6.—The Remitter, on stating that the Order is to be paid only through a Bank, to have the option of giving or withdrawing the name of the Payee, in such case the Order will be crossed in the same way the Cheques are commonly crossed when they are intended to be paid through a Bank.

7.—When an Order is presented through a Bank, a receipt by any person will be sufficient provided the Order be crossed with name of the receiving Bank, and be presented by some Person known to be in the employ of such Bank.

8.—The signature of the Payee of a Money Order to be affixed to the Order in the place provided for the purpose. If the Payee be unable to write he must sign the receipt by making his mark in the presence of a Witness, who must sign his name, with his address in presence of the Officer who pays the Order.

9.—Should the Payee of a Money Order desire to receive payment in the Country in which the Order was issued, at some other Office than that in which the Order was originally drawn, the transfer will be granted, provided the Order be inclosed to the Postmaster of the Office in which it was drawn. In such case a new Order will be issued, the Commission chargeable upon which will be deducted from the amount of the new Order.

10.—In the event of a Money Order miscarrying or being lost, a duplicate will be granted on a written application from the Payee (containing the necessary particulars, and accompanied by an additional Commission) to the Office where the original Order was payable.

11.—On the receipt of a similar application, orders will be given to stop payment of a Money Order, or to renew a lapsed Order. The additional Commission in the last case will be deducted from the amount of the new Order. Lapsed Orders must be presented with the application for a new Order.

12.—But when it is desired that any error in the name of the Remitter or Payee should be corrected, or that the amount of a Money Order should be repaid to the Remitter, or that a Lapsed Order should be renewed for payment in the Country in which the Order was originally drawn, application must be made to the Chief Money Order Office of such Country. This application must be accompanied by an additional Commission, unless it have reference to a Lapsed Order, in which case the Commission will be deducted from the amount of the New Order.

13.—Repayment, whether of an original, or renewed, or a duplicate Order, will not be made to the Remitter until it has been ascertained that the advice has been cancelled at the Office on which the Order was originally drawn.

14.—Payment of an Order must be obtained before the end of the Sixth Calendar Month after that in which it was drawn; for instance, if drawn in January, payment must be obtained before the end of July, otherwise the Order will become lapsed, and a new Order (for which a second Commission, to be deducted from the amount of the Order, will be charged) will become necessary.

15.—If an Order be not paid before the end of the Twelfth Calendar Month after, that in which it was drawn,—for instance, if drawn in January and not paid before the end of the following January—all claim to the Money will be forfeited, unless, under peculiar circumstances, the Post Office of the Country in which the Order was drawn thinks proper to allow it.

16.—After once paying a Money Order, by whomsoever presented, the paying Office will not be liable to any further claim. If a wrong payment, however, be made owing to negligence on the part of any Officer of the Post Office, the Postmaster General of the Country or Colony in which the negligence occurs will, if he see fit, require the Officer in fault to made good the loss.

17.—No Money Order will be paid unless the advice has been previously received.

18.—Additional Rules for greater security against fraud, and for better working of the system generally, will be made as occasion may require.

19.—Should it appear that Money Orders are used by mercantile men, or others, either in the United Kingdom or at Hongkong, Shanghai, or Yokohama, for the transmission of large sums of money, the British or Colonial Post Office, as the case may be, will consider the propriety of increasing the Commission, and will exercise the power of wholly suspending for a time the issue of Money Orders.

By Command,

F. W. MITCHELL,
Postmaster General.

General Post Office, Hongkong, 22nd August, 1868.

1.—With reference to the Notification of the 22nd ultimo, it is hereby further notified by direction of His Excellency The GOVERNOR, that, on and after Monday, the 2nd November next, Money Orders will be granted at this Office on the Post Offices at Shanghae and Yokohama, and in like manner Money Orders will be granted at Shanghae and Yokohama upon this Office, for sums not exceeding Fifty Dollars, at the ruling rates for Dollars, charged with the following rates of Commission, viz:—

    On Orders not exceeding $25,............................15 cents.
    Above $25 and not exceeding $50,...................30 ,,

2.—The Money Orders will in such case be drawn in Dollars and Cents.

3.—All payments for Money Orders, whether by the Public to the Post Office, or by the Post Office to the Public, will be made in Current Dollars.

4.—The stipulations contained in the Notification of the 22nd August last, so far as they are applicable, will be enforced in conducting the local Money Order system between Hongkong, and Shanghae and Yokohama.

F. W. MITCHELL,
Postmaster General.

General Post Office, Hongkong, 9th September, 1868.

OPIUM SALES AT CALCUTTA.
To be held in 1874.

Date.	Behar Chests.	Benares Chests.	Total Chests.
1st Sale on or about Monday,......... 5th January,......	2209	1541	3750
2nd " " Wednesday,....... 4th February,....	2185	1565	3750
3rd " " Thursday,......... 5th March,......	2185	1565	3750
4th " " Monday,......... 6th April,.........	2185	1565	3750
5th " " Monday,......... 4th May,.........	2185	1565	3750
6th " " Thursday,......... 4th June,.........	2185	1565	3750
7th " " Monday,......... 6th July,.........	2185	1565	3750
8th " " Wednesday,......... 5th August,.......	2185	1565	3750
9th " " Monday,......... 7th September,...	2185	1565	3750
10th " " Wednesday,....... 7th October,......	2185	1565	3750
11th " " Friday,......... 6th November,....	2185	1565	3750
12th " " Thursday,......... 3rd December,.....	2185	1565	3750
Total Chests..................	26,244	18,756	45,000

Averages, &c., realised at the Opium Sales in Calcutta, held during the year 1873.

At the Sale of the Month of	Average of Patna.	Average of Benares.	Increase over the Budget Estimate of Rs. 1,200.		Decrease under the Budget Estimate.	
			From Patna.	From Benares.	By Patna.	By Benares.
January	Rs. 1402	Rs. 1267	Rs. 429,250	Rs. 92,125	......	......
February.....	" 1380	" 1269	" 382,500	" 94,875	......	......
March	" 1362	" 1222	" 344,250	" 30,250	......	......
April	" 1330	" 1201	" 276,250	" 1,375	......	......
May	" 1293	" 1176	" 197,625	......	......	Rs. 83,000
June	" 1276	" 1227	" 161,500	" 87,125	......	......
July .,.........	" 1288	" 1246	" 187,000	" 63,250	......	......
August	" 1275	" 1218	" 159,875	" 24,750	......	......
September....	" 1260	" 1208	" 127,500	" 11,000	......	......
October	" 1246	" 1195	" 97,750	......	" 6,875	......
November ...	" 1235	" 1203	" 74,375	" 4,125	......	......
December ...	" 1312	" 1311	" 238,000	" 152,625	......	......
			Rs. 2,675,375	Rs. 511,500	......	Rs. 89,875

The Year of our Lord 1874 corresponds to

The years 5634 of the Jewish Era;
" 7284 since the Creation, according to Hales;
" 2627 since the Foundation of Rome;
" 6587 of the Julian period;
" 1290-91 of the Mohammedan Era;
" 2621 of the Era of Nabonassor;
" 2650 of the Olympiads;
" 98-99 of the Independence of the U. S. of America;
" 1243-44 of the Parsee Era of Yezdejerd;
" 2417-18 of the Religious Era of the Siamese;
" 1236-37 of the Civil Era of the Siamese.

(B 1)

THE STAMP ORDINANCE.

RULES OF THE STAMP OFFICE.

1.—The Office will be open for the transaction of business from 10 A.M. to 3 P.M. every day (Sundays and authorized holidays excepted.)

2.—All applications for Impressed Stamps must be made upon a printed form of Requisition, which will be supplied gratuitously.

3.—Adhesive Stamps can be obtained upon payment, without Requisition.

4.—Payment for Impressed Stamps must be made on presentation of the Requisition, which must be accompanied by the "goods"—i.e. the paper, printed forms, parchment, or documents tendered with it for the purpose of being impressed.

5.—Requisitions for Impressed Stamps will be executed in the order in which they are received, and when it is not possible to complete a requisition in a short time after it is put in, a time will be named at which the "goods" will be ready; in such cases a Receipt on a printed form will be given for the Requisition, and the "goods" will be delivered on presentation of that Receipt only.

6.—All "goods" and money given in change should be counted and examined before they are removed from the counter, as no question as to wrong count of the "goods" or of the weight or goodness of money will be entertained afterwards.

7.—For the present it is not intended to issue Impressed Stamps except upon paper, &c., sent in by the Public.

8.—*Spoiled Stamps on Unexecuted Instruments.*
    1.—Allowance will be made for Stamps on Instruments which have been spoiled by some error in the writing;
    2.—Or defaced by some accident;
    3.—Or which have been rendered useless by some unforeseen circumstances before they have been completed or rendered fit for their intended purpose.

9.—The claim for such stamps must be made by Affidavit by the owner within Six Months after they have been spoiled or rendered useless.

10.—*Spoiled Stamps on Executed Instruments.*
    1.—Allowance will made for Stamps on Instruments which are found unfit for the purpose originally intended by reason of any mistake or error therein;
    2.—Or which cannot be completed in the form proposed by the death of any Person whose signature is necessary;
    3.—Or by reason of the refusal of any Person to sign the same.

11.—The claim for Stamps on executed Instruments must be made within Six Months after they shall have been signed, and the substituted Deeds, if any, must be produced duly stamped.

12.—Stamps on Bills of Exchange or Promissory Notes when signed by the drawer or maker will be allowed—if they have not been out of his hands and have not been accepted or tendered for acceptance.

13.—But Bills, &c., wherein any error or mistake has been made will be allowed also, although they may have been accepted or tendered for acceptance, provided the claimant produces the Bills which have been substituted for them within Six Months after the date of the spoiled ones.

14.—Applications for allowances for Spoiled Stamps will be entertained every Friday between Noon and 3 P.M.

15.—In cases where paper, printed or plain, or parchment, &c., is spoiled in stamping, it will be destroyed, the applicants finding at their own cost the additional paper, &c., required.

16.—The Stamps will be impressed upon any part of the Documents indicated where it may be practicable with security to the Revenue, a point which in case dispute will be decided by the Collector of Stamps.

17.—To prevent inconvenience a few Blank Forms of Bills of Exchange or Bills of Lading may be left at the Stamp Office by persons requiring Impressed Stamps to supply any deficiency which may have occurred in counting, or to re-place any which may have been spoiled in stamping.

18.—All Impressed Stamps will bear the date on which they are impressed.

19.—The Officers of the Stamp Office are not responsible for any loss or damage which may occur to any Deed, Instrument, or Writing sent in for the purpose of being stamped, unless the same occurs wilfully, fraudulently, or by gross negligence.

F. W. MITCHELL,
Collector of Stamp Revenue.

Stamp Office, Hongkong, 4th October, 1867.

SCHEDULE.

CONTAINING A SPECIFICATION OF THE DEEDS, INSTRUMENTS AND WRITINGS WHICH REQUIRE TO BE STAMPED UNDER THIS ORDINANCE, AND OF THE PROPER STAMPS FOR SUCH DEEDS, INSTRUMENTS AND WRITINGS.

1. Agreement, or any Minute or Memorandum of an Agreement not being under seal or of the nature of an Obligation for the payment of Money, and not especially charged with Duty under this Schedule, whether the same be only evidence of a Contract or obligatory upon the parties, and Brokers' Notes or any Document having reference to the sale or purchase of any Merchandize, given by any Broker, ...	50 cents *impressed*.

NOTE.—*If two or more letters are offered in evidence to prove an Agreement between the parties who shall have written such letters, it will be sufficient if any one of such letters be Stamped as an Agreement.*

EXEMPTION.

Label, Slip or Memorandum containing the heads of any Fire or Marine Insurance to be effected.

Memorandum, Letter or Agreement made for or relating to the sale of any Goods, Wares or Merchandize, or to the sale of any Shares in any Public Company not being a Broker's Note or Document given by a Broker.

Seamen's Advance Note or Memorandum or Agreement made between the Master and Mariners of any Ship for Wages.

Emigration Contract. Passage Ticket.

2. Bank Notes, or other Obligations for the payment of Money issued by any Banker or Banking Company in the Colony for Local circulation and payable to bearer on demand, ...	A Stamp Duty of two-thirds per cent per annum per $100 of the average value of such Notes in Circulation, to be collected monthly on a Statement thereof to be furnished by each Banker or Banking Company to the Collector of Stamp Revenue, at the end of each month, and by the Banker or the Manager or Agent and Accountant of such Banking Company.

THE STAMP ORDINANCE.

8. Bills of Exchange, Promissory Notes or other Obligations for the Payment of Money not included in the last preceding Article and not being Cheques or Orders for the payment of money at sight or on demand,....................	*Not exceeding $100—*
	  If drawn singly,........ $0.30
	  If in sets, for each part of a set,........ $0.15
	Exceeding $100 and not exceeding $3,000—
	  If drawn singly,........ $1.00
	  If in sets, for each part of a set,........ $0.50
	Exceeding $3,000—
	  If drawn singly,........ $1.50
	  If in sets, for each part of a set,........ $0.75
	When drawn in the Colony, *impressed.* When drawn out of the Colony, *adhesive.*

Bank Cheques payable on demand to any person, to Bearer or Order,.....................................	2 cents, *impressed* or *adhesive.*
NOTE.—*Cheques drawn out of, but payable in the Colony to be treated as Bills of Exchange.*	
4. Bills of Lading or Ships' Receipts where Bills of Lading are not used, for each part of every set,............	10 cents, *impressed.*

EXEMPTION.

Bills of Lading for any Goods or Effects shipped by any Government Officer on account of Government.

5. Bond or other Obligation concerning Respondentia and Bottomry, and Average Statement or Bond where no Statement is drawn up,..	50 cents for every $1,000 or part of $1,000, *impressed.*
6. Charter Party or any Agreement or Contract for the charter or hiring of any sea-going ship or vessel,.......	*Vessel not exceeding 200 Tons,*........ $2.00 *Exceeding 200 and not exceeding 500 Tons,*........ $3.00 *Exceeding 500 and not exceeding 500 Tons,*........ $4.00 *Exceeding 500 and not exceeding 750 Tons,*........ $5.00 *Exceeding 750 and not exceeding 1,000 Tons,*........ $6.00 *Every 100 Tons over 1,000 Tons,*........ $0.50 *Copy Charter under 200 Tons,*........ $1.00 *Copy Charter above 200 Tons,*........ $2.00 *Duty to be calculated on Registered Tonnage.* *Impressed.*
7. Transfer of Shares or Stock in any Public Company (Scrip Certificate to be exempt),.................................	50 cents for every $500 or fraction of $500, *impressed.*
8. Power of Attorney,..	$2, *impressed.*
9. Note of Protest, by any Commander or Master of a Vessel,..	$25 cents, *impressed.*
10. Any Notarial Act whatsoever not otherwise charged in this Schedule,..	$1, *impressed.*
11. Receipt or Discharge given for the payment of Money or in acquittal of a debt paid in money or otherwise, when the sum received, discharged, or acquitted exceeds $10,..	3 cents, *adhesive.*

EXEMPTIONS.

Letter sent by Post, acknowledging the arrival of a Currency, or Promissory Note, Bill of Exchange, or any security for Money.

Receipt or Discharge written upon or contained in any Bill of Exchange, Promissory Note, Deed or other Instrument charged with duty under this Schedule and duly Stamped, and Receipts for Pay and Allowances of Persons in the service of the Government, whether Civil, Naval or Military.

12. Probates and Letters of Administration with or without the Will annexed (Administration Bonds exempt),	The same *ad valorem* Duty as on a Conveyance, to be calculated upon the value of the Estate and Effects for or in respect of which such Probate or Letters of Administration shall be granted, exclusive of what the deceased shall have been possessed of or entitled to as a Trustee for any other Person or Persons, and not beneficially, *impressed*.
13. Conveyance, Assignment or Instrument of any kind or description whatsoever not specially charged with Duty under this Schedule executed for the transfer for valuable consideration of any Property, moveable or immoveable, or of any Right, Title, Claim, or Interest in, to or upon the same........	25 cents for every $100 or part of $100 of the consideration Money or amount secured up to $1,000; and $2 for every $1,000 or part of $1,000 after the first $1,000, *impressed*.
Deed or other Instrument of Gift, or of Exchange or Settlement where no Money consideration or a merely Nominal Money consideration passes,............	$25, *impressed*.

EXEMPTION.

Transfer by mere Endorsement of a duly Stamped Bill of Exchange, Promissory Note or other Negotiable Instrument, or of a Bill of Lading and Transfer by Assignment of a Policy of Insurance.

14. Mortgage,.....................................	$1, on first $1,000 or part of $1,000 and 50 cents on every other $100 or part thereof, *impressed*.
Where in a Mortgage the sum secured is unlimited,......	$25, *impressed*.
15. Re-assignment of any Mortgaged Property,.........	25 cents on every $5,000 or part of $5,000, *impressed*.
16. Letter or other Instrument of Hypothecation accompanying deposit of Documents of Title to any property,	$1, *impressed*.
17. Duplicate or Counterpart of any Deed, Instrument or Writing of any description whatever chargeable with duty under this Ordinance,............	The same Duty as the Original when such Duty does not exceed $1, *impressed*.
If the Duty chargeable on the Original exceeds $1 but does not exceed $10.............................	$1, *impressed*.
If the Duty chargeable on the Original exceeds $10 but does not exceed $20,...........................	$2, *impressed*.
If the duty on the Original exceeds $20,............	$3, *impressed*.

Provided that such Duplicate or Counterpart Stamp shall be affixed upon the production of the Original Deed, Instrument or Writing bearing its proper Stamp and not otherwise.

18. Lease or Agreement for a Lease made for a term of years or for a period determinable with one or more life or lives or otherwise contingent in consideration of a Sum of Money paid in the way of premium, fine or the like, if without rent,.....................................	The same *ad valorem* Stamp as on a Conveyance. See Article 13.

THE STAMP ORDINANCE.

	1 Year and under	3 Years and under	Over 3 Years
19. Lease or Agreement for a Lease of any Land, House, Building or Tenement at a Rent without any payment of any Sum of Money by way of fine or premium:—	$ c.	$ c.	$ c.
When the Rent for the Year shall not exceed $250,	0.25	0.50	1.00
Above $ 250 and under $ 500,	0.50	1.00	2.00
„ $ 500 „ $1,000,	1.00	2.00	4.00
„ $1,000 „ $2,500,	2.00	4.00	8.00
„ $2,500 „ $5,000,	5.00	10.00	20.00
for every additional $1,000 or part,	1.25	2.50	5.00

Impressed.

Exempt—All Rentals under $50.

20. Lease or Agreement for a Lease of any Land, House, Building or Tenement, stipulating for a Part granted in consideration of a fine or premium, ... } A Stamp of value equal to the joint value of the Stamps for a Conveyance in consideration of the fine and a Lease for the Rent, *impressed.*

NOTE.—*A Lease, executed in pursuance of a duly Stamped Agreement for the same, shall require a Stamp of One Dollar only, to be affixed on production of such Agreement.*

21. Every Instrument in Writing under seal not otherwise specially charged with Duty under this Schedule, } $10, *impressed.*
22. Policies of Marine Insurance and every copy, ... 10 cents each, *impressed.*
23. Articles of Clerkship, or Contract, whereby any person shall first become bound to serve as a Clerk in order to his admission as an Attorney or Solicitor, ... } $50, *impressed.*
24. Warrant of Attorney, ... $5, *impressed.*
25. Copartnership Deed, or other Instrument of .... $5, *impressed.*
26. Cognovit and Arbitration Award, ... $1, *impressed.*
Servant's Security Bond, ... 50 cents, *impressed.*

GENERAL EXEMPTIONS.

Any Deed, Instrument or Writing of any kind whatsoever made or executed by or on behalf of Her Majesty or of any Department of Her Majesty's Service, or whereby any Property or interest is transferred to, or any Contract of any kind whatsoever is made with Her Majesty or any Person for or on behalf of Her Majesty or any such Department as aforesaid.

NOTE.—*The foregoing exemption does not extend to any Deed, Instrument or Writing, executed by the Registrar of the Supreme Court as Official Administrator or by a Receiver appointed by any Court, or to any Deed, Instrument or Writing rendered necessary by any Ordinance or by the order of any Court ; neither does it extend to a sale made for the recovery of an arrear of Revenue or Rent, or in satisfaction of a Decree or Order of Court, in any of which cases the purchaser shall be required to pay in addition to the purchase money the amount of the requisite Stamp.*

EXTRACT OF ORDER

M‘DE BY HIS EXCELLENCY GOVERNC‘S

Sir RICHARD GRAVES MacDONNELL, c.b.,

In Council, this Ninth day of June, 1868.

1.—It is hereby ordered that the Orders of the Governor in Council of the 28th September, 1867; the 4th October, 1867; the 8th October, 1867, and the 9th April, 1868, shall be and they are hereby revoked, from and after the 1st day of July now next ensuing, being the day fixed by Proclamation of the Governor for the coming into operation of Ordinance No. 5 of 1868, and in lieu thereof, it is ordered that the Stamps to be used under Ordinance No. 12 of 1866 and Ordinance No. 5 of 1868 shall be from and after the last mentioned dates:—

2.—First, Adhesive Stamps of the respective values of 2 cents, 8 cents, 25 cents, 30 cents, 50 cents, $1, and $1.50; and Secondly, Impressed or Embossed Stamps of the respective values of 2 cents, 10 cents, 15 cents, 25 cents, 30 cents, 50 cents, 75 cents, $1, $1 50, $2, $2.50, $3, $4, $4.50, $5, $6, $6.50, $8.50, $10, $10.50, $20, $25, $40, $50, and a Stamp bearing the words "Adjudication Fee Paid."

3.—All Impressed Stamps shall be made and impressed in the Stamp Office in the City of Victoria on either paper or parchment, and shall be of the form and size of the specimen Stamps enclosed in a case for Public inspection under the Seal of the Colony, which case shall be kept at the Stamp Office.

4.—Each of the Seven kinds of Adhesive Stamps aforementioned shall be of the form, size, and material of the specimen Stamps enclosed in a case for Public inspection under the Seal of the Colony, which case shall be kept at the Stamp Office.

7.—Stamps shall be impressed or embossed at the Stamp Office, and Adhesive Stamps sold, between the hours of 10 a.m., and 3 p.m., every day, authorized Holidays excepted.

Approved in Council,
RICHARD GRAVES MacDONNELL,
Governor.

L. D'ALMADA E CASTRO,
Clerk of Councils.

A DIGEST OF PENALTIES.

Sec. 7.—For drawing or negociating unstamped or insufficiently stamped Bills of Exchange, Promissory Notes, &c., a sum not exceeding Fifty Dollars, or a sum equal to ten times the value of the Stamp omitted to be used, if the sum so calculated exceed Fifty Dollars.

Sec. 10.—For not obliterating Adhesive Stamps when used by cancelling them in a *bonâ fide* manner, a sum not exceeding Fifty Dollars.

Sec. 12.—For not affixing the proper adhesive Stamps on Bills of Exchange drawn out of the Colony, but payable in, before negociating the same, or failing to cancel the same in a *bonâ fide* manner, a sum not exceeding Fifty Dollars.

Sec. 14.—For drawing Bills purporting to be drawn in a set of two or more, and not drawing the whole number of the set, a sum not exceeding Five Hundred Dollars.

Sec. 16, c. 1.—If any Deed, Instrument, or Writing requiring to be stamped shall have been executed on paper not bearing the proper Stamp, upon the Collector being satisfied that the omission did not arise from any intention to evade payment of the prescribed duty, or to defraud the Government, it may be stamped on payment of the proper Stamp Duty, and as a pen.ty double the amount of the proper Stamp Duty or of the amount required to make up the same. if it be brought to the Collector within six weeks from the date of its execution.

2.—If any Deed shall have been executed on unstamped or insufficiently stamped paper, and brought to be stamped after six weeks of execution, but within four months of that date, treble the amount of the proper Stamp Duty, or of the amount required to make up the same, as the Collector may determine.

If brought after four months, twenty times the amount of such Stamp Duty, or the amount required to make up the same, as the Collector may determine.

Sec. 28.—In default of attaching a receipt stamp to any document given in receipt for money above Ten Dollars, a sum not exceeding Fifty Dollars.

Sec. 27.—For not stating truly, in every Instrument charged under the Schedule annexed to this Ordinance with *ad valorem* duty, the amount of Purchase Money, a sum not exceeding Two Hundred and Fifty Dollars.

Sec. 1, c. 8 (Ordinance 5 of 1868).—In default of placing a 8 cent Stamp on a receipt for any sum exceeding $10: Fifty Dollars.

ADDITIONAL ORDER

Made by His Excellency the Governor in Council, this 28th Day of October, 1878, under Authority of "The Stamp Ordinance, 1866."

IN THE SUPREME COURT, SUMMARY JURISDICTION.

The Stamp Duty payable on Foreign Attachment Bonds shall be as follows :—

In every Case of $500 and upwards, ...$5.00
    "   " $250 and under $500, ... 2.50
    "   "   under $250, ... 1.00

(C)

HYDROGRAPHICAL MEMOS.

(From the China Pilot.)

Tides.—It is high water, full and change, in Hongkong Roads at 10h. 15m., and springs rise about 4½ feet. The tides around the island are irregular, flowing and ebbing without any apparent change of direction at the surface, and sometimes there appear to be only one tide in 24 hours.

Directions.—Hongkong Road is generally approached by sailing vessels from the westward, on which side it is protected by Green Island and Kellett Bank, which extends nearly 1¼ miles northward from the latter island, and carries a depth of 8¼ fathoms. It is sometimes approached from the eastward through the Ly-ee-moon Pass during the N.E. monsoon, but the winds are generally baffling under the high land.

When abreast Green Island, if the vessel be of heavy draught, keep the peak of Lamma Island (Mount Senhouse, 1,140 feet high) open westward of Green Island S. ¾ E. until Devil's Peak (on the mainland near Ly-ee-moon Pass) is in the line with the White rock on the south point of Won-chu-chau, or Stone-cutter's Island, when a S.E. by E. course will lead northward of Kellett Bank, and direct for the anchorage.

Vessels of proper draught can proceed over Kellett Bank or through the 4 fathoms channel between Green Island and the south part of the bank, by passing about 1½ cable northward of the Island and then steering for the road.

The narrow channel between Green Island and Hongkong may be taken if a fresh fair wind blows *right through.** Many sailing vessels have used it, amongst which were H.M.'s ships *Modeste, Wellesley,* and *Vernon.* It has depths of 10 to 12 fathoms in the middle, shoaling to 8, 6, and 4½ fathoms after passing the small islets eastward of Green Island.

Tytam Bay and Harbour.—There are several small bays on the southern shore of Hongkong, all of which are safe for small vessels; but at the south-east part of the island is a deep inlet, named Tytam bay, 2½ miles deep, 1½ miles wide at entrance, free from danger, and carries a depth of 10 to 16 fathoms. Tytam head, the western point of entrance, is a high bluff, with 18 and 14 fathoms near it; from thence the western shore of the bay trends about N. by E. three-quarters of a mile to a small sandy bay, with a rocky islet fronting the beach. About half a mile northward of the islet the land forms a round projecting point, and northward of this point is a large bay with a sandy beach, in which is Tytam village.

Tylong head, or Cape D'Aguilar, off which are two green islets, forms the eastern point of entrance of Tytam bay, and from thence the eastern shore of the bay bends round to the northward for 2 miles, and terminates in a small inlet, called Tytam harbour, carrying 4 to 6 fathoms, but its head, to the northwest, is shoal and rocky. This bay would be useful to a vessel in the event of her being near Wag-lan at the close of the day, with the probability of a dark and tempestuous night, for by running in she will at any rate be snug, even if there should be a typhoon during the night.

Water.—At the head of Tytam harbour there is a rivulet of fresh water, which, however, cannot be procured without inconvenience when the tide is low. Water may be obtained at Tytam village, on the western shore of the bay.

Tides.—There is little tide in Tytam bay, and, like all the places hereabouts, it is difficult to fix the time of high water, owing to the variety of channels, and the wind greatly influencing the tidal streams; but the rise and fall is about 7 or 8 feet at springs, and about 3 or 4 feet at neaps. The ebb sets to the eastward between Lo-chau and Hongkong.

* J. W. King, Master of H. M. S. *Wellesley,* 1842.

PARCEL TARIFFS
FROM HONGKONG.

PENINSULAR & ORIENTAL STEAM NAVIGATION COMPANY.

ORDINARY PARCELS—(*England, Mediterranean and Australia.*)
2 Cubic Inches,..$1.00.
And 20c. additional for every inch up to 2 feet,............. { $3.00, 1 foot.
{ $5.40, 2 feet.
2 to 8 feet. 15c. for every inch, ...$7.20, 8 „

Parcels over $50 value to be charged either by measurement, or at an ad valorem rate, at the option of the Company. Packages exceeding 8 cubic feet will be charged at cargo rates.

MUSTER PARCELS OF NO VALUE.
2 Cubic Inches,..$1.00.
And 15c. for every additional inch up to 8 feet,......... { $2.50, 1 foot.
{ $4.30, 2 feet.
{ $6.10, 8 „

A. MacIVER, *Superintendent*.

P. & O. S. N. Co's Office, January 1, 1872.

SERVICE DES MESSAGERIES MARITIMES.

ORDINARY PARCELS—(*To Marseilles and London.*)
2 Cubic Inches,..$1.00
And 20c. additional for every inch up 2 feet, ... { $3.00, 1 foot.
{ $5.40, 2 feet.
2 to 8 feet, 15c. for every inch, ...$7.20, 8 „

Parcels over $50 value to be charged either by measurement, or at an ad valorem rate, at the option of the Company. Packages exceeding 3 cubic feet will be charged at cargo rates.

MUSTER PARCELS OF NO VALUE.
2 Cubic Inches,..$1.00.
And 15c. for every additional inch up to 8 feet,.................... { $2.50, 1 foot.
{ $4.60, 2 feet.
{ $6.10, 8 „

C. BERTRAND, *Principal Agent*.

Hongkong, January 1, 1872.

PACIFIC MAIL STEAM SHIP COMPANY.

To Yokohama.
Smallest Charge,...................... $0.50
1 ft. 1.00
2 „ 2.00
3 „ 2.50
4 „ 3.00

Valuable goods, 1 % ad valorem.

To Nagasaki and Hiogo.
50 % added to Yokohama rates.

Hongkong, January 1, 1872.

To San Francisco.
Smallest Charge,........................... $1.50
5 to 10 lbs.,.................................. 2.00
11 „ 15 „ 3.00
16 „ 20 „ 4.00
21 „ 25 „ 5.00
26 „ 30 „ 6.00
31 „ 35 „ 7.00
36 „ 40 „ 8.00
41 „ 45 „ 9.00
46 „ 50 „ 10.00
Exceeding 50 pounds, per pound..... 0.20

T. A. HARRIS, *Agent*.

LEGALISED SCALE of FARES for CHAIRS with Two BEARERS, in the COLONY of HONGKONG.

Per day, of Twelve hours,	$1.00
Half day, 6 hours,	70
3 Hours,	50
1 Hour,	20
Half an Hour,	10

In case more than two Bearers are employed, every auditional Bearer to be paid at the rate of half the above scale.

Nothing herein contained prevents special agreements.

CECIL C. SMITH,
Registrar General.

Registrar General's Office, 24th September, 1870.

轎役限價程式
每半點鐘准收工銀十仙
每一點鐘准收工銀二十仙
每三點鐘准收工銀五十仙
每六點鐘准收工銀七十仙
每日計十二點鐘准收工銀一員
如有顧請轎夫過兩名之外
每多一名照上例正工價單
折半交收
倘有別等另行議價者任由
自便與此單內章程無涉

LEGALISED SCALE of FARES for the UNDERMENTIONED BOATS in HONGKONG.

1st Class or Cargo Boats...	per day,	$2.25
	„ trip,	1.50
2nd Class or Cargo Boats..	„ day,	1.25
	„ trip,	75
„ or Hakows,	„ day,	1.25
	„ trip not exceeding one hour,	25
	„ day,	1.00
	„ trip not exceeding one hour,	25
3rd Class or Pulling Boats	„ half trip from shore to ship or *vice versâ*, not to exceed half an hour,	12
	„ „ night trip,	25
	„ day,	50
	„ trip not exceeding one hour,	10
4th Class or Sampans	„ half trip from shore to ship or *vice versâ*, not exceeding half an hour,	6
	„ night trip not exceeding half an hour,	10

(D 1)

CANTON CUSTOM-HOUSE REGULATIONS.

I. Masters must deposit their Ship's Papers and Manifest with their Consul (if they have no Consul, with the Customs,) within 48 hours after entering the Port. — *Ships' Papers.*

II. The Import Manifest must contain a true account of the nature of the Cargo on board, and must be handed to the Customs before any application to break bulk can be attended to. — *Import Manifest.*

III. The Import Manifest having been received, and Ship's Papers duly lodged with the Consul or the Customs, Permits to land goods will be granted, on the receipt of applications specifying the number of packages, with their Marks, Weight, Quantity, and such like particulars. — *Application to land Cargo.*

IV. Before Shipment of goods, Permits to ship must in like manner be obtained. — *Application to ship Cargo.*

V. Cargo for which a Permit has been issued, but which cannot be received on board, must be brought to the Custom House Jetty for examination, before being re-landed. — *Exclusion of Cargo.*

VI. When a vessel has received on board the whole of her Outward Cargo, the Customs must be furnished with an Export Manifest. — *Export Manifest.*

VII. After the examination of goods, Consignees or Shippers will be supplied with a Memorandum, for which early application should be made, of the Duties payable. — *Payment of Duties.*

They may then pay in the amount to the Hae Kwan Bank or Receiving Office, when they will be furnished with a Duty Receipt Chinese, which they must bring to the Custom House.

Import Duties are due upon the landing of Goods, and export Duties on their shipment. Amendment in respect of Weight or Value must be made within 24 hours after the landing or shipment of the goods.

VIII. On application being made for the Customs' Clearance, if the Customs are satisfied that the Import and Export Manifests are correct, and that all Dues and Duties have been paid, the Clearance will be issued. — *Customs' Clearance.*

IX. In all cases of transhipment, application must be made for a Tranship Permit. Goods transhipped before receipt of such Permit, are liable to confiscation. — *Transhipment.*

X. Cargo Boats conveying Goods from Canton to Whampoa for shipment there, must be taken for examination to the Customs' Jetty before the goods can be put on board the Ship. On arrival at Whampoa their permit must be exhibited at the Floating Custom House, for counter-signature. In like manner, the permits of Cargo Boats conveying Goods to Canton from Ships at Whampoa must be Countersigned at the Whampoa Floating Custom House, and on arrival at Canton they must repair to the Customs' Jetty for examination. — *Goods conveyed to and from Whampoa in Cargo Boats.*

RIVER STEAMER REGULATIONS.

Import Manifest.
I. On entering port, Masters of River Steamers must have their Import Manifests in readiness to hand to the Customs' Officer who will board the Vessel on arrival. For Cargo to be discharged at Whampoa, a separate Manifest will be required, to be handed to the Customs' Officer at that place.

The Customs must in all cases be furnished with Import Manifest, before any Cargo can be discharged.

Landing of Cargo.
II. Consignees are not required to make application to the Customs for permission to remove consignments from the steamers, but all Goods imported in such Vessels must on being discharged be taken for examination to the Customs' Jetty.

Shipment of Cargo.
III. All Exports for shipment by River Steamers, must be sent to the Customs' Jetty for examination, on which a Permit to ship will be granted.

Export Manifest.
IV. Manifest of Cargoes exported must be handed to the Customs on the return trip of the Steamers.

Landing or Shipment of Cargo en route.
V. River Steamers must not land or ship Cargo at any other place in the River than Canton and Whampoa. Any breach of these Regulations respecting the shipment or discharge of goods exposes such goods to seizure and confiscation.

Office hours.
VI. The Custom House is open for the transaction of business from 10 A.M. to 4 P.M. and the River Steamer Office from Sunrise to Sunset, Sundays and Holidays excepted.

All applications regarding Customs business should be addressed to
THE COMMISSIONER OF CUSTOMS,
OFFICE OF MARITIME CUSTOMS,
CANTON.

HOLIDAYS observed at the Canton Custom House.

Foreign New Year's Day,	外國元旦日
Chinese New Year's Day (5 or 6 days),	中國新年
Good Friday,	外國禮拜日
23rd Day of 3rd Moon (Emperor's Birthday),	萬壽
5th Day of 5th Moon (Dragon Boat Festival),	端午節
15th Day of 8th Moon (Autumnal Festival),	中秋節
Christmas Day,	耶蘇生日

PHILIPPINE PASSPORT REGULATIONS FOR FOREIGNERS.

GOVERNMENT NOTIFICATION.

Her Majesty's Consul at Manila having forwarded to this Government a Translation of the 3rd, 4th, and 6th Articles of a Royal Decree in reference to the admission and residence of Foreigners in the Territory of the Philippines, His Excellency the Governor has been pleased to order publication thereof for the information of all whom it may concern.

His Excellency has also been pleased to direct it to be notified that all applications for Passports should be addressed to the Colonial Secretary at least 24 hours before they are required, and that all Passports for the Philippine Islands will require to be vised by the Spanish Consul residing at Hongkong.

By Command,

J. GARDINER AUSTIN,
Colonial Secretary.

Colonial Secretary's Office, Hongkong, 15th January, 1869.

DECREE No. 815.

Chapter I.—On the admission and residence of Foreigners in the Territory of the Philippines.

ARTICLE 3.—Every Foreigner desirous of entering the Territory of the Philippine Isles, must present his Passport at the first port at which he arrives viséd by the Diplomatic or Consular Agent of the Spanish Government to whom it may correspond according to the place whence he proceeds, or some other analagous document equivalent to the same by the Police Regulation in force, which shall identify his person.

ARTICLE 4.—The Foreigner who on his arrival within the Territory of the Islands shall fail to present his Passport or some other document which identifies his person, will remain under the surveillance of the authorities and be detained, until his legal position be ascertained. The competent authorities will decide whether he shall be expelled as a vagabond, or confined, or remitted to a third power as a political emigrant; obliging him, in the last case, if he presented himself with arms, to deliver them up immediately, that they may be returned to the country whence he proceeded.

ARTICLE 6.—The Foreigner established in the Philippine Isles, who shall not comply with the obligation of registering himself at the corresponding Provincial Government and at the Consular Agency of his nation, if there be any, shall forfeit all rights with respect to any claim or petition made in his favour by the Consulates of his country, and if he should resolutely refuse to register himself, he shall be treated as a vagabond, and shall not be permitted in any case to continue his residence in the Territory of the Islands.

(F

VICTORIA PEAK, HONGKONG.

THE *Union Jack* will be hoisted at the Mast-head when any vessel is being signalled.

The *Red Ensign* at the Mast-head will denote that a British Functionary of Rank is on board of a Vessel approaching.

The *National* or *House Flag* will be hoisted over the symbol, when either is flying on board the vessel signalled.

The signals of Vessels in the offing will be repeated. In making *signals to Men-of-war*, in the Harbour or in the offing a White Ensign will be hoisted at the Flag Staff, and at the Mast-head, of the Men-of-war.

The *Commercial Code of Signals for all Nations*, will be used at the Staff. All *distance signals* will be made at the *Mast-head*, and all *Compass Bearings* will be made at the Yard.

On a *Steamer* or the *smoke of a Steamer* being sighted, the *Compass bearing over the proper symbol* will be hoisted at the Yard-arm; and the *distance off* in miles will be hoisted at the *Mast-head*. The *Distance Signal* will be kept up ten minutes and the *Compass signal* until the Steamer is made out. When the *Steamer* is made out, if it is an English, French, or American Mail Steamer, a gun will be fired and the *distance off* at that moment will be hoisted under a ball at the *Mast-head*. The Compass Signal will then be hauled down and the proper National or House Flag will be substituted for it. The Mast-head Signal will be kept up ten minutes, and the Yard-arm Signal until the Steamer anchors.

For any other than a Mail steamer, the same signals, will the exception of the gun and ball, will be used.

River Steamers will not be signalled. Other Steamers from Macao and Canton will be made known by shewing the National Flag, and symbol, at West Yard-arm only.

COMPASS SIGNALS.

No.	BEARING.	No.	BEARING.	No.	BEARING.	No.	BEARING.
C. B.	North.	D. B.	East.	F. B.	South.	G. B.	West.
C. F.	N. by E.	D. F.	E. by S.	F. D.	S. by W.	G. D.	W. by N.
C. H.	N. N. E.	D. H.	E. S. E.	F. H.	S. S. W.	G. H.	W. N. W.
C. K.	N. E. by N.	D. K.	S. E. by E.	F. K.	S. W. by S.	G. K.	N. W. by W.
C. M.	N. E.	D. M.	S. E.	F. M.	S. W.	G. M.	N. W.
C. P.	N. E. by E.	D. P.	S. E. by S.	F. P.	S. W. by W.	G. P.	N. W. by N.
C. R.	N. N. E.	D. R.	S. S. E.	F. R.	W. S. W.	G. R.	N. N. W.
C. T.	E. by N.	D. T.	S. by E.	F. T.	W. by S.	G. T.	N. by W.

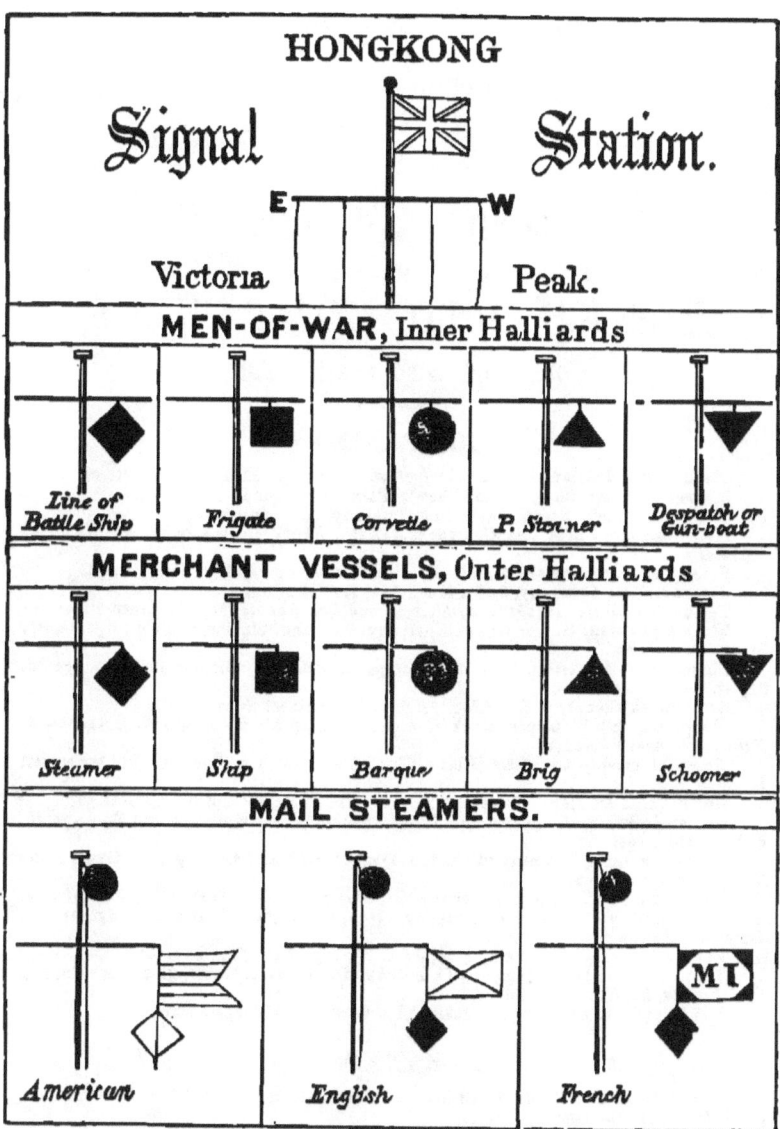

LONDON AGENCIES
OF
BANKS AND COMPANIES
Connected with the Far East.

COMPANIES.

Peninsular and Oriental Steam Navigation Company, 122, Leadenhall-street.
Messageries Maritimes, (Head Office in Paris), 97, Cannon-street.
Netherlands India Steam Navigation Company, 13, Austinfriars.
Hongkong and China Gas Company, 11, Old Jewry Chambers, J. C. Walduck, Secretary.
Singapore Coir Company (Limited), J. M. Little, Agent, 92, Cannon-street.
Singapore Gas Company, 8, St. Mary Axe, Robert King, secretary.
Pacific Saw Mills, Hakodadi, Armitstead and Co., Agents, 21, Old Broad-street.
Singapore Patent Slip and Dock Company, Paterson, Simons, and Co., Agents, 21, St. Swithin's-lane.
Singapore Johore Steam Saw Mills Company, Paterson, Simons and Co., Agents, 21, St. Swithin's-lane.
Amoy Dock Company, John Pook, Agent, Lime-street Square.
Hongkong and Whampoa Dock Company, James Morrison and Co., Agents, 4, Fenchurch-street, London.
Ocean Steamship Company (Holt's Line), John Swire & Sons, 19, Billiter-street, London, E.C.
North China Insurance Company, 25, Cornhill, J. S. Mackintosh, Secretary.
Canton Insurance Company, and Triton Insurance Co., Matheson and Co., Agents, 8, Lombard-street.
Union Insurance Company of Canton, Dent, Palmer and Co., Agents, King's Arms Yard, Moorgate-street.
Hongkong Fire Insurance Company, Gledstanes and Co,, Agents, 26, Austinfriars.
China Traders' Insurance Company, Hongkong, Fearon and Co., Agents, 84, Great St. Helens.
Borneo Company, 7, Mincing-lane, John Harvey, Managing Director.
Tanjong Pagar Dock Company (Limited) of Singapore, Mactaggart, Tidman, and Co., Agents, 34, Great St. Helens.
Silk Supply Association, T. Dickins, President, 25, Moorgate-street.

BANKS.

Chartered Bank of India, Australia, and China, Hatton-court, Threadneedle-street, J. H. Gwyther, Manager.
Chartered Mercantile Bank of India, London, and China, Old Broad-street, D. T. Robertson, General Manager.
Comptoir d'Escompte de Paris, 144, Leadenhall-street, E.C.
Hongkong and Shanghae Banking Corporation, W. H. Vacher, Manager, 24, Lombard-street.
National Bank of India, R. O. Sawers, Chief-manager, 80, King William-street.
Oriental Bank Corporation, Threadneedle-street, C. J. F. Stuart, Chief-manager.

HONGKONG FIRE BRIGADE ESTABLISHMENT.

NAMES AND LOCALITIES OF STATIONS
WHERE ENGINES LADDERS, &C. ARE KEPT.

CENTRAL POLICE STATION.
1 Hand Engine, with Hose, &c., Complete.
1 Fire Ladder
1 Supply Cart, with Hose and Implements for Street Main.

No. 2, POLICE STATION (WANCHAI)
1 Supply Cart, with Hose, &c., for Street Main.

No. 5, POLICE STATION (CROSS ROADS).
2 Steam Engines, with Hose &c., Complete.
1 Hand Engine   Do.
1 Fire-Escape Ladder.
2 Fire Ladders
1 Supply Cart, with Hose and Implements for Street Main.

No. 7, POLICE STATION (WEST POINT).
1 Hand Engine, Hose &c., Complete.
2 Fire Ladders
10 Fire Buckets.

No. 8, POLICE STATION (TAI-PING-SHAN).
1 Supply Cart with Hose and Implements for Street Main.
2 Fire Ladders.
10 Fire Buckets

HARBOUR MASTER'S DEPARTMENT (PRAYA, NEAR THE P. M. S. S. Co.'s PREMISES).
1 Hand Engine, with Hose &c., Complete.
1 Fire-Escape Ladder
2 Fire Ladders.
10 Fire Buckets.

GOVERNMENT HOUSE:
1 Hand Engine, with Hose, &c. Complete.
10 Fire Buckets.

VOLUNTEER FIRE BRIGADE.

HONGKONG FIRE INSURANCE COMPANY PRAYA CENTRAL, NEAR DOUGLAS
LAPRAIK & CO.'S WHARF, (JARDINE, MATHESON & CO., AGENTS.)
1 Steam Engine with Hose and Implements.

IMPERIAL INSURANCE CO.: BURDS' LANE, (GIBB LIVINGSTON & CO. AGENTS.)
1 Hand Engine, with Hose and Implements.

ALLIANCE FIRE INSURANCE: JARDINE BAZAAR, EAST POINT,
(JARDINE, MATHESON & CO. AGENTS.)
1 Hand Engine, with Hose and Implements.

ROYAL INSURANCE COMPANY: PRAYA EAST, (R. S. WALKER & CO. AGENTS.)
1 Hand Engine, with Hose and Implements.

ENGINES OWNED BY CHINESE.

PAWNBROKERS' ASSOCIATION: QUEEN'S ROAD CENTRAL, NEAR HILLIER ST.
1 Hand Engine, with Hose and Implements.

SILK MERCERS' ASSOCIATION: JERVOIS STREET.
1 Hand Engine, with Hose and Implements.

NAM PAK HONG; BONHAM STRAND WEST.
1 Hand Engine, with Hose and Implements.

FIRE ALARMS.

GIVEN FROM THE BELLS AT THE FOLLOWING STATIONS.
Central Police Station.
No. 5 Police Station, (Cross Roads.)
Harbour Master's Department, (Praya Central.)
Hongkong Fire Insurance Co.'s Fire Engine Station, (Praya Central)
Clock Tower.

SIGNALS USED.

EASTERN DISTRICT.
From the East to Murray Barracks . . . by a Single Stroke at a time.

CENTRAL DISTRICT.
From Murray Barracks to the Harbour Masters Office, by a Double Stroke at a time.

WESTERN DISTRICT.
From Harbour Master's Office to the extreme West,—by a Treble Stroke at a time.

C. MAY,
Supt. Fire Brigade.

FIRE BRIGADE DEPARTMENT.
Hongkong, 15th December, 1878.

REPRINTED BY

Ch'eng-wen Publishing Co.
P. O. Box 22605, Taipei, Taiwan,
The Republic of China

1971

發行人：黃　　成　　助
地　址：台北郵政信箱第22605號

發行所：成文出版社有限公司
地　址：台北市羅斯福路3段266—1號

印刷所：東　南　印　製　廠
地　址：台北市和平西路2段70巷83弄29號

中華民國 六十 年五月

內政部登記證內版台業字第1147號

www.ingramcontent.com/pod-product-compliance
Lightning Source LLC
Chambersburg PA
CBHW032014220426
43664CB00006B/245